THE WAR LIST OF THE
UNIVERSITY OF CAMBRIDGE
1914–1918

CAMBRIDGE UNIVERSITY PRESS

C. F. CLAY, Manager

LONDON : FETTER LANE, E.C. 4

NEW YORK : THE MACMILLAN CO.
BOMBAY ⎫
CALCUTTA ⎬ MACMILLAN AND CO., Ltd.
MADRAS ⎭
TORONTO : THE MACMILLAN CO. OF
CANADA, Ltd.
TOKYO : MARUZEN-KABUSHIKI-KAISHA

THE WAR LIST

OF THE

UNIVERSITY OF CAMBRIDGE

1914-1918

EDITED BY

G. V. CAREY, M.A.

FELLOW OF CLARE COLLEGE

LATE MAJOR, RIFLE BRIGADE AND ROYAL AIR FORCE

CAMBRIDGE

AT THE UNIVERSITY PRESS

1921

CONTENTS

INTRODUCTION

DURING the late war no official record was kept by the University of the services of Cambridge men with the Forces. Each College kept touch, so far as was possible, with the doings of its past, and present, members; and the various College records were collated and supplemented in a list initiated by the Executive Committee of *The Cambridge Review* and published by them from time to time. This list, the seventh and last edition of which appeared in April 1917, while the Battle of Arras was at its height, was the product of the patient and arduous work of Mr J. Austin Fabb, printer of *The Cambridge Review*; and, though no edition was published after the date mentioned above, Mr Fabb continued his efforts to keep the list up to date until, in December 1919, the publication of an official list was undertaken by the Syndics of the Press. The present War List is thus founded on the invaluable work of Mr Fabb, and it is fitting that the first words of this book should be a tribute to his labours.

But there remained much to be done. Mr Fabb had at no time had access to the Army List; to keep pace with the lists of casualties and distinctions alone was the utmost that human energy could compass during the war—to extract the promotions daily announced in *The London Gazette* had been quite out of the question. It was therefore obvious in December 1919 that, if anything like accuracy in the mere matter of rank was to be attained, it was necessary that every name should be checked with the official Service lists. This has duly been done, and after a prolonged and painful experience of the Army List and kindred publications the editor finds himself, if not confident of complete accuracy, at any rate conscious of having made some progress towards it.

There were also other problems to be tackled; and not the least of these were the three main questions: what, for the purposes of an official record, should be the definition of a Cambridge man, what should constitute " service," and what date should be regarded as marking the end of the war? Perhaps the chief difficulty in compiling a work of this nature is that of dealing with "border-line cases." No border-line can be drawn which eliminates altogether the doubtful case, nor one which, in some of its exclusions and inclusions, is wholly consistent with individual justice; the best that can be done is to make the line as clean-cut and as intelligible as possible. Before deciding the principles on which the present list should be based, the Syndics of the Press took counsel with representatives of the Colleges, and a general agreement was reached. It is hoped that the following outline, in conjunction with the List of Abbreviations, which has been drawn up with an eye to a generation unfamiliar with the naval and military common-places of to-day, will make plain to every reader both the broad principles and the details of this book.

UNIVERSITY QUALIFICATION. It was felt that, as an official record of the war services of Cambridge men, this list ought to include only those who were Cambridge men at the time of their war service. Thus the names of many hundreds who matriculated after serving in the war have been deliberately omitted, and *residence prior to war service* as a dividing-line has been closely adhered to, with one exception: it was decided to include those who had been admitted for the Michaelmas Term of 1914 and were prevented from coming into residence in that term only by the fact of having joined the Forces at the outbreak of war.

SERVICE QUALIFICATION. Only those who served in some branch of His Majesty's Forces are included in this list. The Army, Navy, and Air Force Lists have formed the criterion throughout, though some latitude has been used in the case of Colonial volunteer units, which, though they do not appear in the Army List, in some instances engaged in actual fighting. This ruling necessarily excludes the names of many who performed valuable, distinguished, and often dangerous services in the war; but it was felt to be the only principle that could afford a comparatively clear dividing-line.

PERIOD OF SERVICE. For the purposes of this record, the war

closes with the armistice of November 11th, 1918. No event which took place after that date has been recorded, except deaths caused by, and honours awarded for, service prior to the armistice.

RANK. The differences between substantive, temporary, and acting rank became somewhat complicated, and the terms themselves altered in meaning, during the war. This list therefore aims at giving the highest rank held for an appreciable period, irrespective of its category—honorary rank is the only kind that is specifically stated. In cases where the service included staff appointments, the highest staff appointment attained is given.

REGIMENT, etc. The individual career of nearly every officer and man in the Army included service, if not in more than one regiment, at least in more than one battalion of the same regiment. To specify each battalion was clearly impracticable; but where transfers to different regiments, or to different arms of the service, took place, they have been recorded, so far as they are known, with the highest rank held in each regiment or arm. The semi-colon is used to separate successive stages of service.

CASUALTIES. All deaths which occurred from any cause whatsoever during service with the Forces previous to the armistice are recorded with a cross against the entry. Wherever possible, the actual date of death is given; a date given in parentheses represents the date of publication of the casualty list in which the death was announced. Deaths which have taken place since the armistice are not recorded, unless they were the result of wounds or other causes directly attributable to service prior to the armistice; in a few cases where death after the armistice may have been indirectly due to war service, a footnote has been added.

Casualties due to gas-poisoning were, for the greater part of the war, included among the "wounded" in the official casualty lists; injuries due to accident, on the other hand, were not so included. The same principle has been adopted in this list.

In cases where a "(W.)" appears against the name of one who died of wounds, it refers to an occasion other than that which resulted in death.

HONOURS AND AWARDS. Distinctions gained for service in the war are shown in italics after the description of rank, regiment, etc., and are, approximately, in order of dignity and not in the order in which they were gained; pre-war distinctions are given in small capitals immediately after the surname and initials.

In compiling the present list I have received assistance from various quarters. My thanks are due first and foremost to my wife, whose patient help alone enabled me to carry through the task of checking each entry with the Army, Navy, or Air Force Lists; in the compilation of the Summary also she has borne a large share of the work. The Index is the work of Mr H. A. Parsons, of the University Press, and others of my colleagues on the staff of the Press have given me valuable advice and help. I am indebted to the Commanding Officer, the Adjutant, and the Headquarters staff of the Cambridge University Officers Training Corps for facilities readily granted to me at all times to consult their documents; and to the Registrar of the India Office for the loan of a copy of the Indian Army List. To the officials of several of the Colleges, whether Master, Fellow, or clerk, my acknowledgments are due for careful co-operation in compiling the portions of the book relating to their respective Colleges; and, last but not least, I wish to thank all those who, in answer to my appeals in the public press, sent me first-hand information of their services. I am only too conscious that, even now, this record must fall far short of completeness and accuracy, and I shall be grateful if those who discover mistakes or omissions will draw my attention to them. Finally, if any lover of statistics should feel tempted to test the accuracy of the Summary, I sincerely hope that the temptation may be too strong for him.

G. V. C.

UNIVERSITY PRESS,
September, 1921.

LIST OF ABBREVIATIONS

(A.) = Aeroplane officer
(A. and S.) = Aeroplane and Seaplane officer
A.A. and Q.M.G. = Assistant Adjutant and Quartermaster-General
A.A.G. = Assistant Adjutant-General
A.B. = Able Seaman
A.C.G. = Assistant Chaplain-General
(Ad.) = Administrative officer
A.D. = Assistant Director
A.D.C. = Aide-de-Camp
A.D.G.T. = Assistant Director-General of Transportation
Adjt. = Adjutant
A.D.M.S. = Assistant Director of Medical Services
A.D.O.S. = Assistant Director of Ordnance Services
A.D.S. and T. = Assistant Director of Supplies and Transport
A.F.C. = Air Force Cross
A.I.G.T. = Assistant Inspector-General of Transportation
A.M.C. = Army Medical Corps
A.M.L.O. = Assistant Military Landing Officer
A.M.S. = Army Medical Service
A.P.M. = Assistant Provost-Marshal
A.Q.M.G. = Assistant Quartermaster-General
attd. = attached
Bde. = Brigade
Bdr. = Bombardier
Bn. = Battalion
B.S.M. = Battery Sergeant-Major
Bt. = Brevet
Bty. = Battery
Capt. = Captain
C.B. = Companion of the Order of the Bath
C.B.E. = Companion of the Order of the British Empire
Cdr. = Commander
C.F. = Chaplain to the Forces
C.I.E. = Companion of the Order of the Indian Empire
cmdg. = commanding
Cmdt. = Commandant
C.M.G. = Companion of the Order of St Michael and St George
Corpl. = Corporal
Coy. = Company
C.P.O. = Chief Petty Officer

C.Q.M.S. = Company Quartermaster-Sergeant
C.R.E. = Commanding Royal Engineers
C.S.I. = Companion of the Order of the Star of India
C.S.M. = Company Sergeant-Major
D. (in "D. of Wellington's," etc.) = Duke
D.A. and Q.M.G. = Deputy Adjutant and Quartermaster-General
D.A.A. and Q.M.G. = Deputy Assistant Adjutant and Quartermaster-General
D.A.A.G. = Deputy Assistant Adjutant-General
D.A.C.G. = Deputy Assistant Chaplain-General
D.A.D. = Deputy Assistant Director
D.A.D.M.S. = Deputy Assistant Director of Medical Services
D.A.D.O.S. = Deputy Assistant Director of Ordnance Services
D.A.D.R.T. = Deputy Assistant Director of Railway Traffic
D.A.D.S.andT. = Deputy Assistant Director of Supplies and Transport
D.A.D.V.S. = Deputy Assistant Director of Veterinary Services
D.A.G. = Deputy Adjutant-General
D.A.M.S. = Deputy Assistant Military Secretary
D.A.P.C. = Deputy Assistant Principal Chaplain
D.A.P.M. = Deputy Assistant Provost-Marshal
D.A.Q.M.G. = Deputy Assistant Quartermaster-General
D.C.M. = Distinguished Conduct Medal
D.D. = Deputy Director
D.D.M.S. = Deputy Director of Medical Services
Dep. = Deputy
Dept. = Department
D.F.C. = Distinguished Flying Cross
D.G.T. = Director-General of Transportation
Div. = Divisional
D.Q.M.G. = Deputy Quartermaster-General
D.S.andT. = Director of Supplies and Transport

D.S.C. = Distinguished Service Cross
D.S.O. = Distinguished Service Order (Companion of)
E. = East, or Eastern
empld. = employed
E.O. = Equipment Officer
Exp. = Expeditionary
F.A. = Field Artillery
Flt. = Flight
Fus. = Fusiliers
G.B.E. = Knight Grand Cross of the Order of the British Empire
G.C.I.E. = Knight Grand Cross of the Order of the Indian Empire
Gds. = Guards
Gen. = General
Gnr. = Gunner
G.S.O. (1, 2, 3) = General Staff Officer (1st, 2nd, 3rd grade)
H.A. = Heavy Artillery
H.A.C. = Honourable Artillery Company
Hdrs. = Highlanders
H.Q. = Headquarters
I.A.R.O. = Indian Army Reserve of Officers
i/c = in charge of
Imp. = Imperial
I.M.S. = Indian Medical Service
Infy. = Infantry
I.O.M. = Inspector of Ordnance Machinery
K. (in "K. Edward's Horse," etc.) = King
(K.B.) = Kite-Balloon officer
K.B.E. = Knight Commander of the Order of the British Empire
K.C.B. = Knight Commander of the Order of the Bath
K.C.M.G. = Knight Commander of the Order of St Michael and St George
K.C.S.I. = Knight Commander of the Order of the Star of India
Lce. = Lance
L.I. = Light Infantry
Lieut. = Lieutenant
Lieut.-Col. = Lieutenant-Colonel
L. of C. = Lines of Communication
L.R.B. = London Rifle Brigade
M., *M*2., etc. = Mentioned in despatches once, twice, etc.
m., *m*2., etc. = mentioned (once, twice, etc.) in the Secretary of State's list, for valuable services in connection with the war
M.B.E. = Member of the Order of the British Empire
M.C. = Military Cross

Mech. = Mechanic
Med. = Medical
M.G. = Machine Gun
M.G.C. = Machine Gun Corps
M.L.O. = Military Landing Officer
M.M. = Military Medal
M.O. = Medical Officer
M.S.M. = Meritorious Service Medal
(M.T.) = Mechanical Transport
Mtd. = Mounted
M.V.O. = Member of the Royal Victorian Order
N. = North, or Northern
(O.) = Observer officer
O.B.E. = Officer of the Order of the British Empire
O.C.B. = Officer Cadet Battalion
O.T.C. = Officers Training Corps
(P.) = Prisoner of War
P. and B.T. = Physical and Bayonet Training
P.O. = Petty Officer
P. of W. Coy. (Camp) = Prisoners of War Company (Camp)
Prob. = Probationer
P.S.Bn. = Public Schools Battalion
Pte. = Private
Q.M. = Quartermaster
Q.M.G. = Quartermaster-General
Q.M.S. = Quartermaster-Sergeant
Q.V.R. = Queen Victoria's Rifles
R. = Royal
R.A. = Royal Artillery
R.A.C.D. = Royal Army Chaplains' Department
R.A.F. = Royal Air Force
R.A.M.C. = Royal Army Medical Corps
R.A.O.C. = Royal Army Ordnance Corps
R.A.S.C. = Royal Army Service Corps
R.A.V.C. = Royal Army Veterinary Corps
R.E. = Royal Engineers
Regt. = Regiment
Res. = Reserve
ret. = retired
R.F.A. = Royal Field Artillery
R.F.C. = Royal Flying Corps
Rfn. = Rifleman
R.G.A. = Royal Garrison Artillery
R.H.A. = Royal Horse Artillery
R.M.A. = Royal Marine Artillery
R.M.A.,Woolwich = Royal Military Academy, Woolwich
R.M.C. = Royal Military College
R.M.L.I. = Royal Marine Light Infantry

R.N. = Royal Navy
R.N.A.S. = Royal Naval Air Service
R.N.D. = Royal Naval Division
R.N.R. = Royal Naval Reserve
R.N.V.R. = Royal Naval Volunteer
  Reserve
R. of O. = Reserve of Officers
R.Q.M.S. = Regimental Quarter-
  master-Sergeant
R.S.M. = Regimental Sergeant-Major
R.T.O. = Railway Traffic Officer, or
  Railway Transport Officer
S. = South, or Southern
(S.) = Seaplane officer
S. and T. Corps. = Supply and Trans-
  port Corps
Sergt. = Sergeant

S.O. (1, 2, 3) = Staff Officer (1st, 2nd,
  3rd Grade)
Spec. = Special
Sqdn. = Squadron
Supt. = Superintendent
(T.) = Technical officer
T.D. = Territorial Decoration
T.F. = Territorial Force
T.M.B. = Trench Mortar Battery
Unattd. = Unattached
V.D. = Volunteer Decoration
Vol. = Volunteer
W. = West, or Western
(W.), (W2.), etc. = Wounded once,
  twice, etc.
Yeo. = Yeomanry

NOTE. The date inserted with each entry is the year of matriculation, except in the following cases:

(i) For those who were admitted for the Michaelmas Term of 1914, but who never actually matriculated, the year is shown as [1914].

(ii) A date marked with an asterisk denotes that the person to whom the entry refers joined the College in that year by some procedure other than matriculation, e.g. by migration from another College or the non-collegiate body.

ADDITIONS AND CORRECTIONS

Page 131   *After* FRASER, D. H. *read as follows*: Capt., R.A.M.C.; attd. R.A.F. *O.B.E. M.C. Médaille de la Reconnaissance Française, 2nd Class, and Médaille des Epidémies.*

150   *For* RIX, R. G. *read* RIX, R. G. B.

260   *For* M'LACHLAN, T. K. *read* MACLACHLAN, T. K.

277   *After* WADHAM, W. F. A., V.D. *read* Lieut.-Col., King's Own (R. Lancaster Regt., T.F.) *m.*

406   *Add* HARWOOD, H. M. Capt., R.A.M.C.(T.F.) 1892

421   *Add* LAWSON, H. B. Lieut., London Regt. (Kensington Bn.); attd. Manchester Regt.(T.F.) *M.C.* 1916

446   *For* PRICE, Rt. Rev. McC. E. *read* PRICE, Rt. Rev. H. McC. E.

538   *For* MURDOCK, A. J. *read* MURDOCH, A. J.

"WE PASS TO THE THOUGHT OF THE MANY WHO WILL NOT RETURN; NOT BECAUSE OF ANY CHANGE OF PLAN, BUT BECAUSE THE OFFER WHICH ALL HAVE MADE HAS IN THEIR CASE BEEN ACCEPTED TO THE FULL....FOR THESE NO PRIVILEGE THAT WE CAN DEVISE AVAILS. YET THE UNIVERSITY BEARS THEM UPON HER HEART, AND WILL NOT, I KNOW, NEGLECT TO PERPETUATE THE MEMORY OF THEM IN SUCH SORT THAT IT MAY SPEAK TO THE YOUTH OF ENGLAND IN TIME TO COME....MANY AND DIVERSE WERE THE HOPES AND EXPECTATIONS WE HAD FORMED FOR THEM, BUT EVERY ONE OF THESE HAS BEEN SURPASSED BY THE EVENT. THEY HAVE ALL BEEN FOUND CAPABLE OF MAKING THE GREATEST DENIAL OF SELF THAT MEN CAN MAKE. τὸ ζῆν ἀνήλωσαν εἰς τὸ τοὺς ἄλλους καλῶς ζῆν: THEY PAID AWAY THEIR OWN LIFE THAT THE LIFE OF THEIR FELLOWS MIGHT BE HAPPY."

Dr M. R. JAMES, *in his Address to the Senate, 1 October* 1915.

CHRIST'S COLLEGE

✠ABBOTT, C. H.   2nd Lieut., Lincolnshire Regt.   1915
  Died 7 May 1917 of wounds received in action
ADAMI, J. G.   Colonel, Canadian A.M.C.; A.D.M.S.   1880
  C.B.E.
ADAMS, F. S.   Capt., R.A.M.C.   (W.)   1903
✠ADCOCK, H. M.   Capt., Lancs. Fus.   1909
  Killed in action 5 July 1916
ADSHEAD, H. E.   2nd Lieut., R.E.   1908
ADSHEAD, M. S.   Lieut., Cheshire Regt.   [1914]
AGER, Rev. A. D.   Chaplain, R.N.   1906
AGIUS, Rev. T. A.   C.F. 4th Class, R.A.C.D.   (W.)   1910
AINSWORTH DAVIS, J. C.   Capt., Rifle Brigade; Hon. Capt.   1914
  (O.), R.A.F.   (W.)   *M.*
✠AIREY, T. A.   Pte., London Regt. (London Scottish)   1913   *Thomas A Westme*
  Killed in action 1 July 1916
AKAM, Rev. J. W.   2nd Lieut., R.A.S.C.   1912
AKERMAN, E. J. B.   Major, Somerset L.I.; D.A.Q.M.G.   1904
  (W.)   *M.C.   French Croix de Guerre*
ALAN-WILLIAMS, A. C.   Capt., Warwickshire Yeo.;   1908
  A.D.C.   (W.)   *M.C.*
ALDRIDGE, C. B. M.   Capt., R.A.M.C.   1896
✠ALLEN, J. S.   Major, Northumberland Fus.   (W.)   *M.C.*   1910
  Killed in action 11 April 1918
ALLEN, R. C.   Lieut.-Col., Auckland Regt., N. Zealand   1899
  Force.   *D.S.O. and Bar.   M.*
ALLEN, W. H.   Major, R.A.M.C.   1887
ANDERSON, H.   2nd Lieut., S. Staffs. Regt.   1910
ANGUS, W. B. G.   Major, R.A.M.C.   *O.B.E.   M.C.   M.*   1903
ARMOUR, J. K. C.   Lieut., R.G.A.   1914
✠ARMSTRONG, F. M.   Major, R.F.A.(T.F.)   *M.*   1896
  Killed in action 25 Sept. 1917

ARNOLD, W. Major, R.F.A.; empld. Ministry of Muni- 1897
tions. (W 3.)
ARTHUR, W. L. Capt., Channel Islands Militia, empld. 1902
R. Jersey Garrison Bn.
ASHLEY, N. D. 2nd Lieut., R.A.S.C.(M.T.) 1913
ASHWORTH, J. Lieut., R.A.S.C. *m.* 1908
ASTBURY, Rev. H. S. C.F. 4th Class, R.A.C.D. *M.C.* 1909
ASTLEY, W. Major, R.E. (W.) 1900
ATCHISON, G. T. Lieut., Bedford Grammar School O.T.C. 1896
AUDEN, G. A. Major, R.A.M.C.(T.F.); D.A.D.M.S. 1890

✠BAINES, A. B. Capt., Oxford and Bucks. L.I. (W.) 1907
Killed in action 3 April 1917
BAINES, D. L. Major, Uganda Vol. Regt. *O.B.E.* 1900
BAKER, T. Y. Instructor Cdr., R.N. *Chevalier, Legion* 1895
of Honour (France)
BAKEWELL, B. Lieut., R.F.A. (W 2.) *M.* 1909
BANISTER, T. E. Capt., R.A.M.C. 1905
BANKS, L. 2nd Lieut., 1st Brahmans, Indian Army 1909
✠BANYARD, J. H. 2nd Lieut., Bedfordshire Regt. *1907
Killed in action 3 Sept. 1916
BAPTIE, N. Pte., London Regt. 1907
BARBER, W. E. Capt., Seaforth Hdrs.; attd. Gen. Staff. *m*2. 1903
BARCLAY, A. E. Capt., R.A.M.C. (2nd W. Gen. Hos- 1894
pital, T.F.)
BARFF, Rev. F. R. Chaplain, R.N. 1907
BARKER, A. Lieut., Worcestershire Regt. (W.) 1915
BARLOW, R. G. Capt., Seaforth Hdrs. (W.) 1911
BARNARD, H. J. Lieut., Gen. List, empld. T.M.B. (W.) [1914]
BARR, G. Lieut. (Ad.), R.A.F. 1904
BARRAN, P. A. Major, R.F.A.(T.F.); empld. Ministry 1897
of Munitions
BARRETT, L. Lieut., R.E. (Fortress, T.F.). 1910
BARRETT, Rev. L. T. S. Chaplain, R.N. 1905
BARTLETT, A. W. Lieut., R.A.M.C. (Sanitary Service, *1902
T.F.)
BARTLEY, Rev. P. R. C.F. 4th Class, R.A.C.D. 1893
BARWICK, R. L. Capt., R.A.M.C. 1897
BASHFORD, P. F. R. Capt., R.N.R. 1904
BATEMAN, W. Lieut., King's Own (Yorkshire L.I.) [1914]
(W.) (P.)
✠BATTY, G. G. H. Capt., Northamptonshire Regt. 1913
Died 27 Sept. 1916 *of wounds received in action 26 Sept.*
1916

BEAUMONT, D. C.   Capt., R.A.M.C.   1912
BEAUMONT, O. A.   Capt., R.A.M.C.   *M.C. M.*   1909
BECK, G. R.   Lieut., London Regt. (Blackheath and   [1914]
   Woolwich Bn.); Capt. (A.), R.A.F.
✠BECKETT, V. L. S.   Major, Yorkshire Regt.   1901
   Died 19 July 1916 of wounds received in action 5 July
   1916
BEDDOW, H. J.   Capt., R.A.M.C.   1897
BEECROFT, A. E.   Capt. and Adjt., R.E.   *M.B.E.*   1906
BEEDHAM, H. W.   Capt., R.A.M.C.(T.F.)   1887
✠BELL, Rev. C. H.   C.F. 4th Class, R.A.C.D.   *M.C.*   1907
   Killed in action 23 Aug. 1918
BELL, Rev. J. A. H.   C.F. 4th Class, R.A.C.D.   *M.C. M.*   1908
BENBOW, H.   Major, E. Surrey Regt.   *1894
BENGOUGH CLARK, J.   *See* CLARK, J. B.
BENNETT, E. B.   Pte., R.A.S.C.(M.T.)   1909
BENNETT, F. G.   Capt., R.A.M.C.(T.F.)   *M.*   1891
BENNETT, G. L.   Hon. Major, Lincolnshire Regt. and 1885
   Labour Corps.   *M* 2.
BENOLY, H. J.   Pte., R.A.M.C.; Sapper, R.E.   1909
BETTERIDGE, B. F.   2nd Lieut., Northamptonshire Regt. 1912
BETTERIDGE, H. G. W.   Pte., R. Fusiliers   1913
BICKNELL, R. P.   2nd Lieut., R. Marines   1893
BIGGAR, C. L. P.   Lieut., Hampshire Regt. (W.)   *M.C.* 1912
   M 2.
BIGG-WITHER, H. S.   Major, R.A.O.C.; D.A.Q.M.G.   1907
   O.B.E. M.
BILDERBECK, A. C. L. O'S.   Capt., I.M.S.   *M.*   1907
BINKS, B. B.   Lieut., R.A.S.C.(T.F.)   1908
BISHOP, R. O.   2nd Lieut., Gen. List, empld. Ministry of 1894
   Munitions.   *M.B.E.*
✠BLACK, M. A.   Major, Dragoon Gds.; attd. R.F.C.   (W.) 1895
   Killed in action 11 Feb. 1917
BLACK, R. A.   Capt., King's (Shropshire L.I.); A.M.L.O. 1896
BLACKBURN, W. H.   Surgeon Lieut., R.N.   1911
BLACKBURNE, Rev. E. V.   C.F. 4th Class, R.A.C.D.   1907
BLACKLEDGE, R. D.   Pte., R. Scots; Capt., Highland L.I. 1910
   (P.)   *M.C.*
BLANCH, N. H.   Lieut., R.F.A.(T.F.)   1914
✠BLIGH, E.   Lieut., E. Lancs. Regt.   1913
   Killed in action 9 May 1915
BLISS, E. W.   Lieut., Labour Corps   1908
BLYTH, A. C.   Capt., Norfolk Regt. (W.)   *M.C.*   1909
BONNALIE, F. E.   Lieut., R.F.A.   1914

✠BONSER, W. J. Capt., Rifle Brigade   1904
    Killed in action 25 Sept. 1915
BOOTH, A. F. Instructor Lieut., R.N.   1912
BOOTY, M. G. R. Pte., H.A.C.   1904
BOTTOME, G. M. Major, R.A.S.C. (Canteens). *M* 2.   1906
BOULTBEE, Rev. H. T. C.F., Australian Chaplains' Dept.   1904
✠BOURNE, J. C. 2nd Lieut., Worcestershire Regt.   *1892
    Killed in action 18 *July* 1915
BOUSFIELD, H. T. W. Lieut., I.A.R.O., attd. 9th Bhopal   1909
    Infy. *M.*
BOWEN, G. Pte., London Regt. (Artists Rifles)   1901
BRANSTON, R. Cadet, O.C.B.   1914
✠BRASNETT, T. J. G. 2nd Lieut., E. Surrey Regt.   1912
    Killed in action at the Hohenzollern Redoubt 13 *Oct.* 1915
BRAWN, J. A. Lieut., R.E.(T.F.)   1912
BRIERLEY, W. B. Sergt., Indian Army   1905
BRIGGS, P. J. Pte., H.A.C. (W.)   1912
BRIGGS, W. R. Capt., Spec. List (Staff Capt.). *O.B.E.*   1901
BRISTOW, C. H. Lieut., I.A.R.O., attd. 4th Gurkha   1906
    Rifles. (W.)
BRITTAIN, A. W. 2nd Lieut., Sherwood Foresters (Notts.   1909
    and Derby Regt.)
BROCKLEHURST, H. 2nd Lieut., Northumberland Fus.   1914
BRODE, Rev. R. T. Pte., London Regt. (Artists Rifles)   1911
BROOMFIELD, R. S. Lieut., Railway Bn., Indian Defence   1901
    Force
BROSTER, E. D. Surgeon Lieut., R.N.   1910
BROWN, A. E. Lieut., Australian A.M.C. *M.*   1907
BROWN, C. A. 2nd Lieut., R. Welsh Fus.   1893
BROWN, G. W. Lieut., Queen's Own (R.W. Kent Regt.);   1912
    Capt., Spec. List (School of Instruction). (W.) *M.B.E.*
BROWN, L. T. Pte., R. Fusiliers   1913
BROWNING, T. C. Lieut.-Col., Supernumerary List,   1888
    Indian Army
BRYCESON, E. Lieut., Canadian A.M.C.; Capt., R.A.M.C.   1876
BUNTING, S. A. S. Lieut., I.A.R.O., attd. Sappers and   1901
    Miners. *M.B.E.*
BURDON, Hon. J. A., C.M.G. Major, Barbados Vols. *m.*   1885
BURKITT, F. T. Capt., The Queen's (R.W. Surrey Regt.)   1911
    (W 2.)
BURKITT, Rev. H. J. C.F. 2nd Class, R.A.C.D.(T.F.)   1888
BURROW, Rev. W. J. A. C.F. 4th Class, R.A.C.D.   1902
✠BURTON-FANNING, N. E. E. Capt., R.M.L.I.   [1914]
    Killed in action at Gavrelle 28 *April* 1917

✠Buszard, S. G. Lieut., Norfolk Yeo.   1908
  Killed in action 8 Dec. 17
Butt, H. T. H. Capt., R.A.M.C.   1902
Butterwick, J. C. 2nd Lieut., Eton College O.T.C.   1909
Butterworth, R. Lieut., R.A.M.C.   1889
Buttery, H. R. Surgeon Lieut., R.N.   1906
Bygrave, W. 2nd Lieut., Blundell's School O.T.C.   1901
Byrne, Rev. J. H. C.F. 4th Class, N. Zealand Chaplains'   *1913
  Dept.

Cadman, H. S. Capt., Denstone College O.T.C.   1896
Caiger, Rev. S. L. C.F. 4th Class, R.A.C.D.   1905
Canney, J. R. C. Capt., R.A.M.C.(T.F.)   1901
Capon, E. O. Lieut., R. Berkshire Regt. and R. Defence   1891
  Corps
Cardwell, H. E. 2nd Lieut. (A.), R.A.F.   1898
Carlton-Williams, E. W. Flt. Sub-Lieut., R.N.A.S.   1909
Carmichael, Rev. D. W. W. C.F. 4th Class, R.A.C.D.   1898
Carr, J. D. 2nd Lieut., Worcestershire Regt.   1897
✠Carrington, E.A. A.B., R.N.V.R.; 2nd Lieut., Wiltshire   1911
  Regt. (W.)
  Killed in action at Gueudecourt 18 Oct. 1916
Carstairs, J. L. Capt., R.E.   1901
✠Carter, G. L. L. Asst. Paymaster, R.N.R.; Instructor   1910
  Lieut., R.N.
  Died 29 July 1918 of pneumonia
Cartwright, S. H. Lieut., R.F.A. (W.)   1915
Castell, S. P. Lieut., R.A.M.C.   1913
Cator, A. N. L. Lieut., Hyderabad Rifles, Indian De-   1899
  fence Force
Cattell, McK. Sergt., United States Army   1912
Chaffey, Rev. L. B. T. Lieut., Eton College O.T.C.   1894
Challoner, J. L. Lieut., Northumberland Fus. and   1913
  M.G.C. (W 2.)
Chapman, H. Corpl., R.E. (Signals); Major, D. of Corn-   1905
  wall's L.I. (W 2.) M 2.
Charlesworth, J. B. 2nd Lieut., R.F.A.   [1914]
Chiene, G. L. Major, R.A.M.C.(T.F.)   1891
Child, F. J. Capt., R.A.M.C.   1893
Child, W. N. Capt., R.A.M.C.   1901
Chivers, W. B. Lieut., Middlesex Regt.   1912
Clark, J. B. Lieut., R. North Devon Yeo.   1877
Clarke, E. B. 2nd Lieut., Gloucestershire Regt. (P.)   1913
Clarke, W. S. Major, Gloucestershire Regt.   *1888

CLEEVE, C. E. Major, R.A.S.C.(M.T.) *O.B.E. M.* 1909
CLOUGH, J. 2nd Lieut., Yorkshire Regt.; Major, Tank 1912
    Corps. (W 3.) *D.S.O. M.C. M.*
CLOUGH, Rev. V. C.F. 4th Class, R.A.C.D. 1908
COCHRAN, G. G. Lieut., R.E. *M.* 1914
COCKTON, J. C. Lieut., Westmorland and Cumberland 1910
    Yeo.
✠COHEN, G. H. Lieut., King's (Liverpool Regt., T.F.) 1897
    Killed in action near La Bassée 16 May 1915
COLEY, C. Lieut., Suffolk Regt. 1909
COLLINGRIDGE, W. Lieut.-Col., R.A.M.C.(T.F.) 1875
COLLINS, G. A. Capt., Rifle Brigade 1907
CONNETT, H. Capt., United States Army 1913
COOK, V. C. Pte., H.A.C.; Capt., R.A.S.C.(M.T.) 1904
    O.B.E. M.
COPE, J. L. Lieut., R.N.R. 1911
✠COPEMAN, E. H. Pte., Middlesex Regt.; 2nd Lieut., 1906
    Queen's Own (R. W. Kent Regt.)
    Killed in action 18 March 1916
CORFIELD, Rev. F. DE LA P. C.F. 4th Class, R.A.C.D. 1893
CORY, J. F. T. Trooper, Berkshire Yeo. *1906
✠COTTERILL, D. Capt., R.A.M.C. 1900
    Died 2 Dec. 1918 of pneumonia contracted on active
    service
COX, G. L. Capt., R.A.M.C 1898
COXWELL, C. B. 2nd Lieut., R.M.A. 1908
CRABTREE, Rev. H. G. C.F. 3rd Class, R.A.C.D. *M.C.* 1898
✠CRANE, H. E. Pte., R. Fusiliers 1903
    Died 27 Oct. 1916
CRAWFORD, G. B. Lieut., Yorkshire Regt. 1910
CRAWSHAW, C. B. H. Capt., R.E. *M.C. M.* 1912
CRAWSHAW, C. H. Major, R.A.M.C (T.F.) *M.* 1906
✠CREED, Rev. A. H. G. Chaplain, R.N. *1884
    Died 21 May 1917
✠CRESSEY, G. E. L. Lieut., Yorkshire Regt. [1914]
    Killed in action 26 Sept. 1915
CROOK, A. H. Surgeon Lieut., R.N.V.R. *M.* 1902
CROSBY, G. J. V. 2nd Lieut., R.E.(T.F.) 1916
CROWDER, G.C.G. Lieut.,Border Regt.and M.G.C. (W.) 1910
CUMBERLIDGE, W. I. Capt., R.A.M.C.(T.F.) 1899
CUNLIFFE, J. H. G. 2nd Lieut., R. Marines 1912

DAVENPORT, H. Lieut., W. Yorks. Regt. (W.) (P.) 1909
DAVENPORT, S. Capt. (Airship), R.A.F. *m.* 1907

DAVIDSON, A. Major, Border Regt. 1894
DAVIDSON, Sir W. E., K.C.M.G. Hon. Colonel, R. New- 1878
foundland Regt.
DAVIES, E. D. D. Surgeon Lieut., R.N.; Surgeon, 1907
R.M.L.I.
DAVIES, Rev. L. C. C.F. 4th Class, R.A.C.D. 1906
DAVIES, Rev. R. E. C.F. 4th Class, R.A.C.D. *1899
DAVIS, J. C. A. *See* AINSWORTH DAVIS, J. C.
DAWES, H. J. Lieut., Spec. List (Dental Surgeon) *1908
DAWSON, Rev. H. P. Chaplain, R.N. 1881
DE BARATHY, S. A. Lieut., Alberta Regt., Canadian Force. *1896
(W.)
DE LA PRYME, W. H. A. Major, W. Yorks. Regt.; Staff 1899
Capt., War Office. (W.) *D.S.O. M. m. Chevalier,*
Order of Leopold (Belgium)
✠DENNES, W. Major, R.F.A. *M.C. and Bar* 1908
Killed in action 21 March 1918
DESOER, A. Sergt., Belgian Artillery 1915
DIBB, R. K. Major, E. Yorks. Regt. (W 2.) *M.* 1913
DICKSON, H. S. Capt., R.A.M.C. (W 2.) 1898
DILLON, H. G. S. Lieut., R.N.V.R. 1907
DIPPIE, H. Major, Worcestershire Regt. (W.) *D.S.O.* *1906
M.
DIXON, A. F. W. Capt., Border Regt.(T.F.) (W.) 1911
DIXON, A. H. Capt., Norfolk Regt. (Cyclist Bn., T.F.) 1911
(W.)
DOBELL, H. Sapper, R.N.D. Engineers; Capt., R. 1901
Marines; Lieut.-Cdr., R.N.V.R.; Major (A.), R.A.F.
(P.)
DODD, A. H. 2nd Lieut., Unattd. List, T.F. 1910
DODDRELL, Rev. E. C. C.F. 4th Class, R.A.C.D. *1890
DODWELL, G. M. Capt., R.F.A. (W.) 1902
DOUGLAS, R. O. Lieut., Queen's Own (R.W. Kent Regt.) [1914]
DOVE, W. B. Capt., R.A.M.C. 1890
✠DOWNIE, J. M. Capt., R.A.M.C. 1911
Died 29 Oct. 1918 *of pneumonia*
DOWSON, W. J. Pte., Nairobi Defence Force 1906
DRUMMOND, J. G. Lieut., I.A.R.O., attd. 42nd Cavalry; 1903
Capt. and Adjt., Hodson's Horse
DUIGAN, W. Capt., R.A.M.C.(3rd S. Gen. Hospital, T.F.) 1883
DUNBAR, R. Capt., R.F.A. (W 2.) *M.C. M.* 1914
✠DYER, C. M. 2nd Lieut., Rifle Brigade 1912
Killed in action 9 April 1915

EARLES, F. J. Capt., Manchester Regt. (W.)   1912
ECKENSTEIN, T. C. Capt., S. Lancs. Regt. (W 2.) *M.C.*   1904
EDDISON, H. W. Surgeon Lieut., R.N.   1911
EDE, J. C. Sergt., E. Surrey Regt.   1903
EDWARDS, D. L. P. Capt., Spec. List (Dental Surgeon)   *1910
✠EDWARDS, D. W. Capt., R.A.S.C.; attd. R.F.C. *M.C.*   *1910
    Killed in action 6 April 1917
EDWARDS, H. W. Capt., R. Warwickshire Regt.; Lieut.-   *1907
    Col.,R.E.; A.D.Signals. *D.S.O. M.C. M*2. *French*
    Croix de Guerre
✠EDWARDS, LL. A. Capt., R. Warwickshire Regt. (W.)   1913
    Died in German hands 21 *March* 1918 *of wounds*
    received in action
EDWARDS, W. N. Pte., R.A.M.C.(T.F.)   1908
ELLIOTT, A. D. Capt., R.E. (Signals)   1902
ELLIOTT, T. R. H. Pte., London Regt.   1912
ELLIS, B. J. Lieut., Worcestershire Regt.; Staff Capt.   *1899
    (W.)
ELLIS, M. F. Capt., R.A.M.C.   1899
ELLISTON, W. R. Major, Suffolk Regt. (Cyclist Bn., T.F.)   1887
EMBLETON, D. Major, R.A.M.C. *M. m.*   1900
ENGLAND,W. B. 2nd Lieut., R. Berkshire Regt.; Lieut.,   1911
    Labour Corps. (W.)
ESCHWEGE, F. S. *See* FOOT, T. J.
ESPIN, C. E. Lieut., Coldstream Gds. (W 2.) *M.C.*   1900
EVISON, R. R. Capt., W. Yorks. Regt.   1904
EWART, G. A. Capt., R.A.M.C. (4th London Gen. Hos-   1906
    pital, T.F.)
EWING, A. W. Capt., R.A.M.C.   1900

✠FAIR, J. C. 2nd Lieut., Coldstream Gds.   1912
    Killed in action 25 *Sept.* 1915
✠FARNHAM, F. J. 2nd Lieut., London Regt. and R.G.A.   1912
    Accidentally killed 15 *April* 1917
FAULCONBRIDGE, F. T. Pte., Worcestershire Regt.   1912
FAWCETT, W. F. Bt. Colonel, cmdg. Depôt, Northamp-   1876
    tonshire Regt.
✠FAWSITT, T. R. Pte., Middlesex Regt. (P. S. Bn.); 2nd   1905
    Lieut., York and Lancaster Regt.
    Killed in action 16 *Sept.* 1916
FAY, C. R. Lieut., The Buffs (E. Kent Regt.); Capt.,   *1909
    M.G.C. and Spec. List (Asst. Instructor). *M.*
FAY, S. J. Capt., R.A.S.C.(M.T.) *M.*   1901
FELLOWS, R. B., C.B. Hon. Colonel, Bedfordshire Regt.   1850

FERGUSON, A. C. W. Lieut., Loyal N. Lancs. Regt. (W.) 1896
FERGUSON, S. C. Major, Northumberland Fus. (R. of O.); 1887
    Embarkation S.O. *O.B.E.* *m.*
FINLAYSON, J. G. Sergt., R.A.M.C. 1904
FISHER, L. G. 2nd Lieut., N. Staffs. Regt. 1914
FISHER-SMITH, E. L. Lieut., R.A.S.C. [1914]
✠FITCH, A. S. 2nd Lieut., R. Sussex Regt. [1914]
    Killed in action 9 *April* 1917
FITCH, E. W. Instructor Cdr., R.N. 1895
FOOT, T. J. Capt., R.A.M.C. 1901
FORBES, J. G. Capt., R.A.M.C. *M.* 1891
FORBES, J. W. F. Capt., Christ's Hospital O.T.C. 1888
FORDER, Rev. F. G. Capt., Charterhouse School O.T.C. 1902
FRANCILLON, F. E. Capt., Gloucestershire Regt. *M.* 1907
FRANCILLON, F. J. Lieut., R. Fusiliers and M.G.C. 1899
FRANCIS, J. A. Capt., R.A.S.C. *M* 2. 1894
FRASER, F. R. Major, R.A.M.C. 1904
FRASER, W. A. Lieut., W. Yorks. Regt. 1911
FREEMAN, H. Lieut. (T.), R.A.F. 1906
FRETZ, W. T. S. Trooper, British S. African Police 1910
FRYER, J. H. Capt., R.A.M.C. 1893
FULTON, E. C. Major, S.O. 2, R.A.F. 1897
FURSE, W. K. 2nd Lieut., R.F.A. 1902

GANDY, E. S. Lieut., Epsom College O.T.C. 1905
GARDINER, A. F. Major, R.F.A. *M.C.* *M.* 1906
GARDINER, O. C. Lieut., R.E.(T.F.) (W.) 1903
✠GARDNER, H. M. Lieut.-Col., Lincolnshire Regt. (W.) 1884
    Died 28 *Oct.* 1918 *of pneumonia*
GASKELL, L. S. Capt., R.A.M.C. 1889
GAY, Rev. J. J. Chaplain, R.N. 1890
✠GIBBONS, A. ST H. Lieut.-Col., R. Fusiliers and King's 1878
    (Liverpool Regt.) *M* 2.
    Died 15 *July* 1916 *of wounds received in action*
GIBSON, I. F. 2nd Lieut., K. Edward's School, Birming- 1909
    ham, O.T.C.
GIBSON, Rev. R. M. C.F. 4th Class, R.A.C.D. 1908
GILBERTSON, W. Capt., R.A.M.C. 1886
GILMORE, A. E. Lieut., Essex Regt. (W.) 1890
GLASER, W. H. 2nd Lieut. (T.), R.A.F. 1910
GLEN, R. A. Lieut., Middlesex Regt. (T.F.Res.) 1894
GLENISTER, D. J. 2nd Lieut., R.G.A. (W.) 1906
GODDARD, F. W. 2nd Lieut., R.F.A. (W.) 1912
GODDARD, J. Major, H.A.C. 1899

GORDON, F. J. Lieut., R.A.M.C.   1900
GOWER-REES, Rev. A. P. C.F. 2nd Class, R.A.C.D. (W.) *1903
  M.C. M.
GRACE, E. M. Capt., R.A.M.C.   1905
GRANT, F. G. Lieut., R.N.V.R.   1902
GRAVES, B. Capt., R.A.M.C. (W.) *M.C.*   1907
GRAY, W. H. Asst. Paymaster, R.N.   1911
GREATHEAD, J. M. Major, R.E. *M.*   1904
✠GREATHEAD, J. R. 2nd Lieut., Rifle Brigade   1914
  Killed in action 23 *Oct.* 1916
GREEN, A. G. N. Lieut., Durham L.I.(T.F.) (P.)   1908
GREEN, GABRIEL. Lieut.-Col., Essex Regt. *M.C.*   *1905
GREEN, GEORGE. Capt., Loyal N. Lancs. Regt.; empld.   1894
  Ministry of Munitions. (W.)
GREENE, L. Capt., Natal and Orange Free State Regt.,   1901
  S. African Force. (W.) *D.S.O. M.C. M.*
GREENWOOD, C. F. 2nd Lieut., Northamptonshire Regt.   1913
  and R.A.S.C.
GRIBBIN, Rev. J. A. C.F. 4th Class, R.A.C.D.   1913
✠GRIFFITH, H. H. Capt. (A.), R.F.C.   1909
  Killed in flying accident 2 *Nov.* 1917
GRIFFITH, J. R. Capt., R.A.M.C.   1905
GROVES, J. D. Capt., Derbyshire Yeo. (W.)   1899
GROVES, W. PEER. Flt.-Cdr., R.N.V.R., attd. R.N.A.S.;   1897
  Major, S.O. 2, R.A.F. *Order of the Rising Sun, 4th
  Class (Japan)*
GUNDRY, P. G. Lieut., R.N.V.R., attd. R.N.A.S.   1900
GUTCH, J. Capt., R.A.M.C.(T.F.)   1889
GUTCH, W. Capt., Yorkshire Hussars; Staff Capt., War   1890
  Office. *m.*

HACKING, A. Major, Gen. List. *O.B.E.*   1896
HADDON, E. B. Hon. Capt., Uganda Carrier Coy.   1901
✠HAIGH, A. G. 2nd Lieut., R.E.   1903
  Killed in action 15 *Feb.* 1916
HALES, G. T. 2nd Lieut., Worcestershire Regt.; empld.   1905
  War Office
HALL, W. Capt., R.E. (Tyne Electrical Engineers, T.F.);   1892
  attd. R. Marines
HAMILTON, A. Capt., R.A.M.C. (W 2.) *Officer, Ordre   1902
  de l'Etoile Noire (France)*
HANCE, J. B. Capt., I.M.S.   1905
HANCOCK, Rev. W. H. M. C.F. 4th Class, R.A.C.D.   1894

HANDCOCK, W. A. S. Lieut., R.A.S.C.   *1904
HANDFORD, Rev. W. B. Chaplain, R.N.R.   1881
HANDS, A. C. Lieut., R. Warwickshire Regt.; Lieut.(Ad.),   1913
   R.A.F.
✠HANNINGTON, G. J. 2nd Lieut., R.A.S.C.(M.T.)   1903
   Accidentally killed 1 *Oct.* 1915
HANSELL, G. F. Lieut., E. Yorks. Regt. and King's Own   1912
   (Yorkshire L.I.) (W.)
HANSON, E. T. 2nd Lieut., R.G.A. (W.)   1901
✠HARDING, Rev. W. J. Pte., R.A.M.C.; Chaplain, R.N.V.R.   1904
   (R.N.D.) *M.C.*
   Killed in action 31 *Oct.* 1917
HARDINGHAM, C. H. Lieut., R.G.A.   1896
HARDY, E. W. D. Capt., R.A.M.C. (W.) *M.C.*   1897
HARE, W. T. Major, R.A.M.C.; D.A.D.M.S. *M.C.*   1907
HARGREAVES, R. Capt., Border Regt. (T.F.)   1910
HARPER, C. H. Major, R.F.A. *M.C. and Bar*   1906
HARRICKS, N. 2nd Lieut., R.A.S.C. and Spec. List   1913
HARRIS, A. A. A.B., R.N.V.R.; Lieut. (K.B.), R.A.F.   1899
HARRIS, E. T. Major, I.M.S. *D.S.O.* *M* 3.   1896
HARRIS, H. E. Capt., R.A.M.C.(T.F.)   1878
HARRIS, H. E. junr. Lieut., King's (Shropshire L.I.);   [1914]
   attd. T.M.B. (W.) *M.C.*
HARRISON, E. M. Capt., Lincolnshire Regt. (W 3.)   1912
HARRISON, P. R.A.M.C.   1893
HARVEY, Rev. C. H. C.F. 4th Class, N. Zealand Chaplains' 1898
   Dept.
✠HARVEY, W. 2nd Lieut., King's (Liverpool Regt.)   1911
   Killed in action 25 *Sept.* 1915
HARVEY, W. H. Capt., R.A.M.C.   1906
✠HARVIE, E. F. Capt., Gordon Hdrs. (W 4.) *M.C.* [1914]
   Killed in action 15 *June* 1918
HARVIE, J. K. Lieut., 3rd Hussars. (W 2.)   1912
HASSARD-SHORT, Rev. F. W. C.F. 4th Class, R.A.C.D. 1892
   (T.F.)
HASTINGS, W. Major, Egyptian A.M.C. *O.B.E.* *M.* 1898
✠HATCH, P. R. Capt., The Buffs (E. Kent Regt.)   1911
   Killed in action 7 *Oct.* 1916
HAWKINS, A. G. J. Lieut., Gen. List (Intelligence). *M* 3. 1906
HAWKINS, R. J. Lieut., R.F.A. (W.)   1911
HAYTON, Rev. J. D. W. C.F. 4th Class, R.A.C.D.   1911
HAYWARD, Rev. G. C.F. 4th Class, R.A.C.D.   *1911
HEATON, R. Capt., R.A.M.C. *M. Serbian Distinguished* 1904
   Service Medal

HENDERSON, J. A. Capt., R.E.   1900
HENDRY, F. H. A. 2nd Lieut., Highland L.I. (W.)   1916
HERKLOTS, H. Lieut., R.A.S.C.   1887
HERRING, J. H. Major (A.), R.A.F. (W.) *D.S.O. M.C.*   1908
  M 2. French Croix de Guerre.
HETT, A. I. Lieut., Bedfordshire Regt. and The Buffs   1912
  (E. Kent Regt.) (W.)
HEYDON, G. A. M. Major, Australian A.M.C. (W.) *M.C.*   1900
✠HINDLE, H. B. Lieut., R.H.A. (W.)   1913
  Killed in action 27 March 1918
HINDLEY, Rev. W. T. C.F. 4th Class, R.A.C.D.(T.F.)   1899
HOBSON, W. W. 2nd Lieut., E. Yorks. Regt.   1913
HODGES, C. E. Major, R.F.A.(T.F.); empld. Ministry   *1903
  of Munitions
HODGSON, A. E. Capt., R.A.M.C. *m.*   1903
HODGSON, T. R. Capt., R.A.S.C.(T.F.)   1901
HODGSON, W. HAMMOND. Capt., R.A.M.C.   1899
HODGSON, W. HARRY. Lieut., King's Own (R. Lancaster   1904
  Regt.) *M.*
HOFFMANN, W. A. *See* ARNOLD, W.
HOGARTH, T. J. Lieut., R.A.S.C.; Major, D.A.D. Labour   1902
HOLLAND, C. C. Capt., R.A.S.C.   1896
HOLLAND, C. E. Lieut., R.N.R.   1884
HOLMES, H. W. H. Major, R.A.M.C. *M*   1913
HOLROYD, G. Capt., I.M.S.   1898
HOLT, R. Pte., R.A.M.C.   1910
HONY, G. B. 2nd Lieut., 4th (R. Irish) Dragoon Gds.;   1912
  Lieut., Res. Regt. of Cavalry. (W.)
HOOD, J. A. 2nd Lieut., R.A.S.C. *M.*   1907
HOOD, Rev. J. C. F. C.F. 4th Class, R.A.C.D.   1902
HOOKER, J. S. Lieut.-Col., 12th Pioneers, Indian Army   1896
✠HORNE, J. A. Pte., London Regt. (Artists Rifles); 2nd   1910
  Lieut., London Regt. (Queen's Westminster Rifles)
  Killed in action 1 July 1916
HORNIMAN, J. E. 2nd Lieut., Essex Regt.   1909
HOSKEN, H. 2nd Lieut., Rifle Brigade; Capt., O.C.B.   1905
HOULTON, J. W. Capt., Suffolk Regt. (W.)   1911
HUDSON, N. B. Lieut.-Col., R. Berkshire Regt. (W 3.)   1912
  D.S.O. and Bar. M.C. and Bar. M 2.
HUMPHREYS, W. H. Cadet, O.C.B.   1905
HURST, W. H. Lieut., R.A.S.C.   1909

INCE, S. R. 2nd Lieut., K. Edward's School, Bath,   1904
  O.T.C.

INNOCENT, A. Trooper, Canadian Mtd. Rifles 1906
INGLES, W. H. S. Pte., Oxford and Bucks. L.I. [1914]
IREDALE, H. C. Lieut., Bedfordshire Regt. (W 2.) 1909

JACKSON, A. C. D. Lieut., E. Lancs. Regt.; Capt., Gen. 1901
  List, empld. Inland Waterways and Docks
JACKSON, Rev. L. J. C.F. 4th Class, R.A.C.D. 1903
JACOB, L. G. Capt., R.A.M.C. 1909
JAMES, A. E. G. Sergt., M.G.C. *1912
JAMES, Rev. T. J. C.F. 4th Class, R.A.C.D. M.C. 1895
✠JAMES, W. M. Capt., Monmouthshire Regt. 1890
  Killed in action 8 Oct. 1918
JARVIS, F. J. Pte., Australian Force *1904
JENKIN, N. W. Capt., R.A.M.C. 1901
JENKINS, J. Capt., Welsh Regt. (W.) M. 1909
JESSOP, G. L. Capt., Manchester Regt. and Gen. List, 1896
  empld. Ministry of National Service
✠JEWITT, D. P. 2nd Lieut., Worcestershire Yeo. 1912
  Killed in action 23 April 1916
JOHNSON, A. V. Capt., Worcestershire Regt. 1912
JONES, E. Capt., R.E. M 2. 1911
JONES, Rev. E. K. C.F. 4th Class, R.A.C.D. 1890
✠JONES, I. C. S. Lieut., King's Own (Yorkshire L.I., T.F.) 1913
  Died 21 Sept. 1916 of wounds received in action
JONES, L. T. P. 2nd Lieut., The Buffs (E. Kent Regt.) 1897
JONES, R. T. P. Capt., R.F.A. 1897
JONES, W. B. Lieut.-Col., Welsh Regt. 1883
JONES, W. H. Surgeon Lieut., R.N. 1900
✠JOSEPH, W. F. G. 2nd Lieut., R. Berkshire Regt. 1901
  Killed in action 27 May 1918
JUPP, A. O. Lieut., Spec. List (Recruiting Staff) 1895

KAPP, E. Lieut., R. Sussex Regt. 1910
✠KARIM KHAN, A. Major, 129th Baluchis, Indian Army 1894
  Killed in action (31 Dec. 1914)
KEARNS, H. W. L. Lieut., R.F.A.(T.F.); Staff Capt. M. 1909
  Belgian Croix de Guerre
✠KELLEHER, H. Pte., Canadian Infy. 1910
  Killed in action April 1915
KEMPSON, Rev. J. H. C.F. 3rd Class, R.A.C.D. M. 1889
✠KENNEDY, R. S. Capt., R.A.M.C. M.C. M. 1906
  Killed in action 17 April 1918
KENT, Rev. N. B. Chaplain, R.N. 1905

KERR, J. G. 2nd Lieut., Cameronians (Scottish Rifles, 1892
T.F.)

✠KITTERMASTER, A. N. C. Capt., Worcestershire Regt. 1890
Killed in action 5 *April* 1916

KNIGHT, R. Lieut., Middlesex Regt.; Capt., T.M.B. 1911
(W 2.) *M.C.*

LADD, L. S. Capt. and Adjt., R.A.S.C. *M.* 1911

LAMBERT, F. 2nd Lieut., R.G.A. 1902

LANE, P. Lieut., R.E.(T.F.) 1912

LANGERMAN, A. H. R. S. African Force 1903

LANGERMAN, E. S. S. African Force 1907

LARYMORE, H. D., C.M.G. Major, R.G.A.; Asst. Inspector, 1903
Woolwich Arsenal

LAW, R. R. Capt., R.A.M.C. 1886

LAZARUS, E. L. Lieut., Worcestershire Regt.; attd. M.G.C. 1910
(W 2.)

LEACH, Rev. N. K. C.F. 4th Class, R.A.C.D. 1900

LEACH, R. W. Capt., Suffolk Regt.; Brigade Major. 1903
(W.)

LEE, A. 2nd Lieut., Unattd. List, T.F. (O.T.C.) 1899

LEE, W. E. Corpl., R.E. 1909

LEECH, E. B. Capt., R.A.M.C. (W.) 1894

LEWIS, F. H. Capt., R. Welsh Fus. (W.) 1908

✠LEWIS, R. C. Capt., R. Berkshire Regt. *M.C.* 1911
Killed in action on the Somme 1 *July* 1916

LEWIS, W. B. A. Lieut., King's (Shropshire L.I.) (W.) 1911

LIPTROT, R. N. Pte., Cheshire Regt.(T.F.); Lieut., 1908
R.F.A.

LIVENS, W. H. Capt., R.E.; Staff Capt. *D.S.O. M.C.* 1908
M 3.

LLEWELLYN, E. E. Surgeon Lieut., R.N. 1912

LLOYD GEORGE, R. Capt., R. Welsh Fus.; Major, R.E. 1907

LOVIBOND, J. L. Major, Northumberland Fus. (T.F.); 1893
empld. P. of W. Coy. (W.) *T.D. M.*

LOW, Rev. W. P. C.F. 4th Class, R.A.C.D. *M.* 1895

LOWE, Rev. C. A. H. C.F. 4th Class, R.A.C.D. *M.* 1909

LUCE, Sir R. H. Major-Gen., A.M.S.(T.F.); Director of 1886
Medical Services. *K.C.M.G. C.B. C.M.G. V.D.*
M 3.

LUMBY, A. F. R. Capt., 69th Punjabis, Indian Army; 1909
G.S.O. 2. (W)

✠LUNDIE, R. C. Major, R.E. (W.) *D.S.O. M* 2. 1904
Killed in action 15 *Oct.* 1918

MAASDORP, V. H. Lieut., R. Fusiliers. (W 2.) 1906
MCALLUM, J. H. Capt., R.A.M.C. 1891
MCARTHUR, R. Lieut., R.F.A.(T.F.) (P.) *M.C.* *1914
MCCALL, H. D. Capt., R.A.M.C. 1907
MACCALLAN, A. F. Major, R.A.M.C., empld. Egyptian 1891
Army. *C.B.E. O.B.E. M.*
MCCOLL, A. M. Sergt., King's Royal Rifle Corps; Cadet, 1913
R.A.F. *M.M. and Bar*
MCCOLL, H. H. 2nd Lieut., Rifle Brigade; Capt., D. of 1912
Wellington's (W. Riding Regt.); Hon. Capt. (O.),
R.A.F. (W 3.) *M.C. M.*
MACDONALD, Rev. H. Chaplain, R.N. 1883
MCDOUGALL, A. Capt., London Yeo. (Middlesex Hussars). 1904
D.S.O.
MCGOWAN, N. S. 2nd Lieut., Sikhs, Indian Army. (W.) 1909
MCINNES, A. N. 2nd Lieut., Northumberland Fus.(T.F.) 1914
MCINTOSH, J. G. H. Capt., Scottish Horse; attd. Cam- 1895
eron Hdrs.
MACK, A. A. Sergt., R.A.S.C.; attd. R.A.M.C. 1894
✠MACKAY, D. R. G. Pte., R. Fusiliers (P. S. Bn.); 2nd [1914]
Lieut., Argyll and Sutherland Hdrs.; Capt. (A.),
R.A.F. (W.) *D.F.C.*
Died 11 Nov. 1918 of wounds received in action
MCLEAN, K. G. Lieut., R.E. [1914]
MACNAB, J. T. Surgeon Lieut., R.N. 1898
✠MCVITTIE, G. H. 2nd Lieut., Border Regt.(T.F.) 1914
*Died on H.M. transport 12 Mar. 1915 of cerebro-spinal
meningitis*
MALIM, J. W. Capt., R.A.M.C.(T.F.). *m.* 1894
MALONE, C. R. R. Lieut.-Col., Hampshire Regt.; Major, 1877
Worcestershire Regt. (R. of O.) *m.*
MANN, F. A. W. Pte., R. Fusiliers (P.S. Bn.); Lieut. (A.), [1914]
R.A.F. (W.)
MANNERS-SMITH, E. V. Cadet, R.M.A., Woolwich [1914]
MARDON, E. J. Major, Devon Regt. and Rifle Brigade 1886
(T.F.) *m 2.*
MARKHAM, E. B. Lieut., Lincolnshire Regt. and Gen. 1912
Staff, empld. British Military Mission
MARQUAND, C. V. B. 2nd Lieut., Tank Corps. 1915
MARRIOTT, Rev. F. G. C.F. 4th Class, R.A.C.D. 1912
MARTIN, R. G. 2nd Lieut., Plymouth College O.T.C. 1909
MASTERMAN, W. S. Major, Welsh Regt. 1897
MASTERS, Rev. T. H. C.F. 1st Class, R.A.C.D.; A.C.G. 1886
C.B.E. M 2.

MAUFE, H. B. Lieut., Rhodesia Motor Vols.   1898
✠MAULE, G. L. Capt., R.A.M.C.   1910
    Died at Baghdad 15 *Nov.* 1918 *of pneumonia*
✠MAULE, R. Lieut., R. Scots(T.F.)   1904
    Killed in action in Gallipoli 27 *May* 1915
MAW, R. P. Lieut., R.G.A.   1886
MAXWELL, W. W. Major, R.G.A.   1896
MAY, A. H. Lieut.-Col. R.E. *O.B.E.* *m.*   1896
MAY, C. P. Pte., Middlesex Regt. (P. S. Bn.); Lieut., The   1909
    Buffs (E. Kent Regt.)
MAYBREY, H. J. Lieut., Wiltshire Regt. and Worcester-   1912
    shire Regt.; empld. Ministry of Munitions
✠MAYER, F. C. Sergt., 52me Regt., French Army. *French*   1911
    Croix de Guerre. M 2.
    Killed in action in Champagne 21 *Sept.* 1915
MAYER, N. E. Pte., R. Fusiliers; 2nd Lieut., Spec. List.   1908
    M.
MAYNE, C. R. G., D.S.O. Major, Highland L.I.; Brig.-   1893
    Gen. (W 2.) *C.M.G.* *Brevet Lieut.-Colonel.*
    M 5. *Osmanieh, 4th Class and Medjidieh, 3rd Class*
    (*Egypt*)
MEE, J. T. M. Capt., Suffolk Yeo. *M.*   1908
MELITUS, P. N. Lieut., R. Warwickshire Regt.; Hon.   1913
    Lieut. (O.), R.A.F.
MELLING, J. S. Pte., Cheshire Regt.; 2nd Lieut., R.   1909
    Welsh Fus.
MERCER, Ven. H. F. Capt., Australian Force; Capt.(Ad.),   1890
    R.A.F.
MERCER, J. Instructor Cdr., R. N.   *1910
✠MERE, C. L. Lieut., King's Own (R. Lancaster Regt.)   1907
    Killed in action in Gallipoli 10 *Aug.* 1915
MIDGLEY, W. A. L. Lieut., R.G.A.   1905
✠MILNE, G. W. Lieut. and Adjt., R.F.A. (W.)   1915
    Died 22 *Oct.* 1917 *of wounds received in action*
MISQUITH, O. G. Lieut., London Regt. (Queen's)   1911
MOBBS, G. F. Pte., London Regt. (Artists Rifles). (W.)   1916
MONCRIEFF, A. Capt., R.E.; S.O. to Chief Engineer.   1912
    (W 2.) *M.C. M.*
MONTGOMERY, J. K. Lieut., Spec. List (Censor's Staff)   1892
MOORE, R. F. Capt., R.A.M.C. *O.B.E. M.*   *1898
✠MOORE, R. T. Trooper, R. Wiltshire Yeo.   1910
    Drowned on S.S. Leinster 10 *Oct.* 1918
MORRIS, G. P. Lieut., Oxford and Bucks L.I.; Major,   1911
    M.G.C.

MORRISON, J. T. J. Lieut.-Col., R.A.M.C.(T.F.)   *1881
MOSLEY, I. H. Lieut., H.A.C.; Capt., Spec. List (Adjt.,   1901
School of Instruction). *M.C.*
MOUNTAIN, H. Lieut.-Col., R.F.A.   1898
MOWLL, G. M. Cadet, O.C.B.   1918
MURRAY, E. G. D. Capt., R.A.M.C. *O.B.E.*   1909
MURRAY, Rev. E. T. C.F. 4th Class, R.A.C.D. (W.)   1895
MUSPRATT, P. K. Capt., R.A.M.C.   1895

NAOROJI, K. A. D. Sergt., Middlesex Regt. (W.)   1912
NAPIER, O. J. W. 2nd Lieut. (T.), R.A.F.   1908
NEEDHAM, E. Lieut., E. Surrey Regt.; Major, M.G.C.   1907
(W.) (P.) *M.*
✠NELDER, G. C. A. 2nd Lieut., Hampshire Regt.   1912
Killed in action at Suvla Bay 6 Aug. 1915
NELSON, E. W. Lieut.-Cdr., R.N.V.R. *M.*   1902
NELSON, R. D. Capt., R.F.A.   1907
NELSON, T. B. 2nd Lieut. (Ad.), R.A.F.   1902
NEWMAN, E. Capt., R.A.O.C.; D.A.D.O.S.; attd.,   1901
R.A.F. *Cavalier, Order of the Crown of Italy*
✠NEWMAN, J. S. 2nd Lieut., E. Yorks. Regt.   1913
Killed in action at Suvla Bay 9 Aug. 1915
NEWTON, G. F. Pte., H.A.C.   *1901
NICHOLAS, A. J. Lieut., R. Welsh Fus.   *1907
NICKAL, G. B. 2nd Lieut., R.A.F.   1909
NIGHTINGALE, H. P. C.Q.M.S., Queen's Own (R. W.   1907
Kent Regt.)
NIXON, Rev. W. H. C.F. 2nd Class, R.A.C.D. *m.*   1883
NOBLE, Rev. R. H. C.F. 4th Class, R.A.C.D.   *1916
NUTTALL, E. D. Lieut., R.G.A.   *1909
NUTTALL, W. L. F. 2nd Lieut. (A.), R.A.F. *D.F.C.*   1916

✠ODELL, R. E. Pte., R. Fusiliers (P.S. Bn.); Lieut., Black 1913
Watch
Died 20 Dec. 1916 *of wounds received in action 18 Dec.*
1916
OGILVIE, J. Capt., R.A.M.C.   1886
O'REILLY, J. B. Major, Durham L.I. and Leinster Regt. 1878
✠ORMESHER, H. Lieut., Lincolnshire Regt.   1913
Killed in action 4 Oct. 1915
ORMSBY, M. H. Lieut., I.A.R.O., attd. S. Provinces Mtd. 1896
Rifles; Major and Cmdt., Clerks Training School
ORTON, W. A. Lieut., Dorset Regt.; attd. T.M.B. (W.) 1916
OSBORNE, D. R. Major, Northumberland Fus.   1901

✠OSBORNE, L. H. Lieut., Lancs. Fus.   1912
   Killed in action in Gallipoli 7 Aug. 1915
OTWAY, J. T. F. Hon. Lieut.-Col., Spec. List   1870
OULTON, E. V. Major, R.A.M.C. *M.*   1900
OWEN, G. Lieut., N. Zealand Rifle Brigade. (W.)   1902
OWEN, P. R. T. 2nd Lieut., The Buffs (E. Kent Regt.)   1907
   (W.)

PAGET, H. E. G. Capt., 46th Punjabis, Indian Army   1905
PARKER, Rev. J. C. Chaplain, R.N. *M.*   1904
PARRY, T. H., M.P. Lieut.-Col., R. Welsh Fus.(T.F.)   1900
   (W 2.) *D.S.O. M. Order of the Nile, 4th Class*
   (*Egypt*)
PARTRIDGE, C. Lieut., Spec. List (R.T.O.)   1892
PATRICK, N. C. Capt., R.A.M.C.   1895
✠PAYTON, R. S. Lieut., R. Warwickshire Regt.   1913
   Killed in action 22 July 1916
PECK, A. H. Lieut., Devon Regt.; Major (A.), R.A.F.   1906
   D.S.O. M.C. and Bar. M.
PECK, E. S. Lieut.-Col., I.M.S.   1885
PEERS, E. A. 2nd Lieut., Felsted School O.T.C.   1909
PEILE, J. Lieut., E. Surrey Regt.; Capt., Gen. List   1897
PETERS, A. J. Pte., Middlesex Regt.(P. S. Bn.); Capt., S.   1911
   Lancs. Regt.
PETERS, M. W. Lieut., King's Royal Rifle Corps and   1907
   M.G.C. (W 2.) *M.C.*
PETTIT, J. R. Lieut., R.A.S.C.(M.T.) *M.*   1912
PEYTON-BURBERY, Rev. R. J. P. Chaplain, R.N.   1901
PHILLIPS, E. S. Major, R.G.A. *D.S.O. M.*   1895
PHILLIPS, J. E. Capt., O.T.C.   1903
✠PICKARD-CAMBRIDGE, H. E. W. Lieut., Sussex Yeo.   1915
   Killed in action 1 Nov. 1917
PIGEON, H. W. Lieut., R.A.M.C. *m.*   1877
[1]PIGEON, J. W. Capt., I.M.S.   1905
PIM, F. H. Capt., R.A.S.C.   1897
PIRKIS, F. C. L. Lieut., R.F.A.; Staff Lieut., War Office.   1895
   (W.)
PITHER, F. E. L. 2nd Lieut., Somerset L.I.   1914
POPE, S. B. Lieut.-Col., 58th (Vaughan's) Rifles, Indian   1898
   Army; G.S.O.1. *D.S.O. Brevet Lieut.-Colonel. M 4.*
   Chevalier, Legion of Honour (France). Order of the
   Nile, 3rd Class (*Egypt*)
PORTER, R. E. Major, R.A.S.C. *M.C.*   [1914]

---

[1] Killed in action in Mesopotamia after the armistice.

PRIESTLEY, R. E. Capt., R.E. (Signals, T.F.). *M.C.* 1913
PUMPHREY, C. E. Capt., Durham L.I. (W.) *M.C. M* 2. 1899
PURDIE, Rev. A. B. C.F. 3rd Class, R.A.C.D. *O.B.E.* 1913
   M. Order of St Sava, 3rd Class (Serbia)
PURTON, G. A. Lce.-Corpl., Training Res. Bn. 1895
PYMAN, W. H. Lieut., R.F.A.; empld. Ministry of Ship- 1905
   ping

QUILLET, L. A. Lieut., R.A.S.C. 1914

RADICE, W. A. Capt. and Adjt., Calcutta Bn., Indian 1901
   Defence Force
RAMSAY, D. 2nd Lieut., The Queen's (R.W. Surrey Regt.) 1906
✠RAMSAY, L. N. G. 2nd Lieut., Gordon Hdrs. 1911
   Killed in action 21 March 1915
RAMSAY, M. G. 2nd Lieut., The Buffs (E. Kent Regt.) 1909
RANSFORD, W. M. Capt., R.E. *M.C.* 1909
RAPPIS, P. A. G. 2nd Lieut., Wireless Corps, Italian Army 1899
READ, R. S. Lieut., Suffolk Regt.; empld. Ministry of 1915
   Labour. (W 2.)
✠REED, B. Lieut., W. Yorks. Regt. (W 2.) *1913
   Killed in action 12 April 1918
REED, C. H. Capt., R.E. (London Electrical Engineers, 1900
   T.F.)
REES, T. J. Lieut., Welsh Regt.(T.F.); attd. R.E. 1908
✠REESE, J. Wireless Telegraphist, R.N. 1915
   Killed in action on H.M. patrol boat 10 *Feb.* 1918
REID, E. D. W. *See* WHITEHEAD REID, E. D.
RENDLE, A. C. Capt., R.A.M.C. *1885
✠RICE-JONES, A. T. Capt., King's (Liverpool Regt.) 1909
   (W 2.)
   Died 23 March 1918 *of wounds received in action*
RICE-JONES, B. R. Lieut., R.G.A.(T.F.) (W.) 1907
RICHARDS, C.T. 2nd Lieut., R.G.A.; Lieut.(Ad.),R.A.F. 1909
RICHARDS, W. G. Major, I.M.S. 1887
RICHARDSON, D. J. A. Gnr., R.G.A. 1908
RICHARDSON, G. P. N. Capt., R.A.M.C. 1914
RICHARDSON, J. H. Asst. Paymaster, Army Pay Dept. 1896
RICHARDSON KUHLMANN, D. *See* RICHARDSON, D. J. A.
✠RIEU, A. Pte., 2me Regt. Etranger, French Army, and 1897
   Middlesex Regt.
   Killed in action 3 *July* 1916
RIGBY, Rev. P. C.F. 4th Class, R.A.C.D. 1904
RILEY, A. Air Mechanic, R.A.F. 1909

ROBERTS, F. H. Lieut., R. Sussex Regt.(T.F.)   1901
ROBERTS, Rev. LL. C. C.F. 4th Class, R.A.C.D.   *1909
ROBERTSON, D. D. A.B., R.N.V.R. (Anti-Aircraft)   1889
ROBINS, J. N. Capt., R.A.M.C.(T.F.). (W.)   1895
ROBINSON, A. C. Lieut.-Col., R.A.S.C.; A.A. and Q.M.G.   1903
    D.S.O. M. *Order of the Nile, 4th Class (Egypt)*
ROBSON, Rev. E. I. Lieut., Spec. List (Intelligence)   1892
ROGERS, J. L. Lieut., R.G.A.   1907
ROMANES, J. Capt., Border Regt.; empld. War Office.   1905
    (W.)
ROSE, C. A. Lieut., R.F.A. (W.) *M.C.*   1905
ROUSE, W. H. D. Lieut., Perse School, Cambridge,   1882
    O.T.C.
RUBINSTEIN, L. Russian Army   1913
RUDKINS, F. P. Lieut., Emanuel School, Wandsworth,   1907
    O.T.C.
RUSSELL, J. 2nd Lieut., Gordon Hdrs. (W 2.)   1915

SANER, F. D. Capt., R.A.M.C.   1902
SAUNDERS, A. H. Instructor Lieut., R.N.   1908
SAUNDERS, J. T. Capt., Durham L.I. (W 2.)   1907
SAUNDERS, Rev. W. D. C.F. 4th Class, R.A.C.D. *m.*   *1911
SCHARFF, G. E. Sapper, R.E.   1909
✠SCHWARZ, R. O. Capt., S. African Infy.; Major, King's   1893
    Royal Rifle Corps; D.A.Q.M.G.; Asst. Controller of
    Salvage. (W.) *M.C. M.*
    *Died 20 Nov. 1918 of influenza contracted on active
    service*
SCOTT, J. H. Capt., York and Lancaster Regt.   1905
SCOTT, L. B. Major, I.M.S.   1894
✠SEABROOKE, A. S. Capt., R.A.M.C.   1903
    Died in Mesopotamia 1 July 1916 of typhoid
SELBY, J. S. E. Capt., R.A.M.C.   1886
SEVERNE, A. DE M. 2nd Lieut., R.F.A.; Lieut. (A.),   1915
    R.A.F. (W.)
SEWELL, H. W. Capt., Border Regt.   1891
SEWELL, R. B. S. Major, I.M.S. *M.*   1899
SHANKS, P. M. 2nd Lieut., St John's School, Leather-   1897
    head, O.T.C.
SHARP, D. G. Lieut., W. Yorks. Regt.; Capt., T.M.B.   1915
    M.C.
SHARPE, G. R. Lieut., Loyal N. Lancs. Regt. (W 3.)   1912
SHELL, Rev. A. Chaplain, R.N.   *1898
SHELLEY, J. Pte., R.A.S.C.   *1905

SHENNAN, W. D. Capt., R.E. *M.C. M.* 1907
SHEPHARD, W. H. Capt., R.A.M.C.; D.A.D.M.S. (W.) 1908
SHEPPARD, W. S. Capt., R.A.M.C. 1889
SHIELDS, T. Major, R. Berkshire Regt.(T.F.) 1881
✠SHILCOCK, J. W. Lieut., The Queen's (R.W. Surrey Regt.) 1907
Killed in action near Baghdad 22–24 Nov. 1915
SHINER, Rev. R. P. C.F. 4th Class, R.A.C.D. *1904
SHUFFLEBOTTOM, E. Pte., Essex Regt.; 2nd Lieut., R. 1915
Fusiliers
SHURLOCK, F. W. Pte., R. Fusiliers (P.S. Bn.); Instructor 1911
Lieut., R.N.
SIMPSON, A. J. G. Major, N.S.W. Bn., Australian Force 1906
SIMPSON, A. W. W. Lieut.-Col., Manchester Regt. (T.F.) 1894
O.B.E. Brevet Lieut.-Colonel. M 3. *Order of the
Nile, 3rd Class (Egypt)*
✠SIMPSON, G. B. G. Pte., Australian Infy. 1906
Killed in action in Gallipoli 6 Aug. 1915
SIMPSON, J. G. Pte., London Regt.(Artists Rifles); Lieut., 1908
R. Sussex Regt. (W 2.) *M.C.*
✠SING, C. M. Pte., R. Fusiliers; 2nd Lieut., R. Sussex Regt. 1907
Died 7 July 1916 *of wounds received in action*
SKYRME, C. R. Capt., R.A.M.C. 1892
SLAUGHTER, C. E. Capt., R.A.S.C.; attd. R.G.A. (W.) *M.* 1913
SLEEMAN, C. M. Lieut., R.N.V.R. 1902
SMALL, D. W. Lieut., R.E. 1914
SMITH, A. C. DENISON. Lieut., E. Yorks. Regt. (W.) *M.C.* 1906
SMITH, A. E. CLARENCE. Capt., S. Lancs. Regt. 1906
SMITH, A. E. S. Lieut., R.A.S.C. 1893
✠SMITH, C. R. B. 2nd Lieut., Bedfordshire Regt. 1915
Killed in action 28 April 1917
SMITH, F. C. Cadet, O.C.B. (R.F.A.) 1917
SMITH, J. Capt., R.F.A. (W.) 1912
SMITH, J. T. Lieut., Sussex Yeo. (W.) 1915
SMITH, W. H. 2nd Lieut., Coldstream Gds. 1905
SMITH-CARINGTON, Rev. A. E. C. C.F. 4th Class, R.A.C.D. 1909
SMITHSON, A. E. Lieut.-Col., R.A.M.C. *1884
SMUTS, Rt Hon. J. C. Lieut.-Gen.; Cmdt.-Gen., S. 1891
African Defence Force; Member of Imp. War Cabinet.
*Companion of Honour. Commander, Legion of Honour
(France). Grand Officer, Order of Leopold (Belgium).
Belgian Croix de Guerre*
SNAPE, H. J. Capt., Repton School O.T.C. 1894
SNOWDEN, A. DE W. Hon. Major, R.A.M.C. (Red Cross 1891
Hospital, Netley). *C.B.E.*

SOWELS, F. Lce.-Corpl., Oxford and Bucks. L.I.; Capt.,   1895
   Gen. Staff (Intelligence). *Chevalier, Order of the*
   Redeemer (*Greece*)
SPENCER, Rev. L. D. W.   C.F. 3rd Class, R.A.C.D.(T.F.)   1896
SPURRELL, R. K.   Capt., D. of Cornwall's L.I. (W 2.)   [1914]
   M.C. M.
SQUIRE, A. M.   2nd Lieut., R.A.O.C.   1901
SQUIRE, S. G.   Lieut., Oundle School O.T.C.   1898
✠STANDEN, L. J. D.   Lieut., Lincolnshire Regt.(T.F.)   1913
   Killed in action 18 *March* 1916
STANTON, H. J. C.   Staff Capt., War Office. *m* 2.   1879
✠STARKEY, V. G.   Pte., R. Fusiliers (P. S. Bn.); Lieut., 1913
   King's Own (Yorkshire L.I.)
   Killed in action 14 *Oct.* 1915
STAVERS, W. M.   Capt., R. Scots Fus. (W.)   1911
STEEN, S. W. P.   2nd Lieut., Rifle Brigade. (W.)   1918
STEPHENS, Rev. H. H.   C.F. 4th Class, R.A.C.D.   1916
STEPHENSON, Rev. H. S.   Senior Chaplain, Indian Army   1894
STEVENS, F. B.   Lieut., Sussex Yeo.; Capt. (K.B.), R.A.F. 1899
   M.
STEWART, C. B.   Capt., R.A.M.C.(T.F.)   1883
STEWART, P. M.   Major, R. Fusiliers (P. S. Bn.) and   1890
   Training Res. Bn.
STILL, H. N.   2nd Lieut., Shropshire Yeo.; Lieut.,   1912
   R.G.A. *m.*
STILL, Rev. W. H.   C.F. 4th Class, R.A.C.D.   1910
STOLTERFORTH, G. H.   Lieut., Cheshire Regt. and   1897
   M.G.C. (W.)
STRACHAN, Rev. R. H.   C.F. 4th Class, R.A.C.D. *m.*   1911
SULLIVAN, Rev. A. M.   C.F. 4th Class, R.A.C.D.(T.F.)   1897
SULLIVAN, J. H. B.   Lieut., I.A.R.O. (Cavalry)   1909
SUTTON, Rev. F. O.   C.F. 4th Class, R.A.C.D.(T.F.) *M.* *1883
SWANN, C. H.   Lieut., R.N.V.R.   *1903

✠TANNER, G. R.   Lieut., Wiltshire Regt. (W 3.) *M.C.* 1913
   Died 8 *April* 1918 *of wounds received in action* 24 *March*
   1918
TANNER, H. R.   Capt., Somerset L.I. (W.)   1911
TANNER, R. R.   Lieut.-Col., Rifle Brigade (T.F.)   1882
TAYLOR, C. H.   Major, York and Lancaster Regt. and   1883
   King's Own (Yorkshire L.I.)
TAYLOR, D. R.   Capt., R.A.M.C.   1898
TAYLOR, G. C.   Major, R.A.M.C.(T.F.); D.A.D.M.S.   1887
   O.B.E. M 2

THEOPHILUS, S. C. Pte., H.A.C.; Lieut., Rifle Brigade ; 1903
  Capt., T.M.B.; Major, Tank Corps. *M.C.*
THOMAS, A. A. Lieut., Welsh Regt. 1911
THOMAS, E. C. Capt., Suffolk Regt. 1894
THOMAS, T. J. Lieut., R. Welsh Fus.; attd. T.M.B. 1902
  (W.) *M.C.*
THOMAS, W. Major, S. African Med. Corps. *O.B.E. M.* 1889
THOMPSON, Rev. A. E. C.F. 4th Class, R.A.C.D. 1898
THOMPSON, A. P. Capt., R.A.S.C. 1912
THOMPSON, G. H. M. Lieut., Spec. List, empld. R.E. 1910
  (Inland Water Transport)
THOMPSON, G. W. Capt., R.A.M.C. 1886
THOMPSON, P. A. Capt., R.A.S.C. 1895
THORNE, H. S. Lieut., R. Scots; attd. Gen. Staff. (W.) 1911
THURSTON, E. T. Lieut., I.A.R.O., attd. Garrison Arty., 1908
  Indian Defence Force
TINDALL, C. Lieut., R.E. 1902
TODD, M. Lieut., R.F.A. (W.) 1908
✠TOWNROE, G. C. Capt., S. Lancs. Regt. 1913
  Killed in action 8 Sept. 1917
TOWNSON, B. A. Lieut., The Buffs (E. Kent Regt., T.F. 1911
  Res.)
✠TREMEARNE, A. J. N. Major, Seaforth Hdrs. 1906
  Killed in action in the Battle of Loos 25 Sept. 1915
✠TREMEARNE, W. C. 2nd Lieut., Seaforth Hdrs. 1910
  Killed in action in the Battle of Loos 26 Sept. 1915
TREND, J. B. Capt., R.A.S.C.; Lieut., R.G.A.; empld. 1906
  War Office. *m.*
TRENDELL, Rev. G. J. W. C.F. 4th Class, R.A.C.D. 1883
TRESTRAIL, A. E. Y. Lieut.-Col., Cheshire Regt. (W.) 1894
  D.S.O. M.
TURKINGTON, J. S. Trooper, R. Canadian Dragoons; 1912
  Lieut., Gen. List, Canadian Force. (W 2.)
TURNBULL, E. L. 2nd Lieut., King's Royal Rifle Corps. (W.) 1907
✠TURNER, E. P. Capt., R.F.A. 1911
  Killed in action 19 March 1917
TURNER, H. W. Lieut., Spec. List (Intelligence) *1906
TURNER, R. L. Lieut., I.A.R.O.; Capt. and Adjt., 3rd 1907
  Gurkha Rifles (attd.) *M.C. M.*
TURNER, W. H. Major, R.F.A.(T.F.) *M.C. M.* 1912
✠TURPIN, J. K. Lieut., R.F.A.(T.F.) 1911
  Killed in action 14 Aug. 1917
TWENTYMAN, J. M. Capt., R.A.M.C. 1888
TWENTYMAN, Rev. W. P. C.F. 4th Class, R.A.C.D. 1897

ULLRICH, E. H.   Pte., Middlesex Regt.; Sapper, R.E.   1914
(Signals)
UNWIN, C. H.   Major, D. of Wellington's (W. Riding   1896
Regt.); empld. O.C.B. (W.) *M.*
UPWARD, H. A.   Capt., R.A.M.C.   1892

VARLEY, G.   Sergt., R. Fusiliers   1893
VEALE, H. P.   Major, S. African Med. Corps.   1883
VINT, A. W.   Capt., Worcestershire Regt. *M.C.*   1915
VINT, M. D.   Capt., R.A.M.C. (W.) *M.*   1912
✠VOELCKER, H. E.   2nd Lieut., S. Lancs. Regt. (W.)   1913
Killed in action 20 *July* 1916

WADDY, R. A.   Pte., London Regt. (Artists Rifles)   [1914]
WADE, R.   Capt., R.A.M.C.   1898
WADHAM, S. M.   Lieut., Durham L.I.; Capt., Spec.   1910
List, empld. R.E. *M.*
WAGNER, R. H.   Capt., London Regt. (R. Fusiliers); attd.   1910
R.E. (Signals). *M.C.*
WAIAPU, Rt Rev. Bishop of.   C.F. 3rd Class, N. Zealand   1879
Chaplains' Dept.
✠WAINWRIGHT, G. L.   Pte., Middlesex Regt. (P. S. Bn.);   1913
2nd Lieut., R. Sussex Regt.
Killed in action 25 *Sept.* 1915
WALKER, D. G.   Capt., Highland L.I. (W.)   1914
WALKER, F. C.   Lieut., Yorkshire Regt. (W.)   1909
WALKER, K. M.   Capt., Suffolk Regt. (W 2.)   [1914]
WALKEY, Rev. J. R.   C.F. 2nd Class, R.A.C.D.; D.A.C.G.   1899
M.
WALLIS, H. H.   Lieut., Trent College O.T.C.   1905
WARD, F. K.   Lieut., I.A.R.O., attd. 116th Mahrattas   1904
WARD, R.   2nd Lieut., R.G.A.   *1906
WARREN, Rev. S.   C.F. 4th Class, R.A.C.D.   1886
WATERWORTH, Rev. H.   C.F. 4th Class, R.A.C.D.   1909
WATKINS, W. F.   Lieut., Suffolk Regt.   [1914]
WATSON, Rev. H.   C.F. 4th Class, N. Zealand Chaplains'   1894
Dept.
WATSON, H. S.   2nd Lieut., R.E. (Tyne Electrical Eng-   1895
ineers, T.F.)
WATSON, Rev. R.   C.F. 4th Class, R.A.C.D. (W.)   1889
WATSON, T. T. B.   Capt., R.A.M.C.   1908
✠WEBB, A. H.   Pte., R. Fusiliers (P. S. Bn.); 2nd Lieut.,   1912
Leicestershire Regt.
Died 4 *May* 1916

WEBB, E. O. Pte., London Regt. (Artists Rifles); 2nd 1911
Lieut., M.G.C.

✠WEBB, H. C. Capt., Border Regt.; attd. T.M.B. 1911
Killed in action 19 *Sept.* 1916

WEDDELL, J. M. Capt., R.A.M.C. *M* 2. 1903

✠WESTWOOD, A. H. Capt., R. Warwickshire Regt. (W 2.) 1910
Killed in action 21 *Sept.* 1918

✠WHALEY, O. S. Pte., R. Fusiliers (P. S. Bn.); 2nd Lieut., 1908
Hampshire Regt.
Killed in action in Gallipoli 10 *Aug.* 1915

WHEAT, E. G. Capt., R.A.M.C. 1897

WHEELER, J. N. Major, R.A.M.C. *M.* 1901

WHEELER, Rev. S. M. C.F. 4th Class, R.A.C.D. 1905

✠WHITE, L. 2nd Lieut., Welsh Regt. *1913
Killed in action 19 *March* 1916

WHITEHEAD, H. M. Capt., Sherwood Foresters (Notts. 1893
and Derby Regt.); A.D.C.; Lieut.-Col., Labour Corps.
O.B.E. *Chevalier, Ordre du Mérite Agricole (France)*

WHITEHEAD, J. H. M. Capt., W. African Frontier Force 1892

WHITEHEAD, R. B. Lieut., King's Royal Rifle Corps; attd. 1908
R.E. (Signals). *M.*

WHITEHEAD REID, E. D. Capt., R.A.M.C. 1902

WHITEMAN, R. J. N. Major, Australian A.M.C. 1907

WILES, H. H. Lieut., Wiltshire Regt.; Capt., Devon 1911
Regt.; Capt. and Adjt., Labour Corps. (W.)

WILES, J. W. Hon. Capt., Serbian Army. *Serbian Royal* *1916
Red Cross

WILKINSON, S. J. Capt., R.A.S.C. *M. m.* 1907

WILKINSON, V. Capt. and Adjt., Border Regt. *M.C.* 1911
M.

WILLIAMS, A. Major, Gen. Staff. O.B.E. *M. Cavalier,* 1882
Order of the Crown of Italy

WILLIAMS, Rev. C. M. C.F. 4th Class, R.A.C.D. *1897

WILLIAMS, D. G. Lieut., 4th (R. Irish) Dragoon Gds. 1912

WILLIAMS, E. C. Capt., R.A.M.C.; D.A.D.M.S. 1885

WILLIAMS, F. L. Capt., Bedfordshire Regt. and Gen. 1910
List. (W.) *M.*

WILLIAMS, H. H. Capt., R.A.S.C. (M.T.) *M.B.E. m.* 1900

WILLIAMS, Rev. J. E. C.F. 4th Class, R.A.C.D. *m* 2. *1909

✠WILLIAMS, K. G. 2nd Lieut., N. Zealand M.G.C. 1906
Killed in action 9 *June* 1917

WILLIAMS, Rev. W. D. C.F. 4th Class, R.A.C.D. *1888

WILLIAMSON, R. S. 2nd Lieut., Yorkshire Regt. 1901

WILLIS, A. G. F. Lieut., The Buffs (E. Kent Regt.) 1909

WILSON, C. J. Capt., E. African Mtd. Rifles and Spec. 1898
List. *M.C.* *M* 2.
WILSON, E. Pte., W. Yorks. Regt. 1914
WILSON, F. A. Capt., Cameronians (Scottish Rifles, 1912
T.F.); 2nd Lieut. (O.), R.A.F. (W.)
WILSON, H. F. Major, R.A.M.C. (W.) *M.C. and Bar.* M. 1904
WOLFE, J. A. Lieut., R.G.A. 1915
WOOD, C. F. Lieut., I.A.R.O.; Capt., Mohmand Militia 1903
WOOD, S. Capt., R.A.M.C. 1901
WOOD, W. L. Major, R.E. (W.) *O.B.E.* *M* 2. 1903
WOODARD, E. A. 2nd Lieut., King's Own (Yorkshire L.I.) 1905
WOODHEAD, H. M. 2nd Lieut., D. of Wellington's (W. 1912
Riding Regt.); Lieut., Cheshire Regt.; attd. T.M.B.
✠WOOLF, W. R. M. 2nd Lieut., Border Regt. 1904
Died 26 Sept. 1915 *of wounds received in action 25 Sept.*
1915
WOOLLEY, E. C. 2nd Lieut., Loyal N. Lancs. Regt. (W.) *1908
WOOLLEY, J. M. Lieut.-Col., I.M.S. 1890
WORRALL, L. 2nd Lieut., R.A.S.C. 1893
WRIGHT, C. R. Pte., R.A.S.C.(M.T.) 1905
WRIGHT, O. K. Lieut.-Col., R.A.M.C.(T.F.) 1900
WRIGHT, P. J. Lieut., R.G.A. 1896
WRIGLEY, A. A.B., R.N.V.R.; Lieut., R.A.S.C. *M.* 1908
WYATT, T. C. Major, R.A.S.C. *O.B.E.* *M.* 1906

✠YARDE, J. T. Capt., Bedfordshire Regt.(T.F.) (W 2.) 1913
M.C. and Bar. *M* 2.
Died 21 Sept. 1918 *of wounds received in action in*
Palestine 19 Sept. 1918
YELVERTON, E. E. C.F. 4th Class, R.A.C.D. *O.B.E.* *M.* 1907
YOUNG, B. W. Lieut., R.G.A.; empld. Ministry of Muni- 1910
tions
✠YOUNG, E. T. Lieut., Manchester Regt. 1903
Killed in action in Gallipoli 10 *June* 1915
YOUNG, F. E. Lieut.-Col., Rifle Brigade. (W.) *M.C.* *M.* 1908
YOUNG, F. F. Capt., London Regt. (Artists Rifles) [1914]
YOUNG, F. P. Capt., R.A.M.C. 1899
YOUNG, J. G. Lieut., Somerset L.I. and M.G.C. 1910
YOUNG, P. C. Colonel, R.E.; A.I.G.T. *C.B.E.* *O.B.E.* 1899
M.
YOUNG, R. F. Capt., R.A.M.C. (W.) *M.C.* *M.* 1898
YOUNG, Rev. S. D. C.F. 3rd Class, R.A.C.D. *D.S.O.* 1905
O.B.E. *M* 2.
YOUNG, S. L. O. Capt., R.A.M.C. 1896

CLARE COLLEGE

ABRAHAMSON, I. *See* LUBBOCK, I.

ADAMS, H. P. Corpl., H.A.C.   1880

ADLER, F. B. Capt., S. African F.A.; Major, R.F.A.   1901
(P.) *M.C. M* 2.

AIKMAN, K. B. Capt., R.A.M.C.; Surgeon Lieut., R.N.;   1907
Capt. (Med.), R.A.F.

AIKMAN, R. B. 2nd Lieut., Lanarkshire Yeo.   1902

ALCOCK, J. F. Lieut. (A.), R.A.F.   1914

ALEXANDER, J. G. Lieut., R. Inniskilling Fus.   1899

ALEXANDER, J. W. Capt., R.A.S.C.   1905

ALEXANDER, R. M. Lieut., E. Yorks. Regt. and T.M.B.;   1903
empld. War Office

✠ALEXANDER, W. G. 2nd Lieut., King's (Liverpool Regt.)   1909
Killed in action at Festubert 15 *May* 1915

ALLAN, P. B. M. Capt., London Regt. (London Scottish);   1903
empld. War Office

ALLEN, W. Trooper, R. Horse Gds.   1908

ALSTON, W. E. Capt., R.A.M.C.(T.F.)   1886

✠AMPHLETT-MORTON, J. F. 2nd Lieut., King's Royal Rifle   1911
Corps. *M.*
Killed in action 10 *Jan.* 1915

ANDERSON, K. B. Lieut., R.G.A.(T.F.)   1900

ANDERSON, R. C. Lieut., R.N.V.R. (Coastal Motor-   1902
boat Service)

ANDERSON, S. M. Brig.-Gen., R.A., Australian Force.   1898
D.S.O. Brevet Lieut.-Colonel. M 2. *Chevalier, Legion
of Honour (France). American Distinguished Service
Medal*

ANDERSON, W. A. Capt., R.A.M.C.(T.F.) *M. French*   1903
Médaille d'Honneur and Médaille des Épidémies

✠ANDERTON, G. E. A. Lieut., Lancs. Fus.; attd. M.G.C. [1914] (W.) *M.*
Killed in action 22 *March* 1918
ANDREW, G. H. Instructor Lieut., R.N. *M.*   1895
✠ANGUS, R. E. Lieut., Ayrshire Yeo.; attd. R.F.C.   [1914]
Killed in action 20 *Nov.* 1917
ANSELL, A. E. Lieut., S. Staffs. Regt.(T.F.); Capt.,   1904
R.A.S.C.
APPLETON, E. L. Lieut., Border Regt. and Training Res. 1897
Bn.
✠APPLEYARD, W. Lieut., Yorkshire Regt.   1912
Killed in action in Gallipoli 22 *Aug.* 1915
ARDERN, L. Lieut., London Regt. (Surrey Rifles); attd. 1906
Durham L.I.
ARMITAGE, W. A. Capt., York and Lancaster Regt.; 1898
Major, M.G.C. (Motor). (W.) *D.S.O. M.*
ARMSTRONG, G. F. Pte., H.A.C.; Lieut., Labour Corps 1901
ARNOLD, L. M. Surgeon Lieut., R.N.   1908
ARNOLD, W. B. Lieut., Rifle Brigade. (W 2.) *M.*   1914
ASPINWALL, G. R. Capt., W. Yorks. Regt. (W 2.)   1911
ATHERTON, Rev. E. C. C.F. 1st Class, R.A.C.D.(T.F.)   1883
ATTERBURY, H. H. Capt., Derbyshire Yeo.; Lieut., Gds.   1895
M.G. Regt. (W.)
AVERY, G. C. Instructor Cdr., R.N. *Chevalier, Legion* 1896
of Honour (*France*)
AYDON, J. Surgeon Lieut., R.N.   1906

BAGGE, H. P. Major, Yorkshire Regt.(T.F.) (W.) *M.C.*   1898
BAIKIE, R. Capt., R.G.A.(T.F.)   1910
BAILEY, B. F. Capt., R.A.M.C. *M.C.*   1909
BAILEY, E. B. Lieut., R.G.A. (W 2.) *M.C. M* 2.   1899
Chevalier, Legion of Honour (*France*). *French Croix*
de Guerre
BAILEY, M. A. Capt., R.F.A. *M.C.*   1908
✠BAILEY, P. G. Major, R.F.A.   1905
Killed in action 26 *April* 1917
¹BAILEY, T. E. G. Capt., Yorkshire Regt. (W.) *M.C.*   1902
BAKER, E. T. L. Lieut., Queen's Own (R.W. Kent Regt.)   1913
(W.)
BAKEWELL, G. V. Major, R.A.M.C. *O.B.E. M* 2.   1906
BALFOUR, R. N. Capt., R.A.S.C. *M.*   1900
BANKS, W. E. H. Surgeon Sub-Lieut., R.N.V.R.   1914
BARBER, H. W. Capt., R.A.M.C.   1905
¹ Killed in action in N. Russia after the armistice.

✠BARHAM, W. S. Capt., The Buffs (E. Kent Regt.) 1914
  Died 10 *Oct.* 1915 *of wounds received in action*
BARKER, K. E. M. Capt., Cambridgeshire Regt.(T.F.Res.) 1896
BARNES, J. E. Lieut., R.A.S.C. *M.* 1910
BARRAN, C. A. Capt., Oxford and Bucks. L.I.; Asst. 1912
  Officer i/c R.F.C. Records. (W.)
BARTLETT, Rev. D. M. M. C.F. 4th Class, R.A.C.D. 1892
BARTON, W. J. Major, Norfolk Regt.(T.F.); Asst. 1893
  Officer i/c R.A.M.C. Records
✠BASS, V. A. 2nd Lieut., R. Fusiliers 1907
  Killed in action 20 *July* 1916
BASSETT, P. R. Lieut., Suffolk Regt. 1897
✠BASTOW, F. Capt., W. Yorks. Regt. (W.) 1912
  Killed in action near Rheims 27 *May* 1918
BATHER, E. J. Major, R.F.A. *D.S.O. M* 3. 1907
✠BAWDON, R. H. 2nd Lieut., S. Wales Borderers 1913
  Died 10 *July* 1915 *of illness contracted on active service*
BAYLY, H. W. Major, R.A.M.C. (W.) *M.C.* 1891
✠BAYNES, D. L. H. Major, R.G.A. *M.C. M.* 1905
  Killed in action near Ypres 14 *Oct.* 1918
BAZETT, S. C. Major, Indian Army; empld. Govt. of 1893
  Burma
BEALEY, R. N. Capt., R. Fusiliers and Training Res. Bn. 1880
BEARD, R. H. 2nd Lieut., R.F.A. (W.) 1915
BEARDMORE, W. J. M. Capt., Gordon Hdrs. (W.) 1913
BECK, B. R. Pte., Australian A.M.C. 1898
BECK, E. W. T. Capt., R. Fusiliers; Staff Capt.; Major, 1905
  S.O. 2, R.A.F. (W 3.) *D.S.O. M.C. M* 2.
BECK, F. G. M. Capt., R.G.A.(T.F.) 1901
✠BECKETT, P. A. Pte., Middlesex Regt.; 2nd Lieut., Queen's 1911
  Own (R.W. Kent Regt.)
  Killed in action 14 *Feb.* 1917
✠BEDALE, Rev. C. L. C.F. 4th Class, R.A.C.D. (W.) 1898
  Died 8 *March* 1919 *of illness contracted on active service*
BEDALE, F. S. Capt., R.A.M.C.(T.F.) (W.) *M.C. M.* 1905
BELL, D. W. Lieut., Worcestershire Regt.; Major, M.G.C. 1905
  M.C.
BELL, J. H. Capt., Hampshire Regt. *M.C.* 1905
✠BEMROSE, R. H. Lieut., R.F.A. *M.C.* 1915
  Died 7 *Nov.* 1918 *of wounds received in action* 25 *Sept.*
  1918
✠BENJAMIN, J. A. Capt., D. of Wellington's (W. Riding 1911
  Regt.)
  Killed in action 5 *July* 1916

BENJAMIN, R. N. Capt., R. Fusiliers. (W 3.) *M.C.*   1912
BENNETT, H. C. L. Capt., N.S.W. Bn., Australian Force 1909
BENNETT, K. L. Sergt., Australian Infy. (W.)   1902
✠BENSON, C. D. Pte., R. Fusiliers   1913
  Died of wounds received in action Feb. 1917
BERNEY-FICKLIN, A. T. M. Major, Norfolk Regt. (W.) [1914]
  M.C. M.
BERRY, H. S. Capt., R.A.M.C. (W.)   1900
BEST, J. Cadet, O.C.B.   1914
✠BEVAN, C. B. Capt., Suffolk Regt. (W.)   1912
  Killed in action 20 *July* 1916
BEVERIDGE, G. 2nd Lieut., Gordon Hdrs.(T.F.) (W.)   1910
BICKET, T. B. Capt., R.F.A.(T.F.); empld. War Office.   1910
  (W.) *M.C.*
BIGGS, E. K. Capt., R.F.A.(T.F.); attd. R.G.A.   1901
BIGNOLD, C. S. Pte., R.A.M.C. (W.)   1907
BILLINTON, H. L. Lieut., Lancs. Fus.; Lieut. (T.), R.A.F.   1913
  (W.)
BILTON, C. H. E. Capt., Highland Cyclist Bn.   1908
✠BILTON, E. B. Capt., King's Own (Yorkshire L.I.) *M.*   1906
  Killed in action at Achiet-le-Petit 14 *March* 1917
BIRCH, J. R. Capt., R.E. (London Electrical Engineers,   1902
  T.F.)
BIRD, S. 2nd Lieut., Dorset Regt.   1906
BIRKBECK, M. Lieut., R.N.A.S.   1910
BIRNSTINGL, C. A. 2nd Lieut., R. Fusiliers   1913
BISCOE, V. F. Capt., London Regt. (L.R.B.)   1905
BISHOP, P. F. Capt., R.A.M.C.   1913
✠BLACK, G. D. A. Lieut., R. Fusiliers   [1914]
  Killed in action 21 *June* 1916
✠BLACK, J. N. Major, Somerset L.I. *M.*   1913
  Killed in action 9 *April* 1917
BLACK, R. B. 2nd Lieut., 3rd Dragoon Gds.; Capt.,   1896
  Middlesex Regt. and Spec. List (Recruiting Staff)
BLACKBURNE, Rev. H. W. C.F. 1st Class, R.A.C.D.;   1897
  A.C.G. *D.S.O. M.C. M* 4.
BLADON, J. W. Pte., London Regt. (Artists Rifles)   1909
BLADON, M. W. B. Sub-Lieut., R.N.V.R.   1913
BLAIR, A. 2nd Lieut., R. Scots(T.F.) (W.)   1897
BLATHERWICK, R. Capt., R. Scots Fus.; Capt. (A.),   1908
  R.A.F. (W 2.)
BLOCKEY, H. S. Capt., S. Staffs. Regt.; Major (Ad.),   1904
  R.A.F. (W.) *m. French Croix de Guerre*
BLOW, A. E. Lieut., Spec. List, empld. Records   1913

BODLEY, A. L.   Capt., R.A.M.C.(T.F.).   *M.C.*   1909
BODVEL-ROBERTS, H. F.   Capt., R.A.M.C.   1892
BOLLAND, J. F.   Cadet, O.C.B.   1917
BOND, G. W.   Major, S. and T. Corps, Indian Army.   1891
D.S.O.   M 2.
BONHOTE, Rev. E. F.   Lieut., Rugby School O.T.C.;   1907
Pte., M.G.C.
✠BOSTON, L.   Lieut., W. Yorks. Regt.; attd. M.G.C.   (W.)   1911
M.
Accidentally killed at Aldershot 9 May 1916
✠BOTHAM, A. F.   Gnr., H.A.C.; 2nd Lieut., R.F.A.   *M.*   1908
Died 18 June 1917 of wounds received in action in E.
Africa
BOTTOMLEY, A. C.   Lieut., R.N.V.R.   1904
BOTTOMLEY, R. A. A.   Lieut.-Col., W. Yorks. Regt. (T.F.   1889
Res.); empld. Ministry of National Service.   *m.*
BOUCHER, R. E.   Capt., Leicestershire Regt.; Capt. and   1913
Adjt., Tank Corps.   *M.*
BOULDERSON, G.   Lieut., S. and T. Corps, E. African Force   1908
BOULTON, H.   Lieut.-Col., I.M.S.; D.A.D.M.S.   *Brevet*   1891
Lieut.-Colonel.   M 3.
BOULTON, R. J.   Capt., Herefordshire Regt. and King's   1911
(Shropshire L.I.)
BOWCHER, F. H.   Lieut., R.G.A.   1895
BOWEN, T. S.   Capt., Welsh Regt.; attd. M.G.C.; empld.   1910
Admiralty
✠BOWLES, R. J. A.   Lieut., R. Welsh Fus.   (W.)   1910
Died 20 July 1916 of wounds received in action
✠BRADSHAW-ISHERWOOD, F. E.   Lieut.-Col., York and Lan-   1887
caster Regt.   *Brevet Lieut.-Colonel.   M.*
Killed in action at Zillebeke 8 May 1915.
✠BREWER, C. H.   2nd Lieut., Lancs. Fus.   1903
Killed in action 4 Oct. 1917
✠BRIGGS, G. C.   Capt., R. Scots Fus.   *M.*   1896
Killed in action on the Aisne 15–16 Oct. 1914
✠BRODIE, H. W.   Capt., The Buffs (E. Kent Regt.)   *M.*   1895
Killed in action 13 Oct. 1915
BRODIE, P.   Lieut., Highland L.I.; Capt., Spec. List   1899
(Bde. Bombing Officer).   (W.)
BROGDEN, G. A.   Capt., R.A.M.C.(T.F.)   1887
✠BROGDEN, I. R. R.   Lieut., R.A.M.C.   1910
Drowned on H.M. transport 15 April 1917
✠BROMET, J. N.   Lieut., R.F.A.   1911
Killed in action 30 Nov. 1917

✠Brooks, L. W. Lieut., W. Yorks. Regt.; attd. Lincoln- 1911
shire Regt.
Killed in action in the Battle of Loos 25 *Sept.* 1915
✠Brothers, M. Capt., E. Lancs. Regt.(T.F.) 1901
Killed in action 28 *May* 1917
✠Brown, G. S. R. J. 2nd Lieut., R. Scots Fus. 1909
Died 22 *May* 1915 *of wounds received in action*
Brown, J. D. 2nd Lieut., Labour Corps 1903
Browse, G. Colonel, I.M.S.; A.D.M.S. *D.S.O. Brevet* 1892
Lieut.-Colonel. M 2.
Brunton, A. Corpl., R.A.S.C.(M.T.) 1901
✠Bucknell, W. W. Trooper, K. Edward's Horse; Lieut., [1914]
R.F.A. (W.)
Killed in action 10 *Aug.* 1917
Burges-Bayly, A. R. Lieut., Herefordshire Regt. 1893
Burlison, J. C. Capt. and Adjt., M.G.C. (Motor). *M* 2. 1892
✠Burnand, G. C. Lieut. (E.O.), R.F.C. 1901
Killed in action 7 *April* 1917
Burn-Callender, F. Capt., R.F.A. *M.C.* 1907
Burnside, B. Surgeon Lieut., R.N. *Mentioned in* 1909
French General Orders for saving life from drowning.
French Silver Medal, 2*nd Class*
Burrell, E. M. Capt., R. Welsh Fus. 1911
Burrell, G. P. Major, Hampshire Regt. *M.C. M.* 1899
Burrell, H. A. Capt., Hampshire Regt. 1900
Burrill-Robinson, W. R. Capt., Yorkshire Regt. 1903
Burton, G. E. Surgeon Lieut., R.N. 1911
Burton, P. M. A.B., R.N.V.R. 1890
Buss, H. S. 2nd Lieut., Rifle Brigade 1913
Butler, E. N. Major, R.A.M.C.(T.F.); Capt., Spec. 1907
List. *M.B.E.*
Buttanshaw, C. Lieut., R.G.A. 1910
✠Byatt, H. V. B. Capt., I.M.S. 1901
Died (11 *March* 1915) *of wounds received in action near*
Neuve Chapelle
Byatt, R. N. B. 2nd Lieut., R.F.A. 1907
Byrne, M. G. M. C. Capt., Middlesex Regt. 1912
✠Byrne-Johnson, J. V. Capt. and Adjt., Rifle Brigade. *M.* 1912
Killed in action at Delville Wood 23 *Aug.* 1916

Campbell, B. P. Capt., R.A.M.C. 1900
Campbell, E. N. McC. Cadet, O.C.B. 1917
Carden-Roe, W. R. Capt., R. Irish Fus.; Major, 1893
G.S.O. 2. *M.C. M.*

CAREY, F. C. S. Lce.-Corpl., R.A.M.C.(T.F.); Major, 1901
R.A.O.C.; D.A.D.O.S.
CARR-FORSTER, E. W. Lieut., R.G.A. 1912
CARTHEW, R. J. Hon. Colonel, R.F.A. (R. of O.);Lieut.- 1882
Col., Gen. Staff. *m.*
CARTMAN, J. P. C. Lieut., Dorset Regt. (W.) 1894
CARVER, A. E. Capt., R.A.M.C. 1891
CARVER, H., T.D. Capt., Cheshire Yeo. 1902
CASEY, H. J. Major, R.G.A.(T.F.) *M.C.* 1903
CASSIDY, M. A. Capt., R.A.M.C.(T.F.) 1898
CAWTHRA, J. J. Capt., Canadian A.M.C. 1897
CAZALET, R. G. Capt., I.A.R.O., attd. 17th Cavalry. *M.* 1909
CHAPPELL, H. S. 2nd Lieut., King s Own (Yorkshire 1906
L.I.); Lieut., Res. Regt. of Cavalry and King's
African Rifles
CHAYTOR, A. H. Capt., London Regt. (Post Office 1888
Rifles); A.D.C.
CHAYTOR, D'A. Lieut.-Col., Canterbury Rifles, N. 1893
Zealand Force; Cmdt., Administrative H.Q., Egypt.
C.M.G. *M* 2. *Order of the Nile, 3rd Class (Egypt)*
CHIBNALL, A. C. Capt., R.A.S.C.; Capt. (A.), R.A.F. 1912
CHIGNELL, N. J. Lieut., Charterhouse School O.T.C. 1902
CHINNECK, S. T. E. 2nd Lieut., Bradfield College O.T.C. 1895
✠CLAIRMONTE, G. E. 2nd Lieut., Gloucestershire Regt. [1914]
Killed in action at Hulluch 25–26 *Sept.* 1915
✠CLARK, G. R. H. 2nd Lieut., R. Fusiliers; Lieut., N. 1914
Staffs. Regt. (W.) *M.*
Killed in action near Baku 26 *Aug.* 1918
CLARK, H. J. Lieut., Durham L.I.; Staff Capt.; empld. 1911
War Office
CLARK, Rev. S. H. C.F. 4th Class, R.A.C.D. 1888
CLARKE, A. S. Major, R. Sussex Regt.; attd. Gen. Staff 1900
✠CLARKE, HAROLD M. Lieut., London Regt. (Poplar and 1907
Stepney Rifles)
Killed in action in the Battle of Loos 26 *Sept.* 1915
CLARKE, HENRY M. Capt., R.A.M.C.(T.F.) *M.* 1897
CLARKE, H. T. Lieut.-Col., Worcestershire Regt. *D.S.O.* 1890
and Bar. M 2.
✠CLAYE, G. W. Lieut., Cheshire Regt. 1912
Died 29 *March* 1917 *of wounds received in action*
CLAYTON, J. Capt., R.A.M.C. (Sanitary Service, T.F.) 1905
M 2. *Chevalier, Ordre du Mérite Agricole (France)*
CLIFFORD, E. C. Major, R.F.A. (W.) *D.S.O. M.C.* 1908
M 2.

CLISSOLD, Rev. C. H. C.F. 4th Class, R.A.C.D. 1887

COCKS, H. S. Lieut., R.A.S.C. 1910

COE, C. G. Major (T.), R.A.F. *M.B.E. M.* 1893

✠COLE, L. S. 2nd Lieut., Cheshire Regt. 1909
Killed in action 3 *Oct.* 1915

COLLIER, A. C. 2nd Lieut., King's Own (R. Lancaster [1914]
Regt.); Lieut. (A.), R.A.F. (P.) *M.*

COLVILLE, N. R. Lieut., Argyll and Sutherland Hdrs.; 1913
Capt., Spec. List, empld. Ministry of Labour. (W.)
M.C. M.

CONSIDINE, H. H. Lieut., R.G.A.; empld. Board of Trade 1905

✠CONSTANTINE, H. N. Capt., Yorkshire Regt.(T.F.) (W.) 1910
M.C.
Killed in action 27 *May* 1918

CONSTANTINE, W. W. Major, Yorkshire Regt.; empld. 1905
Ministry of Shipping. (W 3.) *M.C. M.*

CONWAY, S. V. Lieut., R.G.A. 1903

✠COOPER, A. L. 2nd Lieut., London Regt. (St Pancras Bn.) 1913
Killed in action at High Wood 15 *Sept.* 1916

COPE, J. R. O. Lieut., R.A.S.C. 1897

COPE, W., M.P. Major, Glamorgan Yeo. 1888

CORNELIUS, N. S. Lieut., R.G.A.(T.F.) 1905

COTT, A. M. Lieut. (T.), R.A.F. 1906

COTT, A. W. Lieut. (T.), R.A.F. 1906

COUSENS, R. B. Major, R.F.A.; Lieut.-Col., A.A. and 1898
Q.M.G. *D.S.O. M* 4.

COW, C. S. 2nd Lieut., R.A.S.C. 1898

COX, R. B. 2nd Lieut., King's Own (Yorkshire L.I.); 1912
Capt., Yorkshire Regt.

CRAMPTON, E. B. Lieut. (A.), R.F.C. 1899

CRAMPTON, H. P. Capt., R.A.M.C.(T.F.) 1897

CRICK, Rev. P. C. T. C.F. 2nd Class, R.A.C.D.; D.A.C.G. *1906

CRITCHETT, G. M. Capt., London Regt. (Q.V.R.); empld. 1903
War Office

CROCKER, G. G. Lieut., 6th (Inniskilling) Dragoons; attd. 1912
Gen. Staff (Intelligence). *M.B.E. m.*

CROFTON-ATKINS, W. A. Lieut., R.A.S.C. 1896

CROSFIELD, Rev. A. C. C.F. 4th Class, R.A.C.D. 1887

CROSHAW, F. P. Lieut., Yorkshire Regt.; attd. S. Wales 1900
Borderers

✠CROSS, R. C. Trooper, Strathcona's Horse, Canadian 1911
Force; Lieut., Dorset Yeo.; attd. S. Lancs. Regt.
(W.) *M.*
Killed in action 7 *June* 1918

✠CROSSLEY, A. H. Lieut., Herefordshire Regt. 1897
Died 10 *May* 1917 *of wounds received in action* 9 *April* 1917

CROSSLEY, E. A. Capt., Sherwood Foresters (Notts. and 1899 Derby Regt.) (W.)

CROSSLEY, F. M. Lieut., R.A.S.C. 1904

CROWE, D. M. Lieut., Bedfordshire Regt. and Nigeria 1911 Regt., W. African Frontier Force. (W.) *M.C.*

CROWTHER, H. O. Pte., Queen's Own (R.W. Kent Regt., 1907 T.F.); Capt., I.A.R.O., attd. 119th Infy. *M.B.E. M.*

CRUICKSHANK, G. Lieut., R.F.A.(T.F.); attd. R.E. (Sig- 1913 nals). *M.*

CUMMING, W. Lieut., Highland L.I. (W 2.) *M.* 1897

CUNNINGHAM REID, A. *See* REID, A. CUNNINGHAM

CURLING, W. G. Major, R.F.A.; empld. Ministry of 1898 Munitions

✠CUTHBERTSON, E. H. Lieut., R. Warwickshire Regt. (W.) 1907
Died in Mesopotamia 24 *July* 1917 *of sunstroke*

✠CUTLER, E. T. 2nd Lieut., Essex Regt. 1905
Killed in action 9 *Aug.* 1917

CUTLER, H. A. Capt., R.A.M.C. 1893

DAIN, G. R. Lieut. and Adjt., Sherwood Rangers; 1903 Major, R.G.A.(T.F.) *M.C. M.*

D'ALBUQUERQUE, N. P. Lieut., King's (Shropshire L.I.) 1912 (W.)

✠DALE, A. P. Major, W. Yorks. Regt.(T.F.) 1898
Killed in action 27 *Feb.* 1917

DALTRY, R. W. O. 2nd Lieut., Northamptonshire Regt. 1917 (W.)

DANIELS, Rev. A. P. C.F. 4th Class, R.A.C.D. *M.C.* 1908

DARBISHIRE, H. D. Major, R.F.A.(T.F.) 1900

DARBY, A. J. L. Lieut., R.N.V.R. 1895

DASHWOOD, H. T. A. Lieut., Grenadier Gds. 1896

DAVEY, H. C. Lieut., Essex Regt.(T.F.); Capt., R. 1893 Sussex Regt. (T.F.)

DAVEY, H. N. 2nd Lieut., R.G.A.; Lieut., R.E.; Capt., 1907 G.S.O. 3. *M.*

✠DAVEY, S. G. Major, Norfolk Regt.(T.F.); attd. M.G.C. 1912
Killed in action 25 *March* 1918

DAVID, M. Major, R.E. (R. Monmouth) *D.S.O. M.* 1895

DAVIDSON, Rev. G. M. C.F. 4th Class, R.A.C.D. 1894

✠DAVIES, T. J. C. 2nd Lieut., Welsh Regt. [1914]
Killed in action in the Battle of Loos 2 *Oct.* 1915

Davis, C. E. J. Capt., Rifle Brigade   1898
✠Davis, W. J. Lieut., Northumberland Fus.(T.F.)   1909
    Killed in action 30 June 1916
Dawson, C. P. Lieut.-Col. (ret.), attd. R.A.O.C.   1875
de Courcy Ireland, G. B. *See* Ireland, G. B. de Courcy
De Freitas, D. A. A. 2nd Lieut., Gloucestershire Regt.;   1913
    attd. E. Lancs. Regt. (W 2.)
De Freitas, J. M. Capt., Gloucestershire Regt. (W.)   1909
    O.B.E.
Delius, S. St M. Capt. and Adjt., Yorkshire Dragoons.   1908
    M.
✠Denis Browne, W. C. Sub-Lieut., R.N.V.R. (Hood Bn.,   1907
    R.N.D.) (W.)
    Died 14 June 1915 of wounds received in action in
    Gallipoli
Depree, H. T. Surgeon Lieut., R.N.   1904
Dew, J. W. Major, R.A.M.C. *M.C.* *M 2.*   1906
✠Dewar, A. Lieut., R.E. *M.*   1904
    Died 21 Dec. 1914 of wounds received in action near
    Ypres
Dinn, H. K. Lieut., King's Royal Rifle Corps. (W.)   1903
✠Dolby, H. A. Pte., Middlesex Regt. (P.S. Bn.); Lieut.,   1913
    Leicestershire Regt.
    Killed in action 7 May 1917
✠Donahoo, M. G. Capt., King's Own (Yorkshire L.I.)   1892
    M.C.
    Died 31 Jan. 1917 of wounds received in action
Donnithorne, V. H. 2nd Lieut., Hampshire Regt.   1911
    (W.) *M.C.*
Dorling, Rev. E. E. C.F. 4th Class, R.A.C.D.   1881
Dottridge, C. A. Capt., R.A.M.C.   1903
Doughty, W. H. Lieut., Liverpool Institute O.T.C.   1905
Douthwaite, A. W. S. Lieut., R.G.A.   1907
Downton, A. M. Capt., R.F.A.(T.F.)   1906
✠Drummond-Fraser, H. R. Capt., Cheshire Regt.; attd.   1913
    Herefordshire Regt. *M.C.*
    Killed in action 1 Aug. 1918
Duckham, T. H. Capt., R.F.A.(T.F.)   1906
Duncan, M. M., t.d. Lieut.-Col., R.F.A.(T.F.) *C.M.G.*   1885
    M 2.
✠Dunn, P. M. Capt., R. Welsh Fus.   1908
    Killed in action in India 3 Feb. 1917
Durell, C. V. Lieut., R.G.A.; Staff Capt. *M.*   1900
Dyer, F. N. V. Surgeon Lieut., R.N.   1912

CLARE COLLEGE 37

✠DYSON, H. A. Capt., The Buffs (E. Kent Regt.) (W.) 1912
M.
Killed in action 18 *Nov.* 1916

EDWARDS, H. S. Capt., R.A.S.C.; attd. The Queen's (R.W. 1911
Surrey Regt.) *M.*
EDWARDS, R. H. Lieut., Worcestershire Regt.; empld. 1905
Command Depôt
ELDERTON, M. B. Capt., R.G.A. 1903
ELDERTON, T. H. Lieut., Bedfordshire Regt. (W.) 1905
ELLIOTT, M. L. F. Capt. and Adjt., Gloucestershire 1909
Regt. *M.B.E.*
ELLIOTT, T. R. Colonel, A.M.S. *C.B.E. D.S.O. M* 3. *1908
ELLIS, B. W. Capt., R.F.A. 1901
ELLIS, D. W. Lieut., Scots Gds.; Major, Spec. List 1910
(Chief Instructor, Corps Reinforcement Depôt).
(W.) *Italian Croce di Guerra*
ENGLAND, F. Capt., King's Royal Rifle Corps and Gen. 1902
List (A.P.M.) (W.) *M.*
ENTWISLE, F. W. Capt., Manchester Regt.(T.F.) *M.C.* [1914]
M.
ENYS, C. R. S. Pte., Suffolk Regt. 1916
EVANS, Rev. E. G. C.F. 4th Class, R.A.C.D. 1888
EVANS, H. J. A. Major, R.F.A. and Gen. Staff (O.C.B.) 1898
M.B.E. m.
EVANS, J. R. A. Capt., R.F.A.(T.F.). *M.* 1913
EVERS, Rev. M. S. C.F. 4th Class, R.A.C.D. (W.) 1906
M.C. and Bar
EWEN, J. F. B. Lieut., Gen. List, attd. Sherwood For- 1912
esters (Notts. and Derby Regt.) *M.*
EXSHAW, T. S. N. Lieut., R.A.S.C. 1912

✠FALLOWES, J. T. C. Pte., Canadian Infy.; Lieut., Suffolk 1910
Regt.
Killed in action 15 *Sept.* 1916
FARIE, A. J. C. Major, R.A.S.C. 1901
✠FARMER, J. I. 2nd Lieut., King's Royal Rifle Corps 1913
Killed in action 9 *May* 1915
FASSON, F. H. Capt., Scottish Horse and Remount Ser- 1896
vice. *M* 2.
FAULDER, T. J. Capt., R.A.M.C.(T.F.) 1889
FAUQUET LEMAITRE, P. A. Cuirassiers of the Guard, 1906
French Army

✠FEILDEN, O. H. Capt. and Adjt., Leicestershire Regt.   1907
   Died 29 *Sept.* 1917 *of wounds received in action* 28
   Sept. 1917
FERGUS, A. McF. H. 2nd Lieut., Seaforth Hdrs.   1911
FINDLAY, J. Capt., R. Irish Rifles. (W.) *M.C.*   1913
FISCHER, F. N. 2nd Lieut., R.A.S.C.   1886
✠FISHER, G. H. Pte., Canadian Mtd. Rifles; 2nd Lieut.,   1906
   Sherwood Foresters (Notts. and Derby Regt.)
   Died 25 *Oct.* 1915 *of wounds received in action*
FLEMING-BROWN, G. F. Lieut., Bedfordshire Regt.;   1912
   Capt., O.C.B.
FLETCHER, W. T. Capt., 97th Deccan Infy., Indian Army   1902
   (P.)
FOLLIT, H. H. B. Lieut.-Col., Australian A.M.C.;   1900
   D.A.D.M.S. *M.*
FORBES, J. F. Lieut., Seaforth Hdrs.; Staff Lieut.   1908
FORD, H. J. Pte., London Regt. (Artists Rifles)   1879
FORDE, C. L. Major, R.A.M.C.   1900
FOWLE, Sir H.W. H. Colonel, S. African Defence Force;   1890
   Provost-Marshal and Commissioner for Enemy
   Subjects. *K.B.E. C.B.E.*
✠FOX, R. W. Lieut.-Col. Devon Regt.(T.F.) *M.*   1885
   Killed in action in Mesopotamia 8 *March* 1916
FRANKS, G. L. T. Pte., R.A.M.C.   1908
FRASER, J. H. Lce.-Corpl., Highland L.I.   1897
FRASER, T. Colonel, R.E.; Major-Gen. *C.B. C.S.I.*   1884
   C.M.G. Brevet Colonel. M 7. *Order of the White*
   Eagle, 4*th Class, with swords* (*Serbia*)
FREEBORN, J. H. R. Lieut., York and Lancaster Regt.;   1911
   Capt., Spec. List (Adjt., Vol. Bn.)
FREEMAN, J. E. Lieut., Essex Regt.; Capt., Spec. List   1900
   (Bde. Bombing Officer)
FROST, H. K. Major, R.F.A.(T.F.)   1904
✠FROST, T. L. Capt. and Adjt., Cheshire Regt. *M.*   1907
   Killed in action near Ypres 28 *March* 1915
FRY, K. R. B. 2nd Lieut., King's Royal Rifle Corps   1901
✠FRY, L. H. Lieut., N. Somerset Yeo. and 19th Hussars.   1910
   M.
   Killed in action at Caix 9 *Aug.* 1918
FURSDON, A. A. Capt., Devon Regt.(T.F.)   .   1914

✠GAFFIKIN, G. H. Major, R. Irish Rifles. *M.*   1905
   Killed in action at Thiepval 1 *July* 1916
GALLOWAY, W. D. Surgeon Lieut., R.N. *M.*   1907

GARRARD, G. G. C. Pte., H.A.C.; 2nd Lieut., R.E.(T.F.) 1909
✠GARROD, R. P. 2nd Lieut., London Regt. (Rifles) [1914]
 Killed in action 22 *May* 1915
GARSON, H. L. Capt., R.A.M.C. (W.) *O.B.E. M.C.* 1909
 M 4.
GASCOIGNE, T. 2nd Lieut., Northamptonshire Regt. 1900
GASKELL, J. G. Major, R.F.A.(T.F.); attd. R.G.A. 1903
GASKING, E. B. 2nd Lieut., Labour Corps 1916
GATEHOUSE, H. 2nd Lieut., R.E. and R.A.S.C.; Major, 1890
 Spec. List (Courts-Martial Officer). *O.B.E.*
GAWLER, A. E. J. Lieut., Somerset L.I.(T.F.) 1912
GAY, L. H. Capt., S. Lancs. Regt.; Major, R. Defence 1889
 Corps. *m.*
GAYNE, A. A. A. Capt., Army Pay Dept. 1909
GIBBS, J. W. Pte., London Regt.; 2nd Lieut., R. Sussex 1901
 Regt.
GIBSON, D. K. Lieut., R.G.A.(T.F.); attd. R.A.O.C. 1908
GIBSON, G. M. Pte., Canadian Force 1899
GIBSON, W. F. A.B., R.N.V.R. 1914
GIFFORD, R. E. Capt., Somerset L.I.; Instructor in Mus- 1903
 ketry
GILL, H. L. O. Trooper, Worcestershire Yeo.; 2nd 1913
 Lieut., Staffordshire Yeo.; Lieut., Gloucestershire
 Regt.; attd. R. Welsh Fus. (W 2.) *M.C.*
✠GLENNY, H. Q. Assistant Resident, N. Nigeria 1898
 Died 18 *Nov.* 1914 *of wounds received in action at*
 Gazabu (Cameroons) 16 *Nov.* 1914
GLYNN, E. E. Capt., R.A.M.C. (1st W. Gen. Hospital, 1892
 T.F.). *m.*
GLYNN, E. H. Trooper, K. Edward's Horse 1912
GLYNNE, A. Lieut. (A.), R.A.F. (W.) 1910
GOING, T. H. 2nd Lieut., R.F.A.; Lieut., R.T.O. 1895
✠GOLDTHORPE, A. F. 2nd Lieut., E. Yorks. Regt. 1913
 Killed in action 12 *May* 1917
✠GOODHART, E. J. Sergt., R.E. (Signals). *D.C.M. M.* 1913
 French Médaille Militaire
 Died April 1915 *of typhoid contracted on active service*
✠GORDON, E. P. Lieut., R.E.; attd. 104th Rifles, Indian 1909
 Army
 Killed in action in Mesopotamia Nov. 1915
GORDON, W. B. Capt., R.A.M.C. (W.) *M.* 1908
GORDON BROWNE, H. H. Lieut., Worcestershire Regt.; 1893
 Lieut.-Col., Somerset L.I.(T.F.); Administrative
 Cmdt. *D.S.O. M* 2.

GOULD, E. 2nd Lieut., King's Own (Yorkshire L.I.); 1898
Capt. and Adjt., Lovat's Scouts; attd. 12th Lancers;
Capt., Spec. List (Intelligence Staff)

GOULD, H. C. Trooper, K. Edward's Horse. (W.) 1911

GOWANS, J., D.S.O. Hon. Lieut.-Col. R.A. (R. of O.), 1890
empld. R.F.A. *M* 2.

GRACE, C. R. Lieut., Lovat's Scouts; Hon. Lieut. (A.), 1905
R.A.F.

GRAHAM, G. L. 2nd Lieut., 18th Hussars; Capt. (A.), 1914
R.A.F. *D.F.C. Chevalier, Legion of Honour (France).
French Croix de Guerre*

GRAHAM, G. W. Major, R.G.A.; Instructor of Artil- 1892
lery

✠GRAHAM, R. L. Lieut., R.F.A. and R.F.C. (W.) *M.* 1914
Killed in action 16 Sept. 1917

GRAHAM-HODGSON, H. K. Corpl., R.E. (Signals); Capt., 1910
R.A.M.C.

✠GRANDAGE, W. B. Lieut.-Col., R.F.A.(T.F.) 1899
Died 14 May 1917 *of wounds received in action*

GRANGER, E. H. H. Capt., R.A.M.C. *M.C.* 1909

GRAY, W. Capt., Yorkshire Regt. (W.) (P.) *M.* [1914]

GREEN, B. B. Capt., Essex Regt. 1899

GREEN, Rev. L. N. C.F. 4th Class, R.A.C.D. *m.* 1899

✠GREGORY, S. B. Lieut., Devon Regt.(T.F.); attd. Queen's 1913
Own (R. W. Kent Regt.) (P.)
Died at Mosul 3 June 1916

GREGSON, C. D. Major, 20th Deccan Horse, Indian 1899
Army

GREIG, J. L. Major, Remount Service 1887

GRIEVE, A. B. Instructor Lieut., R.N. 1908

GRIFFITH, A. L. P. Major, R.F.A. (W 3.) *D.S.O. Brevet* 1905
Major. M 4.

GRIFFITH, R. Major, R. Welsh Fus.(T.F.); Lieut.-Col., 1892
R.A.M.C. (W.) *Brevet Lieut.-Colonel. M* 2.

GRONOW, W. H. 2nd Lieut., R. Welsh Fus. 1909

GROSE, T. Capt. and Adjt., R.A.S.C. 1914

GROSE, T. A. Lieut., R.G.A. (W.) 1902

GUILFORD, E. L. 2nd Lieut., Sherwood Foresters (Notts. 1903
and Derby Regt.)

GUSH, C. R. Lieut., R.E. (W.) 1913

GUTHRIE, A. G. Lieut., R.E.(T.F.) 1904

GUTHRIE, N. B. Corpl., R.E. (Signals); Lieut., King's 1913
(Liverpool Regt., Liverpool Scottish, T.F.). (W.)

GYLES, W. H. K. Capt., R.E. (Railways). *M* 2. 1903

HABERSHON, Rev. E. F. C.F. 4th Class, R.A.C.D. (W.) 1904
✠HABERSHON, P. H. 2nd Lieut., King's Royal Rifle Corps 1912
Killed in action 25 Sept. 1915
✠HABERSHON, S. H. 2nd Lieut., Suffolk Regt. (W.) *M.* 1908
Killed in action 8–13 April 1918
HABGOOD, G. Capt., R.A.M.C. 1909
✠HAINES, F. P. Lieut., Leicestershire Regt. 1907
Killed in action 15 June 1917
HALL, A. K. D. Major, Dorset Regt.; G.S.O. 3 1904
HALL, H. Corpl., R.E. (Signals); Lieut., R.F.A. (W.) 1911
HALL, J. A. Lieut.-Cdr., R.N.V.R. 1905
HALL, P. A. Major, Oxford and Bucks. L.I.; Lieut.-Col., 1910
R. Warwickshire Regt. *D.S.O. M.C. M. Italian
Bronze Medal for Military Valour*
HANSEN, J. C. Capt., Hampshire Regt. *M.* 1913
HANSON, C. E. B. Major, D. of Wellington's (W. Riding 1892
Regt.)
✠HARBORD, J. Capt., Norfolk Yeo.; attd. Norfolk Regt. 1911
(W.) *M.C.*
Died 10 July 1918 *of wounds received in action*
HARGREAVES, R. Q.M.S., H.A.C. 1899
HARRIES-JONES, J. S. D. Lieut. (T.), R.A.F. 1910
HARRIS, A. F. S. Major, R.G.A.(T.F.) 1908
HARRISON, W. J. Capt., R.G.A.; Asst. Proof and Ex- 1903
perimental Officer, Woolwich Arsenal. *M.B.E. m.*
HARROWING, W. W. 2nd Lieut., D. of Cornwall's L.I. 1915
HART, S. Major R.F.A.(T.F.) (W.) *M.C.* 1907
HARTCUP, G. H. W. Major, R.G.A. *M.C. M.* 1904
HARTCUP, R. E. 2nd Lieut., R.G.A. 1907
HAWTHORNE, C. B. Capt., R.A.M.C.(T.F.) 1901
HAY, J. A., T.D. Major, Inns of Court O.T.C. *m.* 1884
HAY-ROBERTSON, J. W. Capt., Black Watch (T.F.) (W.) 1908
M.C. and Bar
HEDDERWICK, A. S. Capt., Spec. List, empld. Records; 1904
Staff Capt. *M.*
HEDDERWICK, G. Lieut., R. Scots; Major, Tank Corps. 1912
M.C.
HEDGES, A. D. 2nd Lieut., R.F.A. (W.) [1914]
HEELIS, J. R. Major, Manchester Regt.; attd. Welsh 1898
Regt. (W.) *M.C. M* 3.
HEGARTY, M. B. 2nd Lieut., R.A.S.C. 1915
✠HELE-SHAW, H. R. Pte., R. Fusiliers (P. S. Bn.); 2nd [1914]
Lieut., R.G.A.; Lieut. (A.), R.F.C. (W.)
Killed in action 19 July 1916

✠HEMSWORTH, A. H. 2nd Lieut., King's Own (Yorkshire   1913
L.I.)
Accidentally killed in motor accident 6 June 1915
✠HENDERSON, D. 2nd Lieut., King's Royal Rifle Corps   1912
Killed in action 11 Jan. 1915
✠HENDERSON, N. C. 2nd Lieut., Black Watch   1913
Killed in action 25 Sept. 1915
HENDERSON, R. K. 2nd Lieut., Grenadier Gds.   1903
HENDRICKS, C. A. C. J. Capt. and Adjt., King's Own   1902
(Yorkshire L I.) (W.) *M.C.*
HERRIOT, J. A. Capt., Northumberland Fus.; attd.   1904
M.G.C.
HERRMAN, L. C. Sergt., Middlesex Regt.   1913
HESKETH, G. M. Major, Loyal N. Lancs. Regt.(T.F.)   1906
HICKS, E. J. Sergt., London Regt. (Artists Rifles)   1910
HIGGINS, L. G. Surgeon Lieut., R.N.   1912
HILL, G. M. Capt., D. of Wellington's (W. Riding   1911
Regt.). (W 2.) *M.*
HINDE, S. L. Major, R.A.M.C. *M.*   1881
HODGE, D. S. Capt., R.A.S.C.   1894
HODGE, E. H. V. Capt., I.M.S. *M.*   1902
HODGSON, A. J. Capt., King's (Liverpool Regt.) and   1906
Spec. List (Courts-Martial Officer). (W.) *m.*
HOLLAND, J. E. D. Capt., 5th (Princess Charlotte of   1898
Wales's) Dragoon Gds.; Major, G.S.O. 2. (W.)
D.S.O. M.C. M 3.
HOLMAN, A. F. Capt., D. of Cornwall's L.I.   1888
HOLMES, A. K. Lieut., R. Sussex Regt.   1900
HOLT,H.D.G. Lieut., R. Fusiliers; attd. N. Staffs. Regt.   1913
and R.F.C. (W.)
HOOKER, C. W. R. Lieut., R.N.V.R. *O.B.E.*   1904
HOOPER, F. H. Capt. and Adjt., R.F.A.; Major, R.F.C.   1905
(W.) *M. m* 2.
HOPE, H. N. Lieut.. Grenadier Gds.   1902
HOPKINS, Rev. N. T. C.F. 4th Class, R.A.C.D.; Chap-   1910
lain, R.A.F.
HORSLEY, G. Capt., R.G.A.(T.F.)   [1914]
HORSLEY, S. Major, R.G.A.(T.F.)   1901
✠HOSKYNS, H. C. W. Major, Lincolnshire Regt. *D.S.O.*   1893
M.
Killed in action 25 Sept. 1915
HOTBLACK, H. S. Lieut., R.F.A.(T.F.)   1908
HOUSEMAN, E. A. Major, Indian Defence Force Med.   1891
Corps

HOWARD, J. C. Lieut., Lincolnshire Regt.; Capt., Spec. 1906
List (Courts-Martial Officer)
HOWELL, J. H. Lieut., Pembroke Yeo.; attd. Dragoon 1899
Gds.
HOWITT, A. B. Capt., R.A.M.C. 1898
HUDSON, B. Major, R.A.M.C. 1896
HUDSON, N. Pte., R. Fusiliers (Sportsman's Bn.) (W.) 1911
(P.)
HUGHES, E. C. Capt., R.A.M.C. (2nd London Gen. 1898
Hospital, T.F.) O.B.E.
HUGHES, E. L. Major, Northamptonshire Regt.; Lieut.- 1895
Col., A.A. and Q.M.G.; Base Cmdt., Taranto. D.S.O.
O.B.E. M 4. Officer, Order of St Maurice and St
Lazarus (Italy)
HUGHES, O. Capt. (A.), R.A.F. 1908
HUGHES, T. J. 2nd Lieut., Loyal N. Lancs. Regt. 1913
HULBERT, M. L. Lieut., R. North Devon Yeo.; attd. 1905
M.G.C.
HUMPHRYS, R. P. Capt., King's (Liverpool Regt., T.F.) M. 1909
HUNT, E. G. Lieut., Middlesex Regt. (W.) 1898
HUNTER, E. J. Capt., Suffolk Regt. (Cyclist Bn., T.F.) 1909
HUNTER, M. J. Capt., R.F.A.(T.F.) 1909
✠HUNTER, N. F. Lieut., R. Warwickshire Regt.; attd. R. 1897
Fusiliers
Died 16 June 1915 of wounds received in action
HUSSEY-MACPHERSON, L. F. Capt., Cameron Hdrs.; 1908
empld. War Office and O.C.B. (W 2.) M.
HUTCHINSON, G. C. Capt., Lancs. Fus.(T.F.); (W.) 1912
M.C. M.
✠HUTCHINSON, J. G. Lieut., R.F.A.(T.F.) 1915
Killed in action 10 Nov. 1918
✠HUTCHINSON, L. G. Lieut., E. Yorks. Regt. (W.) 1912
Killed in action 10 Sept. 1918
HUTCHINSON, N. W. 2nd Lieut., R. Jersey Militia; Capt. 1907
and Adjt., R.A.S.C. m.
HUTCHINSON, R. H. Capt., R.A.M.C. 1901

IMBERT-TERRY, F. B. Lieut., Devon Regt. M.C. M 2. 1906
INCHBALD, Rev. C. C. E. C.F. 4th Class, R.A.C.D. 1909
IONIDES, A. G. Lieut., R.N.V.R. 1888
IRELAND, G. B. DE COURCY. Capt. and Adjt., King's Royal 1913
Rifle Corps. (W 2.) M.V.O. M.C.
IRELAND-BLACKBURNE, C. G. C. M. Lieut., R.A.S.C. 1909
ISHERWOOD, F. E. B. See BRADSHAW-ISHERWOOD, F. E.

JACKSON, A. L. Capt., R.A.M.C.   1886
JACKSON, R. W. P. Major, R.A.M.C. *M.C. M. French* 1909
  Croix de Guerre
JAMES, A. M. T. Capt., R.F.A.(T.F.) *M.C.*   1913
✠JEMMETT, C. W. Lieut. and Adjt., The Buffs (E. Kent 1905
  Regt., T.F.) (W.)
  Killed in action 15 *March* 1918
JOHN, D. W. Capt., R.A.M.C. *M.C. M* 2.   1906
JOHNS, S. H. M. Surgeon Lieut., R.N.   1909
JOHNSON, E. S. H. Pte., H.A.C.; Capt., R.A.O.C.   1899
JOHNSON, R. F. Pte., H.A.C.; Capt., R.A.O.C.;   1910
  D.A.D.O.S. *M.*
JOHNSTONE, C. M. Major, Dragoon Gds. (R. of O.)   1883
JONES, H. LL. Major, Hussars; Lieut.-Col., Welsh Regt. 1905
  (W.) *D.S.O. M* 2. *Chevalier, Legion of Honour*
  (*France*)
JONES, T. E. Warrant Schoolmaster, R.N.   1910
JORDAN, A. R. Capt., R.A.M.C.   1901

KEAY, E. D. Capt., R. Warwickshire Regt.(T.F.) (W.) 1908
✠KEAY, J. G. 2nd Lieut., R. Warwickshire Regt.(T.F.) 1914
  Died 2 *July* 1916 *of wounds received in action*
KEIGWIN, W. S. 2nd Lieut., Welsh Regt.; Lieut., Train- 1907
  ing Res. Bn.
✠KELSEY, W. Lieut., R.F.A.   1914
  Died 23 *Sept.* 1916 *of wounds received in action* 14 *July*
  1916
KENNINGTON, J. Major, Lincolnshire Regt.; Lieut.-Col., 1894
  R. Warwickshire Regt. (W.) *D.S.O. M.C. M.*
KENWORTHY, C. H. Sub-Lieut., R.N.V.R.   1911
KERBY, Rev. E. T. C.F. 4th Class, R.A.C.D.(T.F.) (W.) 1896
  M.C. M 2.
KERBY, P. W. Lieut., R.F.A. (T.F.Res.); empld. Army 1898
  and Navy Canteen Board
KERR, J. F. Lieut., Seaforth Hdrs. and Gen. List (Staff 1913
  Lieut.) (W.)
KERR, M. J. D. Major, R.E. (W 2.) *M.*   1903
✠KIDD, J. N. Capt., 6th Dragoon Gds. (Carabiniers). (W.) 1899
  Killed in action 19 *Jan.* 1916
KING, K. Lieut., R.A.S.C.   1911
KING, S. Major, Middlesex Regt.(T.F.) (W.) *M.*   1902
KIRBY, H. 2nd Lieut., The Buffs (E. Kent Regt.); Lieut. 1914
  (A.), R.A.F. (W.) (P.) *M.*
KIRKE, G. G. Capt., Black Watch (T.F.)   1907

CLARE COLLEGE 45

KISCH, E. R. Capt., London Regt. (Kensington Bn.) 1905
M.C.
KITTERMASTER, Rev. D. B. C.F. 3rd Class, R.A.C.D. 1896
M.C. M.
KLUGH, H. Lieut., R.N.V.R. *D.S.C.* 1881
KNOWLES, C. K. Lieut., Dorset Regt. and Tank Corps 1911
KNOX, B. Capt., R.H.A.(T.F.) 1910

LADENBURG, A. L. Capt., R. Fusiliers 1888
LANE, T. W. Lieut., R.F.A. 1912
LANGDALE, K. M. Sapper, R.E. (Signals) 1903
LAUGHLIN, C. E. H. Major, Leinster Regt.; Brigade 1877
Major; Lieut.-Col., Hampshire Regt.(T.F.); empld.
Ministry of Munitions. *Brevet Major. m.*
LEACH, R. C. Capt., King's Own (R. Lancaster Regt.); 1908
empld. O.C.B. (W 2.) *M.C. M.*
LEATHART, P. W. Capt., R.A.M.C. 1895
✠LEES, T. P. Major, London Regt. (Q.V.R.) *M.C.* 1893
Killed in action near Ypres 21 April 1915
LE FLEMING, E. K. Hon. Lieut., R.A.M.C. 1891
LE FLEMING, J. Lieut.-Col., Kent Cyclist Bn.; Major, 1884
Queen's Own (R.W. Kent Regt., T.F.)
LEGGE-CURRIE, J. D. Lieut., R.A.M.C. 1904
LEHMANN, J. R. 2nd Lieut., Northamptonshire Regt. 1909
LEMON, G. T. Capt., I.A.R.O., attd. 30th Punjabis and 1904
104th Wellesley's Rifles; Staff Capt.; Major, D.A.D.
Military Works. (W.) *O.B.E. M 2.*
✠LEON, E. J. 2nd Lieut., London Regt. (Post Office Rifles) 1914
Killed in action 7 Oct. 1916
LEONARD, H. V. Capt. and Adjt., E. Lancs. Regt.; Capt., 1912
Cheshire Regt. (W 3.) *M.C. and Bar. M. French Croix de Guerre*
LEVESON, W. E. Capt., R.G.A. *M.C.* *1892
LEVY, L. A. Lieut., Spec. List.; Capt., R.E. *m.* 1904
LEWIN, H. W. Major, R.A.S.C. *m 2.* 1901
✠LEWIS, H. M. 2nd Lieut., Middlesex Regt. 1913
Killed in action in Gallipoli 4 Nov. 1915
LEWIS, L. H. Major, E. Lancs. Regt. (W.) *D.S.O.* 1912
M.C. M.
✠LINDSAY, F. H. Major, London Regt. (London Scottish). 1895
(W.) *M.*
Killed in action 1 July 1916
LINFORD, W. A. M. Lieut., Northamptonshire Regt. 1911
LIPSCHITZ, J. Capt., R.F.A. (W.) 1912

LLOYD, L. W. Lieut., 21st Lancers; Capt. and Adjt., 1912
Command Depôt. (W.)
✠LLOYD, T. G. Capt., Welsh Regt. 1910
Killed in action 10 *May* 1918
✠LLOYD-WILLIAMS, K. P. 2nd Lieut., Welsh Regt. 1914
Killed in action 17 *Oct.* 1916
LOMBARD, Rev. B. S. C.F. 4th Class, R.A.C.D. 1887
LONGSTAFF, F. V. Major, E. Surrey Regt.(T.F.) 1899
LONGSTAFF, G. C. Lieut., R.N.V.R. (Coastal Motor-boat 1903
Service)
LORING, R. W. Pte., H.A.C. 1905
LOVELL, J. S. Capt., R.G.A. (W 2.) 1888
LOW, A. R. Major (T.), R.A.F. (Aircraft Production 1900
Dept.)
LOWCOCK, D. R. Pte., R. Fusiliers 1903
LOWE, F. G. Lieut., I.A.R.O., attd. 13th Rajputs; Adjt., 1902
17th Infy. Depôt; Staff. Lieut. (Asst. Embarkation
S.O.) *M.*
LOWE, G. B. Surgeon-Lieut., R.N. 1911
LOWNDES, Rev. R. G. C.F. 4th Class, R.A.C.D. 1901
LUARD, S. D'A. 2nd Lieut., Worcestershire Regt.; Lieut., 1912
Cheshire Regt.
LUBBOCK, I. Capt., R.G.A. (W.) 1910
LUCAS, T. C. Major, R.A.M.C. 1895
LUCY, R. S. Lieut., Worcestershire Regt.(T.F.); Major 1912
(A.), R.A.F. *A.F.C.*
✠LUMB, H. Pte., London Regt. (Artists Rifles); Lieut., 1905
R.F.A.
Died 8 *Oct.* 1915 *of illness contracted on active service*
LUPTON, R. H. Capt., R. Sussex Regt. *M.C. M* 2. 1903
LUPTON, W. M. Capt., I.M.S. *M.* 1907
LUSHINGTON, Rev. F. DE W. C.F. 4th Class, R.A.C.D. 1887

MACARTNEY, M. E. Pte., R.A.S.C.(T.F.) 1902
✠MCCLENAGHAN, A. B. P. 2nd Lieut., Wiltshire Regt. [1914]
Killed in action 16 *June* 1915
MCCLURE, I. H. Capt., Spec. List; G.S.O. 3 (Intelli- 1910
gence). *D.S.O. M* 2. *Italian Croce di Guerra*
✠MCCOSH, E. Major, Highland L.I. (W.) *M.C. M* 2. 1910
Died 26 *Sept.* 1918 *of wounds received in action*
MCCRIRICK, D. H. G. Capt., Somerset L.I. 1912
MCGEAGH, J. P. Lieut., Sherwood Foresters (Notts. and 1912
Derby Regt.); attd. Nigeria Regt., W. African Fron-
tier Force

McGown, T. W. M. Major, R.A.O.C.; D.A.Q.M.G. *M.* 1894
Machin, B. W. Lieut., Black Watch 1888
Macintyre, D. L. Capt. and Adjt., Cameron Hdrs. 1912
  M 2.
✠Mackenzie, B. M. S. Capt., The Queen's (R.W. Surrey 1908
  Regt.)
  Killed in action 22 March 1918
Mackenzie-Kennedy, H. C. D. C. Lieut., E. African 1908
  Force; attd. N. Rhodesian Police
✠McKerrow, C. K. Capt., R.A.M.C. 1902
  Died 20 Dec. 1916 of wounds received in action
Mackrill, O. W. Air Mechanic, R.A.F. 1902
Maclaren, A. I. Lieut., R.F.A. *M.C.* 1907
✠McMichael, D. W. Pte., R. Fusiliers (P. S. Bn.); 2nd 1912
  Lieut., Bedfordshire Regt.
  Died 17 April 1916 of wounds received in action
Macnee, E. A. Capt., M.G.C. *M.* 1904
McNeill, A. H. Capt., King's Own Scottish Borderers 1902
  (T.F.) (W.) *Order of Karageorge, 4th Class, with
  swords (Serbia)*
Macpherson, D. G. Lieut., Cameron Hdrs. (W.) 1912
Macqueen, R. H. Capt., R.A.S.C. *O.B.E. M* 2. 1897
✠Makant, A. V. Capt., Loyal N. Lancs. Regt.(T.F.) 1909
  *Died 14 March 1915 of wounds received in action near
  St Eloi 10 March 1915*
Makant, R. K. Capt., Loyal N. Lancs. Regt.(T.F.); [1914]
  A.D.C. (W.) *M.C. and Bar*
✠Malpas, C. C. Seaman, R.N.V.R. (R.N.D.) 1909
  Died 10 March 1915 of cerebro-spinal meningitis
Marriott, C. E. Major, R.A.M.C.(5th N. Gen. Hospital, 1888
  T.F.)
Marriott, C. G. L. Trooper, W. Kent Yeo.; Capt., 1912
  The Queen's (R.W. Surrey Regt., T.F.)
Marriott, C. J. B. Capt., R.A.S.C. *m.* 1880
Marsden, C. H. Major, Yorkshire Regt.; Chief In- 1894
  structor, School of Musketry. *m.*
Marshall, E. A. Lieut., R.N.V.R. 1911
✠Marsland, S. H. Lieut., Manchester Regt. 1910
  Killed in action in Gallipoli 7 Aug. 1915
✠Marten, C. P. Lieut.-Col., W. Yorks. Regt. and King's 1898
  Royal Rifle Corps. *M.*
  Killed in action near Flers 15 Sept. 1916
Martin, Rev. E. W. L. Capt., Labour Corps 1908
Martin, Rev. H. C. C.F. 4th Class, R.A.C.D. 1896

MASSER, B. R. Pte., H.A.C.   1901
MASSER, C. S. 2nd Lieut., Unattd. List, T.F.; A.D.C.   1910
MATHEWS, J. K. Sapper, R.E.   1903
MATRAVERS, F. G. Eng. Lieut.-Cdr., R.N.   1905
MATTHEWS, J. B. Capt., R.A.M.C. *M.C. M.*   1908
MAUFE, F. W. B. Capt., R.F.A.(T.F.) (W 2.) *M.C.* [1914]
    and Bar. M.
✠MAUFE, S. B. Major, W. Yorks. Regt. *M.*   1906
    Killed in action on the Somme 5 July 1916
MAYALL, G. Capt., R.H.A.(T.F.) *M.*   1887
MAYO, T. A. Lieut., R.A.M.C.   1893
MEDLYCOTT, W. Capt., R.A.S.C.   1896
MEERES, Rev. B. H. Chaplain, R.N.   *1892
MELLIN, E. L. 2nd Lieut., Labour Corps   1907
MELLIN, G. L. Capt., London Regt. (W.)   1902
✠MELLIS, G. D. Capt., R.F.A.(T.F.) (W.) *M.*   1907
    Died 11 Dec. 1917 of wounds received in action 30 Nov.
    1917
METHUEN, L. H. Capt., Argyll and Sutherland Hdrs.;   1913
    Staff Capt. (W 2.) *O.B.E. M.C. M.*
MIDWOOD, R. Lieut., Montgomeryshire Yeo. and M.G.C.   1914
    Capt., Spec. List (P. and B.T. Staff). *m.*
✠MILLAR, A. L. Capt., Rifle Brigade   1906
    Killed in action 15 April 1918
MILLER, H. M. Lieut., Spec. List; Staff Lieut. *M 2.*   1896
MILLER, J. C. Major, Gresham's School, Holt, O.T.C.   1887
MILLER, R. M. Capt., R.A.M.C. (W.) *D.S.O. M.*   1896
✠MILLS, C. G. 2nd Lieut., Coldstream Gds. *M.*   1912
    Killed in action near Béthune 26 Jan. 1915
MILLS, F. A. Capt., R.A.M.C.   1888
MILNE, D. D. W. Major, Highland L.I.(T.F.); empld.   1906
    War Office; Major (T.), R.A.F. (Aircraft Production
    Dept.)
MITCHELL, F. J. L. Lieut., R.G.A. (W.)   1914
✠MITCHELL, F. M. Capt., 18th Hussars; attd. Worcester-   1910
    shire Yeo. *M.C.*
    Killed in action 2 May 1918
MITCHELL, G. W. Capt., R.A.M.C. (W.)   1903
MITCHELL, J. R. Capt., R.A.M.C. *M.*   1912
MOGGRIDGE, C. D. Lieut., Spec. List (Graves Registra-   1887
    tion Commission)
MONTGOMERY, H. R. G. Capt., Norfolk Regt. (W 2.)   1909
    M.C.
MONTGOMERY, W. E. Lieut.-Cdr., R.N.V.R. *M.B.E.*   1881

MOORE, F. R. Lieut., R.E. (R. Anglesey). 1907
MOORE, G. Capt., R.A.M.C.(T.F.) *M.C. M.* 1904
MORCOM, A. F. Capt., R.A.M.C. 1903
MORGAN, O. G. Capt., R.A.M.C. 1907
MORGAN, W. P. Capt., R.A.M.C. 1895
✠MORISON, D. R. 2nd Lieut., Wiltshire Regt. 1905
  Killed in action 13 March 1915
MORLAND, D. M. T. Major, R.E.(T.F.) (W.) *M.C. M.* 1911
✠MORRICE, W. W. Capt., Wiltshire Regt.; attd. Labour 1900
  Corps
  Killed in action 30 Dec. 1917
✠MORTIMER, E. Lieut., Northumberland Fus.(T.F.) 1898
  Killed in action at Ypres 26 April 1915
✠MORTON, E. A. Lieut., R.F.A. (R. of O.) 1897
  Died 6 Nov. 1918
MORTON, J. F. A. *See* AMPHLETT-MORTON, J. F.
MOURILYAN, Rev. C. A. C.F. 4th Class, R.A.C.D. 1901
MUMFORD, C. G. 2nd Lieut., Essex Regt.(T.F.) 1912
MUNDAY, E. Major, Lancs. Fus. (W 2.) *M.* 1909
MUNRO, R. M. C. 2nd Lieut., R. Welsh Fus.; attd. King's 1893
  (Liverpool Regt.)
MURDOCH, A. J. Capt., Rifle Brigade. (W.) 1912

NATHAN, J. Capt., R. Sussex Regt.(T.F.) 1907
NEILD, W. C. Capt., Essex Regt.; empld. Ministry of 1910
  Labour. (W 2.) *M.C. and Bar. M.*
NEILSON, W. Capt., Highland L.I.; Major, Tank Corps. 1891
  (W.) (P.)
✠NESS, G. S. Lieut., R. Scots Fus. 1904
  Killed in action 10 Nov. 1914
NEWNES, Sir F. H., Bart. Capt., Bedfordshire Regt. 1894
NEWTON CLARE, E. T. Major (A.), R.A.F. *D.S.O.* 1901
  O.B.E. Chevalier, Order of Leopold (Belgium)
NEWTON CLARE, H. J. Major, S.O. 2, R.A.F. *M 2.* 1906
NEWTON CLARE, W. S. Capt. (Ad.), R.A.F. *M.B.E.* 1906
NICHOLSON, G. B. Capt., R.A.M.C. 1890
✠NICHOLSON, G. C. N. Capt. (A.), R.F.C. 1904
  Killed in flying accident 11 March 1916
NICHOLSON, R. S. Lieut., Spec. List (Recruiting Staff) 1889
NIELSEN, E. E. M. 2nd Lieut., Norfolk Regt. (W.) 1911
NOBLE, A. H. Lieut., King's (Liverpool Regt., Liverpool 1906
  Scottish, T.F.) and M.G.C. (W.)
✠NORMAN, C. Capt., N. Irish Horse (R. of O.) 1898
  Killed in action 12 Feb. 1917

NORMAN, R. E. Lce.-Sergt., London Regt. (Artists Rifles);   1908
Lieut., Oxford and Bucks. L.I. (W.)

✠NORTHROP, J. E. Flt. Sub-Lieut., R.N.A.S.   1913
Killed in flying accident 2 March 1917

✠NOYES, J. C. Pte., Hertfordshire Regt.   1912
Killed in action 16 Sept. 1916

ODLING, F. C. Surgeon Lieut., R.N.   1912

OGILVIE, N. Pte., H.A.C.   1909

OLDNALL, R. W. Major, R. Munster Fus.; Capt., Gen.   1889
List (Town Major). (W.)

OLIVE, G. W. Lieut., Oundle School O.T.C.   1904

OLIVER, W. S. V. Lieut., Lancs. Fus.; Lieut. (A.), R.A.F.   1910
(W.)

OPPENHEIM, W., T.D. Hon. Major, R.E. (Signals, T.F. Res.)   1890
M.

✠ORFORD, W. K. Pte., R. Fusiliers (P. S. Bn.); 2nd Lieut.,   1913
Manchester Regt. and Gen. List (T.M.B.)
Killed in action on the Somme 1 *July* 1916

ORPEN-PALMER, R. A. H. Lieut.-Col., Leinster Regt.   1896
(W 2.) *D.S.O. M.*

OSBORN, E. B., T.D. Major, R.F.A. (T.F.) *M* 2.   1889

OVENS, A. B. Capt. (A.), R.A.F.   1910

✠OWEN, W. H. K. Lieut., Welsh Regt.   1913
Died 1 *Oct.* 1915 *of wounds received in action*

PAGE, C. C. Capt., R.A.O.C.   1902

PALMER, C. Major, R.A.O.C.   1904

PALMER, N. ST C. Lieut., Hertfordshire Regt.; Capt.,   1900
N. Staffs. Regt. (W.) (P.)

PAM, E. A. 2nd Lieut., The Queen's (R.W. Surrey Regt.)   1911
(W.)

PANTER, A. E. Surgeon-Lieut., R.N.; Capt. (Med.),   1907
R.A.F. (W.)

PAREZ, C. C. T. Lieut., Spec. List (Staff Lieut.)   1884

PARKIN, R. C. Lieut., London Regt. (Blackheath and   1905
Woolwich Bn.)

PARKIN, R. T. Lieut., Rifle Brigade; empld. War Office.   1900
(W.)

PARNELL-SMITH, W. Capt., Victoria College, Jersey,   1902
O.T.C.

PARRINGTON, N. Capt., W. Yorks. Regt. (W 3.) *M.*   1905

PARRINGTON, W. F. Major, R.F.A. *M.C. M* 2.   1908

PARRY, A. H. Capt., Rifle Brigade; Staff. Capt.; empld. 1910
  Ministry of Munitions. (W.) *O.B.E.*
PARRY, D. B. Lieut.-Col., London Regt. (London Irish 1896
  Rifles) and M.G.C. (W.) *D.S.O.* *M* 3.
PARTON, E. G. Capt., London Regt. (Kensington Bn.) 1897
  and Gen. Staff (Draft Conducting Officer)
PATERSON, K. Lieut., Suffolk Regt. and 9th Gurkha 1912
  Rifles, Indian Army
✠PATERSON, R. D. Lieut., King's (Liverpool Regt.). (W.) 1911
  Killed in action 12 *Oct.* 1916
PATON, W. Capt., King's (Liverpool Regt.); empld. War 1911
  Office. (W 2.)
PAUL, R. Lieut., Cheshire Regt.; attd. T.M.B. (W.) 1915
PAVEY SMITH, A. B. Capt., R.A.M.C.(T.F.) *M.* 1905
PEACEY, Rev. C. C. C.F. 4th Class, R.A.C.D. 1898
PEACOCK, G. Capt., R.A.S.C. 1910
PEACOCK, G. H. Lieut., Eastbourne College O.T.C. 1884
PEAKE, E. G. Capt., R.A.S.C.; Major, R.E. *M.* 1895
PEARCE, A. H. Surgeon Lieut., R.N. *M.* 1911
✠PEARLESS, H. N. Sergt., British Columbia Regt., Can- 1903
  adian Force. *D.C.M.*
  Killed in action near Ypres 24 *April* 1915
PEGG, J. 2nd Lieut., R.A.S.C.; Capt. (T.), R.A.F. 1908
PELLIER, C. DU C. Capt., R.A.M.C. 1892
PELLING, Rev. S. B. C.F. 4th Class, R.A.C.D. *M* 2. 1904
PELLY, Rev. R. L. C.F. 4th Class, R.A.C.D. *m.* 1905
PEMBERTON, J. Lieut., Cheshire Regt.(T.F.) *M* 2. 1912
PENISTAN, Rev. E. J. C.F. 4th Class, R.A.C.D. 1895
PENNINGTON, Rev. C. G. T. S. C.F. 4th Class, R.A.C.D. 1893
  (T.F.)
PHELPS, G. I. DE B. Capt. and Adjt., R.E. *m.* 1895
PILCHER, E. M., D.S.O. Colonel, R.A.M.C.; Hon. Sur- 1884
  geon to the King; Professor of Military Surgery, R.
  Army Medical College. *C.B.* *C.B.E.* *M.V.O.*
  M 3. *m.*
✠PINFIELD, G. V. Lieut., 8th (King's R. Irish) Hussars 1913
  Killed in the Irish rebellion 24 *April* 1916
PINKS, E. D. P. Lieut.-Cdr., R.N.V.R. 1906
PITT, G. NEWTON. Major, R.A.M.C. (2nd London Gen. 1872
  Hospital, T.F.) *O.B.E.*
PITT, R. B. Lieut.-Col., R.E. *M.C.* *M* 3. *Cavalier,* 1907
  Order of the Redeemer (*Greece*)
PLAYER, H. Lieut., Montgomeryshire Yeo. and M.G.C. 1890
  (Cavalry).

PLEWS, H. W. Lieut., R.N.V.R. 1907
PLOWDEN, H. R. Capt., 17th Lancers. *M* 2. 1907
POLLARD, H. J. A. R.A.M.C. 1911
POTTER, W. M. Lieut., Seaforth Hdrs.; Capt., Lanark- 1908
shire Yeo. (W.)
POWELL, H. M. Lieut., R.F.A. *M.C.* 1888
✠POWER-CLUTTERBUCK, J. E. Corpl., R.E. (Signals); 2nd 1913
Lieut., R.F.A.; attd. R.F.C. (W.)
Killed in action 25 June 1917
POYNDER, E. G. T. Capt., R.A.M.C.(T.F.) 1903
PRANCE, Rev. E. R. C.F. 4th Class, R.A.C.D. 1890
✠PRANKERD, R. P. Lieut., Warwickshire Yeo. and M.G.C. 1914
Killed in action 10 Nov. 1918
✠PREESTON, R. S. Gnr., H.A.C.; Cadet, O.C.B. 1904
Died April 1916 of septic pneumonia
PRICHARD, A. A. Capt., R.A.M.C. 1909
PRICHARD, R. G. Major, R.E. *M* 2. 1907
PRINGLE, J. S. Capt., R. Scots (T.F.) *French Croix de* 1901
Guerre
PROCTER, J. A. Lieut., Sherwood Foresters (Notts. and 1900
Derby Regt.) and Gen. List (T.M.B.)
PROCTER, R. A. W. Capt., R.A.M.C. (W.) *M.C.* 1909
PRYCE JONES, A. W. Major, R. Welsh Fus. (T.F. Res.); 1889
Lieut.-Col., Saskatchewan Regt., Canadian Force;
attd. Gen. Staff. *O.B.E. M.*
✠PUCKRIDGE, C. F. H. Pte., R. Fusiliers (P. S. Bn.); Capt., 1913
D. of Cornwall's L.I.
Killed in action 28 March 1917
PULMAN, W. P. Lieut., Somerset L.I.; A.D.C. *M.* 1907
✠PYMAN, A. Lieut., Yorkshire Regt. 1913
Killed in action 15 June 1915
PYMAN, R. L. Gnr., R.G.A.(T.F.) 1900

QUILL, J. J. Lieut., M.G.C. (Motor) 1902

RADFORD, R. L. Capt., R.A.S.C. and R.F.A. (W.) 1908
RAMSAY, J. G. Major, Cameron Hdrs.; Lieut.-Col., 1900
A.A. and Q.M.G. (W.) *D.S.O. O.B.E. M* 2. *Bel-*
gian Croix de Guerre
RAMSBOTHAM, W. H. Capt., W. Yorks. Regt. 1908
RANKIN, R. Corpl., R. Fusiliers (P. S. Bn.); 2nd Lieut., 1898
S. Staffs. Regt. *M.C. M.M.*
RAVENSHEAR, E. W. Major, R. Berkshire Regt. *M* 2. 1912

CLARE COLLEGE 53

RAWCLIFFE, D. M. Capt., Manchester Regt.(T.F.); Lieut. 1907
(A.), R.A.F.
RAWLENCE, A. R. Major, R.A.S.C. *M.* 1907
READ, H. M. Lieut., R.E. (W 2.) *M.C. M.* 1911
READE, J. A. D. 2nd Lieut., St Edmund's School, Canter- 1893
bury, O.T.C.
REBSCH, R. F. W. Capt., S. Wales Borderers and Un- 1901
attd. List, T.F. (W.) *M.C.*
REED, H. L. Capt. and Adjt., Middlesex Regt.; Major, 1903
Gen. List (Staff Capt.)
REES, A. G. T. Lieut., R.F.A. *M.C.* 1911
REES, G. M. T. Major, S.O. 2, R.A.F. *O.B.E.* 1905
REEVE, A. E. 2nd Lieut., Norfolk Regt. (W.) (P.) 1909
REID, A. A. 2nd Lieut., R.E. 1904
REID, A. CUNNINGHAM. 2nd Lieut., R.E.; Capt. (A. and 1913
S.) R.A.F.; S.O. 3. (W.) *D.F.C. A.F.C. M.*
REID, E. B. Lieut., R.F.A. (W 2.) 1914
RHODES, F. A. Lieut., D. of Wellington's (W. Riding 1915
Regt.) (W.)
RICHARDS, H. A. Capt., R.A.M.C. 1903
✠RICHARDSON, E. B. 2nd Lieut., R.E. 1903
*Died 28 Oct. 1915 of wounds received in action in
Gallipoli*
RICHARDSON, T. Capt., Gen. List, empld. Ministry of 1899
National Service. *O.B.E.*
RILEY, J. H. 2nd Lieut., Yorkshire Regt. 1879
RINTOUL, A. J. Capt., Spec. List, empld. P. of W. Camp 1902
ROBERTS, A. C. Pte., R.A.S.C. 1914
✠ROBERTS, C.Q. Corpl., R.E. (Signals); 2nd Lieut., R.F.A. 1912
M. French Médaille Militaire
Killed in action 16 May 1915
ROBERTS, FF. Capt., R.A.M.C.(T.F.); attd. R.A.F. 1907
ROBERTS, H. T. LL. Capt., R.A.M.C. *m 2. Order of* 1901
St Stanislas, 2nd Class (Russia)
✠ROBERTS, R. B. Trooper, Denbigh Yeo.; Capt., West- 1900
morland and Cumberland Yeo.
Died 13 Jan. 1918 of illness contracted on active service
ROBERTSON, J. W. H. *See* HAY-ROBERTSON, J. W.
ROBINSON, Rev. A. H. R. Chaplain, R.N. 1897
ROBINSON, L. D. Lieut., R.G.A. 1902
✠ROBSON, Rev. E. G. U. Chaplain, R.N. 1901
Drowned on H.M.S. Aboukir 22 Sept. 1914
RODDAM, R. J. Lieut.-Col., Northumberland Fus. and 1876
Spec. List (Staff Lieut.) *O.B.E. M. m.*

Roe, J. C. Lieut., Lincolnshire Yeo.   1887
Rogers, A. L. Major, R.F.A. (W 3.) *D.S.O M.*   1900
Ropner, L. Major, R.G.A. *M.C.*   [1914]
✠Roscoe, T. le B. Pte., S. African Infy.   1897
 Killed in action 18 *Sept.* 1917
Rowe, E. F. Capt., Suffolk Regt. (R. of O.)   1884
✠Rutherford, J. D. Surgeon Lieut., R.N.   1908
 Died 13 *Sept.* 1917 *of tuberculosis contracted on active
 service*
Ruthven, J. St C. 2nd Lieut., R.E.   1917

Sadler, P. H. Lieut. (A.), R.A.F.   1914
Salter, M. A. Lieut., R.A.S.C.(M.T.)   1915
Salter, R. E. Capt., R.A.S.C.   1911
Samuel, C. H. Capt., Lancs. Fus.   1910
✠Sassoon, H. W. 2nd Lieut., R.E.   1905
 Died 1 *Nov.* 1915 *of wounds received in action in
 Gallipoli*
Sassoon, S. L. Capt., Montgomeryshire Yeo. and R.   1905
 Welsh Fus. (W 2.) *M.C.*
Saul, C. L. Lieut., Tank Corps. (W 2.)   1913
Saunders, A. G. Major, Bedfordshire Regt.; attd. Essex   1908
 Regt. (W). *m. French Croix de Guerre*
Saunders, D.M. Capt. and Adjt., Bedfordshire Regt. *M.C.*   1912
Saunders, F. P. Capt., R.A.M.C.   1904
Sawtell, H. D. Lieut., R.A.O.C.; I.O.M. 3rd Class   1909
✠Scholey, C. H. N. Capt., Rifle Brigade   1912
 Killed in action 25 *Sept.* 1915
Sclater, F. A. Capt., R.E. (Signals). *O.B.E. M.C. M 2.*   1912
 Italian Croce di Guerra
Scott, J. H. Lieut., Scottish Horse; Major, Gen. Staff.   1892
 O.B.E. M. Order of the Nile, 4th *Class (Egypt)*
Scott, H. W. Surgeon, R.N.   1902
Scott, W. L. Lieut., R.N.V.R. *D.S.C.*   1910
Scowcroft, H. D. Lieut., R.F.A.; Lieut. (O.), R.A.F.   1912
Scutt, C. A. 2nd Lieut., Spec. List (Interpreter)   1908
Seddon, G. N. Capt., Suffolk Regt. (W.) *M.C.*   1912
Seddon, W. D'A. 2nd Lieut., Worcestershire Regt.   1910
Sedgwick, H. R. Capt., R.A.M.C. *m 2.*   1888
✠Semple, W. D. Pte., R. Fusiliers (P. S. Bn.); 2nd Lieut.,   1913
 King's Royal Rifle Corps
 Killed in action 29 *June* 1916
✠Senior, J. Lieut., W. Yorks. Regt.; attd. R.F.C.   1911
 Died 9 *May* 1917 *of wounds received in action*

SESSIONS, L. F. Capt., R.A.M.C. (W.) *Italian Silver* 1911
Medal for Military Valour
SESSIONS, R. V. Pte., London Regt. (Artists Rifles); 1914
Lieut. (A.), R.A.F.
SETH-SMITH, K. J. Capt., R.F.A.; Staff Capt. *O.B.E.* 1900
SEWILL, J. W. 2nd Lieut., Army Cyclist Corps; Lieut., 1908
R.E. (Spec. Bde.); empld. Ministry of Munitions
SEWILL, R. W. Capt., R.A.S.C. 1911
SHACKLETON, A. G. Hon. Capt. and Q.M., London Regt. 1914
(R. Fus.) *O.B.E. M.*
SHAW, C. R. Major, Loyal N. Lancs. Regt.(T.F.) 1899
SHAXBY, R. U. Major, R.A.O.C.; I.O.M. 1st Class 1898
SHEARD, M. H. Lieut., R.N.V.R. *Officer, Order of* 1908
Nichan-Iftikhar (Tunis)
✠SHEARMAN, V. Pte., R. Fusiliers(P.S.Bn.); Capt., R. Scots 1907
Killed in action 25 March 1918
SHEPHERDSON, J. F. 2nd Lieut., Leys School O.T.C. 1913
SHERLOCK, E. L. Lieut., R.N.V.R. 1898
SHOLL, A. E. Lieut., Loyal N. Lancs. Regt.(T.F.). 1912
(W.)
SIDEBOTHAM, F. N. Capt., R.A.M.C. 1911
✠SIDEBOTHAM, J. N. W. Capt., Manchester Regt. 1909
Killed in action 12 Oct. 1916
SIDGWICK, H. C. Lieut.-Col., R.A.M.C. *O.B.E. M* 2. 1896
✠SILVERTOP, W. A. Capt., 20th Hussars. (W.) *M.C. M* 2. 1903
Killed in action 27 Nov. 1917
SIMPSON-HAYWARD, G. H. Capt., Oxford and Bucks. 1894
L.I. (T.F.)
✠SISSON, G. Lieut., R.G.A. [1914]
Died in Germany 20 Dec. 1917 of wounds received in
action near Cambrai 30 Nov. 1917
SISSON, H. A. Major, R.E.; D.A.D. Gas Services. *O.B.E.* 1904
M 2.
✠SKIRROW, G. Capt., W. Yorks. Regt.(T.F.) *French Croix* 1914
de Guerre
Killed in action 27 Aug. 1918
✠SLACKE, R. C. Major, The Buffs (E. Kent Regt.); attd. 1899
The Queen's (R.W. Surrey Regt.) *M.*
Killed in action 16 May 1915
SLADE, E. A. Capt., R. Warwickshire Regt. and Labour [1914]
Corps
SLADE, J. G. Capt. and Adjt., R.A.M.C. 1895
SLANEY, J. N. Lieut., King's (Shropshire L.I.) and 1913
M.G.C. (W.)

SMITH, A. B. P. *See* PAVEY SMITH, A. B.

SMITH, J. F. H. Capt. and Adjt., R.F.A. (W.) 1906

SMITH, N. H. Capt., R.A.M.C.; Surgeon Lieut., R.N. 1908
D.S.C.

SMITH, S. Pioneer, R.E. (Spec. Bde.) 1910

✠SMITH, W. G. F. Pte., R. Fusiliers (P. S. Bn.); Lieut., 1907
N. Staffs. Regt.
Died 5 July 1915 of wounds received in action

SOMERVILLE, Rev. K. B. C.F. 4th Class, R.A.C.D.; attd. 1909
R.A.F.

SORLEY, G. M. Capt., London Regt. (R. Fus.); R.T.O. 1910
(W.) *O.B.E. M* 2.

SOUTHWELL, H. M. 2nd Lieut., Highland L.I. 1910

SPENCER, R. Capt., Denbighshire Yeo. and Tank Corps. 1901
M.C. M 2. *Chevalier, Legion of Honour (France)*

✠SPITTLE, T. S. Capt., Monmouthshire Regt. 1903
Died 2 Oct. 1917 of wounds received in action

SPURRELL, H. W. Pte., R. Fusiliers (P. S. Bn.); Capt. 1913
M.G.C. (W 2.) *M.C.*

✠STANFIELD, A. V. 2nd Lieut., The Queen's (R.W. Surrey 1903
Regt.)
Killed in action 16 Aug. 1916

STAVELEY, Rev. C. H. C.F. 4th Class, R.A.C.D. 1907

STEEDMAN, M. T. W. Capt., R.A.M.C. 1907

STEPHEN, A. F. Lieut., R.G.A. *M.* 1907

✠STERNBERG, R. O. Corpl., R.E. (Signals); 2nd Lieut., 1911
R.F.A. (W.)
Died 1 July 1916 of wounds received in action

STIRLING, F. Lieut., Hampshire Regt. 1897

✠STIRLING, G. S. Capt., Argyll and Sutherland Hdrs. 1905
(R. of O.) and King's African Rifles. *D.S.O. M.C.
M.*
Died 26 Dec. 1916 of wounds received in action

✠STOODLEY, P. B. 2nd Lieut., Wiltshire Regt. 1912
Died 9 Nov. 1916

STORER, R. S. 2nd Lieut., Hertfordshire Regt. 1908

STOREY, C. B. C. 2nd Lieut., Lancs. Fus.(T.F.) 1887

✠STORRS, J. P. 2nd Lieut., Cheshire Regt.(T.F.) 1908
Died 8 Aug. 1917 of wounds received in action

STRAIN, L. H. Lieut.-Col. (A.), R.A.F.; S.O. 1. *D.S.C.* 1894
M 3. *Order of the Redeemer, 4th Class (Greece)*

STRINGER, C. H. Capt., Suffolk Regt. (Cyclist Bn., T.F.) 1905
m.

SWETE-EVANS, W. B. Major, R.A.M.C. 1891

SWINSTEAD, N. H.   Lieut., R.E. (Signals); empld. War   1911
Office. *M.B.E. m.*
SYME, D. A.   Lieut., K. Edward's Horse; Capt., Tank   1913
Corps. (W.) *M.*
SYMINGTON, A. W.   Lieut., King's Royal Rifle Corps;   1911
Lieut.(A.), R.A.F.   (W.) *M.C. M.*

✠TALBOT, C. E. C.   2nd Lieut., Somerset L.I.   1913
Killed in action 25 Sept. 1915
✠TANBURN, W. L.   Lieut., I.A.R.O., attd. 2nd Gurkhas   [1914]
Killed in action 13 April 1917
TATHAM, C. F.   Lieut., R.A.S.C.   1906
TAYLOR, C. P.   Corpl., R.A.S.C.(M.T.)   1900
TAYLOR, J. T.   2nd Lieut., Dorset Yeo.   1914
TELFER, Rev. W.   C.F. 3rd Class, R.A.C.D.; Cadet,   1905
O.C.B. *M.C.*
✠TEMPERLEY, A. R.   Pte., Northumberland Fus.(T.F.)   1907
Died of injuries accidentally received while on duty
26 *Aug.* 1914
TEMPERLEY, H. R.   Lieut., R.F.A. (W.)   1899
THA, R. R. H. O.   Lieut., I.M.S.   1905
THIRKILL, H.   Major, R.E. (Signals). *M.C.*   1905
THOMAS, H. J.   Capt., King's (Liverpool Regt.) (W 2.) *1904
M.C.
THOMAS-PETER, G. F.   Capt., D. of Cornwall L.I.(T.F.)   1901
THOMPSON, S. W.   Lieut., R. Scots Fus.; Capt. (A.),   1911
R.A.F.
✠THORNE, C.   Capt., E. Surrey Regt. *M.C. M.*   1911
Killed in action on the Somme 30 Sept. 1916
✠THORNTON, A. C.   Pte., Canadian Force   1904
Died at Bailleul 22 Nov. 1915 *of wounds received in*
action
THORNYCROFT, O.   Lieut., R.N.V.R.   1903
THURSBY, P. H.   Capt., R.F.A. *M* 2.   1913
TIMINS, Rev. F. C.   C.F. 3rd Class, R.A.C.D. *D.S.O.*   1884
M.
TIPPER, G. H.   Lieut., I.A.R.O.   1900
TOLLER, T. E.   2nd Lieut., Leicestershire Regt.; Capt.,   1904
R. Munster Fus. *M.*
✠TOOLIS, J. H.   Lieut., Lincolnshire Regt.   1912
Killed in action 1 July 1916
TOONE,C.L. Capt.,Cheshire Regt.and Gen. List(A.P.M.)   1896
TOOTAL, F. E. O.   Lieut., R.F.A.; Capt., Spec. List.   1895
Chevalier, Military Order of Avis (Portugal)

✠Topham, H. A. C. 2nd Lieut., Indian Army, attd. Welsh   1910
  Regt.
  Died 25 May 1915 of wounds received in action 24 May
  1915
Tozer, W. Capt., York and Lancaster Regt. (T.F.);   1913
  empld. War Office. (W 4.) *M.*
Treadgold, C. H. Capt., R.A.M.C.   1899
Trechman, O. L. Major, R.G.A. *M.*   1902
✠Trevor-Jones, E. E. 2nd Lieut., Rifle Brigade   1914
  Killed in action on the Somme 1 July 1916
✠Trevor-Jones, J. E. Capt. and Adjt., Rifle Brigade.   1914
  M.C.
  Killed in action 22 April 1918
✠Trevor-Roper, C. C. Capt., Hampshire Regt.(T.F.)   1904
  Died 3 Aug. 1917 of wounds received in action
✠Trier, N. E. Pte., London Regt. (Artists Rifles); 2nd   1907
  Lieut., E. Yorks. Regt.; attd. Yorkshire Regt.
  Died 6 Oct. 1915 of wounds received in action at the
  Hohenzollern Redoubt   1913
Tringham, Rev. H. R. P. C.F. 4th Class, R.A.C.D.   1894
Trotter, J. Capt., Highland L.I. (W.) *M.*   1913
Trotter, L. B. C. Capt., R.A.M.C.   1902
Trubshaw, A. R. Lieut., R.F.A.(T.F.); Staff Lieut.   1913
Trubshaw, C. S. Capt. and Adjt., R. Welsh Fus.   1908
Trubshaw, H. E. Major, R.E.(T.F.). *M.*   1901
Tufnell-Klug, M. W. T. Capt., R.A.S.C.(T.F.)   1903
Turner, J. T. Capt., I.A.R.O., attd. 28th Light Cavalry   1899
Tweddell, J. R. M. Lieut., Leicestershire Regt.; attd.   1899
  R. Defence Corps; Capt. (Ad.), R.A.F.

Unwin, W. N. Lieut., R.F.A.(T.F.)   1897

van der Byl, C. F. Capt., 16th Lancers (R. of O.);   1894
  Major, Army Cyclist Corps. *M.*
Vane, Hon. W. L. Hon. Colonel, Durham L.I.(T.F.) *m.*   1877
Vanrenen, J. E. Lieut.-Col., R.E.; C.R.E. *Brevet*   1884
  Colonel. M.
Vatcher, H. M. Lieut., R.E. and R. Jersey Militia.   1905
  M.C.
Vaux, R. W. Pte., The Buffs (E. Kent Regt.)   1910
Vestey, F. 2nd Lieut., Border Regt.   1911
Vestey, P. C. Lieut., Suffolk Regt.   1911
Vey, D. C. L. Capt., R.A.M.C. *M.C. M.*   1908
Vey, F. H. Surgeon Lieut., R.N.   1907

✠WAINWRIGHT, G. C. 2nd Lieut., Northamptonshire Regt. 1913
    Died 22 Dec. 1914 of wounds received in action
WALKER, C. E. Major, R.G.A.(T.F.) *M.C.* 1904
WALKER, C. V. Cadet, O.C.B. 1905
WALKER, G. A. C. Lieut., Inniskilling Fus. and Gen. 1912
    List, empld. R.E. (Signals). *M.C. M.*
WALKER, J. Major, R.A.M.C.(T.F.) (W.) *M.C. M* 4. 1902
WALKER, V. A. Capt., Res. Regt. of Cavalry and Spec. 1901
    List; A.M.L.O.; D.A.D.R.T. *Brevet Major*
WALLACE, H. L. Pte., Worcestershire Regt. 1917
✠WALLEY, G. S. Lieut. King's Royal Rifle Corps. (W 2.) 1911
    Died 20 Aug. 1916 of wounds received in action
WALLINGER, E. A. Lieut.-Col., R.F.A.; G.S.O. 2. (W.) 1897
    D.S.O. M 4. *Chevalier, Legion of Honour (France).*
    Officer, Ordre de la Couronne (Belgium). Belgian
    Croix de Guerre
✠WALLIS, E. P. Capt., R. Sussex Regt. 1912
    Killed in action 18 Oct. 1916
WALLIS, W. E. Capt., R.A.M.C. (W.) 1902
WALTERS, W. J. Capt., R.A.M.C. 1909
WANE, H. B. 2nd Lieut., Labour Corps 1909
✠WARD, F. W. Capt., Gloucestershire Regt.(T.F.) 1904
    Killed in action 9 Oct. 1917
WARD, H. M. A. Major, R.G.A.; A.D.C. *D.S.O. T.D.* 1903
    M.
WARD, W. H. 2nd Lieut., W. Yorks. Regt. 1884
WARLOW, N. F. Pte., King's Own (Yorkshire L.I.) 1915
WATSON, A. W. H. Capt., King's Royal Rifle Corps and 1911
    Gen. List (Brigade Major). *D.S.O. M.C. M* 2.
WATSON, D. H. Lieut., 1st Dragoons 1912
WAUTON, A. D. B. Lieut., R.A.S.C.; Capt., R.T.O. 1903
WEAVER, F. W. H. Naval Transport Officer. *O.B.E.* 1898
WEBB, J. C. Major, R.A.M.C. 1887
WEBER, D. McR. Lieut., Middlesex Regt. 1906
WEBER, H. G. Lieut., Bombay Garrison Arty., Indian 1903
    Defence Force
✠WEBSTER, J. R. Pte., H.A.C.; Capt. and Adjt., London 1899
    Regt. (R. Fus.)
    Killed in action 9 Sept. 1916
WELLER, C. A. Capt., R.A.M.C. *M.* 1907
WHATHAM, A. Capt., King's Own (R. Lancaster Regt.) 1910
    and R. Defence Corps
WHITAKER, G. H. 2nd Lieut., King's (Liverpool Regt.); 1908
    Lieut., M.G.C.; Hon. Lieut. (T.), R.A.F. (W.)

WHITE, A. K. G. Major, R.F.A.; G.S.O. 2. *D.S.O.* 1900
M 2.

WHITE, L. T. 2nd Lieut., R.G.A. 1907

WHITEHEAD, B. Major, R.A.M.C.; D.A.D.M.S. *M.C.* 1907

WHITEHEAD, C. M. Capt., King's Own (R. Lancaster 1900
Regt.) *D.S.O. M.C. M* 2. *Chevalier, Legion of
Honour* (*France*)

✠WHITEHEAD, P. N. Trooper, S. African Light Horse; 1907
Capt., R.E. (W 2.) *M.C. M.S.M.*
Killed in action 21 *March* 1918

WHITEHEAD, R. H. H. Capt., R.H.A.; Courts-Martial 1899
Officer. *M.C.*

WHITFIELD, J. G. Capt., R. Warwickshire Regt.(T.F.); 1895
Major, Spec. List (Cmdt., Reception Camp)

WILCOX, Rev. A. G. C.F. 4th Class, R.A.C.D. *M.* *1881

WILES, J. J. Capt. and Adjt., Wiltshire Regt.(T.F.) 1909

WILKINSON, C. L. G. Capt., King's Royal Rifle Corps 1914

WILKINSON, R. DU C. Lieut., R.A.S.C. 1913

WILKINSON, S. Capt., King's Own (Yorkshire L.I.) *M.C.* 1910

✠WILLIAMS, C. J. Lieut., Bedfordshire Regt. 1906
Died 19 *Dec.* 1915 *of gas-poisoning received near Ypres*

WILLIAMS, E. H. Y. Lieut., King's (Liverpool Regt.) 1902
(W.)

WILLIAMS, Rev. H. F. F. Junior Chaplain, Indian Army 1904

WILLIAMS, N. S. Lieut., R.A.M.C. 1904

WILLIAMS, W. F. Lieut., R.E. (Signals). *M.B.E. M.* 1903

WILLOX, A. G. Lieut., Gordon Hdrs.; empld. War Office. 1910
(W.) *M.*

WILSON, A. Capt., W. Yorks. Regt.(T.F.) (W.) 1903

✠WILSON, A. E. Capt., R. Warwickshire Regt. 1908
Died 3 *Dec.* 1918 *of pneumonia contracted on active
service*

WILSON, A. E. J. Major, Somerset L.I.; Lieut.-Col., 1898
A. A. and Q. M. G. *D.S.O. M* 3. *Medjidieh, 4th
Class*

WILSON, Rev. E. C. C.F. 4th Class, R.A.C.D. 1888

WILSON, G. H. A. Major, Unattd. List, T.F.; G.S.O. 3, 1892
War Office. *O.B.E. M.B.E. Brevet Lieut.-Colonel.*
m 2.

WILSON, Rev. K. F. C.F. 4th Class, R.A.C.D. 1906

WILSON, W. H. Pte., London Regt. (London Scottish); 1914
Lieut., Devon Regt.(T.F.) *M.*

WILTSHIRE, H. W. Major, R.A.M.C. *D.S.O. O.B.E.* 1897
M 2. *Order of St Sava, 4th Class* (*Serbia*)

WINTER, B. E.   Lieut.-Col., Army Pay Corps; Staff   1875
    Paymaster
WINTER, C. E. G.   Capt., R.A.M.C.   1889
WINTER, W.   Pte., H.A.C.   1915
✠WINTON, E. W.   2nd Lieut., R.G.A.   1915
    Killed in action 15 *Dec.* 1917
WOOD, A. R.   Lieut., R.G.A.(T.F.); Capt. (T.), R.A.F.   1914
✠WOOD, P B.   Lieut., R. Fusiliers   1904
    Killed in action 23 *April* 1917
WOOD, S. R.   Lieut., R.G.A. (W.)   1905
WOOD, W. V.   Lieut.-Col., R.A.M.C. *M.C.*   1893
✠WOODHOUSE, Rev. D. C.   C.F. 4th Class, R.A.C.D.   1902
    Died on active service 6 *Oct.* 1916
WOODHOUSE, G. W.   Surgeon Lieut., R.N.   1909
WOOTTON, H. A.   Capt., Spec. List; empld. Ministry of   1902
    Munitions. *M.B.E. m.*
WORKMAN, R.   Major, R. Irish Rifles. (W.)   1902
WORSLEY, Rev. F. W.   C.F. 4th Class, R.A.C.D.   1910
✠WRAGG, N. J.   Lieut., S. Staffs. Regt. (W.)   1909
    Died 18 *July* 1916 *of wounds received in action* 16 *July*
    1916
WRIGHT, A. J.   Capt., R.A.O.C.; I.O.M., 2nd Class.   1909
    O.B.E.
WRIGHT, F. T.   Lieut., R.E. (W.) *M.C.*   1909
WYER, F. F.   Lieut., R.F.A. (W.)   1910
WYNNE, R. O.   Capt., Bedfordshire Regt.; Lieut.-Col.,   1912
    King's (Liverpool Regt.). (W.) *D.S.O. M* 3.

YEATMAN, F. D.   Lieut., Middlesex Regt. (W.)   1908
YOULL, G. B.   Lieut., Northumberland Fus. (W.)   1897
YOUNG, C. S.   Major, R.F.A.; Inspector, Woolwich   1897
    Arsenal. *Brevet Lieut.-Colonel. m.*
YOUNG, K. R.   2nd Lieut., Lancs. Fus.; Lieut., R. Welsh   1913
    Fus.
✠YOUNG, P. M.   Lieut., King's (Liverpool Regt.) *M.*   1911
    Killed in action at Givenchy 10 *March* 1915

CORPUS CHRISTI COLLEGE

ADAM, D. BRUCE. *See* BRUCE ADAM, D.
ADAMS, Rev. N. P. C.F. 4th Class, R.A.C.D.   1895
ALFORD, Rev. C. S. L. C.F. 4th Class, R.A.C.D.   1903
ALFORD, Rev. J. G., v.d. C.F. 1st Class, R.A.C.D.   1866
   C.B.E. m 2.
ARNOLD, A. J., d.s.o. Bt. Colonel, Manchester Regt. and   1884
   R. Welsh Fus. *C.B.E. m.*

✠BARKER, W. Major, Worcestershire Regt.   1894
   Died 15 *Aug.* 1918 *of wounds received in action*
✠BARNES, J. E. T. Capt., Gloucestershire Regt.   [1914]
   Killed in action 3 *Feb.* 1917
BELL, R. H. Capt., Oxford and Bucks. L.I. (W.) *M.C.*   1906
   and Bar
BERNARD, D. V. 2nd Lieut., D. of Wellington's (W. Rid-   1913
   ing Regt.); Lieut., The Queen's (R.W. Surrey Regt.)
BOLD, T. A. 2nd Lieut., Loyal N. Lancs. Regt.   1914
BOOTH, W. R. Lieut., R.F.A.   1910
BOULTBEE, B. ST J. 2nd Lieut., E. Yorks. Regt.; Lieut.,   1913
   Northamptonshire Regt.; Capt. (A.), R.A.F. *M.C.*
   M.
BOURNES, G. H. Corpl., R.E.   1893
✠BOWER, C. F. Capt., Sherwood Foresters (Notts. and   1910
   Derby Regt.)
   Killed in action 13 *Sept.* 1917
✠BRAY, E. F. Lieut., R.N.A.S.   [1914]
   Missing, presumed killed in action, 19 *July* 1917
✠BROWNLEE, W. M. 2nd Lieut., Dorset Regt.   1915
   Died 12 *Oct.* 1914 *of pneumonia*

BRUCE ADAM, D. Lieut., Argyll and Sutherland Hdrs. 1911
and M.G.C.; attd. R.E. (Signals)

✠BRUCE LOCKHART, N. D. S. Lieut., Seaforth Hdrs. 1913
Killed in action 25 *Sept.* 1915

BUCK, G. R. Lieut., Bedfordshire Regt.(T.F.) 1909

✠BUDGEN, R. G. Lieut., King's (Shropshire L.I.) 1913
Killed in action 24 *Aug.* 1915

✠BULLOCK, G. F. 2nd Lieut., S. Wales Borderers 1900
Killed in action 31 *July* 1917

✠BURGESS, D. Lieut.-Col., R.A.M.C.(3rd N. Gen. Hospital, 1872
T.F.)
Died 17 *Jan.* 1917

BUTLER, R. L. G. Capt., Spec. List; Town Major, Ypres. *1913
(W.)

CAREY, R. S. Surgeon Lieut., R.N. *O.B.E. M.* 1901

CASSIDI, F. L. Surgeon Lieut., R.N. 1907

CAVE, T. S. Capt., R.G.A.; empld. Ministry of Muni- 1910
tions

CHADWICK, Rev. C. E. C.F. 2nd Class, R.A.C.D.; 1905
D.A.C.G.; Senior Chaplain, R.A.F. (W.) *M.C.*
M. m.

CHAPPELL, F. E. Major, R.A.S.C. *M.* 1900

CHRISTIE, R. G. Capt., R.E. *M* 3. 1913

CHURCHILL, G. S. Capt., E. Surrey Regt. 1898

CHURCHILL, H. E. Lieut., R.A.S.C.(M.T.) 1912

CHURCHWARD, Rev. B. C.F. 4th Class, R.A.C.D. 1908

✠CHURCHWARD, H. A. 2nd Lieut., London Yeo. (West- 1911
minster Dragoons); attd. R.F.C.
Killed in action 16 *Aug.* 1917

CLARK KENNEDY, A. E. Lieut., The Queen's (R. W. 1911
Surrey Regt.); Capt., R.A.M.C.

✠CLARKE, J. P. D. Lieut., Worcestershire Regt. 1910
Accidentally killed 1915

COLLETT, W. G. Major, Rifle Brigade 1888

COLLINS, E. G. W. Lieut., Wiltshire Regt. (W2.) *M.C.* 1913

CONNINGHAM, W. F. M. 2nd Lieut., R.A.S.C.(M.T.) 1909

COOPER, H. O. Lieut., R.F.A.; Staff Capt. *O.B.E.* 1907
M 2. *French Croix de Guerre*

✠COOPER, H. W. F. 2nd Lieut., R. Fusiliers 1899
Died 28 *April* 1917 *of wounds received in action*

COPEMAN, S. A. M., T.D. Lieut.-Col., R.A.M.C. (Sani- 1879
tary Service, T.F.Res.) *Order of St John of Jeru-*
salem

COULCHER, G. B. Pte., Durham L.I.; Lieut., R.A.S.C. 1901
M.
CRAFT, H. B. Sergt., R.A.M.C.(T.F.)   1904
CRICK, G. H. Lieut., R. Scots; Asst. Instructor in Gun- 1913
nery; Capt. (T.), R.A.F.
CRISPIN, A. E. Pte., London Regt. (Artists Rifles)   1894
✠CROSSE, R. G. Lieut., Queen's Own (R.W. Kent Regt.) 1913
    Died 14 July 1916 of wounds received in action
CROWTHER, W. C. Lieut., London Regt. (St Pancras Bn.) 1904
CULLEN, W. G. 2nd Lieut. (T.), R.A.F.   1914
CULLEY, G.C.H. Capt., Norfolk Regt.; Capt. (A.), R.A.F. 1911
✠CUNNINGTON, E. C. Capt., R.A.M.C. M.   1908
    Killed in action 23 March 1918

DARE, A. G. 2nd Lieut., St Lawrence College, Rams- 1902
gate, O.T.C.
DAVIES, Rev. P. M. C.F. 4th Class, R.A.C.D.   1908
✠DAVIES, T. A. M. Lieut., R.F.A.(T.F.)   1912
    Killed in action 1 July 1916
DAWBARN, G. R. Lce.-Corpl., R. Fusiliers   1912
DAWES, Rev. A. W. C.F. 2nd Class, R.A.C.D.   1891
✠DAY, N. L. 2nd Lieut., King's (Liverpool Regt.)   1913
    Killed in action 14 Sept. 1916
✠DEVEREUX, H. W. Lieut., S. Staffs. Regt.(T.F.) (W.) 1913
    Killed in action 26 June 1916
✠DIXON WRIGHT, Rev. H. D., M.V.O. Chaplain, R.N. 1889
    *Died 31 May 1916 of wounds received in action in the
    Battle of Jutland*
DONALDSON, C. H. Rfn., London Regt.(L.R.B.) (W.) 1903
(P.)
✠DOUDNEY, Rev. C. E. C.F. 4th Class, R.A.C.D.   1889
    Died 16 Oct. 1915 of wounds received in action
DOUGHTY, E. C. Major, Suffolk Regt.; empld. War Office 1888
DRURY, Rev. W. C.F. 2nd Class, R.A.C.D. M.C. M 4. 1895
✠DUCKWORTH, W. C. 2nd Lieut., Welsh Regt.; attd. King's *1910
(Shropshire L.I.)
    Killed in action 8 Oct. 1918
DUNLOP, C. C. Lieut., R. Scots   1907
DURNFORD, Rev. F. H. C.F. 4th Class, Australian Chap- 1901
lains' Dept. M.C.
✠DYER, H. F. 2nd Lieut., D. of Wellington's (W. Riding 1904
Regt.)
    *Died 28 Aug. 1917 of wounds received in action 8 Aug.
    1917*

EDDOWES, Rev. H. C. C.F. 4th Class, R.A.C.D.; attd. 1899
R.A.F.
ELWIN, W. D. Capt., R.E.(T.F.) 1899
EVERETT, C. E. F. Pte., R. Fusiliers [1914]

FARNSWORTH, Rev. C. R. C.F. 4th Class, R.A.C.D. 1910
FARRER, E. R. B. Capt., R.A.S.C.; Major, D.A.D. Supplies. 1910
M.C. M 4.
FINDLAY, J. G. Lieut., Bedfordshire Regt. 1902
FISON, E. T. Capt., R.A.M.C. (Sanitary Service, T.F.) 1888
FORSE, Rev. L. N. C.F. 4th Class, R.A.C.D. (P.) 1903
FOULSTON, S. V. Corpl., R.E. (Spec. Bde.) 1912

GAITSKELL, M. H. Lieut., R.E. 1914
GALER, F. B. Capt. and Adjt., London Regt. (Queen's) 1892
GALER, R. V. Capt., London Regt. (Queen's) 1898
GALLOWAY, A. Capt., Cameronians (Scottish Rifles); [1914]
G.S.O. 3. M.C. M.
GARDNER, J. Lieut., R.G.A. 1899
GATES, S. B. Pte., R. Fusiliers (P. S. Bn.) 1911
GELL, Rev. E. A. S. Lieut., R. Fusiliers; Lieut.-Col., 1894
Lancs. Fus. (W 2.) (P.) D.S.O. M.C. M.
GILLIBRAND, A. Pte., R. Fusiliers (P. S. Bn.); Lieut., D. 1904
of Wellington's (W. Riding Regt.) (W 2.)
GLEDHILL, A. Lieut., Monmouthshire Regt. (W.) M.C. 1914
✠GLEGG, A. L. 2nd Lieut., King's Royal Rifle Corps 1914
Killed in action 10 Aug. 1915
GOOLDEN, D. C. 2nd Lieut., R. Fusiliers [1914]
GRABURN, G. N. Lieut., R.F.A.(T.F.) (W 2.) 1903
GREEN, T. R. Pte., R. Fusiliers; Lieut. (K.B.), R.A.F. 1910
GRIFFITHS, Rev. R. C.F. 4th Class, R.A.C.D. M. 1893

HALL, A. F. Lce.-Corpl., Gloucestershire Regt. 1911
HALL, A. L. Pte., Kent Cyclist Bn.; Lieut., Lancs. Fus. 1908
HALL, J. T. Lieut., Loyal N. Lancs. Regt.; attd. King's 1912
Royal Rifle Corps. (W 2.) m.
✠HAMILTON, J. 2nd Lieut., Border Regt.(T.F.) 1898
Killed in action 5 Nov. 1916
✠HANNA, J. H. 2nd Lieut., London Regt. (St Pancras Bn.) 1901
Killed in action 20 Sept. 1917
HARPER-SMITH, S. W. Q.M.S., R. Fusiliers; 2nd Lieut., 1892
Labour Corps
HARRISON, F. E. Capt. and Adjt., R.F.A. M.C. and 1911
Bar. M.

✠HARSTON, F. N. Capt., E. Lancs. Regt.; Brigade Major. 1909
M.C. M 2.
Killed in action 22 April 1918
HART, B. H. L. Capt. and Adjt., King's Own (Yorkshire 1913
L.I.) (W 2.)
HARVEY, G. T. B. Lieut., I.A.R.O., attd. Corps of 1910
Guides; Major, Calcutta Bn., Indian Defence Force
HARVEY, H. M. 2nd Lieut., Northamptonshire Regt. and 1913
R.G.A.
HAVERS, C. R. Lieut., Hampshire Regt.; Capt. and Adjt., 1908
Tank Corps. (W.) M.
HEATON, R. Lieut., R.F.A. (W.) 1915
✠HEWITT, Rev. F. W. C.F. 4th Class, R.A.C.D. 1893
Killed in action near Vermelles 28 Sept. 1915
✠HILL, W. R. Lieut., Durham L.I. (W.) M.C. and 1915
Bar
Died at Stralsund, Germany, 6 Nov. 1918 of blood
poisoning
HINDERLICH, A. A. W. Capt. and Adjt., R.G.A. (W.) 1912
M.
HODDER, F. E. Lce.-Corpl., R. Munster Fus. 1902
HOLT, F. N. Capt., Queen's Own (R. W. Kent Regt.); 1912
empld. Ministry of Labour
HOOLEY, L. J. Corpl., R.E. (W.) 1912
HOSKYNS, Rev. E. C. C.F. 3rd Class, R.A.C.D. (W.) *1915
M.C. M.
HUNTER, C. J. Lieut., N. Staffs. Regt. (W.) M.C. 1907
HUTCHINSON, J. H. Air Mechanic, R.A.F. 1912

ILLINGWORTH, O. Capt., W. Yorks. Regt. (W.) (P.) 1906
ISON, A. J. Lieut., Northumberland Fus. and Welsh 1911
Gds.; attd. Gds. M.G. Regt.; Cmdt., School of
Instruction

JACKS, M. Lieut., E. Lancs. Regt.; Lieut. (Ad.) R.A.F. 1913
✠JAMES, E. S. P. K. Capt., King's Royal Rifle Corps 1906
Killed in action 17 March 1915
JAMESON, Rev. C. W. C.F. 4th Class, R.A.C.D. 1909
JEEVES, Rev. L. L. G. C.F. 4th Class, R.A.C.D. m. *1910
JENKINS, G. E. Lieut., E. Yorks. Regt. and The Queen's 1913
(R.W. Surrey Regt.)
JOMARON, A. C. Capt., R.F.A. (W.) 1912
JONES, B. C. Capt. (A.), R.A.F. (W.) M. 1911
JONES, R. R. P. Instructor Lieut., R.N. 1905

JORDAN, G. P. 2nd Lieut., Essex Regt.(T.F.); Lieut., 1908
Labour Corps

KAIN, H. G. Lieut., R.G.A. 1913
✠KEATING, G. H. Pte., Middlesex Regt. (P.S. Bn.); Lieut., 1911
Cambridgeshire Regt.; Instructor in Bombing
Killed in action 18 Sept. 1918
KELHAM, M. H. C. Lieut., Durham L.I.; attd. R. Defence 1907
Corps. (W.)
KEMP, K. M. Capt., I.A.R.O., attd. Baluchistan Infy. 1903
KEMPE, Rev. W. N. C.F. 4th Class, R.A.C.D. 1907
KENDALL, J. M. A. Capt., Norfolk Yeo. 1911
KIRKCALDY, G. I. Lieut., R.A.S.C. 1913
KIRKPATRICK, R. M. Capt., Rifle Brigade and Gen. Staff. 1909
(W.)
✠KNIGHT, E. A. 2nd Lieut., M.G.C. 1905
Killed in action 24 Sept. 1917

LA BROOY, M. V. T. J. Lieut., R.G.A.; empld. Ministry 1913
of Munitions
✠LAING, A. T. Capt., Northumberland Fus. 1907
Died 24 July 1916 of wounds received in action
LAMBERT, W. Capt., R. Fusiliers; Major (K.B.), R.A.F. 1909
m.
LA MOTHE, H. D. Nigeria Regt., W. African Frontier 1909
Force
✠LANG, H. A. Major, Worcestershire Regt. *M.* 1893
Killed in action in Gallipoli 9 June 1915
LAPORTE PAYNE, A. A. Major, R.F.A. (W.) *M 2.* 1909
LAPORTE PAYNE, Rev. R. M. C.F. 4th Class, R.A.C.D. 1910
LART, C. E. Capt., Devon Regt.(T.F.) *T.D.* 1886
LAST, F. W. 2nd Lieut., Lincolnshire Regt. 1910
✠LA TOUCHE, D. D. 2nd Lieut., King's (Shropshire L.I.); [1914]
Capt., Welsh Regt.
Killed in action in Gallipoli 8 Aug. 1915
LATTEY, W. T. Lieut., R.F.A. 1904
LAWRENCE, Rev. G. H. R.A.M.C. 1892
LEAKEY, R. A. Capt., Indian Army; R.T.O. 1905
✠LEEKE, H. A. Lieut., R. Warwickshire Regt. 1899
Died 29 May 1915 of fever
✠LEEMING, A. J. Capt., R. Fusiliers. *M.* 1908
Killed in action 31 July 1917
L'ESTRANGE FAWCETT, A. W. Capt., Gloucestershire 1913
Regt.; Major, M.G.C. (W.) *M.C.*

[1]LEWIS, A. M. Pte., R. Fusiliers (P.S. Bn.); Lieut., Devon   1913
    Regt.; Capt., 52nd Sikhs, Indian Army. (W 2.) *M* 2.

✠LING, L. S. 2nd Lieut., Norfolk Regt.   1915
    Killed in action 4 May 1917

LITTLE, A. H. Capt., R.A.M.C.   1909

LOFT, Rev. E. W. B. C.F. 4th Class, R.A.C.D.   1884

LUCAS, Rev. R. H. C.F. 4th Class, R.A.C.D.   1892

LYLE, R. C. Capt. and Adjt., R.A.S.C. *M.C. M.*   1906

✠MACINTOSH, H. M. Capt., Argyll and Sutherland Hdrs.   1911
    Died 26 July 1918 *of wounds received in action*

✠MACKAY, C. L. 2nd Lieut., Worcestershire Regt.   1913
    Died 7 June 1915 *of wounds received in action 28 May*
    1915

MACLEOD, J. D. Capt., Cameron Hdrs. and M.G.C.   1913

MAINWARING, C. L. Lieut., R.G.A.   1906

MANSFIELD, Rev. J. Sergt., R.A.M.C. (2nd S. Gen. Hos-   1894
    pital, T.F.)

✠MARRIOTT, J. F. L. 2nd Lieut., D. of Cornwall's L.I.   1907
    Died 26 Jan. 1915 *of spotted fever*

MARSHALL, A. T. Lieut., Suffolk Regt.(T.F.)   1899

✠MARTIN, E. N. M. 2nd Lieut., 5th (R. Irish) Lancers   1898
    Killed in action 30 Sept. 1916

MARTINDALE, R. G. Lce.-Corpl., R.E. (Fortress, T.F.);   1907
    2nd Lieut., R.G.A.

MASTERS, Rev. F. G. C.F. 4th Class, Australian Chaplains'   1890
    Dept.

✠MATHEWS, A. Lieut., Cheshire Regt.   1913
    Died 14 April 1916 *of wounds received in action*

MAUNDRELL, Rev. W. H. Chaplain, R.N.   1895

MAWDESLEY, J. L. Sergt., London Regt.; Capt., R.A.O.C.   1911

MERRIMAN, Rev. H. S. C.F. 4th Class, R.A.C.D.   1905

MICHELL, Rev. E. W. C.F. 4th Class, R.A.C.D.   1896

MILLS, E. Lieut., Bedfordshire Regt. and Northampton-   1910
    shire Regt.; Staff Capt.; Major, Military Governor
    of Gaza. (W.) *O.B.E. M.*

MONTAGU, G. H. S. Lieut., London Regt. (W.)   1911

[2]MORTON, H. S. Capt., R.A.S.C.; Major, D.A.D. Quar-   1908
    tering, War Office. *O.B.E.*

MOUNSEY, J. P. Lieut., Lancs. Fus. and King's African   1906
    Rifles

MURRAY, D. C. L. Lieut., Middlesex Regt. *M.C.*   1908

---

[1] Killed in action against the Kurds after the armistice.
[2] Died of influenza shortly after demobilisation.

NEALE, F. S.   Pte., R. Fusiliers; Lieut., M.G.C.   1913
✠NELSON, E. B.   2nd Lieut., I.A.R.O., attd. Indian Infy.   1909
    Died 15 March 1916 of wounds received in action
NEVINSON, G. R. G.   Sergt., R. Fusiliers   1907
NISBET, A. T.   2nd Lieut., R.A.S.C.   1913
NORRIS, W. H. H.   Lieut., R.E.; empld. Ministry of   1903
    Munitions. (W.)

✠OKE, R. W. L.   Capt., R. Berkshire Regt.   *1904
    Killed in action 25 Sept. 1915
OLDFIELD, Rev. H. D.   C.F. 3rd Class, R.A.C.D.   *M.C.*   1899
    M 3.
ONYON, R. R.   Capt., E. Surrey Regt.(T.F.)   1906

PAGE, C. H. W.   Capt., R.A.M.C.   1896
PALLISER, W. F.   Lieut., Worcestershire Regt.   1911
PALMER, Rev. S.   C.F. 1st Class, R.A.C.D.; A.C.G.   1874
    D.S.O. M.C.
PARKER, Rev. H. L.   C.F. 4th Class, R.A.C.D.   1894
✠PATCH, N. J. S.   Pte., Australian Force   1892
    Killed in action 11 Oct. 1917
PATTESON, C.   Major (A.), R.A.F. (W.)   *M.C. M* 2.   1909
PAYNE, A. A.   *See* LAPORTE PAYNE, A. A.   1909
PEARSON, L.   Pte., London Regt. (Artists Rifles); 2nd   1895
    Lieut., S. Staffs. Regt.
PENZER, N. M.   2nd Lieut., Essex Regt.   1911
PEROWNE, J. T. W., V.D.   Lieut.-Col., R.F.A.(T.F.)   1882
PETTY, W.   Lieut.-Col., Seaforth Hdrs. (W 2.)   *D.S.O.*   1894
    M 2.
PICKTHORN, K. W. M.   Capt., London Regt. (Civil Ser-   *1914
    vice Rifles); empld. War Office; Capt. (O.), R.A.F.
    (W 2.)
✠PIERSON, L. D.   Lieut., E. Yorks. Regt.   *M.*   [1914]
    Killed in action 30 Oct. 1916
POIGNAND, G. C. I.   2nd Lieut., Leinster Regt.; Capt.   1910
    R.A.S.C.
POOK, J. DE C.   Lieut., I.A.R.O., attd. S. and T. Corps   1906
PRYOR, G. H. D.   Lieut., King's Royal Rifle Corps. (W.)   1912
PULLINGER, S. R.   Capt., Leicestershire Regt.(T.F.)   1910

QUENTIN, G. A. F.   Lieut., King's Royal Rifle Corps;   1900
    Asst. Officer i/c Records.   *m.*

RAVEN, G. E.   Lieut., W. Yorks. Regt.; A.D.C. (W.)   1912
    M.C.

✠READ, Rev. E. O.   C.F. 4th Class, R.A.C.D.   1909
   Killed in action 3 Oct. 1918
RECKITT, F. N.   Lieut., Middlesex Regt.; Capt., Labour   1891
   Corps
RESKER, Rev. B. A.   Lce.-Corpl., London Regt. (Artists   1908
   Rifles)
RICHARDSON, J. A. ST C.   Lieut., E. Yorks. Regt.   1914
RINTOUL, D.   Colonel, Clifton College O.T.C.   1882
RODGERS, Rev. H. N.   C.F. 4th Class, R.A.C.D.   1906
ROWAN, A.   Lieut., Spec. List (Staff Lieut.)   1905
✠ROXBURGH, J. H.   Major, M.G.C.   *M.C. M.*   [1914]
   Killed in action 2 Oct. 1918
ROYLANCE, P.   Lieut., D. of Lancaster's Own Yeo.   1910
RYOTT, T. G.   Pte., M.G.C.   1899

✠SANDFORD, C. R. F.   Capt., King's Own (Yorkshire L.I.,   1913
   T.F.) (W.) *M.C.*
   Killed in action 22 Feb. 1917
✠SANKEY, W. M.   Lieut., Monmouthshire Regt.   (W.)   1914
   M.C.
   Died 23 March 1918 *of wounds received in action*
SAYERS, L. D. W.   Lieut.-Col., R.A.S.C.   1897
SEDDON, A. D.   Capt., King's Own (R. Lancaster Regt.)   1908
   (W.) (P.)
SELWYN, Rev. E. G.   C.F. 4th Class, R.A.C.D. *M.*   *1909
SELWYN, J.   Capt., R.F.A.; A.D.C.; Staff Capt.; Major,   1911
   S.O. 2, R.A.F. (W.)
SHARP, Rev. G. F.   C.F. 4th Class, R.A.C.D.   1905
✠SHAW, R.   Capt., King's (Liverpool Regt., T.F.)   1910
   Killed in action 20 Sept. 1917
SKINNER, E. F.   Capt., R.A.M.C.(T.F.)   1899
SMITH, Rev. F. S.   C.F. 4th Class, R.A.C.D.   1893
✠SMITH, G. R.   Lieut., Canadian Infy.   1902
   Killed in action 6 May 1917
SMITH, W. CAMPBELL.   Lieut.-Col., London Regt.(Artists   1906
   Rifles); attd. R.E. (Spec. Bde.) *M.C. M* 2.
SMYTH, Rev. J. W. W.   C.F. 4th Class, R.A.C.D. *M.*   1893
STEPHENS, A. R.   Corpl., R.A.S.C.; Staff Capt. (W.)   1897
STEPHENS, E. A.   Corpl., Middlesex Regt. and M.G.C.   1901
   (W.)
STEVENS, J. A.   Lieut.-Col., Rangoon Bn., Indian Defence   1891
   Force. *C.I.E. O.B.E.*
STUART PRINCE, D.   Capt., I.A.R.O., attd. Indian Army   [1914]
   Clothing Dept.

SWANSTON, E. R. Lieut., R.E. 1911

TEBBS, J. A. Lieut., R.F.A. 1910
TELFER, R. G. Lieut., Border Regt.; Draft Conducting 1896
Officer
✠TERRELL, F. W. Lieut., Gloucestershire Regt.; attd. Wor- 1912
cestershire Regt. (W.)
Killed in action 3 *Sept.* 1916
THOMAS, T. G. Lieut., King's (Liverpool Regt.); Capt., 1904
Spec. List (Bombing Officer)
THOMPSON, J. C. Capt., Cameron Hdrs. (W.) 1899
THOMSON, G. P. Capt., The Queen's (R.W. Surrey *1914
Regt.); empld. British Military Mission; attd. R.A.F.
m.
THOULESS, R. H. 2nd Lieut., R.E. (Signals) 1912
TOOGOOD, Rev. J. H. C.F. 4th Class, R.A.C.D.(T.F.) 1890

VAUGHAN, J. H. Lieut., R. Inniskilling Fus.; attd. R.E. 1911
(Signals). (W.) *M.C.*
VIGGERS, Rev. S. C.F. 4th Class, R.A.C.D. *M.* 1909

WARD, Rev. A. C.F. 4th Class, R.A.C.D. 1887
WARD, D. C. L. Capt., London Regt.; Staff Capt. (W.) 1910
M. m.
WEATHERHEAD, R. Instructor Cdr., R.N. 1895
✠WEBB, A. H. 2nd Lieut., The Buffs (E. Kent Regt., T.F.) 1911
Killed in action 23 *June* 1917
WELLS, H. M. Lieut., R.E.; empld. Ministry of Muni- *1912
tions
✠WHITTAM, M. J. G. Lieut., D. of Wellington's (W. 1912
Riding Regt.)
Died 11 *Aug.* 1915 *of wounds received in action in*
Gallipoli
WILBERFORCE, H. H. Lieut.-Col., R.A.S.C.(T.F.) *D.S.O.* 1900
M.
WILLIAMS, G. D. Pte., London Regt. (Artists Rifles); 1901
Lieut., Essex Regt.
WILLIAMSON, Rev. F. L. C.F. 4th Class, R.A.C.D. 1900
WILLS, A. G. P. Capt., R.A.M.C. *M.C.* 1910
✠WILSON, R. E. 2nd Lieut., Bombay Vol. Rifles 1904
Killed in action in E. Africa 11 *March* 1916
WILSON, Rev. T. Pte., King's Own (Yorkshire L.I.) 1912

✠WYNNE, E. E.   Pte., R. Fusiliers (P.S. Bn.); Capt., Leicester-   1913
    shire Regt.(T.F.) (W.)
    Killed in action 8 June 1917

YENCKEN, A. F.   Major, R.F.A.(T.F.)   *M.C. M.*   1912
YENCKEN, E. D.   Capt., R.A.S.C.   *M.*   1912

DOWNING COLLEGE

A-BECKETT, A. H.   Capt., Australian Light Horse   1887
ADAMS, E. T.   Hon. Lieut., R.N.V.R.   1900
AHMAD, A. M.   Capt., R.A.M.C.   1910
AINSWORTH, C. G.   Surgeon Lieut., R.N.   1907
ALLEN, Rev. C. A. B.   Chaplain, R.N.   1906
ALLEN, W. L.   Lieut., King's School, Chester, O.T.C.   1909
ANDERSON, A. C.   Capt., I.M.S.   1902
ANDREWS, T. E.   Lieut., R.F.A.   1914
APPLETON, A. B.   Capt., R.A.M.C.   1907
✠ASTON, W. D.   Capt., Cambridgeshire Regt.   1901
     Died 2 Nov. 1917 of wounds received in action
ATKINSON, J. L.   Capt., Quebec Regt., Canadian Force   1907

BACK, N.   Capt., R.F.A.(T.F.); attd. 2nd Dragoons   1910
     (R. Scots Greys)
BALDWIN, T. H.   Lieut., Essex Regt.   1915
BAINES, W.   2nd Lieut., R.F.A.   1906
BALL, G. R.   Lieut., W. Yorks. Regt.; empld. Ministry   1910
     of Munitions. (W.)
BARLOW, P.   Capt., Spec. List (Recruiting Staff)   *1893
BARNARD, E. C.   Lieut., Hertfordshire Regt.   1907
BEDWORTH, A. C.   Capt., R. Warwickshire Regt.   1913
BELL, J. A.   Capt., Durham L.I.(T.F.); Staff Capt. (W 3.) 1913
     M.C.
✠BENNETT, S. G.   2nd Lieut., Suffolk Regt.   1907
     Killed in action 20 July 1916
BENNETT-EVANS, G. L.   Capt., S. Staffs. Regt. (W.)   1905
BOURNE, A. W.   Capt., R.A.M.C.   1905
BOWEN-DAVIES, J.   Capt., Pembroke Yeo.; attd. R. North   1894
     Devon Yeo.; Courts-Martial Officer

BOYER, G. W. B.   Lieut., R.G.A.   [1914]
BRADBURY, J. B.   Lieut.-Col., R.A.M.C. (1st E. Gen.   *1865
    Hospital, T.F.)
BRAILEY, A. R.   Surgeon Lieut.-Cdr., R.N.V.R.   1896
BRAIMBRIDGE, C. V.   Capt., R.A.M.C.   1911
BREWIS, C. C.   Capt., R.A.M.C.   1908
BRINTON, R. D.   Capt., R.A.M.C.   1879
BROOK, R.   Lieut., Manchester Regt.; empld. Board of   1914
    Trade. (W.)
BROWN, H.   Lieut. (A.), R.A.F.   1916
✠BROWN, I. M.   Capt., R.A.M.C.   1907
    Killed in action 15 *Nov.* 1916
BROWN, S. V.   Lieut., Liverpool Institute O.T.C.   1909
✠BRYAN BROWN, Rev. G. S.   C.F., N. Zealand Chaplains'   1904
    Dept. (W.)
    Killed in action 4 *Oct.* 1917
BRYANT, V. S.   Major, Wellington College O.T.C.   *m.*   1897
✠BUCHANAN, A.   Pte., King's (Liverpool Regt., Liverpool   1910
    Scottish, T.F.)
    Killed in action near Ypres 16 *June* 1915
✠BURGESS, W. C.   2nd Lieut., Somerset L.I.(T.F.)   1909
    Killed in action 22 *Aug.* 1917
BYRDE, E. H.   Capt., Monmouthshire Regt.; Major, Gen.   1905
    Staff. (W.) *m.*

CHAPMAN, E. H.   Capt., R.E.   *M.*   1905
CHOPRA, R. N.   Major, I.M.S.   1903
CLARK, O. A. P.   Lieut., Northumberland Fus. (T.F.);   1913
    attd. R.E. (Spec. Bde.) (W.)
CLARKE, E.   Capt., R.A.M.C.   1879
CLARKE, G. A. C.   Capt., R.G.A. (W.) *M.C.*   1909
CLIFTON, G. F.   Capt., R.A.M.C.   1908
COLE, Rev. T. E. F.   C.F. 4th Class, R.A.C.D.   *1884
COLLINGWOOD, C. A.   Lieut., Northumberland Fus.;   1909
    Capt., Spec. List (Courts-Martial Officer). (W.)
✠CORKE, G. H.   2nd Lieut., Northumberland Fus. *M.*   1909
    Killed in action 17 *Sept.* 1916
COTTON, C. K.   Capt. and Adjt., Cheshire Regt.   1906
COWELL, J.   Pte., R.A.M.C.   1912
CRAMPTON, G. P.   Capt., Northamptonshire Regt.; attd.   1912
    9th Gurkha Rifles, Indian Army
CROUCH, H. A.   Capt., R.A.M.C. *M.C.*   1909
CUNNINGHAM, L.   Capt., R.A.M.C.   1911
CURL, S. W.   Capt., R.A.M.C.(T.F.)   1893

CURZON, C. T. B. Paymaster Sub-Lieut., R.N.V.R. 1909

DARE, A. J. Lieut., R.E. 1905
DAVIES, D. G. Lieut., Welsh Horse and M.G.C. (Cavalry) 1910
✠DAVIES, F. C. Capt., R.A.M.C. 1903
    Killed in action 17 Oct. 1917
DAVIES, G. B. Capt. and Adjt., 48th Pioneers, Indian 1902
    Army
DAVIES, J. B. *See* BOWEN-DAVIES, J.
DAVIES, J. T. Bdr., R.G.A. *1914
DAVIES, LL. J. Lieut., R.Warwickshire Regt.(T.F.) (W2.) 1913
DAVIES, R. L. Lieut., King's (Liverpool Regt., T.F.) 1909
    (W.)
✠DAWE, A. H. 2nd Lieut., King's Royal Rifle Corps 1913
    Killed in action 11 April 1917
DAY, C. D. Capt., R.A.M.C. 1908
DEKKERS, L. A. Lieut., R.F.A. 1896
✠DEWAR, D. Lieut., W. Yorks. Regt. and M.G.C. *M.* 1912
    Killed in action 22 March 1918
DICK, J. R. Capt., R.A.M.C. 1903
DICKSON, A. N. Capt., I.M.S. *M.C.* 1907
DIGBY-JOHNSON, N. Lieut., R.A.S.C. (W.) *1907
DIXON, W. E. Surgeon Lieut., R.N. *m.* 1902
DODSON, F. K. Capt., E. Lancs. Regt. (W.) 1909
DOUGLAS-HAMILTON, Rev. W.A. C.F.4th Class, R.A.C.D. 1887
DUFFIELD, C. A. W. Lieut., Queen's Own (R.W. Kent *1909
    Regt.) *M.C.*
✠DUNKERLEY, H. Major, R.A.M.C. (W.) 1907
    Died 23 March 1918 of wounds received in action
DUNSCOMBE, C. Pte., R.A.M.C.(T.F.) 1914
DUNSCOMBE, N. D. Surgeon Sub-Lieut., R.N.V.R. 1915

ECCLES, G. T. Capt., R.A.M.C. *1885
EDMUNDS, C.H. Lieut., London Regt.(Surrey Rifles). (W.) 1908
EHRHARDT, W. H. Capt., R. Warwickshire Regt. (W.) 1911
ELLISON, J. Capt., R.A.M.C. 1904
✠EMINSON, R. A. F. 2nd Lieut., King's Royal Rifle Corps; 1909
    attd. M.G.C.
    Killed in action 20 July 1916
EVANS, D. A. 2nd Lieut., Norfolk Regt. (W.) 1913
EVANS, G. Colonel, I.A.R.O. (Agricultural Directorate). 1901
    C.I.E. M.
EVANS, G. L. B. *See* BENNETT-EVANS, G. L.
EVANS, G. H. Pioneer, R.E. (Spec. Bde.) 1903

✠EVERETT, W. W.   Capt. and Adjt., Norfolk Regt.   1910
  Killed in action near Brancourt 8 *Oct.* 1918

FIELDHOUSE, E. E.   A.B.,R.N.V.R.(Hawke Bn., R.N.D.);   1908
  Paymaster Sub-Lieut., R.N.R.   *Cavalier, Order of
  the Crown of Italy*

FISHER, J., D.S.O.   Lieut.-Col., I.M.S.   *m.*   1893

FONTAINE DE MAZINGHEN, A.   Cpl., French Infy.; 2nd   1912
  Lieut., R.G.A.   (W.)   *French Croix de Guerre*

FORDHAM, W. H.   Capt., R.F.A.   1902

FORSYTH, A. B.   Lieut., Bedfordshire Regt.; Capt., Army   1912
  Cyclist Corps

FOSTER, A. W.   2nd Lieut., R. Warwickshire Regt.   1912

FREEMAN, P.   Lieut., R.G.A.   (W.)   1905

GABB, H. S.   Lieut., R.A.M.C.   1895

GAINSBOROUGH, H.   Capt., R.A.M.C.   1912

GARDNER, C. G.   Lieut., Suffolk Regt.   (W 2.)   *M.C.*   1908

GIBSON, N.   Lieut., E. Yorks. Regt.(T.F.)   (P.)   1910

GILL, Rev. H. V.   C.F. 3rd Class, R.A.C.D.   *D.S.O.*   1907
  M.C.   M 2.

GINSBURG, H. H.   *See* GAINSBOROUGH, H.

GIRARD, D. L. M.   Liaison Officer, French Army.   *French*   1908
  Croix de Guerre

GORDON-VAUDIN, Rev. C. G.   Chaplain, R.N.   *1881

GOULDEN, C. B.   Capt., R.A.M.C.   *O.B.E.   M.*   1906

GOULDEN, D.   Lieut., N. Staffs. Regt.   (W.)   1914

GOULDEN, E. O.   Lieut., Queen's Own (R.W. Kent Regt.)   1913
  (W 2.)   *M.C.*

GOWER, L. C.   2nd Lieut., S. Wales Borderers; Gnr.,   1909
  R.F.A.   (W.)

GRANT, C. V.   Pte., R.A.M.C.; Lce.-Corpl., R.E. (Meteoro-   1914
  logical Section)

GRANTHAM, J.   Lce.-Corpl., Malay Vol. Rifles   1909

✠GREEN, J. L.   Capt., R.A.M.C.(T.F.)   (W.)   1907
  V.C.   "For most conspicuous devotion to duty. Although himself wounded, he went to the assistance of an
  officer who had been wounded and was hung up on the
  enemy's wire entanglements, and succeeded in dragging
  him to a shell hole, where he dressed his wounds, not-
  withstanding that bombs and rifle grenades were thrown
  at him the whole time. Captain Green then endeavoured
  to bring the wounded officer into safe cover, and had
  nearly succeeded in doing so when he was himself killed."
  Supplement to *The London Gazette,* 5 Aug. 1916.
  Killed in action 1 *July* 1916

GREEN, S. J. Lieut., R.N.V.R.   1908
GREENE, G. W. Major, R.A.M.C.(T.F.)   1895
GREGORY, C. C. L. Sapper, R.E. (Meteorological and   1913
Sound-ranging Sections)
GRELLIER, E. F. W. Capt., R.A.M.C.   1905
GRICE, J. E. Pte., R.A.S.C.(M.T.)   1912
GUDGIN, S. H. Capt. (K.B.), R.A.F.   1907

HALL, R. 2nd Lieut., Loyal N. Lancs. Regt.   1911
HAM, P. S. Capt., R.A.S.C.; attd. S. and T. Corps,   1910
Indian Army
HAMILTON, J. L. Capt., R.A.M.C.(T.F.). (W.) *M.C.*   1908
HAMMOND, J. Capt., Norfolk Regt. (W 2.)   1907
HARDMAN, W. H. Pte., R.A.S.C.   1907
✠HARMER, G. 2nd Lieut., N. Staffs. Regt.   1914
Killed in action 11 *Aug.* 1916
HARRISON, F. Capt., R.G.A. *M.*   1912
HART, N. B. Capt., I.A.R.O., attd. 6th Gurkha Rifles.   1909
M.
HARVEY, H. W. Lieut., R.N.V.R. *M.*   1906
HAYNES, H. G. L. Lieut.-Col., R.A.M.C.(T.F.)   1896
✠HILLIARD, G. W. R.N.A.S.   *1906
Died Aug. 1915 *of wounds received in action*
HILLS, T. W. S. Capt., R.A.M.C.(T.F.) (W.)   1897
HIRSCH, F. B. 2nd Lieut., Durham L.I.   1917
HONE, P. F. Capt., Welsh Regt.; Staff Capt.; Lieut.-Col.,   1897
Middlesex Regt. *D.S.O. and Bar. M.C. and Bar.*
M.
HOWLETT, J. M. Capt., Norfolk Regt.(T.F.); empld.   1907
O.C.B. (W 2.) *M.C.*
✠HUCKLE, H. W. 2nd Lieut., Cambridgeshire Regt.   1907
Killed in action 5 *Sept.* 1918
HUNT, R. V. Major, R.A.S.C. and Outram's Rifles,   *1892
Indian Army. *M* 2.
HURST, N. V. Lieut., R.F.A.(T.F.)   1914
HYDE, H. A. 2nd Lieut., R.G.A.   1910

ISAACS, M. G. 2nd Lieut., R. Warwickshire Regt.   1911

JARDINE, R. F. Capt., R. Warwickshire Regt. (W.)   1913
JARVIS, H. E. G. A.B., R.N.V.R.   1909
✠JENKINS, D. J. C. Sergt., Canadian Infy.   1912
Killed in action 8 *April* 1916
JENKINS, W. L. Capt., R.E. *M.*   1915

JOHNSON, N. D. *See* DIGBY-JOHNSON, N.
JOHNSON, O. G. Lieut., Middlesex Regt. (W.)   [1914]
✠JOLLY, B. O. 2nd Lieut., Yorkshire Regt.   1913
   Died 9 Feb. 1917 of wounds received in action
JONES, C. McC. Capt., R. Welsh Fus.   1911
JONES, C. S. Lieut., Suffolk Regt.   1914
JONES, E. LLOYD. Major, R.A.M.C. (1st E. Gen. Hospital,   1892
   T.F.)

KAMINSKI, V. Aviation Corps, Russian Army. (W.)   1914
KARN, Rev. J. C. Chaplain, R.N.   1908
✠KEARNEY, J. J. Trooper, Gloucestershire Yeo.   1902
   Killed in action in Gallipoli 21 Aug. 1915
✠KEESEY, G. E. H. Capt., Rifle Brigade. (W.) *M.*   1905
   Killed in action on the Somme 24 Aug. 1916
✠KEITH, A. J. 2nd Lieut., Middlesex Regt.   1912
   Killed in action on the Somme 14 July 1916
KELLY, D. P. J. Capt., Connaught Rangers; empld. War   1906
   Office. *M.C. Belgian Croix de Guerre*
KERBY, W. M. Pte., Middlesex Regt.   1906
KIRKMAN, R. W. Capt. Lancs. Fus.; Asst. Officer i/c   1909
   Records
KNOWLES, R. Capt., I.M.S. (W 2.) *M* 2.   1902

LAKER, W. N. 2nd Lieut., Suffolk Regt. and R. War-   1915
   wickshire Regt.
LAMB, Rev. P. C. C. C.F. 4th Class, R.A.C.D.; Chaplain,   1907
   R.A.F. *m.*
LAMBERT, J. Surgeon Lieut., R.N. *O.B.E. M.*   1898
LANDER, P. E. Capt., R.A.M.C. (Sanitary Service, T.F.)   1907
   M.
LANGLEY, A. S. Lieut.-Cdr., R.N.V.R. *C.M.G. M.*   1905
LANSBERRY, H. G. Pte., R.A.M.C.   1910
LAW, H. S. Lieut., R.F.A.(T.F.)   1892
LAYTON, D. H. Capt., E. Yorks. Regt. (W 2.) *M.C.*   1907
LAZARUS-BARLOW, P. Lce.-Sergt., W. Kent Yeo.; Pte.,   1913
   R.A.M.C.; 2nd Lieut., Dorset Regt. and Tank
   Corps
LAZARUS-BARLOW, W. S. Capt., R.A.M.C.   1884
LEADER, H. E. Lieut.. Sherwood Foresters (Notts. and   1908
   Derby Regt.). (W.)
LEGGE, R. J. Lieut., R.A.S.C. and R.F.A.   1906
LEIGH, F. 2nd Lieut., S. Lancs. Regt.   1911
LEIGHTON, Rev. J. W. C.F. 4th Class, R.A.C.D.   1907

LEWIS, J. B. S. Capt., R.A.M.C.   1912
LEWIS, M. M. Capt., R. Welsh Fus. and Gen. List (Asst. 1910
Instructor, Command Depôt). *M.C. and Bar*
LEWIS, W. A. H. 2nd Lieut., R.G.A.   1909
LIDDLE, H. W. 2nd Lieut., King's Royal Rifle Corps. 1909
(W.) (P.)
✠LINE, J. Y. A. 2nd Lieut., N. Staffs. Regt.   ·   1914
Died 13 March 1916 of wounds received in action near
Neuve Chapelle 12 March 1916
LINFOOT, G. C. Gnr., R.N.   1914
LITTLEWOOD, A. Lieut., St Elizabeth College, Guernsey, 1908
O.T.C.
LLEWELYN, Rev. D. E. K. C.F. 4th Class, R.A.C.D.   1910
LOGAN, M. J. S. Lieut., S. Lancs. Regt. and King's Own 1900
(R. Lancaster Regt.)
LONDON, G. E. Lieut., Gloucestershire Regt. (W.)   1908
LONG, R. A. Lieut., R. Fusiliers; empld. Ministry of [1914]
Munitions. (W.)

MACDONALD BROWN, I. *See* BROWN, I. M.
MACKENZIE, J. W. Lieut., R. Fusiliers; empld. Army 1912
and Navy Canteen Board. (W 2.)
McKERGOW, R. W. Major, Sussex Yeo.; Lieut.-Col., 1889
Queen's Own (R.W. Kent Regt., T.F.) *O.B.E. T.D.*
✠McLAREN, A. D. Pte., R. Scots   1908
Killed in action 9 April 1917
MACTIER, J. C. Lieut., R. Glasgow Yeo.   1899
MALLETT, F. J. Capt., R.E. *M.C. and Bar*   1909
MARSH, C. J. Major, R.A.M.C.   *1912
✠MARSH, F. HOWARD. Hon. Colonel, R.A.M.C.(T.F.) *1907
Died 24 June 1915
MATHEWS, E. V. D. Lieut., D. of Cornwall's L.I.; 1913
Lieut. (A), R.A.F.
MATTHEWS, J. C. Capt., R.A.M.C. *M.C.*   1896
MILLER, D. C. Major (A.), R.A.F.   1912
MILLER-WILLIAMS, E. J. Lieut., R.F.A.(T.F.) (W.) 1910
MILLWARD, G. D. Lieut., R.A.S.C. *M.*   1906
MILWARD, H. H. Lieut., Worcestershire Regt. and M.G.C. 1913
(W 2.)
MONCKTON, F. H. Capt., R.E.   1911
MORGAN, D. A. Trooper, Welsh Horse   1909
MORGAN, D. F. Lieut., St Edward's School, Oxford, 1912
O.T.C.
MORGAN, H. A. Lieut., R.A.O.C.   1912

MOWLAM, H. J. Capt., Durham L.I.(T.F.); attd. Sher- 1907
wood Foresters (Notts. and Derby Regt.) (W.) (P.)

NEWMAN, F. C. Surgeon Lieut., R.N. *M.* 1902
NEWMAN, L. F. Capt., R.A.S.C. *m.* 1906
NICHOLLS, G. S. 2nd Lieut., R.E.; Staff Lieut. (Draft 1909
Conducting Officer)
NICHOLLS, L. Capt., R.A.M.C. 1904
NICOLSON, L. G. Lieut., R.A.F. 1910
NORMAN, N. F. Major, R.A.M.C. *1905
NORTH, J. F. A. Lieut., Northamptonshire Regt. 1913

OLIVER, E. G. Major, Essex Regt. and Gen. Staff. (W.) 1898
OLLARD, J. W. A. Capt., Cambridgeshire Regt.; Capt., 1916
and Adjt. Northamptonshire Regt.
ONTANON, C. 2nd Lieut., R.G.A. 1905
✠O'REILLY, H. D. R. Pte., R. Fusiliers; Capt., The Queen's [1914]
(R.W. Surrey Regt.)
Died 31 *May* 1919 *of wounds received in action in*
Mesopotamia
ORMROD, W. Capt., Lancs. Fus.; Brigade Major. *M.C.* 1909
M 3.

PASSANT, Rev. E. J. C.F. 4th Class, R.A.C.D. 1908
PEAD, J. H. Surgeon Cdr., R.N. *M. Chevalier, Legion* *1890
of Honour (France). Order of St Stanislas, 2nd Class,
with swords (Russia)
PECKOVER, H. D. Cadet, O.C.B. 1917
PETTY, M. J. Lieut., R.A.M.C. 1906
PHELPS, Rev. P. B. Lieut., R.N.V.R. 1908
PHILLIPS, D. I. W. Pte., R. Fusiliers (P. S. Bn.) 1909
PHILLIPS, W. D. Pte., R.A.S.C.(M.T.) 1911
PITT, W. J. Pte., Gold Coast Vol. Force 1906
PORTEOUS, N. W. Capt., Palmer's School, Grays, O.T.C. 1910
PORTWAY, D. Major, R.E. (Signals) 1906
PREVOST, P. G. C.F. 4th Class, R.A.C.D.; Cadet, R.G.A. 1902
PRICE, A. F. M. Pte., Malay States Vol. Force 1901

REA, D. Lieut., Suffolk Regt. *M.B.E.* 1913
REDFERN, W. A. K. Capt., R.F.A. and Spec. List (Adjt., *1907
Graves Registration Units); Staff Capt.
REECE, R. J. Surgeon Lieut.-Col., R.F.A.; Hon. Surgeon- 1888
Colonel, H.A.C. *C.B. m.*

REES, R. A. T.   Major, Loyal N. Lancs. Regt.; attd. S.   1904
   Staffs. Regt.(T.F.) (W.)
REID, W. L.   2nd Lieut., R.A.S.C.   1913
ROBINSON, A. D.   Capt., R.A.S.C.   1895
ROBINSON, W. H.   Lieut., R.A.M.C.   1898
ROTHFIELD, I.   Lieut., King's (Liverpool Regt.) (W 2.)   1911
   M.C.
✠ROUND, W. H.   Capt., Sherwood Foresters (Notts. and   1913
   Derby Regt., T.F.)
   Killed in action 1 *July* 1916
✠ROWLAND, S. D.   Major, R.A.M.C.   1889
   Died 6 *March* 1917 *of illness contracted on active*
   service
ROWSE, A. A.   Lieut., R.E.   1907
RUMSEY, C. F.   Capt., R.A.M.C.   1908
RUSHTON, W. F.   Lieut., King's (Liverpool Regt.)   1907
RUTHVEN, J.   Capt., Monmouthshire Regt.   1910

SAINT, A. P.   Major, R.A.M.C.; D.A.D.M.S. *M.C. M.*   1908
SAUNDERS, H. F.   Capt., Railway Bn., Indian Defence   1904
   Force. (W.)
SAVAGE, E. G.   Major, Queen's Own (R.W. Kent Regt.);   1903
   empld. Ministry of Munitions. (W.)
SELBY, E. J.   Major, R.A.M.C.; D.A.D.M.S.   *O B.E.*   1909
   M 3.
SHELTON, Rev. R. N.   C.F. 4th Class, R.A.C.D.   1903
SHRUBBS, C. A.   Lieut., R.A.S.C.   1907
SIMONS, E.   Capt., S. Wales Borderers.   *M.C. and Bar*   1904
SINCLAIR, W. M.   A.B., R.N.V.R.   1894
SMITH, D. W.   Corpl., R.A.F.   1917
SOLVAY, M. A.   Gnr., 2me Regt. d'Artillerie, Belgian   1916
   Army. *Belgian Croix de Guerre*
SPERO, L. H.   Rfn., London Regt. (L.R.B.)   1914
SPOWART, W. C.   Lieut., I.A.R.O., attd. S. and T.   **1910
   Corps. (W.)
SPRAKE, G. G.   2nd Lieut., R.G.A.   1915
SPROAT, R. H.   Lieut., S. Staffs. Regt.; attd. R.E.; Capt., 1913
   Spec. List (Cmdt., Anti-Gas School). *Italian Croce di*
   Guerra
STARKEY, H. S. C.   Capt., R.A.M.C.(T.F.) *O.B.E. M.*   1904
STENNING, Rev. E. H.   Capt., K. William's College, I. of   1906
   Man, O.T.C.
✠STERCKEMAN, P.   Cpl., French Infy. (W.) (P.)   1909
   Died 15 *Feb.* 1917 *of wounds received in action*

STEVENS, H. L.   Lieut. (A.), R.A.F.   1911
STEWARD, S. J.   Capt., R.A.M.C. *D.S.O. M.*   1897
✠STRATFORD, E. P.   Lieut., R.A.M.C.   *1903
  Died 20 April 1915 of wounds received in action near
  Neuve Chapelle 17 March 1915
✠STRINGER, G. M.   2nd Lieut., Cheshire Regt.   1911
  Accidentally killed 15 March 1915
SURRIDGE, B. J.   Lieut., Loyal N. Lancs. Regt.; empld.   1912
  Recruiting Staff
SUTTON, W. H. R.   Major, S. African Med. Service.   1900
  M 2.

TAFFS, L. H.   Lieut., 84th Punjabis, Indian Army   1904
TALPUR, MIR G. A.   2nd Lieut., Imp. Service Cavalry   1910
  Staff, Egyptian Army
TAYLOR, A. E.   Capt., Australian A.M.C.   1898
TAYLOR, R. S.   Major, E. African Med. Service   1899
THACKER, C. R. A.   Lieut., R.A.M.C.   1908
THODAY, F. A.   Major, Devon Regt.(T.F.)   1907
THOMAS, G. P.   Pte., Welsh Regt.   1914
THOMAS, H. H.   Lieut., R.F.A.; Capt. (T.), R.A.F.   1904
  M.B.E. *M 2.* *Order of the Nile, 4th Class*
  (Egypt)
THOMAS, M. E.   Lieut., R.E.(T.F.) (W.) *M.C. and*   1913
  Bar
THOMAS, N. L.   Capt., London Regt. (R. Fus.) (W.)   1911
THOMSON, M. S.   Lieut., R.A.M.C.   1914
✠TOPHAM, M.   Sergt., R. Fusiliers (P.S. Bn.); 2nd Lieut., [1914]
  R.F.C.
  Killed in action 13 April 1917
TREADGOLD, H. A.   Capt., R.A.M.C.   1903
TURNER, H. J.   Lieut., R. Welsh Fus.   1906
TURNER, J. W.   Lieut., Indian Army; Capt., Sherwood *1905
  Foresters (Notts. and Derby Regt.). *M.C.* *M.*

VIGURS, C. C.   Capt., R.A.M.C.   *1892

WAITE, W. F.   Lieut., Lancs. Fus. and Spec. List (Re-   1904
  cruiting Staff); empld. Ministry of Food. (W.) *M.*
WALKER, B.   Sub-Lieut., R.N.V.R.   1892
WALKER, R.   Capt., The Buffs (E. Kent Regt., T.F.)   1908
WALLIS, R. L. M.   Capt., R.A.M.C.   1904
WALSH, E. S.   Capt., D. of Wellington's (W. Riding Regt.)   1913
  and R.E. (W.)

WATTS, A. E. Capt. and Adjt., London Regt. (Kensing- 1909
ton Bn.)
WAUGH, G. E. Major, R.A.M.C. 1894
WEBB, F. E. A. Lieut.-Col., R.A.M.C.(T.F.) *O.B.E.* 1895
Brevet Lieut.-Colonel. M 2.
WEBB, F. H. Lieut., R. Warwickshire Regt. (W.) 1912
WHERRY, G. E. Lieut.-Col., R.A.M.C. (1st E. Gen. Hos- 1878
pital, T.F.). *m.*
WHITBY, L. E. H. Capt., Queen's Own (R.W. Kent [1914]
Regt.); Major, M.G.C. (W.) *M.C.*
WHITING, M. H. Capt., R.A.M.C. *O.B.E. M.* 1904
WHITMORE, C. J. R. Major, R.G.A. (W.) *M.C. M.* 1907
WHITTINGDALE, J. Lieut., R.A.M.C. 1913
✠WHITWORTH, A. G. R. 2nd Lieut., Northumberland 1914
Fus.
Died of wounds received in action 21 *March* 1918
WIDDICOMBE, E. P. Lieut., I.A.R.O. attd. Sappers and *1898
Miners; Capt., Spec. List; Major, R.E. *M.*
WILCOCK, J. A. 2nd Lieut., R.F.A. (W.) *M.C.* 1911
WILDERSPIN, B. C. Lieut., Worksop College O.T.C. 1908
WILKS, E. L. 2nd Lieut., York and Lancaster Regt. 1912
(W.)
✠WILL, J. G. Lieut., Leinster Regt.; attd. R.F.C. (W 2.) 1911
Killed in action 25 *March* 1917
WILLIAMS, Rev. H. C.F. 3rd Class, R.A.C.D.(T.F.) *1892
M.
WILLIAMS, T. P. 2nd Lieut., Suffolk Regt.; Lieut., Welsh 1914
Regt.
WILLIAMS, W. J. P.O. Telegraphist, R.N.V.R. 1915
WILLIAMS, W. P. G. Capt., I.M.S. 1899
WILLIS, R. E. Lieut.-Col., British W. Indies Regt. 1906
✠WILTON, S. B. Capt., N. Staffs. Regt. (W 2.) *M.C.* 1911
Killed in action 14 *March* 1917
WINFIELD, A. Lieut., R.A.M.C. 1905
WINFIELD, F. B. Major, R.A.M.C.; D.A.D.M.S. (W.) 1909
O.B.E. M 2. *French Croix de Guerre*
WITHINSHAW, J. W. Lieut., R. Scots and M.G.C. 1910
WOOD, F. E. Capt., Malay States Guides Med. Service 1895
WOOD, Rev. W. C.F. 4th Class, R.A.C.D. 1910
WOODHOUSE, R. A. Capt., R.A.M.C. 1911
WOODS, R. S. Capt., R.A.M.C. *M.* 1911
WORSTER-DROUGHT, C. C. Capt., R.A.M.C. 1906
WORTLEY, H. A. S. Capt., R.G.A. *M. m.* 1904

YORKE, G. O. 2nd Lieut., Army Cyclist Corps; Staff 1908
Lieut.
YOUNG, V. C. Lieut., R. Irish Rifles. (W 3.) *M.* 1914

ZAN, M. B. Subadar, Indian Army 1908

EMMANUEL COLLEGE

ABRAHAMS, A. Major, R.A.M.C. *O.B.E. m.*   1903
ADDISON, N. H. Lieut., R. Fusiliers (R. of O.)   1900
ADKIN, B. C. Capt., R.A.S.C.; attd. Suffolk Regt.   1911
AINSWORTH, J. M. Corpl., R.A.M.C. and R.E.(Spec. Bde.)   1912
ALLAN, F. L. Capt., Northumberland Fus. (W.) *M.C.*   1912
  M.
ALLEN, Rev. F. B. C.F. 4th Class, R.A.C.D.   1906
ALLEN, Rev. J. M. C.F. 4th Class, R.A.C.D.   1907
ALLSOPP, Rev. F. G. C.F. 4th Class, R.A.C.D. (W.)   1895
ALMOND, J. Capt. and Adjt., I.A.R.O., attd. Mohmand   1910
  Militia
ALTOUNYAN, E. H. R. Capt., R.A.M.C. (W.) *M.C.*   1908
ANDERSON, G. B. Capt., Middlesex Regt.; Major, R.   [1914]
  Berkshire Regt. (W.) *M.C. M.*
ANDERSON, L. A. P. Capt., I.M.S. (P.) *M.*   1906
ANDRADE, E. N. DA C. Capt., R.G.A.; empld. Ministry   1912
  of Munitions. *M.*
ANDREW, G. W. M. Capt., R.A.M.C.(T.F.) *M.*   1904
ANGAS, D. T. Sub-Lieut., R.N.A.S. (W.)   1912
✠APPLEGARTH, T. W. Pte., R.A.S.C.; 2nd Lieut., Dur-   1912
  ham L.I.
  *Died in Germany 9 Aug. 1918 of wounds received in
  action 3 June 1918*
ARMITAGE, W. J., T.D. Major, York and Lancaster Regt.   1886
  (T.F.); Garrison Musketry S.O.
ARNOLD, E. C. 2nd Lieut., Eastbourne College O.T.C.   1887
ARROWSMITH, R. Driver, H.A.C.   1912
ARUNDEL, F. D. Capt., R.G.A. *M.*   1908
✠ASHBY, K. H. Corpl., R.E. (Signals)   1910
  Missing, presumed killed in action at Mons, 1 Sept. 1914

✠ASHCROFT, F. Lieut., King's (Liverpool Regt.) 1905
Killed in action at Armentières 9 *April* 1917
ATKINSON, J. C. Lieut., R.E. (Signals, T.F.) *M.C.* 1914
✠ATKINSON, M.L. Pte., M.G.C.(Motor); 2nd Lieut., Tank 1907
Corps
Killed in action near Cambrai 20 *Nov.* 1917
✠ATKINSON, R. E. Lieut., Durham L.I.(T.F.) (W.) 1910
Killed in action at Armentières 20 *Feb.* 1916
ATTFIELD, W. H. Lieut., Hampshire Regt.; attd. King's 1907
Royal Rifle Corps
ATTLEE, C. K. Capt., R.A.M.C. 1894
ATTNEAVE, A. L. Sapper, R.E. 1914
AYLWIN, W. E. Pte., R. Fusiliers (P. S. Bn.); Capt., [1914]
Bedfordshire Regt. (W 2.) *M.C. M.B.E. m.*

BAINBRIDGE-BELL, L. H. Lieut., R. Munster Fus.; attd. 1912
R.E.; Hon. Lieut. (T.), R.A.F. *M.C.*
BAKER, Rev. A. T. B. Chaplain, R.N. 1897
BALDWIN, H. J. Capt. and Adjt., R.A.M.C. (Sanitary 1899
Service, T.F.)
BALL, Rev. W. A. R. C.F. 4th Class, Canadian Chaplains' 1904
Dept. (W.)
BALLINGALL, D.C.G. Major, R.A.M.C. (W.) *M.C. M*2. 1907
BALY, H. Sergt., Canadian Hdrs.; attd. Army Pay Corps 1893
BAMFORD, A. J. Lieut. and Adjt., Armoured Motor Bty.; 1904
Capt., Gen. List, empld. R.E. (Field Survey Coy.)
M.C. M 2.
BAMPFIELD, L. A. 2nd Lieut., W. Yorks. Regt.; Capt., 1901
Gen. List; A.D.C. *M.B.E. M* 3. *Italian Croce di
Guerra*
BANKS, E. H. Capt., Cheshire Regt. 1903
BARK, G. M. Lieut., R. Warwickshire Regt.; empld. War 1901
Office. (W.)
BARKER, F. A. Capt., I.M.S. *O.B.E. M.* 1900
BARLOW, Rev. C. W. Chaplain, R.N. 1898
BARNETT, F. S. G. Trooper, Gloucestershire Yeo.; Capt. 1910
and Adjt., R.F.A. *M.C. M.*
BARRETT, F. G. Lieut., London Regt. (Surrey Rifles) 1906
BARRITT, J. L. 2nd Lieut., W. Yorks. Regt.; Capt., R.E. 1911
M.
BARROW, H. E. Capt., King's (Liverpool Regt.) and [1914]
T.M.B. *M.C.*
BARROW-IN-FURNESS, Rt Rev. Bishop of. C.F. 4th Class, 1896
R.A.C.D.

BARTLETT, A. C. Corpl., R.E. (Signals) 1912
BATCHELOR, B. W. Capt., Rifle Brigade. (W.) 1914
BATES, Rev. H. R. C.F. 4th Class, R.A.C.D. (W.) 1900
BATHURST, C.R. Lieut., Northamptonshire Regt.; empld. 1898
Ministry of Labour. (W.) *M.*
BAWDON, W. S. Pte., Australian Infy. 1910
BAXTER, F.H. Capt., Portsmouth Grammar School O.T.C. 1892
BEAMISH, Rev. C. N. B. C.F. 4th Class, R.A.C.D. 1896
BEEVOR, R. B. Pte., London Regt.; 2nd Lieut., Bedford- [1914]
shire Regt. and R. Irish Fus.; Lieut. (A.), R.A.F.
Italian Croce di Guerra
BELL, A. W. Lieut., R.F.A.(T.F.) *M.C.* 1914
BELLERBY, Rev. A. C. B. C.F. 4th Class, R.A.C.D. 1907
BELLHOUSE, S. Lieut., W. Yorks. Regt.(T.F.) (W 2.) 1913
French Croix de Guerre
BELLWARD, G. W. F. Lieut., Essex Regt. (T.F.) and 1910
R.A.S.C.
✠BENGOUGH, J. C. Capt., Gloucestershire Yeo.; A.D.C. 1908
M.
Killed in action in Egypt 26 Feb. 1916
BENNETT, H. H. G. Lieut., Worcestershire Regt.(T.F.); 1910
empld. O.C.B.
BENNETT, W. P. Lieut., Border Regt.; Capt., R.G.A. 1909
(W.)
BENSLY, Rev. W. J. Capt., Dorset Regt.; Major, British 1893
W. India Regt. *D.S.O. M* 2.
BENSON, Rev. H. W. Cadet, O.C.B. 1910
BENTLEY, J. D. Lieut., R.F.A.(T.F.) (W.) 1910
BENTON, D. Lieut., Manchester Regt. 1910
BERGHEIM, P. Capt., R.G.A.; empld. War Office. 1904
O.B.E. M.C.
BESCOBY, A. C. Capt., R.A.M.C. (Sanitary Service, T.F.) 1905
✠BETTINGTON, A. F. Sqdn. Cdr., R.N.A.S. [1914]
Killed in flying accident 12 Sept. 1917
BEVAN-BROWN, C. M. Sergt., N. Zealand Med. Service 1909
BIENEMANN, G. A. J. 2nd Lieut., Nigeria Regt., W. 1909
African Frontier Force
BIGGER, W. K. Capt., R.A.M.C. *M.C.* 1909
BIRD, A. K. Capt., Suffolk Regt.; empld. O.C.B. (W.) 1912
BIRD, M. W. K. Capt., R.A.M.C.(T.F.) 1908
BISPHAM, J. W. Capt., R.E. *O.B.E. M* 2. 1902
BISS, H. C. J. Major, R. Irish Regt. 1889
BISSETT, C. C. Lieut. (T.), R.A.F. (Aircraft Production 1913
Dept.)

✠BLAKE, C. 2nd Lieut., Bedfordshire Regt.   1910
   Killed in action on the Somme 4 Sept. 1916
BLAKISTON, A. F. Trooper, K. Edward's Horse; Lieut., 1909
   R.F.A. (W.) *M.C.*
BLANCHARD, J. F. J. Corpl., K. Edward's Horse; Capt., 1911
   Canadian F.A. (W.)
BLAND, B. S. Capt., W. Yorks. Regt.(T.F.) (W 2.)   1909
BLAND, C. Major, Leicestershire Regt.   1892
BLOXHAM, L. A. Lieut., London Regt. (Kensington Bn.) 1914
   and Gen. Staff (Intelligence). (W.)
BLUETT, D. C. Pte., R. Fusiliers; Capt., R.A.M.C.   1902
BLUETT, T. L. C. Pte., R.A.M.C.   1903
BOARDMAN, H. Pte., Queen's Own (R.W. Kent Regt.)   1914
✠BODDINGTON, O. W. Lieut., N. Staffs. Regt.(T.F.)   1907
   Killed in action 13 Oct. 1915
BODDY, J. A. V. Lieut., Durham L.I.; Lieut. (A.), [1914]
   R.A.F. (W.)
BOLINGBROKE, C. B. Capt., Norfolk Regt.; attd. Man- 1909
   chester Regt. (W.)
BOND, J. S. Instructor Lieut., R.N.   1905
BONNER, C. A. J. Capt., Lancs. Fus.; empld. Ministry of 1905
   Labour. (W.) *M.*
✠BOOTE, C. W. Capt., Cheshire Regt.   1908
   Killed in action 4-5 April 1916
✠BOSTOCK, G. E. Capt., R. Munster Fus.   1913
   Killed in action at Loos 30 Jan. 1916
BOTTING, C. G. 2nd Lieut., St Paul's School O.T.C.   1889
BOURDILLON, T. E. Lieut., R. Sussex Regt. (W.) (P.) [1914]
BOWER, H. J. Capt., R.A.M.C. (W.)   1907
BOWES, G. B. Major, Cambridgeshire Regt. and Labour 1892
   Corps. *T.D.*
BOWKER, R. C. S. 2nd Lieut., R.F.A.; Lieut. (A.), R.A.F. 1911
BOWLE-EVANS, C.H. Colonel, I.M.S.; A.D.M.S. *C.M.G.* 1886
   C.B.E. M 3.
BOYD, Rev. H. J. C.F. 4th Class, R.A.C.D.   1895
BRAUNHOLTZ, G. E. K. Corpl., Manchester Regt.   1906
BRAYNE, W. F. Major, I.M.S.   1894
✠BREARLEY, A. J. Capt., Devon Regt.(T.F.) and R.E.   1909
   Killed in action 20 June 1917
BREWER, J. Lieut., R.A.M.C.   1906
BRIGGS, H. W. 2nd Lieut., Gloucestershire Regt.; Lieut., 1913
   R.A.F.
✠BRIGGS, R. S. Lieut., W. Yorks. Regt.(T.F.)   1913
   Killed in action 29 July 1915

BROOKE, J. 2nd Lieut., Dorset Regt.   1904
BROOKES, H. V. Pte., Middlesex Regt.   1915
✠BROUGH, Rev. J. S. B. C.F. 3rd Class, R.A.C.D. *M.*   1897
  Died 11 Nov. 1918 *of pneumonia*
BROWN, A.W. Lieut., Cameronians (Scottish Rifles, T.F.) 1913
  (W.)
BROWN, H. C. Major, I.M.S. *C.I.E.*   1895
BROWN, H. G. Surgeon Lieut., R.N.   1896
BROWN, O. N. Pte., R.A.M.C.; attd. R.F.A.   [1914]
BROWNE, C. R. Lieut.-Cdr., R.N.V.R. (R.N.D. and   1912
  Coastal Motor-boat Service). *M.*
BROWNE, R. D. H. Cadet, O.C.B.   1887
BRUTTON, J. C. Lieut., 8th Hussars (R. of O.); Capt., 1894
  Res. Regt. of Cavalry
BRYANT, G. W. Lieut., Malay Vol. Force   1906
✠BUCKNILL, J. C. 2nd Lieut., Hampshire Regt.(T.F.)   1898
  M.C. M.
  Killed in action in Mesopotamia 21 Jan. 1916
BURBIDGE, E. D'A. Capt., R.F.A. *M.*   1891
✠BURCH, R. S. Lieut. (A.), R.A.F.   1911
  Killed in action 28 June 1918
BURKITT, F. Lieut., Lincolnshire Regt.; attd. R. Irish 1913
  Rifles. (W.)
BURN, J. H. Capt., R.E. (Signals)   1909
BURROWS, C. Major, R.A.M.C. (T.F.)   *1894
BURTON, D. F. Lieut., Suffolk Regt.; Lieut. (A.), R.A.F. 1906
  (P.)
BURTON, Rev. W. 2nd Lieut., Sir R. Manwood's School,   1904
  Sandwich, O.T.C.
BUTLER, G. G. Capt., R.A.M.C. *M.B.E.*   1899
BUTLIN, Rev. T. H. C.F. 4th Class, R.A.C.D.   1909
BYRON, H. Pte., R. Fusiliers; 2nd Lieut., R.E.   1893

CARNEGY, P. L. ST C. Pte., R.A.M.C.   1894
✠CASS, L. F. Capt., R. Sussex Regt.   1897
  Killed in action 21 Dec. 1915
CAUSTON, E. P. G. Surgeon Lieut., R.N.; Major,   1894
  R.A.M.C. *O.B.E. m.*
CAVE-ORME, G. A. R. Capt., Spec. List, empld. Ministry 1886
  of National Service
CHALLANDS, R. S. 2nd Lieut., Worcestershire Yeo.;   1899
  Lieut. Grenadier Gds.; attd. Gds. M.G. Regt.
✠CHALMERS, H. S. Capt., R.F.A.(T.F.)   1913
  Died 29 Sept. 1917 *of wounds received in action*

CHAMBERS, E. L. Capt., Bedfordshire Regt.; Major, 1901
Northumberland Fus.; Lieut.-Col., King's Own
(Yorkshire L.I.) *M.*

✠CHANING-PEARCE, W. T. Capt., R.A.M.C. *M.C.* 1904
Killed in action 1 *Oct.* 1917

CHAPMAN, E. J. C. Lieut., Spec. List (R.T.O.) *M.C. M.* 1896

CHARTER, H. R. Lieut., E. Surrey Regt.; Major, R.E. 1909
(Spec. Bde.); Chemical Adviser. *M.C.*

CHAWNER, W. R. Capt., R.E. 1908

CHEETHAM, C. E. Capt., R.G.A.(T.F.Res.); empld. Min- 1899
istry of National Service

CHILDS, A. E. 2nd Lieut., Somerset L.I.; Capt., R.E. 1914
(W.)

CHRYSTALL,H.M. Lieut.,R.N.V.R.(Howe Bn.,R.N.D.); 1912
Staff Capt.; Capt., R.E. (W.) *M.*

CHUBB, C. Capt., R.A.S.C. 1903

CLARKE, Rev. H. S. S. C.F. 4th Class, R.A.C.D. 1895

CLARKE, L. B. Capt., R.A.M.C.(T.F.) *M.* 1905

✠CLIFFORD, A. C. 2nd Lieut., 3rd Dragoon Gds. (R. of O.) 1906
Killed in action at Ypres 2 *June* 1915

COBB, Rev. F. W. C.F. 4th Class, R.A.C.D. 1892

✠COBHAM, Rev. E. Pte., R.A.M.C.; C.F. 4th Class, 1900
R.A.C.D. *M.C.*
Died 19 *Sept.* 1917 *of wounds received in action in E.*
Africa

COHEN, Rev. A. C.F. 4th Class, R.A.C.D. 1906

COLLEY, W. H. Major, Yorkshire Regt.; Lieut.-Col., 1907
Manchester Regt. (W.) *O.B.E. M. Chevalier,*
Order of Leopold (Belgium). Belgian Croix de Guerre

COLLIE, A. E. Lieut., R.A.M.C. 1906

COLLINS, Rev. R. L. C.F. 4th Class, R.A.C.D. *m.* 1900

COLSON, Rev. F. S. C.F. 4th Class, R.A.C.D. 1908

✠COLTMAN, R. L. 2nd Lieut., Coldstream Gds.; attd. Gds. 1914
M.G. Regt. (W.)
Killed in action near Cambrai 27 *Nov.* 1917

CONACHER, H. 2nd Lieut., R.A.S.C.; Major, D.A.D. 1900
Army Printing and Stationery Services

COOKE, E. R. C. Capt., R.A.M.C. *M.C.* 1905

COOKE, H. L. Lieut., R.E. 1903

COOKSON, H. A. Major, R.A.M.C.(T.F.) 1915

COOMBS, H. M. McC. Capt., R.A.M.C.(T.F.) *M* 2. 1901

COOPER, A. L. Lieut., Fettes College O.T.C. 1906

COOPER, H. Surgeon Lieut.-Cdr., R.N.; Lieut.-Col. 1896
(Med.), R.A.F. *D.S.O. Belgian Croix de Guerre*

COOPER-HUNT, Rev. C. L.   C.F. 4th Class, R.A.C.D.   1908
COOPER-HUNT, D. L.   Lieut., Hampshire Regt.(T.F.)   1908
COOTE, A.   Lieut., R.A.S.C.   1895
CORNWALL, G.   Lieut., Suffolk Regt.; Capt., Gen. List 1914
    (T.M.B.); Lieut. (K.B.), R.A.F. (W.)
CORSER, J. S.   Pte., R. Fusiliers (P.S. Bn.); Lieut., Hamp- 1897
    shire Regt.
COTTINGHAM, J. W.   Pte., W. Yorks. Regt. (W.)   1912
COWELL, Rev. J. B.   C.F. 3rd Class, R.A.C.D. M 2.   1909
COWIE, D. H.   Lieut., R.G.A.   1910
COXE, K. H.   Capt., I.A.R.O., attd. 2nd Gurkha Rifles. 1909
    M.C.
COXON, T.   Pte., R. Fusiliers (P.S. Bn.); Capt., S. Lancs. 1913
    Regt. (W.) M.
✠COYNE, C. T.   Capt., W. Yorks. Regt. (W.)   1913
    Killed in action 27 Aug. 1917
COZENS, F. C.   Surgeon Sub-Lieut., R.N.V.R.   1911
CRAIG, G. W.   Lieut.-Col., R.A.M.C.(T.F.) m.   1898
CREIGHTON, W. R.   Capt., R.A.S.C. M.C. M 2.   1896
CREW, F. D.   Capt., R.A.M.C.   1897
CRISFORD, Rev. K. N.   C.F. 4th Class, R.A.C.D. (W.)   1906
    M.C.
CROFTS, J. M.   Capt., E. Lancs. Regt.; Major, Spec. List 1893
    (Chemical Adviser). M.
CROMPTON, R. A.   2nd Lieut., K. Edward's Horse   1913
CROOKE, R. H.   A.B., R.N.V.R. (Hawke Bn., R.N.D.)   1907
    (W.)
CROWTHER, H. N.   Pte., Wiltshire Regt.   1902
✠CRUIKSHANK, G. L.   Capt., Gordon Hdrs.; attd. R.F.C. 1908
    D.S.O. M.C. M 2.
    Killed in action 15 Sept. 1916
✠CUBITT, V. M.   Lieut., Norfolk Regt.   1906
    Killed in action at Suvla Bay 12 Aug. 1915
CUCKNEY, J.   Lieut., R.E. (Spec. Bde.)   1913
CUMBERLEGE, B. S.   Major, R.A.S.C.(M.T.) O.B.E.   1910
    M 2.
CUMMING, J. E.   Capt., R.F.A.(T.F.) M.C.   1913
CUTHBERTSON, Rev. J. H.   C.F. 4th Class, R.A.C.D.   1900
CUTTS, Rev. F. J.   Hon. Chaplain, R.N.   1906

DAMAN, T. W. A.   Major, R.A.M.C. (4th N. Gen. Hos-   1887
    pital, T.F.)
✠DANDRIDGE, W. L.   Lieut., R.A.M.C.   1912
    Died 5 Oct. 1918 of wounds received in action 3 Oct. 1918

DANIELL, J. Pte., R. Fusiliers; Capt., R.A.S.C.(T.F.) 1897
DAVENPORT, T. 2nd Lieut., Loyal N. Lancs. Regt. 1913
and M.G.C.; Lieut., 40th Pathans, Indian Army.
(W 2.)
DAVIDSON, W. W. Pte., Malay Vol. Rifles; Lieut., R.E. 1903
(W.) *M.C.*
DAVIES, Rev. J. C. C.F. 4th Class, R.A.C.D. (W.) (P.) 1904
✠DAVIES, J. G. Capt., Welsh Regt. 1910
Died 11 Feb. 1916 of wounds received in action
✠DAVIES, J. LL. Major, Essex Regt. 1901
*Died at Wesel, Germany, of wounds received in action
in the Battle of Loos 26 Sept. 1915*
DAVIES, J. LL. Capt., R.A.M.C. *M.* 1909
DAVIES, J. S. H. Pioneer, R.E. (Spec. Bde.) 1913
✠DAVIES, L. F. ST J. Lieut., Norfolk Regt.; Major, M.G.C. 1911
(W 2.) *M.C. M.*
Died 10 Nov. 1918
DAVIES-COLLEY, R. Colonel, A.M.S. *C.M.G. m* 2. 1899
✠DAVIS, H. N. 2nd Lieut., R.E. 1909
*Died 22 Feb. 1915 of wounds received in action 21 Feb.
1915*
DAWE, L. S. Lieut., Hampshire Regt. 1909
DAWKINS, R. McG. Lieut., R.N.V.R. *Cavalier, Order* 1898
of the Redeemer (Greece)
✠DAY, G. R. Lieut., Bedfordshire Regt.; Capt., R. War- *1912
wickshire Regt. (W.)
Killed in action on the Somme 27 Aug. 1916
DEED, N. G. Lieut., R.F.A. (W.) *M.C.* 1907
DENNEHY, H. G. Lieut., I.A.R.O., attd. 10th Gurkha 1909
Rifles
DENNISTON, J. G. Lieut., K. Edward's Horse, empld. 1912
Corps Cavalry Regt.
DENTON-THOMPSON, B. J. 2nd Lieut., Gloucestershire 1913
Regt.; Capt., Manchester Regt. (W 2.) *M.C.*
DICKSON, F. J. C. Trooper, Essex Yeo.; Lieut., R.A.S.C. 1908
DOBSON, A. T. A. 2nd Lieut., Hampshire Regt.; Staff 1904
Capt.; Major, S.O. 2, R.A.F.
DODDS, Rev. M. T. C.F. 4th Class, R.A.C.D.(T.F.) 1902
DODWELL, H. B. 2nd Lieut., R. Sussex Regt.; Capt., 1911
R.A.M.C.
DOGGART, H. Pte., R.A.S.C. 1904
DONALDSON, Rev. J. T. Cadet, O.C.B. 1912
✠DORRELL, H. G. H. 2nd Lieut., Durham L.I. (W 2.) 1910
Killed in action 3 April 1916

DREW, V. Lieut., Serbian Army. *Order of St Sava, 5th* 1910
Class (Serbia)
DUCKET, A. A. 2nd Lieut., R.E. 1909
DUNCANSON, E. F. Lieut., R.N.V.R. (Coastal Motor-boat 1898
Service)
DUNCANSON, T. J. G. Lieut., R.N.V.R. (Coastal Motor- 1892
boat Service)
DURAND, P. F. 2nd Lieut., I.A.R.O., attd. Sikhs. (W.) 1907
M.C. M.
DURIE, J. A. Capt., Black Watch; Staff Capt.; Lieut.- 1907
Col., Argyll and Sutherland Hdrs. (W.) *M.C.*
Brevet Major. M 2.
DURLING, J. A. Lieut., The Buffs (E. Kent Regt.) (W.) 1914
DVORKOVITZ, V. Driver, Armoured Cars, Russian Army 1911
DYER, A. C. Lieut., King's (Shropshire L.I.) *M.* 1907

EARDLEY-SIMPSON, L. E. Capt., R.F.A.(T.F.) 1898
✠EAST, G. D. Capt., R.A.M.C. 1907
Killed in action in the Third Battle of Ypres 31 *July*
1917
EDDOWES, W. B. Lieut.-Col., Manchester Regt., North- 1896
umberland Fus., Yorkshire Regt., and Spec. List. *M.*
EDMONDS, J. Capt., Wilson's School, Camberwell,O.T.C. *1901
EDWARDS, Rev. T. G. C.F. 4th Class, R.A.C.D. 1906
ELLIOTT, A. F. Capt., R.A.M.C. 1896
ELLIOTT, Rev. E. C. C.F. 4th Class, R.A.C.D. 1907
ELLIS, J. M. 2nd Lieut., R. Warwickshire Regt. (W.) 1914
ELLIS, Rev.P.D. C.F. 4th Class, R.A.C.D.; Pte., London 1899
Regt. (Artists Rifles); Lieut., R.A.O.C.
ELLISON, W. J. Capt., R.F.A.; empld. Ministry of 1910
Labour. (W 2.) *M.*
ELWORTHY, C. W. Capt., R.A.S.C. 1897
ENGLAND, E. M. Asst. Paymaster, R.N.V.R. 1913
EVANS, C. H. *See* BOWLE-EVANS, C. H.
EVANS, J. LL. Lieut., S. Wales Borderers. (W.) 1913
EVITT, Rev. E. U. C.F. 4th Class, R.A.C.D. 1904

FARMERY, J. W. Pioneer, R.E. (Spec. Bde.) (W.) 1914
FARMILOE, K. M. Pte., London Regt.; 2nd Lieut., Rifle 1913
Brigade
✠FAWCETT, R. H. 2nd Lieut., Bedfordshire Regt. 1912
Killed in action near Ypres 26 *April* 1915
FAWCETT, T. G. Lieut., W. Yorks. Regt.(T.F.); Lieut. 1914
(O.), R.A.F. (W.)

✠Fayle, B. J. L. Capt., R.A.M.C. 1908
Killed in action 24 *Oct.* 1916
Fell, F. J. 2nd Lieut., Black Watch. (W.) 1914
✠Fenn, E. G. P. 2nd Lieut., R. Welsh Fus.; attd. Essex 1914
Regt.
Killed in action 19 *Sept.* 1918
Fenwick, W. Pte., R. Fusiliers (P. S. Bn.); Lieut., 1911
Durham L.I.; Staff Capt. *M.*
✠Ferguson, J. C. M. Capt., Bedfordshire Regt. (W.) 1907
Died 19 *Nov.* 1918 *of illness contracted on active service*
Fiddian, E. A. Surgeon Lieut., R.N. *Bronze Medal for* 1911
gallantry in saving life at sea
Fiddian, J. V. Capt., R.A.M.C. 1907
Finch, G. 2nd Lieut., R.G.A. 1912
Finter, F. B. Lieut., R.E. (W.) 1912
Fisher, E. G. Surgeon Lieut., R.N. 1902
✠Fisher, E. H. Pte., London Regt. (Artists Rifles); 2nd 1902
Lieut., Yorkshire Regt.
Killed in action near Festubert 19 *May* 1915
Fisher, W. H. Major, R.A.M.C.(T.F.) *O.B.E. M.* 1895
Fletcher, A. W. Capt., Loyal N. Lancs. Regt. (W.) 1912
✠Foley, M. J. A. Capt. and Adjt., Middlesex Regt.(T.F.) 1900
Killed in action in Gallipoli 10 *Aug.* 1915
Foot, S. H. Capt., R.E.; Major, G.S.O. 2, empld. Tank 1906
Corps. *D.S.O. Brevet Major. M* 2.
Fothergill, C. F. Lieut., R.A.M.C. 1898
Frampton, H. H. C. Pte., Army Pay Corps 1889
Frazier-Upton, Rev. G. Chaplain, R.A.F. *m.* 1900
Freeman, H. Pte., R. Fusiliers (Sportsman's Bn.) 1898
Fry, C. R. M. 2nd Lieut., R. Sussex Regt. (W.) 1914
✠Fulford, Rev. R. H. C.F. 4th Class, R.A.C.D. 1905
Killed in action 15 *Dec.* 1916

Gabriel, E. V., c.s.i., c.v.o. Lieut.-Col., Gen List., 1893
Indian Army; attd. Gen. Staff, War Office, Italian
Army, and Palestine. *C.M.G. C.B.E. M*2. *m.*
Officer, Order of the Crown of Italy. Officer, Order
of St Maurice and St Lazarus (*Italy*). *Italian Croce di*
Guerra
Gabriel, J. B. S. Capt., R.E. (London Electrical Eng- 1907
ineers, T.F.) *m.*
Gabriel, O. B. Major, R.A.S.C.(M.T.) 1909
Gandy, E. W. Lieut.-Cdr., R.N.V.R. *O.B.E. M.* 1898
Chevalier, Legion of Honour (*France*)

GARDNER, G. H.   2nd Lieut., Gen. List; Lieut., Army   1901
Printing and Stationery Services
GARDNER, R.   Lieut.-Col., King's Own (R. Lancaster   1908
Regt., T.F.) *M.C.* *M* 2.
GARDNER, Rev. R. T.   C.F. 4th Class, R.A.C.D.   1882
GARNETT, R. T.   Lieut., R.G.A.   1907
GARRETT, D. T.   Lieut., R.N.V.R.   1902
✠GARROD, A. N.   Lieut., R.A.M.C.   1906
Killed in action 25 Jan. 1916
✠GAULD, A. G.   Capt., London Regt.   1912
Killed in action on the Somme 15 Sept. 1916
GERMAN, R. L.   Lieut., Hampshire Regt.; attd. Tank   1911
Corps
GIBB, P.   Major, R.A.S.C. *M.C.* *M.*   1906
GILBERT, H.   Major, York and Lancaster Regt. and   1912
M.G.C. *M.C.* *M* 2.
GIMSON, B. L.   2nd Lieut., R.A.S.C.   1909
GIMSON, C.   2nd Lieut., I.A.R.O., attd. 18th Infy.   1906
GIRLING, Rev. F. B.   C.F. 4th Class, R.A.C.D.   1900
GLEN-BOTT, C. L.   Engineer Lieut., R.N.V.R.   1902
GLENDAY, R. G.   Lieut., King's African Rifles. (W.)   1908
M.C. *M.*
GOODALL, J. F.   2nd Lieut., E. Lancs. Regt.   1910
GOODWIN, E.   Staff Lieut., Ministry of Munitions; Capt.,   1896
Spec. List. *O.B.E.* *m* 2.
GOOLDEN, C. E.   2nd Lieut., R. Munster Fus.; Lieut.,   1911
Labour Corps
GORDON, G. A.   Lieut., 2nd Dragoon Gds. (Queen's Bays).   1907
(W.)
GOSSLING, F. N.   Major, R.E. (Postal Section). *M.C.* *M.*   1908
GOUGH, D. L.   Capt., Somerset L.I. (W 2.) *M.C.*   [1914]
GOUGH, H. A.   Major, W. Yorks. Regt. (W 2.) *M.C.*   1907
M 2.
GOVER, J. E. B.   Air Mechanic, R.N.A.S.   1913
✠GOW, C. H.   Surgeon Lieut., R.N.V.R. (R.N.D.)   1909
Killed in action on the Somme 13 Nov. 1916
GRAHAM HOBSON, W. J.   Lieut., R.F.A.; attd. R.G.A.   1913
GRAHAM-JONES, J. L.   Capt., R.A.M.C.   1899
GRANGE, E. L., T.D.   Hon. Colonel, R.F.A.(T.F. Res.) *m.*   1877
GRAY, A. H.   Lieut., R.G.A. *M.*   1914
GRAY, N.   Capt., R.A.M.C. *M.*   1907
GREAVES, H. G.   Lieut., R.A.M.C.   1903
GREEN, Rev. A. G.   C.F. 4th Class, R.A.C.D.   1887
GREEN, C. C.   Pte., Middlesex Regt.   1915

GREEN, E. A. Surgeon Lieut., R.N. *M.*   1910
GREENBERG, B. M. *See* GREENHILL, B. M.
GREENE, C. W. Capt., R.A.M.C.(T.F.) (W.) *M* 3.   1900
GREENHILL, B. M. 2nd Lieut., Buckinghamshire Yeo.;   1911
    Lieut., R. Horse Gds. (W.) (P.)
GREGORY, C. H. Capt., R.A.M.C.(T.F.)   1896
GREGORY-JONES, E. Lieut., R.F.A. (W.) *M.C.*   1907
GRIBBLE, H. W. G. Pte., London Regt.   1910
GRIFFITH-WILLIAMS, G. C. Lieut., R.F.A.(T.F.) (W.)   1913
    M.
GROVE, A. J. Hon. Lieut., Spec. List (Entomologist)   1910
GUINNESS, Rev. P. W. C.F. 2nd Class, R.A.C.D. *D.S.O.*   1895
    M.C. *M* 2.
✠GUNTON, J. W. 2nd Lieut., Somerset L.I.; attd. R.F.C.   1914
    Killed in action 9 *Aug.* 1916
GURNEY, B. T. Sergt., R.E.   1913
GURNHILL, Rev. C. J. C.F. 4th Class, R.A.C.D.; Pte.,   1908
    R.A.M.C.
GWINN, R. F. Lieut., Cambridgeshire Regt.; attd. North-   1913
    amptonshire Regt.; Capt., King's (Liverpool Regt.)
    (W.)
GWYN, R. F. 2nd Lieut., S. Wales Borderers; Lieut.,   1906
    Army Cyclist Corps

HAHN, F. M. 2nd Lieut., E. Yorks. Regt. and N. Staffs.   1911
    Regt.; Capt., R.A.O.C.; I.O.M. 3rd Class. (W.)
HAINES, H. Y. Lieut., Canadian Infy.   1911
HALE, G. D. Lieut.-Col., Loyal N. Lancs. Regt.(T.F.)   1886
HALL, D. G. Major, R.A.M.C. (2nd E. Gen. Hospital,   1894
    T.F.)
HALL, G. V. 2nd Lieut., R. Welsh Fus.   1917
HALL, J. Capt., R. Scots; empld. P. and B.T. Staff   1900
HANSON, Rev. R. E. V. C.F. 2nd Class, R.A.C.D.; Dep.   1885
    Chaplain-in-Chief, R.A.F. *O.B.E.* *m.*
HARDING, Rev. N. S. C.F. 4th Class, R.A.C.D.   1906
HARLAND, Rev. H. C. C.F. 3rd Class, R.A.C.D. *M.C.*   1907
HARLAND, R. E. C. Lieut., The Queen's (R.W. Surrey   1910
    Regt.); Liaison Officer with Portuguese Army. (W.)
HARRIES, A. T. Lieut., R. Welsh Fus.; Brigade Major.   1914
    M 2.
HARRIS, A. D. Lieut., R.F.A.   1905
HARRIS, Rev. H. C.F. 4th Class, R.A.C.D. *M.C.* *M.*   1896
✠HARRIS, H. A. Capt., R.A.M.C. (W.)   1896
    Killed in action 31 *July* 1917

HARRIS, T. Lieut., R.E. (Meteorological Section) 1909
✠HARRISON, D. H. Lieut., R.F.A.(T.F.) 1912
  Killed in action 16 *Sept.* 1918
HARRISON, L. Hon. Lieut., Spec. List (Entomologist) 1914
HARTMAN, R. T. Capt., London Regt. (R. Fus.); Asst. 1912
  Supt., Ordnance Factories
HATTERSLEY, S. M. Major, R.A.M.C.; D.A.D.M.S. (P.) 1906
  M.C. M. French Croix de Guerre
HAWKINS, A. G. 2nd Lieut., Worcestershire Regt.(T.F.) 1898
HAWKINS, C. L. Lieut., R.A.M.C. 1893
HAYTER, G. K. H. Lieut., R.F.A.; Staff Capt. *M.* 1906
HEAD, Rev. F. W. C.F. 3rd Class, R.A.C.D. *M.C. and* 1893
  Bar
HEANY, W. P. Lieut., E. Yorks. Regt. (W.) 1912
✠HEARN, J. S. 2nd Lieut., Suffolk Regt. 1908
  Killed in action at Gueudecourt 12 *Oct.* 1916
HEATH, C. N. Capt., R.E. 1906
HELE, T. S. Capt., R.A.M.C.(T.F.) *O.B.E. M* 2. 1900
HEMPSON, E. R. 2nd Lieut., R. Fusiliers [1914]
✠HENSLEY, W.H. Pte.,R.Fusiliers (P.S. Bn.); Capt., Som- 1913
  erset L.I. (W.)
  Killed in action at Amiens 21 *March* 1918
HEPWORTH, Rev. B. G. Lce.-Corpl., Australian Infy. 1905
HERBERT, Rev. F. F. C.F. 4th Class, R.A.C.D. 1898
HEYWOOD, W. B. Capt., R.A.M.C. 1889
HIGGINS, Rev. W. N. C.F. 4th Class, R.A.C.D. 1898
HIGHFIELD, A. 2nd Lieut., R.E. (Spec. Bde.) 1913
HILL, A. Capt., R.G.A.(T.F.) *M* 2. 1897
HILL, A. T. 2nd Lieut., Berkhamsted School O.T.C. 1906
HILL, H. L. Trooper, N. Somerset Yeo.; 2nd Lieut., 1911
  Loyal N. Lancs. Regt.; Lieut.,N.Somerset Yeo.; attd.
  Dragoon Gds.
HILL, R. Pioneer, R.E. (Spec. Bde.) 1917
✠HILLBROOK, W. Capt. (M. O.), Congo Carrier Corps, 1910
  E. African Force
  Died at Nairobi 22 *July* 1916
HIND, A. M. Capt., R.A.S.C.; Major, D.A.Q.M.G. 1899
  O.B.E. M 3.
HINDE, Rev. B. F. C.F. 4th Class, R.A.C.D. *M.C.* 1905
HINDE, E. B. Capt., R.A.M.C.(T.F. Res.) *M.* 1900
HINDE, Rev. P. M. C.F. 4th Class, R.A.C.D. *M.C.* 1903
HOBSON, W. J. G. *See* GRAHAM HOBSON, W. J.
HODGES, Rev. L. N. C.F. 4th Class, R.A.C.D. 1905
HOLE, H. W. 2nd Lieut., Hampshire Regt. 1911

✠HOLLINS, E. R. L.　Capt., King's Own (R. Lancaster　1903
Regt.)
Died 3 March 1916 of wounds received in action 2 March 1916

HOOLE, N.　Lieut., W. Yorks. Regt. and Labour Corps.　1911
(W.)　M.

HOOPER, A. N.　Capt., R.A.M.C. (W.)　M.　1907

HOOPER, A. W.　Capt. and Adjt., R.G.A.　M.C.　1908

✠HOOPER, L. J.　2nd Lieut., Dorset Regt.　1913
Killed in action 26 Sept. 1916

HOPE, Rev. B. L.　C.F. 4th Class, R.A.C.D.　1899

HOPKINSON, H. C.　2nd Lieut., King's (Shropshire L.I.)　1911
and R.F.C.

HORDER, C. A.　Surgeon Sub-Lieut., R.N.V.R.　1915

HORNER, P. W. M.　Capt., R.A.S.C.　1913

HORNSBY-WRIGHT, G. J.　Lieut.-Col., Essex Regt. (T.F.)　1893
D.S.O.　M.　m.

HORTON, E. F.　Capt., Dorset Regt. (W.)　M.　1903

HOSTE, T. B.　Sergt., King's Royal Rifle Corps　1914

HOWARD, C. G.　Lieut., Nigeria Regt., W. African Frontier　1911
Force

HOWARD, T. H.　Major, Hampshire Regt.; Staff Capt.　1902

HOWELL, E. B.　Lieut.-Col., Spec. List (Censor's Dept.);　1895
Military Governor of Baghdad.　C.I.E.　C.S.I.　M 5.

HOWELL, R. A.　Lieut., R.A.S.C.　1908

HOWELL, R. G. D.　2nd Lieut., R.A.S.C.　1896

HOWLAND, R. C. J.　Gnr., R.G.A.　1915

✠HUDDART, L. H. L.　Lieut., R.E.; attd. Nigeria Regt., W.　1898
African Frontier Force
Died 12 Feb. 1917

HUGHES, L. W.　Lieut., R.A.S.C.　1911

HULL, H. C.　Major, Gen. Staff, attd. S.W. African Field　1905
Force

HUMPHREYS, I. H. M.　Capt., Border Regt. (T.F.); empld.　1912
Air Ministry. (W.)

HUNT, Rev. J. B.　Lieut., R. Fusiliers; empld. Ministry of　1909
Munitions. (W.)　M.C.

HUNTBACH, G. W.　Capt., King's (Shropshire L.I.);　1907
attd. R.F.C.; Major, Tank Corps. (W.)

✠HUSSEY, E. T.　Pte., R. Fusiliers (P. S. Bn.); 2nd Lieut.,　[1914]
R. Munster Fus. (W.)
Killed in action 7 June 1917

HUTCHINGS, C. E.　2nd Lieut., R. Berkshire Regt.; Capt.,　1908
Army Cyclist Corps.　M.

HUTCHINGS, Rev. H. W. Pte., London Regt. C.F. 4th 1906
Class, R.A.C.D. (W 2.) *M.C*

✠ILIFFE, C. A. M. Pte., R. Fusiliers 1911
Killed in action on the Somme July 1916
IMLAY, A. D. 2nd Lieut., Clifton College O.T.C. 1904
✠INGOLDBY, Rev. R. H. Trooper, Alberta Dragoons, Can- 1905
adian Force; 2nd Lieut., R. Dublin Fus.
Killed in action on the Somme 1 July 1916
IRVINE, L. C. D. Surgeon Lieut., R.N.V.R. 1905

✠JACOT, E. Lieut. (A.), R.F.C. 1910
Killed in action 6 June 1917
JAFFÉ, A. C. Major, London Yeo. (Westminster Dragoons); 1902
Lieut.-Col., Remount Service
JAGO, E. O. Lieut., Gloucestershire Regt.(T.F.) (W.) 1905
JAMES, L. H. Capt., Worcestershire Regt. 1909
JAMES, T. M. 2nd Lieut., Sutton Valence School O.T.C. 1910
JAMESON, F. R. W. Corpl., H.A.C.; Lieut., R.E. (Signals) 1912
D.S.O. M.C. and two Bars. M 2.
JAMESON, Rev. W. L. C.F. 4th Class, R.A.C.D. (W.) 1905
M.
JAMIE, J. P. W. Capt., Leicestershire Regt.(T.F.) *M.C.* 1913
JAQUET, Rev. D. A. C.F. 4th Class, R.A.C.D. 1906
JARVIE, J. M. Capt., R.A.M.C. 1903
JENKINS, W. A., Pte., W. Yorks. Regt. 1912
JOHN, Rev. W. R. C.F. 4th Class, R.A.C.D. 1894
JOHNS, N. A. 2nd Lieut., Queen's Own (R. W. Kent 1908
Regt.); Major, M.G.C. *M.C. and Bar*
✠JOHNS, O. LL. 2nd Lieut., R.F.A. *M.C.* 1911
Killed in action 25 June 1916
✠JOHNSON, D. F. G. Lieut., Manchester Regt. 1911
*Died 15 July 1916 of wounds received in action on the
Somme*
JOLLY, Rev. R. B. C.F. 4th Class, R.A.C.D. 1905
JONES, B. M. Lieut.-Col. (T.), R.A.F. (Aircraft Production 1906
Dept.) *A.F.C. M. m.*
JONES, C. J. Capt., R. Welsh Fus. and R.E.; Staff Capt. 1910
JONES, E. GREGORY. *See* GREGORY-JONES, E.
JONES, Rev. F. H. Chaplain, R.N. *O.B.E.* 1897
JONES, I. F. H. Lieut., Hampshire Regt.(T.F.); Capt., 1906
S. Staffs. Regt.(T.F.)
JONES, L. W. Capt., R.A.M.C. 1910
JONES, W. E. D. Corpl., R.E. (Spec. Bde.) 1912

JONES, W. N.   Capt. (T.), R.A.F.   1903
JORDAN, J. H.   Major, R.A.M.C. (W.) *M.C.*   1908
JOYNER, C. B.   Capt., Essex Regt. and Gen. List, empld.   1901
   Ministry of Munitions. *O.B.E.   M.B.E.   m.*
✠JUNOR, P. B.   Pte., E. African Rifles   1900
   Killed in action in E. Africa Sept. 1914

KANN, E. A.   Pte., R. Sussex Regt.   1908
KEETON, G. H.   2nd Lieut., Reading School O.T.C.   1897
KELLAND, W. H. C.   Capt., R.E.(T.F.)   1912
✠KELLOCK, H. P.   Lieut., N. Irish Horse; attd. R.F.A.   [1914]
   Died 6 *Oct.* 1918 *of wounds received in action*
KELLOCK, T. H.   Capt., R.A.M.C. (3rd London Gen.   1880
   Hospital, T.F., and R. Army Med. College)
KENT, A. G.   Lieut., Coldstream Gds.   1893
KENT, T. P. P.   Lieut., Devon Regt.   1910
KILNER, S. D.   Surgeon Lieut., R.N.   1908
KING, H.   Lieut., Seaforth Hdrs.; attd. R.E. (Signals).   1906
   (W.) *M.C. and Bar*
KINGHAM, B. V.   Lieut., Oundle School O.T.C.   1908
✠KIRBY, W. E.   2nd Lieut., I.A.R.O., attd. 15th Sikhs   1902
   Wounded and missing, presumed killed in action in Galli-
   poli (10 *July* 1915)
KIRKLAND, Rev. A. E.   C.F. 4th Class, R.A.C.D.   1908
✠KIRKLAND, F. W.   2nd Lieut., Rifle Brigade   1914
   Killed in action on the Somme 1 *July* 1916
✠KNIGHT, W. F.   Lieut., W. Yorks. Regt.   1908
   Killed in action 27 *Feb.* 1917
KNIGHTS, Rev. H. J. W.   C.F. 4th Class, R.A.C.D.   1899
KNIGHTS, K. M. W.   Corpl., Canadian Engineers. (W.)   1904

LANG, A.   Trooper, Scottish Horse; Corpl., R.E.(Signals);   1902
   2nd Lieut., Bedfordshire Regt.; attd. Cambridgeshire
   Regt.
LANGMEAD, L. G. N.   Major, Rifle Brigade. *M.C.   M.*   1911
LANGTRY, R. L.   Lieut., Welsh Regt. (W.)   1897
LANKESTER, Rev. R. F.   2nd Lieut., Labour Corps   1907
LASBREY, Rev. E. W.   C.F. 4th Class, R.A.C.D.   1903
LATHBURY, R. J.   Capt., London Regt. (Rifles). (W 2.)   1912
LEA, Rev. H. A. H.   Lieut., Labour Corps   1896
LEE, R. O.   Capt., R.A.M.C.   1895
LEES, A. A.   Capt., R.A.M.C. *M.C.   M.*   1908
LESLEY, J. W.   Capt., Yorkshire Regt.(T.F.) and King's   1907
   Royal Rifle Corps. (W.) (P.) *M.C.*

LEVIEN, Rev. E. G. Lieut., R.N.V.R. 1898
LEWIS, C. B. Lieut., R.G.A. 1900
LEWIS, J. H. 2nd Lieut., E. Surrey Regt.; Lieut., 1914
Middlesex Regt.; attd. T.M.B.
✠LEWIS, W. H. 2nd Lieut., R.F.A. *M.* 1913
Died (15 *Aug.* 1917) *of wounds received in action*
✠LIDGETT, J. C. Lieut., S. Lancs. Regt. 1904
Killed in action 23 *March* 1918
✠LILLIE, F. S. Major, R. Irish Regt. 1892
Killed in action at St Eloi 15 *March* 1915
LINE, J. Capt., R.A.S.C.; Hon. Capt. (A.), R.A.F. 1912
A.F.C.
LLOYD, H. I. Lieut., Northamptonshire Regt.; Capt., 1913
King's Own (R. Lancaster Regt.) *M.C.*
LLOYD, R. B. Capt., I.M.S. *M.* 1900
✠LLOYD-JONES, E. W. Capt., R. Welsh Fus.(T.F.) *M.* 1907
Killed in action in Gallipoli 10 *Aug.* 1915
✠LLOYD-JONES, J. Pte., London Regt. (Artists Rifles); 1910
Capt., Yorkshire Regt. (W.) *M.C. M.*
Died 11 *March* 1916 *of septic pneumonia and pleurisy*
LONGDEN, J. M. Lieut.-Col., Durham L.I. and Gen. 1892
Staff
LONSDALE, H. Lieut., Suffolk Regt. (W 2.) *M.* 1904
LOSEBY, Rev. P. J. Pte., R.A.M.C.; C.F. 4th Class, 1894
R.A.C.D. (W.)
LUCAS, E. Pte., R.A.M.C. 1906
LUSH, H. Pte., R. Warwickshire Regt.; Lieut., W. Yorks. 1913
Regt. (W.) *M.B.E.*
LYON-SMITH, G. Lieut. and Adjt., R.F.A.(T.F.); Brigade 1912
Major. (W.) *M.*

McCOMBE, F. W. W. Corpl., Army Pay Corps; 2nd 1913
Lieut., R.G.A.
McCREA, E. D. Capt., R.A.M.C. 1917
MACDONALD, C. L. Lieut.-Col., Manchester Regt.; attd. 1900
Devon Regt. and King's (Liverpool Regt.). *D.S.O.*
and Bar. M 2.
MACKENZIE, C. Major, R.A.M.C. *O.B.E. M.* 1901
MACKENZIE, H. W. G. Capt., R.A.M.C. (2nd London 1876
Gen. Hospital, T.F.)
MACLEAN, E. W. Capt., N. Zealand M.G.C. 1904
MACLEOD, D. J. Capt., King's (Shropshire L.I.); Bri- 1914
gade Major; empld. O.C.B. (W.) *M.*
MACLEOD, N. D. Capt., Black Watch. *M.C. and Bar* 1913

MacMaster, H. V. Capt., Spec. List   1898
McNair, A. J. Capt., R.A.M.C.   1905
Macrae, L. Capt., Cameron Hdrs.(T.F.)   1911
Madge, Q. Capt., R.A.M.C. *O.B.E.* *M.*   1906
Makepeace, F. L. Lieut. and Adjt., Suffolk Regt.; Lieut.,   1901
  Labour Corps
Malaher, Rev. H. T. C.F. 4th Class, R.A.C.D. *m.*   1906
✠Malcomson, L. Corpl., R.E. (Spec. Bde.)   1910
  Killed in action Nov. 1916
Malcomson, W. T. Lce.-Corpl., R. Dublin Fus.; 2nd   1908
  Lieut., R.E. *M.C.*
Malleson, W. M. Pte., R. Fusiliers   1908
Man, Rev. M. L. C.F. 4th Class, R.A.C.D.   1896
✠Manley, J. D. 2nd Lieut., R.E.   1910
  Killed in action at Vendresse 26 *Sept.* 1914
Mann, R. 2nd Lieut., Lancs. Fus.; Lieut., M.G.C.   1900
  (Motor)
Mann, T. C. Asst. Paymaster, Army Pay Dept.; Capt.,   1907
  R.E. (London Electrical Engineers, T.F.) *M.B.E.* *m.*
Mansell, R. A. Capt., R.A.M.C.; Major, D.A.D.M.S.   1909
  M.B.E. *M.* *Order of the White Eagle, 5th Class*
  (Serbia)
Mansfield, H. Y. Capt., R.A.M.C.   1907
Mansfield, W. S. Lieut., 8th (King's R. Irish) Hussars   1912
  (R. of O.) *Chevalier, Ordre du Mérite Agricole*
  (France)
Marriott, F.W.P. Pte., R.A.M.C.; Capt., R.G.A. *M.C.*   1897
Marris, E. D. Lieut., R.Warwickshire Regt.(T.F.); Capt.   1910
  R.E. (Signals)
Marsden, W. G. Capt., R.A.M.C.   1905
Marshall, A. R. Major, R.E. (Signals) and Spec. List   1905
  (Chief Instructor, Training Centre.) *D.S.O.* *M.C.*
  M 2.
Marshall, Rev. H. G. C.F. 2nd Class, R.A.C.D. *M.*   1901
Marshall, Rev. N. E. 2nd Lieut., Nagpur Rifles, Indian   1908
  Defence Force; Junior Chaplain, Indian Army
Martin, H. W. L. 2nd Lieut., Northumberland Fus.;   1915
  Lieut., York and Lancaster Regt.; attd. S. Notts.
  Hussars. (W.)
Martin, J. H. B. Surgeon Lieut.-Cdr., R.N. *M.*   1900
Martin, T. L. Lieut., Cheshire Regt.(T.F.) and Gen.   1912
  Staff
Mason, G. H. 2nd Lieut., R. Warwickshire Regt.;   1903
  Lieut., M.G.C.

MATTHEWS, H. DE C. 2nd Lieut., Nigeria Regt., W. 1891
African Frontier Force
MAUDE-ROXBY, Rev. J. H. T. C.F. 4th Class, R.A.C.D. 1902
(T.F.)
✠MAYNARD, A. F. Lieut., R.N.V.R. (Howe Bn., R.N.D.) 1912
(W.)
Killed in action on the Somme 13 *Nov.* 1916
MAYNARD, H. A. Capt., Middlesex Regt. and Gen. List; 1911
Staff Capt. (W 2.) *M.C. and Bar. M.*
✠MELHUISH, I. V. B. 2nd Lieut., Somerset L.I. [1914]
Killed in action 27 *Oct.* 1915
MELLIS-SMITH, D. B. Lieut., Cameronians (Scottish 1905
Rifles) and Seaforth Hdrs.; A.D.C. (W 2.)
MENENDEZ, Sir M. R. Major, Spec. List, empld. Ministry 1887
of National Service. *m.*
METCALF, Rev. F. W. R. Chaplain and Instructor Cdr., 1894
R.N.
METCALFE-GIBSON, R. A. 2nd Lieut., R.A.S.C. 1905
✠MILBURN, W. H. 2nd Lieut., Suffolk Regt.(T.F.) 1910
Killed in action on the Somme 15 *July* 1916
MILLARD, C. S. 2nd Lieut., Gloucestershire Regt.(T.F.); 1911
Gnr., R.G.A.
MILLER, J. W. E. Capt. and Adjt., Argyll and Sutherland 1913
Hdrs.; Staff Capt. *M. French Croix de Guerre*
MILLION, Rev. A. B. C.F. 4th Class, R.A.C.D. 1909
MILLION, C. H. S. Gnr., H.A.C. 1914
MILNER, Rev. G. R. C.F. 4th Class, R.A.C.D. 1909
MILROY, G. W. W. W. Pte., R.A.O.C.; 2nd Lieut., 1906
Labour Corps
✠MITCHELL, Rev. C. W. C.F. 4th Class, R.A.C.D. *M.* 1902
Died 3 *May* 1917 *of wounds received in action*
MITCHELL, Rev. H. C.F. 4th Class, R.A.C.D. *1892
MOERAN, Rev. W. G. C.F. 4th Class, R.A.C.D. *M.C.* 1908
MOLINE, R. W. H. Capt., Rifle Brigade; Major, M.G.C. 1909
(W 2.) (P.) *M.C.*
MOLSON, J. E. Major, R.A.M.C.(T.F.) 1882
MONEY, Rev. W. T. C.F. 4th Class, R.A.C.D. *1893
✠MOORCOCK, F. A. Lce.-Corpl., R.A.M.C.; 2nd Lieut., 1913
King's Own (Yorkshire L.I.)
Killed in action 3 *May* 1917
MOORE, A. W. Lieut.-Col., R.A.M.C.(T.F.) *O.B.E.* 1899
M 3. *Order of the Nile,* 3*rd Class* (*Egypt*)
MORGAN, E. H. Lieut., R.A.O.C. 1898
MORGAN, Rev. W. E. C.F. 4th Class, R.A.C.D. 1906

MORIER, C. E. Capt., D. of Wellington's (W. Riding   1908
Regt.) (W 2.)

MORITZ, M. Capt., R.A.M.C. (2nd W. Gen. Hospital,   1905
T.F.)

✠MORRIS, J. O. Corpl., London Regt.   1905
Killed in action 31 *Oct.* 1917

MORRIS, W. Lieut., Lancs. Fus. (W.)   1914

MORSE, C. G. H. Major, R.A.M.C.   1904

MORTON, H. T. Lieut., Mtd. Rifles and M.G.C., N.   1909
Zealand Force. (W.)

MOULD, R. C. L. Capt., Leicestershire Regt.(T.F.)   1913

MOULSDALE, J. R. B. Cadet, O.C.B.   1917

MOUNTFORT, Rev. C. C. Capt., Uppingham School   1902
O.T.C.

MOUSLEY, E. O. Capt., R.F.A.; A.D.C. (W.) (P.) *M.* 1912

MUIR, J. C. Capt., R.A.M.C. (P.)   1891

MULLER, Rev. H. C. A. S. Chaplain, R.N.   1896

MURRAY, Rev. D. W. C.F. 4th Class, R.A.C.D. *M.C.*   1905
and Bar

MUSSON, F. W. Capt., Loyal N. Lancs. Regt.; Capt.   1913
(T.), R.A.F. (W.) *A.F.C.*

MYLES, D. 2nd Lieut., Northumberland Fus.; Capt., R.E. 1912
(Tyne Electrical Engineers, T.F.) *M. French Croix
de Guerre*

NAISBY, J. V. Capt., R.G.A. (W.) *M.C.*   1913

NAISH, W. V. Capt., R.A.M.C.   1892

NATERS, Rev. C. C. T. C.F. 4th Class, R.A.C.D.(T.F.) 1900

NAYLOR, Rev. A. T. A. C.F. 2nd Class, R.A.C.D.; A.C.G. 1908
(W.) *O.B.E. M* 2.

NETHERSOLE, F. R. Lieut.-Col., Supernumerary List,   1884
Indian Army. *C.I.E.*

NEVETT, Rev. R. B. Cadet, O.C.B.   1909

NEVILLE, E. G. M. Lieut., Essex Regt.(T.F.)   1913

NEVILLE, H. A. D. Capt., R.E.(T.F.); empld. Ministry 1911
of Munitions. *m.*

NEW, F. O. W. Lieut., Leicestershire Regt. (W 2.)   1907

NEWTON, T. H. Lieut., R.N.V.R.; Capt. (A. and S.),   1902
R.A.F. *D.S.C. M.*

NEWTON, W. H. Lieut., R.A.M.C. (W.)   1897

NICHOLAS, F. Capt., Worcestershire Regt.(T.F.) (W.) 1910
M.

NICHOLS, C. W. Sergt., R.E. (Spec. Bde.)   1909

NIHILL, J. H. B. Capt., R. Munster Fus. (W.) *M.C.* 1911

NOBBS, S. W. 2nd Lieut., R.E. (W.) 1914
NORMAN, D. T. Capt., R.E. *M.C. Chevalier, Order of* 1908
Leopold (Belgium). Belgian Croix de Guerre
✠NORMAN, J. Sub-Lieut., R.N.V.R. (Howe Bn., R.N.D.) 1912
(W.)
Killed in action in Gallipoli 7 June 1915
NORMAN, N. F. Major, R.A.M.C. 1902
NORQUOY, F. Pte., R. Fusiliers 1901
NORTHCOTE, T. F. Lieut., K. Edward's Horse and Res. 1913
Regt. of Cavalry; 2nd Lieut. (T.), R.A.F. (W.)
NORTON, Rev. V. E. B. C.F. 4th Class, R.A.C.D. 1906
✠NOTT, H. P. Lieut., Gloucestershire Regt.(T.F.) (W.) 1913
M.
Killed in action 27 April 1916
✠NOTT, L. C. Capt. and Adjt., Gloucestershire Regt. 1912
(T.F.) *M.C.*
Killed in action on the Somme 18 April 1917
✠NOTT, T. W. Lieut.-Col., Gloucestershire Regt.(T.F.) 1907
D.S.O. M 2.
Killed in action on the Somme 18 April 1917

OAKES, M. W. Lieut., Nigeria Regt., W. African Frontier 1909
Force
OGDEN, H. 2nd Lieut., N. Staffs. Regt. and Gen. List, 1913
empld. Ministry of Munitions
OLDHAM, R. S. Capt., R.A.M.C. 1899
OLIPHANT, J. Major, Canadian A.S.C. *M. French* 1904
Croix de Guerre
OSBORNE, W. M. Capt., R.A.S.C.; attd. R. Scots. (W.) 1908
OSMASTON, U. E. Major, R.F.A.; Instructor in Gunnery. 1903
M.C. M. m.
OSMOND, T. E. Capt., R.A.M.C. (P.) *M.* 1903
OWST, G. R. Sergt., R.E. (Signals) 1913

PADWICK, H. B. Surgeon Lieut., R.N. *D.S.O. M.* 1908
PAGE, S. W. Capt., R.A.M.C. 1912
PAGE, W. E. 2nd Lieut., Wellington School, Somerset, 1910
O.T.C.
PAIN, B. H. Surgeon Cdr., R.N. 1897
PAINE, B. W. F. Pte., Middlesex Regt. 1917
PARES, B. Surgeon-Major, 2nd Life Gds.; A.D.M.S. 1887
C.M.G. D.S.O. M 2.
PARKER, G. M. Capt., Australian A.M.C. 1903
PARRY, Rev. T. J. C.F. 4th Class, R.A.C.D. 1897

PATERSON, A. R. Major, R.A.M.C.(T.F.) 1890
PAYNE, D. N. 2nd Lieut., R.A.S.C. 1902
✠PAYNE, J. W. 2nd Lieut., Durham L.I.(T.F.) 1911
   Killed in action 14 *April* 1917
PEACOCK, F. W., T.D. Major, Derbyshire Yeo. *C.B.* 1879
PEARCE, T. Lieut., I.A.R.O., attd. 48th Pioneers 1904
PEARD, C. J. Lieut.-Col., Somerset L.I. (W.) *D.S.O.* 1908
M.
PEARD, J. C. N. Capt., Somerset L.I. (W 4.) *M.C. M.* 1909
PEARMAN-SMITH, P. B. Pte., R. Fusiliers 1907
✠PEARSALL, H. G. Capt., Tank Corps. *M.C.* 1907
   Died 19 *March* 1919 *of pneumonia following gas-poisoning*
PEARSON, E. E. Capt., Suffolk Regt. (P.) 1898
PEARSON, J. W. Capt., Unattd. List, T.F. 1901
PEARSON, L. H. Capt., Leicestershire Regt.(T.F.) (W 3.) 1913
   (P.) *M. French Croix de Guerre*
PEEL, Rev. H. D. C.F. 4th Class, Australian Chaplains' 1904
   Dept.
PELLY, Rev. D. R., V.D. C.F. 3rd Class, R.A.C.D. *D.S.O.* 1883
M 3.
PERKINS, F. A. Lieut., R.E. 1907
PERKINS, J. J. Capt., R.A.M.C.(T.F.) 1885
PERRY, C. G. Pte., R. Fusiliers; Lieut., Spec. List 1893
PHILLIPS, P. Lieut., R.E. *M.* 1904
PHILP, F. E. L. 2nd Lieut., Res. Regt. of Cavalry; Capt., 1896
   R.A.S.C. *M.*
PHILPOT, A. J. Capt., R.E. *O.B.E. M.* 1914
PHIPPS, W. T. Lieut., W. Yorks. Regt. (W.) 1901
PICTON-WARLOW, Rev. F. T. C.F. 4th Class, R.A.C.D. 1898
✠PIGGOTT, F. C. H. Capt., R.A.M.C. 1878
   Died 26 *June* 1917
PILTER, R. 2nd Lieut., Interpreter, Indian Army; 1904
   Lieut., R.A.S.C.; Capt., Spec. List (Directorate of
   Requisitions and Hirings)
✠PINKERTON, Rev. J. Lce.-Corpl., R. Scots 1909
   Killed in action (1 *Oct.* 1916)
PITT, T. G. Trooper, Imperial Light Horse, W. Africa. 1903
   (W.)
PITTS, Rev. B. T. C.F. 4th Class, R.A.C.D. 1905
✠PLAYER, G. A.B., R.N.V.R. (Coastal Motor-boat Service); 1892
   2nd Lieut., Durham L.I.
   Died 30 *July* 1916 *of wounds received in action* 28 *July*
   1916

✠PLUMPTRE, Rev. B. P. C.F. 4th Class, R.A.C.D. *M.C.* 1902
  Killed in action 16 *July* 1917
PONDER, C. W. Capt., R.A.M.C. (Sanitary Service, T.F.) 1898
PORTER, S. L. Capt., Spec. List, empld. Ministry of 1899
  National Service
POSTLETHWAITE, J. M. Capt., R.A.M.C.(T.F. Res.) 1898
POTTER, A. R. Capt., R.A.S.C. 1901
POWELL, D. W. Major, Northamptonshire Regt.; Lieut.- 1896
  Col., R. Berkshire Regt.; Capt. (A.), R.F.C. (W.)
  D.S.O. M.
POWELL, J. M. S. Pte., H.A.C.; Sapper, R.E. 1911
POWELL, R. R. Capt., R.A.M.C.(T.F.) 1909
POWER, A. G. Capt., R. Munster Fus.; Major, M.G.C. *M.* 1905
PRALL, S. R. Surgeon Prob., R.N.V.R.; Capt., R.A.M.C. 1910
PRESTON, R. W. D. Pte., Grenadier Gds. 1908
✠PRINCE, A. L. Capt., Loyal N. Lancs. Regt. *M.* 1896
  Killed in action 8 *Nov.* 1914
✠PRINGLE, W. R. Lieut., S. Lancs. Regt. 1912
  Killed in action on the Somme 22 *July* 1916
PRIOR, B. C. Lieut., Essex Regt.(T.F.) 1902
PRIOR, H. A. S. Lieut.-Col., Yorkshire Regt. and Train- 1893
  ing Res. Bn. *D.S.O. O.B.E. M* 2. *m.*
PUNCHARD, C. Capt. and Adjt., R.F.A.(T.F.); A.D.C. 1915
PUTNAM, P. W. Lieut., R.A.M.C. 1913
PUTTOCK, R. Capt., R.A.M.C. (W.) 1897

RAMSBOTTOM, J. Lieut., Spec. List (Pathologist). *O.B.E.* 1905
  M.B.E. M 3.
RAMSBOTTOM, W. H. Lieut., R.G.A. (W.) *M.C.* 1914
  M.B.E. M.
RAVEN, Rev. C. E. C.F. 4th Class, R.A.C.D. *1910
RAVEN, H. P. Capt., R.F.A.(T.F.) 1896
RAWLINSON, H. G. Major, Madras and S. Mahratta 1899
  Railway Rifles, Indian Defence Force
RAYNER, S. Capt., Durham L.I.(T.F. Res.) 1905
✠READE, R. W. Lieut., R. Warwickshire Regt. (W.) 1911
  Killed in action at Kut 5 *April* 1916
READE, W. P. Major, Cheshire Regt.(T.F.) and Gen. 1893
  Staff. *T.D. M.*
REEVE, G. T. 2nd Lieut., Bridlington Grammar School 1906
  O.T.C.
REID, D. M. Major, R.F.A.(T.F.) (W 2.) *M.C.* 1913
RENNIE, W. B. Major, Spec. List; Lieut.-Col., A.A. 1895
  and Q.M.G. *D.S.O. M.C. M* 3.

REYNOLDS, G. D.   Corpl., Suffolk Regt. and Bedford-   1914
shire Regt.
REYNOLDS, K.   Lieut., Bedfordshire Regt.   1910
RICHARDS, C. J.   Capt., Dorset Regt.; attd. D. of Welling-   1913
ton's (W. Riding Regt.)
RICHARDSON, C.   Major, Worcestershire Regt.   (W.)   1897
Brevet Lieut.-Colonel
✠RICHARDSON, V.   Lieut., R. Sussex Regt.(T.F.); attd. [1914]
King's Royal Rifle Corps.   *M.C.*
Died 9 June 1917 of wounds received in action 9 April
1917
RICKMAN, J.   2nd Lieut., E. African Force, attd. Road   1893
Corps.   *M.*
✠RIGBY, J. R. A.   Lieut., Yorkshire Regt.   1909
Killed in action in the Battle of Loos 26 Sept. 1915
RIGG, J. H.   Pte., Border Regt.; Lieut., I.A.R.O., attd.   1912
93rd Burma Infy.   (W.)
ROBERTON, J. A. W.   Lieut., Gordon Hdrs.   (W.)   1912
ROBERTON, J. B. W.   Capt., Northumberland Fus.   (W 2.) [1914]
D.S.O.
ROBERTS, B. F.   Lieut., Oxford and Bucks. L.I.   1913
ROBERTSON, C. J. T.   Lieut.-Col., R.A.O.C.; A.D.O.S.   1897
O.B.E.   M.C.   M.
ROBERTSON, W. R. D.   Trooper, K. Edward's Horse;   1911
Major, R.F.A.   *M.C.   M.*
ROBINSON, A. S.   Lieut., R.A.M.C.   1889
ROBINSON, C. S.   Pte., R.A.S.C.   1907
ROBINSON, F. J.   Corpl., S. African F.A.   1900
RODERICK, H. B.   Lieut.-Col., R.A.M.C.(T.F.)   *O.B.E.* *1892
M 2.
RODICK, R. L.   Major, R.A.S.C.   1910
ROGERS, F. E. W.   Major, R.A.M.C. (Sanitary Service,   1904
T.F.)   *M.C.   M.*
ROSE, H. A.   Hon. Lieut.-Col., Indian Army   1886
ROSE, R. DE R.   Major, R. Irish Rifles.   (W.)   *M.C. and*   1897
Bar.   M.
✠ROTHERA, A. C. H.   Capt., Australian A.M.C.   1899
Died 3 Oct. 1915 of pneumonia
ROXBY, Rev. J. H. T. M.   *See* MAUDE-ROXBY, Rev. J. H. T.
ROY, P. L.   Pte., H.A.C.   1912
RUDD, N. B.   Lieut., Norfolk Regt. and I.A.R.O., attd.   1905
48th Pioneers
RULE, Rev. G. S.   C.F. 4th Class, R.A.C.D.   1909
RUMBOLL, N.   Capt. (Med.), R.A.F.   1913

RUSCOE, R. G. Lieut., R.A.S.C.(T.F.) *M.* 1912
RUSHTON, E. R. Lieut., Middlesex Regt. (W.) (P.) 1910
RUSSELL, W. A. Capt., R.A.M.C. *M.* 1905
RYLEY, C. M. Surgeon Lieut., R.N. 1904

SALISBURY, Rev. C. E. C.F. 4th Class, R.A.C.D. 1907
SALMON, B. A. Capt., London Regt. (Poplar and Stepney [1914]
  Rifles)
SAUNDERS, W. H. Lieut., Suffolk Regt. [1914]
✠SAVILE, G. K. 2nd Lieut., Gloucestershire Regt.(T.F.) 1909
  Killed in action 20 *June* 1915
SCHOLTZ, C. J. Capt., R.A.M.C. 1907
SCHUDDEKOPF, W. G. A. *See* SHUTTLEWORTH, W. G. A.
SCLATER, Rev. J. R. P. C.F. 4th Class, R.A.C.D.(T.F.) 1895
  m.
SCOTT, J. E. Capt., R. Munster Fus. and Gen. List 1910
  (O.C.B.) (W.) *M.C.*
SCOTT, J. S. Lieut., Durham L.I.(T.F.); Interpreter. 1900
  M. Cavalier, Order of the Redeemer, 5th Class
  (*Greece*)
SCOTT, W. D. Pte., London Regt. (Artists Rifles); Lieut., 1912
  R.G.A. and Gen. Staff (Intelligence)
✠SEAVER, C. Capt., R. Inniskilling Fus. (W.) 1912
  Died 3 *Oct.* 1916 *of wounds received in action* 13 *Sept.*
  1916
SELLWOOD, F. G. Major, R.A.S.C. *O.B.E. M.C. M.* 1912
SELWYN, Rev. W. M. C.F. 4th Class, R.A.C.D.(T.F.) 1898
SHAKESPEARE, G. H. Capt., Norfolk Regt.(T.F.); attd. 1912
  The Queen's (R.W. Surrey Regt.)
SHARP, E. W. L. Capt., R.A.M.C. *M.* 1909
SHARPE, A. G. Lieut., R.A.S.C.(T.F.) and 4th Cavalry, 1914
  Indian Army
SHAW, Rev. K. E. C.F. 4th Class, R.A.C.D. 1902
SHELDON, T. W. Capt., R.A.M.C. 1907
SHELFORD, Rev. L. McN. C.F. 4th Class, R.A.C.D. 1890
SHENSTONE, A. G. Capt., R.E. *M.C. M.* 1914
SHERA, A. G. Capt., R.A.M.C. 1908
SHERLOCK, J. H. Lieut., R.E. 1912
SHERWOOD, G. D. Capt., R.A.M.C. 1906
SHIELDS, C. ST B. Capt., R.G.A. (W.) 1908
SHILDRICK, L. R. Major, R. Munster Fus. *M.* 1906
SHIPTON, W. Capt., R.A.M.C. 1902
SHONE, H. J. Major, R.A.M.C. (W.) *M.* 1896
SHUCKBURGH, R. S. 2nd Lieut., R.G.A. 1899

SHUTTLEWORTH, W. G. A. 2nd Lieut., W. Yorks. Regt. 1910
(T.F.); Lieut., R.A.M.C.
SIBLEY, F. H. Lieut., R.F.A.(T.F.); Hon. Lieut. (O.), [1914]
R.A.F.
SIM, P. W. Lieut., R.F.A.; Lieut. (A.), R.A.F. *M.* [1914]
SINDALL, R. D. Cadet, O.C.B. 1918
SISSON, B. H. 2nd Lieut., R.G.A.; Capt. (K.B.), R.A.F. 1906
m.
SLATER, J. A. Capt., R.F.A. 1903
SMETHAM, S. J. Corpl., R.E. 1914
SMITH, C. S. Capt., R.E. (Signals, T.F.) 1910
SMITH, D. B. M. *See* MELLIS-SMITH, D. B.
SMITH, H. Instructor Lieut., R.N. *m.* 1912
SMITH, Rev. L. C.F. 4th Class, R.A.C.D. 1904
SMITH, R. E. Surgeon Lieut., R.N. *O.B.E.* 1899
SMITH-REWSE, H. G. Capt., Suffolk Regt. 1907
✠SMYTH, W. H. Lieut., Devon Regt. and Worcestershire 1897
Regt.
Killed in action 17 April 1918
SMYTHE, G. A. Capt., R.A.M.C. 1906
SOOTHILL, V. F. Major, R.A.M.C. *M.* 1906
SOPWITH, S. S. 2nd Lieut., Shrewsbury School O.T.C. 1905
SOUTAR, A. K. Capt. (Med.), R.A.F. 1905
SOUTH, F. W. Lieut., Singapore Vol. Force 1904
SPARK, D. S. Capt., Somerset L.I. *M.C.* 1911
✠SPEARING, E. Lieut., King's Own (R. Lancaster Regt., 1908
T.F.) (W.)
Killed in action at Ginchy 11 Sept. 1916
SPILSBURY, L. J. Lieut., R.E. *M.C.* 1905
STALEY, H. S. Lieut., Unattd. List, T.F. 1903
STANCOMB, Rev. J. M. D. C.F. 4th Class, R.A.C.D.; Capt., 1908
Devon Regt. (T.F.) and Somerset L.I. (T.F.) *M.*
STAPLES-BROWNE, R. C. Capt. and Q.M., N. Zealand 1899
Med. Corps. *M.B.E.*
STEEL, O. W. D. Staff Capt.; Major, R. Monmouthshire 1905
Regt.; Lieut.-Col., R.A.M.C.(T.F.) *M.C.* *M* 2.
✠STEPHEN, F. C. Lieut., Gordon Hdrs.(T.F.) 1909
Killed in action in the Battle of Loos 25 Sept. 1915
STEVENS, C. G. B. Pte., N. Bengal Mtd. Rifles, Indian 1908
Defence Force
STIMSON, W. B. Sergt., R. Fusiliers; Lieut., Bedfordshire 1912
Regt. (W 2.) *M.C.*
STINSON, H. J. E. Major, R.G.A. *M.C. and Bar* 1905
STOKES, W. A. Capt., R.A.M.C.(T.F.) *m.* 1905

STONE, B. J. V. 2nd Lieut., Leicestershire Regt.; Lieut.,   1912
    Cheshire Regt. (W.)
STONE, E. R. Capt., R.A.M.C.   1901
STORRS, K. S. Capt., R.A.M.C. (T.F. Res.)   1888
✠STRACHAN, H. Lieut., Durham L.I.(T.F.) (W 2.)   1914
    Died 29 *July* 1918 *of wounds received in action*
STRAHAN,W.R. Capt.,London Regt.(London Irish Rifles)   1909
STREETEN, Rev. A. H. C.F. 4th Class, R.A.C.D. (W 2.)   1904
    M.C.
STRINGER, C. E. W. Lieut., Canadian H.A.   1902
STRONG, J. P. Lieut., Loyal N. Lancs. Regt. (W.)   1914
STURGES, Rev. E. L. Chaplain, R.N.   1903
STURTON, K. M. Capt. (T.), R.A.F. (Aircraft Production   1905
    Dept.)
STURTON, S. D. Surgeon Sub-Lieut., R.N.V.R.   1915
STYLE, A. H. Capt., R.A.M.C.   1893
SUFFERN, C. Surgeon Sub-Lieut., R.N.V.R.   1911
SUMMERHAYES, C. H. Capt., Durham L.I. and Glouces- [1914]
    tershire Regt. (W.)
SUMMERS, F. Lieut.-Col., R.E.; C.R.E. *D.S.O. M.C.*   1913
    M 4.
SUTCLIFFE, A. Capt., R.A.M.C.(T.F.) *M* 2.   1905
SUTCLIFFE, P. T. Surgeon Cdr., R.N.   1892
SYKES, W. S. Surgeon Lieut., R.N.   1913

TABBERER, C. O. Pte., R.A.M.C.; Sergt., Leicestershire   1908
    Regt.; Capt., London Regt. (L.R.B.) *M.C.*
TAGGART, W. Q. Pte., R. Fusiliers (P. S. Bn.); Capt.,   1911
    King's (Liverpool Regt.) *M.C.*
TALBOT, Very Rev. A. E. C.F. 1st Class, Australian   1902
    Chaplains' Dept. (W.)
TANNER, Rev. E. V. C.F. 4th Class, R.A.C.D. (W.)   1905
    M.C. and Bar
TEALE, Rev. K. W. P. C.F. 4th Class, R.A.C.D.   1894
TEUTEN, Rev. L. M. C.F. 4th Class, R.A.C.D.   1907
THEOBALD, G. W. Surgeon Prob., R.N.V.R.   1914
THOMAS, E. F. Corpl., R.E.   1912
THOMAS, E. R. Capt., R.A.O.C.; Major, D.A.Q.M.G.   1911
    M.
THOMPSON, A. B. Capt., Northumberland Fus.(T.F.);   1907
    Staff Capt. (W.) *m.*
THOMSON, N. G. Surgeon Prob., R.N.V.R.   1914
THORNTON, C. G. Lieut., R. Inniskilling Fus.; Capt.,   1907
    O.C.B.

THORNTON, L. H. D. Capt., R.A.M.C. *M.*   1907
THORNTON, V. S. 2nd Lieut., Essex Regt. (W.)   1908
THORP, C. F. Lieut., Northumberland Fus. and King's   1898
Royal Rifle Corps
THORP, H. C. Capt., R.A.M.C.   1891
✠TIDY, T. Signalman, R.N.V.R.   1913
Killed in explosion on H.M.S. Bulwark 28 Nov. 1914
TILLY, R. L. Lieut., The Queen's (R.W. Surrey Regt.);   1912
Hon. Lieut. (A.), R.A.F.
TOMLINSON, A. E. Lieut., S. Staffs. Regt.; empld. War   1912
Office. (W.)
TOMLINSON, W. A. Corpl., R.G.A.   1897
TOOVEY, T. P. Capt., The Queen's (R.W. Surrey Regt.)   1915
(W.) *M.C. and Bar*
TOULMIN-SMITH, A. K.   Capt. (T.), R.A.F. (Aircraft   1899
Production Dept.)
TRACY, G. D. C. Lieut., Gordon Hdrs. (T.F.); Pte.,   1912
R.A.S.C.
TRAUTMANN, H. F. *See* TREWMAN, H. F.
TREWMAN, H. F. Lieut., Bedfordshire Regt. (W 2.)   1911
TRIBE, K. W. Lieut., N. China Vol. Force   1909
TRIPP, N. F. Pte., R. Fusiliers (P. S. Bn.); Lieut.,   1911
R.A.S.C.; attd. R. Fusiliers and R. Warwickshire
Regt. (W 2.) *M.C.*
TUNMER, E. J. E. Capt., King's (Shropshire L.I.) (W 2.)   1902
TURNBULL, J. B. Lieut., Shropshire Yeo.; attd. R. Welsh   1913
Fus. (W.)
✠TURNBULL, W. A. Lieut., Bedfordshire Regt.   1912
Killed in action 13 Nov. 1916
TURNER, A. C. Lieut., R. Fusiliers and Gen. List; In-   1911
spector, Woolwich Arsenal. *M.B.E.*
TURNER, H. C. Major, London Regt. (Queen's). *M.*   1898
French Croix de Guerre
✠TWINING, R. W. Trooper, Devon Yeo.; 2nd Lieut.,   1913
Dragoon Gds. and Devon Regt.
Killed in action on the Somme 1 July 1916

URLING-SMITH, F. M. Lieut., Nigeria Regt., W. African   1897
Frontier Force
✠URQUHART, J. L. Lieut., Northamptonshire Regt.   1910
Killed in action 2 Nov. 1915

VALLÉ-POPE, E. 2nd Lieut., King's Own (R. Lancaster   1892
Regt.)

VERNIQUET, W. G. Capt., R.A.M.C.   1911
VERRALL, F. H. Artificer, R.N.V.R.   1902
VICKERS, V. C. W. Capt., R.A.M.C. *M.*   1907
VINING, Rev. L. G. C.F. 3rd Class, R.A.C.D. *M* 2.   1907
VISCHER, H. 2nd Lieut., Nigeria Regt., W. African   1896
    Frontier Force; Major, Spec. List; G.S.O. 3 (Intelli-
    gence). *C.B.E. Chevalier, Legion of Honour (France).
    Officer, Ordre de l'Etoile Noire (France). Chevalier,
    Ordre de la Couronne (Belgium). Cavalier, Order of
    the Crown of Italy*
VISCHER, Rev. M. M. C.F. 3rd Class, R.A.C.D. *M.*   1898

WADDINGTON, J. E. 2nd Lieut., R.A.S.C.   [1914]
WAILES, F. G. Capt. and Adjt., R.G.A. *M.*   1906
WALDEGRAVE, Rev. G. T. Hon. Chaplain, R.N.   1908
WALDEGRAVE, Rev. S. C. C.F. 4th Class, R.A.C.D. *M.C.*   1907
WALKER, A. Capt., R.A.M.C.(T.F.) *D.S.O. Brevet*   1897
    Major. M.
WALKER, A. R. Lieut., Welsh Regt.   1911
✠WALKER, E. B. 2nd Lieut., Dorset Regt. and Queen's   1907
    Own (R.W. Kent Regt.) *M.*
    Killed in action 18 *April* 1915
WALKER, E. R. C. 2nd Lieut., Black Watch. (W.)   1916
WALKER, L. P. Lieut., R.A.O.C.; Major (Ad.), R.A.F.   1900
WALKER, Rev. L. W. L. Chaplain, R.N.   1893
WALKER, S. W. Lieut., Nigeria Regt., W. African Frontier   1911
    Force
WALLACE, F.W. 2nd Lieut., Cameronians (Scottish Rifles);   1909
    Lieut., R.E. (Signals). (W.)
WALLACE, J. C. Capt., R.E.; Hon. Capt. (T.), R.A.F.   1909
    M.C. M.
WALLER, N. H. Major, Gloucestershire Regt. (T.F.)   1899
    M.C. M.
WALLIS, O. B. Capt., Herefordshire Regt.; attd. King's   1907
    (Shropshire L.I.) (W 2.)
WALTHALL, H. D. D. Capt., R.A.S.C. *O.B.E. M.*   1899
WARREN, A. C. Lieut., R.A.M.C.   1894
WARRINGTON, T. Capt., R.A.M.C.   *1907
WATERER, C. R. Corpl., R.E. (London Electrical En-   1906
    gineers, T.F.)
WATKINS, C.R. Capt., Bengal Vol. Rifles, Indian Defence   1901
    Force. *C.I.E.*
✠WATKINS, E. L. C. Lieut., R.F.A.   1910
    Died 17 *March* 1917 *of wounds received in action*

WATKINS, W. F.　Lieut., Gloucestershire Regt.　(W.)　1906
M.C. M.
WATTS, Rev. B. H.　C.F. 4th Class, R.A.C.D.　1894
WAYET, Rev. J. W. F.　Lieut., Lincolnshire Regt. and　1901
Gen. Staff
WAYMAN, G. B.　Pte., Devon Regt.(T.F.)　1913
WEATHERELL, R. K.　Lieut., Suffolk Regt.; attd. Essex　1905
Regt. (W.)
WEBSTER, V. T. P.　Capt., R.A.M.C.　1901
WEIGALL, G. J. V.　Capt., Kent Cyclist Bn.　1889
WELBOURNE, E.　Major, Durham L.I.; attd. W. Yorks.　1912
Regt. (W.)　*M.C. m.*
WELD, C. G.　Lieut., Worcestershire Regt.　(W.)　1896
WELLS, C.A.　Major, Hampshire Regt.; Staff Capt. *O.B.E.*　1900
Brevet Major. M 2.
✠WELLS, C. D.　Lieut., King's Own (R. Lancaster Regt.); [1914]
Lieut. (O.), R.A.F.　*M.C. M.*
Killed in action 16 May 1918
WELLS, R. C.　Capt., R.E.; attd. R. Irish Regt. (W.) (P.)　1904
WERNICKE, W. G.　*See* VERNIQUET, W. G.
WESTBROOK, H. W.　2nd Lieut., Cheshire Regt.　1899
WEST-WATSON, C.　*See* BARROW-IN-FURNESS, Rt Rev.
Bishop of
WHISTLER, F.　Major, R. Scots; Staff Capt.; empld. High-　*1877
land L.I. Depôt
WHISTLER, Rev. W. W.　C.F. 2nd Class, R.A.C.D. *m.*　1888
WHITAKER, G. M.　Pte., London Regt. (Artists Rifles);　1915
Lieut., R.G.A.; attd. R.E. (Signals). *M.*
WHITE, F.　Capt., Cheshire Regt.(T.F.) and 25th Pun-　1912
jabis, Indian Army.　(W.)
WHITEHEAD, R. F.　Air Mechanic, R.A.F.　1900
WHITLEY, N. H. P.　Capt., Manchester Regt.(T.F.);　1901
G.S.O. 3.　(W.)　*M.C. M 3. Cavalier, Order of
the Crown of Italy.　French Croix de Guerre*
WHITWILL, T. N.　Capt., Gloucestershire Regt.(T.F.); attd.　1912
Suffolk Regt.
WIGLEY, W. C. S.　Sergt.-Instructor, R.E. (Signals)　1909
WILCOX, Rev. A. J.　C.F. 4th Class, R.A.C.D.　(P.)　1909
WILKINSON, G.　Major, R.A.M.C. (3rd N. Gen. Hospital,　1885
T.F.)
WILLAN, G.T.　Lieut.-Col., R.A.M.C.(T.F.) *D.S.O. M.*　1893
WILLANS, E. T.　Capt., R.A.M.C.　1903
WILLIAMS, G.　Capt., Welsh Regt.(T.F.); Cmdt., Anti-　1912
Gas School

WILLIAMS, H. A. Capt., R.A.M.C.　1904
WILLIAMS, H. P. W. B. Major, R.A.S.C. *M.C.*　1906
WILLIAMS, Rev. O. ST M. C.F. 4th Class, R.A.C.D.　1902
WILLIAMSON, F. Lieut., Middlesex Regt.(T.F.); Capt., 1909
　I.A.R.O., attd. 1st and 11th Gurkha Rifles. (W.) *M.*
✠WILLIAMSON, G. H. Capt., King's Royal Rifle Corps. 1910
　M.C. M.
　Died 12 April 1917 of wounds received in action
WILLIS, A. G. DE L. Lieut., R.N.V.R. (Howe Bn., 1913
　R.N.D.); Capt., R.G.A. (W.)
WILLS, A. S. Capt., 18th Hussars (R. of O.)　1896
WILLS, J. P. Lieut., R.F.A. (W.) *M.C.*　1909
✠WILLSON, F. J. Lieut., Sappers and Miners, Indian Army 1907
　Died 10 Jan. 1917 of wounds received in action
WILSON, Rev. H. Sergt., King's Royal Rifle Corps　1912
WILSON, H. G. Lieut.-Col., Lincolnshire Regt.(T.F.) 1901
　(W.) *D.S.O. T.D. M* 2.
✠WILSON, H. V. Lieut., Hampshire Regt.　1914
　Died 15 Dec. 1919 of wounds received in action in the
　Struma Valley 30 Sept. 1916
WILSON, L. E. Lieut., Queen's Own (R.W. Kent Regt.,
　T.F.); attd. 27th Punjabis, Indian Army
✠WILSON, W. R. Lieut., R.A.M.C.　1909
　Died 12 July 1916 of wounds received in action 11 July
　1916
WILTSHIRE, H. G. Capt., R.A.M.C.　1908
WIMBERLEY, D. N. Capt., Cameron Hdrs.; Major, M.G.C. 1914
　(W.) *M.C.*
WINDSOR, F. N. Lieut.-Col., I.M.S.　1887
WINSER, E. F. Capt., Sherwood Foresters (Notts. and 1903
　Derby Regt., T.F.); Major, N. Staffs. Regt.(T.F.)
　M.C. M.
WINTER, A. W. B. Air Mechanic, R.A.F.　1914
✠WINTER, J. F. Lieut., R.E. (Field Survey Coy.)　1903
　Killed in action 28 Oct. 1918
WITHERINGTON, A. S. Lieut., R.F.A.(T.F.) (P.)　1908
WOMERSLEY, W. D. 2nd Lieut., D. of Wellington's (W. 1912
　Riding Regt.); Lieut., R.E. (Signals, T.F.); attd.
　R.A.F. *M.*
WOOD, F. E. Pte., R.A.S.C.　1909
WOOD, J. I. Pte., R. Fusiliers; Lieut., Border Regt.; 1913
　empld. War Office. (W 2.)
WOODS, D. Pte., R.A.M.C.　[1914]
WOOLF, A. E. M. Capt., R.A.M.C.　1902

WORDLEY, E. Capt., R.A.M.C. *M.C.*   1905
WORLEY, N. A. Lieut., Malay Vol. Force   1910
WORTHINGTON, E. H. B. S. African Force   1890
✠WORTHINGTON, R. F. Capt., Gloucestershire Regt.(T.F.)   1900
    Died 4 May 1917 of wounds received in action 7 April
    1917
WRIGHT, C. S. E. Major, R.A.M.C. *M* 2. *French Croix*   1902
    de Guerre
WRIGHT, H. L. Major, King's (Liverpool Regt.); empld.   1897
    R.A.M.C. (W 2.)
WRIGHT, R. B. Lieut., R.F.A.(T.F.)   1895
WURTZBURG, C. E. Capt. and Adjt., King's (Liverpool   1910
    Regt.); Brigade Major. *M.C.*
WYATT, H. E. Lieut., Worcestershire Regt.; empld.   1914
    O.C.B. (W.) *M.C.*
WYER, J. F. W. Capt., R.A.M.C.(T.F.) (W.)   1902

YEO, K. J. Capt., R.A.M.C.   .   1907
YOUNG, H. G. K. Capt., R.A.M.C.   1894
YOUNG, Rev. H. P. C.F. 4th Class, R.A.C.D.   1913
YUSUF, Z. M. Lce.-Corpl., R.E. (Signals)   1911

GONVILLE AND CAIUS COLLEGE

ABERCROMBIE, G. F. Surgeon Sub-Lieut., R.N.V.R. *M.* 1914
ABERCROMBIE, R. G. Capt., R.A.M.C. (W.) 1891
ABRAHAMS, A. 2nd Lieut., Border Regt.; Lieut., M.G.C. [1914]
ABRAM, G. S. Major, R.A.M.C.(T.F.) *m.* 1885
ACKROYD, E. Lieut., King's (Liverpool Regt.) and R. 1894
Defence Corps
✠ACKROYD, H. Capt., R.A.M.C. (W.) *M.C.* 1896
V.C. " For most conspicuous bravery. During recent
operations Capt. Ackroyd displayed the greatest gallantry
and devotion to duty. Utterly regardless of danger, he
worked continuously for many hours up and down and
in front of the line tending the wounded and saving the
lives of officers and men. In so doing he had to move
across the open under heavy machine gun, rifle and shell
fire. He carried a wounded officer to a place of safety
under very heavy fire. On another occasion he went
some way in front of our advanced line and brought in
a wounded man under continuous rifle and machine gun
fire. His heroism was the means of saving many lives,
and provided a magnificent example of courage, cheer-
fulness and determination to the fighting men in whose
midst he was carrying out his splendid work. This
gallant officer has since been killed in action."—Supplement to *The London Gazette*, 6 Sept. 1917.
Killed in action 11 *Aug.* 1917
ADAMS, J. W. Lieut., Singapore Field Ambulance 1903
AERON-THOMAS, G. E. Capt., R.F.A.; Staff Capt. *M* 4. 1904
AINSLEY, A. C. Capt., R.A.M.C.(T.F.) (W.) *M.C.* 1909
AINSLIE, M. A. Instructor Cdr., R.N. 1888
ALDERSON, G. G. Capt., R.A.M.C. 1903

118   GONVILLE AND CAIUS COLLEGE

✠ALDRICH, C. P. G. 2nd Lieut., R. Fusiliers   1914
    Killed in action 7 Oct. 1916
ALEXANDER, E. Hon. Capt., R. Marines   1905
ALEXANDER, W. A. Capt., R.A.M.C.   1899
ALLBUTT, Rt Hon. Sir T. C., K.C.B. Hon. Colonel,   1855
    R.A.M.C.(T.F.)
ALLEN, F. D. C. Capt., R.G.A.; Instructor in Gunnery.   1911
    (W.) *M.*
✠ALLEN, P. H. C. Lieut., E. Lancs. Regt.   1909
    Killed in action 9 May 1915
ANDERSON, A. R. S. Lieut.-Col., I.M.S.   1879
ANDERSON, W. L. Capt. (S.), R.A.F. *D.S.C.*   1911
ARMSTRONG, J. C. Major, R.A.S.C.(M.T.) *M.C. M.*   1906
ARNELL, O. R. Lieut., R.E.   1907
✠ARNOT, D. W. Lieut., R. Warwickshire Regt. (W.)   1903
    Killed in action 3 Sept. 1916
✠ARON, F. A. Lieut., S. Lancs. Regt.   1906
    Killed in action 23 Aug. 1918
ARROWSMITH, Rev. W. G. C.F. 4th Class, R.A.C.D.   1908
ASCOLI, G. H. D. Lieut., 2nd Dragoon Gds. (Queen's   1906
    Bays); attd. R.E. (Signals). (W.) *M.C.*
ASERMAN, C. Lieut., R.G.A. *M.C.*   1915
ASHCROFT, A. H. Major, S. Staffs. Regt. *D.S.O. M* 3.   1906
    Officer, Order of the Crown of Italy
ASHCROFT, J. M. Lieut., I.A.R.O., attd. 19th Lancers   1902
ASHCROFT, R. L. Capt. and Adjt., King's Own (R. Lan-   1911
    caster Regt.) *M.C.*
✠ASHCROFT, W. Lieut. and Adjt., King's (Liverpool Regt.)   1900
    (W.)
    Killed in action 22 March 1918
ASTON, R. L. Lieut., Tonbridge School O.T.C.   1888
ATHERTON, T. J., C.B. Bt. Colonel, Res. Regt. of Cavalry   1875
    and Labour Corps. *C.M.G. M* 2.
ATKIN, C. S. Lieut., R.A.M.C.   1906
ATKIN, E. E. Capt., R.A.M.C.   1899
ATKINS, B. S. Capt., 11th Rajputs, Indian Army; attd.   1903
    R.F.C. (W.) (P.) *M.*
ATKINSON, E. W. Capt., R.A.M.C.   1900
ATTWOOD, H. C. Lieut., R.A.M.C.   1905
AUDRA, E. Lieut., 279me Regt., French Army, and   1908
    French Mission with British Third Army. *M.C.*
    French Croix de Guerre
AVENT, Rev. E. C.F. 3rd Class, R.A.C.D. *M.*   1894
AVENT, M. Capt., R.A.M.C. (W.)   1906

✠BACHE, H. G.   Pte., Lincolnshire Regt.; 2nd Lieut., Lancs.   1908
Fus.
Killed in action 15 *Feb.* 1916
BACK, G. A.   Capt., R.A.M.C.   1910
✠BACK, H. A. W.   Chaplain, R.N.   1909
Accidentally killed on H.M.S. Vanguard 9 *July* 1917
BAGNALL-WILD, R. K.   Brig.-Gen., R.A.F. (Aircraft Pro-   1864
duction Dept.) *C.M.G.*
✠BAILEY, C. M.   Pte., R. Fusiliers; 2nd Lieut. (A.), R.F.C.   1913
Killed in action 3 *Aug.* 1917
BAILEY, T. B.   Capt., R.A.M.C.   1909
BAIRD, R. F.   Lieut.-Col., I.M.S.   1889
BAKER, F. R.   C.S.M., Transvaal Scottish and 4th S.   1897
African Infy. (W.) (P.)
BAKER, S.   Lieut., The Buffs (E. Kent Regt., T.F.);   1909
Capt. (A.), R.A.F.   *M.*
BALFOUR, A., C.M.G.   Lieut.-Col., R.A.M.C.   *C.B. M.*   1896
BALFOUR-BROWNE, W. A. F.   Capt., R.A.M.C. (Sanitary   *1913
Service, T.F.)
✠BANNATYNE, E. J.   Lieut., 19th Hussars; Major (A.),   1910
R.F.C. *D.S.O. M.*
Died 11 *Sept.* 1917 *of injuries received while flying*
30 *Aug.* 1917
BARBER, P. E.   Major, R.A.M.C.   1880
BARCLAY, E. D.   Lieut., Worcestershire Regt. (W.) *M.C.*   1913
BARKER, L. E. H. R.   Capt., R.A.M.C.(T.F.)   1895
BARKER, R. W.   Capt., Unattd. List, Indian Army   1901
BARNETT, R. O.   Capt., London Regt. (Kensington Bn.)   1896
BARNETT, S. H.   Lieut., Highland L.I. (W.)   1910
BARRACLOUGH, J. N.   Capt., King's Own (Yorkshire L.I.)   1909
and Spec. List, attd. Egyptian Army
BARRETT, R. S.   Hon. Capt., R.E. (Signals, T.F. Res.)   1902
BARRINGTON, F. E. P.   Capt. (A.), R.A.F.   1911
BARRIS, J. D.   Capt., R.A.M.C.   1898
BARRON, G. D.   Lieut., Connaught Rangers   1910
BARRY, Sir E., Bart.   Lieut.-Col., Berkshire Yeo. (T.F.   1881
Res.)
BARTLETT, H. S.   Lieut., R.F.A.; attd. R.E.   *M.C.*   1906
BATTEN, W. D. G.   Capt., 3rd Gurkha Rifles, Indian   1909
Army. *Order of El Nahda, 3rd Class (Hedjaz)*
BATTERHAM, D. J.   Capt., R.A.M.C.   1912
BATTY-SMITH, S. H.   Capt., Loyal N. Lancs. Regt. (W.)   1909
(P.)
BAYER, S. F.   Pte., R.A.S.C.(M.T.)   1901

BAYNES, F. W. W. United Provinces Horse, Indian De- 1908
fence Force

✠BEALE, C. W. Pte., R. Fusiliers (P. S. Bn.); Lieut., R. 1911
Sussex Regt.; attd. T.M.B.
Killed in action 3 March 1916

BEAMISH, R. DE B. Major, R.G.A. 1896

BEAN, C. V. Lieut., Devon Regt. 1916

BEATTIE, L. H. Capt. and Adjt., R.F.A. 1898

BECKETT, C. M. Lieut., R.E. (Signals) 1912

✠BEDFORD, S. H. 2nd Lieut., R. Berkshire Regt. (W.) 1907
Killed in action 1 July 1916

✠BEECH, J. Lieut., S. Staffs. Regt.; Capt., R.E. (W.) 1906
Killed in action 12 May 1918

✠BEER, H. O. 2nd Lieut., Queen's Own (R.W. Kent Regt.) [1914]
Killed in action near Hulluch 26 Sept. 1915

BEGG, M. G. Capt., Rifle Brigade; Lieut. (A.), R.A.F. 1914
(P.) *M.C. and Bar*

BELFIELD, S. ST G. C. Major (K.B.), R.A.F. 1906

✠BELL, J. D. Lieut., R.F.A. 1906
Died 30 Oct. 1918 of influenza

BENEST, E. E. Sub-Lieut., R.N.V.R. 1910

BENNETT, E. K. Pte., Worcestershire Regt.; 2nd Lieut., 1914
Spec. List (Intelligence)

✠BENNETT, H. R. Capt., King's (Liverpool Regt.) (W.) *M.* 1912
Killed in action 23 March 1918

✠BENSON, A. H. Major, R.A.M.C. 1882
Died 24 Sept. 1916

BENTALL, C. E. Capt., R.A.S.C.(T.F.) *M.* 1904

✠BERRY, A. J. Pte., R. Fusiliers (P. S. Bn.); 2nd Lieut., [1914]
Lancs. Fus.(T.F.) (W.)
Killed in action 21 Aug. 1916

BERRY, H. V. Lieut., R.A.S.C.; attd. Somerset L.I. (W.) 1910

BERRY, W. L. Surgeon Lieut., R.N. 1913

BESANT, G. B. Lieut., Somerset L.I. *M.* 1898

BESLY, E. M. Capt., R.E. (P.) *M. Belgian Croix de* 1907
Guerre

BEVAN, J. M. Capt., R.F.A.; Staff Capt. *M.C.* 1905

✠BEWLEY, E. N. 2nd Lieut., Sherwood Foresters (Notts. 1903
and Derby Regt., T.F.)
Killed in action 26 June 1917

BICKERDIKE, R. B. Major, R.F.A.(T.F.) *D.S.O. M* 3. 1902

BICKFORD-SMITH, W. N. Capt., D. of Cornwall's L.I. 1900
(T.F.)

BIGLAND, A. D. Capt., R.A.M.C. 1905

BILLING, E. Capt., R.A.M.C.   1903
BILLINGTON, C. M. Capt., E. Yorks. Regt.   1913
BIRKS, A. H. Capt., R.A.M.C.   1903
BLACK, J. A. Pte., Cambridgeshire Regt.; Lieut., Sea- 1912
    forth Hdrs.; Capt., M.G.C. (W.)
BLACK, P. Capt., R.A.M.C.   1898
BLACKETT, G. E. Capt., Durham L.I. (P.)   1912
BLAIKIE, C. J. Capt., R.A.M.C.   1903
BLANCHARD, N. Pte., London Regt.; 2nd Lieut., R.A.S.C. 1898
BLANDY, R. Major, 11th Gurkha Rifles, Indian Army.   1902
    (W.) *M.C. and Bar. M* 2.
BLEW, C. L. Capt., Worcestershire Yeo.; Major, Wilt- 1900
    shire Regt. (W.)
✠BOARDMAN, J. H. Major, Oxford and Bucks. L.I.; attd. 1910
    Rifle Brigade. (W.) *M* 2.
    *Died in German hands 25 April 1918 of wounds received
    in action*
BOCK, E. N. Capt., S. Lancs. Regt.   1911
✠BODEY, A. R. Lieut., King's (Liverpool Regt., T.F.)   1913
    Killed in action 28 June 1916
BOMFORD, J. F. Capt., Worcestershire Regt. *M.C.*   [1914]
BOND, C. E. Capt., R.A.M.C.   1911
BOUSFIELD, J. K. Lieut., R.E.; attd. R.F.C. (P. *Escaped* 1912
    from Germany.) *M.C. and Bar*
BOUSFIELD, R. B. Pte., 9th Bn., Australian Infy.   1905
BOUSFIELD, S. Hon. Major, R.A.M.C.   1889
BOUSFIELD, W. E. Lieut. (T.), R.A.F.   1900
BOWER, C. W. 2nd Lieut., Middlesex Regt.(T.F.)   [1914]
BOYSON, H. A. Lieut., 15th Hussars   1912
BOYSON, J. C. Capt., Coldstream Gds. *M.C.*   1906
BRACKEN, R. J. M. E. Capt., R. Welsh Fus.(T.F.);   1896
    Lieut.-Col., M.G.C. *M.C. M.*
BRADBURY, J. B. Lieut.-Col., R.A.M.C. (1st E. Gen. Hos- 1862
    pital, T.F.)
BRADFIELD, L. G. Lieut., R.F.A.   1905
BRADFIELD, R. Major, R.E. (Electric Lights, T.F.)   1905
BRADLEY, A. S. Capt., R.A.M.C.   1905
BRADLEY, S. B. Lieut. (A.), R.A.F. *M.*   1910
BRAILSFORD, R. W. Capt., R.F.A.(T.F.)   1913
BRAITHWAITE, C. F. 2nd Lieut., R.F.A.(T.F.); empld.   1898
    Ministry of Labour. (W.)
✠BRAITHWAITE, P. P. Capt., I.A.R.O., attd. 36th Cavalry 1899
    (Jacob's Horse). (W.)
    Killed in action in Palestine 23 Sept. 1918

BRATTON, A. B.   Capt., Loyal N. Lancs. Regt.   (W.)   1909
  D.S.O.   M.C.   M 2.
BRETT, J. H.   Major, Suffolk Regt.   M 2.   1911
BREWER, F. G.   2nd Lieut., R.G.A.(T.F.)   1912
BRIGGS GOODERHAM, E. J. R.   See GOODERHAM, Rev.
  E. J. R. B.
BRIGHT, W. A.   Capt., R.A.S.C.   1898
✠BRISLEY, C. E.   Major (A.), R.A.F.   1905
  Killed in flying accident 30 July 1918
BRITTAIN, E. S.   Capt., R.F.A.   1910
✠BROAD, A. M.   Lieut., R. Fusiliers; attd. M.G.C.   1914
  Killed in action 12 July 1916
✠BROADBENT, E. R.   Major, 8th (King's R. Irish) Hussars;   1898
  D.A.Q.M.G.   M.C.   M.
  Died 31 Oct. 1918 of influenza
BROADMEAD, H. H.   Lieut., Somerset L.I.; Staff Capt.   1907
BROCKMAN, E. P.   Surgeon Sub-Lieut., R.N.V.R.   M.   1913
BROCKMAN, R. ST L.   Surgeon Lieut., R.N.   1907
BROCKMAN, W. D.   Lieut., Rifle Brigade(T.F.) and M.G.C.   1910
  (W.)
BROMET, E.   Capt., R.A.M.C.(T.F.)   M.   1885
BROMLEY, L.   Capt., R.A.M.C.   1903
BROOKE, J. C.   Capt. (S.), R.A.F.   D.S.C.   1912
BROOKE, Z. N.   Capt., E. Surrey Regt. and Gen. List *1908
  (Intelligence)
BROUGHTON, A. D.   2nd Lieut., Res. Regt. of Cavalry;   1910
  Capt. (A.), R.A.F.
✠BROWN, A. A.   Capt., R.F.A.; Staff Capt.   M.C.   1905
  Died 4 March 1918 of heart failure
✠BROWN, A. R.   2nd Lieut., R.F.A.; attd. R.F.C.   1913
  Killed in action 6 April 1917
✠BROWN, A. W. S.   Lieut., Rifle Brigade   1900
  Killed in action 18 Aug. 1916
BROWN, C. B.   Lieut., R. Fusiliers (P. S. Bn.) and Gen.   1906
  List (Staff Capt.)   M.C.   M.
BROWN, E. B.   Capt., Loyal N. Lancs. Regt.   1912
BROWN, G. D.   Capt., R. Fusiliers   1888
BROWN, H. H.   Capt., I.M.S.; D.A.D.M.S.   M 3.   Order   1904
  of the Nile, 4th Class (Egypt)
✠BROWN, H. M.   Trooper, Natal Light Horse; 2nd Lieut.,   1906
  E. Lancs. Regt.
  Killed in action in Mesopotamia 9 April 1916
✠BROWN, R. W.   Capt., Wiltshire Regt.   (W.)   [1914]
  Killed in action 9 April 1917

✠BROWN, T. Sergt., R. Fusiliers (P. S. Bn.); 2nd Lieut., 1908
Norfolk Regt.
Killed in action near Guillemont 4 Sept. 1916

✠BROWN, W. S. Capt., R.A.M.C. 1911
Died while returning from Mesopotamia 27 March 1919
of illness contracted on active service

✠BROWNE, G. BUCKSTON. Lieut.-Col., R.F.A.(T.F.) (W.) 1895
D.S.O. M 3.
Died 6 Jan. 1919 *of pneumonia contracted on active*
service

✠BROWNSWORD, D. A. Capt., R.A.S.C.(T.F.) and King's 1909
Royal Rifle Corps
Died 25 Dec. 1917 *of wounds received in action on*
Passchendaele Ridge

BUCKELL, E. R. Strathcona's Horse, Canadian Force 1908
BULL, H. C. H. Capt., King's Own (Yorkshire L.I.) 1909
(W.) *M.C.*
BULL, W. E. H. Major, R.A.M.C.(T.F.) *M.C.* 1908
BULLOCK, J. C. Paymaster Sub-Lieut., R.N.V.R. 1911
BULLOUGH, E. Lieut., R.N.V.R., empld. Admiralty *1911
BURGESS, A. S. Capt., R.A.M.C. 1898
BURGESS, R. Lieut.-Col., R.A.M.C.(T.F.) (W.) *D.S.O.* 1899
M.C. M 2. *French Croix de Guerre*
BURGOYNE JOHNSON, F. W. Capt., Durham L.I.; attd. 1911
M.G.C.

✠BURN, C. J. Lieut., Leicestershire Regt. (W 2.) 1912
Killed in action 1 *Oct.* 1917
BURNELL, Rev. E. W. C.F. 4th Class, R.A.C.D. 1898
BURNET, J. R. W. Lieut., Spec. List, empld. Ministry of 1905
National Service
BURNETT, F. E. Lieut., R.E. (Electric Lights, T.F.) [1914]
BURTON, E. T. D. Capt., R.F.A. (W.) *M.* [1914]
BURWELL, W. K. Lieut., E. Yorks. Regt.; Capt., R.E. (W.) 1901
BUSH, F. R. 2nd Lieut., E. Surrey Regt.; Lieut., Rifle 1895
Brigade; Major (Ad.), R.A.F.
BUSWELL, H. L. F. United States Signal Corps. *French* 1905
Croix de Guerre

✠CAIGER, F. H. S. 2nd Lieut., R.F.A. 1915
Killed in action 11 *Nov.* 1916
CAIGER, G. H. Lieut., R.F.A.(T.F.) (W.) 1915
CALDERWOOD, J. L. Capt., King's (Liverpool Regt.) *M.* 1906
CALDWELL, H. G. Lieut., Cameronians (Scottish Rifles). 1914
(W.)

CAM, W. H. Capt., R.A.M.C. 1902
CAMERON, D. W. Instructor Lieut., R.N. 1912
CAMPBELL, G. Sub-Lieut., R.N.V.R. (R.N.D.); Lieut., 1914
R.M.A.
CAMPBELL, W. H. Major, R.A.S.C. *M.* 1905
CANDY, K. E. Lieut., Lancs. Fus.; Capt., Labour Corps 1910
(P. of W. Coy.) (W.) *M.C.*
CANNINGTON, A. S. Capt., R.A.S.C. 1905
CANT, F. V. Capt., R.A.M.C. 1909
CARDWELL, C. R. Capt., Dorset Regt.(T.F.) 1907
CARDWELL, W. Lieut., Spec. List (Censor's Staff) 1901
CAREY, G. V. Major, Rifle Brigade; Major (Ad.), R.A.F.; 1906
S.O. 3, Air Ministry. (W.) *M. Belgian Croix de Guerre*
CARR, G. D'R. Lieut.-Col., R.A.M.C. (W 3.) *M.C. and* 1908
two Bars. Brevet Major. M.
CARSBERG, A. E. Capt., R.A.M.C. 1891
CARTER, G. S. Capt., Leicestershire Regt. and R.E. 1912
(W 2.)
CARVER, A. E. A. Capt., R.A.M.C. 1902
CASTELLAN, C. E., T.D. Major, R.F.A.(T.F.) 1894
CAVE, H. W. Lieut., R.F.A.(T.F.) *M.C.* 1910
CAVE, W. T. C. Capt., London Regt. (P.) 1901
CAVE-MOYLE, Rev. G. E. P. C.F. 4th Class, R.A.C.D. 1894
✠CECIL, C. Pte., R. Fusiliers (P. S. Bn.); 2nd Lieut., R. 1894
Berkshire Regt.(T.F.)
Killed in action on the Somme 16 *July* 1916
✠CHALLONER, A. C. 2nd Lieut., D. of Cornwall's L.I. 1911
Killed in action 30 *July* 1915
CHAMBERLAIN, D. A. Capt., R.A.M.C. 1898
CHANCELLOR, R. B. 2nd Lieut., 5th (R. Irish) Lancers [1914]
✠CHAPMAN, G. M. Lieut., R.A.M.C. *French Medal for* 1907
saving life at sea
Killed in action 13 *May* 1915
CHAPPEL, B. H. Lieut., D. of Cornwall's L.I.; attd. [1914]
107th Pioneers, Indian Army; Capt., Norfolk Regt.
(W 2.)
CHAPPEL, G. P. Major, R.A.M.C.(T.F.) 1886
CHARLES, J. R. Capt., R.A.M.C. (2nd S. Gen. Hospital, 1891
T.F.)
✠CHEAPE, J. DE C. Lieut., R. Sussex Regt. 1913
Killed in action 3 *Sept.* 1916
CHEFFAUD, P. H. M. Capt. 295me Regt., French Army. 1910
(W.)

✠Chessex, R. E. A. Lieut., R.N.V.R.   1896
Accidentally killed on H.M.S. Vanguard 9 *July* 1917
✠Child, G. J. Lieut., King's Own (Yorkshire L.I.)   1911
Killed in action 18 *April* 1915
Chisholm, D. C. H. Major, Worcestershire Regt. (R.   1897
of O.); A.P.M. *M.*
Chittick, H. S. Capt., R.E.(T.F.) *M.*   1904
Christie, J. F. Capt., Hertfordshire Regt. and Bedford-   1911
shire Regt. (W 2.) *M.C.*
Christie, S. O. K. Hon. Capt., R. Marines, empld.   1911
Admiralty
Churcher, W. D. Lieut., E. Surrey Regt.(T.F.); Capt.,   1912
67th Punjabis, Indian Army
Churchill, A. R. Capt., London Regt. (Cyclist Bn.) and   1902
Middlesex Regt.(T.F.)
Churton, W. A. V. Lieut.-Col., Cheshire Regt.(T.F.)   1895
D.S.O. T.D. M 3.
Clarence-Smith, K. W. Lieut., R.F.A.   1909
Clark, G. W. Pte., R. Fusiliers   1896
Clarke, A. G. A. Lieut., R.A.S.C.   1890
Clarke, A. J. M. *See* Michell-Clarke, A. J.
Clarke, A. V. Colonel, A.M.S. (T.F. Res.); A.D.M.S.   1889
Clarke, J. M. *See* Michell-Clarke, J.
Clarke, J. S. Capt., R.A.M.C.(T.F.) *M.C.*   1892
Clarke, R. H. Surgeon Sub-Lieut., R.N.V.R.   1908
Clarke, S. H. Capt., R.A.M.C.(T.F.)   1897
Clarkson, J. F. Lieut.-Col., R.G.A. (R. of O.)   1879
Claudet, B. J. A. Capt., R.N.V.R. (R.N.D.); Capt. [1914]
(Ad.), R.A.F.
Claudet, F. H. B. Pte., H.A.C.; Lieut., R.F.A. (T.F.);   1908
(W.)
Claudet, R. A. O. Pte., H.A.C.; Lieut., 2nd Dragoon [1914]
Gds. (Queen's Bays). (W.)
Claye, H. Capt., Sherwood Foresters (Notts. and Derby   1907
Regt., T.F.); Hon. Capt. (O.), R.A.F. (W 2.) (P.)
Clayton, E. B. Capt., R.A.M.C. (4th London Gen.   1900
Hospital, T.F.)
Cleminson, F. J. Capt., R.A.M.C.   1897
✠Cloudesley,H. Lieut.,The Queen's(R.W. Surrey Regt.)   1902
Killed in action 1 *July* 1916
Coast, W. Corpl., R.A.M.C.   1916
✠Coates, A. D. Lieut., London Regt. (R. Fus.)   1912
Killed in action in Gallipoli 27–28 *April* 1915
Coates, N. H. Lieut., R.A.S.C.   1910

COATES, V. H. M.   Capt., R.A.M.C. *M.C.*   1907
COBBOLD, A. W.   Capt., Remount Service   1874
✠COBBOLD, C. T.   2nd Lieut., R.F.A.   1912
   Killed in action 3 *Oct.* 1916
COBBOLD, J. V.   2nd Lieut., Yorkshire Regt.(T.F.)   1916
✠COCHRAN, F. A.   2nd Lieut., Gordon Hdrs.   [1914]
   Killed in action 25 *Sept.* 1915
COCKAYNE, A. A.   Surgeon Lieut., R.N. *D.S.C.*   1909
COCKIN, M. S.   Capt., E. Yorks. Regt.; empld. Ministry   1900
   of Munitions. (W.) *M.*
COCKIN, R. P.   Lieut., R.A.M.C.   1898
COCKSEDGE, T. A. B.   Major, R.A.V.C.(T.F.) *M.*   1902
COLBECK, E. H.   Major, N. Zealand Med. Corps   1884
COLCUTT, A. M.   Capt., R.A.M.C. (2nd E. Gen. Hospital,   1887
   T.F.)
COLLEDGE, L.   Capt., R.A.M.C.(T.F.) *M.*   1901
COLLINGWOOD, B. J.   Major, R.A.M.C. *O.B.E.*   1890
✠COLLINSON, G. E. C.   Lieut., Cameron Hdrs.; attd.   [1914]
   R.F.C.
   Killed in flying accident 13 *April* 1917
✠COLLOT, T. A.   2nd Lieut., Dorset Regt. and R. Berk-   1912
   shire Regt.
   Killed in action 1 *July* 1916
COLQUHOUN, J. C.   Capt., Highland L.I. and Gen. List   1913
   (P. and B.T. Staff). (W.) *M.B.E. M.*
COMBE, E. P.   Capt., R. Scots; Brigade Major. *M.C. and*   1909
   Bar. M 2.
COMPTON, A. G. W.   Capt., R.A.M.C. (W.) *M.C. M.*   1903
CONNOLLY, B. B., C.B.   Colonel, A.M.S.; A.D.M.S. *m.*   1863
CONNOP, H.   Major, R.A.M.C.(T.F.)   1885
COOKE, W. I.   Corpl., R.E. (Signals)   1906
COOMBE, R.   Major, R.A.M.C. (4th S. Gen. Hospital, T.F.)   1879
COOPER, H. C.   Lieut., R.A.S.C.(M.T.)   1914
COOPER, H. J.   Capt., R.A.M.C.   1882
CORBET-SINGLETON, M. G.   Lieut., R. Dublin Fus. and   [1914]
   Gen. List
CORBETT, R. S.   Capt., R.A.M.C.   1912
✠CORY, C. W.   2nd Lieut., Suffolk Regt.(T.F.)   1906
   Killed in action 12 *Aug.* 1915
CORY, R. F. P.   Surgeon Lieut., R.N.   1904
COSTIGAN, R. H.   Lieut., R. Warwickshire Regt. (W.)   1909
COSTOBADIE, L. P.   Capt., R.A.M.C.   1908
✠COTTAM, H. C. B.   Capt., Hampshire Regt.(T.F.) *M.C.*   1909
   Killed in action 30 *Sept.* 1918

COUCHMAN, H. J. Capt., R.A.M.C. *M.*   1904
COULSON, R. N. Major, Cameronians (Scottish Rifles);   1898
Lieut.-Col., King's Own Scottish Borderers. *D.S.O.*
M 2. *French Croix de Guerre*
COWAN-DOUGLAS, H. Capt., Rifle Brigade   1914
✠COWIE, A. G. Capt., Seaforth Hdrs. (W.)   1909
Died 6 April 1916 of wounds received in action
COX, D. H. Capt., Scottish Horse and R.E. (Signals)   1900
✠COX, E. Fleet-Surgeon, R.N.   1892
Accidentally killed on H.M.S. Vanguard 9 July 1917
COX, R. Capt., R.A.M.C.   1902
CRAIG, M. Lieut.-Col., R.A.M.C. *C.B.E.*   1884
CRAIGIE, R. C. Capt., King's (Shropshire L.I.) (W.) [1914]
M.C. and Bar
CRAWHALL, T. L. Lieut., R.A.M.C.   1912
✠CREAN, T. Capt., Northamptonshire Regt.; attd. R.F.C.   1899
Killed in flying accident 26 Oct. 1914
CREED, Rev. J. M. C.F. 4th Class, R.A.C.D.   1908
CRESWELL, H. E. Capt., R.A.M.C. (W.) *M.C. and Bar*   1907
CRIMP, G. L. Lieut., R.A.M.C.   1894
CROMIE, B. P. 2nd Lieut., London Regt.; Lieut., R.F.A. [1914]
M.C. M.
CROMPTON, J. Capt., 10th Jats, Indian Army. *O.B.E.*   1905
CROSS, W. E. Capt., R. Sussex Regt.; attd. Lovat's Scouts   1892
✠CROSSE, T. L. Capt., Border Regt. (W 2.)   1908
Killed in action 3 July 1916
CROYSDALE, J. H. 2nd Lieut., R.A.S.C.   1897
CROZIER, J. E. D. 2nd Lieut., Coldstream Gds.   1917
CRUMP, N. E. Lieut., Middlesex Regt. (T.F.); attd. R.E. [1914]
(Signals)
✠CRUNDWELL, A. Lieut., King's (Liverpool Regt.)   [1914]
Killed in action 23 April 1918
CULLIMORE, C. Capt., R.F.A.(T.F.) (W.)   1909
CULLIMORE, JAMES. Lieut., R.F.A.(T.F.)   1904
✠CULLIMORE, JOHN. Lieut., Cheshire Regt. *M* 2.   1912
Died 16 April 1916 of wounds received in action
CULLIMORE, W. Lieut., Cheshire Regt.(T.F.)   1906
CUMMING, J. B. 2nd Lieut., Scottish Horse; Lieut. and [1914]
Adjt., R.F.A.(T.F.)
CURME, D. E. Lieut.-Col., R.A.M.C.   1889
CURNOW. A. T. Pte., Middlesex Regt.; 2nd Lieut., E.   1916
Riding of Yorkshire Yeo.
CURSETJEE, H. J. M. Capt., I.M.S. (W.) *D.S.O. M* 2.   1908
Order of the White Eagle, 5th Class (Serbia)

CURWEN, B. M. Major, Rifle Brigade   1909
✠CURWEN, C. N. Lieut., King's Royal Rifle Corps   1908
Killed in action 15 Sept. 1916   ·

DALY, I. DE B. Flt. Lieut., R.N.A.S.; Capt. (Med.), R.A.F. 1911
(W.)
DALY, U. DE B. Capt., R. Dublin Fus.; Major, Spec. List   1911
(Cmdt., Bombing School). (W.) *M.*
DARLEY, C. B. 2nd Lieut., R.F.A. (W.) (P.)   1906
DAUKES, S. H. Capt., R.A.M.C. (Sanitary Service, T.F.)   1897
O.B.E. *M.*
DAVENPORT, W. H. Lieut.-Col., R. Warwickshire Regt.,   1885
attd. R.A.O.C.
DAVIDSON, G. E. Capt., R.A.M.C.   1896
✠DAVIES, I. T. 2nd Lieut., Oxford and Bucks. L.I.   1913
Killed in action 22 June 1915
✠DAVIES, J. R. 2nd Lieut., London Regt.   1899
Died 28 Nov. 1917 of wounds received in action
DAVIES, R. E. L. Lieut. (A. and S.), R.A.F. *D.F.C.* *M.* 1913
✠DAVIS, C. J. B. Capt., R.E.(T.F.)   1913
Died 29 Sept. 1917 of wounds received in action 25 Sept.
1917
DAVIS, F. M. Capt., London Regt. (W 2.) (P.)   1908
DAVIS, F. P. Capt., R.A.S.C. and M.G.C. (P.)   1905
DAVY, G. H. Capt., R.A.M.C. *O.B.E.* *M.*   1901
DAWBARN, J. R. Lieut., Northamptonshire Regt. and   1914
Bedfordshire Regt.
DAWSON, H. H. Major, 75th Carnatic Infy., Indian   1895
Army; D.A.A.G. *M.*
DAY, E. C. Major, Remount Service   1892
DAY, G. 2nd Lieut., R.E. *M.C.*   1907
DAY, W. F. L. Lieut., R.A.M.C.   1895
DEARDEN, H. Hon. Capt., R.A.M.C. (W 2.)   1901
DEBAILLEUL, A. Pte., French Army; Interpreter with   1904
British Exp. Force
DEBENHAM, F. Major, Oxford and Bucks. L.I. (W.)   1913
O.B.E.
DENDY, E. H. Capt., R.A.M.C.   1910
✠DEVITT, G. F. O. 2nd Lieut., Rifle Brigade   1912
Killed in action at Hooge 30 July 1915
✠DICKSON, A. F. Lieut., I.A.R.O., attd. 14th Murray's   1909
Jat Lancers and 34th Poona Horse
Killed in action in Palestine 14 July 1918

✠DIETRICHSEN, F. C. Capt., Sherwood Foresters (Notts.   1901
and Derby Regt., T.F.) *M.*
Killed in the Irish rebellion 1 *May* 1916
DILL, J. F. GORDON. Surgeon Major, Norfolk Yeo. *O.B.E.*   1877
T.D. m.
DISNEY, H. A. P.   Capt.,   Cambridgeshire   Regt.;   1912
D.A.Q.M.G.; Lieut.-Col. (T.), R.A.F.; S.O. 1. *M.*
m 2. *Officer, Order of the Crown of Italy*
✠DIXON, T. H. Capt., Manchester Regt. (W.) *M.C.*   1913
Killed in action 25 *Aug.* 1918
DOAK, J. K. R. Lieut., Cameron Hdrs. (W 3.)   1909
DOBIE, J. N. Major, R.A.M.C.   1885
✠DOBIE, W. M. Lieut., Queen's Own (R. W. Kent Regt.) [1914]
Killed in action 9 *April* 1916
DOBSON, D. R. 2nd Lieut., R.A.S.C.   1898
DOBSON, G. M. B. Capt. (T.), R.A.F. *m.*   1907
DOBSON, H. D. Lieut., R.A.S.C.   1909
DONALDSON, E. A. Chaplain, R.N.   1892
✠DONALDSON, G. B. Capt., R. Warwickshire Regt.(T.F.)   1912
Died in German hands 19 *July* 1916 *of wounds received*
in action
DONNELL, J. H. Capt., R.A.M.C.(T.F.)   1896
DRACUP, A. H. 2nd Lieut., I.A.R.O.   1907
DREWRY, G. H. Lieut., R.F.A.(T.F.)   1907
DRUMMOND, J. M. F. Lieut., Highland L.I.   1900
DRURY, A. N. Major, R.A.M.C.(T.F.); D.A.D.M.S.   1909
DRYLAND, G. W. Lieut., R.A.M.C.   1900
DUCKWORTH, L. Capt., Loyal N. Lancs. Regt.(T.F.);   1910
Major, King's (Liverpool Regt., T.F.) *M.*
DUDDELL, A. G. Lieut., R. Warwickshire Regt.; Capt.,   1912
Spec. List (Bde. Bombing Officer). (W.)
DUKA, A. T., D.S.O. Major, R.A.M.C. *M.*   1884
DUKE, H. L. Capt., Spec. List, empld. E. African Force   1902
DUNCAN, J. H. Major, R.A.S.C. *M.*   1905
✠DUNLOP, J. G. M. 2nd Lieut., R. Dublin Fus.   1905
Killed in action at Clary 27 *Aug.* 1914
DUNLOP, W. N. U. Lieut., London Regt. (Kensington   1912
Bn.); Capt. and Adjt., M.G.C. *M.*
DUNN, T. W. N. Capt., R.A.M.C.   1898
DURST, A. Capt., R.E.(T.F.); attd. Labour Corps. *M.*   1894
DYAS, G. E. Capt., R.A.M.C. *M.C.*   1905
DYKES, K. Major, Queen's Own (R. W. Kent Regt.);   1913
D.A.Q.M.G. (W.) *O.B.E. M.C. M. Order of St*
Stanislas, 3*rd Class (Russia). Belgian Croix de Guerre*

EALAND, V. F.   Lieut., R.F.A.   1913
EAMES, W. L'E., c.b., v.d.   Bt. Colonel, R.A.M.C.   *C.B.E.*   1882
  M 2.   *Commander, Military Order of Avis (Portugal)*
EBDEN, J. W.   Capt., I.A.R.O.; Staff Capt.   1901
EBDEN, W. S.   2nd Lieut., King's (Shropshire L.I.)   (W 2.)   1906
  (P.)
ECCLES, R.   Bt. Colonel, Durham L.I. and King's (Liver-   1872
  pool Regt.)
EDGEWORTH, F. H.   Major, R.A.M.C. (2nd S. Gen.   1883
  Hospital, T.F.)
EDWARDS, C. G.   Capt., R.A.S.C.   (W.)   *m.*   1911
EISDELL, H. M.   Lieut., R.N.V.R.   1901
ELAM, J. E.   2nd Lieut., Monmouthshire Regt.   1914
ELEY, H. G.   Lieut., E. Surrey Regt.; Major, R.E.   (W.)   1906
  M.B.E.
ELLISON, H. B.   Capt., R.A.M.C.   1900
ELTON, H. B.   Capt., R.A.M.C.   1901
ELTRINGHAM, H. C.   2nd Lieut., D. of Wellington's (W.   1911
  Riding Regt.); attd. R.F.C.
✠ELWORTHY, T.   2nd Lieut., R.E.; Lieut., King's Own   1911
  (R. Lancaster Regt.)   *M.*
  Killed in action 3 May 1917
ELWORTHY, W. R.   Lieut., R.G.A.   1915
EMRYS-JONES, M. F.   Capt., R.A.M.C.   1900
ENGLAND, H.   Capt., R.A.M.C.(T.F.)   1884
EVANS, M. W. H.   Flt. Lieut., R.N.A.S.   1914
✠EVATT, J. M.   Capt., R.A.M.C.   1908
  Killed in action 21 *March* 1918
EVE, H. F. H.   Capt. and Adjt., R.A.S.C.   *M.C.*   1911
EVERETT, Rev. B. C. S.   C.F. 4th Class, R.A.C.D.   *M.*   1894
EVERITT, H. L.   Capt. (A.), R.A.F.   *A.F.C.*   1910
EVERSHED, Rev. F. T. P.   C.F. 4th Class, R.A.C.D.   1888
EWENS, B. C.   Capt., R.A.M.C.   *Order of St Sava, 5th*   1907
  Class (Serbia)
EWING, W. T.   Lieut.-Col., R. Scots (T.F.)   *D.S.O. and*   1906
  Bar. M.   French Croix de Guerre
EYRE, L. B.   Lieut., E. Surrey Regt.(T.F.)   1909

FAGAN, C. H. J.   Major, R.A.M.C.(T.F.)   *O.B.E.*   1897
FAIRBROTHER, J.   Surgeon Lieut., R.N.   1908
✠FAWCETT, R. W.   Surgeon Prob., R.N.V.R.; 2nd Lieut.,   1910
  S. Staffs. Regt.
  Died 26 *Sept.* 1915 *of wounds received in action*
FEARFIELD, C. J.   Major, R.E.   *M.C.   M.*   1910

FELTON, D. G. W.   2nd Lieut., Hereford School O.T.C.   1905
FENWICK, J. S.   Lieut., Oxford and Bucks. L.I. (W.)   1912
FERRAND, J. B. P.   Major (S.), R.A.F. (P.) *D.S.O.*   [1914]
FERRERS, E. B.   Major, Cameronians (Scottish Rifles);   1897
Lieut.-Col., Spec. List (Cmdt., School of Instruction).
(W.) *D.S.O. M* 2.
FEUERHEERD, L. M.   R. Fusiliers   1894
✠FIELDING, E. F.   Lieut., W. African Frontier Force   1898
Killed in action in the Cameroons 24 *Oct.* 1915
FINLAY, R. V. K.   Lieut., R.N.V.R.   1902
✠FISCHER, A. W.   Pte., London Regt.(Artists Rifles); Lieut.,   [1914]
Devon Regt. (W.) *M.*
Died 17 *May* 1916 *of wounds received in action*
FITTON, R.   Capt., R.F.A.; Lieut. (O.), R.A.F. (W.)   1909
M.C. M.
FITZGERALD, H. S.   Lieut., Northumberland Fus.; attd.   1902
W. African Frontier Force. (W.)
FITZJOHN, T.   Lieut.-Col., Worcestershire Regt. (W.)   1898
D.S.O. and Bar. M 3. *French Croix de Guerre*
FLEMMING, M. G.   Corpl., R.E. (Signals); Lieut., R.G.A.   1911
FLETCHER, A. B.   Capt., 10th Jats, Indian Army   *M* 2.   1912
FLETCHER, W.   Capt., R.A.M.C.   1890
FORMAN, D. P.   Capt., Sherwood Foresters (Notts. and   1906
Derby Regt., T.F.); attd. R.E. (Signals). *M.*
FORMOY, R. R.   Pte., London Regt. (Artists Rifles)   1905
FORSTER, C. M.   Capt., R.A.M.C. (W.) *M. Order of*   1905
St Sava, 5*th Class* (*Serbia*)
✠FORSTER-BROWN, J. C.   Lieut., Rifle Brigade   1911
Died 27 *Aug.* 1916 *of wounds received in action*
FORSYTH, G.   Lieut., London Regt. (Q.V.R.); A.D.C.   1899
FORSYTH, L. W.   Capt., R.A.M.C.   1893
FOWLER, Sir J. K., K.C.V.O.   Colonel, A.M.S. *C.M.G. M.*   1876
FOWLER, T. G.   Sub-Lieut., R.N.V.R. (Coastal Motor-   1910
boat Service)
FOX, H. M.   Capt., R.A.S.C.   1908
FRANCIS, G. L. B.   Capt., Monmouthshire Regt.; Major,   1904
R.A.S.C.(T.F.)
FRANKLIN, C. D. G.   Lieut., Rifle Brigade and M.G.C.   1903
(Motor)
FRASER, D. H.   Capt., R.A.M.C.; attd. R.A.F. *M.C.*   1896
*M.B.E. French Médaille d'Honneur and Médaille des
Epidémies*
✠FREEMAN, G. C.   Capt., R. Berkshire Regt.   1910
Killed in action 1 *Oct.* 1916

FRENCH, E. N. Major, Lincolnshire Regt.; Lieut.-Col.,   1897
London Regt. (W.)
FROST, T. F. C. Lieut., 15th Hussars. (W.)   1913
FRUHE-SUTCLIFFE, R. Major, R.E.(T.F.) *m.*   1909
✠FRY, J. D. Lieut., London Regt. (R. Fus.)   1913
Killed in action 15 *Sept.* 1916
FUCHS, H. M. *See* FOX, H. M.
FYFFE, W. K. Major, N. Zealand Med. Corps. (W.)   1882

GABB, J. D. Capt., The Queen's (R. W. Surrey Regt.,   1910
T.F.); attd. 74th Punjabis, Indian Army. *M.*
GALBRAITH, H. G. Lieut., R.G.A. (W.)   1911
GAMLEN, R. L. Capt., R.A.M.C.   1899
GARDINER, A. L. 2nd Lieut., Norfolk Regt.; Lieut.,   1912
I.A.R.O., attd. 23rd Cavalry
GARDINER, H. H. Capt., R.F.A.; A.D.C. (W 3.) *M.C.*   1910
M 2.
GARDNER, E. Capt., R.A.M.C. *M.*   1896
GARDNER, E. A. Lieut.-Cdr., R.N.V.R. *Officer, Order*   1880
of the Redeemer (*Greece*)
GARDNER, R. C. B. Lieut., R.G.A.; attd. Gen. Staff. *M.*   1908
GARNSEY, E. Major, H.A.C. and Gen. Staff; A.P.M. *M.*   1898
French Croix de Guerre
GASKELL, J. F. Capt., R.A.M.C.(T.F.) *M.*   1897
GATER, B. A. R. Lieut., R. Fusiliers and Gen. List. (W.)   1914
GAVIN, N. D. I. Lieut., King's Own Scottish Borderers;   1913
Lieut. (A.), R.A.F.
GAYE, A. W. Lieut., R.A.M.C.   1904
GELL, W. C. C. Lieut.-Col., R. Warwickshire Regt.   1907
(T.F.) (W.) *D.S.O. and Bar. M.C. M* 3. *Italian*
Silver Medal for Military Valour
✠GEORGE, A. K. D. Lieut., Dorset Regt.   1905
Died 14 *Sept.* 1914 *of wounds received in action*
GERARD, R. J. L. Lieut., Gordon Hdrs. (T.F.); Capt.   1913
(Ad.), R.A.F.
✠GETTY, J. H. Capt., W. Yorks. Regt. *M.*   1907
Killed in action 3 *May* 1917
GIBSON, A. M. Lieut., R.G.A. and Spec. List (Intelli-   1914
gence). *Italian Croce di Guerra*
GILLIES, H. D. Major, R.A.M.C. *C.B.E. m.*   1901
GIMBLETT, C. L. Surgeon Lieut., R.N.   1908
GIMLETTE, C. H. M. Surgeon Lieut., R.N.   1908
GINGELL, W. C. Lieut., R.A.S.C.(M.T.)   1908
GLANVILLE, W. J. Major, R.A.O.C.; I.O.M. 1st Class. *M.*   1901

GLENDINNING, H. W. Capt., Cheshire Regt.(T.F.) (W.) [1914]
✠GLOSTER, H. C. Lieut., Gordon Hdrs.(T.F.)   1913
    Killed in action at Neuve Chapelle 13 *March* 1915
GLOVER, G. H. Lieut., 20th Hussars. (W.)   1914
GLOVER, H. P. McC. Major, R.F.A. (W 2.) *M.C.*   [1914]
GLYN, J. P. 2nd Lieut., N. Irish Horse; Lieut., R.   1905
    Horse Gds.
GOODALL, C. C. Hon. Capt., R.A.M.C.   1909
✠GOODCHILD, E. L. Pte., Norfolk Regt.   1910
    Killed in action 28 *April* 1916
✠GOODERHAM, Rev. E. J. R. B. 2nd Lieut., R. Irish Regt. 1908
    and M.G.C.
    Killed in action 13 *Dec.* 1916
GOODHUE, F. W. J. Lce.-Corpl., R. Fusiliers (Sportsman's 1885
    Bn.)
GOODWIN, E. ST G. S. Surgeon Lieut., R.N. *M.*   1904
GORDON, A. Capt., Border Regt. and Tank Corps. (W.) [1914]
✠GORDON, G. Lieut., 12th Lancers   1904
    Killed in action at Ypres 30 *April* 1915
✠GORDON, H. Lieut., King's Own Scottish Borderers. (W.) [1914]
    Died 19 *Dec.* 1915 *of wounds received in action in
    Gallipoli*
GOSSE, A. H. Major, R.A.M.C.(T.F.) *Brevet Major. M* 4. 1903
GOSSE, R. W. Lieut., Northamptonshire Regt.(T.F.);   1910
    Lieut. (A.), R.A.F.
GOSSET, A. C. V. Lieut., Oxford and Bucks. L.I. (W 2.) 1913
GOSTLING, E. V. Colonel, R.A.M.C.(T.F.); A.D.M.S.   1891
    (W.) *D.S.O. M. m.*
✠GOTCH, D. H. Pte., London Regt. (Artists Rifles); 2nd 1910
    Lieut., Worcestershire Regt.
    Killed in action at Neuve Chapelle 11 *March* 1915
GOULD, L. McL. Sergt., 2nd Central Ontario Regt.,   1897
    Canadian Force. *Belgian Croix de Guerre*
GOULLET, A. S. C. Lieut., Middlesex Regt.   1913
GRAHAM, Rev. C. Chaplain, R.N. *O.B.E.*   1897
GRAHAM, L. A. Capt., R.A.M.C.   1906
GRAHAM, W. P. G. Lieut.-Col., R.A.M.C.   1880
GRANTHAM-HILL, C. Lieut., 3rd Hussars. (W.)   1909
GRAY, W. A. 2nd Lieut., Rangoon Bn., Indian Defence 1904
    Force
GRAZEBROOK, O. F. Lieut., Worcestershire Regt.(T.F.Res.) 1904
GREENBERG, A. W. *See* GREENHILL, A. W.
GREENE, G. E. 2nd Lieut., Natal Carabineers. (W.)   1899
GREENHILL, A. W. Pte., R.A.S.C.(M.T.)   1911

GREENISH, F. H. S. Surgeon Lieut., R.N.   1908
GRETTON, G. F. Major, 7th Hariana Lancers, Indian   1896
    Army
GRIFFITH, C. Capt., W. Yorks. Regt. (W 2.)   [1914]
GRIFFITH, F. L. 2nd Lieut., R.F.A.; empld. Ministry of   1915
    Labour. (W.)
GRIFFITH-JONES, C. Surgeon Sub-Lieut., R.N.V.R.   1913
GRIFFITHS, P. D. Pte., London Regt. (Artists Rifles)   1917
GRIFFITHS, Rev. T. T. Chaplain and Instructor Cdr., R.N.   1882
GRIFFITHS, W. L. Capt., R.A.M.C.(T.F.)   1890
✠GRIMWADE, E. E. 2nd Lieut., Lancs. Fus.   1906
    Killed in action 17 Sept. 1916
✠GROWSE, R. H. Major, R.A.S.C.   1905
    Died 12 Feb. 1919 *of pneumonia contracted on active*
    service
GRUMMITT, C. C. Capt., R.A.M.C.(T.F.)   1888
GRYLLS, E. A. H. Capt., R.F.A. *M.*   1911
GUINNESS, J. F. G. Lieut., R.F.A.; empld. Ordnance   1908
    College. (W.) *M.*
✠GULLILAND, J. H. Capt., Essex Regt. (W.)   1911
    Died 18 July 1916 *of wounds received in action*
GUNTER, Rev. W. H. C.F. 4th Class, R.A.C.D.   1904
GURNEY, K. T. C. Lieut., R.F.A. and Spec. List (Intelli- 1914
    gence)

HADFIELD, P. H. Capt., R.A.M.C.   1887
HAIGH, B. Capt., R.A.M.C.   1897
HAINES, R. T. M. Capt., R.G.A.   1910
HALE, J. Surgeon Lieut., R.N.   1911
HALE, R. E. V. Capt., R.A.M.C.; Capt. (Med.), R.A.F.   1897
HALL, A. J. Lieut.-Col., R.A.M.C. (3rd N. Gen. Hos-   1884
    pital, T.F.)
✠HALL, E. W. Capt., Lincolnshire Regt. *M.B.E.*   1912
    Killed in action 26 Sept. 1917
HALLIWELL, A. C. Surgeon Sub-Lieut., R.N.V.R.   1914
HALLIWELL, C. C. 2nd Lieut., Welsh Gds. and Gds.   1917
    M.G. Regt.
HAMBLIN, E. C. C. Lieut., R.E.   1910
HAMMOND SEARLE, A. C. Lieut.-Col., R.A.M.C.;   1899
    D.A.D.M.S.
HARDIE, E. E. 2nd Lieut., Gordon Hdrs. (W.)   1912
HARDING, E. W. Lieut., R.N.V.R.   1902
HARDY, F. K. Major, York and Lancaster Regt.; empld. 1900
    Ministry of Labour. *D.S.O. M* 2.

✠HARDY, J.   2nd Lieut., R.A.S.C.(M.T.)   1908
   Died 21 *Oct.* 1918 *of pneumonia*
HARE, A. C.   Lieut., R.E. (Signals, T.F.)   1910
HARE, Rev. S. H.   C.F. 4th Class, R.A.C.D.   1904
HARGREAVES, R.   Capt., R.A.M.C.(T.F.)   1908
HARPER, E. R.   Capt. and Adjt., Monmouthshire Regt.   1904
   M.C.
HARPER-SMITH, G. H.   Capt., R.A.M.C.(T.F.)   1896
HARREY, C. O.   2nd Lieut., R.A.S.C.; Lieut., Gen. List   1913
   (Intelligence). *M* 2. *French Croix de Guerre*
HARRIS, Rt Hon. F. LEVERTON,M.P.   Hon. Cdr., R.N.V.R.   1881
HARRIS, R. T.   Lieut., R. North Devon Yeo. (T.F. Res.)   1883
HARRIS, W. J.   Capt., R.A.M.C.   1888
HARRISON, C. E.   Capt., R.A.S.C.   1888
HARRISON, C. F.   2nd Lieut., K. Edward's Horse; Capt.,   1911
   Dorset Regt.
HARRISON, G. A.   Capt., R.A.M.C.   1913
HARRISON, L. K.   Colonel, R.A.M.C. (5th N. Gen.   1890
   Hospital, T.F.) *C.B.E. Brevet Colonel. m* 2.
HARRISON, T. S.   Surgeon Lieut., R.N.   1894
HART, H. E.   Major, R.F.A.; A.D.C. (W 3.) *M.C.*   1911
HART-SMITH, H. M.   Capt., R.A.M.C. *M.*   1891
✠HARTREE, C.   2nd Lieut., R.G.A.   1897
   Killed in action 29 *May* 1918
HARTREE, K.   Capt., Queen's Own (R. W. Kent Regt.,   1908
   T.F.)
HARWOOD, A. H. F.   Capt., Essex Regt.(T.F.) and   1911
   M.G.C.
HATCH, K.   2nd Lieut., R.A.S.C.; Lieut., 34th Poona [1914]
   Horse, Indian Army
HATCH, M. L.   Lieut., R.F.A.   1913
✠HATHORN, C. N.   2nd Lieut., Loyal N. Lancs. Regt.   1913
   Killed in action 10 *Aug.* 1915
HATHORN, W. B.   Lieut., 6th Dragoon Gds. (Carabiniers).   1912
   (W.) *M.*
HATTEN, G.   Pte., Essex Regt. and Labour Corps   1902
HATTON, G. A. L.   Capt., Queen's Own (R. W. Kent   1907
   Regt.) (P.)
HAULTAIN, W. F. T.   Capt., R.A.M.C. *O.B.E. M.C. M.*   1911
HAWKER, G. P. D.   Major, R.A.M.C.(T.F.) *M. m.*   1894
HAWKER, H. L. L.   Sergt.-Instructor, R.E.   1914
HAWKINS, C. H. G. W.   Lieut., R.A.S.C.   1908
HAWLEY, A. T.   Surgeon Sub-Lieut., R.N.V.R.   1914
HAYDON, A. D.   Capt., R.A.M.C.   1907

HAYDON, T. H.   Colonel, R.A.M.C.(T.F.)   *Brevet Colonel.*   1884
m.

HAYWARD, L. G.   Lieut., Suffolk Regt.(T.F.); attd. Lon-   1913
don Regt.

✠HAYWARD, M. C.   Capt., R.A.M.C.(T.F.)   (W.)   1889
Died 23 Aug. 1916 of septic pneumonia

HAZELDINE, D.   Lieut., R.E.   (W.)   1910

HEALD, C. B.   Lieut.-Col., R.A.M.C.; Lieut.-Col. (Med.),   1902
R.A.F.; S.O. 1, Air Ministry.   *C.B.E.*

HEALD, W. M.   2nd Lieut., Suffolk Regt.; Capt.,   1904
R.A.O.C.   *m.*

HEARD, Rev. A. ST J.   C.F. 4th Class, R.A.C.D.   *M.*   1904

HENDLEY, H. J. H.   Lieut., R.F.A.(T.F.)   (W.)   1914

HERBERT, P. L. W.   Colonel, Sherwood Foresters (Notts.   1901
and Derby Regt.); Brig.-Gen., R.A.F.   *C.M.G.*
Brevet Major. M 4. m. Order of St Anne, 3rd Class,
with swords (Russia). Grand Commander, Order of St
Saviour (Greece). Order of the Nile, 3rd Class (Egypt)

HERBERT, S.   Capt., R.A.M.C.   1884

HEREFORD, J. C.   Lieut., R.N.V.R.   1905

✠HERMANN, J.   Pte., London Regt. (Q.V.R.)   1884
Killed in action 25 Sept. 1916

HERRIOT, D. R.   Capt., Northumberland Fus.   (W 2.)   1912

HESKETH-WRIGHT, J. H.   Lieut., Spec. List, empld. Min-   1892
istry of National Service

HEURTLEY, W. A.   Capt., E. Lancs. Regt.; Major, Gen.   1902
List (Dep. Governor of Military Prison).   *O.B.E.*
M 2.

HEWETT, F. S., M.V.O.   Surgeon Lieut., R.N.V.R.   1898

HEWITT, R. C.   Capt., R.A.M.C.   1909

HEY, C. E. M.   Capt., R.A.M.C.(T.F.)   1882

✠HICKMAN, W. C.   2nd Lieut., R.F.A.   1906
Killed in action 1 July 1916

HICKS, E. H.   Hon. Major, R.A.M.C.   *M. Chevalier*   1877
Order of Leopold (Belgium)

HIGGINS, S. J.   Lieut.-Col., R.A.M.C.   1903

HIGGINS, W. R.   Capt., R.A.M.C.(T.F.)   1896

HIGGINSON, G.   Capt., R.A.M.C.(T.F.)   1888

HIGSON, G. H.   2nd Lieut., Manchester Regt. (T.F. Res.)   1888

✠HILL, P. A.   Capt., S. Wales Borderers (T.F.)   1891
Killed in action 23 April 1917

HILL, R. A. P.   Major, R.A.M.C.   1899

✠HILLS, A. H.   2nd Lieut., Hampshire Regt.(T.F.)   1902
Killed in action 19 April 1917.

HILPERN, W. T. H. Lieut., E. Lancs. Regt. (P.) 1909
HINCHCLIFFE, J. W. Pte., R. Fusiliers; Capt., North- 1912
amptonshire Regt.; attd. Gloucestershire Regt.
HINDLEY, N. L. Lieut., Sherwood Foresters (Notts. and 1913
Derby Regt.); Capt., Gen. Staff. (W 2.) *M.*
HIRST, G. G. Major, I.M.S.; D.A.D.M.S. *M.* 1896
HIRST, J. W. Lieut., D. of Wellington's (W. Riding Regt., 1914
T.F.) (W.)
HISLOP, T. C. A. Capt., Wellington Regt., N. Zealand 1907
Force
✠HOBSON, A. F. Major, R.E. *D.S.O.* M 2. 1911
Killed in action 28 *Aug.* 1916
✠HOBSON, L. F. 2nd Lieut., York and Lancaster Regt. (T.F.) [1914]
Died 12 *July* 1915 *of wounds received in action*
HOFF, H. G. Lieut., Lincolnshire Regt.(T.F.) (W.) 1908
HOFFMEISTER, C. J. R. Lieut., R.A.M.C. 1899
HOLDEN, E. G. Lieut., Welsh Regt. and M.G.C. (W.) 1914
HOLDEN, G. H. R. Capt., R.A.M.C.(T.F.) *m.* 1882
✠HOLLAND, W. D. A. Lieut., 9th Lancers; Capt., Cavalry, 1911
Indian Army. (W.)
Died 13 *Aug.* 1917 *of illness contracted on the Mahsud
expedition*
HOLLIS, Rev. W. C.F. 4th Class, R.A.C.D. 1900
HOLMAN, C. C. Capt., R.A.M.C. 1903
✠HOLMAN, G. H. W. Lieut., Wiltshire Regt. (W.) [1914]
Died 6 *July* 1916 *of wounds received in action near
Thiepval* 5 *July* 1916
HOLMES, G. Capt., R.A.M.C.(T.F.) 1903
HOLMES, T. E. Major, R.A.M.C. *m.* 1894
✠HOOD, G. C. Lce.-Corpl., Middlesex Regt. (P. S. Bn.) 1913
Died 19 *Feb.* 1916 *of wounds received in action* 15 *Feb.*
1916
HOPE, G. M. Lieut., R.N.V.R. 1901
HOPE, S. J. C.P.O., R.N.A.S. 1900
HORNER, N. G. Capt., R.A.M.C. 1899
✠HORSEY, A. M. Surgeon Prob., R.N.V.R. 1913
Killed in action 9 *Aug.* 1917
HORSLEY, C. D. Lieut.-Col., 21st Lancers; D.A.Q.M.G. 1894
(W.) *M.C.* *M.* *French Croix de Guerre*
HOTBLACK, G. V. Capt., Welsh Regt. and Gen. List 1909
(Brigade Major). (W.) *M.C.*
✠HOWARTH, H. V. Lieut., Devon Regt.(T.F.) (W.) 1914
Died 2 *May* 1918 *of wounds received in action*
HOWELL, C. G. 2nd Lieut., R.F.A. (W.) 1913

Howes, A. G. Capt., Remount Service   1889
Howse, T. F. Cadet, O.C.B.   1892
Hudson, R. J. Lieut., R. Fusiliers; Major (A.), R.A.F.   1905
M.C.
Huelin, E. S. B.S.M., H.A.C.   1907
Hulbert, H. B. Lieut., Worcestershire Regt. (W.)   1911
Hullah, J. Nagpur Rifles, Indian Defence Force   1895
Humfrey, S. H. G. Lieut., R.F.A.(T.F.)   1913
Humphrys, H. E. Capt., R.A.M.C.   1901
Hunkin, Rev. J. W.   C.F. 2nd Class, R.A.C.D.;   1906
D.A.C.G. (W.) O.B.E. M.C. and Bar. M 2.
Hunter, J. F. S. Capt., R.E. (Tyne Electrical Engineers,   1913
T.F.) M.B.E. M.
Hunter, J. H. 2nd Lieut., Rangoon Bn., Indian Defence   1908
Force
Hutchence, B. L. Capt., R.A.M.C.   1907
Hutchence, W. G. Major, Durham L.I. and S. Staffs.   1903
Regt. (W.)

Iles, J. H. Capt., R.A.M.C.   1896
✠Iles, J. O. Lieut., S. Staffs. Regt.; attd. R. Welsh Fus.   1912
Killed in action 25 Sept. 1915
Ilott, C. H. T. Capt., R.A.M.C. (W.)   1898
Irving, W. Lieut., R.A.M.C.   1887
Irwin, A. P. B. Lieut.-Col., E. Surrey Regt. (W 3.)   1906
D.S.O. and two Bars. Brevet Major. M 3.

✠Jackson, A. J. 2nd Lieut., Middlesex Regt.   1913
Killed in action 27 April 1915
Jackson, H.S. Lieut.-Col., R.F.A. (W 2.) D.S.O. M 3.   1898
Jacob, A. C. Lieut., R.F.A.   1909
✠James, C. K.   Major, Border Regt.; Lieut.-Col., W.   1910
Yorks. Regt. (W 2.) D.S.O. and Bar. Brevet Major.
M 6.
Killed in action 19 May 1918
James, E. H. Capt., R. North Devon Yeo.; attd. Dorset   1909
Regt. M.C. and Bar
James, Rev. J. A. C.F. 4th Class, R.A.C.D. (W.) M.   1912
Jarvis, Rev. F. C.F. 4th Class, R.A.C.D.   1906
Jasper, R. F. T. Lieut., Essex Regt.; empld. Ministry of   1909
Munitions. (W.)
✠Jennings, F. M. Capt., 8th (King's R. Irish) Hussars   1892
Died 11 Nov. 1918 of wounds received in action
Jephcott, C. Capt., R.A.M.C.(T.F.)   1907

JEPHCOTT, Rev. E. W. C.F. 4th Class, R.A.C.D.   1907
JEPSON, Rev. G. C.F. 4th Class, R.A.C.D.   1875
JERRAM, R. M. Lieut., Hampshire Regt. and Tank Corps. [1914]
M.C.
✠JEUDWINE, S. H. Capt., Lincolnshire Regt. (W 2.)   [1914]
    Killed in action 1 *July* 1916
JOHNSON, F. W. B. *See* BURGOYNE JOHNSON, F. W.
JOHNSON, H. C. J. Major, R.A.O.C.; D.A.D.O.S. *M.*   1902
JOHNSON, H. P. Major, R.A.M.C. (R. of O.)   1882
JOHNSON, L. O. Lieut., King's Own (Yorkshire L.I.)   1913
    (W 2.)
JOHNSON, R. E. Lieut., The Queen's (R.W. Surrey Regt.) 1913
    (W 2.)
JOHNSTON, H. B. 2nd Lieut., Suffolk Regt. and Spec.   1911
    List, empld. Sudan Govt.
JONES, T. A. Capt., R.A.M.C.   1899
✠JONES-BATEMAN, F. Capt., R. Welsh Fus. (W.) *M.*   1914
    Killed in action near Englefontaine 4 *Nov.* 1918
JUPE, H. M. Surgeon Lieut., R.N.   1912

KAUFFMANN, A. L. Ensign, United States Naval Res.   1912
    Flying Corps
KAY, R. L. Capt., Cheshire Regt. *M.C. M.*   1913
KEATING, J. H. Capt., Cambridgeshire Regt. (W 2.)   1912
KEIR, L. 2nd Lieut., R.G.A.   1903
✠KELLIE, K. H. A. Capt.. R.A.M.C.   1893
    Killed in action 25 *June* 1916
KELLOW, W. Engineers, S. African Force.   1912
KELWAY, K. S. Corpl., R.E. (Signals); Lieut., R.A.S.C. 1912
    (M.T.)
KEMPSON, Rev. F. C   Capt,. R.A.M.C.(T.F.); Capt.   1886
    (Med.), R.A.F.
✠KENDALL, L. F. W. A.   Lieut., Norfolk Regt.; attd.   1911
    M.G.C. (Cavalry)
    Died 22 *Nov.* 1917 *of wounds received in action* 21 *Nov.*
    1917
KENNEDY, A. Capt.. I.M.S.   1905
KENNEDY, M. W. Lieut., R. Scots Fus.   [1914]
KENT, H. H. Lieut.-Col., Northumberland Fus. *m.*   1882
✠KINDER, T. H. Capt., Suffolk Regt.   1912
    Killed in action 3 *July* 1916
KING, E. F. H. Capt., R.F.A.(T.F.) (W.)   1911
KING, F. H. Flt. Sub-Lieut., R.N.A.S.   1915
KING, G. C. Capt., R.A.M.C.(T.F.) *M.*   1905

✠King, S. W. T. 2nd Lieut., Cheshire Regt.(T.F.)   [1914]
  Killed in action 10 *Aug.* 1915
Kingsford, G. T. Major, R.E.(T.F.) *D.S.O. M.*   1900
Kingsley-Smith, C. H. Lieut., R. Sussex Regt.   1914
Knaggs, R. L. Major, R.A.M.C. (2nd N. Gen. Hospital, 1876
  T.F.)
Knight, E. F. Major, R.E. (W.) *M.C. and Bar*   1907
Knight, H. F. Lieut., Spec. List (R.T.O.)   1905
Knox, R. W. Lieut.-Col., I.M.S. *D.S.O. M* 4. *Order* 1890
  of the White Eagle, 4th Class, with swords (Serbia).
  Officer, Order of the Crown of Italy
✠Knox, W. Capt., Cameron Hdrs.; attd. R.F.C.   1906
  Killed in action 20 *Feb.* 1916
✠Kohn, W. A. Pte., R. Fusiliers; 2nd Lieut., E. Lancs. Regt. 1912
  Killed in action 1 *July* 1916
Kon, G. A. R. Lieut., R.A.M.C.; Capt., R.E. *m.*   1909
Koop, G. G. Lieut., R.F.A.   1903

La Fontaine, J. S. Lieut., R.N.V.R. (W.)   1912
La Fontaine, S. H. Capt., E. African Force. *D.S.O.* 1905
  M.C. M.
Lake, W. I. Sergt., The Queen's (R. W. Surrey Regt.) 1907
  and Middlesex Regt.
Landau, H. Capt., R.F.A. and Spec. List. *O.B.E.*   1910
Lane, H. J. Lieut., R.G.A.; attd. R.E. *M.*   1905
✠Lang, H. Lieut., N. Zealand Rifle Brigade   1910
  Killed in action 20 *July* 1916
Langdale, A. H. Lieut., York and Lancaster Regt. *M.* 1909
✠Langdale, H. C. Pte., H.A.C.; Capt., R. Sussex Regt. 1912
  (W 2.)
  Killed in action 26 *Sept.* 1917
Langdon, H. C. T. Capt., R.A.M.C.; Lieut.-Col.(Med.), 1890
  R.A.F. *O.B.E. M.*
Langley, E. R. Lieut., Spec. List (Carrier Corps)   1908
Langley, F. O. Capt., S. Staffs. Regt.(T.F.); Major, 1902
  Asst. Military Attaché. *M.C. M. Chevalier, Legion*
  of Honour (France)
Lankester, E. A. Major, H.A.C. (W.) *M.*   1886
Lauderdale, E. M. Surgeon Lieut., R.N.   1902
Laurie, F. G. Capt., Loyal N. Lancs. Regt. (W 2.) *M.C.* 1912
Laurie, H. C. Lieut., King's Royal Rifle Corps   1913
Lawrence, J. S. G. Lieut., R.E.; Asst. Inspector of R.E. 1911
  Machinery
Lea, M. Capt. and Adjt., York and Lancaster Regt. (W.) 1903

LEACH LEWIS, W. Lieut., R.F.A.   1902
LEE, C. S. Capt., R.A.M.C.(T.F.)   1898
LEES, K. Lieut., Manchester Regt. (W.)   1913
✠LEETE, W. J. H. Capt., Lancs. Fus.   1905
   Killed in action 21 Jan. 1916
LEIGHTON, A. F. Lieut., R.F.A. *M.C. M.*   1907
LENEY, R. J. B. Capt., R.A.M.C.   1902
✠LENNY, L. A. Pte., R. Fusiliers (P. S. Bn.); 2nd Lieut., S. [1914]
   Staffs. Regt.; Lieut., R. Irish Fus.
   Killed in action 20 Dec. 1917
LESCHER, F. G. Major, R.A.M.C. (P.) *M.C. and two Bars* 1907
LESTER, Rev. C. V. C.F. 4th Class, Canadian Force   1900
LEWIS, G. A., T.D.   Lieut.-Col., Sherwood Foresters   1888
   (Notts. and Derby Regt., T.F.) *C.M.G. M. m.*
LEWIS, H. H. Major, R.F.A.(T.F.); Brigade Major   1907
✠LEWIS, T. E. Capt., S. Wales Borderers   1906
   Killed in bombing accident 28 Aug. 1915
LEWIS, W. H. Lce.-Corpl., Bihar Light Horse, Indian   1907
   Defence Force
LEWTAS, F. G. Pte., R. Fusiliers (P. S. Bn.); Surgeon   1910
   Lieut., R.N.
LEYTON, A. S. F. Major, R.A.M.C.(T.F.)   1887
LILLY, G. A. Capt., R.A.M.C. *M.C. M.*   1907
LINLEY-HOWLDEN, R. C. Lieut., R.G.A. (W.)   1902
LIPP, G. A. S. Lieut., M.G.C. (W.) *M.C.* French   1914
   Croix de Guerre
LITTLE, J. C. Capt., Queensland and Tasmania Bn.,   1905
   Australian Force. *M.C.*
LITTLE, R. A. Lieut., R.F.A. (W.)   1914
LITTLEJOHNS, A. S. Major, R.A.M.C. *D.S.O. M.*   1896
LLOYD, A. H. Capt., Calcutta Bn., Indian Defence Force   1902
LLOYD, I. G. Major, Rangoon Bn., Indian Defence Force   1897
✠LLOYD-JONES, I. T. Capt., R. Welsh Fus.(T.F.)   [1914]
   Killed in action 26 March 1917
LLOYD-JONES, P. Capt., R. Welsh Fus.   1903
✠LLOYD-PRICE, LL. O. Rfn., King's Royal Rifle Corps   1903
   Killed in action 10 Jan. 1915
LOCK, N. F. Capt., R.A.M.C.   1904
LOCK, P. G. Capt., R.A.M.C.   1893
✠LODGE, J. W. Colonel, Yorkshire Regt.   1874
   Died 23 Aug. 1917
✠LONG, B. A. Capt., S. Lancs. Regt. and King's Own (R.   1894
   Lancaster Regt.)
   Died 10 Feb. 1917

Long, C.W. Capt., London Regt.(L.R.B.) and Spec. List   1911
(Adjt., Vol. Bn.)
Loveband, F. R. Bt. Colonel, W. India Regt. and W.   1882
Yorks. Regt. *m.*
Loveday, G. E. Capt., R.A.M.C.(T.F.) *M.*   1895
Lovelock, A. R. Capt., Cameron Hdrs. (W.) *M.*   1908
Low, A. J. Instructor Lieut., R.N.   1914
Low, H. Capt., R.A.M.C. (5th London Gen. Hospital,   1882
T.F.)
✠Lowry, W. A. H. 2nd Lieut., I.A.R.O., attd. 14th Sikhs   1908
Killed in action in Gallipoli 4 June 1915
Lumb, T. F. Capt., R.A.M.C. *M.*   1899
Lunniss, S. F. 2nd Lieut., R.A.S.C.   1904

Mabane, W. Lieut., E. Yorks. Regt.; Capt., Spec. List.   1914
(W.) *M.*
McBride, L. G. 2nd Lieut., Seaforth Hdrs. (W.)   1911
McCardie, W. J Capt., R.A.M.C. (1st S. Gen. Hos-   1885
pital, T.F.)
McCaskie, H. B. Capt., R.A.M.C.   1896
McCaskie, N. J. Lieut., R.A.M.C.   1893
McCaw, O. C. 2nd Lieut., Middlesex Regt.   1908
✠McClenaghan, G. M. Capt., Queen's Own (R. W. Kent   [1914]
Regt.) (W.)
Died 8 Nov. 1918 *of wounds received in action*
✠MacCombie, W. J. Capt., King's Own Scottish Borderers.   1910
(W.) *M.*
Killed in action 17 July 1916
MacDonald, J. N. Major, K. Edward's Horse. (W.)   1906
M.
Macfarlane, C. B. Lieut., Gordon Hdrs. (W.)   1905
Macfie, R. A. S. R.Q.M.S., King's (Liverpool Regt.,   1886
Liverpool Scottish, T.F.)
McGeagh, G. R. D. Capt., R.A.M.C. *M.C.*   1906
✠Macgregor, A. H. Capt., Seaforth Hdrs. (T.F.) *M.*   1909
Killed in action 13 Nov. 1916
Mackenzie, A. V. Lieut., King's (Shropshire L.I.) (W.)   1915
M.C.
McKerrow, G. Capt. (T.), R.A.F. *m.*   1910
MacLean, H. Driver, R.G.A.   1898
Macleod, D. N. Capt., R.A.M.C.   1905
✠MacMullen, A. R. Surgeon Lieut., R.N., attd. R.N.D.   1907
D.S.C. and Bar
Died 7 Sept. 1918 *of wounds received in action*

McNair, W. L.   Lieut., R. Warwickshire Regt.; Capt.,   1911
O.C.B. (W.) *m*.
Macpherson, Rev. D. G.   C.F. 4th Class, R.A.C.D.   1898
O.B.E. M.
MacQuarrie, H.   Lieut., R.F.A.; empld. Ministry of   1911
Munitions
MacRury, E.   Capt., Spec. List (Intelligence).   *M* 2.   1907
Cavalier, Order of the Crown of Italy. Order of the
Nile 4th Class (Egypt)
McTaggart, H. A.   Hon. Capt., Gen. List, Canadian   1913
Force
Mairis, E. S.   Lieut.-Col., R.M.L.I.; empld. Admiralty   1914
Makin, E. L.   Major, Wiltshire Regt.; G.S.O. 2. *D.S.O.*   1896
M 3. *m*.
Malcolm, A. S. L.   Capt., R.A.M.C. *M*.   1906
Malden, E. C.   Capt., R.A.M.C. *M*.   1909
✠Malet, H. A. G.   Lieut., King's Own Scottish Borderers   1910
Killed in action at Hill 60 18 April 1915
Marchant, W. F.   Capt., London Regt. (Blackheath and   1892
Woolwich Bn.); empld. Infy. Base Depôt. *O.B.E. M*.
Marett Tims, R. D.   *See* Tims, R. D. Marett
Marklove, J. C.   Major, R.A.M.C.(T.F.) *M* 2.   1901
Marriott, G. A.   Capt., King's Royal Rifle Corps and   1911
Gen. List
Marris, H. F.   Major, R.A.M.C. *Brevet Major. M*.   1897
Marsden, Rev. T.   C.F. 4th Class, Canadian Force   1903
✠Marsh, A. S.   Capt., Somerset L.I.   *1913
Killed in action 6 Jan. 1916
✠Marshall, A. R.   Corpl. R.E. (Signals); Capt. and Adjt.,   1909
R.G.A.
Died 2 Feb. 1918 of wounds received in action 8 Dec. 1917
Marshall, D.   Capt., Manchester Regt. *M.C.*   1910
✠Marshall, F.   Capt., King's (Liverpool Regt.)   1896
Died 30 Sept. 1914 of wounds received in action on the
Aisne 20 Sept. 1914
✠Marten, H. H.   2nd Lieut., King's Royal Rifle Corps and   1912
Manchester Regt. *M*.
Killed in action 13 Aug. 1915
Marten, R. H.   Major, R.A.S.C. *M* 2. *Italian Silver*   1909
Medal for Military Valour
Martin, N. T.   Lieut., R.F.A.   1914
Martin, R. C.   Pte., R. Fusiliers   1913
Martin, W. E.   Lieut., Devon Regt. and Gen. List   [1914]
(Adjt., Base Depôt). (W.)

Mason, H. B.   Capt., R. Warwickshire Regt.(T.F.);   1913
empld. Ministry of Munitions. (W.)
Mason, J. H.   Capt., R.E. (Fortress, T.F.)   1906
Mason, J. W.   2nd Lieut., R.G.A. *M.C. M.*   1910
Master, A. E.   Lieut.-Col., R.A.M.C. *m.*   1887
Matthews, R. W. Y.   Lieut., R.F.A.(T.F.)   [1914]
Mattingly, H.   Pte., London Regt. (Artists Rifles)   1903
Maturin, F. H.   Lieut.-Col., Hampshire Regt. (T.F.) and   1889
R.A.M.C.
Maunsell, L. B.   Lieut., S. Staffs. Regt. and M.G.C.;   1914
empld. Ministry of Labour. (W 2.) *M.C.*
Mawer, A.   Lieut., Durham Univ. O.T.C.   1901
Maxwell, L. B.   Hon. Capt., Gen. List. *O.B.E. Chevalier,*   1913
Ordre de la Couronne (Belgium). Order of St John of
Jerusalem. French Croix de Guerre
May, E.   Capt., R.G.A.   1913
Mayfield, E.   Hon. Lieut.-Col., R.F.A.   1888
Maynard, H. A. V.   Lieut., R. Welsh Fus. (W.)   1911
Mayne, C. F.   Surgeon Lieut., R.N. *O.B.E. M.*   1907
Mayo, H. R.   Capt., R.A.M.C.   1893
✠Meadowcroft, J.   2nd Lieut., R.E.   1917
Died 7 Nov. 1918 of pneumonia
Medley, R. P.   Capt., Felsted School O.T.C.   1900
Meggeson, R. R. H.   Lieut., R.G.A.   1906
Melvill, L. V.   Lieut., Signal Corps, S. African Force   1906
Mercer, W. B.   Lieut., R.A.M.C.(T.F.)   1886
Messiter, C. C.   Capt., R.A.M.C.(T.F. Res.)   1902
Metcalfe, G. C.   Capt., R.A.M.C.   1906
Metcalfe-Gibson, A. E.   Lieut., R.A.S.C.(M.T.)   1906
Methven, M. D.   Capt., London Regt. (Hackney Bn.);   1909
Lieut.-Col. (T.), R.A.F. *O.B.E. M. m.*
✠Michell, R. W.   Capt., R.A.M.C. *M.*   1880
Died 19 July 1916 of wounds received in action
Michell-Clarke, A. J.   Major, Gloucestershire Regt.;   1913
Major (A.), R.A.F. *M.C.*
Michell-Clarke, J.   Lieut.-Col., R.A.M.C. (2nd S. Gen.   1879
Hospital, T.F.)
Miller, A. T.   Capt., Sherwood Foresters (Notts. and   1906
Derby Regt.); Major, G.S.O. 2. *M.C. and Bar.*
Brevet Major. M 3. French Croix de Guerre
Miller, C. A. M.   Lieut., R.H.A.   1912
Milligan, D. W.   Lieut., Cameron Hdrs.   1912
✠Milner-Barry, E. L.   Lieut.-Cdr., R.N.V.R.   1887
Died 7 May 1917 of heart failure following bronchitis

MISKIN, G. 2nd Lieut., Coldstream Gds.   1908
MITCHELL, A. L.   Capt., Spec. List (Inland Water Trans-   1900
port)
MITCHELL, A. W. C. Lieut., R.G.A.   1909
MITCHELL, F. R.F.A.   1893
MOIR, A. Capt., R.E.·   1913
✠MOIR, R. Lieut., R.E.   1911
Died 9 Nov. 1915 of illness contracted on active service
MOLLER, N. H. Capt., Middlesex Regt. (W.)   1911
MONCKTON, J. F. E. Lieut., Northamptonshire Regt.   1912
MONRO, C. G. Capt., R.A.M.C.   1886
MONRO, H. E. Lieut., R.G.A.; empld. War Office   1898
✠MONTAGUE, P. D. Lieut., Rifle Brigade; attd. R.F.C.   1909
Killed in action 13 Nov. 1917
MOORE, C. G. H. Major, R.A.M.C. *m.*   1903
MOORE, J. H. E   Capt., R.A.M.C.   1913
MOORE, M. Lieut., York and Lancaster Regt.; attd. [1914]
R.F.C. (P.)
MOORE, W. G. Major (S.), R.A.F. *D.S.C.*   1911
MOORHOUSE, S. Major, Argyll and Sutherland Hdrs.   1897
MORE, T. 2nd Lieut., Cameron Hdrs.   1904
MORETON, T. W. E. Capt., R.A.M.C.   1882
MORGAN, F. J. 2nd Lieut., S. Wales Borderers; Capt.,   1907
Norfolk Regt. *D.S.O. M.C. M.*
MORGAN, H. T. Lieut., Welsh Regt.(T.F.); Capt. and   1912
Adjt., Wiltshire Regt. *M.C. M.*
MORIARTY, G. H. Lieut., R.F.A. and Spec. List (Intelli-   1912
gence). (W.)
MORRIS, A. Capt., R.A.M.C. (W 2.)   1896
MORRIS, C. A., C.V.O. Major, R.A.M.C.(T.F.)   1878
MORRISON, E. O. Surgeon Lieut., R.N.   1910
MORRISON, H. Surgeon Lieut., R.N.   1913
MOSSE, C. G. T. Capt., R.A.M.C. *Order of St Sava,*   1909
5th Class (Serbia). Serbian Royal Red Cross
MOSSOP, M. C. Lieut. (A.), R.A.F. *A.F.C.*   1906
MOSSOP, N. R. Capt., Suffolk Regt.; Hon. Capt. (K.B.),   1913
R.A.F. (W.) *M.*
MOTION, D. G. 2nd Lieut., R.F.A.   1917
✠MOTION, S. H. Lieut., Northamptonshire Regt. (W.) *M.*   1913
*Died 1 Aug. 1917 of wounds received in action 31 July
1917*
✠MOWATT, O. Lieut., 10th Hussars   1899
*Died 22 April 1917 of wounds received in action at
Monchy-le-Preux 11th April 1917*

MOWLL, C. K.   Capt., R.A.M.C.   1911
✠MOYSEY, L.   Capt., R.A.M.C.(T.F.)   1887
    *Drowned on H.M. hospital ship Glenart Castle 26
    Feb.* 1918
MUIRHEAD, J. A. O.   Lieut., Clifton College O.T.C.   1909
✠MURPHY, J. K.   Staff Surgeon, R.N.V.R.   1888
    Died 13 Sept. 1916
MYERS, C. S.   Lieut.-Col., R.A.M.C.   *C.B.E.   M* 2.   1891
✠MYLES, W. W.   2nd Lieut., Cameronians (Scottish Rifles);   1914
    attd. T.M.B.
    Died 20 Sept. 1916 *of wounds received in action*
✠MYLREA, W. P. G.   Lieut.-Col., R.F.A.(T.F.)   1889
    Died 25 Aug. 1915 *of illness contracted on active
    service*

✠NANGLE, E. J.   Capt., R.A.M.C.   1906
    Killed in action 26 Sept. 1915
NEAME, T.   Lieut., Worcestershire Regt. and Gen. List.   1904
    (W.)   *M.B.E.*
NEILSON, H. V.   2nd Lieut., Sherwood Foresters (Notts.   1909
    and Derby Regt.) and Gen. List (Asst. Officer i/c
    Records).   (W.)
✠NELSON, W.   Foreign Legion, French Army; 2nd Lieut.,   1889
    S. Staffs. Regt.(T.F.)
    Killed in action at the Hohenzollern Redoubt 13 Oct.
    1915
NEWBOLD, C. J.   Lieut.-Col., R.E.   *D.S.O.   M* 3.   1900
NEWINGTON, H. A. H.   Capt., London Regt. (London   1895
    Scottish); Lieut.-Col., Deputy Controller of Labour.
    D.S.O.   M 5.
NEWMAN, E. A. R.   Lieut.-Col., I.M.S.   *C.I.E.*   1884
NICHOL, R. W.   Major (A.), R.A.F.   (P.)   *M.*   1911
NICHOLLS, S. H.   Lieut., R.A.S.C.   1899
NICHOLSON, C. J.   Capt., R.A.M.C.   1902
NICKELS, R. N.   Lieut., R.F.A.(T.F.)   (W 2.)   1908
NICOLL, H. M. D.   Capt., R.A.M.C.   1903
NIXON, J. A.   Colonel, A.M.S.   *C.M.G.   M* 2.   1893
✠NORTH, W. G. B.   Corpl., R. Fusiliers   1901
    Killed in action 10 *June* 1916
NORTON, D. G.   Major, Lancs. Fus. and Labour Corps.   1905
    (W.)
NORTON, E. H. P.   2nd Lieut., R.F.A.   1917
NORTON, G. P.   Lieut.-Col., D. of Wellington's (W.   1900
    Riding Regt., T.F.)   *D.S.O. and Bar.   M* 2.

✠NOYES, H. F. G.   Capt., R.A.M.C.   1899
Died 5 Sept. 1916

OATS, W.   2nd Lieut., The Buffs (E. Kent Regt.)   1901
O'BRIEN, J. C. P.   Major, R. Irish Fus. (W 3.)   *M.C.*   1903
✠OKE, R. W. L.   Capt., R. Berkshire Regt.   1902
Killed in action 25 Sept. 1915
OLIVER, F. R.   Surgeon Sub-Lieut., R.N.V.R.   1914
OLIVER, H. G.   Capt., R.A.M.C. (W.) *M.C. M.*   1908
OLIVER, T. H.   Major, R.A.M.C.   1906
OLPHERT, R. A.   Capt., R.A.M.C.   1913
OPIE, P. A.   Major, R.A.M.C.; D.A.D.M.S. *M* 2.   1904
ORCHARD, S.   Lieut., R.F.A.(T.F.) (W.)   1914
OWEN, H. B.   Capt., E. African Force. *D.S.O.*   1897

PAGE, D. S.   Capt., R.A.M.C.   1907
PAGE, Rev. F. G. J.   C.F. 4th Class, R.A.C.D.   1881
PAGE, J.   Capt. (T.), R.A.F.   1903
PAGET, O. F.   Major, Australian A.M.C.   1891
PAIGE, J. F.   Lieut., R.E. *M.C. M.*   1910
PALMER, C. E.   Major, I.M.S.   1898
PANK, P. E. D.   Capt., R.A.M.C.   1910
PARISH, G. W.   2nd Lieut., Westmorland and Cumber-   1905
land Yeo. (W.)
PARKER, R. D.   Capt., S. African Med. Corps   1890
PARSONS, H.   Major, R.A.M.C.   1902
PATERSON, T. W. S.   Major, R.A.M.C.(T.F.)   1893
PATRICK, C. V.   Surgeon Sub-Lieut., R.N.V.R.   1916
PAUL, H.   Lieut., D. of Wellington's (W. Riding Regt.);   1910
attd. R.E. (Spec. Bde.)
PAWLE, H.   Capt., R. Berkshire Regt.; Staff Capt. *M* 2.   1904
French Croix de Guerre
✠PEARKES, A. M.   Pte.,London Regt.(Artists Rifles); Capt.,   1906
W. Yorks. Regt.
Killed in action in Gallipoli 7 Aug. 1915
✠PEARMAN, J. O'H.   2nd Lieut., R. Warwickshire Regt.   1901
Killed in action 25 Jan. 1917
PEARS, R.   Capt., Middlesex Regt.; empld. O.C.B.   1909
PECK, J. N.   Lieut.-Col., King's (Liverpool Regt.) (W.)   1905
(P.) *M.C.*
PEGGE, A. V.   Capt., R.A.M.C. *M.C.*   1912
PENDERED, J. H.   Major, R.A.M.C.; D.A.D.M.S. *M.C.*   1906
French Médaille des Epidémies

PENTLAND, G. C. C.   Lieut., R. Dublin Fus.; attd. M.G.C.   1908
(Motor); Capt. (T.), R.A.F.
PERCIVAL, A. F.   Lieut., R.G.A.   1905
PERKINS, B. M. N.   2nd Lieut., Spec. List (Interpreter)   1907
PERRIN, W. S.   Lieut., R.A.M.C.   1901
PERRY, E. W.   Capt., I.A.R.O., attd. 114th Mahrattas,   1910
110th Mahratta L.I., and Gwalior Imp. Service Infy.
PERTH (Australia), ARCHBISHOP OF.   Chaplain-General,   1874
Australian Force
PESHALL, S. F.   Lieut., King's Royal Rifle Corps; empld.   1902
War Office. (W.) *M.C.*
PETCH, D. B.   Capt., Leicestershire Regt. (W 3.) *M.C.*   1915
and Bar
PETERS, E. A.   Capt., R.A.M.C. *M.*   1887
PETERS, R. A.   Capt., R.A.M.C.; empld. Ministry of Muni-   1908
tions. *M.C. and Bar. m.*
PHEAR, H. W.   Lieut., R.F.A.; Lieut. (A)., R.A.F. (W 2.)   1912
PHILLIPS, L. C. P.   Lieut.-Col., R.A.M.C. *M* 2.   1889
PICKERING, B. M.   2nd Lieut., The Queen's (R.W. Surrey   1910
Regt.)
PICKETT, A. C.   Capt., R.A.M.C. *O.B.E. m* 2.   1903
PICTON-WARLOW, A. J.   P.O., R.N.V.R.   (P.)   1892
PIKE, H. H.   Lieut., W. Yorks. Regt.   1909
PINKHAM, C.   Capt., Middlesex Regt. and Spec. List   1908
PINTO-LEITE, H.M.   Capt., R.A.M.C.(T.F.); D.A.D.M.S.   1899
m.
PLATT, A. H.   Capt., R.A.M.C.(T.F.)   1901
✠PLATTS, A. L.   Capt., Suffolk Regt.   1910
Killed in action 20 *July* 1916
PLATTS, S. G.   Capt., R.A.M.C.   1907
PLAYFAIR, K.   Capt., R.A.M.C. *M.*   1909
POIGNAND, Rev. C. W.   Chaplain, R.N.   1898
✠POLLAK, H. L.   Lieut., R. Marines and Rifle Brigade   1904
Killed in action 23 *Oct.* 1916
POOLEY, G. H.   Major, R.A.M.C.(T.F.)   1886
POPE, H. B.   Major, R.A.M.C.(T.F.) *M.C. M. French*   1905
Croix de Guerre
PORRITT, R. N.   Capt., R.A.M.C.   (W.)   1908
PORTER, C. E. V.   Capt., Essex Regt.(T.F.); Hon. Capt.   1912
(A.), R.A.F.
✠PORTER, G. H.   Lieut., R. Welsh Fus.   1912
Killed in action 3 *Oct.* 1916
✠PORTER, J. E.   2nd Lieut., S. Lancs. Regt.   1914
Killed in action 23 *July* 1916

PORTER, W. N., C.I.E., V.D.   Major, R. Sussex Regt.; Presi-   1869
   dent, Central Quartering Committee.   (W.)   *M.*
POTTS, J. L.   Lieut., R.N.V.R.   1914
POWEL SMITH, L. J.   Lieut., Durham L.I.   1911
POWELL, G. G.   Capt., Gordon Hdrs.   1907
✠POWELL, L. M.   2nd Lieut., Gordon Hdrs.   1913
   Killed in action 17 June 1915
PRESTIGE, A. R.   Capt., R.A.S.C.(M.T.)   1910
PRIDDLE, A. E.   Major, R. Welsh Fus.(T.F. Res.)   1889
PRIDHAM, C. F.   Capt., R.A.M.C.   (W.)   1885
PRIEST, R. C.   Capt., R.A.M.C.   1901
PRING, J. G.   Lieut., R.G.A.   1899
PRIOR, H. B.   Major (A.), R.A.F.   1905
PURVIS, J. H.   Lieut.-Col., Highland L.I.   *D.S.O.   M* 2.   1883
PYE-SMITH, T. E. B.   Capt., Wiltshire Regt.(T.F.)   *M.*   1905
PYMAN, F. C.   Capt., Yorkshire Regt.; empld. Ministry   1907
   of Munitions.   (W.)   *M.*
PYTCHES, G. J.   Capt., Suffolk Regt. (T.F.); attd. M.G.C.   1900

QUIGGIN, E. C.   Lieut., Spec. List (Censor's Dept.);   1893
   Lieut., R.N.V.R., empld. Admiralty

RABY, G. H   Lieut., Oxford and Bucks. L.I.(T.F.)   1912
RADFORD, A. C.   Lieut., R.A.S.C.(T.F.)   1901
RAE, A. J.   Capt., R.A.M.C.   1900
RAIKES, W. O.   Lieut., The Buffs (E. Kent Regt.); Capt.   1907
   (A.), R.A.F.; Lieut.-Col., S.O. 1, Air Ministry.
   O.B.E.   M.B.E
✠RAIMES, Rev. L.   Capt., Durham L.I.(T.F.)   1906
   Died 1 June 1916 of wounds received in action 31 May
   1916
✠RAMSAY, A.   2nd Lieut., R. Fusiliers; Lieut., R. War-   1906
   wickshire Regt.
   Killed in action 25 April 1915
RATTRAY, I. M.   2nd Lieut., R. Inniskilling Fus.   1910
RAVEN, Rev. C. E.   C.F. 4th Class, R.A.C.D.   1904
RAWLING, L. B.   Major, R.A.M.C. (T.F.)   1890
RAYMOND, C.   Hon. Capt., I.M.S.   1900
RAYNER, A. E.   Major, R.A.M.C. (Sanitary Service, T.F.)   1902
   O.B.E.   M 2.
RAYNER, E. C.   Capt., R.A.M.C.   1904
REA, R. H. T.   2nd Lieut., R.F.A.   1917
READ, Rev. H. C.   C.F. 4th Class, R.A.C.D.   1909
READ, R. I.   2nd Lieut., R.A.S.C.   1907

REDDAWAY, H. Lieut., R. Fusiliers; Hon. Lieut. (O.),   1910
R.A.F. (W.)
REID, C. B. Canadian Force   1908
✠RENTON, T. Pte., London Regt. (Kensington Bn.)   1910
Killed in action at Fromelles 9 *May* 1915
REYNOLDS, E. P. Major, R.E. (Signals). (W.) *M.C.* 1906
REYNOLDS, T. W. Capt., Suffolk Regt.   1907
RHODES, S. H. Capt., R.F.A.(T.F.)   1908
RHODES, W. A. Pte., R. Berkshire Regt.; Corpl., Devon 1902
Regt. and Labour Corps
RICHARDS, C. S. Lieut., R.E. (W.)   1904
RICHARDS, F. S. Capt., Spec. List (Survey Coy., R.E.) 1905
M 2.
RICHARDS, F. W. Major, R.E. (W 2.) *D.S.O. M.C. M.* 1913
✠RICHARDSON, A. S. Sergt., R.A.M.C.; 2nd Lieut., R.G.A. 1912
Killed in action 25 *June* 1917
RICHARDSON, C. Sub-Lieut., R.N.V.R.   1909
RICHARDSON, D. E. E. Capt., R.E.(T.F.) (W.)   1912
RICHARDSON, D. W. R. Surgeon Lieut., R.N.   1912
RICHARDSON, F. K. Capt., E. Yorks. Regt. (W 2.) *M* 2. 1910
✠RIEU, H. Pte., Middlesex Regt. (P. S. Bn.)   1897
Killed in action 30 *Jan.* 1916
✠RIGBY, F. J. Capt., Seaforth Hdrs. (W.) *M.C. M.* 1906
Killed in action in Mesopotamia 21 *Jan.* 1916
RIGBY, J. C. A. Major, S. African Med. Corps   1890
RIGG, R. Major, Border Regt. *O.B.E.*   1897
RILEY, Rev. C. L. C.F. 4th Class, Australian Chaplains' 1906
Dept.
RILEY, Rt. Rev. C. O. L. *See* PERTH, ARCHBISHOP OF
RIPLEY, H. E. R. Lieut., R.A.S.C. *m.*   1902
RIX, R. G. Gnr., H.A.C.   1903
ROBATHAN, K. M. Capt., I.A.R.O., attd. 2nd Gurkha 1908
Rifles
ROBERTS, A. D. Pte., R. Fusiliers (P. S. Bn.); Capt., 1907
Welsh Regt. (W.) *M.C.*
ROBERTS, C. J. Lieut., R. Welsh Fus.   1915
ROBERTS, F. M. 2nd Lieut. (T.), R.A.F.   1893
✠ROBERTS, F. P. Pte., R.A.S.C.   1897
Died 25 *Aug.* 1915
ROBERTSON-SHERSBY-HARVIE, R. Lieut., R.N.V.R.   1909
ROBINSON, C. A. Capt., R.A.M.C.(T.F.)   1890
ROBINSON, H. D. Paymaster Sub-Lieut., R.N.R.   1907
✠ROGERS, E. H. 2nd Lieut., R. Warwickshire Regt.   1910
Killed in action 3 *July* 1916

ROGERS, G. F. Capt., R.A.M.C. (1st E. Gen. Hospital, 1885
T.F.)

ROLSTON, A. C. Lieut., R.E.(T.F.) 1906

ROMER, C. Capt., R.E., attd. Gen. Staff. *M.C. M. m.* 1902

ROOKE, C. P. Major, Middlesex Regt.; Lieut.-Col., R. 1893
Warwickshire Regt.; Lieut.-Col. (T.), R.A.F. (W.)
D.S.O. M.

ROSCOE, W. Lieut., S. Lancs. Regt.; Major, M.G.C. 1907
(W.) *M.*

ROTH, G. J. Lieut., 166me Regt., French Army; Capt., 1911
155me Regt. (W 2.) *Chevalier, Legion of Honour
(France). French Croix de Guérre. M* 2.

ROUTH, L. M. Capt., R.A.M.C. (P.) 1902

RUSHFORTH, F. V. Lieut., I.A.R.O.; Controller of War 1907
Accounts

RUSSELL, E. C. Major, London Regt. (Blackheath and 1896
Woolwich Bn., T.F. Res.); G.S.O. 3. *m.*

RUSSELL, J. C. Major, R.F.A. *M.C. Belgian Croix de* 1907
Guerre

✠RUTHERFORD, W. McC. Pte., R.A.M.C.; 2nd Lieut., E. 1908
Yorks. Regt.
Died 19 *April* 1918 *of wounds received in action*

RYAN, J. Major, R.E. (Signals). (W.) *M.C. M.* 1913

SABIN, J. H. Capt., R. Welsh Fus.(T.F.) (W.) 1911

SALOMONS, Sir D., Bart. Hon. Colonel, R.E. (Fortress, 1870
T.F.)

✠SALOMONS, D. R. H. P. Capt., R.E. (Fortress, T.F.) 1904
Drowned on H.M.S. Hythe 28 *Oct.* 1915

SANCTUARY, A. G. E. Lieut., R.F.A.(T.F.); empld. War 1910
Office

SANCTUARY, C. T. Capt., R.F.A.(T.F.); Hon. Capt. (A.), 1908
R.A.F.

✠SANDERSON, F. B. 2nd Lieut., R.F.A.(T.F.) 1907
Died 10 *Aug.* 1916 *of wounds received in action*

SANDERSON, R. E. R. Surgeon Sub-Lieut., R.N.V.R. 1914

SANFORD, D. W. Capt., R.E. *M. Greek Medal for* 1909
Military Merit, 3rd Class

SARGEAUNT, G. M. 2nd Lieut., Marlborough College 1902
O.T.C.

SAUNDER, D. A. Lieut., N. Staffs. Regt.; attd. R.E. (Sig- 1910
nals). *M.C.*

SAUNDERS, E. G. S. Capt., R.A.M.C. (4th S. Gen. Hos- 1883
pital, T.F.)

SAUNDERS, H.   Capt., R.A.M.C.   1879
SAVILE, W. S.   Capt., Dorset Yeo.   1874
✠SCHAEFER, T. S. H.   Lieut., Northumberland Fus.   1910
   Killed in action in the Battle of Loos 26 Sept. 1915
SCHLESINGER, G. L.   Capt., Somerset L.I.   (W 2.)   1908
SCHOLFIELD, J. A.   Capt. and Adjt., Manchester Regt.   1907
   (T.F.) (W.) (P.)
SCHONLAND, B. F. J.   Capt., R.E.   *O.B.E.   M.*   1915
SCHURR, C. G.   Capt., R.A.M.C.   1911
SCOTT, J.   Capt., R.A.M.C.   1875
SCOTT, R. S.   Major., R.A.M.C.   *M.*   1906
SCOWCROFT, H. E.   Surgeon Lieut., R.N.   1890
SCRIMGEOUR, G. C.   Major, R.F.A.(T.F.)   *D.S.O.   M.C.*   1905
   and Bar.   M.
SEDGWICK, R.E.   Capt., R.A.M.C.   1893
SELL, F. W.   Capt., Med. Res. Corps, United States Army   1888
✠SELLARS, E. F.   Capt., Cheshire Regt.   (W 2.)   *M.C.   M.* 1914
   Killed in action in Macedonia 18 Sept. 1918
SEPHTON, R.   Lieut.-Col., R.E.   *M* 2.   *Order of the Rising* 1901
   Sun, 4th Class (Japan)
SHANN, S. E. T.   Hon. Capt., R.A.M.C.   1901
SHARP, J. E.   Capt., R.A.M.C.   1907
SHARP, L. W.   Hon. Capt., R.A.M.C.   1901
SHAW, A. G.   Lieut.-Col., The Queen's (R. W. Surrey   1884
   Regt.)   *Brevet Colonel.   m* 2.
SHAW, R. D.   Capt., Hampshire Regt.   *M.C.*   1913
SHELDON, H. F.   Capt., R.A.M.C.   1890
SHELLEY, L. W.   Capt., R.A.M.C.   1906
SHEPPARD, G.   Capt., R.G.A.   *M.C.*   1895
✠SHERMAN, R.   Capt., R.A.M.C.   1906
   Died 10 Oct. 1917 of wounds received in action
SHOWELL-ROGERS, E. N.   Lieut., 5th (R. Irish) Lancers;   1909
   A.D.C.
SHUTTE, M. W.   Capt., R.A.M.C.   1892
SIDEBOTHAM, F. L.   Major, R.E.(T.F.)   (W.)   *M.C.*   1912
SIDEBOTHAM, J. B.   Lieut., R.E.(T.F.); Lieut. (E.O.),   1911
   R.F.C.   (W.)
SILBURN, L.   Lieut., R.A.S.C.(T.F.); attd. Durham L.I.   1910
✠SIMON, Sir R. M.   Lieut.-Col., R.A.M.C.(T.F.)   1870
   Died 22 Dec. 1914
SIMONDS, C. C. B.   Lieut., R.E.(T.F.)   1910
SIMPSON, Rev. J. B.   C.F. 4th Class, R.A.C.D.   *M.*   1899
SIMPSON, J. C.   Capt., R.A.M.C. (1st E. Gen. Hospital,   1898
   T.F.)

SIMPSON, W. H.   Pte., Cambridgeshire Regt.; Lce.-Corpl.,   1897
Northamptonshire Regt.; Capt., R.G.A.   *m.*
SINGTON, H. S.   Surgeon Lieut., R.N.   1896
SKELDING, H.   Major, R.A.M.C.(T.F.)   1879
SKINNER, J. A. D.   Surgeon Lieut., R.N.   1910
SLATER, F. C.   Lieut., King's Own (R. Lancaster Regt.)   1913
SMALLEY, S.   Lieut., Cambridgeshire Regt. and I.A.R.O.,   1912
attd. 69th Punjabis
SMALLWOOD, A. McN.   Lieut., Northumberland Fus.;   1914
Capt., Spec. List (P. and B.T. Staff)
SMART, A. H. J.   Surgeon Lieut., R.N.   1913
SMITH, Rev. E. W.   C.F. 4th Class, R.A.C.D.   *M.C.   M.*   1901
SMITH, G. B., C.M.G.   Colonel (Chief Paymaster), Army   1879
Pay Dept.   *C.B.   M* 3.
SMITH, H. E.   Lieut., The Queen's (R.W. Surrey Regt.)   1910
(W 2.)
SMITH, K. P.   Capt., Northamptonshire Regt.   *M.C.   M.*   1912
SMITH, S. H.   Lieut., Cheshire Regt.; Major, Gen. Staff.   1907
M.C.   M 2.   *French Croix de Guerre*
✠SMITH, S. P.   Capt., S. Staffs. Regt.(T.F.)   (W.)   1907
Killed in action 28 *Feb.* 1917
SMITH, T. L.   Corpl., R. Fusiliers (P.S.Bn.); Lieut., Black   1911
Watch
SMITH, W. E.   Capt., R.A.S.C.   1911
SNELL, H. C.   Capt., R.A.M.C. (3rd N. Gen. Hospital,   1901
T.F.)
SNELL, J. A. B.   Surgeon Lieut., R.N.   1908
✠SOLLY, A. N.   Sergt., R. Fusiliers (P.S. Bn.); 2nd Lieut.,   1913
Manchester Regt.; Capt. (A.), R.F.C.   (W.)
Killed in action 11 *Aug.* 1917
SOMERS-CLARKE, G.   Major (T.), R.A.F.   *O.B.E.   M.*   1899
SOMERVELL, T. H.   Capt., R.A.M.C.(T.F.)   *M.*   1909
✠SPARENBORG, H. R.   Capt., King's Own (R. Lancaster   1894
Regt.)
Killed in action at Le Cateau 26 *Aug.* 1914
SPARKS, C. E.   Hon. Lieut., R.A.M.C.   1888
SPARROW, G.   Surgeon Lieut., R.N.; attd. R.N.D.   *M.C.*   1905
SPEAKMAN, L. A.   Lieut., Haileybury College O.T.C.   1903
SPEARMAN, B.   Med. Officer, E. African Force   1896
SPEARMAN, W.   Lieut., Devon Regt.; Capt., Gen. List   1900
(Courts-Martial Officer)
SPENCE, R. B.   Major, 96th Berar Infy., Indian Army;   1901
D.A.A. and Q.M.G.   *O.B.E.   M* 3.
SQUIRES, F. V.   Lieut., R.F.A.   (W.)   1913

STAFFORD, H. N. Capt., R.A.M.C. (W.) *M.C. M.* 1909
STANLEY-CLARK, C. Capt., R.A.M.C. 1898
STEPHENS, J. W. W. Lieut.-Col., R.A.M.C. 1884
STEPHENSON, H. M. Capt., R.A.M.C. (W.) *M.C.* 1906
STEVENS, G. H. Lieut., R.F.A.; attd. R.E. *M.* 1908
STEVENS, L. B. Capt., R.F.A.; Staff Capt. *M.C.* 1904
STEWART, F. H. Major, I.M.S. 1900
STEWART, W. H. E. Capt., R.A.M.C.(T.F.) *M.C.* 1893
STEWART-SAVILE, W. S. *See* SAVILE, W. S.
STIFF, H. H. Capt., R.A.M.C. 1892
STIRLING, E. M. Capt.. London Regt. (London Scottish); 1901
  Major, R.E. (W.)
STOREY, H. H. Lieut., R.E.(T.F.); Lieut. (A.), R.A.F. 1913
STOREY, L. H. T. Lieut., R.N.V.R. 1907
STRADLING, A. R. Capt., R.A.S.C. *M.* 1905
STRATTON, F. J. M. Capt., Unattd. List, T.F.; Lieut.- 1901
  Col., R.E. (Signals); A. D. Signals. *D.S.O. Brevet*
  Lieut.-Colonel. M 5. *Chevalier, Legion of Honour*
  (*France*)
STRETTON, J. W. Capt., R.A.M.C. (1st S. Gen. Hospital, 1906
  T.F.) *m.*
STRICKLAND, A. F. P.O., R.N.V.R. (R.N.D.); Capt., 1905
  R.G.A. (W.) *M.C.*
STRICKLAND, C. Capt., N. Zealand Med. Corps 1899
STUART, A. A. P. R. Capt. and Adjt., Manchester Regt.; 1899
  Major, Sherwood Foresters (Notts. and Derby Regt.)
STUART, R. S. D. Capt., Gloucestershire Regt.(T.F.) 1910
  (W 2.)
STURGESS, J. Capt., R.F.A.(T.F.) 1908
SUHR, A. C. H. *See* HAMMOND SEARLE, A. C. 1899
SUMMERS, G. Lieut., R.E.(T.F.); Capt., Spec. List 1910
SUTCLIFFE, J. H. Lieut., Essex Regt. 1904
SUTHERLAND, F. B. Lieut., Durham L.I.; Major, M.G.C. 1912
SUTHERLAND, J. F. Lieut., R.G.A.(T.F.) 1908
SVENSSON, R. Lieut.-Col., R.A.M.C. *D.S.O.   M.C.* 1900
  M 2. *French Croix de Guerre*
SWAINSON, E. A. C. Capt., R.A.M.C. 1886
SWANN, M. B. R. Surgeon Lieut., R.N. 1912
SWIFT, B. H. Capt., R.A.M.C. *M.C.* 1911
SWINDLEHURST, J. E. Lieut., R.E.(T.F.) 1908
SWINDLEHURST, T. R. Lieut., R.F.A.; attd. T.M.B. *M.* 1913
✠SYKES, E. T. Capt., D. of Wellington's (W. Riding Regt., 1913
  T.F.) (W.)
  Killed in action 3 *May* 1917

SYKES, S. W.   Capt., Spec. List (Intelligence).   *O.B.E.*   1903
M.C. M 3.
SYME, G. W.   2nd Lieut., Gordon Hdrs.; Lieut., R.F.A.;   1908
empld. Ministry of Munitions.   (W 2.)
SYMNS, J. LL. M.   Major, R.A.M.C.(T.F.)   1904
SYMNS, J. M.   Major, I.A.R.O.; G.S.O. 2   1898
SYMONDS, F. C.   Capt., Cambridgeshire Regt.   1906
SYMPSON, E. M.   Lieut.-Col., R.A.M.C. (4th N. Gen.   1879
Hospital, T.F.)

TAIT, W. H.   2nd Lieut., R.E.   (W.)   *French Médaille* [1914]
Militaire
TALLERMAN, K. H.   Capt., R.F.A.   (W.)   *M.C.*   1913
✠TAPP, T. A.   Capt., Coldstream Gds. and M.G.C.   (W.)   1902
M.C. and Bar. M.
Died 21 *Oct.* 1917 *of wounds received in action* 11 *Oct.*
1917
TAYLOR, A. R.   Capt., Dulwich College O.T.C.   1900
TAYLOR, C. H. S.   Lieut.-Col. (Med.), R.A.F.; S.O. 2,   1901
Air Ministry. *M.*
✠TAYLOR, C. P.   Capt., E. Yorks. Regt. *M.*   1914
Killed in action 28 *Oct.* 1916
TAYLOR, C. R.   Capt., R.A.M.C. *O.B.E. M.*   1906
TAYLOR, E. J. D.   Major, R.A.M.C. (5th S. Gen. Hos-   1892
pital, T.F.)
TAYLOR, E. L. T.   Lieut., R.G.A.   1897
TAYLOR, Rev. G. H.   C.F. 4th Class, R.A.C.D.   1910
TAYLOR, S. H. S.   Capt., R.A.M.C.   1897
TEICHMANN, O.   Capt., R.A.M.C.(T.F.)   (W 3.) *D.S.O.*   1898
M.C. M 2. *French Croix de Guerre. Italian Croce*
di Guerra
TELFORD, E. D.   Capt., R.A.M.C.(T.F.)   1894
TEWSON, E. G.   Lieut., R.G.A.   1905
✠THOMAS, D. C. W.   Capt., Argyll and Sutherland Hdrs.;   1908
attd. Gordon Hdrs.
Killed in action 12 *Nov.* 1914
THOMAS, F. G.   Major, R.A.M.C. (3rd W. Gen. Hos-   1890
pital, T.F.)
THOMAS, G. E. A.   *See* AERON-THOMAS, G. E.
THOMAS, J. G. T.   Capt., R.A.M.C. *M.C.*   1910
THOMAS, T. P.   Capt., R.A.M.C.(T.F.)   1893
✠THOMASSET, G. T.   Lieut., London Regt. (Blackheath   1913
and Woolwich Bn.)
Killed in action 25 *Sept.* 1915

THOMPSON, J. H. G. Cadet, O.C.B.   191'
THOMPSON, O. S. Surgeon Lieut., R.N.   191(
THOMPSON, R. C. Capt., Spec. List (Intelligence). *M* 3.   189!
THOMPSON, R. M. Lieut., R.G.A.   191:
THOMPSON, T. W. Capt., R.E. *M.*   189(
✠THOMPSTONE, R. Lieut., S. Staffs. Regt. (W.)   [1914
    Died 25 Jan. 1921 of illness contracted on active service
    during the war
THOMSON, G. D. Pte., London Regt. (Artists Rifles);   191:
    Lieut., R.A.S.C.; attd. R.A.F.
✠THORBURN, E. F. Lieut., Manchester Regt.(T.F.)   191:
    Killed in action in Gallipoli 10 June 1915
THORNTON, L. H. Colonel, Rifle Brigade; A.Q.M.G. *1911
    C.M.G. D.S.O. M 4.
THORP, R. C. 2nd Lieut., R.F.A.   1914
THRELFALL, C. R. F. Capt., R.E. (Signals). *M.C.*   191:
THRELFALL, R. E. Lieut., R.E. (Signals); empld. Ministry   191c
    of Munitions
THRELFALL, W. B. Lieut., R.N.V.R.   1914
THRESHER, W. H. Capt., R.A.M.C.   189(
✠THURLOW, A. G. 2nd Lieut., D. of Wellington's (W.   1911
    Riding Regt.)
    Died 29 Aug. 1918 of wounds received in action in
    Gallipoli 21 Aug. 1918
TIDMAN, O. P. Lieut., R.N.A.S. and Naval Transport   1902
    Service
TIMS, R. D. MARETT. Lieut., London Regt.; Capt.,   1909
    Northumberland Fus. and Training Res. Bn. (W.)
✠TODD, A. F. Capt., Norfolk Regt. *M.*   1892
    Killed in action at Hill 60 21 April 1915
TODHUNTER, J. R. A. D. Capt., R.A.M.C.   1904
TONKS, J. W. Capt., R.A.M.C.   1906
TOPHAM, D. B. Lieut., Middlesex Regt.(T.F.) and Grena-   1910
    dier Gds.
✠TOPPIN, S. M. Major, R.G.A. *M.C. M*.   1896
    Died 27 Sept. 1917 of wounds received in action
TORREY, J. Corpl. R.E. (Signals)   191:
TOTTENHAM, C. E. L. 2nd Lieut., Middlesex Regt.   1906
TOWNSEND, A. L. H. E. African Force   1904
✠TRAFFORD, G. T. Lieut., Life Gds.; Capt., Tank Corps. [1914]
    (W 2.) *M.*
    Killed in action 23 July 1918
TRAPNELL, H. Capt., Gloucestershire Regt. (T.F.); attd.   1913
    R.E.

TRAVIS-CLEGG, G. R.   2nd Lieut., Loyal N. Lancs. Regt   1913
(T.F.)

✠TREGELLES, G. P.   Capt., Devon Regt.   *M.*   1911
Killed in action 1 July 1916

TREVES, F. B.   Major, R.A.M.C.(T.F.)   *O.B.E. M.*   1898

TREVES, W. W.   Major, R.A.M.C.   *O.B.E. M* 4.   1901

TROLLOPE, T. A.   Lieut., R.A.S.C.(T.F.); attd. Rifle   1912
Brigade

TUCKER, E. G.   Pte., R. Fusiliers; Sapper, R.E. (Signals);   1904
attd. Intelligence Staff.   *M.M. and Bar*

TUCKETT, J. E. S., T.D.   Major, Marlborough College   1889
O.T.C.

TURCAN, J. S.   Major, Seaforth Hdrs.   (W 4.)   *M.C.*   1909

TURNER, Rev. H. A.   C.F. 4th Class, R.A.C.D.   1895

TWEEDIE, F. I. G.   Capt., Manchester Regt.(T.F.)   (W.)   1911

TWEEDIE, J. M.   Capt., R.A.S.C.; Major, D.A.D.Canteens,   1903
War Office.   *M* 2.

✠TWEEDIE, L. K.   2nd Lieut., R.F.A.   1908
Killed in action 17 Jan. 1916

TWEEDY, O. M.   Capt., Leinster Regt. and Gen. Staff.   1908
(W.)   *M.*

TWEEDY, R. J.   Capt., 19th Lancers, Indian Army; Staff   1907
Capt.

✠TWEEN, A. S.   Major, Essex Regt.   *D.S.O. M* 2.   1910
Died 23 March 1918 of wounds received in action at Rouez

TWIGG, G. W.   Capt., R.A.M.C.   *M.*   1901

TYSON, W.   Capt., R.A.M.C. (1st E. Gen. Hospital, T.F.   1889
Res.)

UHTHOFF, R. K.   Capt., R.E.   (W.)   *M.C.*   1906

UNDERHILL FAITHORNE, C. F.   Major, Connaught Rangers;   1898
Lieut.-Col., Spec. List (Cmdt., School of Musketry).
(W.)

USHER, C. T.   Major, R.A.M.C.(T.F.)   1883

VAUDREY, W. E.   Major, R.G.A.   (W 2.)   *M.C. and Bar*   1912

VERNON, R. J.   Major, R.A.M.C.   *M.*   1899

VICKERS, S.   Major, R.F.A.(T.F.)   (W.)   *D.S.O. M.*   1910

VIVIAN, C. ST A.   Capt., R.A.M.C.   1901

VOS, P.   Lieut., Norfolk Regt.; empld. War Office.   (W.)   1909
French Croix de Guerre

VYVYAN, M. C.   Lieut., Natal Carabineers and M.G.C.   1910
(W.)

WADDY, A. C. Lieut., R.F.A.(T.F.); Staff Capt. *O.B.E.*   1911
M.

WADSON, F. P. Lce.-Corpl., Lincolnshire Regt.   1895
WAINWRIGHT, C. B. Capt., R.A.M.C.   1905
WALFORD, H. H. Lieut., R.A.S.C.(T.F.)   1906
WALKER, A. C. Major, R.F.A. (W.) *M.C.*   1911
WALKER, C. A. P. Lieut., Highland L.I.; attd. 44th Infy.,   1912
Indian Army
WALKER, D. Lieut., King's (Liverpool Regt.); Capt.,   1913
M.G.C. (W.) *M. Belgian Croix de Guerre*
WALKER, K. M. Capt., R.A.M.C. *O.B.E. M* 3.   1901
WALKER, W. J. Sergt., Army Pay Corps; attd. R.E.   1913
WALKER, W. M. Lieut., King's (Liverpool Regt.). (W.)   1911
M.C.
WALLACE, R. W. J. Lieut., R.F.A. (W 2.)   1908
WANKLYN, W.McC. Capt.,R.A.M.C.(T.F.);D.A.D.M.S.   1885
WARD, G. H. Surgeon Sub-Lieut., R.N.V.R.   1911
WARDEN, A. R. S. Surgeon Lieut., R.N.   1906
WARDEN, G. Pte., King's Own (Yorkshire L.I.) and   1913
Wiltshire Regt.; Sergt., Devon Regt.
WARDLE, Rev. W. L. C.F. 4th Class, R.A.C.D.   1895
WARNER, Rev. M. C.F. 4th Class, R.A.C.D.   1897
✠WARNER, T. L. Major, Leicestershire Regt. (W 2.)   1913
D.S.O. M 3.
Died 27 *Dec.* 1917 *of wounds received in action*
WARNES, G. G. Capt., Suffolk Regt.(T.F.) (W.)   1911
WATERMEYER, E. F. Lieut., Cape Garrison Artillery   1899
WATERMEYER, H. A. Capt., R.A.M.C.   1906
WATERWORTH, S. Capt., Loyal N. Lancs. Regt. (W 2.)   1912
M.C.
WATKINS, D. J. G. Major, R.A.M.C. (4th N. Gen. Hos-   1886
pital, T.F.)
WATKINS, W. B. Capt., R.F.A.(T.F.) (W.)   1910
WATSON, F. H. Surgeon Lieut., R.N.V.R.   1904
WATSON, W. G. Surgeon Lieut., R.N.   1905
WATSON WILLIAMS, E. Major, R.A.M.C. *M.C.*   1909
WATT, G. T. C. Lieut., King's College School, Wimble-   1905
don, O.T.C.
WATTS, E. M. Capt., R.F.A. (W.) *M.C.*   1912
WEAVER-ADAMS, E. R. Lieut., R.E. (Signals). *M.*   1913
WEBB, T. L. Capt., Yorkshire Regt.   1903
✠WEDD, E. P. W. Capt., Essex Yeo.; Staff Capt.; Capt.,   1902
R.A.M.C. *M.C. M.*
Killed in action 13 *July* 1918

✠WEDGWOOD, A.   2nd Lieut., Northumberland Fus.   1911
    Killed in action 19 *Aug.* 1915
WEEKS, LL. M.   Major, R.A.M.C. (W.) *M.C.*   1905
WEEKS, R. M.   Major, Rifle Brigade; G.S.O.2. *D.S.O.*   1909
    M.C. and Bar.   Brevet Major.   M 3.   *French Croix
    de Guerre*
✠WEGG, H. N.   Capt., Middlesex Regt.   1900
    Killed in action 25 *March* 1918
WEGG, W. H. J.   2nd Lieut., R.G.A.   1895
✠WELLS, N. L.   Lieut., Loyal N. Lancs. Regt.   1906
    Killed in action in Gallipoli 10 *Aug.* 1915
WELLS-COLE, G. C.   Capt., R.A.M.C.   1913
WELSFORD, A. G.   Capt., R.A.M.C. *m.*   1883
✠WELSFORD, G. J. L.   2nd Lieut., Middlesex Regt. and   1913
    R.F.C. (W.)
    Killed in action 30 *March* 1916
WEST, F. R.   2nd Lieut., King's Royal Rifle Corps   1912
WEST, P. C.   Capt., R.A.M.C.   1896
WESTON, G. H.   Capt., R.A.M.C. (Sanitary Service, T.F.)   1879
✠WETENHALL, W. T.   Capt., Leicestershire Regt.   1907
    Killed in action 16 *July* 1916
WHELDON, E. J.   2nd Lieut., R.E.   1907
✠WHITAKER, T. S.   2nd Lieut., D. of Wellington's (W.   1911
    Riding Regt., T.F.)
    Killed in action 7 *Nov.* 1915
✠WHITBY, J. H.   Capt., London Regt. (St Pancras Bn.)   1912
    M.
    Died 16 *March* 1916 *of illness contracted on active
    service*
WHITCOMBE, E. P.   Lieut., Worcestershire Regt. (W.)   1913
WHITCOMBE, R. H., V.D.   Major, R.A.S.C.(T.F.) *D.S.O.* *1880
    M 2.
✠WHITE, C. W. M.   2nd Lieut., Norfolk Regt.   [1914]
    Killed in action 26 *Sept.* 1915
WHITE, G. F.   Air Mechanic, R.A.F.   1894
✠WHITEHEAD, A. G.   2nd Lieut., W. Yorks. Regt.(T.F.);   1911
    Capt. (A.), R.F.C.
    Killed in action 29 *Jan.* 1918
WHITEHEAD, C. E.   Capt., R.A.M.C.(T.F.) (W 2.)   1901
WHITFIELD, E. O.   2nd Lieut., S. Staffs. Regt.   1912
WHITING, E. R. S. M.   Pte., R.A.M.C.   1912
WHITMORE, A.   Major, I.M.S.   1894
WHITTALL, H. C.   Lieut.-Cdr., R.N.V.R. *O.B.E. Officer,*   1907
    Order of the Redeemer (*Greece*)

WHITTY, H. N. Capt., London Regt. (Kensington Bn.) 1901
(W 2.)
WHITWORTH, J. Lieut., R. 1st Devon Yeo.; attd. Devon 1902
Regt.(T.F.)
WIDDICOMBE, E. P. Lieut., I.A.R.O., attd. Sappers and *1899
Miners; Capt., Spec. List; Major, R.E. *M.*
✠WIGGIN, N. H. Lieut., R.F.A. *M.* 1914
Died 11 *Jan.* 1917 *of wounds received in action*
WIGMORE, J. B. A. Lieut.-Col., R.A.M.C. *M* 2. 1905
✠WILEMAN, G. W. B. Capt., S. Wales Borderers. (W.) 1909
Killed in action 8 *Sept.* 1916
✠WILKINSON, G. J. Sergt., Middlesex Regt. 1905
Killed in action 1 *July* 1916
WILKINSON, N. Lieut., Bombay Garrison Artillery, In- 1909
dian Defence Force
WILKS, J. H. Capt., R.A.M.C. 1884
WILLCOCKS, R. W. Capt., R.A.M.C. *M.* 1905
WILLEY, H. L. Capt., King's Own (Yorkshire L.I.) (W.) 1913
✠WILLEY, R. H. D. Pte., R.A.M.C. and R. Fusiliers (P. S. 1905
Bn.); Capt., 13th Hussars
Died at Amadia 14 *July* 1919 *of wounds received in action*
WILLIAMS, A. C. 2nd Lieut., R.E.; Capt., Corps of 1889
Military Accountants
WILLIAMS, A. D. J. B. Major, E. African Med. Service. 1902
O.B.E. M 4.
WILLIAMS, A. F. Lieut., R.E.(T.F.); empld. Ministry of 1913
Labour
WILLIAMS, A. G. Surgeon Lieut., R.N. (W.) *O.B.E.* 1907
M. French Croix de Guerre
WILLIAMS, Rev. A. J. Chaplain, R.N. 1902
WILLIAMS, Rev. C. C.F. 4th Class, R.A.C.D. 1900
WILLIAMS, C. E. Lieut.-Col., I.M.S. 1884
WILLIAMS, E. K. Capt., R.A.M.C. 1896
WILLIAMS, G. C. Capt., R.A.M.C.(T.F.) 1910
WILLIAMS, J. C. S. Capt., R.A.S.C. 1902
WILLIAMS, J. L. C. Capt., R. Welsh Fus. (W.) 1910
WILLIAMS, J. S. Capt., R.F.A. and Gen. Staff. (W.) 1914
M.C. M.
WILLIAMS, M. B. Major, Welsh Regt. (W.) 1899
WILLIAMS, N. A. Lieut., M.G.C. (Motor) [1914]
✠WILLIAMS, R. B. Capt., R.E. *M.C. M.* 1905
Killed in action 19 *Sept.* 1916
WILLIAMS, R. F. Capt., R.A.M.C. (W.) *M.C. M* 2. 1894
WILLIAMS, R. G. Lieut., W. African Frontier Force 1902

✠Williams, S. C. Lieut., R.F.A.   1912
Killed in action 18 *Jan.* 1917
Williams, S. R. K. Edward's Horse   1912
Williams, Rev. T. B. C.F. 4th Class, R.A.C.D.   1905
Williams, W. P. Lieut., R. Fusiliers; empld. War Office   1914
✠Williamson, J. M. Pte., London Regt. (Artists Rifles);   1908
2nd Lieut., Gordon Hdrs.
Killed in action 16 *May* 1915
✠Willink, H. J. L. Pte., R. Fusiliers (P. S. Bn.); Capt.,   1903
D. of Wellington's (W. Riding Regt.)
Died 5 *Nov.* 1918 *of wounds received in action* 1 *Nov.*
1918
Wilson, A. G. Capt., R.A.M.C.(T.F.) *M.*   1892
Wilson, Rev. J. V. C.F. 4th Class, R.A.C.D.   1900
Wimbush, G. S. H.A.C.   1908
Wimbush, Rev. R. C.F. 4th Class, R.A.C.D.   1905
Wimperis, H. E. Lieut.-Cdr., R.N.V.R.; Major (T.),   1898
R.A.F. (Aircraft Production Dept.) *O.B.E.*
Winder, J. F. E. Lieut., Oxford and Bucks. L.I.   1894
Winslow, W. Capt., R.A.M.C.   1883
Winter, P. G. D. Capt., R. Defence Corps   1892
Winter, W. H. Capt., Herefordshire Regt. and M.G.C.   1901
Winterbotham, F. P. Lieut., R.G.A. *M.*   1904
Wolff, L. Soldat-Secrétaire, French Army   1906
Wood, C. S. Lce.-Corpl., R.E.   1907
Wood, D. E. Lieut.-Col., Remount Service; Inspector of   1871
Remounts. *C.B. M.*
Wood, E. C. Corpl., R.E. (Signals)   1913
✠Wood, E. H. 2nd Lieut., Hampshire Regt.   1904
Killed in action 23 *Oct.* 1916
✠Wood, J. W. M., m.v.o. Lieut.-Col., Remount Service;   1873
D.A.D. Remounts
Died 9 *Dec.* 1916
Woodhouse, G. F. Capt., Unattd. List, T.F.   1893
Woodruff, G. G. Lieut., R.F.A.; empld. Ministry of   1905
Munitions. *M.*
Woodsend, P. D. Capt., R.A.S.C.   1910
Woolf, H. M. A. 2nd Lieut., R.A.S.C.; Hon. Capt.,   1907
Spec. List
Woollcombe-Boyce, K. W. Sergt., R. Fusiliers; attd.   1907
Infy. Bde. H.Q. *M.S.M. M.*
Woolward, A. T. Lieut., R.F.A.; Capt., R.A.M.C. *M.*   1909
✠Wordsworth, J. L. Lieut., 5th (R. Irish) Lancers   1901
Killed in action 4 *Nov.* 1914

WORSLEY-WORSWICK, C. F. 2nd Lieut., R. Welsh Fus.; 1904
Lieut., Leicestershire Regt.
WORTHINGTON, C. R. Capt., Canadian A.M.C. 1895
WORTLEY, Rev. R. W. C.F. 4th Class, R.A.C.D. 1897
WRIGHT, C. S. Capt., R.E.; G.S.O. 3. *O.B.E. M.C.* 1908
M 2. *Chevalier, Legion of Honour (France)*
WRIGHT, H. M. Lieut., Black Watch; attd. King's African 1906
Rifles. (W.) *M.C.*
WRIGHT, M. E. A. Major (T.), R.A.F. (Aircraft Produc- 1912
tion Dept.) *A.F.C. M. Belgian Croix de Guerre*
WYLLIE, A. K., C.B. Hon. Colonel, D. of Wellington's 1874
(W. Riding Regt.)
WYMAN, B. Lieut., Cheshire Regt. (T.F.); attd. R.E. (W.) 1902
WYNNE-YORKE, B. A. Y. Lieut., E. Yorks. Regt.; empld. 1907
P. and B.T. Staff

YEATS, B. E. 2nd Lieut., R. Scots (T.F.) 1905
YEOMANS, F. A. Capt., N. Staffs. Regt.(T.F.) 1913
YOLLAND, R. H. Capt., R.A.M.C. *M.* 1909
YOUNG, M. L. 2nd Lieut., R. Sussex Regt. (W.) 1913

ZIEGLER, G. G. Capt., R. Fusiliers. (W 2.) *M.C. M.* 1913

JESUS COLLEGE

ADAMI, J. G. Colonel, Canadian A.M.C.; A.D.M.S. *1891
C.B.E.

ADDY, R. Capt., E. Yorks. Regt. 1910

AINLEY, J. A. G. Lieut., Durham L.I. and M.G.C. 1911

✠AINLEY, Rev. W. P. C.F. 4th Class, R.A.C.D. 1906
Died 12 Oct. 1915 of cerebro-spinal meningitis

AKHURST, A. F. Instructor Lieut., R.N. 1912

✠ALDERSON, A. E. Lieut., The Queen's (R. W. Surrey 1902
Regt.); Capt., King's Own (Yorkshire L.I.)
Accidentally drowned 11 March 1918

✠ALDOUS, A. E. Trooper, 12th Lancers; 2nd Lieut., Bor- 1911
der Regt. (W.)
Killed in action 3 July 1916

ALDOUS, F. C. Major, Manchester Regt. (T.F.); Lieut.- 1898
Col., M.G.C. (W.) D.S.O. M 2.

✠ALLEN, J. H. Lieut., Worcestershire Regt. 1907
Killed in action in Gallipoli 21 June 1915

✠ALLEN, R. G. R. 2nd Lieut., W. Yorks. Regt.(T.F.); 1908
attd. R.F.C.
Killed in action 16 Nov. 1916

✠ALLISON, H. S. Major, R. Irish Rifles. M. 1911
Killed in action 7 Aug. 1917

ALLISON, W. W. Lieut., R. Sussex Regt., M.G.C., and 1914
R.G.A. M.

ALSTON, C. R. 2nd Lieut., S. Lancs. Regt.; Capt. (A.), 1912
R.A.F. (W.)

ANDERSON, Rev. F. I. C.F. 1st Class, R.A.C.D. C.M.G. 1893
M 5. Officer, Order of the Crown of Italy

ANDREW, R. H. Lce.-Sergt., R.H.A.; Capt., Suffolk 1903
Regt.; Lieut.-Col., Spec. List (D.A.M.S.) O.B.E.
M.C. M. Order of the Nile, 3rd Class (Egypt)

ANSTEY, A. Major, Devon Regt. *T.D.*   1892
✠ARMSTRONG, C. 2nd Lieut., R. Fusiliers; attd. Loyal N.   1907
    Lancs. Regt. *M.*
    Killed in action in Mesopotamia 9 April 1916
ARNOLD, B. M. Major, R.G.A.(T.F.) *D.S.O. M.*   1903
✠ARON, E. M. Sub-Lieut., R.N.V.R. (R.N.D.)   1910
    Killed in action 13 *Nov.* 1916
ASTBURY, W. T. Lce.-Corpl., R.A.M.C.   1916
✠ATKIN, K. Capt., R.A.M.C. (P.)   1911
    Died 6 *June* 1918 *of wounds received in action*
✠AYRE, B. P. Capt., Norfolk Regt.   1911
    Killed in action 1 *July* 1916

BAILLIEU, H. L. Lieut., R.G.A. (W.) *M.C.*   1911
BALDWIN, F. E. W. Major, 121st Pioneers, Indian Army;   1898
    D.A.A.G. *M. Order of the Nile, 4th Class*
    (*Egypt*)
✠BANISTER, C. W. 2nd Lieut., R. Fusiliers   1911
    Killed in action 16 *June* 1915
BANISTER, J. B. Capt., R.A.M.C.   1898
BANNING, H. B. S. 2nd Lieut., R.G.A.(T.F.)   1898
BARDWELL, T. G. N. Capt., E. Riding of Yorkshire Yeo.   1903
    and Spec. List, empld. Egyptian Army. *T.D.*
✠BARNARD, H. D. 2nd Lieut., Rifle Brigade   1911
    Killed in action 21 *Aug.* 1916
BARTON, C. H. Pte., S. Staffs. Regt.   1916
BATTY, W. R. Capt., Manchester Regt. *M.C.*   1907
BAYNHAM, C. T. Major, R.H.A. *D.S.O. M* 3.   1908
BAYNHAM, Rev. J.H. C.F. 2nd Class, R.A.C.D.; D.A.C.G.   1893
    M.
BEASLEY, H. O. C. 2nd Lieut., R. Welsh Fus.; Capt.,   1896
    Cameronians (Scottish Rifles); Major, Labour Corps;
    Asst. Controller of Labour. *O.B.E. M.*
BECK, A. C. T., M.P. Hon. Lieut., R.N.V.R.   1895
✠BECKH, R. H. Pte., R. Fusiliers (P.S. Bn.); 2nd Lieut.,   1913
    E. Yorks. Regt.
    Killed in action 16 *Aug.* 1916
BELL, A. C. Capt., R.F.A. (W 2.) *M.C. French Croix*   1911
    de Guerre
BELL, H. A. Capt., R.A.M.C.(T.F.)   1906
BELL, W. B. Capt., 12th Lancers; Major, G.S.O. 2.   1900
    (W.) *Brevet Major. m.*
BELLAMY, J. Sergt., London Regt. (London Scottish);   1903
    Instructor, School of Musketry

BELLHOUSE, A. P. Capt., Welsh Regt.; Lieut., 8th Raj- 1913
puts, Indian Army
BENEY, C. C. Lieut., I.M.S.; Surgeon Lieut., R.N.   1911
BENHAM, J. H. F. Trooper, E. African Mtd. Rifles   1903
BERNEY-FICKLIN, H. P. M. Lieut., Norfolk Regt.; Capt., 1911
Spec. List. (W 2.) (P.) M.C. Brevet Major on pro-
motion to Captain. M 2. Chevalier, Legion of Honour
(France)
BETTERIDGE, C. D. Lieut., R.E.   1910
BETTERIDGE, J. E. H. Pte., R.A.M.C.   1909
BEVAN, Rev. J. C.F. 4th Class, R.A.C.D.   1911
BEVAN, W. H. 2nd Lieut., King's Royal Rifle Corps; 1914
Capt., Gen. List (R.T.O.) (W.)
BICKNELL, C. H., T.D. Capt., Unattd. List, T.F.   1882
BINDLOSS, W. Capt., King's (Liverpool Regt.) and R. 1887
Defence Corps
BLAKER, R. N. R. Lce.-Corpl., Queen's Own (R. W. 1898
Kent Regt.); Lieut., Rifle Brigade. M.C.
BLAND, E. C. 2nd Lieut., Essex Regt. M.   [1914]
BODEN, Rev. J. F. W. Lieut., I.A.R.O., attd. S. and T. 1905
Corps. M.
BOOT, J. C. Capt., Sherwood Foresters (Notts. and 1907
Derby Regt.), and Gen. Staff
BOUQUET, Rev. A. C. C.F. 4th Class, R.A.C.D. m.   *1905
BOWE, J. H. Major, Border Regt. and Gen. List. (W.) 1900
M.
BOWLES, H. F. Hon. Colonel, Middlesex Regt.   1877
✠BOYTON, H. J. Capt., R. Fusiliers; Lieut., Grenadier Gds. 1910
(W.)
Killed in action 14 Dec. 1916
BRACECAMP, F. W. Lieut., R.F.A. M.C.   1910
BRADLEY, E. J. Major, R.A.M.C. (W.) M.C. and Bar. 1908
M.
✠BRADLEY, G. M. Lieut., Rifle Brigade; attd. Welsh Regt. 1911
M.
Killed in action near Festubert 21 Dec. 1914
BRADLEY, V. M. Capt., R.F.A.; Staff Capt.   [1914]
BRADLEY, W. DE W. H. Capt., Wiltshire Regt. (W.) 1907
BRADSTOCK, G. Major, R.F.A. (W.) D.S.O. M.C. and 1907
Bar. M.
BREED, F. G. 2nd Lieut., Suffolk Regt.   1913
BRIGGS, G. R. Major, R.F.A. (W 2.) M.   1908
BROOK, A. K. Lieut., R.A.S.C.   1887
BROOKS, Rev. D. G. Chaplain, R.N.   1893

Brown, G. L. Pte., R.A.M.C.; Lieut., R.A.S.C.; Capt., 1910
Connaught Rangers
✠Brown, G. M. Lieut., 12th Lancers. *M.C.* *M.* 1907
Killed in action 27 Nov. 1917
✠Brown, H. Major, Yorkshire Regt.(T.F.) (W3.) *D.S.O.* 1899
M.C. Brevet Major. M 2. French Croix de Guerre
Killed in action 23 March 1918
✠Brown, K. A. Capt., Cameronians (Scottish Rifles). 1905
(W.) *M.*
Killed in action 14 April 1917
Brown, M. L. C. Capt., M.G.C. [1914]
Brown, V. S. Major (T.), R.A.F. (Aircraft Production 1907
Dept.) *m. French Croix de Guerre*
✠Brunwin-Hales, G. O. Capt., Essex Regt.; Capt. and 1907
Flt. Cdr., R.F.C.
Killed in action 24 March 1917
Brunwin-Hales, Rev. G. T. C.F. 4th Class, R.A.C.D. 1878
m.
Bruty, W. G. Capt., Spec. List (A.P.M.) *M.B.E.* *m 2.* 1888
Brydone, P. 2nd Lieut., R.A.S.C. 1895
✠Bullen, R. E. Capt., King's Royal Rifle Corps. (W 2.) 1911
M.
Died 19 April 1916 *of wounds received in action*
✠Bullough, J. L. Lieut., Argyll and Sutherland Hdrs. 1912
Killed in action 25 Sept. 1915
Bulmer, A. C. Lieut., E. Yorks. Regt.; attd. R.E. (Signals). 1909
M.
Burnard, C. F., d.s.o. Major, R. Warwickshire Regt. and 1894
Labour Corps
Burrough, Rev. J. C.F. 3rd Class, R.A.C.D. 1892
Burton, D. C. F. Lieut., Northumberland Fus.; empld. 1906
Foreign Office
✠Butt, H. A. Capt., Gloucestershire Regt. 1887
Killed in action 8 June 1916

Calthorpe, Hon. F. S. G. *See* Gough-Calthorpe, Hon.
F. S.
Calvert-Jones, H. F. Capt., R.F.A. and Gen. Staff. *M.* 1912
Cameron, A. G. Capt., Argyll and Sutherland Hdrs. and 1913
Tank Corps. *M.C.*
Campbell, F. R. M. Capt., 91st Punjabis, Indian Army 1902
Cane, E. G. S. Capt., R.A.M.C. (P.) *D.S.O.* *M.* 1904
Card, F. W. F. Lieut., 1st Dragoon Gds. *M.C.* 1909

✠CARMICHAEL, D. Capt., Rifle Brigade 1911
Killed in action in the Ypres Salient 25 Sept. 1915
CARROLL, F. H. Capt., Devon Regt. 1907
CARTER, J. L. Pte., King's (Liverpool Regt.); Lieut., 1913
Manchester Regt. (W.)
✠CARTWRIGHT, E. Lce.-Corpl., Canadian Infy. 1904
Died 11 Oct. 1916 of wounds received in action
✠CARVER, L. H. L. 2nd Lieut., Irish Gds. 1902
Killed in action 26 May 1918
CAZALET, G. L. Capt., R. Fusiliers; Brigade Major. 1909
(W 2.) *D.S.O. M.C. M* 2.
CHAMPION, R. E. Cadet, O.C.B. 1910
✠CHANDLER, E. S. 2nd Lieut., Sherwood Foresters (Notts. 1914
and Derby Regt.)
Killed in action near Ypres 14 Feb. 1916
CHANDLER, F. G. Capt., R.A.M.C. 1905
CHANDLER, K. S. Capt., Cheshire Regt.(T.F.) (W.) [1914]
CHANDLER, R. A. Major, King's (Liverpool Regt., T.F.); 1910
empld. War Office
CHARLESWORTH, M. P. 2nd Lieut., Labour Corps 1914
CHIVERS, J. S. Lieut., R.F.A.(T.F.) 1911
CHUDLEIGH, C. A. E. Capt. and Adjt., Leicestershire 1908
Regt. and R. Defence Corps. (W.)
CLARK, A. G. Lieut., Highland L.I.(T.F.) (W 2.) 1909
CLARK, G. L. Capt., W. Yorks. Regt. (Leeds Rifles, T.F.) 1910
(W.)
CLARK, N. M. Lieut., Highland L.I. 1910
CLARKE, A. B. Lieut., I.A.R.O., attd. Indian Labour 1896
Corps
CLAYDEN, H. K. Capt., R.A.S.C. 1905
CLEGG, M. T. Capt., R.A.M.C.(T.F.) *M.* 1907
COAKS, H. C. Pte., R. Fusiliers (P. S. Bn.); Lieut., E. 1909
Lancs. Regt. (W.)
✠COLEMAN, H. N. 2nd Lieut., N. Zealand Infy. 1903
Killed in action 13 April 1918
✠COLES, C. 2nd Lieut., E. Lancs. Regt.(T.F.) 1907
Killed in action in Gallipoli 4 June 1915
COLES, W. T. Lieut., R.A.S.C. 1914
COLLIER, Rev. A. G. C.F. 4th Class, R.A.C.D. 1903
COODE, A. T. Cdr., R.N.V.R. *Order of St Anne (Russia)* 1895
COOPER, J. S. Capt., R.A.M.C.(T.F. Res.) 1896
✠COOPER-MARSDIN, Rev. A. C. C.F. 4th Class, R.A.C.D. 1887
Died Aug. 1918
COPLESTONE, W. D. Capt., R.A.M.C. 1898

CORFIELD, B. C.   Lieut., R.F.A.   *M* 2.   1909
COX, F. B. H.   Lieut., Fife and Forfar Yeo.   1906
COX, P. H.   Pte., R. Fusiliers (P. S. Bn.); Lieut., Durham [1914]
   L.I. and Grenadier Gds.   (W.)   (P.)
✠COY, J. C.   2nd Lieut., Durham L.I.; Capt., North-   1909
   umberland Fus.
   Killed in action 27 Sept. 1918
CRAVEN, A. E. L.   Lieut., Wiltshire Regt. and Labour   1912
   Corps.   (W.)
CRAVEN, W. L.   Pte., R.A.M.C.; Corpl., Labour Corps;   1906
   Cadet, O.C.B.
✠CREYKE, E. R.   Capt., King's Own (Yorkshire L.I., T.F.)   1905
   M.
   Killed in action 5 July 1916
CRONK, H. L.   Capt., R.A.M.C.   1908
✠CROOKHAM, H. A. R.   Lieut., Cambridgeshire Regt.   1912
   Died 4 Aug. 1915 *of meningitis following wounds re-*
   ceived in action
✠CROWE, T. M.   Sub-Lieut., R.N.V.R.,(Anson Bn.,R.N.D.)   1905
   Killed in action in Gallipoli 11 *June* 1915
CUFFE, G. E.   Capt., R.E. (Signals).   *M.*   1911
CURRIE, J. H.   Instructor Lieut., R.N.   1914
CUTTER, R. C.   Capt. and Adjt., R. Fusiliers and Gen.   1905
   List (Courts-Martial Officer).   (W.)

DAVID, R. S. R.   Lieut., Welsh Regt.(T.F.)   (W.)   1915
DAVIDSON, W. E. F.   Major, E. Yorks. Regt.; Major (A.),   1911
   R.A.F.   (W.)
DAVIES, C. E. H.   *See* HUGHES DAVIES, C. E.
DAVIES, Rev. C. E. S.   C.F. 4th Class, R.A.C.D.   1899
DAVIES, Rev. J. B.   C.F. 4th Class, R.A.C.D.   1897
DAVIES, J. P. H.   Hon. Capt., R.A.M.C.(T.F.)   1902
✠DAVIES, K. G.   Lieut., R.E.   1914
   Killed in action 19 *May* 1917
DAVIES, W. E.   Lieut., R.E.   1912
DAVIS, E. M.   Lieut., Middlesex Regt.(T.F.)   1911
DAVY, G.   Pte., R. Fusiliers (P. S. Bn.); Major, R.E.; 1908
   D.A.D. Roads.   *M.C.   M.*
DAY, E. C.   Capt., King's (Shropshire L.I.)   *M.C. and*   1909
   Bar.   M.
DEEDES, J.   Capt., King's (Shropshire L.I.)   (P.)   1912
DEEDES, W.   2nd Lieut., Spec. List (Asst. Officer i/c   1875
   Records)
DELAFIELD, M. E. C.   Capt., R.A.M.C.   *M.C.*   1904

✠DENT, A. C. Sergt., R.A.M.C.   1910
  Killed in action in Gallipoli 19 *July* 1915
DE VINE, Rev. C. N. C.F. 4th Class, R.A.C.D. (W.) 1902
  M.C. M.
✠DE VINE, Rev. H. B. ST J. C.F. 4th Class, R.A.C.D.   1910
  Killed in action 27 *April* 1916
DEXTER, E. N. Trooper, W. Kent Yeo.; Lieut., R.F.A. 1911
DEXTER, J. E. Trooper, W. Kent Yeo.; Capt., R. Fusiliers 1909
  and Training Res. Bn. (W.)
DEXTER, R. M. Major, R.F.A. *M.C.*   1910
DIGBY-JOHNSON, N. Lieut., R.A.S.C. (W.)   1905
DIXON, J. G. Pte., R. Fusiliers (P. S. Bn.); Capt., Wor- [1914]
  cestershire Regt.(T.F.) *M.C.*
DONALDSON, A. Capt., 34th Sikh Pioneers, Indian Army 1905
DORE, A. S. W.   Major, Worcestershire Regt.(T.F.); 1901
  Lieut.-Col. (A.), R.A.F. (W.) *D.S.O. M* 2.
DOWER, E. L. Flt. Sub-Lieut., R.N.A.S.   1913
DOWNMAN, Rev. L. C. C.F. 4th Class, R.A.C.D. *M.* 1905
DRYSDALE, J. E. Major, R.A.S.C. *M.C.*   1906
DRYSDALE, T. Capt., R.A.M.C.   1898
DUCKWORTH, W. L. H. Capt., R.A.M.C.(T.F.)   1889
DUTFIELD, D. Capt., London Regt. (R. Fus.) *M.*   1911
✠DWYER, C. H. Capt., Worcestershire Regt. *M.*   [1914]
  Killed in action 17 *Nov.* 1916
DYSON, E. A. Capt., R.A.M.C.   1903

EASON, E. K. Lieut., R. Dublin Fus.   1903
EDGE, A. S. 2nd Lieut., S. Lancs. Regt.; Lieut., R.F.A. 1911
  (T.F.) *M.*
EDMUNDS, Rev. H. V. C.F. 4th Class, R.A.C.D.   1905
ELLIOT, R. H. 2nd Lieut., R. Scots   [1914]
✠ELLIOTT, C. A. B. 2nd Lieut., Norfolk Regt. and Somer- 1913
  set L.I. (W.)
  Killed in action in the Battle of Arras 12 *April* 1917
ELLIS ROBERTS, R. Cadet, O.C.B.   1907
ELMSLIE, G. F. Capt., E. Surrey Regt.(T.F.)   1908
✠ELVERSON, R. W. Lieut., E. Surrey Regt.   1909
  Killed in action 25 *Sept.* 1915
ENSELL, Rev. C. S. C.F. 2nd Class, R.A.C.D. *M.*   1889
✠EVERS, B. S. Capt., W. Yorks. Regt. (W.)   1910
  Killed in action 14 *Sept.* 1916
EVORS, C. A., T.D. Capt., Middlesex Regt.(T.F.) and 1879
  Highgate School O.T.C.
EWING, J. R. Capt., R. Sussex Regt.   1880

FABER, L. E. Lieut., R. Fusiliers; Major, M.G.C. (P.)   1896
M.C. M.

FAIRBAIRN, C. O. Capt., Loyal N. Lancs. Regt.; Major   1912
(A.), R.A.F. (W.) *A.F.C.*

FAIRBAIRN, C. P. Lieut., Scots Gds.   1905

FAIRBAIRN, G. A. Lieut., 18th Hussars; Capt., Spec.   1911
List, empld. Egyptian Army. (W.)

✠FAIRBAIRN, G. E. 2nd Lieut., Durham L.I.   1906
Killed in action 20 June 1915

FARRELL, W. J. Lieut., R.F.A.; Capt., Gen. Staff (In- 1901
telligence). *M.C.*

FAUNCE-DE-LAUNE, E. 2nd Lieut., R. East Kent Yeo.   1894

✠FELL, D. M. 2nd Lieut., R.F.A.   1914
Killed in action 17 July 1916

FINCH, A. Capt., Norfolk Regt., R.E., and Gen. List   1890
(Military Port Assistant). (W.)

✠FINDLAY, I. C. 2nd Lieut., York and Lancaster Regt. 1914
Died 10 Aug. 1915 of wounds received in action

FINLOW, L. W. Capt., Loyal N. Lancs. Regt. and   1911
M.G.C. (W.) *M.*

FIRTH, M. M. Lieut., R. Wiltshire Yeo. and R.F.A.   1914

FISHER, B. O. F. DE C. Capt., Norfolk Regt.   *1912

FISHER, G. A. Lieut., King's Royal Rifle Corps. (W 2.) 1910
M.C. M.

✠FISHER, G. W. 2nd Lieut., Suffolk Regt.   1910
Killed in action 18 Nov. 1917

FITCH, C. E. Major, Worcestershire Regt.; Lieut.-Col., 1889
R. Welsh Fus.(T.F.)

FLETCHER, E. Lieut., R.A.S.C.(T.F.) (W.)   1897

FLOOD, C. B. Capt., Derbyshire Yeo. *O.B.E. M 2.*   1900

✠FLOWER, O. S. Brigade Major; Lieut.-Col., R. Welsh   1890
Fus. *M.*
Died 24 July 1916 of wounds received in action at Mametz Wood

FORMAN, G. E. G. Capt., Black Watch   1911

FORSTER, Rev. G. W. C.F. 4th Class, R.A.C.D.   1910

FOSTER, J. D. Capt., Australian A.S.C.   1887

FOSTER, J. H. Pte., Middlesex Regt. (P. S. Bn.); Capt., 1900
R. Fusiliers; Major, King's Own (R. Lancaster
Regt.); Lieut.-Col., Highland L.I. and Northamp-
tonshire Regt. (W 3.) *M 2.*

FRASER, J. H. P. Lieut.-Col., R.A.M.C.(T.F.) *D.S.O.* 1891
M.C. and Bar. M 3. French Croix de Guerre

✠FURZE, C. Capt., London Regt. (L.R.B.) (W.)   1910
Died 6 *April* 1918 *of wounds received in action*

GALLOWAY, Rev. S. J. C.F. 4th Class, R.A.C.D.   1905
GARNE, T. Lieut., Connaught Rangers; attd. R.F.C.   1902
GARRETT, T. R. H. Lieut.-Cdr., R.N.V.R. *O.B.E.*   1899
GIBSON, R. W. B. Capt., R.A.M.C.   1903
GIFFARD, J. S. 2nd Lieut., Manchester Regt.; Capt.   1908
(K.B.), R.A.F. *M. Belgian Croix de Guerre*
GILLSON, G. Brig.-Gen., R.A. (W.) *C.M.G. D.S.O.*   1886
Brevet Colonel. M & . Order of Danilo, 3rd Class
(Montenegro)
GILMAN, J. Major, R.A.S.C. *M.*   1898
✠GOLDSMITH, H. M. Lieut., Devon Regt.; attd. Lincoln-   1904
shire Regt.
Killed in action at Fromelles 9 *May* 1915
GOODACRE, Rev. J. C.F. 3rd Class, R.A.C.D.(T.F.)   1894
M.C. M.
GOODCHILD, H. N. Lieut., R.F.A.; Lieut. (Ad.), R.A.F.   1908
GOODMAN, E. L. Lieut., R.N.A.S.   1905
GOODWIN, H. A. C. Capt., S. Lancs. Regt. and Gen. List   1907
(T.F. Res.); Instructor, School of Musketry
✠GOODWIN, H. J. 2nd Lieut., R.G.A.   1905
Killed in action 24 *April* 1917
GOSS, J. Capt., R.A.M.C.   1896
GOUGH CALTHORPE, Hon. F. S. Lieut., Staffordshire   1911
Yeo.; Capt., Spec. List (P. and B.T. Staff)
GOULD, R. Gnr., H.A.C.; Capt., R.F.A. *M.*   1911
GRAHAM, H. E. Capt., R.A.M.C.   1896
✠GRAHAM-MONTGOMERY, G. J. E. Capt., Hampshire Regt.   1912
Killed in action 24 *April* 1917
✠GRASETT, E. B. Lieut., 28th, attd. 33rd, Punjabis, Indian   *1908
Army
Killed in action 25 *Sept.* 1915
GRAY, A. K. Capt., Spec. List (Graves Registration   1907
Commission)
GRAY, Rev. R. H. C.F. 4th Class, R.A.C.D.   1915
GRAY, S. T. Capt., I.A.R.O., attd. 58th Vaughan's Rifles.   1909
(W.)
GREEN, W. R. C. Capt., The Queen's (R. W. Surrey   1913
Regt.) (P.)
GREENHAM, R. G. H. Lieut., Army Pay Dept.   1905
GRENFELL, E. B. Capt., D. of Cornwall's L.I. (T.F.);   1911
Capt. (A.), R.A.F.

GRIGG, G. H. Trooper, R. North Devon Yeo.; Lieut., [1914]
N. Irish Horse and R.F.A.

GRIGG, J. H. Trooper, R. North Devon Yeo.; Lieut., [1914]
N. Irish Horse

GRIPPER, A. G. Sergt., R.E.   1913

GROGAN, E. S. Major, E. African Field Force. *D.S.O.*   1893
M 2. *Officer, Order of Leopold (Belgium)*

GROSS, W. S. Sergt., Middlesex Regt.; 2nd Lieut., Wor-   1911
cestershire Regt.; Lieut., R.A.M.C. (W.)

GRUBB, H. C. S. Pte., R. Fusiliers (P. S. Bn.); Lieut., R.   1912
Irish Fus. and R.E. (Signals). *ᐟM.C. and Bar*

GULLICK, C. D. Capt., The Buffs (E. Kent Regt.) (W 4.)   1911
M.C. and Bar

GUY, O. V. Capt., W. Yorks. Regt.; Major, Tank Corps.   1910
(W 2.) *D.S.O. M.C. and Bar. M. Chevalier,
Legion of Honour (France)*

HABGOOD, A. H. Major, R.A.M.C. *D.S.O. M.*   1900

HACKWORTH, A. Gnr., H.A.C.; Lieut., R.F.A.; attd.   1909
T.M.B. (W.) *M.*

✠HALDANE, J. O. 2nd Lieut., Rifle Brigade   1898
Killed in action 18 *Aug.* 1916

HALDANE, M. M. Major, R. Scots (R. of O.); G.S.O. 2,   1896
War Office. *Brevet Lieut.-Colonel. m.*

HALES, Rev. J. P. C.F. 2nd Class, R.A.C.D.; D.A.C.G.   1888
D.S.O. M 2.

✠HAMILTON, N. C. Pte., London Regt. (Artists Rifles);   1912
2nd Lieut., Northamptonshire Regt. (W.)
Killed in action 14 *July* 1916

HANDS, W. J. G. Major, R.A.S.C.   1911

HANSARD, L. A. S. Sub-Lieut., R.N.V.R.   1913

HARCOURT, Rev. G. H. Chaplain, R.N.   1903

HARDWICK, F. 2nd Lieut., London Regt. (Post Office   1910
Rifles); Major, R.E. (Postal Section). *M.B.E.
M.*

HARDY, F. W. Colonel, R.A.M.C. *M* 2.   1883

HARRIS, A. L. S. 2nd Lieut., Oxford and Bucks. L.I.   1913
(T.F.); Lieut., R. Marines

HARRISON, W. P. 2nd Lieut., W. Kent Yeo.; Lieut., Life   1904
Gds.

HARRY, N. G. Capt., Worcestershire Regt.(T.F.) and   1896
R.A.M.C.

HARTLEY, B. C. Lieut., Hertfordshire Regt.; empld. War   1897
Office. (W.)

✠HARVEST, G. L. Lieut., London Regt. (L.R.B.) *M.C.* [1914]
Killed in action 20 *June* 1917
HAWDON, H. W. Lieut., Durham L.I. (W.) 1909
✠HAWDON, Rev. N. E. C.F. 4th Class, R.A.C.D. 1905
Died 16 *Nov.* 1918 *of pneumonia contracted on active
service*
HAWKINS, O. C. Major, R.E. (T.F.); Staff Capt., War 1908
Office. (W.) *m.*
✠HAWKINS, O. L. 2nd Lieut., E. Yorks. Regt. 1912
Died 26 *April* 1915 *of wounds received in action*
HAY, A. C. Capt., Loyal N. Lancs. Regt. (W.) 1907
HEAD, H. G. Capt., London Regt. and Tank Corps. *M.C.* 1907
HEARFIELD, J. 2nd Lieut., R.A.S.C. 1898
HEARN, R. J. Capt., R.A.M.C.; Capt. (Med.), R.A.F. 1908
(W.) *m.*
HEARSEY, G. A. C. Lieut., I.A.R.O. (Cavalry) 1905
HEATHCOTE, G. S. Capt., Sherwood Foresters (Notts. 1902
and Derby Regt.); Major, Camp Cmdt. *M.V.O.*
M 2.
HENDERSON, J. A. Major, 8th (King's R. Irish) Hussars 1883
(R. of O.); A.P.M. *D.S.O. O.B.E. M* 4.
HENTY, E. C. Capt., R.A.S.C.; Lieut., R.F.A. (W.) *M.* 1906
HIGGINS, W. G. Capt., 2nd Dragoon Gds. (Queen's Bays). 1913
M.
HIGSON, F. Lieut.-Col., Norfolk Regt. *O.B.E. M.* 1899
HILL, H. P. Major, Hampshire Regt. (T.F.) 1907
HOBBS, C. R. Trooper, K. Edward's Horse; Major, 1910
R.F.A. (W.) *M.*
HOBSON, F. W. E. 2nd Lieut., Labour Corps 1902
HOBSON, R. L. Lieut., London Regt. (Civil Service 1890
Rifles); empld. Admiralty
HODGSON, C. L. Major, King's Own (R. Lancaster Regt.) 1898
and Gen. Staff (O.C.B.) (W.) *m*
HODGSON, E. J. Lieut., S. Staffs. Regt.; attd. Leicester- 1913
shire Regt.; Lieut., M.G.C. (W.)
HOLLAND, Rev. P. F. Pte., R.A.M.C. 1905
✠HOLLOWAY, B. H. Capt., R. Sussex Regt. 1907
Killed in action 27 *Sept.* 1915
HOLLOWAY, N. J. Lieut., R. Fusiliers (P.S. Bn.); Capt., 1909
R.E.
HOLMAN, A. H. Lieut., R.N.V.R. 1908
✠HOLMAN, P. Pte., H.A.C. 1910
Killed in action 17 *Feb.* 1915
HOLMDEN, F. A. A., D.S.O. Major, R.A.M.C. 1889

HOLME, H. R.   Lieut., King's Royal Rifle Corps.; Capt.,   1908
M.G.C. (W.)
HOLMES, J. C.   Capt., R.E. *M.C. M.*   1910
HOLT, E.   Lieut., Oxford and Bucks. L.I.; Capt., R. [1914]
Warwickshire Regt. (W 2.) *M.C.*
HOOD, H. M.   Capt., I.A.R.O., attd. 28th Light Cavalry   1903
✠HOPCRAFT, E. G. DE L.   Lieut., Middlesex Regt.   1906
Killed in action 27 Sept. 1918
HOSKYNS, Rev. E. C.   C.F. 3rd Class, R.A.C.D. (W.)   1903
M.C. M.
HOVIL, R.   Major, R.F.A. *D.S.O.* *M* 2.   1898
HOWARD, J.   Capt., R.E.(T.F.)   1912
HOYTE, W. N.   Lieut., Sherwood Foresters (Notts. and   1913
Derby Regt.) *M.C. and Bar*
HUDSON, H. C. H.   Major, 11th Hussars; Lieut.-Col.,   1906
A.Q.M.G. (W.) *M.V.O.   Brevet Major.   M* 2.
Chevalier, Legion of Honour (France). French Croix de
Guerre. Chevalier, Ordre de la Couronne (Belgium).
Belgian Croix de Guerre
HUGHES, J. W. C.   Paymaster Sub-Lieut., R.N.V.R.   1913
HUGHES DAVIES, C. E.   Capt., R.F.A.; Staff Lieut. (W.)   1909
M.C.
HUGHES-HALLETT, N. M.   2nd Lieut., Worcestershire [1914]
Regt.; Capt., King's (Shropshire L.I.) (W.)
HULTON-SAMS, K. A.   Pte., Oxford and Bucks. L.I.   1903
HUTCHINSON, G.   Capt., R. Inniskilling Fus.   1908

INGLES, Ven. C. W. C.   Chaplain of the Fleet, R.N.   1887
IREMONGER, E. A.   Lieut.-Col., Suffolk Regt.; Colonel   1881
i/c Records; empld. Ministry of National Service.
C.B.E. m.
IRONS, W. H.   Sergt., R.E.   1891

JACKSON, A.   Lieut., E. Yorks. Regt.   1915
✠JACKSON, D. F.   Lieut., Lanarkshire Yeo. (W.) *M* 2.   1906
Killed in action 11 *Oct.* 1918
JACOBY, A. H. M.   2nd Lieut.(T.), R.A.F.   1903
JAMES, H. M.   Capt. and Adjt., Middlesex Regt. (W.)   1903
M.C.
JAQUET, Rev. E. G.   C.F. 4th Class, R.A.C.D.   1908
✠JEFFCOCK, H. C. F.   Lieut., Sherwood Foresters (Notts.   1904
and Derby Regt.)
Died 30 *May* 1917 *of wounds received in action* 28 *May*
1917

JEFFCOCK, P. E. Lieut. (T.), R.A.F.   1906
JEFFCOCK, W. H. C. 2nd Lieut., York and Lancaster 1907
  Regt; Lieut., W. Yorks. Regt. (W.)
JENKIN, R. T. Lieut., I.A.R.O., attd. S. and T. Corps   1906
JENKINS, Rev. C. E. C.F. 4th Class, R.A.C.D.(T.F.)   *1896
JENKINS, R. E. Capt., Hampshire Regt.(T.F.)   1909
JENNINGS, A. R. Capt., R.A.M.C. *M. Order of St Sava,* 1904
  4th Class (Serbia)
✠JENNINGS, R. W. Lieut., Worcestershire Regt. *M.*   1907
  Died 3 July 1916 of wounds received in action at La
  Boisselle
JERWOOD, Rev. F. H. Capt., Oakham School O.T.C.   1905
✠JERWOOD, J. H. Pte., London Regt. (Artists Rifles);   1909
  Capt., Durham L.I.; Major, Somerset L.I. (W 2.)
  M.C.   `
  Killed in action 21 March 1918
✠JOHNSON, G. B. Capt., Norfolk Regt.   1912
  Killed in action 22 Nov. 1915
JOHNSON, N. D. *See* DIGBY-JOHNSON, N.
JOHNSTONE, C. C. G. Capt., Argyll and Sutherland Hdrs.; 1908
  Major, R. Scots. (W.)
JOHNSTONE, W. Lieut., Coldstream Gds. (W.)   1907
JOICEY, J. Major, N. Somerset Yeo.   1880
JOICEY, Hon. J. A. Major, Northumberland Fus.(T.F.) *m.* 1898
JONES, C. E. Lieut., I.A.R.O.   1910
✠JONES, E. W. 2nd Lieut., Welsh Regt.   [1914]
  Died 9 Nov. 1915 of dysentery contracted on active
  service
JONES, H. A. Lieut.-Col., R.A.S.C.; Brig.-Gen., D.Q.M.G. 1898
  Brevet Lieut.-Colonel. m. Chevalier, Legion of Honour
  (France)
JONES, J. W. B. 2nd Lieut., Labour Corps   1900

KEATS, J. R. Capt., Suffolk Yeo. (W 2.) *M.C.*   1912
KEBLE, T. H. Lieut., The Buffs (E. Kent Regt.); Capt., [1914]
  G.S.O. 3. *M.*
KEMP, Sir K. H., Bart. Colonel, Norfolk Regt. *C.B.E.* 1871
  m.
KENNEDY, Rev. D. J. C.F. 3rd Class, R.A.C.D.   1900
KIDD, W. A. T. Lieut., R. Sussex Regt.; Capt., R.E. *M.* 1907
KING, W. B. R. Capt., R. Welsh Fus.(T.F.); S.O. to   1908
  Engineer-in-Chief. *O.B.E. M 2.*
KIRKPATRICK, J. B. Capt., Rifle Brigade; empld. O.C.B. 1912
  (W.)

KITCHING, A. E. E. African Field Force	1909
KITCHING, G. C.   Capt., London Regt.(L.R.B.)   (W.)   1911
(P.)
KNIGHT, C. E. Capt., R.F.A.	1908
✠KOETTGEN, E. A.   Pte., London Regt. (London Scottish)   1892
Killed in action 30 *June* 1917
KRAUSE, E. H.   Lieut., Durham L.I. and Gen. List.   1911
(W 2.)
KUTNOW, H. S. Lieut., R.A.O.C.	1907

LAISTNER, M. L. W. Pte., Middlesex Regt.	1909
LANG, R.   Pte., R. Fusiliers (P.S. Bn.); Lieut. (A.), R.A.F.   [1914]
(W.)
✠LAUDER, J. C.   Capt., Argyll and Sutherland Hdrs. (W 3.)   1910
Killed in action 29 *Dec.* 1916
LEA, D. H. Pte., M.G.C. (W.)	1900
LEALE, R. J. Capt., R. Guernsey Militia	1910
✠LEARY, G. G. W. Lieut., Gloucestershire Regt.	1910
Killed in action 25 *Sept.* 1915
LEES, J.   Capt., Queen's Own (R. W. Kent Regt.) and   1878
Spec. List (Adjt., Rest Camp).   *M.*
LE GROS, F. G.   2nd Lieut., R. Jersey Militia; Lieut.,   1912
R.G.A.
LE NEVE FOSTER, B. A. J. C.   Sergt., R. Fusiliers   1912
LETTS, C. F. C. Major, Rifle Brigade. (W 3.)	1907
✠LEVICK, P. Capt., R.A.M.C.	1892
Accidentally killed on active service 21 *March* 1918
LIAS, W. J. Capt., Lancs. Fus. and R.E. *M.*	1886
LIGHT, P. Capt., Cheshire Regt. *M.C.*	1901
LILLY, C. O.   Capt., Dorset Regt.; G.S.O. 3; Hon. Capt.   1908
(A.), R.A.F.   (W 2.)   *D.S.O.   M.*
LIVINGSTON, P. C.   Surgeon Prob., R.N.V.R.; Capt.   1912
(Med.), R.A.F.
LLOYD, B. S. Lieut., R.G.A.	1915
LLOYD, H. W. C.   Capt., Wiltshire Regt.; G.S.O. 3.   (P.)   1910
D.S.O.   M.C.   M.   French Croix de Guerre
LLOYD-BARROW, R. A. Capt., R.F.A.	1909
LLOYD GEORGE, G.   Lieut., R. Welsh Fus.; A.D.C.;   1913
Major, R.G.A.   *M.*
LOCKHART, J. H. B.   2nd Lieut., Seaforth Hdrs. and Gen.   1908
Staff.   *M.*
LOEWE, L. L.   Lieut., Oxford and Bucks. L.I. (T.F.) and   1911
R. Sussex Regt.   (W.)
LOVEBAND, G. Y. Capt., R. Dublin Fus. *M.*	1911

Low, A. Capt., R. Irish Fus.; Major, M.G.C. (W.) 1912
  M.C. M.
Lowe, P. R. Capt., R.A.M.C. *M.*   1887
Luce, H. W. Capt., R.F.A.(T.F.)   1913
✠Lunn, H. C. Sergt., R. Fusiliers (P. S. Bn.); Lieut., 1908
  Northumberland Fus. and R. Scots. (W.)
  Killed in action 22 March 1917

Macalpine, J. L. Lieut., 9th Lancers. (W.) *M.C.*   1904
McBain, N. S. Capt., R.F.A.(T.F.)   1913
✠MacBryan, E. C. Lieut., Somerset L.I. (W.)   1912
  Killed in action 1 *July* 1916
McCaughey, S. Lieut., R.F.A.   1912
McConnell, A. E. Capt., R. Irish Rifles. *M.*   1899
McCorquodale, K. Capt., Lovat's Scouts. *M.C.*   1913
McGowan, I. A. W. Capt., R.F.A.(T.F.) *M.C.*   1904
McIlroy, H. D. Surgeon Prob., R.N.V.R.; Capt.,   1910
  R.A.M.C. (W.)
✠Mack, I. A. Capt., Suffolk Regt.; attd. T.M.B.   1911
  Killed in action 1 *July* 1916
Mackay, A. S. Major, 7th Gurkha Rifles, Indian Army. 1909
  M.C. M.
Mackie, E. D. Pte., R. Fusiliers (Sportsman's Bn.)   1888
✠McLaughlin, A. Lieut., R. Irish Rifles   1913
  Killed in action 9 *May* 1915
Maclean, F. S. Trooper, K. Edward's Horse; Lieut.,   1911
  R.F.A. (W.)
McNeil, J. Sub-Lieut., R.N.V.R.   1907
Macnutt, Rev. A. C. C.F. 3rd Class, R.A.C.D.   1898
Mainprice, H. Capt., King's Royal Rifle Corps and Gen. 1902
  Staff. *m.*
✠Maitland, J. D. Pte., R. Fusiliers (P.S. Bn.); 2nd Lieut., 1910
  D. of Wellington's (W. Riding Regt.)
  Killed in action 22 Feb. 1916
Manderson, J. R. 2nd Lieut., Devon Regt.(T.F.); Capt., 1890
  Argyll and Sutherland Hdrs.
Manduell, M. D. Capt., R.F.A. *M.C. French Croix* 1896
  de Guerre
Manifold, E. W. Lieut., R.F.A. *M.C.*   1911
Manifold, J. Lieut., R.F.A.   1907
✠Mann, R. L. Lieut., 7th Dragoon Gds.   1910
  Killed in action at Festubert 23 Dec. 1914
Manning, R. Capt., Buckinghamshire Yeo. and M.G.C. 1908
  M.C. M. French Croix de Guerre

MANNING, T. E. Major, Northamptonshire Yeo. *M.*   1902
MARNHAM, A. E. Lieut.-Col., R.G.A. *M.C. M.*   1909
  *Chevalier, Order of Leopold (Belgium). Belgian Croix
  de Guerre*
MARSHALL, G. T. Sergt., R. Welsh Fus.   1913
MARSHALL, Rev. H. A. C.F. 3rd Class, R.A.C.D. (W.) *M.*   1902
MARTIN, B. S. Lieut., M.G.C. (Motor) and Tank Corps.   1910
  (W.)
MASEFIELD, Rev. W. B. Chaplain, R.N.   1904
✠MASON, K. R. 2nd Lieut., Suffolk Regt.(T.F.)   1909
  Killed in action 21 June 1915
✠MASON, R. S. 2nd Lieut., Rifle Brigade   1912
  Killed in action 14 March 1915
✠MASSEY, J. H. Capt., R.F.A. (W.) *M.C. French Croix*   1912
  de Guerre
  Killed in action 27 May 1918
MATTHEWS, N. H., T.D. Major, R. Defence Corps   1870
MEAKIN, F. G. Lieut., R.F.A.(T.F.)   1903
✠MEERES, H. W. H. Lce.-Corpl., R. Fusiliers   1899
  Killed in action 19 March 1915
MELLOR, J. E. Capt., Leys School O.T.C.; empld. O.C.B.   1903
✠MEREDITH, O. W. W. H. 2nd Lieut. (A.), R.F.C.   1914
  Killed in action near Cambrai 20 Nov. 1917
MILBURN, B. Capt., Hertfordshire Regt. and Coldstream   1907
  Gds. (W 2.) *D.S.O. M.C. M* 3.
MILBURN, W. H. Capt., Yorkshire Regt.; Major, Em-   1902
  barkation S.O.
MILLER, C. P. Lieut., Yorkshire Regt.   1909
MILLS, H. J. F. Capt., King's Royal Rifle Corps. (W.)   1913
  (P.)
✠MITCHELL, A. C. O. 2nd Lieut., S. Wales Borderers. *M.*   1905
  Killed in action in Mesopotamia 30 April 1917
MITCHELL, S. Major, Fife and Forfar Yeo.(T.F. Res.)   1903
  and Gen. Staff. *m.*
MITCHELSON, Rev. J. K. C.F. 4th Class, R.A.C.D. (P.)   1907
MITFORD, A. H. Capt., York and Lancaster Regt. and   1884
  Gen. List. (W.)
MITFORD, C. W. 2nd Lieut., Shrewsbury School O.T.C.   1904
✠MOFFITT, J. P. Capt., Durham L.I. *M.C.*   1911
  Killed in action 3 Dec. 1917
MONKS, G. Lieut., R. Scots. (W.)   1908
MONTGOMERY, H. K. Lieut., Black Watch. (W.)   1914
MOORE, H. M. M. Lieut., R.G.A.   1906
MOORE, N. Lieut., Intelligence Dept., Uganda Force   1907

MORGAN, R. T. Lieut., R.F.A.(T.F.); attd. Ordnance 1897
  College
MORGAN, T. D. Capt., R.A.M.C. 1909
MORLEY, G. C. Trooper, Gloucestershire Yeo. 1913
✠MORRIS, A. C. Trooper, 12th Lancers; Pte., R. Munster 1912
  Fus.
  Killed in action 27 Nov. 1915
MORRIS, G. G. 2nd Lieut., Sherborne School O.T.C. *1911
MORRISON, M. J. Capt., Durham L.I.(T.F.) (W.) *M.C.* 1912
MORTLOCK, Rev. C. B. C.F. 4th Class, R.A.C.D. *1911
MORUM, S. D. Capt., Rifle Brigade. (W.) 1914
✠MOSS, F. W. Pte., Suffolk Regt.; 2nd Lieut., Leicester- 1913
  shire Regt.; attd. R.E.
  Killed in action 28 May 1918
MOSSE, Rev. C. H. C.F. 4th Class, R.A.C.D. 1908
MUIR-MACKENZIE, K. J. Pte., H.A.C.; Lieut., R. Munster 1901
  Fus.
✠MUIR-MACKENZIE, Sir R. C., Bart. Lieut., Durham L.I. 1910
  M.C.
  Killed in action 12 April 1918
MUMFORD, P. S. Capt., London Yeo. (Westminster 1912
  Dragoons); Hon. Capt. (Ad.), R.A.F.
✠MURRAY, M. A. Pte., Middlesex Regt. (P.S. Bn.); Lieut., [1914]
  Essex Regt.
  Killed in action in the Battle of Loos 25 Sept. 1915
✠MURRAY, R. L. Capt., Northamptonshire Regt.(T.F.) 1912
  (W.) *M* 2.
  Killed in action 19 April 1917
MUSSON, T. M. B. Pte., King's (Liverpool Regt., Liver- 1910
  pool Scottish, T.F.); Lieut., R. Welsh Fus. and Essex
  Regt. (W.)
✠MYDDELTON, E. G. 2nd Lieut., Suffolk Regt. 1912
  Killed in action at Le Cateau 26 Aug. 1914

NALDER, F. W. Lieut., Somerset L.I. 1913
NALDRETT, H. C. Lieut., Essex Regt. (T.F.); Lieut. (A.), 1912
  R.A.F. (W.)
NAPIER, Sir J. W. L., Bart. Pte., London Regt. (London 1913
  Scottish); Lieut., S. Wales Borderers. (W 2.) (P.)
✠NAPIER, Sir W. L., Bart. Major, S. Wales Borderers 1886
  Killed in action in Gallipoli 13 Aug. 1915
NATHAN, A. A. Capt., Hampshire Yeo.; Major, R.A.F.; 1905
  S.O. 2, Air Ministry. *M. m.*
NEALE, J. B. Capt., R.A.S.C. *M.* 1909

✠NEVILL, W.P. Capt., E. Surrey Regt.; attd. E. Yorks. Regt. 1913
Killed in action 1 *July* 1916
NEVILLE, G. J. E. P. O., R.N.V.R.; 2nd Lieut., R.A.S.C. 1904
(M.T.)
NEWHAM, C. E. Capt., Army Cyclist Corps. (W.) 1912
NEWLING, A. J. Lieut., London Regt. (Finsbury Rifles); 1915
Hon. Lieut. (T.), R.A.F.
NEWMAN, F. H. C. Capt., R.A.S.C. 1899
NICHOLAS, F. P. Surgeon Sub-Lieut., R.N.V.R. 1909
✠NICHOLS, W. H. Major, Somerset L.I. 1892
Died in Germany 15 *Oct.* 1915 *of wounds received in
action in the Battle of Loos* 26 *Sept.* 1915
NORMAN, T. V. 2nd Lieut., Northamptonshire Regt. (W.) 1911
NORTH, G. D. Lieut., Life Gds. (W.) 1912
NOWELL-USTICKE, G. W. Capt., R.F.A. *M.C.* 1913
NUTMAN, B. K. Lieut., R.A.M.C. 1900

OLDHAM, E. A. S. Gnr., H.A.C.; Capt. and Adjt., Sea- 1912
forth Hdrs.(T.F.) (W.)
OLIVER, H. C. Instructor Lieut., R.N. 1913
OPPENHEIMER, K. M. 2nd Lieut., Durham L.I.; Lieut., 1911
I.A.R.O.
ORR, H. R. Pte., Canadian Force, empld. Records 1885
OSBORNE, E. C. Lieut., Black Watch. (W.) 1891
OWEN, T. Surgeon Lieut., R.N. 1906
OWSTON, C. S. 2nd Lieut., King's Royal Rifle Corps; 1908
Lieut., R.F.A.; empld. Records

PALMER, A. S. M. Capt., R.A.M.C. 1897
PALMER, F. W. M. Capt., R.A.M.C. 1896
✠PARKE, A. Capt., Lancs. Fus. (W 2.) *M.C.* 1911
Killed in action 27 *Sept.* 1918
PARKER, H. V. Capt. and Adjt., R.F.A. (W.) *M.C.* 1910
PARKES, E. B. H. Capt., R.A.S.C. (W.) 1886
PARMENTER, Rev. G. E. P. Chaplain, R.N. 1911
✠PASSINGHAM, E. G. Pte., London Regt. (Artists Rifles); 1913
Capt., Northumberland Fus. (W.) *M.C.*
Killed in action at Monchy-le-Preux 3 *May* 1917
PATERSON, G. A. R. Capt., Gordon Hdrs.(T.F.) *M.C.* 1911
✠PATTERSON, R. A. Capt., Rifle Brigade. (W.) 1914
Killed in action 12 *April* 1917
PATTINSON, L. A. Lieut., Durham L.I.(T.F.) and R. Fusi- 1909
liers; Lieut.-Col. (A.), R.A.F. *D.S.O. M.C. D.F.C.*
M.

✠PAYNE, G. H.   Lieut., Suffolk Regt.   1911
Killed in action at Le Cateau 26 Aug. 1914
PEACOCK, W. M.   Capt., Leicestershire Regt.(T.F.) (W.)   1909
PEACOCK, W. T.   Lieut., R.A.S.C.(M.T.)   1894
✠PEASE, M. R.   Lieut., E. Yorks. Regt.   [1914]
Killed in action 20 Oct. 1914
PEDLEY, C. F.   Lieut., R.A.M.C.   1907
PEGG, H. G.   Pte., London Regt. (Artists Rifles); Capt.,   1909
Argyll and Sutherland Hdrs. and Gen. List. (W.)
PENNELL, K. E. L.   Capt., R.E. *M.C. M* 2.   1908
PENNY, C. J.   Surgeon Prob., R.N.V.R.; Capt., R.A.M.C.   1911
O.B.E. M.
PENNY, G. S.   Capt., Spec. List (Intelligence)   1904
PENNY, W. M.   Capt., R.A.M.C. (W.) *M.C.*   1903
PETERS, B. A. I.   Lieut., R.A.M.C.   1901
¹PETERS, J. H. G.   Lieut., The Buffs (E. Kent Regt., T.F.);   1913
Capt., 51st Sikhs, attd. 152nd Punjabis, Indian Army.
(W.)
PETRO, J. A. W.   Capt., R.F.A.(T.F.); Cmdt., P. of W.   1913
Camp; empld. War Office
PHAYRE, Sir A.   Lieut.-Gen., Indian Army. *K.C.B.*   1876
PHELPS, M. N.   Capt., R. Warwickshire Regt.(T.F.);   1889
A.P.M. *M. Officer, Ordre de l'Étoile Noire (France)*
PHIPPS, C. E.   Lieut.-Col., R.G.A.; Dep. Chief Inspector,   1884
Woolwich Arsenal. *C.B. m.*
✠PIGG, B. W.   Sergt., H.A.C.; 2nd Lieut., Worcestershire   1907
Regt.
Killed in action at La Boisselle 3 July 1916
PIGG, C. H.   Capt., Worcestershire Regt. and Gen. List;   1906
Brigade Major. (W.) *M.C. m.*
PINK, H. S.   A.B., R.N.V.R. (R.N.D.); Capt., Sherwood   1906
Foresters (Notts. and Derby Regt.)
✠PLUMMER, W. F.   2nd Lieut., London Regt. (London Irish   1914
Rifles)
Killed in action 15 Sept. 1916
POLHILL, S. F. P.   Corpl., R.E.; Lieut. (A.), R.A.F. *M* 2.   1910
✠PREEDY, A.   Capt., Devon Regt.   1911
Killed in action 11 July 1916
PRIOR, Rev. C. B.   C.F. 4th Class, R.A.C.D. *M.C.*   1909
PRYCE, E. O.   Trooper, K. Edward's Horse; Capt., R.F.A.   1913
(W.) *M.C.*
PRYCE-JONES, Sir E., Bart.   Hon. Colonel, R. Welsh Fus.   1880
PRYCE-JONES, P.V.   Capt., Welsh Horse; attd. Cheshire Yeo.   1906

¹ Killed in action on the N.W. Indian frontier after the armistice.

PRYOR, J. W.   Lieut., S. Lancs. Regt. (W.) (P.)   [1914]
PURDY, T. W.   Major, Norfolk Regt.(T.F.) (W.) *T.D. m.*   1893
✠PYMAN, R. L.   Lieut., Middlesex Regt.   1905
    Killed in action 3 *May* 1917
PYPER, J. R.   Capt., London Regt. (R. Fus.); attd. M.G.C.   1911
    (W.) *M.C. and Bar. M.*

QUILLER-COUCH, Sir A. T.   Capt., D. of Cornwall's L.I.   *1912

RAIMES, E. A.   Lieut., Staffordshire Yeo. and W. Yorks.   1911
    Regt.; empld. War Office
RAIMES, G. H.   Lieut., Yorkshire Dragoons; attd. 21st   1914
    Lancers and 14th Hussars
RATCLIFF, R. F., M.P., V.D.   Lieut.-Col., N. Staffs. Regt.   1886
    (T.F. Res.) *C.M.G. m* 2.
RAVENSCROFT, P. D.   Corpl., R. Fusiliers; Capt., King's   1908
    Royal Rifle Corps. (W.) *M.C. M.*
RAWES, P. L.   Lieut., R.A.S.C. *M. Chevalier, Military*   1902
    Order of Avis (*Portugal*)
RAWSTORN, J. O.   Capt., R. Welsh Fus.(T.F.) (W.)   1910
REA, J. G. G.   Capt., Northumberland Yeo. and Labour   1904
    Corps. (W.) *D.S.O. M* 2. *Officer, Ordre du Mérite*
    Agricole (*France*)
READ, C. F.   2nd Lieut., R. Sussex Regt.   [1914]
READ, J. W.   Lieut., R. Sussex Regt.   1912
READ, W. R.   Capt., 1st Dragoon Gds.; Major (A.), R.A.F.   1905
    (W.) *M.C. D.F.C. A.F.C. M.*
REED, D. H.   Capt., Devon Regt.(T.F.) (W.)   1913
REID, C. H.   Lieut., 5th Dragoon Gds.; Capt., M.G.C.   1909
    (Cavalry). *M.C. M.*
REID, J. S. C.   Lieut., R. Scots; Major, M.G.C.   1908
RENDELL, W. R.   Capt., Cambridge Univ. O.T.C., attd.   1887
    Gen. Staff, War Office
RICARDO, A. ST Q., D.S.O.   Lieut.-Col., R. Inniskilling   1886
    Fus.; Brig.-Gen.; Colonel, Gen. Staff (Base Cmdt.)
    C.M.G. C.B.E. Brevet Lieut.-Colonel. M 7.
RICHARDSON, A.   Gnr., R.H.A.; Lieut., R.F.A. *M.C.*   1915
RICHARDSON, A. J. M.   Capt., N. Somerset Yeo.   1913
RICHARDSON, P. J.   Corpl., Calcutta Vol. Artillery; Capt.,   1910
    King's African Rifles. *M.*
RIDLEY, A. H.   Lieut., Northumberland Yeo.   1910
✠RIDLEY, C. N.   Capt., Northumberland Yeo.   1904
    Died 7 *Oct.* 1915 *of wounds received in action* 30 *Sept.*
    1915

✠RIDLEY, L. E. Lieut., R. Berkshire Regt. 1910
Killed in action 18 *Aug.* 1916
RIDOUT, P. M. Capt., Oxford and Bucks. L.I. (W.) 1913
ROBERTS, A. H. Lieut., Middlesex Regt. and Gen. List, 1909
empld. Inland Waterways and Docks. (W.)
ROBERTS, A. J. R. Lieut., Mill Hill School O.T.C. 1900
✠ROBERTS, F. B. Capt., Rifle Brigade 1901
Killed in action 8 *Feb.* 1916
ROBERTS, R. E. Major, Manchester Regt. 1900
ROBINSON, G. H. Pte., R. Fusiliers (Sportsman's Bn.) 1887
RODERICK, D. B. 2nd Lieut., Rifle Brigade 1916
ROLFE, W. J. L. Lieut., R.E. (Signals) 1915
ROSCOE, G. T. Lieut., R.A.S.C.(T.F.); attd. Worcester- 1913
shire Regt.
ROSS, O. F. Capt., N. Staffs. Regt. (W.) 1913
✠ROWE, H. P. Capt., R.E. (Signals) 1908
Died 6 *Nov.* 1918 *of pneumonia*
ROWE, W. H. C. Lieut.-Col., R.A.S.C. *C.B.E. O.B.E* 1902
M 5.
✠ROWSELL, H. G. Pte., R. Fusiliers (P. S. Bn.); Capt., 1907
Hampshire Regt.
Killed in action 11 *Sept.* 1916
✠ROYLE, J. B. Major, S. Wales Borderers 1892
Killed in action 15 *Jan.* 1917
RUBIE, T. A. C. Lieut., Uganda Protectorate Force and 1911
Unattd. List, T.F.
✠RUCK-KEENE, R. E. Lieut., R. Welsh Fus. 1907
Accidentally killed 24 *Jan.* 1916
✠RUDD, K. S. Pte., King's (Shropshire L.I.); Capt. and 1913
Adjt., W. Yorks. Regt. (W.)
Killed in action 10 *Oct.* 1918
RUSSELL, A. Major, R.G.A. (W.) *M.C.* 1912
RUTHERFORD, G. L. Capt., Durham L.I.(T.F.) (W.) 1910
M.C. M.
RYAN, C. M., D.S.O. Colonel, R.A.S.C.; Brig.-Gen., 1885
Director of Supplies and Transport. *C.M.G. C.B.E.*
M 2. *Officer, Legion of Honour* (*France*)

SADLER, H. Major, 6th Dragoon Gds. (Carabiniers); 1909
G.S.O. 2. *French Croix de Guerre*
SALE, H. G. Lieut., Northumberland Fus. (W.) 1912
SALMON, H. B. 2nd Lieut., R.G.A.; Staff Lieut. 1910
SALMON, L. H. Sergt., King's Royal Rifle Corps; Capt., 1901
Worcestershire Regt.

✠Sanderson, G. E.   Pte., R. Fusiliers (P.S. Bn.); Lieut.,   1907
   R. Irish Rifles; attd. M.G.C.
   Killed in action 15 *July* 1916
Saner, J. D. J.   Capt., R.E. (Signals, T.F.)   *M.C. M.*   1913
✠Sarsby, R. A.   2nd Lieut., Norfolk Regt.   1912
   Killed in action 31 *Dec.* 1915
✠Saunders, C. P. G.   Capt., Loyal N. Lancs. Regt.   1914
   Killed in action at Eaucourt l'Abbaye 28 *Sept.* 1916
✠Savory, H. L. S.   2nd Lieut., Durham L.I. and Suffolk Regt.   1916
   Killed in action 26 *April* 1918
✠Schiff, M. E. H.   Capt., Suffolk Regt.   1907
   Killed in action at Gouzeaucourt 25 *Sept.* 1917
Scott, D. A.   2nd Lieut., King's Royal Rifle Corps   1905
Scott, Rev. F. E.   C.F. 4th Class, R.A.C.D.   1904
Scott, Rev. H. P. F.   Chaplain, R.N.   1902
Scott, S. C.   Pte., R. Fusiliers (P. S. Bn.); Capt., Essex   1912
   Regt. and I.A.R.O., attd. 109th Infy. (W.) *M.C.*
Scott, W.   Capt., R.A.S.C. *m* 2.   1913
Sendell, C. H.   Pte., London Regt. (Artists Rifles);   1913
   Lieut., R.F.A. (W.)
Senior, F. G.   Capt., E. Yorks. Regt.; A.M.L.O. *M.*   1891
Seymour, Rev. A. G.   Chaplain, R.N.   1905
Shackle, S. A.   Capt., Spec. List (Remount Service)   1896
Sharp, Rev. J. S.   C.F. 4th Class, R.A.C.D.   1901
Sharpe, Rev. E.   C.F. 4th Class, R.A.C.D.   1906
Shelmerdine, Rev. T. G.   C.F. 4th Class, R.A.C.D.   1905
Shelton, O. W. M.   Lieut., R.A.S.C.; attd. King's Own   1909
   (Yorkshire L.I.)
Shenton, Rev. J. S.   C.F. 4th Class, R.A.C.D.   1909
Shera, F. H.   Capt., Malvern College O.T.C.   1901
✠Shields, H. J. S.   Lieut., R.A.M.C. *M.*   1906
   Killed in action 25 *Oct.* 1914
Shurlock, A. G.   Capt., R.A.M.C.   1913
Shuter, A. E.   Major, R.F.A.(T.F.) (W.)   1891
Shuter, C. H.   Major, H.A.C. and R.F.A.(T.F.)   1893
Sidney, P.   Capt., Northumberland Fus.; Lieut.-Col.,   1900
   S.O. 1, R.A.F. *m.*
✠Simson, J.   Lieut., Australian F.A.   1910
   Killed in action 31 *July* 1917
✠Skinner, H. S.   Pte., London Regt.   1914
   Died 13 *Sept.* 1916 *of wounds received in action*
Sleigh, G. P.   Capt., D. of Wellington's (W. Riding   1912
   Regt.); empld. O.C.B.; attd. Embarkation Staff,
   Indian Army

SMITH, A. S. D. 2nd Lieut., Forest School, Waltham- 1902
  stow, O.T.C.
SMITH, Rev. B. T. D. C.F. 4th Class, R.A.C.D. *1906
SMITH, F. B. Lieut., R.A.S.C. 1910
SMITH, Rev. G. A. C. C.F. 4th Class, R.A.C.D. 1899
SMITH, J. P. F. H. 2nd Lieut., R.A.S.C. (W.) 1905
SMITH, W. H. Capt., King's Own (Yorkshire L.I.) (W.) 1898
SMITH-CARINGTON, M. C. H. Capt., R.F.A.(T.F.) M. 1905
SMYTH, S. S. Lieut., King's (Liverpool Regt.) 1911
SMYTHE, D. Pte., Black Watch; Lieut., Seaforth Hdrs. 1910
  (W.)
SNELL, Rev. C. C. C.F. 4th Class, R.A.C.D. M. 1893
SOLE, B. J. B. Pte., Middlesex Regt. (P. S. Bn.); 2nd 1913
  Lieut., King's Royal Rifle Corps
✠SOLOMONS, M. Cadet, O.C.B. 1915
  Died 16 July 1916 of appendicitis
SOMERSET, A. P. F. C. Lieut., R. Fusiliers 1908
SOPER, F. P. P. Major, R.A.S.C.(T.F. Res.) 1894
SPENCER, T. B. W. Lieut. (Ad.), R.A.F. 1902
SPICER, H. W. Lieut., R.E. (Signals) 1909
STAFFORD, G. B. Capt. and Adjt., Durham L.I. (W.) 1908
STAFFORD, R. S. H. Lieut.-Col., King's Royal Rifle Corps; 1909
  attd. Middlesex Regt. and Gen. Staff. *D.S.O. and*
  Bar. M.C. M 4.
STAMPER, E. P. F. Capt., R. Welsh Fus. M. 1905
STANSFELD, C. A. Lieut., R.A.S.C. and 11th Bengal 1910
  Lancers, Indian Army
STARLING, E. C. W. Major, R.A.M.C. (W.) *M.C.* 1907
✠STAVELEY, H. S. Lieut., E. Yorks. Regt. 1907
  Killed in action 3 May 1917
STEDALL, G. ST G. Capt., London Yeo. (Sharpshooters); 1911
  Hon. Capt. (A.), R.A.F.
STEWART, D. H. Lieut., S. African Force 1890
✠STOBART, W. Lieut., Durham L.I.; attd. R.F.C. (W 2.) 1912
  Killed in action 24 Aug. 1916
STODDARD, J. W. Lieut., W. Yorks. Regt. (T.F.); Capt., 1902
  Spec. List (School of Instruction). *M.B.E.*
STORRS, B. ST J. Lieut., R.F.A. *1906
✠STORRS, F. E. Lieut., R.N.V.R. 1902
  Died 10 Nov. 1918 of pneumonia
✠STRACHAN, E. S. 2nd Lieut., Sherwood Foresters (Notts. 1898
  and Derby Regt., T.F.)
  Killed in action 14 Oct. 1915
STRAKER, A. C. Lieut., 15th Hussars; empld. Records 1911

STRAKER, G. H. Capt., 15th Hussars; A.D.C. *D.S.O.* 1910
M.C. Brevet Major. M 5. Chevalier, Legion of Honour (France). French Croix de Guerre. Order of St Anne, 4th Class (Russia)

STRAKER, L. S. Lieut., Irish Gds.; Capt., Gds. M.G. 1910
Regt. and Gen. Staff. (W.) *M.*

STROYAN, J. R. A. Major, R.F.A. 1909

SUTTON, Rev. F. O. C.F. 4th Class, R.A.C.D.(T.F.) *M.* *1883

SWAINSON, F. E. Lieut.-Col., Middlesex Regt. (W.) *m.* 1891

SWANSTON, H. E. Capt., R.F.A.(T.F.) 1906

SWAYNE, P. C. Lieut., D. of Wellington's (W. Riding 1896
Regt.); Capt., W. Yorks. Regt.

✠SWEARS, H. M. Sergt., R. Fusiliers (P. S. Bn.); Lieut., 1912
M.G.C.
Killed in action 11 *April* 1917

SYER, H. B. Major, R. Irish Rifles 1878

SYKES, A. H. C. 2nd Lieut., D. of Wellington's (W. Riding 1911
Regt.); Lieut., R.A.S.C.(M.T.)

SYKES, Sir M., Bart., M.P. Hon. Colonel, E. Yorks. 1897
Regt. and Gen. Staff. *m. Order of St Stanislas, 2nd Class (Russia). Commander, Order of the Star of Roumania*

SYMONS, H. J. Capt., E. Yorks. Regt.; Major, Tank Corps. 1897
M.

TANNER, H. O'S. F. Major, 19th Hussars and Gen. Staff. 1894
(W.) *M.*

TATE, J. E. Lieut., R.F.A. *M.* 1911

✠TAYLOR, E. F. H. 2nd Lieut., R. Fusiliers , 1909
Killed in action 27 *July* 1916

TAYLOR, R. H. H. Pte., R.A.S.C. 1916

TAYLOR, W. R. Lieut., The Buffs (E. Kent Regt.) 1910
(W 2.) (P.)

TELFER, Rev. W. C.F. 3rd Class, R.A.C.D.; Cadet, *1908
O.C.B. *M.C.*

THOMAS, A. L. Capt., R.G.A. 1887

✠THOMAS, O. V. 2nd Lieut., R. Welsh Fus.; Capt. (A.), 1912
R.A.F. *M* 2.
Died 29 *July* 1918 *of injuries received in flying accident*

THOMPSON, W. Capt., Durham L.I. 1895

THORBURN, K. D. S. M. Pte., R. Fusiliers (P. S. Bn.); 1895
Capt., Northumberland Fus.

THORNE, F. J. Major, R.A.M.C. *M.B.E. M.* 1904

THORNTON, W. H. J.   Major,   R.F.A.;   Lieut.-Col.,   1907
A.Q.M.G.   *M.C.   Brevet Major.   Brevet Lieut.-*
Colonel on promotion to substantive Major.   M 3.
Order of the Nile, 4th Class (Egypt)
TILLYARD, E. M. W.   Capt., King's Own (R. Lancaster   1908
Regt.) and Gen. Staff (Intelligence).   *O.B.E.   M 3.*
Greek Military Cross
✠TODD, J. G.   Pte., R. Fusiliers (P.S. Bn.); Capt., North-   1901
umberland Fus.
Killed in action 1 July 1916
✠TOMLIN, C. G.   2nd Lieut., London Regt. (W.)   1910
Died 9 July 1916 of wounds received in action
✠TOWN, C. A.   Capt., W. Yorks. Regt. (W 2.)   *M.C.   M.*   1903
Killed in action 20 Sept. 1917
TRACY, S. J.   Capt., R. Marines. (W.)   1913
TREE, H. B. LE D.   Capt., 112th Infy., Indian Army;   1900
Brigade Major.   *M 2.   Order of the Nile, 4th Class*
(Egypt)
TURNER, H. F. A.   Capt., Loyal N. Lancs. Regt.   *M.*   1913
✠TURNER, R. B.   2nd Lieut., Cheshire Regt.(T.F.)   1914
Killed in action 9 April 1916
TWYFORD, H.   Major, Sherwood Foresters (Notts. and   1893
Derby Regt.) and Gen. List (A.P.M.)
TYNDALE-BISCOE, C. J.   Lieut., R.F.A.; Staff Lieut. (W.) [1914]
M.C.
TYNDALE-BISCOE, H. L'E.   Capt. (A.), R.A.F.   1911
✠TYRRELL-GREEN, D. N.   Capt., R. Sussex Regt.(T.F.)   1913
Killed in action 26 March 1917

UBSDELL, T. R.   Major, R.F.A.(T.F.); Staff Capt.   *D.S.O.*   1891
M 4.   Officer, Legion of Honour (France)
UPTON, R.   Lieut., London Regt. (Cyclist Bn.)   1899

✠VAN SCHAICK, J. B.   M.G. Bn., American Army   1884
Died 9 Dec. 1918 of influenza contracted on active service
✠VANN, A. H. A.   Capt. and Adjt., W. Yorks. Regt.   1909
Killed in action 25 Sept. 1915
✠VANN, Rev. B. W.   Lieut.-Col., Sherwood Foresters   1907
(Notts. and Derby Regt.)   (W 5.)   *M.C. and Bar.*
M 2.   French Croix de Guerre
𝒱.𝕮.   "For most conspicuous bravery, devotion to
duty and fine leadership during the attack at Bellenglise
and Lehaucourt on September 19th, 1918. He led his
battalion with great skill across the Canal du Nord

through a very thick fog and under heavy fire from field and machine guns. On reaching the high ground above Bellenglise the whole attack was held up by fire of all descriptions from the front and right flank. Realising that everything depended on the advance going forward with the barrage, Col. Vann rushed up to the firing line and with the greatest gallantry led the line forward. By his prompt action and absolute contempt for danger the whole situation was changed, the men were encouraged and the line swept forward. Later, he rushed a field gun single-handed and knocked out three of the detachment. The success of the day was in no small degree due to the splendid gallantry and fine leadership displayed by this officer. Lieut.-Col. Vann, who had on all occasions set the highest example of valour, was killed near Ramicourt on 3rd October, 1918, when leading his battalion in attack."—Supplement to *The London Gazette* of 14 Dec. 1918.

Killed in action 3 Oct. 1918

VERDON, P.   Capt., R.A.M.C.; Lieut., I.M.S.   1905
VICK, G. R.   Capt., Durham L.I. and Gen. List (O.C.B.   1910
VICK, R. M.   Major, R.A.M.C.(T.F.) *O.B.E.* M 3.   1902
VINCENT, H. G.   Lieut., London Regt. (L.R.B.); attd.   1911
   R.E. (Signals)

WADSWORTH, S.   Lieut., Madras Gds., Indian Defence   1908
   Force
WAILES-FAIRBAIRN, N. W. F.   Capt., Yorkshire Hussars;   1911
   Lieut., R.E.(T.F.)
WAILES-FAIRBAIRN, W. F.   Major, S. Notts. Hussars.   1879
   (W.)
WAIT, R. J.   Corpl., R.E. (Signals); Lieut., R.G.A.   (W.) 1912
WAKEFIELD, W. V.   Capt., R. Warwickshire Regt.(T.F.   1910
   Res.); empld. War Office
WALKER, A. E. J.   2nd Lieut., Labour Corps; Lieut.,   1908
   Gen. List (Claims Commission)
WALKER, H.   Capt., R.A.M.C. *M.C. M.*   1905
WALKER, H. C.   Capt., Canadian F.A.   1914
WARE, B. O.   Lieut., Loyal N. Lancs. Regt.   (W.)   1914
WARREN, C. K. W.   2nd Lieut., Monkton Combe School   1912
   O.T.C.; Air Mechanic, R.A.F.
WARREN, L. A.   2nd Lieut., S. Lancs. Regt.; Lieut.,   1906
   Cheshire Regt.
WATERALL, L. S.   Lieut., Suffolk Regt. and Rifle Brigade. 1904
   (W.)

WATSON, J. A.   Lieut., W. Yorks. Regt.; attd. Durham L.I.   1910
WATSON, Hon. T. H.   Capt., R.A.S.C.   1887
WATT, A. F.   Lieut.-Col., Yorkshire Hussars; A.D.C.   1890
  D.S.O.   T.D.   *Brevet Lieut.-Colonel.   M.   Chevalier,*
  Legion of Honour (France)
WAYLEN, D. C.   Capt. (K.B.), R.A.F.; S.O. 3, Air Ministry.   1911
  M.B.E.   M 2.
✠WEBB, J. C.   Pte., R. Fusiliers (P.S. Bn.); 2nd Lieut.,   1912
  Leicestershire Regt.
  Killed in action 15 Sept. 1916
WELCH, D.   2nd Lieut., Cameronians (Scottish Rifles);   1905
  Lieut. (A), R.A.F.
✠WELINKAR, S. C.   Lieut. (A.), R.A.F.   1915
  Died in German hands 30 June 1918 of wounds received
  in action
WENLEY, J. A. S.   2nd Lieut., R.F.A.   1911
WHALE, G. H. L.   Capt., R.A.M.C. (T.F.)   1895
WHELPTON, L. G.   Lieut., R. Berkshire Regt. (T.F. Res.);   1910
  attd. King's Own (Yorkshire L.I.)
WHITE, G. G.   Capt., E. Surrey Regt.; attd. Gen. Staff.   1911
  O.B.E.   m.
WHITE, J.   Lieut., Northamptonshire Regt. (T.F.)   1912
✠WHITE, M.   Trooper, S. African Horse   1890
  Died May 1916
WILD, J. A. P.   Capt., Yorkshire Regt.; empld. O.C.B.   (W.)   1901
WILDE, C. A. G.   2nd Lieut., London Regt. (Kensington   1911
  Bn.)   M.C.
WILKINSON, F. C.   2nd Lieut., Argyll and Sutherland Hdrs.;   1906
  Capt. (T.), R.A.F. (Aircraft Production Dept.)   (W.)
WILLIAMS, A. L.   Pte., R.A.S.C.; Capt., R. Fusiliers   1911
WILLIAMS, C. S., v.D.   Hon. Colonel, Queen's Own (R.W.   1868
  Kent Regt., T.F.)   m.
WILLIAMS, Rev. F. F. S.   Lieut., Eastbourne College O.T.C.   1889
WILLIAMS, Rev. H. F. F.   Junior Chaplain, Indian Army   *1907
WILLIAMS, L.   Capt., Welsh Regt.   1913
✠WILSON, D. R.   Lieut., The Queen's (R.W. Surrey Regt.)   1910
  Killed in action near Ypres 30 Oct. 1914
✠WILSON-BARKWORTH, K. A.   Capt., E. Yorks. Regt.   (W 2.)   1902
  M.C.
  Killed in action 25 Oct. 1917
WILTON, J. P.   Capt., Spec. List; Bdr., R.G.A.   1902
WILTON, T. R.   Capt., R.E. (Fortress, T.F.)   M.   1897
WINDLEY, Rev. F. M.   C.F. 3rd Class, R.A.C.D.   (W.)   1908
WINGATE, W. M. R.   Lieut., R. Fusiliers; Capt., Spec.   1905
  List (Recruiting Staff).   m.

WINNICOTT, D. W. Surgeon Sub-Lieut., R.N.V.R. 1914
✠WISEMAN, P. H. F. Pte., R. Fusiliers (P. S. Bn.); Lieut., 1906
Loyal N. Lancs. Regt. (W.)
Died 27 Oct. 1917 of wounds received in action
WISEMAN, Sir W. G. E., Bart. Lieut.-Col., Gen. List. 1904
C.B. m.
✠WOLRYCHE-WHITMORE, P. M. 2nd Lieut., Lincolnshire 1910
Yeo.; Lieut., R.F.A.
Killed in action 1 Aug. 1918
WOOD, C. J. Lieut., The Buffs (E. Kent Regt.); Capt. 1913
and Adjt., Queen's Own (R. W. Kent Regt.) *M.C.*
WOOD, E. W. Capt., S. Staffs. Regt. (W.) *M.C. and* 1911
Bar
WOOD, FRANKLIN G. Surgeon Lieut., R.N. 1910
WOOD, F. GORDON. Leading Telegraphist, R.N.V.R. 1907
WOOD, G. H. A. Pte., R. Fusiliers (P. S. Bn.); Lieut., 1913
Border Regt.; attd. Wiltshire Regt.; empld. Ministry
of Munitions. (W 2.)
WOOD, J. Cadet, R.A.F. 1908
WOOD, W. B. Capt., R.A.M.C. *M.* 1902
WOODARD, E. H. J. Lieut., R. Warwickshire Regt.; 1894
Capt., Gen. List (R.T.O.) (W.)
WOODARD, Rev. F. A. Capt., Forest School, Waltham- 1908
stow, O.T.C.
WOODROFFE, L. W. Capt., R. Marines; M.L.O. 1913
WOODS, S. M. J. Lieut., Somerset L.I., R. Warwickshire 1888
Regt., and Devon Regt.; Capt., Labour Corps
✠WRAY, K. C. G. Capt., S. Lancs. Regt.(T.F.) 1910
Killed in action 9 Aug. 1916
✠WRENFORD, A. L. Major, Worcestershire Regt.; attd. R. 1900
Inniskilling Fus.; Lieut.-Col., E. Lancs. Regt. (W.)
M.
Killed in action 21 March 1918
WRIGHT, A. J. Capt. and Adjt., Northamptonshire Regt. 1908
(T.F.); Brigade Major. *D.S.O. M.C. M* 3.
WYLD, E. J. M. Capt., Wiltshire Regt.(T.F.) 1913
WYLEY, D. H. F. Capt., R.F.A.; Staff Capt. *O.B.E.* 1906
M.C.
WYNN, Rev. H. E. C.F. 3rd Class, R.A.C.D. *M.* *1910
Italian Croce di Guerra
WYNNE, H. F. D. Pte., R. Fusiliers (P. S. Bn.) and 1913
R.A.M.C.

✠YATES, H. B. Lieut.-Col., Canadian A.M.C. 1883
Died 22 Jan. 1916 of illness contracted on active service

KING'S COLLEGE

ACLAND, T. W. G. Capt., R.E. (London Electrical En-   1909
gineers, T.F.); empld. Ministry of Munitions
ADAM, C. G. FORBES. *See* FORBES ADAM, C. G.
ADAMS, W. T. Lieut., E. Yorks. Regt. *M.C.*   1913
ADCOCK, F. E. Lieut.-Cdr., R.N.V.R., empld. Admiralty.   1905
O.B.E.
AGAR, W. E. Capt., Highland L.I. (T.F.)   1900
AGNEW, G. C. 2nd Lieut., Gen. List (Intelligence)   1901
✠AINGER, T. E. 2nd Lieut., Berkshire Yeo.   1903
Killed in action in Gallipoli 21 Aug. 1915
ALEXANDER, R. D. Flt. Cadet, R.A.F.   1917
ALFORD, E. J. G. Lieut., Spec. List (R.T.O.)   1909
ALLBOOK, W. Pte., Middlesex Regt.   1915
ALLEN, H. S. Capt., King's (Liverpool Regt., Liverpool   1914
Scottish, T.F.) (W.)
AMPS, L. W. Lieut., R.E.; empld. Ministry of Munitions.   1910
(W.) *M.*
ANNAN, J. G. Capt., R.G.A.; empld. Foreign Office.   1905
Chevalier, Legion of Honour (France)
✠ARBUTHNOT, M. A. Capt., 16th Lancers; A.D.C.; Staff   1908
Capt. *M.C. M* 2. *French Croix de Guerre*
Died 14 Oct. 1918 *of septic pneumonia*
ARCHER, J. F. Major, King's Own (Yorkshire L.I., T.F.   1900
Res.)
ARIS, H. Major, Winchester College O.T.C. *m.*   1887
ARMBRUSTER, C. H. Major, Gen. Staff. *O.B.E. M* 4.   1893
Order of the Nile, 3rd Class (Egypt)
✠ARMSTRONG, E. W. 2nd Lieut., Rifle Brigade   1911
Died 11 *July* 1915 *of wounds received in action* 10 *July*
1915

✠ASHINGTON, H. S. O. Capt., E. Yorks. Regt. (W.)   1910
Killed in action near Combles 31 *Jan.* 1917

✠BACON, D. F. C. 2nd Lieut., Durham L.I.; attd. North- [1914]
umberland Fus.
Died 1 *Nov.* 1915 *of wounds received in action* 2 *Oct.*
1915 *at the Hohenzollern Redoubt*
BAGENAL, N. B. Lieut., Irish Gds.; empld. Ministry of   1910
Labour. (W 4.)
BAGGE, Sir A. W. F., Bart. Lieut., Norfolk Regt. (T.F.);   1894
Capt., King's (Liverpool Regt.)
BAGSHAWE, H. V. Lieut.-Col., R.A.M.C.; A.D.M.S.   1893
C.B.E. D.S.O. Brevet Lieut.-Colonel. M 3. *Order
of the Nile,* 3*rd Class* (*Egypt*)
BAILEY, R. F. 2nd Lieut., Shrewsbury School O.T.C.   1903
BAINBRIDGE, O. J. Lieut., Sherwood Rangers   1898
BALL, R. G. Capt., R. Inniskilling Fus.; Major, M.G.C.   1900
(W.)
BALL, W. V. A.B., R.N.V.R. (Anti-Aircraft). *O.B.E.*   1893
BANHAM, Rev. V. G. C.F. 4th Class, R.A.C.D. *M.C.*   1900
and Bar
BANNATYNE, A. G. Capt., R.A.S.C. *M.B.E. m.*   1904
BARKER, G. P. Major, Suffolk Yeo. (W.)   1906
BARKER, R. I. P. Capt., R.A.S.C.(T.F.); Capt. (A.),   1908
R.A.F.
BARNARD, F. A. B. Capt., R. Fusiliers; attd. T.M.B. (W.) 1911
M.
BARNES, J. S. 2nd Lieut., R. Horse Gds.; Major (A. and   1913
S.), R.A.F. (W.)
BARRACLOUGH, N. E. Capt. (A.), R.A.F. *M.C.*   1913
BARROW, R. M. Cadet, O.C.B.   1912
BARTHOLOMEW, Rev. G. T. C.F. 4th Class, R.A.C.D.   1900
(T.F.)
BATE, A. G. Capt., R.A.M.C. (2nd E. Gen. Hospital,   1894
T.F.)
BATEMAN, R. J. S. Lieut. Essex Regt.(T.F.)   1901
BATHER, Rev. A. G. Capt., Winchester College O.T.C.   1887
BAXTER, T. H. 2nd Lieut. (T.), R.A.F.   1904
✠BAYLEY, C. H. Capt., S. Lancs. Regt.   1899
Died 7 *Aug.* 1917 *of wounds received in action*
BAYLISS, C. W. Capt., Welsh Regt. (Cyclist Bn., T.F.);   1913
attd. R.E. (Sound-ranging Section)
BEALE, E. V. Capt., R.A.M.C.   1912
BECK, H. M. Lieut., Aldenham School O.T.C.   1887

BEDDINGTON, F. Lieut., King's Royal Rifle Corps [1914]
BENSON, C. T. V. Major, R.A.M.C. 1901
BENTHALL, E. C. Capt., Devon Regt.; empld. War Office. 1912
(W.)
BERESFORD, J. B. Lieut., R.A.S.C. *M.B.E.* 1907
BERRY, A. 2nd Lieut., Spec. List (Intelligence). *O.B.E.* 1882
✠BERRY, P. H. Lieut., R.A.M.C. 1907
Drowned 17 March 1916 on the Egyptian coast in the
attempt to rescue a comrade
✠BERRY, W. Lieut., R.A.S.C. 1902
Died 5 July 1917 of gas poisoning and shell shock
BEVAN, A. E. Major, M.G.C. (W.) 1911
✠BEVAN, F. H. V. Capt., S. Wales Borderers; attd. R.F.C. 1913
Killed in action April 1917
BEVAN-BROWN, R. E. Sergt., R.A.M.C. *M.S.M.* 1911
BEVAN-PETMAN, B. A. Trooper, Punjab Light Horse, In- 1889
dian Defence Force
BEVAN-PETMAN, B. H. Lieut., 21st Cavalry, Indian Army [1914]
BEVERIDGE, E. W. Lieut., R. Dublin Fus.; attd. R.E. (Sig- [1914]
nals). *M.*
BIRCH, F. L. Lieut.-Cdr., R.N.V.R.; empld. Admiralty. 1909
O.B.E.
BIRCH, W. C. Sapper, R.E. (Signals) 1904
BIRD, C. K. Lieut., R.E. 1911.
✠BLAIR, P. C. B. 2nd Lieut., Rifle Brigade 1910
Killed in action 6 July 1915
BLAKE, A. G. Capt., Essex Regt.; attd. 79th Punjabis, [1914]
Indian Army. (W.)
✠BLECH, E. L. 2nd Lieut., E. Surrey Regt. and M.G.C. [1914]
Killed in action near Guillemont 18 Aug. 1916
✠BLISS, F. K. Pte., London Regt. (Artists Rifles); 2nd 1911
Lieut., R.F.A.
Killed in action at Thiepval 28 Sept. 1916
BLUNT, Rev. A. S. V. C.F. 4th Class, R.A.C.D. *O.B.E.* 1889
BLUNT, D. L. Lieut., R.A.S.C. 1909
BOLTON, P. Lieut., Oundle School O.T.C. 1908
BOOTH, C. H. B. Capt., R.A.M.C. *M.* 1905
BOSANQUET, W. S. B. Capt., Coldstream Gds. (W.) 1911
D.S.O. M.
✠BOTTOMLEY, E. W. Capt., London Regt. (R. Fus.) [1914]
Killed in action 15 June 1917
BOULENGER, C. L. Hon. Lieut., Spec. List 1903
BOWEN, A. G. W. Fleet-Surgeon, R.N. 1881
BOWRING, H. Capt., R.A.M.C. 1901

BRADBURY, J. F. Major, R.A.S.C.(T.F.) *m.* 1903
BRAITHWAITE, J. G. Lieut., R.N.V.R. [1914]
BRAUNHOLTZ, E. J. K. Pte., The Buffs (E. Kent Regt.), 1909
The Queen's (R. W. Surrey Regt.), and Middlesex
Regt.
BREWSTER, G. W. 2nd Lieut., Oundle School O.T.C. 1899
BRISTED, G. T. Capt., R.E. *M.* 1913
✠BROOKE, R. C. Sub-Lieut., R.N.V.R. (Howe Bn., R.N.D.) 1906
Died at Scyros 23 April 1915 of blood-poisoning follow-
ing sunstroke
✠BROOKE, W. A. C. 2nd Lieut., London Regt. (Post Office 1909
Rifles)
Killed in action 14 June 1915
BROOKS, C. D. Capt. and Adjt., R.G.A. *M.* 1905
BROOKS, D. C. M. Capt. (A.), R.A.F. *M.C. A.F.C.* 1914
BROWN, A. C. Lieut., R.F.A. (W.) 1902
BROWN, G. B. 2nd Lieut., Tank Corps. (W.) 1905
BROWN, G. M. Capt. and Adjt., Suffolk Regt.; Staff 1910
Capt. *O.B.E. M. m.*
BROWN, W. B. Lieut., Northumberland Fus. (W.) 1912
BRUNDRIT, J. C. Capt., R. Welsh Fus.(T.F.) 1897
BRUNDRIT, P. W. Cadet, O.C.B. 1894
BRUNWIN, A. H. Lieut., King's Own (R. Lancaster [1914]
Regt.) (W 2.) *M.C.*
BRYAN, F. Capt., R.A.M.C.; Asst. Embarkation S.O. 1895
BUCKLE, C. L. Capt., R.A.S.C. 1904
BUCKLEY, Hon. B. B. Lieut., London Regt. (Rangers, 1909
T.F. Res.); empld. Admiralty
✠BURGOYNE JOHNSON, L. V. Capt., Durham L.I.(T.F.) 1909
Killed in action 26 April 1915
BURKE, H. F. Capt., R.F.A.; Staff Capt. *M.C.* 1902
BURKE, M. L. Lieut., K. Edward's Horse; Capt., Tank 1907
Corps
BURR, Rev. A. L. C.F. 4th Class, R.A.C.D. 1909
BURTON, A. Capt., R.A.M.C. 1889
BURY, E. B. Lieut., Suffolk Regt.; Staff Lieut. (W.) 1909
BUSHELL, W. F. Capt., Unattd. List, T.F.; Lieut., Here- 1903
fordshire Regt.
✠BUSK, E. T. 2nd Lieut., R.E. ٠ 1904
Killed in flying accident 5 Nov. 1914
✠BUSK, H. A. Flt. Cdr., R.N.A.S. 1912
Killed in action over Gallipoli 6 Jan. 1916
✠BYTHWAY, M. H. P.O., R.N.A.S. 1899
Died 9 Dec. 1915 of wounds received in action

✠CAMPBELL, R. C. C.   Capt., King's Own Scottish Bor-   1907
derers
Died 20 *May* 1915 *of wounds received in action*
CANE, A. S.   Major, R.A.M.C.; D.A.D.M.S.   (P.)   1903
D.S.O. O.B.E. M 4.
CANE, L. B.   Capt., R.A.M.C.   1900
CANE, M. H.   Major, R.A.M.C.   *O.B.E.*   1906
CARLISLE, H. B.   Capt., Lancs. Fus.(T.F.); Major, M.G.C.   1910
CARNEGIE, J. D.   Lieut., Hampshire Yeo. and Hampshire   1913
Regt.; attd. 6th (Inniskilling) Dragoons.   (W.)
CARROW, R. B.   Lieut., The Buffs (E. Kent Regt.)   (W.)   1911
(P.)
✠CARTER, J. S.   Capt., Grenadier Gds.   1900
Killed in action at Hesquières 27 *Sept.* 1918
CARTWRIGHT, J. L.   2nd Lieut., Labour Corps; attd. R.   1915
Sussex Regt.
CARVER, N. C.   Surgeon Lieut., R.N.   1895
CHAMBERS, H. T.   Major, R.A.S.C.; D.A.D.S. and T.   1913
O.B.E. M 2.
CHAMPION, H. H.   Capt., Uppingham School O.T.C.   1892
✠CHESTER, H. K.   Capt., Essex Regt.   1913
Died 28 *March* 1917 *of wounds received in action at*
Gaza
CHITTY, J. W.   Capt., Essex Regt.(T.F.)   1913
✠CHUBB, E. G.   Capt., The Queen's (R.W. Surrey Regt.)   1887
Killed in action at Hill 60 12 *July* 1915
✠CHUBB, F. J. M.   Lieut., King's Own (Yorkshire L.I.)   1912
Killed in action near Ypres 18 *April* 1915   •
CLARK, A. J.   Hon. Capt., R.A.M.C.   *M.C. M.*   1903
CLARK, Rev. P. N.   Capt., Spec. List.   *1889
CLARK, W. M.   Lieut., King's Own Scottish Borderers.   1903
(W.)
CLARKE, R. S.   Capt., Sussex Yeo.; attd. R. Sussex Regt.;   1911
A.D.C.   (W.)
✠CLAUGHTON, I. D.   Lieut., Suffolk Regt.   1909
Killed in action 4 *March* 1916
CLIFFORD, F. A.   Capt., R.E.   (W.)   1903
CLOUT, C. W.   Capt., London Regt. (Blackheath and   1913
Woolwich Bn.); Staff .Capt., War Office.   (W.)
M.B.E. M.
COHEN, A. M.   Major, Queen's Own (R. W. Kent Regt.,   1895
T.F.)
COHEN, Sir H. B., Bart.   Major, Queen's Own (R. W.   1892
Kent Regt., T.F.); Embarkation S.O.   *O.B.E. m.*

✠COLBECK, L. G. 2nd Lieut., R.F.A. *M.C.*   1903
    Died at sea 3 Jan. 1918
COLE, G. H. 2nd Lieut., Somerset L.I.   1915
COLE, Rev. H. B. C.F. 4th Class, R.A.C.D. *M.C.* 1894
COLE, L. B. 2nd Lieut., R.F.A.   1916
COLLIN, E. P. C. Lieut., I.A.R.O., attd. 18th Lancers 1909
COLLINGHAM, D. H. Capt., R.A.M.C. *M.*   1897
COMEAU, E. A. Lieut. (T.), R.A.F.   1912
✠COMPTON-BURNETT, N. 2nd Lieut., Leicestershire Regt. 1907
    Killed in action 14 July 1916
COMYN, H. F. Capt., R.A.M.C.   1903
✠CONCANON, G. L. B. Capt., Australian Infy. *M.* 1900
    Killed in action in Gallipoli 25 March 1915
CONYBEARE, A. E. Capt., Eton College O.T.C.   1894
✠COOKE, A. W. H. Capt., Durham L.I. (W.) *M.*   1906
    Killed in action 24 March 1918
COOKE, C. H. Capt., R. Berkshire Regt.; Brigade Major. 1902
    M.C. M 2.
COOKE, S. R. Capt., London Regt. (Post Office Rifles); 1911
    G.S.O. 3, War Office. (W.) *m.*
COPEMAN, C. E. F. Lieut.-Col., Cambridgeshire Regt. *1906
    and Northamptonshire Regt.(T.F.) *C.M.G. T.D.*
    m 3.
CORBETT, G. H. U. Capt., R.A.M.C.   1898
CORRIE, G. T. A.B., R.N.V.R. (R.N.D.); Lieut., R. 1907
    Warwickshire Regt.; empld. Ministry of Munitions.
    (W.)
CORYTON, W. A. Lieut., Rifle Brigade; Hon. Lieut. (A.), 1913
    R.A.F. (W.)
COURTAULD, J. S. Major, Gen. List; D.A.A.G. *M.C.* 1899
    M 3. *French Croix de Guerre*
COURTAULD, S. L. Capt., Worcestershire Regt.; Major, 1901
    M.G.C. *M.C. M* 2.
COWAN, J. M. Colonel, A.M.S. *M.*   1888
✠COWARD, H. Lieut., Border Regt.   1906
    Died 20 April 1917 of wounds received in action
CRACE, J. F. Lieut., Eton College O.T.C.   1897
✠CRACROFT, R. B. Lieut., E. Yorks. Regt. (W.)   [1914]
    Killed in action near Mametz Wood 10 July 1916
✠CRAIGMILE, A. M. Capt., Rifle Brigade. (W.) *M.C.* 1914
    Killed in action 29 March 1918
✠CREASY, R. L. Major, R.F.A. (W 2.) *M.C. M.*   1911
    *Died 22 Oct. 1918 of wounds received in action at
    Cambrai*

CREWDSON, B. F. 2nd Lieut., Rifle Brigade; Major, 1905
Border Regt.; Capt., Irish Gds. (W.) *C.B.E. m.*
CREWDSON, R. B. Capt., R.F.A. *M* 2. 1912
✠CROMPTON, N. G. Lieut., R.E. (W.) *M.* 1907
Killed in action near Armentières 5 Nov. 1915
✠CROWE, H. A. 2nd Lieut., London Regt. (R. Fus.) [1914]
Died 30 May 1915 of wounds received in action
CUSHION, E. J. Corpl., R.A.M.C. 1905

DALRYMPLE, C. M. Lieut., University College School 1895
O.T.C.
DALTON, C. H. C. 2nd Lieut., Northamptonshire Regt.; 1914
Lieut., Manchester Regt.
DALTON, E. H. J. N. Lieut., R.G.A. *Italian Bronze* 1906
Medal for Military Valour
✠DARLEY, D. J. 2nd Lieut., Suffolk Regt. 1914
Killed in action at La Boisselle 1 July 1916
DAVIES, D. Lieut.-Col., R. Welsh Fus.(T.F.) *Order of* 1899
St Stanislas, 2nd Class, with swords (Russia)
DAVIES, G. F. Capt., Gloucestershire Regt.(T.F.); 1894
Major, Spec. List (Asst. Cmdt., Reinforcement Camp)
DAVIES, R. G. R. Lieut., 16th Lancers; Major, M.G.C. 1909
(Cavalry). (W.) *M.C. M* 4.
DAVIES, T. M. Lieut., R. Sussex Regt.(T.F.); Capt., 1899
R.G.A. (W.)
DAVIS, G. F. S. Lieut., R.A.S.C.; attd. R.G.A. (W.) 1905
DAVIS, K. J. A. Capt., R.A.M.C. 1902
✠DAWSWELL, G. A. 2nd Lieut., London Regt. (St Pancras 1912
Bn.)
Killed in action 20 March 1916
DE HAMEL, H. G. Sergt., London Regt. (London Scot- 1899
tish). (W.)
✠DEIGHTON, G. W. Capt., Suffolk Regt. *M.C. M.* 1911
Chevalier, Legion of Honour (France)
Killed in action at Ovillers 3 July 1916
DE LINDE, C. A. Corpl., London Regt. (London Scot- [1914]
tish); 2nd Lieut., R.E. (W.)
DEUCHAR, J. L. Lieut., Tank Corps. (W.) 1905
DEXTER, J. Pte., N. Staffs. Regt. (W.) 1916
DICKINSON, P. P. Paymaster Sub-Lieut., R.N.V.R. 1902
DILKE, C. W. 2nd Lieut., Surrey Yeo. 1896
DOBBS, A. F. Major, R.G.A. *M.* 1895
DOBSON, E. L. Capt., H.A.C. and R.A.M.C. 1906
DOGGART, J. H. Surgeon Sub-Lieut., R.N.V.R. 1917

DOHERTY, W. D. Capt., R.A.S.C   1912
DOUGLAS, C. K. M. Lieut., R. Scots; Capt. (A.), R.A.F.   1912
    (W.) *A.F.C.*
✠DOWSON, H. Pte., H.A.C.; Capt., King's Royal Rifle   1908
    Corps. *M.C. M.*
    Killed in action 15 *Sept.* 1916
DRINKWATER, J. R. Major, R.F.A. (W.)   1906
DUNN, Rev. C. S. C.F. 4th Class, R.A.C.D. (W.)   1892
DURHAM, H.E. Hon. Lieut., R.A.M.C.; Major, Spec. List   1884
DURNFORD, H. G. E. Capt., R.F.A. (P. *Escaped from*   1905
    Germany.) *M.C.*
✠DURNFORD, R. C. Capt., Hampshire Regt.(T.F.) (W.) [1914]
    D.S.O. M.
    Killed in action in Mesopotamia 21 *June* 1918
✠DURNFORD, R. S. Capt., King's Royal Rifle Corps   1904
    Killed in action at Hooge 30 *July* 1915
✠DUVAL, M. R. Capt., 66me Regt., French Army. *French*   1887
    Croix de Guerre
    Killed in action 5 *May* 1916
DYNE, H. E. L. Lieut., The Queen's (R.W. Surrey Regt.)   1904
DYNE, J. B. Cadet, O.C.B.   1894
✠DYSON, W. H. 2nd Lieut., London Regt. (Queen's West-   1910
    minster Rifles)
    Died in German hands 14 *July* 1916 *of wounds received*
    in action

EATON, J. E. C. Sergt., London Regt. (Artists Rifles);   1892
    2nd Lieut., Spec. List (Intelligence)
ECKHARD, O. P. Capt., Manchester Regt.; empld. O.C.B.   1907
    (W.)
EDE, C. Lieut., R.A.M.C.   1905
EDE, M. C. Lieut., S. Wales Borderers. (W.)   1912
EDMUNDS, P. M. L. Lieut., 12th Lancers; Capt. (A.),   1912
    R.A.F. (W.) *M.*
EDWARDS, C. J. Capt., Northumberland Fus. and Gen.   1905
    Staff (O.C.B.) (W.) *M.B.E. m*
✠EDWARDS, G. T. Capt., R. Fusiliers   1909
    Killed in action at Delville Wood 31 *July* 1916
✠EICKE, O. M. Lieut., R.F.A. *M.C.*   1913
    Killed in action 5 *Nov.* 1916
ELLINGTON, N. B. Major, Cheshire Regt.(T.F.) (W.)   1899
    M.C. M.
ELLIOTT, C. A. B. Capt., Leicestershire Regt. (W 2.)   1913
ELLIOTT-COOPER, M. Lieut., R.E.   1900

KING'S COLLEGE 199

ELLIS, C. D. B. Lieut., R.H.A (T.F.) (W.) *M.C. M.* 1913
✠ELMSLIE, K. W. Lieut., 4th (R. Irish) Dragoon Gds. 1906
Killed in action near Messines 4 *Nov.* 1914
✠ELWIN, F. H. Pte., King's (Shropshire L.I.); 2nd Lieut., [1914]
Wiltshire Regt.
Killed in action at Neuve Chapelle 14 *March* 1915
EMRYS-EVANS, P. V. Lieut., Suffolk Regt.; empld. Foreign 1912
Office. (W.)
ENGLISH, B. A. Lieut., Garrison Artillery, Indian Defence 1904
Force
ERRERA, A. J. J. H. Lieut., Artillery and Field Survey, 1904
Belgian Army
EVANS, C. L. Capt., Dover College O.T.C. 1900
EVANS, D. D. Capt., R.A.M.C. *M.C.* 1908
✠EVANS, D. L. Capt., Northamptonshire Regt. 1913
Died 26 *Sept.* 1916 *of wounds received in action*
EVANS, E., T.D. Surgeon Lieut.-Col., Welsh Regt.(T.F.) *1881
EVANS, G. F. F. Capt., R.E.; Staff Capt., War Office; 1907
Major, R.A.F.; S.O. 2, Air Ministry. (W.) *m.*
EVANS, U. R. Pte., London Regt. (Artists Rifles); Lieut., 1907
E. Surrey Regt.; attd. R.E. (Signals)

FALK, H. Major, I.M.S. *M. Order of the White Eagle,* 1897
5*th Class, with swords* (*Serbia*)
FARNELL, H. L. Lieut., Bedfordshire Regt. and Gen. List 1907
(Intelligence). *M.*
FAULKNER, A. K. Lieut., Hampshire Regt. and Nigeria 1906
Regt., W. African Frontier Force
FAY, C. R. Lieut., The Buffs (E. Kent Regt.); Capt., 1902
M.G.C. and Spec. List (Asst. Instructor). *M.*
FELKIN, A. E. Lieut., Spec. List (Interpreter) 1911
FEW, J. E. Capt., Suffolk Regt. and Spec. List, empld. 1896
British Military Mission
FIDDIAN, C. M. 2nd Lieut., S. Staffs. Regt. 1909
FIDDIAN, W. M. Lieut., Suffolk Regt. 1908
FILON, L. N. G. Major, London Regt. (R. Fus., T.F. 1898
Res.); Hon. Major (T.), R.A.F. *m* 2.
✠FINLAY, E. L. 2nd Lieut., London Regt. (Post Office 1910
Rifles) and Devon Regt.(T.F.)
Died 20 *March* 1916 *of wounds received in action in*
Mesopotamia
✠FIRTH, R. B. 2nd Lieut., London Regt. (L.R.B.) 1906
Died 26 *Sept.* 1917 *of wounds received in action near*
St Julien 21 *Sept.* 1917

FISHWICK, J. F.   Lieut., R. Sussex Regt.   1894
✠FITZGERALD, G. T.   Capt., Durham L.I.   (W.)   1902
   Killed in action near Armentières 30 Dec. 1915
FLEMING, G. B.   Capt., R.A.M.C.(T.F.)   (W.)   *M.B.E.*   1900
m.
FLITCH, J. E. C.   Capt., R.F.A.; attd. T.M.B.   (W.)   *M.C.*   1900
M.
FORBES, B. C.   Major, I.A.R.O.; Divisional Recruiting   1900
  Officer
FORBES ADAM, C. G.   Lieut., I.A.R.O., attd. 34th Sikh   1908
  Pioneers
FOSTER, H. P. R.   Lieut., D. of Cornwall's L.I.   1905
FOSTER, R. L. V.   Lieut.-Col., R.A.M.C.   *M.*   1893
FOSTER, V. LE N.   Lieut., Eton College O.T.C.   1894
FOULKES JONES, W.   Surgeon Lieut., R.N.   1901
FOX, C. L.   Major, R.E.(T.F.)   *M.C.*   1903
FRANKLIN, G. D.   Major, I.M.S.   *O.B.E.   M.*   1895
✠FRY, A. H.   2nd Lieut., London Regt. (Queen's)   1904
  Died 30 *Oct.* 1916 *of wounds received in action* 10 *Oct.*
  1916
FRY, L. S.   Surgeon Lieut., R.N.   1908
FRY, T. P.   Capt., Durham L.I.(T.F.)   (W.)   1910
FUNDUKLIAN, A. A.   Corpl., 22nd Infy., United States Army   1911

✠GALLIMORE, H. B.   Capt., R.F.A.(T.F.)   1904
  Killed in action 26 *May* 1917
GARDNER, A.   Paymaster Sub-Lieut., R.N.V.R.   1897
GARDNER, C.   Lieut., R.M.A.   1899
GARDNER, H.   Lieut., R.M.A.   *M.*   1911
GARROD, L. P.   Surgeon Sub-Lieut., R.N.V.R.   1914
✠GASELEE, A. M.   2nd Lieut., 15th Hussars   1912
  Killed in action near Ypres 24 *May* 1915
GEARY, A. B.   Capt., Spec. List (Intelligence)   1897
GELDART, H. R.   Lieut., Northamptonshire Regt.; attd.   1914
  Norfolk Regt.   (W.)   *M.*
GEMMELL, A. A.   2nd Lieut., King's (Liverpool Regt.,   1911
  Liverpool Scottish, T.F.); Capt. and Adjt., Cameron
  Hdrs.   (W.)   *M.C.   M.   Greek Military Cross*
✠GENT, F. E.   Lieut., W. Yorks. Regt.   1912
  Killed in action in Gallipoli 7 *Aug.* 1915
✠GIBBINS, R. B.   Capt., R. Warwickshire Regt.   1904
  Killed in action 4 *Dec.* 1917
GIBLIN, L. F.   Major, 40th (Tasmania) Bn., Australian   1893
  Force.   (W 3.)   *D.S.O.   M.C.   M.*

GILES, G. C. T. 2nd Lieut., King's (Liverpool Regt.); 1910
Capt., Army Cyclist Corps
GILL, C. I. C. Capt., Manchester Regt.(T.F.) 1912
GILLUM, S. J. Trooper, Bombay Light Horse, Indian 1895
Defence Force
GOODDEN, C. P. Capt., R. Marines 1899
GORDON, C. A. Lieut., Grenadier Gds.; Capt., T.M.B. 1904
(W.) *M.C. Belgian Croix de Guerre*
GRANT-IVES, J. C. (*formerly* GRANT). Capt., Rifle Brigade. 1908
M.
GRAY, J. Capt., The Queen's (R.W. Surrey Regt., T.F.) 1909
M.C. French Croix de Guerre
GRAY, J. M. Capt., Sherwood Foresters (Notts. and 1908
Derby Regt., T.F.); empld. Recruiting Staff. (W.)
GREEN, J. R. E. 2nd Lieut., R.F.A. 1903
GREENWOOD, J. E. Pte., London Regt. (Artists Rifles); 1910
Capt., E. Surrey Regt.(T.F.); Lieut., Grenadier Gds.
(W.) *M.*
GRICE, J. W. Capt., R.A.M.C. 1900
GRIFFIN, F. W. W. Capt., R.A.M.C. 1900
GRIFFITH, H. C. Lieut., R.G.A. 1895
GRIFFITHS, J., T.D. Colonel, R.A.M.C. (1st E. Gen. Hos- *1890
pital, T. F.) *C.M.G. m* 3.
GRITTON, H. J. 2nd Lieut., R.A.S.C. 1899
✠GUTHRIE, R. F. Capt., King's (Liverpool Regt.) 1910
Killed in action 9 Aug. 1916
GUTTERIDGE, H. C. Capt., R.A.O.C. *M.* 1895
✠GUY, C. G. Lieut., Northamptonshire Regt. and R.F.C. 1913
*Died in Germany 12 Aug. 1917 of wounds received in
action*
GWATKIN, Sir W. G., C.B. Major-Gen., Chief of Gen. 1879
Staff in Canada. *K.C.M.G. m. Commander, Legion
of Honour (France). Commander, Ordre de la Couronne
(Belgium). Order of St Sava, 2nd Class (Serbia)*

HADLEY, O. H. Capt., Loyal N. Lancs. Regt. (W 2.) [1914]
HADOW, R. H. Capt., Argyll and Sutherland Hdrs.; attd. [1914]
Seaforth Hdrs. (W 2.) *M.C. M.*
HAGGARD, A. J. R. Lieut., The Queen's (R. W. Surrey 1908
Regt.) (W 2.)
HALL, F. G. Lieut., Dorset Regt.; Capt., Spec. List 1907
(Asst. Base Cmdt.) *M.*
✠HALL, Rev. W. Chaplain and Instructor, R.N. 1886
Died 11 Nov. 1916

✠HALLIDAY, C. W. A. 2nd Lieut., R.F.A.   1904
   Died 17 *Nov.* 1916 *of wounds received in action* 8 *Nov.*
   1917
HAMILTON, G. C. H.   Lieut., Manchester Regt.(T.F.)   1906
   (W.)
HAMILTON, J. A. DE C.   Capt., Hampshire Regt.(T.F.)   1914
   (W.) *M.C.*
HAMILTON, J. L.   Lieut., R.F.A.; Staff Lieut. *M.*   1915
HAMMERSLEY, S. S.   Lieut., E. Lancs. Regt.; Capt., Tank   1912
   Corps. (W.)
✠HAMMOND-CHAMBERS, H. B. B.   Capt., King s Own (R.   1905
   Lancaster Regt.)
   Killed in action on the Somme 20 *July* 1916
HAPPELL, A. C.   Capt., Suffolk Regt.   1911
HARBORD, V.   Capt., R.E. (Fortress, T.F.); empld. Min-   1913
   istry of Munitions. (W.)
✠HARDMAN, F. M.   2nd Lieut., R. Fusiliers   1909
   Killed in action at Neuve Chapelle 29 *Oct.* 1914
HARMAN, C. E.   Lieut., Middlesex Regt. (W.) (P.)   1913
HARMER, W. D.   Capt., R.A.M.C. (1st London Gen.   1892
   Hospital, T.F.)
HARPER, F. A.   Capt. (T.), R.A.F.   1907
HARRISON, E. P.   Lieut., R.F.A.   1903
HARTLEY, L. B.   Surgeon Lieut., R.N.   1912
HARTRIDGE, H.   Lieut., R.N.V.R.   1905
HASLAM, W.H.   Hon. Lieut., R.N.V.R. *O.B.E. Cavalier,* 1908
   Order of the Crown of Italy
HAVILAND, W. P.   Capt., Argyll and Sutherland Hdrs.   1899
   (T.F.); G.S.O. 3. *M.B.E. m* 2.
HAWARD, T. W.   Lieut. and Adjt., Inns of Court O.T.C.   1903
   m 2.
HAWES, E. L.   Capt., E. Surrey Regt.(T.F.)   1913
HAYNES, G. S.   Capt., R.A.M.C. (1st E. Gen. Hospital,   1899
   T.F.)
HEALEY, F. G.   2nd Lieut., R.E. (Signals). (W.)   1911
HEAP, F. G.   Corpl., R.E. (Signals); Lieut., Tank Corps.   1911
   M.C.
HEARSON, H. F. P.   2nd Lieut., Bombay Light Horse,   1904
   Indian Defence Force
✠HEBBLETHWAITE, A. R.   Trooper, 18th Hussars; 2nd   1913
   Lieut., R.F.A.
   Killed in action 3 *Oct.* 1915
HEDLEY, E. W.   Capt., R.A.M.C. (5th London Gen.   1892
   Hospital, T.F.) *M.B.E.*

KING'S COLLEGE 203

HEDLEY, I. M. Lieut., 17th Lancers. *M.*   1910
HEDLEY, J. P.   Capt., R.A.M.C. (5th London Gen. Hos- 1895
pital, T.F.)
HEDLEY, W. Major, R.G.A. *D.S.O. M.*   1898
HEELAS, R. J. Capt., R.G.A. (W.) *M.*   1902
HELM, C. Lieut.-Col., R.A.M.C. *D.S.O. M.C. M.*   1907
HENDERSON, I. M. Capt., London Regt. (London Scot- 1896
tish). (W.) (P.) *M.B.E. Brevet Major*
HENSLEY, E. H. V. Capt., R.A.M.C.   1910
✠HERBERT, Hon. E. J. B.   Capt., Gloucestershire Yeo.; 1899
attd. M.G.C. *Order of the White Eagle, 5th Class
(Serbia)
Killed in action 12 Nov. 1917*
HERMAN, A. E. Surgeon Lieut., R.N. *O.B.E.*   1905
HERMAN, G. L. Capt., Queen's Own (R. W. Kent Regt.); 1905
Staff Capt.
HEYCOCK, C. T., V.D. Lieut.-Col., Cambridgeshire Regt. 1877
(T.F. Res.) *m.*
HEYWORTH, E. L. Lieut., Manchester Regt.; Lieut.(Ad.), 1910
R.A.F. (W.) (P.)
HIBBERT, J. P. M. Major, R.F.A.(T.F.) *M.C.*   1903
✠HICKMAN, T. Pte., H.A.C.; Lieut., Leinster Regt. (W.) 1907
Killed in action near Armentières 26–27 June 1916
HICKS, R. J. B. Pte., Gloucestershire Regt.   1916
✠HIGSON, F. S. Capt., Welsh Regt. *M.C.*   1914
Killed in action 31 Aug. 1917
HILL, A. V. Capt., Cambridgeshire Regt.; empld. *1916
Ministry of Munitions. *O.B.E. Brevet Major. m 2.*
HILL, A. W. Hon. Capt., Spec. List (Graves Registration 1894
Commission). *m 2.*
HINE, T. G. M. Hon. Major, R.A.M.C. *C.B.E. O.B.E.* 1892
m 2.
HOARE, C. G. Lieut., Essex Yeo., R. Horse Gds., and 1901
Gds. M.G. Regt. *M.C.*
HOARE, L. G. Capt., Durham L.I.; Staff Capt. *M.*   1898
HOBBS, F. D. Lieut., Life Gds.; Lieut. (A.), R.A.F.   1911
HODDER, A.E. Lieut.-Col.,R.A.M.C.(T.F.) (W.) *D.S.O.* 1895
M 2.
HODGES, A. G. A. Capt., Northamptonshire Regt.(T.F.); 1912
Hon. Capt. (K.B. and Ad.), R.A.F. (W.)
HOLLAND, F. Capt. and Adjt., King's (Liverpool Regt., 1900
Liverpool Scottish, T.F.) *M.B.E.*
HOLLINS, E. M. Capt., R.A.S.C.(M.T.)   1901
HOLLOND, R. C. Capt., Rifle Brigade. (W.) *M.*   1910

✠HOLMES, T. S. 2nd Lieut., The Queen's (R.W. Surrey　1912
　　Regt.); attd. The Buffs (E. Kent Regt.)
　　Killed in action 12 *Nov.* 1914
✠HOLT, H. W. 2nd Lieut., R.E.　　　　　　　　　　　1907
　　Killed in action 23 *Aug.* 1914
HOMFRAY, S. G. Lieut., R.N.V.R.　　　　　　　　　1906
HOPE-JOHNSTONE, C. J. 2nd Lieut., Gen. List (T.F. Res.)　1903
HOPE-JONES, W. Lieut., R.G.A.; attd., R.E.　　　　1903
✠HOPKINSON, B., F.R.S. Major, Unattd. List, T.F.; Colonel,　*1914
　　D.A.D., Air Ministry. *C.M.G. m* 2.
　　Killed in flying accident 26 *Aug.* 1918
HORNE, H. F. Major, R.A.M.C. (Sanitary Section, T.F.);　1897
　　Lieut.-Col. (Med.), R.A.F. *T.D. Brevet Lieut.-
　　Colonel. Brevet Major*
✠HORNUNG, A. O. 2nd Lieut., Essex Regt.　　　　　[1914]
　　Killed in action at Ypres 6 *July* 1915
✠HORSFALL, C. F. Capt., D. of Wellington's (W. Riding　1908
　　Regt.) (W.)
　　Killed in action 18 *Sept.* 1916
✠HORSFALL, R. E. Capt., King's (Liverpool Regt.) (W.)　1912
　　Killed in action at La Vacquerie 20 *Nov.* 1917
✠HOWARD, A. J. Lieut., Bedfordshire Regt.　　　　　1911
　　Killed in action 4 *Sept.* 1916
HOWARTH, W. G. Capt., R.A.M.C. (2nd London Gen.　1897
　　Hospital, T.F.)
HOWELL, G. F. Lieut., The Buffs (E. Kent Regt.)　　1908
HOWSON, H. E. E. Lieut., Shrewsbury School O.T.C.　1907
　　and Eton College O.T.C.
HUNTINGTON, Sir C. P., Bart. Lieut., R. Irish Regt. (W.)　1907
HURST, G. H. J. Capt., R.G.A.; Major, Gen. Staff　　1890

INFELD, H. Capt., London Regt. (Rangers); Major, Spec.　1912
　　List (cmdg. Spec. Coy., R.E.) (W 2.) *M.C.*
INGLE, L. M. Capt., R.A.M.C. (W.)　　　　　　　　1909
INGLIS, A. E. J. Lieut., Army Printing and Stationery　1906
　　Services
INGLIS, C. E. Major, R.E.; Staff Capt., War Office.　1894
　　O.B.E. Brevet Major. m.
INGLIS, G. S. Lieut., Connaught Rangers and R.F.C.;　1913
　　Staff Lieut. *M.C.*
INGRAM, E. M. B. Capt., Spec. List; G.S.O. 3, War　1909
　　Office. *O.B.E. m. Order of the White Eagle, 5th
　　Class (Serbia)*
INSKIP, J. H. Lieut. (K.B.), R.A.F.　　　　　　　　1898

✠IRVING, A. G. 2nd Lieut., R.E. and R.F.C. 1908
Killed in flying accident 15 *March* 1915

JAFFÉ, A. D. Capt., London Regt. (London Irish Rifles) 1899
JARDINE, J. W. Major (K.B.), R.A.F. (W.) *M.* 1899
JEBB, R. D. Capt., R. Sussex Regt.(T.F.) *M.C. M.* 1903
JENKIN, C. O. F. 2nd Lieut., Suffolk Regt.; Lieut., Gen. 1909
  List, empld. Ministry of Munitions. (W.)
✠JENKINS, E. E. Capt., R. Warwickshire Regt.; attd. 1906
  Lancs. Fus.(T.F.) (W 2.) *M.C.*
  Killed in action 25 *March* 1918
JOHN, J. C. Capt., I.M.S. *O.B.E. M.* 1905
JOHNSON, C. Capt., Cheshire Regt. (T.F.); empld. Min- 1911
  istry of Munitions. (W.) *M.B.E. Brevet Major.* *m*3.
JOHNSON, E. H. Capt., R.F.A.(T.F.) (W 2.) *M.C. M.* 1911
JOHNSON, G. F. Major, R.F.A.(T.F.) (W.) *M* 2. 1913
JOHNSON, G. G. F. Capt., Essex Regt. and King's African 1909
  Rifles
✠JOHNSON, R. L. Capt., R.F.A. (W.) 1908
  Killed in action 28 *May* 1917
JOHNSTON, F. B. Pte., King's (Liverpool Regt., Liver- 1912
  pool Scottish, T.F.); Capt., Northumberland Fus.
  (T.F.); attd. Highland L.I.
JOHNSTONE, G. G. Capt., R.A.M.C. (Sanitary Service, 1905
  T.F.) *M.C. M.*
JONES, A. P. Capt., King's (Liverpool Regt., T.F.) 1910
✠JONES, A. V. Pte., H.A.C. 1906
  Killed in action 25 *Nov.* 1914
JONES, C. E. M. Capt., R.A.M.C.(T.F.) (P.) 1900
✠JONES, R. A. Major, R. Warwickshire Regt. 1901
  Killed in action 21 *May* 1916
JONES, R. L. A.B., R.N.V.R. (Anti-Aircraft); Lieut., 1896
  R.G.A.
JOSEPH, H. H. Capt., Durham L.I.(T.F.) (P.) 1903
JOYCE, J. L. Major, R.A.M.C.(T.F.) *Brevet Major. m.* 1901

KARPELES, A. R. Lieut., Gen. List (T.M.B.) (W.) [1914]
KEDDIE, C. M. Lieut., I.A.R.O., attd. 36th Sikhs and 1909
  82nd Punjabis
✠KEELE, C. A. Capt., Rifle Brigade 1913
  Killed in action in the Ypres Salient 12 *July* 1916
KEMPSEY, F. Lieut., R.G.A. 1910
✠KEMP-WELCH, M. 2nd Lieut., Yorkshire Regt. 1899
  Killed in action 11 *April* 1917

KENDALL, E. A. Capt., King's Own (R. Lancaster Regt.)   1906
(W 2.) *M.C. M.*
KENNEDY, J. S. Surgeon Lieut., R.N.   1906
KING, H. H. Capt., London Regt. (Post Office Rifles);   1908
attd. R.E. (Signals, T.F.) (W.)
KINGHORN, E. C. Lieut., Border Regt.; attd. Oxford and   1910
Bucks. L.I.; Lieut. (O.), R.A.F. (W 2.)
KIRK, J. W. C. Lieut.-Col., D. of Cornwall's L.I. *D.S.O.*   1896
M 2.
KNOX, A. D. Lieut., R.N.V.R., empld. Admiralty   1903

LACEY, A. T. Major, M.G.C. (W.) *M* 2.   1911
LAMBART, J. H. L. Capt., R.F.A.; A.D.C.; Staff Capt.   1912
(W.) *M* 2. *French Croix de Guerre*
LANCE, H. W. Lieut., Norfolk Yeo.; Capt., R.A.M.C.   1889
M.
LANCHESTER, W. F. Capt., R.A.M.C. (Sanitary Service,   1893
T.F.)
LANGDON, Rev. A. G. C.F. 4th Class, R.A.C.D.   1887
LAPAGE, F. C. Capt., R.A.M.C.   1907
✠LARKING, R. G. Capt., R.E. (Signals). *M.C. and Bar*   1910
Accidentally killed on active service 1 *April* 1918
LARKWORTHY, F. G. C. Lieut., R. Welsh Fus.   [1914]
LAYARD, A. H. Lieut., R. Sussex Regt.; attd. E. Surrey   1913
Regt.
LAZARUS, G. M. Lieut., R.G.A.   1900
LEE, E. O. Lieut., I.A.R.O., attd. 34th Sikh Pioneers   1910
✠LEGG, H. G. Pte., H.A.C.; Lieut., Durham L.I. (W 2.)   1900
Killed in action on the Somme 25 *March* 1918
✠LEGGATT, L. C. 2nd Lieut., Rifle Brigade and Cold-   1913
stream Gds.
Killed in action at Pilkam Ridge 31 *July* 1917
LEWIN, E. O. Lieut.-Col., R.F.A.; G.S.O. 1. *C.B.*   1897
C.M.G. D.S.O. Brevet Lieut.-Colonel. M 6.
*Chevalier, Legion of Honour (France). French Croix
de Guerre. Commander, Military Order of Avis
(Portugal)*
LEWIS, A. D. Capt., R.E.; Major, D.A.D. Inland Water   1902
Transport
LIAS, A. G. Capt., D. of Wellington's (W. Riding Regt.)   1907
and Gen. List, empld. R.M.C., Sandhurst
LING, G. A. Capt., Suffolk Regt. (W.)   1898
LIVESEY, T. R. M. Lieut., I.A.R.O., attd. Cavalry   1910
LLOYD, J. R. Lieut., R.A.F.   1912

Lob, H. Lieut., E. Lancs. Regt. and R.E. (Field Survey   1905
Bn.)

Loch, D. H. Capt., Spec. List. *Order of the Redeemer,*   1902
*5th Class (Greece). Order of St Sava, 5th Class
(Serbia)*

✠Longworth, E. C. Pte., R. Fusiliers (P.S. Bn.); Capt.,   1908
Lancs. Fus.
Killed in action at Thiepval 26 Sept. 1916

✠Loring, W. Capt., Scottish Horse. *M.*   1885
Died 24 Oct. 1915 *of wounds received in action in
Gallipoli*

✠Lupton, G. A. Lce.-Corpl., R. Fusiliers   1912
Killed in action 17 Feb. 1917

Lupton, Rev. J. M. Capt., Marlborough College O.T.C.   1886

Lyon, Rev. W. T. C.F. 4th Class, R.A.C.D.(T.F.)   1905

McArthur, A. G. F. Capt., R.A.M.C.   1912

✠McDonnell, J. Major, D.A.Q.M.G.; Lieut.-Col., Lein-   1897
ster Regt.
Killed in action 29 Sept. 1918

✠McDougall, S. Lieut., Manchester Regt.(T.F.)   1895
Killed in action in Gallipoli 7 Aug. 1915

✠Machell, H. G. 2nd Lieut., Border Regt.   1906
Died 12 June 1918 *of wounds received in action*

McIntyre, J. Capt., R.A.M.C. *M.C.*   1899

Mackay, R. F. B. Capt., Essex Regt.(T.F.) *m.*   1910

Mackenzie, C. M. Lieut.-Col., London Regt. *D.S.O.*   1895
O.B.E. M. m.

Mackeson, G. P. Lieut., London Regt. (R. Fus.)   1911

McLean, C. F. Surgeon Lieut., R.N.V.R.   1914

Macmillan, W. E. F. Capt., Cameronians (Scottish   1899
Rifles, T.F. Res.) and Gen. Staff

Macmorran, K. M. Lieut., E. Surrey Regt. (T.F.); attd.   1902
R. Sussex Regt.; Capt., Spec. List (Judge-Advocate-
General). *M.*

✠Maddrell, J. D. H. Lieut., D. of Cornwall's L.I.   1914
Died 13 Dec. 1916 *of wounds received in action 22 Nov.*
1916

Mahaffy, R. P. Capt., Devon Regt. and Gen. List,   1890
empld. Egyptian Army. (W.)

Malden, Rev. R. H. Chaplain, R.N.   1898

Mansell-Moullin, O. Lieut. (A.), R.A.F. (P.)   1906

Marett Tims, H. W. *See* Tims, H. W. Marett

Marsden, A. T. Major, Loyal N. Lancs. Regt. *M.C. M.*   1913

MARSEILLE, R. K. G.   Capt., Loyal N. Lancs. Regt.;   191~
empld. Ministry of Pensions. (W.) (P.)

✠MARSH, F. HOWARD.   Hon. Colonel, R.A.M.C.(T.F.)   *190~
Died 24 June 1915

MARSHALL, H. G.   Lieut., Border Regt.(T.F.); Staff Capt.,   190~
Indian Army

MARTIN, O. L.   Capt., York and Lancaster Regt.;   1911
G.S.O. 3. (W 2.) *m. French Croix de Guerre*

MARTIN, R. E.   Lieut.-Col., Leicestershire Regt.(T.F.)   189~
(W 2.) *C.M.G. M.*

✠MARTIN, S. S.   Corpl., Middlesex Regt.   191~
Killed in action 13 *Aug.* 1917

MASON, F. L. L.   Lieut., Rifle Brigade; empld. War Office   190~

MASSEY, B. W. A.   Lieut., R.F.A.; Interpreter. (W.)   190~

MASSON, K.   Surgeon Prob., R.N.V.R.; Capt., R.A.M.C.   190~

MATHIAS, H. H.   Capt., R.A.M.C.   190~

MAWE, E. S.   Capt., R.A.M.C.   190~

MAWE, Rev. M. D.   Major, R.F.A. and R.G.A.   1905

MAYOR, H. B.   Capt., Clifton College O.T.C.   189~

MEISTER, G. C.   Lieut., Sedbergh School O.T.C.   1895

MEISTER, G. E. W.   Pte., R. Fusiliers; Lieut., R. Defence   189~
Corps

MERCER, J. L. C.   Capt., The Queen's (R. W. Surrey Regt.)   190~

MEREDITH, H. O.   Lieut., Belfast Univ. O.T.C.; empld.   1897
Ministry of Munitions

MILNE HOME, C. A.   Lieut., King's Own Scottish Bor-   190~
derers. (W.)

MILNER, G.   Capt., R.E.; empld. Egyptian Army   1912

MILNER-WHITE, Rev. E.   C.F. 3rd Class, R.A.C.D.   1903
D.S.O. M.

MOBERLY, A. H.   Capt., London Regt. (Surrey Rifles) and   1903
Gen. Staff (O.C.B.) (W.) *m.*

MOIR, K. M.   Lieut., E. Surrey Regt.(T.F.); Capt. and   [1914]
Adjt., M.G.C. *M.C. M.*

✠MOND, F. L.   Lieut., R.F.A.(T.F.); Staff Lieut.; Lieut.   1912
(A.), R.A.F.
Killed in action at Bouzencourt 15 *May* 1918

MONRO, K. N.   Major, R.E.   1897

✠MOORE, M. E. J.   Lieut., R. Irish Rifles. (W 2.) *M.C.*   1913
Died in German hands 27 *March* 1918 *of wounds received
in action* 24 *March* 1918

MOORSOM, J.   Lieut., Life Gds. and Gds. M.G. Regt.   1899

MOORSOM, R. S.   Capt., Westmorland and Cumberland   1911
Yeo.; attd. Border Regt. (W.)

MORRISON, Rev. A. C.F. 4th Class, R.A.C.D. 1894
MORSE, F. A. V. Capt., R.E. (London Electrical Engin- 1897
eers, T.F.)
MORSE, L. G. E. Capt., R.E. (London Electrical Engin- 1904
eers, T.F.) *M.B.E.*
[1]MORTON, H. S. Capt., R.A.S.C.; Major, D.A.D. Quar- *1915
tering, War Office. *O.B.E.*
MORTON, J.A.F. Capt., Northamptonshire Regt.; empld. 1912
Ministry of Labour
MOULTON, H. F. 2nd Lieut., R.F.A. (W.) 1895
✠MOULTON, W. R. O. 2nd Lieut., Manchester Regt. 1910
Killed in action 5 *Aug.* 1916
MOWLL, Rev. H. W. K. C.F. 4th Class, R.A.C.D. 1909
MOZLEY, B. C. Capt., Dorset Regt.; empld. O.C.B. (W2.) 1912
D.S.O. M.
MOZLEY, J. H. Capt., R.F.A. (W.) 1906
MUDIE, R. F. Capt., I.A.R.O.; Asst. Instructor, School 1908
of Musketry. *O.B.E.*
MUMMERY, R. T. Lieut., R.G.A. 1914

✠NANCARROW, J. V. Capt., Yorkshire Regt.(T.F.) 1903
Killed in action near Ypres 25 *April* 1915
NAPIER, L. P. Lieut., Canadian Hdrs.; Capt., Canadian 1909
F.A.; Staff Capt. *M.C.*
NATHAN, E. J. Capt., Spec. List (Directorate of Railways 1907
and Roads, War Office). *O.B.E. m.*
NAUMANN, J. H. Capt., Rifle Brigade and Nigeria Regt., 1912
W. African Frontier Force; Staff Capt. (W.)
NEAL, A. W. Lieut., R.F.A. *M.C.* 1912
NEAL, J. Major, R.G.A. *M.C.* 1907
✠NEWBERRY, J. D. Flt. Cdr., R.N.A.S. *French Croix de* 1913
Guerre
Killed in flying accident 28 *Sept.* 1917
NEWTON, H. W. G. 2nd Lieut., Somerset L.I. (W.) (P.) 1902
NOBLE, H. B. Capt., Northumberland Yeo.; G.S.O. 3. 1911
M.C. M 2. *Chevalier, Order of Leopold (Belgium).*
Belgian Croix de Guerre
NORTON, R. H. Lieut., Coldstream Gds. 1896

OATFIELD, W. J. Capt., King's (Liverpool Regt., T.F.) 1910
(W 2.)
✠O'CALLAGHAN, T. F. 2nd Lieut., Leicestershire Regt. 1913
(T.F.)
Killed in action 13 *Oct.* 1915

[1] Died of influenza shortly after demobilisation.

OGILVIE, H. Lieut., R.E. (W.)   1900
OGILVY, L. W. Trooper, Calcutta Light Horse, Indian   1896
    Defence Force
✠ORD, O. R. Lieut., Rifle Brigade   1914
    Killed in action at Lesbœufs 16 Sept. 1916
OSMASTON, D. F. Capt., R.E. *M.*   1911

✠PAGE, R. B. Colonel, Lancs. Fus.   1877
    *Died 11 Nov. 1914 of injuries accidentally received on
    active service*
PARKER SMITH, A. C. H. Capt., Argyll and Sutherland   1902
    Hdrs.
✠PARKER SMITH, W. B. Lieut., Scottish Horse   1904
    *Died 11 Sept. 1915 of wounds received in action in
    Gallipoli 2 Sept. 1915*
PARTRIDGE, H. W. Lieut., Gresham's School, Holt,   1906
    O.T.C.
PASS, A. D. Capt., Dorset Yeo. (W.) (P.)   1904
✠PATERSON, I. R. 2nd Lieut., Cameron Hdrs.   1916
    Killed in action 12 Oct. 1917
PEACEY, H. M. Lieut., R. Sussex Regt.   1899
PEARSALL, R. H. Capt. and Adjt., R.E.(T.F.) *M.*   1902
PERRIN, M. Capt., Loyal N. Lancs. Regt. *M.C.*   1908
PILKINGTON, L. E. Lieut.-Col., S. Lancs. Regt.(T.F. Res.) 1892
    C.M.G. M. m 2.
✠PILTER, C. Lieut., 18th Hussars. (W.)   1906
    Died 30 May 1915 of wounds received in action
✠PLAYFAIR, P. L. Capt., Black Watch(T.F.) (W.)   1912
    *Died 11 April 1918 of wounds received in action at
    Lestrem*
PLOWDEN-WARDLAW, Rev. J. T. C.F. 4th Class, R.A.C.D.   1892
✠POCHIN, A. C. 2nd Lieut., Essex Regt. (W.)   1914
    Killed in action 26 Sept. 1916
POCOCK, S. E. Major, R.A.S.C. *O.B.E. m.*   1904
✠POLACK, B. J. Pte., R. Fusiliers; 2nd Lieut., Worcester- 1909
    shire Regt. *M.*
    Killed in action 9 April 1916
POLLAK, L. A. Capt., London Regt. (St Pancras Bn.);   1908
    Major, M.G.C. (W 2.) *M.C. and Bar. M. French
    Croix de Guerre*
POPHAM, A. E. Capt. (S.), R.A.F. *M. French Croix de*   1908
    Guerre
✠POWELL, K. Pte., H.A.C.   1904
    Killed in action 18 Feb. 1915

✠POWELL, P. 2nd Lieut., Rifle Brigade   1898
   Killed in action at Ypres 2 Aug. 1915
PRETTY, K. Capt., R.A.M.C. *M.*   1902
PRIOR, H.C. Lieut., I.A.R.O., attd. 1st Gurkha Rifles. *M.*   1909
PUCKLE, F. H. Capt., I.A.R.O., attd. N. Waziristan Mil-   1908
   itia
PURVES, C. L. Capt., E. Lancs. Regt   1909

QUIRK, Rev. R. C.F. 4th Class, R.A.C.D.   1901

RAIMES, A. L. Major, Durham L.I.(T.F.) (W3.) *D.S.O.*   1904
   M 2.
RAND, H. M. Capt., R.E. (Signals, T.F.) *M.*   1911
RANSFORD, F. B. Capt., London Regt. (Cyclist Bn.)   1904
RAWLINS, A. Lieut., 5th (R. Irish) Lancers; Lieut. (Ad.),   1908
   R.A.F. (W.)
RAYMOND, E. L. Lieut., Rossall School O.T.C.   1911
READING, E. W. Capt., N. Staffs. Regt.; D.A.A.G. *M.*   1911
RECKITT, A. Capt., E. Yorks. Regt.; Capt. and Adjt.,   1892
   Durham L.I. *m.*
REDDEN, F. A. C. 2nd Lieut., Worcestershire Regt.   1887
REECE, R. H. Surgeon Lieut., R.N.   1913
REED, Rev. L. G. C.F. 2nd Class, R.A.C.D.; D.A.C.G.   1902
   M.C.
REES, J. R. Capt., R.A.M.C. *Chevalier, Ordre de la*   1908
   Couronne (Belgium)
REID, K. G. Lieut., R.N.V.R.   1899
REINERT, E. L. *See* RAYMOND, E. L.
RENWICK, J. E. Lieut., Cheshire Regt.   1904
✠RENWICK, T. B. Lieut., Rifle Brigade; attd. Middlesex   1912
   Regt.
   Killed in action 29 April 1915
REVILLON, J. W. 2nd Lieut., R.E. *O.B.E.* *M.*   1905
RHODES, H. E. Capt., R.A.M.C.   1910
✠RICARD, F. 2nd Lieut., R. Warwickshire Regt.   1906
   Killed in action near Ypres 25 April 1915
RICE, Rev. C. M. C.F. 4th Class, R.A.C.D.   *1905
RICHARDSON, P. W., v.d. Bt. Lieut.-Col., T.F.Res.; Chief   1883
   Instructor, School of Musketry. *O.B.E.* *m.*
RICHMOND, O. L. 2nd Lieut., London Regt.; Capt.,   1900
   Spec. List. *m. Cavalier, Order of the Crown of Italy*
✠RICKEARD, C. W. Lieut., London Regt. (St Pancras Bn.)   1913
   Killed in action 25 Sept. 1915
RICKETT, G.R. Lieut.-Col., R.A.M.C.(T.F.) *O.B.E.* *M*3.   1896

RIDDIOUGH, S. Lieut., R.A.M.C. (W.)   1910
RIGGALL, H. B. Capt., Lincolnshire Regt.(T.F.) (W 2.)   1913
RIPMAN, C. H. Capt., R.A.M.C.   1898
¹RITCHIE, S. E. Capt. (A.), R.A.F.   1914
✠ROBERTS, C. H. Pte., R. Fusiliers   1915
  Killed in action at Thiepval Sept. 1916
ROBERTSON SMITH, N. M. Capt., Cameronians (Scottish   1905
  Rifles, T.F.)
ROBINSON, R. H. O. B. Surgeon Lieut., R.N.   1914
✠ROLLESTON, F. L. Lieut., London Regt. (R. Fus.)   [1914]
  Killed in action at Armentières 26 *April* 1915
ROOTH, A. V. Capt., I.A.R.O. (W.) *M.C. M* 2.   1905
✠ROSCOE, A. 2nd Lieut., Queen's Own (R.W. Kent Regt.)   1909
  M.C.
  Died 5 *Sept.* 1916 *of wounds received in action*
ROSE, G. K. Major, Oxford and Bucks. L.I. (W.) *M.C.*   1908
  and Bar. M 2.
ROSS, C. M. Cadet, O.C.B.   1906
ROWLATT, A. Capt., D. of Cornwall's L.I.   1912
✠ROWNTREE, L. E. 2nd Lieut., R.F.A. (W.)   1913
  Killed in action 25 *Nov.* 1917
ROWNTREE, M. 2nd Lieut., R.E.   1908
RUBENS, H. V. Pte., R. Fusiliers   1897
RUMSEY, Rev. H. ST J. 2nd Lieut., Epsom College O.T.C.   1906
RUSSELL, G. G. Lieut.-Col., K. Edward's Horse. *D.S.O.*   1900
  M 3.
RUSSELL, P. D. Lieut., N. Zealand M.G.C.   1901
RUSSELL, S. C. Lieut., Cameron Hdrs. (W 2.)   1913

SAINSBURY, W. T. Pte., R. Fusiliers (P. S. Bn.); Capt.   1911
  and Adjt., W. Yorks. Regt. (W.) *M.C. and Bar*
SAMBROOK, H. F. Major, R.E. (Postal Section)   1905
SAXTON, W. I. Instructor Lieut., R.N.   1911
✠SCHOLES, W. P. 2nd Lieut., Leicestershire Regt.(T.F.)   1913
  Killed in action 13 *Oct.* 1915
SCHOLFIELD, A. F. Pte., Calcutta Port Defence, attd.   1903
  Sappers and Miners, Indian Army
SCHWANN, H. *See* SWANN, H.
SCOTT, W. M. Major, R.E.(T.F.)   1905
✠SCRUTTON, H. U. Corpl., R.E. (Signals); Capt., North-   1913
  umberland Fus. (W.) *M.C. M* 3.
  Died in a Bulgarian hospital 10 *Sept.* 1916 *of wounds
  received in action on the Struma*

¹ Killed in flying accident after the armistice.

SCRUTTON, Rev. T. B. C.F. 4th Class, R.A.C.D. (W.) 1906
SECONDÉ, E. C. Capt., 16th Rajputs, Indian Army 1902
SEDDON, A. E. Capt., Suffolk Regt. (W.) 1910
SELWYN, Rev. E. G. C.F. 4th Class, R.A.C.D. *M.* 1904
✠SEYRIG, J. R. Pte., 1re Régt. Etranger, French Army 1913
Killed in action in the Champagne 25 Sept. 1915
SHAND, P. M. Gnr., R.F.A. 1906
SHARPE, W. H. S. Capt. (K.B.), R.A.F. 1903
SHAW, E. A. Surgeon Cdr., R.N. *O.B.E.* 1886
SHAW, G. R. D. 2nd Lieut., E. Riding of Yorkshire Yeo.; [1914]
attd. Essex Regt.(T.F.)
✠SHINGLETON-SMITH, F. Capt., I.M.S. 1898
Killed in action at Ctesiphon 22–24 Nov. 1915
SIMEY, A. I. Lieut., R.A.M.C. 1892
✠SIMON, H. H. Major, R.F.A.(T.F.) 1899
Died 8 Sept. 1917 of wounds received in action 1 Sept.
1917
SIMPKINSON, F. V. Capt., R.E. (W 2.) 1907
SINCLAIR, G. W. Lieut., Manchester Regt.(T.F.); empld. 1908
Ministry of Labour
SMART, F. W. B. Major, Charterhouse School O.T.C. 1892
T.D. Brevet Lieut.-Colonel. m.
✠SMITH, A. F. Corpl., Suffolk Regt. and R. Irish Rifles 1915
Missing, presumed killed in action, 16–17 Aug. 1916
SMITH, C. E. G. Capt., Army Cyclist Corps and M.G.C. 1914
SMITH, E. F. Lieut., E. Lancs. Regt.; empld. Command 1909
Depôt. (W.)
SMITH, E. M. Capt., R.E. *M.C. M 2. Military Order* 1909
of Avis, 3rd Class (Portugal)
SMITH, F. B. Capt., R.A.M.C.(T.F.) *M.C. Chevalier,* 1906
Military Order of Avis (Portugal)
SMITH, W.W. Lieut., R.A.S.C. and R.E. (Sound-ranging 1911
Section)
✠SNELL, F. S. Pte., R. Fusiliers (P.S. Bn.); 2nd Lieut., 1906
R. Berkshire Regt.
Killed in action 11 July 1916
SOMERVELL, A. C. Major, R.A.S.C.; D. A. D. Supplies. 1902
O.B.E. M 2.
SOMERVELL, L. C. Capt., R.A.M.C. *M.* 1906
✠SOMERVILLE, M. A. 2nd Lieut., Rifle Brigade; attd. Lon- 1917
don Regt.
Died 21 Sept. 1918 of wounds received in action at Wadi
Kanah
SOUTHERN, N. Major, R.F.A. (W.) (P.) *M.C.* 1903

✠Spencer, J. M. J. Gnr., R.F.A.(T.F.); Lieut., North- [1914]
umberland Fus.; attd. R.F.C.
Killed in action 3 Nov. 1916
Spens, H. B. Lieut.-Col., Cameronians (Scottish Rifles, 1904
T.F.) (W.) *D.S.O. and Bar. Brevet Major. M* 4.
French Croix de Guerre
Spielman, C. M. Major, R.E. *M.C. Brevet Major.* 1907
French Médaille d'Honneur
Stackard, S. F. C. Corpl., R.E. (Signals); Capt., R.A.S.C. 1911
M.
Stanley, E. S. Lieut., R.G.A. (W.) 1910
Stead, J. Lieut., R.E. 1903
Stephen, A. M. Major, R.G.A. (P.) *M.C. M* 1911
✠Stephen, J. H. F. Lieut., Highland L.I. (W.) 1913
Killed in action in Mesopotamia 11 Jan. 1917
Stocks, P. Lieut., R.A.M.C. 1908
Stockwell, G. E. St C. Major, W. Yorks. Regt.(T.F.) 1895
and R.A.M.C.(T.F.) *M.*
Stokes, E. F. Capt., Northamptonshire Regt. (W.) 1911
✠Stone, A. Lieut.-Col., Lancs. Fus. *D.S.O. M.* 1896
Killed in action 2 Oct. 1918
✠Stone, H. B. Lieut., R.E.(T.F.) 1909
Killed in action 18 Feb. 1915
Storrs, B. St J. Lieut., R.F.A. 1903
Streatfeild, H. G. C. Capt., Hampshire Regt.(T.F.) [1914]
Streeten, Rev. E. R. C.F. 4th Class, R.A.C.D. 1901
✠Stroud, H. C. Capt., R.E.(T.F.); attd. R.F.C. (W.) 1913
*Killed 7 March 1918 in defence of London during an air
raid*
Sturdy, A. E. Lieut., 19th Hussars; Capt., Leicester- 1913
shire Regt.; G.S.O. 3. (W.) *M.B.E. M. Order of
St Stanislas, 2nd Class (Russia). Order of St Anne,
3rd Class (Russia)*
✠Swainson, J. L. Lieut.-Col., D. of Cornwall's L.I. and 1896
King's Own (R. Lancaster Regt.) (W.) *D.S.O.
M* 2.
*Died 9 Aug. 1916 of wounds received in action 8 Aug.
1916*
Swann, H. Major, K. Edward's Horse 1904
Swift, C. T. Capt., Grenadier Gds. (W.) *m* 2. 1905
✠Symington, P. G. Lieut., Highland L.I. [1914]
Killed in action 1 July 1916
Symonds, W. P. Cadet, O.C.B. 1918

TAIT, G. B. Capt., Middlesex Regt.(T.F.); Major, M.G.C. 1911
(W.) *M* 3.
TAYLOR, A. J. Major, R.A.S.C.; D.A.D.S. and T. *O.B.E.* 1912
M 2. *Officer, Ordre de l'Etoile Noire (France)*
TAYLOR, E. S. Capt., R.A.M.C.(T.F.) *O.B.E.* *M* 2. 1907
French Médaille des Epidémies
✠TEBBUTT, R. J. Capt., Cambridgeshire Regt.; attd. Essex 1912
Regt. (W 2.)
Killed in action 23 Aug. 1918
TEMPERLEY, H. W. V. Capt., Fife and Forfar Yeo.; Major, 1898
G.S.O. 2; Asst. Military Attaché, Belgrade. *O.B.E.*
m 2. *Officer, Order of the Crown of Roumania, with
swords. Order of the White Eagle, 5th Class, with
swords (Serbia)*
✠THOMAS, H. W. Lieut., Rifle Brigade 1909
Killed in action 3 Sept. 1916
THOMPSON, B. W. Surgeon Sub-Lieut., R.N.V.R. 1911
THOMPSON, H. Lieut., R.N.V.R. 1908
THOMPSON, J. Lieut., R.E. *M.* 1913
✠THOMPSON, W. F. Lieut., R.A.M.C. 1906
Died 1 Jan. 1916 *of wounds received in action*
THORNHILL, N. Lieut., Grenadier Gds. (W.) *M.C.* 1901
✠THORP, R. O. V. Lce.-Corpl., R. Fusiliers (P. S. Bn.); 1897
Lieut., Northumberland Fus.; attd. T.M.B. (W 2.)
M.C.
Killed in action 22 March 1918
✠TILLEY, J. Capt., Norfolk Regt. (W.) [1914]
Killed in action near Arras 28 Nov. 1916
TIMS, H. W. MARETT. Lieut.-Col., R.A.M.C. *O.B.E.* 1899
m. Order of St Sava, 3rd Class (Czecho-Slovakia)
✠TIPPET, A. A. 2nd Lieut., King's (Shropshire L.I.) [1914]
Died 19 Aug. 1915 *of wounds received in action*
TODD, L. Major, Eton College O.T.C. 1894
TOMKINSON, G. S. Capt., Worcestershire Regt.; Lieut.- 1902
Col., R.E.; C.R.E. (W 2.) *O.B.E.* *M.C.* *M.*
TRAPNELL, F. C. Capt., R.A.M.C. 1898
TROTTER, J. M. Y. Lieut., E. African Force; Capt., Spec. 1907
List (O.C.B.)
TROWER, G. S. Capt., R.A.M.C. (W.) 1909
TRUSCOTT, R. F. Capt., Sherwood Foresters (Notts. and 1899
and Derby Regt.) and Gen. List; Staff Capt. *O.B.E.*
M 2.
TUCK, D. A. Capt., French Flying Corps; Capt. (A.), 1907
R.A.F. (W.) *French Croix de Guerre*

TUCK, G. L. J. Lieut.-Col., Suffolk Regt.(T.F.) (W 2.) 1909
C.M.G. D.S.O. and Bar. M 4. Chevalier, Legion of
Honour (France)
TUDSBERY, F. C. T. Lieut., Middlesex Regt.; Major, 1906
D.A.D. Lands, War Office. C.B.E. O.B.E. m 3.
✠TURNBULL, W. E. Lieut., R. Scots 1907
Killed in action in Gallipoli 28 April 1915
TURNER, J. R. Capt., Rangoon Bn., Indian Defence Force 1901
TURNER, L. B. Capt., Spec. List. m. 1904
TYER, A. A. Capt. and Adjt., R.F.A. M.V.O. M 3. 1906

VACHELL, E. T. Capt., R.E. (R. Monmouth). M. 1912
VAN GRUTTEN, W.N.C. Capt., R.F.A.; Staff Capt. O.B.E. 1914
M.C. M 5. French Croix de Guerre
VULLIAMY, E.O. Capt., Cambridge Univ. O.T.C.; empld. 1895
O.C.B.; Lieut., Spec. List (Intelligence)

WALEY, F. R. Capt., S. Lancs. Regt. M.C. 1912
✠WALKER, B. S. 2nd Lieut., Cheshire Regt. 1908
Killed in action 10 May 1915
WALKER, E. A. Lieut., R.A.S.C. 1914
WALKER, Rev. H. C. C.F. 4th Class, R.A.C.D. 1899
WALKER, H. R. Capt., King's Own (R. Lancaster Regt.) 1912
(W.)
WALKER, J. 2nd Lieut., R.F.A. 1914
✠WALKER, T. C. 2nd Lieut., Manchester Regt.(T.F.) [1914]
Killed in action in Gallipoli 5 June 1915
✠WALLACE, W. M. 2nd Lieut., Rifle Brigade; attd. R.F.C. 1912
Killed in action 30 Aug. 1915
WALLER, J. C. 2nd Lieut., E. Surrey Regt. 1910
WALLICE, P. Capt., R.A.M.C. 1908
WALLS, F. R. Capt., R.E. (W.) M.C. M. Chevalier, 1910
Ordre de la Couronne (Belgium). Belgian Croix de Guerre
WALTON, J. H. Lieut., I.A.R.O., attd. 7th Gurkha Rifles 1909
✠WARRE-CORNISH, G. W. Major, Somerset L.I. 1894
Killed in action at Flers 16 Sept. 1916
WARRE-CORNISH, W.H. Lieut., N.Somerset Yeo.; empld. 1892
War Office
✠WATKINS, I. E. M. Capt., Monmouthshire Regt. 1908
Killed in action near Ypres 7 May 1915
WATSON, A. P. Major, R.A.M.C.(T.F.) O.B.E. M. 1898
✠WATSON, C. C. Lieut., R.F.A.(T.F.) M. 1908
Died 1 June 1917 of wounds received in action near Lens
31 May 1917

WATSON, F.W. Capt. and Adjt., R.F.A.(T.F.) (W.) *M.C.* 1911
and Bar
✠WATSON, G. C. Capt., Devon Regt. 1906
Killed in action in Mesopotamia 8 March 1916
✠WATSON, R. W. Lieut., King's Royal Rifle Corps 1912
Killed in action at Hooge 30 July 1915
WAYLEN, G. H. H. Capt., R.A.M.C.(T.F.) *M.C. M.* 1899
WEBSTER, C. K. Capt., Spec. List; G.S.O. 3, War Office 1904
✠WEINBERG, P. D. Lieut., Black Watch (T.F.) [1914]
Killed in action 9 May 1915
✠WELCH, J. S. L. Lieut., King's Own (Yorkshire L.I.) *M.* [1914]
Killed in action on the Somme 1 July 1916
WENHAM, R. A. Capt., R.A.S.C. (Canteens). *M.* 1892
✠WERNER, C. A. Capt., Rifle Brigade 1896
Killed in action at the Aubers Ridge 9 May 1915
WEST, R. R. F. Capt., Spec. List (Intelligence). *D.S.O.* 1910
M 2.
✠WESTON, J. C. 2nd Lieut., London Regt. (Queen's West- 1901
minster Rifles)
*Died 6 June 1917 of wounds received in action 21 May
1917*
WHELON, C. E. Lieut., R.E. (Signals, T.F. Res.) 1906
WHITCOMBE, R. C. P. Surgeon Lieut., R.N. 1911
WHITE, A. H. Capt., S.O. 3, R.A.F. 1906
WHITE, A. S. Lieut., Manchester Regt. 1902
✠WHITE, M. G. Lieut., Rifle Brigade 1905
Killed in action 1 July 1916
WHITE, R. HALE. Lieut., R.A.S.C.; attd. King's Own 1913
(Yorkshire L.I., T.F.) (W.) *M.C.*
WHITTING, R. E. Capt., R.A.M.C. *M.C.* 1897
WIDGERY, G. H. Lieut., R.F.A. *M.C.* 1908
WIGGANS, J. T. V. Capt., Northumberland Fus. (W.) 1914
(P.)
✠WIGLESWORTH, G. 2nd Lieut. (A.), R.F.C. 1913
Killed in flying accident 8 July 1916
WILDE, E. H. N. Gnr., R.F.A. 1898
WILKIN, A. Capt., R.A.M.C. *M* 2. 1898
WILLCOCKS, R. H. Sergt., H.A.C. 1907
WILLEY, H. Major, R.G.A. 1899
WILLIAMS, H. G. E. Capt., R.A.M.C. 1911
WILLIAMS, I. A. Lieut., Yorkshire Regt.(T.F.) and Gen. 1910
Staff (Directorate of Requisitions and Hirings)
✠WILLIAMS, R. A. W. Lieut., King's Own (Yorkshire L.I.) 1912
Killed in action at Ypres 18 April 1915

WILLIAMSON, R. H. W.   Capt., R.A.S.C.   1911
WILLINK, A. J. W.   Lieut., Border Regt.   1909
✠WILLOCK, G. C. B.   Capt., London Regt. (London Irish   1910
Rifles)
Killed in action in the Battle of Loos 25 Sept. 1915
WILLS, A. G.   Pte., Transvaal Scottish, S. African Force;   1910
Capt., Cambridgeshire Regt. and M.G.C.   (W 2.)
M.C.
✠WILSON, H. S.   Lieut., Worcestershire Regt.   1904
Killed in action 15 Sept. 1915
WILSON, J. S.   Capt., King's Royal Rifle Corps.   (W 2.)   1908
Cavalier, Order of the Crown of Italy
✠WILSON, T. I. W.   Capt., Manchester Regt.   (W.)   *M.C.*   1901
Killed in action near Beaumont-Hamel 28 Nov. 1916
WILSON, W. G.   Lieut., R.N.V.R.; Major, Tank Corps.   1894
C.M.G. m 2.
WINGFIELD-STRATFORD, E. C.   Capt., Queen's Own (R.W.   1900
Kent Regt., T.F.)
WINKFIELD, W. B.   Lieut.-Col., R.A.M.C.   1891
WINTERBOTHAM, W.   Lieut., R.G.A.   1897
WOLLASTON, A. F. R.   Surgeon Lieut., R.N.   *D.S.C.*   1893
M 2.
✠WOMERSLEY, S. P.   2nd Lieut., M.G.C.   1910
Killed in action 15 April 1918
✠WOOD, P. L.   2nd Lieut. (A.), R.F.C.   1914
Killed in action 4 March 1917
WOODHEAD, Sir G. S., v.d.   Colonel, R.A.M.C. (Sanitary *1899
Service, T.F.)   *K.B.E. O.B.E. Brevet Colonel. m* 2.
WOOLLEY, V. J.   Capt., R.A.M.C.   1896
✠WRIGHT, E. M.   Capt., E. Lancs. Regt.(T.F.)   1910
Killed in action at Monchy-le-Preux 10 April 1917
WRIGHT, F. W.   Capt. (T.), R.A.F.   1901

[1]YORKE, F.   Trooper, Cheshire Yeo.; Lieut., Cheshire   1912
Regt.(T.F.); Lieut. (A.), R.A.F.   (W 2.)
YOUNG, M. A.   Capt., Rifle Brigade.   (W 2.)   (P.)   1905
YOUNG, R. A.   Capt., Yorkshire Regt. and Northumber-   1904
land Fus.

---

[1] Killed in flying accident after the armistice.

MAGDALENE COLLEGE

ACKERLEY, J. R.   Capt., E. Surrey Regt.   (W.) (P.)   [1914]
AGAR-ROBARTES, Hon. C. E.   Lieut., Rifle Brigade; Capt.,   1911
    Tank Corps
✠ALLIN, H. W.   Lieut., King's (Shropshire L.I.)   1908
    Died 29 Dec. 1917 *of wounds received in action*
ALLSOPP, R.   Capt., E. African Mtd. Infy.   1894
ARCHDALE, R. M.   Lieut., 19th Hussars.   (W.)   *M.C.*   1911
ARMSTRONG, H. M.   Pte., Canadian Infy.; Gnr., Cana-   1909
    dian F.A.
✠ARNOLD, A. C. P.   2nd Lieut., R. Fusiliers (P.S. Bn.)   1911
    Killed in action 7 July 1916
ATKINSON, Rev. A. V.   Chaplain, R.N.   1905

BAGNALL, R. O. G.   2nd Lieut., R. Berkshire Regt.   1912
BAGOT-CHESTER, H. A.   Capt., Staffordshire Yeo. (T.F.   1890
    Res.); A.D.C.
✠BAILLIE, A. H.   Major, Norfolk Regt.   1886
    Died 18 Oct. 1918
BAIN, P. W.   Capt. and Adjt., Connaught Rangers;   1905
    Capt., R. Munster Fus.   (W 2.)
BARBER, Rev. R. W.   C.F. 4th Class, R.A.C.D.(T.F.)   1872
BARBER-STARKEY, C. C.   Air Mechanic, R.A.F.   1909
BARKWORTH, R. C.   Capt., R. Fusiliers.   (W 3.)   *M.C.*   1914
    and Bar. M.
BARNES, F. P.   Lieut.-Col., R.A.S.C.(M.T.)   *D.S.O.*   1899
    O.B.E. M 2.
✠BARROW, A. J.   Capt., Lancs. Fus.   (W.)   *M.C.*   1902
    Died in Germany 24 *June* 1918 *of wounds received in*
    action
BARSTOW, J. N.   Capt., R.F.A. (T.F.); A.D.C.; Brigade   1909
    Major.   *D.S.O.   M.C.   M* 3.

BASSET, A. F.   Lieut., Gen. List (T.F. Res.); Lieut. (Ad.),   1891
R.A.F.
BATHURST, P. L.   Capt., E. Lancs. Regt.; empld. War   1911
Office. (W.) *M.*
BAYLISS, B. H.   Pte., London Regt. (Queen's Westminster   1907
Rifles); 2nd Lieut. (T.), R.A.F.
BEAUMONT, H. R.   Capt., Gen. List (T.F. Res.)   1885
BELLARS, A. E.   Lieut., Rangoon Bn., Indian Defence   1899
Force
✠BERLEIN, L. H.   Lieut., R. Berkshire Regt.   1912
  Killed in action 25 *Sept.* 1915
BEVIR, W. 2nd Lieut., Roysse's School, Abingdon, O.T.C.   1898
BISS, J. C. DE V.   Capt., I.A.R.O. (Cavalry); attd. Gen.   1911
Staff. (W.)
BLAKISTON, Rev. B. R.   Chaplain, R.N.   1895
BLAKISTON, Rev. J. N.   C.F. 4th Class, R.A.C.D.   1898
BLAMIRE-BROWN, C.   Lieut., Christ's Hospital O.T.C.   1904
BLAXTER, K. W.   Lieut., R.A.S.C. and R.F.A.   (W.)   1914
BOND, D.   Lieut., R.N.V.R.   1899
BOOKER, G. H.   Lieut. Spec. List, empld. War Office   1912
BORRETT, P. R.   Capt., Scots Gds. (W.)   1908
BOYNE, Viscount.   Hon. Colonel, Durham L.I.(T.F.)   1883
BROADBENT, F. M.   Instructor Cdr., R.N.   1886
BROPHY, G. M.   Capt., R.G.A. *M.*   1910
BUCKLEY, H. H. C.   Lieut., Coldstream Gds.   1907
✠BULL, G. J. O.   Lieut., R.E.(T.F.) (W.)   1908
  Killed in action in Gallipoli 8 *July* 1915
BUNDY, H. P.   Lieut., Worcestershire Regt.(T.F.) *M.C.*   1914
BURTON, Rev. H. J. C.   C.F. 4th Class, R.A.C.D. *M.B.E.*   1897
BUTLER, H. M.   2nd Lieut., Denstone College O.T.C.   1908

CANHAM, W. D.   2nd Lieut., Norfolk Regt.; Lieut., M.G.C.   1914
(W.) *M.C.*
CARLILE, C.   Capt., R. Scots   1897
CARLILE, E.   Lieut., R.G.A.   1894
✠CARRACK, C. J. R. Fusiliers   [1914]
  Killed in action 17 *Feb.* 1917
CARTER, H. G.   Major, R. Welsh Fus. (W 2.) *M.C.*   1912
✠CAVE, W. H. C.   2nd Lieut., Dorset Regt.   [1914]
  Killed in action 16 *March* 1915
CHAI CHAN, M. R.   Interpreter, Siamese Exp. Force   1916
✠CHARLESWORTH, W. H.   Major, King's Own (Yorkshire   1903
L.I.) (W.)
  Killed in action 15 *Sept.* 1916

CHILDE, C. P.   Lieut.-Col., R.A.M.C. (5th S. Gen. Hos-   1877
    pital, T.F.) *m* 2.
✠CLAPTON, A.   2nd Lieut., R. Fusiliers   1912
    Killed in action 5 Sept. 1916
CLARKE, J. S.   2nd Lieut., W. Yorks. Regt.   1907
CLARKE, W. K.   C.S.M., R. Fusiliers (P. S. Bn.); Lieut.,   1913
    Bedfordshire Regt.; empld. O.C.B. (W.)
CLEMENTS, W. G.   Capt. and Adjt., R.F.A.(T.F.) *M.C.*   1913
COATES, A. S.   Capt., London Regt. (St Pancras Bn.);   1909
    attd. Rifle Brigade
✠COLES, E. R.   Capt., 3rd Dragoon Gds.   1907
    Killed in action 12 May 1915
COLLIER, A. E.   Capt., R.E. *M.C.*   1910
COLLINS, A. J.   2nd Lieut., London Regt. (L.R.B.); Capt.   1912
    and Adjt., R. North Devon Yeo.
COLONNA, Don MARIO.   Italian Army   1908
CORYTON, A. F.   Capt., Hampshire Yeo.; attd. Hamp-   1911
    shire Regt.; Lieut., 18th Hussars
COTTON, V. E.   Major, R.F.A.(T.F.) and Spec. List   1907
    (T.M.B.) *O.B.E.* *M* 3.   *French Croix de Guerre.*
    Italian Croce di Guerra
COUCH, A. W.   Lieut., Hampshire Regt.(T.F.); attd.   1904
    W. Yorks. Regt.
COURTHOPE, R.   Pte., R.A.M.C.   1911
COXON, A. C. M.   Capt., Norfolk Regt.(T.F.) (W.) (P.)   1907
✠CRAWFORD, C. N.   2nd Lieut., Northamptonshire Regt.   1914
    Killed in action 8 April 1916
CRICHTON-BROWNE, H. W. A. F.   Lieut.-Col., King's Own   1884
    Scottish Borderers. *m.*
CRICK, L. C.   Capt., Lincolnshire Regt. (W.) *M.C. M.*   1910
CRISP, J. F.   Capt., Suffolk Yeo.   1913
CROSBIE-OATES, E. C.   Pte., R. Fusiliers (P. S. Bn.);   1912
    Lieut., M.G.C.; attd. R.E., Signals
CULLINAN, M. W. F.   Capt. and Adjt., King's Royal Rifle   1912
    Corps; empld. O.C.B. *M.C. M.*
CUNINGHAME, R. J.   Lieut., Gen. List. *M.C.*   1890
CURTIS, E. D.   Lieut., United States Arty.; attd. Intelli-   1914
    gence Dept.

DAISH, T.   Capt., R.E. *M.C. M.*   1911
DASHWOOD, C. E.   Lieut., R.A.M.C.   1889
DASHWOOD, Rev. R. C.   C.F. 3rd Class, R.A.C.D. *m.*   1887
DAVIDSON, A. H. G.   2nd Lieut., Highland L.I.; empld.   1916
    P. of W. Camp

DAVIDSON, A. J. Capt., Gordon Hdrs.; empld Command 1908
Depôt
DAVIDSON, J. C. F. Paymaster Sub-Lieut., R.N.V.R.; 1911
empld. Admiralty
DAVIES, T. H. Lieut., King's (Shropshire L.I., T.F.) 1896
and Labour Corps
DAVIS, J. O. Major (K.B.), R.A.F. *M.C.* *M. French* 1908
Croix de Guerre
DAWES, E. S. Capt. R. East Kent Yeo. 1912
DE HOXAR, C. F. M. Capt., Spec. List 1883
DE LAS CASAS, M. Lieut., R. North Devon Yeo. (T.F. 1889
Res.); A.D.C.
DE LEDESMA, A. F. Lieut., R.F.A. 1910
✠DENNIS, J. N. Lieut., N. Staffs. Regt.; attd. M.G.C. *M.C.* 1912
Died 15 *Oct.* 1917 *of wounds received in action*
DE PROSPERI, F. C. Italian Army 1905
DE WINDT, H. W. D. Capt., Spec. List (cmdg. P. of W. 1875
Camp)
DIBBLE, T. E. 2nd Lieut., Wellington School, Somerset, 1911
O.T.C.
DICKINS, B. 2nd Lieut., Lincolnshire Regt., King's Own 1909
(Yorkshire L.I.), and Hampshire Regt.
DOVE, C. K. Lieut., R.G.A.; Asst. Officer i/c Records 1905
DOYNE, R. W. Capt., Westmorland and Cumberland Yeo. 1887
DRUCE, A. F. Lieut., Surrey Yeo. *M.C.* *M. French* 1913
Croix de Guerre
DUKE, M. 2nd Lieut., R.E.; empld. Ministry of Labour 1909
DULEEP-SINGH, H.H. Prince F. V., M.V.O. Major, Norfolk 1887
Yeo. and Gen. Staff
DUNCAN, C. W. Lieut., Welsh Gds. and Gds. M.G. Regt. 1912
✠DURRANT, W. B. W. 2nd Lieut., Rifle Brigade 1913
Killed in action 9 *May* 1915

ECCLES, A. G. Capt., King's (Liverpool Regt., T.F.) 1910
(W.) *M.C.*
EDWARDS, Rev. A. L. C.F. 4th Class, R.A.C.D. 1899
ELLIOTT, A. G. Lieut., Grenadier Gds. (W 2.) *M.C.* 1898
ELLIS, V. L. R.A.M.C. 1897
ENGLAND, J. A. Lieut., Bedfordshire Regt.; attd. Durham 1912
L.I. (W.)
✠ESTCOURT, A. C. SOTHERON. Lieut., Wiltshire Regt. and 1912
Gloucestershire Regt.; Capt., T.M.B.; Lieut. (O.),
R.A.F. (W 2.) *M.C.*
Killed in action 8 *Aug.* 1918

ESTCOURT, W. B. SOTHERON. Lieut., E. African Force   1909
EUSTACE, W. R. G. Capt., R.G.A.   1910
EVANS, O. L. J. Lieut.-Col., R. Welsh Fus. *m.*   1875
EXETER, Marquess of. Lieut.-Col., R.F.A.(T.F.) *M* 2.   1897

FAIRBOURN, A. N. Lieut., R.E. (W.)   1908
FAIRLEY, W. Capt. and Adjt., E. Surrey Regt.(T.F.);   1910
   Capt., King's African Rifles. (W.) *M.*
FERGUSSON, N. M. Major, R.A.M.C.(T.F.) *M* 2.   1901
FIXSEN, B. A. Lieut., Rifle Brigade   1912
FLETCHER, A. M. T. Capt., R.A.S.C.   1899
FLETCHER, E. T. D. Lieut., London Yeo. (Middlesex   1908
   Hussars); Surgeon Lieut., R.N.
FOWKE, L. A. Lieut., Leicestershire Regt. (W.) *M.*   1906
FREAKE, F. M. Capt., R.F.A.; A.D.C. *M.*   1894
FREND, J. P. N. Zealand Rifle Brigade   1896
FREWEN, S. Lieut.-Col., A.A. and Q.M.G.   *1877
FRIEDERICHS, L. H. T. Capt., Cheshire Regt. and Spec.   1893
   List
FURNESS, W. Capt., Loyal N. Lancs. Regt. (W.)   1906

✠GARNETT, I. W. 2nd Lieut., King's (Shropshire L.I.)   1912
   (W.)
   Killed in action 12 *Feb.* 1916
GIBBS, A. R. Pte., Hampshire Regt.; Lieut., Worcester-   1904
   shire Regt.
GIBSON, F. A. S. Capt., N. Staffs. Regt. (W 3.) *M.C.*   1912
GILES, C. C. T. 2nd Lieut., Devon Regt.; Lieut., Gren-   1913
   adier Gds. (W.)
GISSING, A. C. Lieut., R.G.A.; attd. Indian Army   [1914]
GLASBROOK, J. H. L. Lieut., Welsh Regt.; attd. R. Welsh   1914
   Fus. (W.) *M.*
GLASSPOOL, R. T. B. Capt., Durham L.I.(T.F.) *M.C.*   1899
   M 2.
✠GOODFORD, C. J. H. Lieut., Hampshire Regt. *M.C.*   [1914]
   M.
   Killed in action 1 *July* 1916
GOODWIN, A. C. Pte., Suffolk Regt.; Lce-Sergt., Suffolk   1914
   Yeo.; Lieut., Labour Corps
GORDON, E. B. 2nd Lieut., Lancing College O.T.C.   1912
GORE, I. ST J. Capt., Gloucestershire Regt. (W.)   1900
GRANT, D. W. Lieut., Lovat's Scouts; attd. Cameron   1913
   Hdrs.

✠GRAY, A. F. Lieut., Wiltshire Regt. and Cambridgeshire 1911
Regt. (W.)
Killed in action 26 Aug. 1918
GRAY, Rev. P. C.F. 4th Class, R.A.C.D. 1907
GREAR, A.T.L. Capt., Gloucestershire Regt.(T.F.) (W 2.) 1906
GREEN, F. N. Lieut., R. Welsh Fus. *m.* [1914]
GREENWOOD, Rev. F. B. C.F. 4th Class, R.A.C.D. 1903
GROOM, H. L. Lieut. (A.), R.A.F. 1915
GROOM, Rev. R. W. C.F. 4th Class, R.A.C.D. 1911
GUBBINS, C. F. R. Major, London Yeo. (Middlesex 1898
Hussars)
GWYER, Rev. H. L. C.F. 4th Class, R.A.C.D. 1902

HAIG, D. P. Lieut.-Col., Cameron Hdrs. and Cameron- 1886
ians (Scottish Rifles). *O.B.E. m.*
✠HALL, H. 2nd Lieut., Lincolnshire Regt. 1913
Killed in action 15 Feb. 1916
HALL, V. C. Lieut.-Col., R.E. (Postal Section). *O.B.E.* 1900
M 2.
HALLOWS, R. W. Major, R.G.A. 1904
HAMMOND, F. W. Lieut., King's Own Scottish Borderers. 1912
(W.)
HANCOCK, D. M. Lieut., Gen. List (T.F. Res.), empld. 1893
Ministry of National Service
HANKIN, G. T. Capt., Oxford and Bucks L.I.(T.F.) 1896
and Gen. Staff. *M. m.*
HANSON, Sir G. S., Bart. Capt., R.F.A and Suffolk Regt. 1886
HARDCASTLE, A. E. L. Capt., The Buffs (E. Kent Regt., 1913
T.F.) (W.)
HARDING, A. M. Capt. (K.B.), R.A.F. 1908
HARLEY, R. G. G. Capt., R. Fusiliers and Gen. List 1900
(A.P.M.)
✠HARRISON, G.H. 2nd Lieut., Loyal N.Lancs. Regt. *M.C.* 1914
Died 21 Aug. 1916 of wounds received in action
HARRISON-BROADLEY, J. Capt., E. Yorks. Regt. 1900
HARRISSON, A. E. Capt., R.A.M.C. *M.* 1890
✠HARTER, J. C. F. 2nd Lieut., Res. Regt. of Cavalry, attd. 1908
Nottinghamshire Yeo.
Killed in action 28 Nov. 1917
✠HARVEY, R. V. Capt., British Columbia Regt., Canadian 1891
Force
*Died in Germany 8 May 1915 of wounds received in
action near Ypres 24 April 1915*

HENN, W. F.   Capt., R. Munster Fus.; attd. R. Irish   1911
Regt. and Gen. Staff (Intelligence). (W.)
HENRYSON-CAIRD, A. J.   Capt., King's Own Scottish   1902
Borderers. (W.) *M.C. M.*
✠HEPBURN, M. A.   2nd Lieut., Seaforth Hdrs.   1910
Killed in action 30 Nov. 1914
✠HEPBURN, R. P.   2nd Lieut., R.E. (Signals). (W.) *M.C.*   1911
Died 3 Aug. 1917 *of wounds received in action*
HIGGS, H. J.   Lieut.-Col., R.E.; A. D. Labour.   (W.)   1905
O.B.E. Albert Medal, 1st *Class. M* 3.
✠HILL, B. W.   Lieut., Rifle Brigade and R.F.C.   (W.)   1911
Killed in action 4 March 1917
✠HILL, M. C.   Lieut., Leicestershire Regt.   (W.)   1913
Killed in action 17 July 1916
HINDLE, E.   Capt., R.E.(T.F.)   1910
HINDLEY-SMITH, J. D.   Lieut. and Adjt., R.F.A.   1912
HOLLINGS, J. H. B.   Lieut., 21st Lancers.   (W.)   1906
HOPEWELL, E. R.   Capt., Worcestershire Regt. (T.F.)   1908
(W.) *M.C.*
HORE, C. W. C.   R.A.F.   1908
HORNSBY, J. A.   Capt., 5th Lancers; A.D.C.   (W.)   1909
HUGHES, H. C.   Lieut., R.E.   1911
HUNT, R.   Major, London Yeo.(T.F. Res.)   1879
HUNTER, G. J.   Capt., Worcestershire Yeo.   1907
HUNTER-MUSKETT, R. G.   Major, Middlesex Regt   1893
HYDE PARKER, W. S.   *See* PARKER, W. S. H.

ISHERWOOD, W.   Lieut., R.G.A.   (W.)   1915

JACKSON, C. R.   Capt., Rifle Brigade; empld. O.C.B.;   1912
Major, M.G.C.   (W.)
JEPSON, R. W.   Lieut., Cheshire Regt.; Capt. (T.), R.A.F.   1907
✠JOHNS, B. C.   2nd Lieut., R.G.A.   1899
Died 22 Oct. 1918 *of pneumonia*
JOHNSON, C. R. I.   Lieut., Northumberland Fus.(T.F.)   1901
(W.)
JOHNSTONE, C. A.   Lieut., King's (Shropshire L.I.)   (W.)   1905
JOLLY, A. F.   Lieut., R. Fusiliers.   (W.) *M.C.*   [1914]
JONSSON, A. T.   Capt., R. Irish Rifles. (P.)   1899
JOURDAIN, R. O.   Capt., R. Fusiliers; Staff Capt., War   1889
Office. (W.) *Brevet Major. m. Cavalier, Order of
the Crown of Italy*
JOYNSON, R.   Capt., King's Own Scottish Borderers.   1906
(P.) *m.*

JUDD, L. A. Capt., Highland L.I. and R. Scots. (W.)   1913

KAY, Rev. A. I. 2nd Lieut., I.A.R.O.   1907
KEABLE, Rev. R. Chaplain, S. African Native Labour   1905
Contingent
✠KELK, A. F. H. 2nd Lieut., Welsh Regt. (W.) *M.C.*   1910
Killed in action 9 *March* 1917
KELSEY, A. R. Lieut., Coldstream Gds.; Capt., Spec.   1909
List (School of Instruction). *M.C. Italian Croce di
Guerra*
✠KEMP, N. 2nd Lieut., Lancs. Fus.(T.F.) (W.)   [1914]
Killed in action 9 *Sept.* 1916
KINDERSLEY, C. E. Surgeon Lieut., R.N.   1909
KINDERSLEY, G. W. Capt., Cameronians (Scottish Rifles); [1914]
attd. Suffolk Regt. (W 2.) *M.*
KING, Rev. F. J. C.F. 3rd Class, R.A.C.D.; D.A.C.G.   1891
(W.) *M* 2.
KIRKBRIDE, G. Capt., R.A.S.C.; Lieut., Imp. Service   1913
Cavalry and 27th Punjabis, Indian Army
KNAPPETT, P. G. Lieut., R.F.A.; Staff Lieut. *M.*   1907
KNOTT, P. G. Capt. and Adjt., R.G.A.   1913
KNUBLEY, C. Corpl., Australian A.M.C.   1907
✠KNUBLEY, R. L. Capt., Wiltshire Regt. (W.) *M.C. M.*   1906
Died 9 *July* 1916 *of wounds received in action*

LAMBE, J. L. P. Sub-Lieut., R.N.V.R.   1913
LAMBTON, J. F. Capt., Northumberland Fus.(T.F.)   1905
✠LANE, J. E. 2nd Lieut., The Buffs (E. Kent Regt., T.F.)   1915
Killed in action 3 *May* 1917
LAWSON-JOHNSTON, E. A. Lieut., 2nd Dragoons (R.   1897
Scots Greys). (W 3.) *M.*
✠LEACH, G. K. Lieut., Border Regt.   1902
Killed in action in Gallipoli 10 *Aug.* 1915
LEE-WILLIAMS, O. LL. Lce.-Corpl., Gloucestershire Regt.   1910
LE FLEMING, G. F. A. H. Hon. Colonel, Spec. List   1878
(Draft Conducting Officer)
LE FLEMING, M. R. Lieut., Queen's Own (R. W. Kent   1913
Regt., T.F.); Capt. and Adjt., M.G.C. (W.) *M.*
LEIGH-MALLORY, G. H. Lieut., R.G.A.   1905
LEIGH-MALLORY, T. Lieut., Lancs. Fus.; Major (A.),   1911
R.A.F. (W.) *D.S.O. M.*
LE ROUGETEL, I. H. Lieut., Northamptonshire Regt.;   1913
Capt., M.G.C. *M.C. and Bar*
LINTHORNE, E. L. R. Seaman, R.N.V.R.   1912

✠LLOYD, M. E. Capt., R. Welsh Fus. 1898
  Killed in action 23 Oct. 1914
✠LONG, F. E. Pte., Hampshire Regt.; Capt., King's 1911
  (Liverpool Regt.) *M.C.*
  Killed in action at Hooge 24 Aug. 1917
LOVEDAY, D. G. 2nd Lieut., Oxford and Bucks. L.I. 1915
LOWRY, G. C. Capt., Cheshire Regt. and Gen. List 1913
  (School of Instruction). (W 2.)
LOWTHER, Hon. L. E. Capt., Gen. Staff. *O.B.E. Order* 1885
  of the Nile, 4th Class (Egypt)
LUCAS, W. R. Major, R.A.S.C. *D.S.O. M* 2. 1903
LUMBY, C. D. R. Lieut., Manchester Regt. (W 2.) 1907
LUSON, T. G. L. Capt. and Adjt., R.A.S.C. *O.B.E. M.* 1913
LYON, R. C. G. Capt., R.F.A.(T.F.); Staff Capt. 1909

McCONNELL, W. E. Capt. (T.), R.A.F. 1907
MACKENZIE, C. Lieut., King's Own (Yorkshire L.I.) 1914
MACKENZIE, L. H. M. Capt., Northamptonshire Regt. *M.* 1913
MacMICHAEL, H. A. Capt., Spec. List, empld. Egyptian 1901
  Army. *D.S.O. M.*
MacMICHAEL, H. C. Capt., Border Regt. (W.) 1909
MACNAB, C. Lieut., Highland L.I. (W.) *m.* 1914
MACPHERSON, A. S. 2nd Lieut., Labour Corps 1915
McPHILLAMY, J. M. 2nd Lieut., R.G.A. 1915
McWILLIAM, J. Lieut., King's (Liverpool Regt.) (W.) 1911
  M.C.
MALLORY, G. H. L. *See* LEIGH-MALLORY, G. H.
MALLORY, T. L. *See* LEIGH-MALLORY, T.
MARGESSON, H. D. R. Capt. and Adjt., 11th Hussars. 1908
  M.C. M.
MATTHEWS, A. S. Lieut., 8th (King's R. Irish) Hussars 1906
MAULE, W. H. F. Capt., Loyal N. Lancs. Regt. (W 3.) 1908
  D.S.O. M.B.E. M.
MAYO, R. H. Capt. (A.), R.F.C.; Major (T.), R.A.F. 1909
  (Aircraft Production Dept.) *O.B.E.*
METHVEN, C. M. Lieut., Black Watch (T.F.) (W.) 1908
MONSON, C. S. Lieut., Lovat's Scouts; Capt., Cameron 1902
  Hdrs. (W.)
✠MORGAN, H. R. Lieut., D. of Lancaster's Own Yeo.; attd. 1905
  R.F.C.
  Killed in action 8 Nov. 1917
MORLEY, J. Lieut., R. Wiltshire Yeo. 1907
✠MORLEY, M. R. H. Lieut., King's Own (Yorkshire L.I.) 1913
  Killed in action at Ovillers 1 July 1916

✠Morris, J. C. Lieut., Welsh Regt. 1911
  Killed in action in Gallipoli 8 Aug. 1915
Morshead, O. F. Capt., R.E.; Major, G.S.O. 2. *D.S.O.* 1913
  M.C. Brevet Major. M 5. *Italian Croce di Guerra*
Mortimer, H. S. Capt., King's Royal Rifle Corps and 1896
  Gen. List (A.P.M.) *M* 2. *French Croix de Guerre*
Mountbatten, Lord L. A. L., g.c.v.o. Capt., King's 1907
  Royal Rifle Corps
Murray, K. R. 2nd Lieut., Cameron Hdrs.; Capt., Wilt- 1907
  shire Regt.(T.F.); attd. Oxford and Bucks L.I.;
  A.D.C.; Staff Capt.
Murray Smith, J. E. Major, R. Horse Gds. (W.) 1909
✠Musgrave, T. Lieut., Irish Gds. *M.* 1908
  Killed in action 6 Feb. 1915

✠Nash, G. 2nd Lieut., Worcestershire Regt. 1909
  Died 20 June 1915 *of wounds received in action*
Neville, A. G. Major, R.H.A.; A.D.C. *M.C. M.* 1909
Neville, H. S. Capt. (A.), R.A.F.; S.O. 3, Air Ministry 1914
Newman, J. C. Lieut., Res. Regt. of Cavalry; A.D.C. 1899
  French Croix de Guerre
Newton, H. A. A.B., R.N.V.R. 1880
Nicholson, O. W. Lieut., R.E. (Signals). *m.* 1910

Oldroyd, F. N. Lieut., R.A.S.C.(M.T.) 1913
Oliver, G. Y. Hon. Major, R.F.A.(T.F. Res.) 1908
Ollerenshaw, F. 2nd Lieut., Cheshire Regt.(T.F.); 1910
  Asst. Paymaster, R.N.V.R.
Orlebar, J. A. A. Capt., R.A.M.C. 1897
✠Orme, F. R. 2nd Lieut., R. Welsh Fus. 1911
  Killed in action 7 Nov. 1914
Otter, W. W. Capt. and Adjt., Sussex Yeo. 1897

Packe, E. C. Major, R. Fusiliers; Lieut.-Col., A.A. and 1896
  Q.M.G. *D.S.O. O.B.E. M* 3.
Palmer, Sir E. G. B., Bart. Major, Leicestershire Regt. 1882
Pape, A. G. 2nd Lieut., Worcestershire Regt. (W.) 1912
Parker, W. D. Hon. Lieut., A.S.C. (T.F. Res.) 1898
Parker, W. S. H. Lieut., 1st Dragoon Gds. 1910
Parker-Jervis, G. Lieut., N. Staffs. Regt.(T.F.); empld. 1914
  O.C.B. *M.*
Parkinson, G. R. 2nd Lieut., King's School, Rochester, 1895
  O.T.C.

PATERSON, W. H. Lieut., Gordon Hdrs. *M.C. M.*   1912
PEEK, B. M. Lieut., Hampshire Regt.   1910
PEEL, W. H. G. 2nd Lieut., R. Guernsey Militia   1892
PERKS, J. N. R. Lieut., R.E.   1911
PERRINS, C. F. D. Capt., R.F.A.(T.F.)   1911
✠PHILLIPPS, R. W. 2nd Lieut., Grenadier Gds   1914
     Killed in action 26 *Oct.* 1915
PLANT, Rev. A. W. Chaplain, R.N.   1878
POLLOK, A. B. Major, 7th Hussars and Gen. Staff   1892
     (cmdg. Cadet Sqdn.) *O.B.E. m* 2.
POPE, P. M. Capt. and Adjt., King's Royal Rifle Corps   1910
     (W.) (P.) *M.*
POYSER, A. V. Major, R.A.M.C. *M.*   1901
PRICHARD, H. C. Major, Glamorgan Yeo.; Lieut.-Col.,   1883
     Spec. List (Cmdt., P. of W. Camp). *C.B.E. m* 2.
PRYDE, A. M. Pte., Norfolk Regt. (W 2.)   1914

RANSOM, P. L. Capt., Hertfordshire Regt.   1911
REECE, C. M. Lieut., Cheshire Regt.; Lieut. (A.), R.A.F.   1913
     (W.) (P.)
✠REEVES, V. C. M. Major, Dorset Yeo. (W.) *M.*   1906
     Killed in action in Egypt 26 *Feb.* 1916
RIDLEY, G. A. Lieut., E. Yorks. Regt.; attd. 30th Lan-   [1914]
     cers, Indian Army
✠RITSON, F. Capt., Dorset Regt.   1909
     Killed in action 17 *June* 1917
ROBERTS, J. H. Lieut., Welsh Regt.; Capt., King's (Liver-   1903
     pool Regt.) and King's African Rifles
ROXBURGH, T. J. Y. Capt., I.A.R.O.   1910

SALTER, F. R. Lieut., Rifle Brigade; Capt. G.S.O. 3, *1910
     Irish Command. (W.)
SANDILANDS, R. B. Capt., The Buffs (E. Kent Regt.)   1912
     M.C.
SARTORIS, G. U. L. 2nd Lieut., R.A.S.C.; Lieut., R.N.V.R.   1913
SAVILL, E. H. Capt., Devon Regt. (W.) *M.C.*   1913
SCARLETT, C. H. Lieut. R.G.A.   1907
SCHOLFIELD, J. L. Capt., R. Fusiliers; R.T.O.   1912
✠SCUDAMORE, R. C. Capt., R. Fusiliers. *M.C.*   [1914]
     Killed in action 11 *March* 1918
✠SHAW, J. R. Lieut.-Col., King's Own (Yorkshire L.I.)   1886
     Died 5 *Nov.* 1916
SHAW-YATES, E. B. 2nd Lieut., R.E. (Signals, T.F. Res.)   1889
SHEPLEY, R. G. S. Lieut., 3rd Dragoon Gds.   1912

SHEPPARD-JONES, J. E. Capt., R.A.M.C.   1902
SIDNEY, R. J. H. Capt., King's (Liverpool Regt.)   1912
SIFFKEN, B. C. DE W. 2nd Lieut., R.A.S.C. (W.) *M.*   1901
SLADE, P. C. A. Capt. and Adjt., R. Defence Corps   1899
✠SMITH, A. G. Capt., Loyal N. Lancs. Regt. (W.) *M.C.*   1909
    Killed in action 18 *April* 1918
SMITH, Rev. J. J. Chaplain and Instructor Cdr., R.N.   1880
SMITH, S. C. KAINES. Major, Gen. Staff (Censor's Dept.)   1895
    M.B.E. M. Officer, Order of the Redeemer (*Greece*).
    Greek Medal for Military Merit
SMITH, W. A. N. Lieut., R.E.(T.F.)   1912
SNAITH, E. G. Capt., Leicestershire Regt.(T.F.) (W.)   1911
    M.C. M.
SNEYD, R. Hon. Lieut.-Col., Spec. List (A.P.M.)   1884
STEDALL, C. P. Major, London Yeo. (Rough Riders) and   1892
    M.G.C.
✠STERN, L. H. 2nd Lieut., London Regt. (Kensington Bn.)   1910
    Killed in action 9 *May* 1915
STOPFORD, R. J. Lieut., R.A.S.C. *M.*   [1914]
SYMONS, S. J. Major, Bedfordshire Regt.(T.F.)   1887

TANQUERAY, T. Capt., The Queen's (R.W. Surrey Regt.);   1907
    empld. O.C.B. (W.)
TAYLOR, G. C. R. Capt., Essex Regt.(T.F.); attd. Devon   1899
    Regt. (W.)
TEDDER, A. W. Capt., Dorset Regt.; Major (A.), R.A.F.   1909
    M 2. *Italian Silver Medal for Military Valour*
TERRY, C. E. Lieut.-Col., E. Yorks. Regt.(T.F.)   1885
THOMPSON, D. H. 2nd Lieut., R.A.S.C.; Lieut., Gen.   1905
    List, attd. R.E. (P.)
TICKELL, G. W. Lieut., Argyll and Sutherland Hdrs.   1914
    (T.F.); attd. 36th Sikhs, Indian Army
TINKER, B. Capt., Yorkshire Dragoons   1910
✠TOLLEMACHE, J. E. Lieut., The Queen's (R. W. Surrey   1911
    Regt.)
    Killed in action 21 *Aug.* 1916
✠TONKING, D. W. Pte., R. Fusiliers (P.S. Bn.); 2nd Lieut.,   1909
    D. of Cornwall's L.I.; Capt., R. Warwickshire Regt.
    Died 29 *May* 1917 *of wounds received in action*
TRINGHAM, H. G. 2nd Lieut., Wiltshire Regt.; Lieut.,   1886
    R.A.S.C.
TYRWHITT, Rev. the Hon. L. F., M.V.O. C.F. 2nd Class,   1882
    R.A.C.D. (W.) *O.B.E. M* 2.

VALENTINE, W. H.   2nd Lieut., King's Own Scottish   1914
    Borderers; Lieut. (A.), R.A.F. (W.)
VARVILL, J. K.   Capt., E. Lancs. Regt. (W.) *M.C. M.*   1910
VERNER, G. W. H.   Lieut., R. Marines   1900

WAITHMAN, J. C.   Capt., R.A.M.C.   1877
✠WALKER, G. S.   Lieut., R.F.A.   1910
    Died 20 Nov. 1917 of wounds received in action
✠WALMESLEY, R.   Lieut., Yorkshire Regt.   1908
    Killed in action 23 Oct. 1914
WALPOLE, R. H.   Lieut., Rifle Brigade. (W 2.)   1911
WALTER, G. L.   Pte., Rhodesian Regt., S. African Force   1909
✠WATSON, C. B.   2nd Lieut., S. Staffs. Regt.; Lieut.,   1913
    M.G.C. *M.C.*
    Died 12 July 1918 of wounds received in action
✠WATSON, K. F.   Flt. Lieut., R.N.A.S.   1912
    Missing, presumed drowned, 3 Aug. 1915
WAUGH, A. D.   Lieut., R.E. *M.*   1908
WAYNE, Rev. ST J.   C.F. 4th Class, R.A.C.D.   1895
WESTALL, D. C.   Lieut., R. Sussex Regt. (W.)   1909
WESTON, G. E.   Capt. and Adjt., R.E.   1906
WHARTON, W. H. A., V.D.   Lieut.-Col., Yorkshire Regt.   1878
    (T.F. Res.) *O.B.E. m.*
WHITCHURCH, R. H. S. G.   Major, Military Accounts   1897
    Dept., Indian Army
WHITEFIELD, C. G.   Lieut., Suffolk Regt.; Capt., Gen.   1910
    Staff
WHITTOME, L.   Capt., Hampshire Regt. (W.)   [1914]
WILKINSON, W. R.   Pte., London Regt. (Artists Rifles);   1912
    2nd Lieut., King's Own (Yorkshire L.I.)
WILLIAMS, G. A.   Capt., Gen. List (T.F. Res.)   1875
✠WILLIAMS, R.   2nd Lieut., Grenadier Gds.   1909
    Killed in action 8 Oct. 1915
WILLIAMSON, C. G.   2nd Lieut., R.A.S.C. (Canteens)   1908
WILSON, A. S., M.P.   Capt., E. Riding of Yorkshire Yeo.   1887
    (T.F. Res.) and Gen. Staff. (P.)
WILSON, R.   Capt., Lancs. Fus. *M.C.*   1873
WINTERBOTHAM, G. L.   Rangoon Bn., Indian Defence   1908
    Force
✠WINTON, H. B.   Pte., Middlesex Regt. (P. S. Bn.); Lieut.   1912
    (A.), R.A.F. (W.)
    Killed in flying accident 21 April 1918
WOMERSLEY, F. G.   Lieut., R. Welsh Fus.; attd. R. Irish   1914
    Fus.; Capt., Gen. List (Asst. Embarkation S.O.)

WOODHOUSE, C. H. Capt., Dorset Regt. (P.) *M.C. M.*   1909
WOODHOUSE, W. E.   2nd Lieut., Worcestershire Regt.   1910
(T.F.)
✠WYNDHAM, G. H.   2nd Lieut., Devon Regt.; attd. North-   1912
umberland Fus.
Killed in action 24 *March* 1915

YERBURGH, R. E. R.   2nd Lieut., Norfolk Regt.   1910
YERBURGH, R. G. C.   Capt., Irish Gds.; Major,   1911
D.A.Q.M.G. *O.B.E. M. Belgian Croix de Guerre.
Italian Croce di Guerra*
YOUNG, R. K.   Lieut., Queen's Own (R. W. Kent Regt.)   1910
(W.)
YOUNG, W.   Sergt., R. Fusiliers; Capt., W. Yorks. Regt.   1890
(W.) *M.C.*

PEMBROKE COLLEGE

ABRAHAM, L. M.   Lieut., R.F.A.   (W.)   1912
AINSLIE, Rev. R. M., T.D.   C.F. 1st Class, R.A.C.D.(T.F.)   1877
ALEXANDER, D. L.   2nd Lieut., Gds. M.G. Regt.   1917
✠ALISON, L. H.   2nd Lieut., R. Berkshire Regt.   1909
   Killed in action 15 May 1915
ALLEN, H. R.   Instructor Lieut., R.N.   1913
ALLEN, S. S.   Lieut.-Col., Auckland Regt., N. Zealand   1901
   Force. (W 2.) *C.M.G. D.S.O. and Bar. M* 3.
ALLEN, W.S.   Lieut., R.E.; Hon. Lieut. (T.), R.A.F. (W.)   1913
✠AMBLER, G.   Lieut., W. Yorks. Regt.(T.F.) (W.)   1912
   Died 3 Aug. 1917 of wounds received in action July 1917
AMES, Rev. E. F. W.   C.F. 4th Class, R.A.C.D.(T.F.)   1905
✠ANDERSON, C. A. K.   2nd Lieut., R. Scots Fus. and   1911
   King's Royal Rifle Corps.
   Killed in action 10 Nov. 1914
ANDERSON, D. C.   Capt., Rifle Brigade. (W.)   1913
ANDERSON, K.   Major, R.F.A. *M.C. M* 2.   1906
✠ANDREWS, C. N.   2nd Lieut., Loyal N. Lancs. Regt.   1913
   Killed in action 24 March 1915
ANNAND, A. W.   Capt., Gordon Hdrs. (W 2.) *M.C.*   1901
APPLEBY, D.   Major, Welsh Regt. *M. m.*   1900
APPLETON, A. J.   Capt. and Adjt., R.A.S.C. *M.C. M* 2.   1899
✠ARMITAGE, D. W.   R. Fusiliers (P. S. Bn.); 2nd Lieut.,   1912
   R. Sussex Regt.
   Killed in action in the Battle of Loos 25 Sept. 1915
ARMITAGE, E. G. H.   Lieut., King's Royal Rifle Corps;   1914
   Capt., Spec. List, empld. Ministry of National
   Service. (W.)
✠ARMITAGE, F. R.   Capt., R.A.M.C.(T.F.) (W.) *D.S.O. M.* 1902
   Killed in action 30 July 1917

ARMITAGE, V. H. Capt., Sherwood Foresters (Notts. and 1907
    Derby Regt., T.F.) (W.) *M.C. Chevalier, Ordre
    de la Couronne (Belgium). Belgian Croix de Guerre*
ARMSTRONG, M. D. Lieut., Middlesex Regt. 1902
ARMSTRONG, V. Pte., R.A.S.C.(M.T.) 1904
ASH, H. A. Capt., R.A.M.C. 1902
✠ASTON, F. M. Capt., D. of Cornwall's L.I. 1886
    Killed in action 30 *July* 1915
✠ATKEY, F. A. H. Capt., Yorkshire Regt. 1901
    Killed in action 5 *July* 1916
ATKEY, J. F. H. Capt., R.F.A.(T.F.) (W.) 1895
ATTERBURY, F. W. Lieut., R.N.V R.; empld. Admiralty. 1909
    m.
ATTWATER, A. L. Capt. and Adjt., R. Welsh Fus. (W.) 1911
ATTWATER, G. L. Surgeon Lieut., R.N. 1907
ATTWATER, H. L. Capt., R.A.M.C. 1903
✠ATTWATER, H. ST J. Capt., Northamptonshire Regt. (W.) 1912
    Killed in action 26 *June* 1916
ATTWATER, W. F. Surgeon Sub-Lieut., R.N.V.R. 1913
AUSTIN, S. P. Lieut., Northumberland Yeo. 1890
AVERILL, A. S. Lieut., R.F.A. 1912
AYKROYD, H. H. Capt. and Adjt., D. of Wellington's [1914]
    (W. Riding Regt.) *M.C.*

BADCOCK, G. E. Lieut.-Col., R.A.S.C.; A. D. Transport. 1901
    C.B.E. D.S.O. Brevet Lieut.-Colonel. M 4.
✠BAGLEY, A. B. Lieut. (A.), R.F.C.; Capt., R. Dublin Fus. 1909
    (W 2.) *M.C.*
    Died 29 *Oct.* 1918 *of wounds received in action*
✠BAGNALL, G. B. 2nd Lieut., Rifle Brigade 1905
    Killed in action 23 *April* 1917
BAGSHAW, W. H., T.D. Major, E. Surrey Regt.(T.F.) 1884
BAILY, R. E. H. Capt., Herefordshire Regt. *M.* 1904
BAINBRIDGE-BELL, Rev. W. D. C.F. 4th Class, R.A.C.D. 1881
BANKS, D. J. Capt., Oxford and Bucks. L.I. (P.) 1895
BANKS, R. G. Capt., R.A.S.C. 1901
BARCLAY, J. A. Capt., London Regt. (Queen's West- 1911
    minster Rifles)
BARKWORTH, H. B. 2nd Lieut., Labour Corps 1897
BARLOW, C. N. Capt., King's Royal Rifle Corps. (W 2.) 1912
    (P.)
BARLOW, E. M. Lieut., R. Fusiliers; Major, Gen. Staff 1911
    (Instructor, British Military Mission). (W.) *M.*

BARLOW, P. Capt., Spec. List (Recruiting Staff)   1885
✠BARNETT, R. W. Capt., King's Royal Rifle Corps; Major,   1911
   G.S.O. 2. (W.) *M.C. and Bar*
   Killed in action 12 Aug. 1918
BARNICOT, H. 2nd Lieut., Labour Corps   1901
BARNINGHAM, V. Lieut., R.A.S.C.   1911
BARRAN, H. B. Capt., R.F.A.(T.F.) (W.) *M.C. M.*   1908
BARRELL, F. M. Lieut., Gloucestershire Regt.(T.F.)   1911
BARRELL, K. C. Lieut., R.E.(T.F.) (P.)   1914
BARRETT, Rev. W. E. C. C.F. 4th Class, R.A.C.D.   1898
BARROW, P. L. Capt., Worcestershire Regt. and Gen.   1911
   Staff (Intelligence). *M.*
BARROW, R. L. Lieut., I.A.R.O., attd. 41st Cavalry   1907
BARRY, A. G. Capt., Manchester Regt.; Lieut.-Col.,   1905
   M.G.C. D.S.O. M.C. M 3.
BARRY, C. B. Capt., I.A.R.O., attd. 17th Cavalry   1905
[1]BARSTOW, J. E. J. Capt., N. Somerset Yeo.; A.D.C.;   [1914]
   Hon. Capt. (A.), R.A.F. (W.)
✠BARTON, C. G. Capt., R. Inniskilling Fus. *M.C. M* 2. 1909
   Killed in action 17 Oct. 1918
✠BARWELL, F. L. Capt., London Regt. (Queen's West-   [1914]
   minster Rifles); attd. R.F.C. (W.)
   Killed in action 29 April 1917
BATES, J. V. Major, R.A.M.C. *M.C. m.*   1910
BATHURST, H. A. 2nd Lieut., R.G.A.   1901
✠BAXTER,W.H.B. Capt.,R.Warwickshire Regt.(T.F.) (W.) 1911
   Killed in action 27 Aug. 1917
BEAUMONT, J. W. F. Lieut., R.G.A.   1896
✠BECK, C. B. H. 2nd Lieut., Cheshire Regt.(T.F.)   1910
   Died 18 Aug. 1915 *of wounds received in action in*
   Gallipoli 17 Aug. 1915
BECKER, W. T. L. 2nd Lieut., Manchester Regt.; Major, 1910
   York and Lancaster Regt.
✠BELL, A. F. Pte., London Regt. (L.R.B.); 2nd Lieut., [1914]
   S. Wales Borderers
   Killed in action 12 Aug. 1915
BELL, A. T. Pte., R.A.S.C.   1909
BELLWOOD, K. B. Surgeon Lieut., R.N. *O.B.E.*   1909
✠BENNETT, S. L. R.N.V.R. (Armoured Car Section); Flt. 1910
   Sub-Lieut., R.N.A.S.
   Killed in action 29 April 1917
BENNION, C. F. Capt., R.H.A.(T.F.)   1903
BENNITT, F. W. Pte., R.A.M.C.   1892

[1] Killed in flying accident after the armistice.

BENSTED-SMITH, W. F.   Capt., R.A.M.C.(T.F.)   *M.*   1906
✠BERKELEY, M. K. F.   Canadian F.A.   1912
   Died 1 May 1915 of wounds received in action
BERRINGTON, K. C.   Pte., R.A.S.C.(M.T.)   1902
✠BEVERIDGE, D. A.   2nd Lieut., R.F.A.   1905
   *Died 13 Sept. 1915 of dysentery contracted on active
   service in Gallipoli*
✠BEVIR, C. E. F.   Lieut., R.F.A.   (W.)   1909
   Killed in action 29 Sept. 1915
BEYTS, C. A.   Capt., Poona Bn., Indian Defence Force   1895
✠BIBBY, R. E.   Sergt., R.F.A.   1904
   *Died in Egypt 23 Oct. 1918 of pneumonia contracted on
   active service*
BICKERTON, J. M.   Surgeon Sub-Lieut., R.N.V.R.   1913
BICKFORD-SMITH, W. N. V.   Capt. and Adjt., S. Wales   1911
   Borderers. (W.) *M.C.*
✠BICKLEY, G.H.   Lieut., Devon Regt.; Capt., M.G.C. (W.)   1911
   Killed in action 4 Oct. 1917
BICKNELL, R. A. W.   Capt., Grenadier Gds. *M.C.*   [1914]
BIRD, C. B.   Capt., King's Own Scottish Borderers. (W.)   1912
   M.C.
✠BISHOP, C. G.   Major, R.E.(T.F.) *D.S.O. M.*   1898
   Killed in action 30 Oct. 1917
BLACK, F. G.   Lieut., Middlesex Regt. *M.C.*   1909
✠BLACKBURNE-DANIELL, G. F.   2nd Lieut., R. Fusiliers   1897
   Killed in action 24 April 1917
BLAINE, H. D.   Lieut., S. African Mtd. Bde.   1904
✠BLAIR, G. Y.   2nd Lieut., R.F.A.   1913
   Killed in action 24 July 1915
BLAIR-IMRIE, H. F.   Major, Black Watch; D.A.Q.M.G.,   1891
   N. Command. *C.M.G. O.B.E. M. m.*
BLAKE, A. L.   Capt., Somerset L.I.(T.F.); attd. R.E.   [1914]
   (Signals). *O.B.E. M.*
BLAKE, P. J.   2nd Lieut., R.G.A.   1898
BLAKE, T. R. H.   Capt., R.A.M.C. *M.C. M.*   1899
BLANDFORD, J. J. G.   Lieut.-Col., R.A.M.C. *m* 2.   1886
BLATHWAYT, F. W.   2nd Lieut., R.G.A.   1898
✠BLEW, K.   Pte., N. Zealand Force; 2nd Lieut., Queen's   1912
   Own (R. W. Kent Regt.)
   Killed in action 12 April 1918
✠BLIGH, E. H. S.   Lieut. R.N.V.R. (Blake Bn., R.N.D.)   1902
   Killed in action in Gallipoli 10 Sept. 1915
BLISS, A. E. D.   Capt., R. Fusiliers; Lieut., Grenadier   1910
   Gds. (W 2.) *M.*

BODLEY, D. H. Lieut., N. Staffs. Regt.(T.F.) and Sher- 1911
wood Foresters (Notts. and Derby Regt., T.F.)

✠BOLTON, M. B. Capt., Manchester Regt. and E. Lancs. 1912
Regt.(T.F.) *M.C.*
*Died in German hands 26 March 1918 of wounds
received in action 21 March 1918*

BOMPAS, H. S. Capt. (K.B.), R.A.F. 1900

✠BOSWELL, D. ST G. K. Capt., D. of Cornwall's L.I.; 1912
Major, M.G.C. (W.) *M* 2.
Died 28 Sept. 1918

BOUSFIELD, L. Capt., R.A.M.C. (T.F. Res.) *Medjidieh*, 1894
4th Class (Egypt)

✠BOVILL, E. H. 2nd Lieut., London Regt. (Queen's West- 1906
minster Rifles)
Killed in action 1 *July* 1916

✠BOVILL, J. E. 2nd Lieut., 6th Dragoon Gds. (Carabiniers) 1913
Killed in action 23 Jan. 1916

✠BOWDEN, E. R. Lieut., Northumberland Fus.(T.F.) 1907
Died 29 April 1915 *of wounds received in action*

BRADFORD, E. C. Capt., R.A.M.C. (1st S. Gen. Hospital, 1907
T.F.) *m.*

✠BRADLEY, E. J. Rfn., London Regt. (L.R.B.) 1911
Killed in action 5 Dec. 1914

BRADLEY, H. E. 2nd Lieut., E. Lancs. Regt. 1912

BRADSHAW, T. B. Capt., R. Defence Corps 1884

BRAMALL, E. H. Major, R.F.A.; empld. War Office 1908

BRAYNE, F. L. Lieut.-Col., Spec. List (Embarkation Staff). 1909
*M.C. Order of the Nile, 4th Class (Egypt). Order of
St Sava, 5th Class (Serbia)*

BRISCOE, F. E. T. Major, R.A.S.C. 1893

BROAD, C. N. F. Major, R.F.A.; Lieut.-Col., G.S.O. 1. 1903
D.S.O. Brevet Lieut.-Colonel. M 3. *Chevalier,
Legion of Honour (France). Belgian Croix de Guerre*

BROCK, A. G. Lieut., The Buffs (E. Kent Regt.) *M.C.* 1903
M.

✠BRÖLEMANN, P. W. A. Sous-Lieut., 12me Cuirassiers à 1913
Pied, French Army. (W.) *French Croix de Guerre.
M* 2.
Killed in action near Moreuil 5 April 1918

BROOKE, F. N. Lieut., King's Own (Yorkshire L.I.) 1912

BROOKE TAYLOR, G. P. Capt. and Adjt., R.F.A. *M.C.* [1914]

BROOKER, R. H. G. Capt. and Adjt., R.A.S.C.(M.T.) 1910
M 2.

BROWN, E. M. Capt., R.A.M.C. 1897

✠Brown, J. C. D. 2nd Lieut., Durham L.I.(T.F.) 1912
Died 29 *April* 1915 *of wounds received in action near Ypres* 25 *April* 1915
✠Brown, O. H. Rfn., Rifle Brigade; Capt., Suffolk Regt. 1910
(W.) *D.S.O. M.C. M.*
Killed in action 1 *Nov.* 1916
Brown, T. H. Lieut., R.A.M.C. 1890
Browne, G. H. S. Bt. Colonel, Gen. Staff; Deputy 1884
Director-Gen., Ministry of Munitions. *C.B. m.*
Browne, R. C. S. *See* Seymour-Browne, R. C.
✠Buchanan, F. C. 2nd Lieut., R. Scots. (W.) 1912
Killed in action 9 *April* 1917
Buckton, W. W. Capt., R.E. 1894
Bullock, Rev. G. G. A. C.F. 4th Class, R.A.C.D. 1896
Bulstrode, Rev. R. C.F. 2nd Class, R.A.C.D. (W.) 1897
M 2.
Bulwer, E. A. E. Lieut.-Col., S. Staffs. Regt. 1883
[1]Burbury, F. W. Lieut.-Col., Queen's Own (R.W. Kent 1884
Regt.) and Rifle Brigade
✠Burdett, H. G. Capt., London Yeo. (Westminster 1895
Dragoons); A.P.M.
Died 3 *March* 1916
Burges-Short, H. G. R. Major, Somerset L.I.; Lieut.- 1893
Col., D. of Cornwall's L.I. (W.) (P.) *D S.O. M.*
Burn, D. C. Lieut., Oxford and Bucks. L.I.; Lieut. (A.), 1914
R.A.F. (W.)
✠Burton, A. H. W. Capt., Lincolnshire Regt. (W.) 1911
Killed in action 23 *Oct.* 1916
Burton, G. J. L. Capt., King's Royal Rifle Corps. [1914]
(W 2.) *M.C. and Bar*
Buss, L. C. Madras Artillery, Indian Defence Force 1908
Butler, E P. Capt., Gloucestershire Yeo. 1905
Butson, H. S. G. *See* Gould Butson, H. S.
Buxton, W. L. Lieut., York and Lancaster Regt.; Capt., 1913
Gen. List. (W.) *M.*
Byers, J. 2nd Lieut., R. Fusiliers 1899

Caley, F. G. Capt., R.A.M.C. (Sanitary Service, T.F.) 1902
M. m.
✠Caley, H. W. Capt., R.A.S.C. *M.* 1904
Died 16 *Sept.* 1918
Calvert, L. M. Capt., London Regt. 1912

---

[1] Died on service in India since the armistice.

CAMPBELL, K. J. Major, Black Watch. (W.)   1897
✠CAMPBELL, R. W. F. Capt., R. Fusiliers   1906
    Died 11 *Aug.* 1916 *of wounds received in action* 15 *July* 1916
CAPRON, N. H. Lieut., London Regt. (Post Office Rifles) 1903
CARDEN, Rev. S. R. C.F. 4th Class, R.A.C.D.   1892
✠CAREY, A. J. E. 2nd Lieut., Gordon Hdrs. (W.)   [1914]
    Killed in action 22 *Aug.* 1917
CARLILE, H. G. Lieut., R.A.O.C.   1900
CARLILE, R. C. Lieut., R.A.S.C. and Spec. List, empld. 1903
    Directorate of Requisitions and Hirings
CARLISLE, F. M. M. Capt., Highland L.I.; Brigade 1908
    Major. (W 2.) *M.C.* *M.*
CARLYON, E. T. R. Capt., Sherwood Foresters (Notts. 1912
    and Derby Regt.) (W.) (P.)
CARPMAEL, A. Lieut., R.G.A.   1895
CARR, F. R. 2nd Lieut., R.G.A.   [1914]
CARR, P. R. Pte., H.A.C.; Capt., R.F.A.(T.F.) (W.)   1911
CARR, R. N. Major, Border Regt. and S. Staffs. Regt. 1913
    (W 2.) *M.C.* *M* 2.
CARRICK, A. D. Capt., Northumberland Fus. (W.)   1913
CARSLAKE, W. B. Capt. and Adjt., The Queen's (R.W. 1912
    Surrey Regt.); empld. Ministry of Pensions. (W 4.)
    M.C.
CARTER, Rev. J. F. Capt., Rifle Brigade and Gen. List 1896
    (O.C.B.) *m* 2.
CARTER, P. Capt., Worcestershire Regt.(T.F.) (W 2.)   1913
    M.C. Italian Croce di Guerra
CARTER, W. R. Hon. Capt., R.A.M.C.   1881
CARTWRIGHT, Rev. G. F. C.F. 4th Class, R.A.C.D.   1895
CARVER, E. T. Major, R.A.S.C. *M.*   1903
✠CASE, G. R. A. 2nd Lieut., S. Lancs. Regt.   1914
    Killed in action 25 *Sept.* 1915
CASEY, S. N. Lieut., R.F.A.   [1914]
✠CASSWELL, E. D. S. Lieut., Rifle Brigade; attd. Army 1913
    Cyclist Corps; attd. R.F.C. (W 2.)
    Killed in action 7 *Nov.* 1917
CAUSTON, Rev. L. J. C.F. 4th Class, R.A.C.D.   1892
CAVENDISH-BUTLER, H. H. Capt., R. Inniskilling Fus.; 1903
    empld. Ministry of Munitions
CAWSTON, E. P. Lieut.-Col., London Regt.(Q.V.R.) (W.) 1901
    M 2.
CAYLEY, N. Lieut., R.G.A.; A.D.C.   1893
CAZALET, M. H. Capt., R.A. (R. of O.); R.T.O.   1890

CHADWICK, C. R. Lieut., Queen's Own (R. W. Kent 1906
Regt.) and Gen. Staff
CHADWICK, J. Instructor Lieut., R.N. 1897
CHAMPION, C. C. Lieut.-Col., S. Lancs. Regt. (W 2.) 1906
D.S.O. M 3.
CHARLES, R. D. S. Capt., London Regt. (L.R.B.); empld. 1908
War Office. (W 2.)
CHASE, Rev. F. A. C.F. 4th Class, R.A.C.D. 1898
CHESTER-MASTER, A. G. 2nd Lieut., R.A.S.C. *M.B.E.* 1909
M.
CHICHESTER, S. R. 2nd Lieut., R. Marines 1902
CHILD, S. Capt., R.A.M.C.(T.F.) 1894
✠CHILDE, C. M. Capt., Gloucestershire Regt. 1913
Died 22 March 1916 *of wounds received in action*
✠CHRISTMAS, D. V. Lieut., Suffolk Regt.; Staff Capt. 1905
Accidentally killed while on duty 25 *Oct.* 1915
CHRISTOPHER, C. M. DE A. Lieut., R.F.A. 1907
✠CHURCHMAN, C. H. Capt., Suffolk Regt. (Cyclist Bn., 1913
T.F.); attd. W. Yorks. Regt.
Killed in action 3 *May* 1917
CLARK, C. S. Capt., Suffolk Regt.; R.T.O. 1911
✠CLARKE, A. P. 2nd Lieut., London Regt. 1913
Died 24 *July* 1915 *of wounds received in action* 22 *July*
1915
CLARKE, E. RUSSELL. Capt., Spec. List (Expert Adviser 1890
to Naval Staff on Wireless Telegraphy). *C.B.E.*
CLARKE, G. T. K. Capt., R.A.S.C. 1898
CLARKE-WILLIAMS, F. Lieut., R.F.A. 1913
CLAYTON, Rev. G. H. C.F. 4th Class, R.A.C.D. *M.* 1903
CLAYTON, L. J. Lieut., Gloucestershire Regt.(T.F.); 1898
empld. Recruiting Staff. (W.)
CLAYTON, T. W. Lieut., R.F.A.(T.F.) 1896
CLEMENTS, Rev. W. D. Chaplain, R.N. 1899
COATES, R. A. Lieut., R.F.A.(T.F.) (W.) 1914
COBBOLD, F. A. W. Major, R.G.A. (W.) *D.S.O. M.* 1901
COBBOLD, G. W. N. 2nd Lieut., R.E. 1911
COCHRANE, R. D. Lieut., London Regt. (Post Office 1911
Rifles). (W.)
COKE, R. A. S. Capt., Lancs. Fus. (W 2.) *M.C.* 1909
COLAM, H. N. Lieut., R.N.V.R. 1900
COLE, C. L. 2nd Lieut., R.A.S.C. 1904
COLE, Rev. G. L. C.F. 4th Class, R.A.C.D. 1906
✠COLEMAN, E. C. Lieut., R.F.A.(T.F.) 1910
Killed in action 2 *April* 1917

COLLETT, G. F. Lieut.-Col., Gloucestershire Regt.(T.F.) 1898
  D.S.O. M 3.
COLLETT, H. A. A. Lieut., Irish Gds. *M.C.* 1916
COLLIER, Rev. F. H. S. C.F. 4th Class, R.A.C.D. 1901
COLLINS, E. D. Capt., King's (Shropshire L.I.); empld. 1912
  Ministry of National Service. (W.)
✠COLLINS, V. ST B. Lieut. (O.), R.A.F. 1912
  Missing, presumed killed in action, 18 *Sept.* 1918
COLMAN, D. M. Capt. and Adjt., R.G.A. 1904
COLMAN, L. M. Major, R.F.A.(T.F.) 1904
COLVILLE, D. Capt., Fife and Forfar Yeo. *M.* 1909
COMBER, H. G. Major, Unattd. List, T.F.; G.S.O. 3 1890
  (Intelligence). *D.S.O. M* 3. *Chevalier, Legion of
  Honour (France). Chevalier, Order of Leopold
  (Belgium). Order of St Stanislas, 2nd Class, with
  crossed swords (Russia). Officer, Order of the Crown of
  Roumania, with swords*
COMYN, A. F. Capt., R.A.M.C.(T.F.) 1899
CONNOLLY, J. S. D'A. 2nd Lieut., Cheshire Regt. (W.) 1913
COOK, J. W. 2nd Lieut., R.G.A. 1917
COOKE, F. F. Capt., Essex Regt. (W 2.) 1909
COOKE, H. D'A. M. Capt., The Queen's (R. W. Surrey 1895
  Regt., T.F. Res.) and Gen. List (R. of O.)
COOMBS, P. G. Capt., Northamptonshire Regt.(T.F.); 1910
  attd. M.G.C.; Lieut., R.G.A.
COPELAND, A. J. Surgeon Lieut., R.N. 1913
✠CORDEUX, E. H. N. Lieut., Sherwood Foresters (Notts. [1914]
  and Derby Regt., T.F.)
  Killed in action 1 *Oct.* 1915
CORNAH, J. R. Lieut., Baluchistan Coy., Indian Defence 1888
  Force
COSSAR, J. M. Capt., Middlesex Regt.(T.F.); empld. 1907
  Ministry of Munitions. *Brevet Major. m.*
COULSON, N. Lieut., 8th (King's R. Irish) Hussars 1910
COURTIS, A. O. Surgeon Lieut., R.N. 1909
COURTNEY, G. B. Capt., R.A.M.C. *m.* 1880
COUSINS, B. D. Cadet Sergt.-Instructor, R.E. (Signals) 1915
✠COWAN, C. J. A. Capt., R. Scots 1912
  Died 5 March 1918 *of wounds received in action*
✠COWAN, R. C. 2nd Lieut., R. Scots 1913
  Killed in action 24 *Oct.* 1914
COWLEY, R. B. Capt., York and Lancaster Regt. (W.) 1907
CRESSWELL, C. E. Lieut., Herefordshire Regt. *m.* 1907
CRICK, Rev. P. C. T. C.F. 2nd Class, R.A.C.D.; D.A.C.G. 1901

CROCKFORD, L. C. Capt., R. Warwickshire Regt.; Major, 1906
D.A.Q.M.G. *M.C. Brevet Major. M* 2. *Italian
Croce di Guerra*

CROFTON, J. H. Capt., R.A.M.C. 1902

CROGHAN, E. H. Lieut., R.F.A. *M.C. M* 2. 1911

CROSBIE, R. E. H. Capt. and Adjt., R.A.S.C. 1905

✠CROSBY, J. C. P. 2nd Lieut., King's (Liverpool Regt.) 1900
Died 21 *Jan.* 1918 *of wounds received in action*

CROSSE, S. S. Capt., R.A.M.C. *M.C.* 1906

CROW, P. Major, R.F.A.(T.F.) (W 4.) *D.S.O. M.C.* 1909
M.

CRUM-EWING, N. R. Lieut., R. Fusiliers and M.G.C.; 1893
attd. Section Sanitaire, French Army. *French Croix
de Guerre*

CRUMP, H. C. Lieut., Gloucestershire Regt.(T.F.) (W.) 1913

CUMBERLAND, R. B. L. Capt., R.E. 1903

CUMMING, J. H. Capt., R.A.M.C.(T.F.) 1903

✠CURNOCK, G. A. Lieut., Rifle Brigade 1912
Killed in action at Langemarck 14 *Aug.* 1917

CUTHBERTSON, M. Major, R. Fusiliers and Gen. List 1900
(Staff Capt.) *M.C. M* 2.

CUTLACK, W. P. Lieut.-Col., Cambridgeshire Regt. 1900

DALE, G. F. 2nd Lieut., 2nd Dragoon Gds. (Queen's 1917
Bays)

DALGLEISH, J. P. Lieut., R.G.A. *M.* 1912

DALLEY, R. P. Lieut., I.A.R.O., attd. Sappers and Miners 1908

DALTON, R. F. Corpl., R.E. [1914]

DAMMERS, B. F. H. A.B., R.N.V.R. 1895

DAMMERS, E. F. H. Capt., Dorset Regt.(T.F.) 1910

DANIEL, T. W. Lieut.-Col., Sherwood Foresters (Notts. 1914
and Derby Regt.) (W.) *D.S.O. and Bar. M.C. M* 2.

DARBYSHIRE, N. A. Lieut., R.E.(T.F.) 1915

✠DASHWOOD, C. B. L. Major, Northumberland Fus. 1891
Died 26 *April* 1916 *of wounds received in action* 24 *April*
1916

DAVID, L. W. Capt., Glamorgan Yeo.; Capt. (Ad.), R.A.F. 1896

DAVIDSON, J. Major, I.A.R.O.; Director of Blockade, 1897
Mesopotamia. *O.B.E.*

DAVIES, H. B. Capt., Manchester Regt. (W.) 1910

DAVIES, R. G. M. Capt., Norfolk Regt. and Labour 1906
Corps. (W.) *M.C.*

DAVIES, T. H. Lieut. (A.), R.A.F. 1901

DAW, W. F. B. 2nd Lieut., R.G.A. 1908

DAWES, E. 2nd Lieut., Norfolk Yeo. 1915
DAWES, M. S. Cadet Sergt.-Instructor, R.E. (Signals) 1908
DAWSON, Rev. E. C. Chaplain, R.N. 1908
DAWSON, F. G. T. Flt. Lieut., R.N.A.S. 1911
DAWSON, J. H. T. Lieut., Worcestershire Yeo. (P.) 1905
DAY, G. W. L. Lieut., R.E.; Hon. Lieut. (O.), R.A.F. [1914]
DAY, M. F. Lieut.-Col., King's Own (Yorkshire L.I.) and 1897
Gen. Staff. *M.C. Brevet Lieut.-Colonel. M* 4. *m.*
✠DEAN, J. H. E. Capt., Cheshire Regt. (W.) *M.C. and* 1913
Bar
Killed in action 27 May 1918
DEAS, P. B. Major, R.A.S.C.(T.F.) *O.B.E. M* 2. 1893
DE CHAZAL, Vicomte P. E. Lieut., R.A.S.C. and King's 1914
African Rifles
DE JERSEY, Rev. N. S. Hon. Chaplain, R.N.V.R. 1886
✠DE LA MOTHE, C. D. F. Lieut., R.N.V.R. (R.N.D.) *M.* 1907
Killed in action at Beaumont Hamel 13 *Nov.* 1916
DE PASS, E. A. Capt., London Yeo. (Sharpshooters); 1911
Capt. (A.), R.A.F. (W.)
DE SLUBICKI, J. M. M.G. Bty., Canadian Force; 2nd 1911
Lieut., R.G.A.
DEWEY, H. G. Major, R.F.A. (W 3.) *M.C. M.* 1913
✠DICKINSON, A. P. Capt., King's (Liverpool Regt., 1910
Liverpool Scottish, T.F.) *M.C.*
Died 1 *June* 1918 *of wounds received in action*
DICKINSON, G. F. Major, King's (Liverpool Regt., 1904
Liverpool Scottish, T.F.); attd. Rifle Brigade. (W.)
DICKSON, F. P. Capt., R.A.S.C. 1907
DIRCKS, L. R. A. Capt., London Regt. (London Irish [1914]
Rifles); Hon. Capt. (K.B.), R.A.F. (W 2.)
DIXON, H. H. Lieut., Dulwich College O.T.C. 1906
DOBB, G. C. Capt., R.F.A. (W.) 1911
DOBB, H. R. Major, R.A.S.C. *O.B.E. M.* 1909
✠DOBB, R. A. 2nd Lieut., R.H.A.; A.D.C.; Capt. and 1912
Adjt., R.F.A. (W.)
Died at Baghdad 22 *Dec.* 1917 *of dysentery*
DODSON, A. D. H. Capt., Queen's Own (R. W. Kent 1913
Regt.) (W.)
DORESA, B. S. Capt., R.F.A.(T.F.) (W 2.) 1915
✠DOUGALL, E. S. Capt., R.F.A. (W.) *M.C.* 1905
𝖁.𝕮. "For most conspicuous bravery and skilful leader-
ship in the field when in command of his battery. Captain
Dougall maintained his guns in action from early morning
throughout a heavy concentration of gas and high-ex-

plosive shell. Finding that he could not clear the crest owing to the withdrawal of our line, Captain Dougall ran his guns on to the top of the ridge to fire over open sights. By this time our infantry had been pressed back in line with the guns. Captain Dougall at once assumed command of the situation, rallied and organised the infantry, supplied them with Lewis guns, and armed as many gunners as he could spare with rifles. With these he formed a line in front of his battery, which during this period was harassing the advancing enemy with a rapid rate of fire. Although exposed to both rifle and machine gun fire, this officer fearlessly walked about as though on parade, calmly giving orders and encouraging everybody. He inspired the infantry with his assurance that "So long as you stick to your trenches I will keep my guns here." This line was maintained throughout the day, thereby delaying the enemy's advance for over twelve hours. In the evening, having expended all its ammunition, the battery received orders to withdraw. This was done by man-handling the guns over a distance of about 800 yards of shell-cratered country, an almost impossible feat considering the ground and the intense machine gun fire. Owing to Captain Dougall's personality and skilful leadership throughout this trying day there is no doubt that a serious breach in our line was averted. This gallant officer was killed four days later whilst directing the fire of his battery."—Supplement to *The London Gazette*, 4 June 1918.

Killed in action 14 *April* 1918

DOUGLAS, C. H. Capt., R.E.(T.F.); Major, R.A.F. (Technical Res.) — 190

✠DOUGLAS, H. K. Lieut.-Cdr., R.N.V.R. (Anson Bn., R.N.D.) (W.) *m.* — 190

Died 21 *May* 1919 *of illness contracted on active service*

DOUGLAS, Rev. R. H. C.F. 4th Class, R.A.C.D. — 190

✠DOUGLASS-JAMES, W. Lieut., R.G.A. — 191

Died 25 *Sept.* 1915 *of wounds received in action*

DOWNING, C. C. R. Surgeon Lieut., R.N. — 191

DRAKE, A. W. C. Capt., R.A.M.C. — 190

DRAKE, F. 2nd Lieut., Devon Regt. — 189

DREW, R. S. Capt., R.A.M.C. — 189

✠DRUMMOND, N. F. Capt., King's Royal Rifle Corps. *M.* — 191

Accidentally killed 20 *Dec.* 1916

DU BERN, G. E. Lieut., R.G.A. — 191

DUKE, Rev. E. H. C.F. 4th Class, R.A.C.D. (W.) — 188

DUKES, C. Sergt.-Major, Army Pay Corps — 189

DUNBAR, Sir A. E., Bart. Major, W. Yorks. Regt. *M.C.* 1907
M.
DUNCAN, G. B. Major, 158th Bn., attd. 7th Bn., Cana- 1899
dian Infy. (W.)
DUNCAN, J. G. Capt., I.A.R.O., attd. 50th Kumaon Rifles 1901
DUNKLEY, G. W. Capt., R. Marines; empld. Ordnance 1911
Committee. *O.B.E.*
✠DUNSMURE, C. H. T. 2nd Lieut., Cameron Hdrs. 1913
Killed in action in the Battle of Loos 25 Sept. 1915
DUNSTAN, V. J. 2nd Lieut., R.G.A. 1917
DURRANT, H. B. *See* LAHORE, Bishop of
DURST, C. S. Capt., R.E. (Fortress, T.F.) 1907

EADE, C. Lieut., Res. Regt. of Cavalry and M.G.C. (Cav- 1909
alry). *M.C.*
✠EDDISON, J. R. 2nd Lieut., Sherwood Foresters (Notts. 1908
and Derby Regt., T.F.)
Killed in action 22 April 1915
EDEN, J. R. Lieut., S. Wales Borderers; Capt. R. Welsh 1911
Fus.
EDWARDS, J. S. Lieut., Fettes College O.T.C. 1899
ELDER, A. L. Pte., London Regt. (W.) 1909
ELIOT, E. F. Lieut.-Col., R.A.M.C. *Cavalier, Order of* 1880
the Crown of Italy
ELISCHER, M. H. 2nd Lieut., Unattd. List, T.F. 1904
ELLIOTT, C. P. Capt., Sherwood Foresters (Notts. and 1914
Derby Regt.) (W 2.) *M.C. M.*
ELLIS, T. P. Capt., R.A.S.C. 1910
ELPHINSTON, A. Lieut.-Col., Argyll and Sutherland Hdrs. 1898
ELRINGTON-BISSET, Rev. M. C.F. 4th Class, R.A.C.D. 1878
✠ELRINGTON-BISSET, W. F. 2nd Lieut., Gordon Hdrs. 1907
Killed in action 25 Sept. 1915
ELVERSON, J. H. Major, R.F.A.; empld. Ministry of 1900
Munitions
✠ERSKINE, F. A. 2nd Lieut., R.M.L.I. *M.* [1914]
Killed in action in Gallipoli 10 May 1915
✠EVANS, C. H. 2nd Lieut., Border Regt. 1910
Died in German hands 26 Oct. 1914 of wounds received
in action
EVANS, F. R. Instructor Lieut., R.N. 1910
EVANS, P. D. Lieut., Northumberland Fus.; Capt., Labour 1900
Corps
EVANS, R. DU B. Capt., King's (Shropshire L.I.) (W.) 1910
(P.)

EVE, A. S. Colonel, Quebec Regt., Canadian Force. 1881
C.B.E.

EVERY-HALSTED, C. E. Major, King's Own (R. Lancaster 1877
Regt.) and Spec. List (Recruiting Staff)

✠EYRE, C. H. Capt., King's Royal Rifle Corps 1902
Killed in action 25 Sept. 1915

✠FAGAN, N. 2nd Lieut., Rifle Brigade 1914
*Died 20 July 1916 of wounds received in action 1 July
1916*

FAIR, C. H. Lieut.-Col., London Regt. (St Pancras Bn.); 1904
empld. O.C.B. *D.S.O. M.*

FALCON, J. H. Capt., R.F.A.(T.F.) *M.* 1911

FALCON, M. Major, R.F.A.(T.F.) *M.* 1907

FALLE, Sir B. G., Bart., M.P. Major, R.F.A. and Spec. 1879
List; Staff Lieut.

FARGUS, Rev. A. H. C. Chaplain, R.N. 1898

FARRAR, Rev. E. M. C.F. 4th Class, R.A.C.D. 1885

FARRAR, F. P. Foreign Legion, French Army 1894

FAVELL, N. B. Capt., Rifle Brigade; attd. R.E. *M.* 1905

FAWELL, C. L. Lieut., R.N.V.R. (Coastal Motor-boat 1901
Service). *D.S.C.*

FAWELL, S. H. 2nd Lieut., R.G.A. 1904

FEILING, A. Capt., R.A.M.C. *M.* 1903

FERNIE, Rev. E. H. C.F. 4th Class, Australian Chaplains' 1901
Dept. *M* 2.

FFRENCH, W. K. P. Lieut.-Col., S. Wales Borderers. 1898
M.C. Brevet Major. M 3.

✠FIELDING-JOHNSON, H. G. Corpl., R.E. (Signals) 1913
Missing, presumed killed in action, 23 *Aug.* 1914

✠FIENNES, J. E. Capt., Gordon Hdrs. (W.) [1914]
*Died 18 June 1917 of wounds received in action 17 June
1917*

FIGGIS, B. E. Capt., R.A.S.C. 1888

FIGGIS, J. M. Capt., Labour Corps. *M.* 1896

FINDLAY, C. W. McD. Major and Adjt., Gordon Hdrs. 1891
(R. of O.) *m.*

FISK, A. A. Capt., Cheshire Regt. *M.* 1902

FLEMING, A. L. Lieut., D. of Cornwall's L.I.; Capt. (A.), 1910
R.A.F. (W 2.) *M.C.*

FLETCHER, W. G. Major, R.F.A. (W.) 1908

FLINN, O. S. Lce.-Corpl., R. Fusiliers (P. S. Bn.); Capt., 1902
The Queen's (R. W. Surrey Regt.) and Gen. Staff
(Intelligence). (W.)

✠FOORD, G. H. 2nd Lieut., R.A.S.C.   1903
  *Died 13 Oct. 1915 of wounds received in action in
  Gallipoli 12 Oct. 1915*
FORMAN, H. Lieut., S. Wales Borderers. (W.) (P.)   1907
FORMAN, Rev. T. P. G. C.F. 4th Class, R.A.C.D.   1904
✠FOSDICK, J. H. Lieut., Rifle Brigade   1913
  *Died 31 July 1915 of wounds received in action at Hooge
  30 July 1915*
FOULGER, H. C. Capt., R. Fusiliers; attd. King's African   1910
  Rifles
✠FOWLIE, J. L. Lieut., Highland L.I.   [1914]
  Killed in action 23 April 1917
✠FOX, A. S. 2nd Lieut., N. Staffs. Regt.(T.F.)   1912
  Killed in action 13 Oct. 1915
FOX, D. S. Capt., Sherwood Foresters (Notts. and   [1914]
  Derby Regt.); Hon. Lieut. (O.), R.A.F. (W 2.) (P.)
FOX-STRANGWAYS, W. A. Suez Local Rifles   1906
FRANCIS, J. C. W. Major, 19th Hussars. (W 2.) M 3.   1907
  Belgian Croix de Guerre
FRANCIS, K. Capt., King's Royal Rifle Corps   1903
FRANCIS, R. Cadet Sergt.-Instructor, R.E. (Signals)   1902
FRANKLIN, C. R. Instructor, Australian Navy   1907
FRANKLIN, F. B. Lieut., R.G.A.; empld. Admiralty   1892
FRANKLIN, R. P. 2nd Lieut., Australian F.A.   1904
FRASER, A. A. Capt. and Adjt., R.A.S.C. M.C.   1913
✠FRASER, A. L. 2nd Lieut., R.G.A.   1907
  Died 1 July 1917 of wounds received in action
FRASER, D. P. Capt., Canterbury Regt., N. Zealand   1896
  Force. M.
✠FRASER, R. Capt., Rifle Brigade   1908
  Killed in action 1 July 1916
FRECHEVILLE, G. Capt. (T.), R.A.F.   1908
FREEMAN, C. R. Major, Northumberland Fus. (W 2.)   1912
  D.S.O. M.C. M 3.
FREEMAN, H. Capt., W. Yorks. Regt. (W.)   1912
FREEMAN, W. H. Major, W. Yorks. Regt. M.C. and Bar   1910
FRERE, J. E. Capt., R.A.M.C. M.   1895
FRITH, Rev. J. B. C.F. 4th Class, R.A.C.D.   1902
FROST, Rev. N. P. C.F. 4th Class, R.A.C.D.   1898
FULLALOVE, A. L. Sub-Lieut., R.N.V.R.   1909

✠GABAIN, W. G. Corpl., R.E. (Signals); Capt., Spec. List   1909
  (Intelligence); attd. Rifle Brigade. M.C. M 2.
  Killed in action 24 March 1918

GAMMELL, J. A. H.   Major, R.F.A.; G.S.O. 2, War   1911
Office; Lieut.-Col., S.O. 1, R.A.F. (W 2.) *D.S.O.*
M.C. M 7. *Cavalier, Order of the Crown of Italy.*
Order of Karageorge, 4th Class, with swords (Serbia)
GAMMELL, S. J. Capt., R.G.A.   1886
GARDINER-HILL, C. Surgeon Lieut., R.N.   1910
GARDINER-HILL, H. Capt., R.A.M.C.; attd. R.A.F.   1909
O.B.E. M.
GARDNER, J. H. Capt., Loyal N. Lancs. Regt.; Major, 1907
M.G.C. (W.)
GARDNER-BROWN, Rev. F. S. G. C.F. 4th Class, R.A.C.D. 1900
(W.)
✠GARDNER-BROWN, J. G. G. Indian Defence Force   1895
Died 18 May 1917 of small-pox
GARNETT, C. 2nd Lieut., Labour Corps   1888
GARNETT, D. G. Surgeon Prob., R.N.V.R.   1915
GARNETT, J. N. Lieut., R.F.A.(T.F.); Lieut.(A.), R.A.F. 1909
(P.)
✠GARNETT, W. P.   Lieut., R. Berkshire Regt.; attd. 1913
R.F.C.
Killed in action 30 March 1917
GARRARD, N. Capt., R.A.M.C.   1906
GARRETT, G. D.   Lieut., R.N.V.R.   (W.)   *Chevalier,* 1909
Military Order of Avis (Portugal)
✠GARRETT, H. F. Capt., E. Yorks. Regt.   1904
Killed in action at Suvla Bay 22 Aug. 1915
✠GARRETT-SMITH, L. 2nd Lieut., R.E.   1905
Died 31 July 1915 of wounds received in action in the
Ypres Salient 30 July 1915
GASKELL, C. H. Capt., Wiltshire Regt. (W.) *M.C.* 1905
Chevalier, Ordre du Mérite Agricole (France)
GATES, C. Lieut., R.F.A.   1913
GEARE, J. W. A. Capt., London Yeo. (Middlesex Hussars); 1908
A.D.C. *M.*
GEAVES, W. L. Cadet, O.C.B.   1914
GEDGE, Rev. A. A. L. C.F. 1st Class, R.A.C.D.   1876
GEMMELL, K. T. Capt., Spec. List (Intelligence). *M.C.* 1902
M 2. *Chevalier, Legion of Honour (France)*
GETHING, J. E. Lieut., R.A.M.C.   1903
GIBBINS, N. M. Lieut., R. Dublin Fus. and Gen. Staff. 1900
(W.)
✠GIBBS, B. 2nd Lieut., Rifle Brigade. *M.C. M.*   1912
Killed in action 6 July 1915
GIBERNE, H. B. Capt., R.A.S.C.   1903

✠GIBSON, J. G. 2nd Lieut., Cameron Hdrs. (W.)   1911
  Died in Germany 12 Sept. 1917 of wounds received in
  action 31 July 1917
GIBSON, R. J. T. Lieut., Devon Regt.(T.F.)   1902
GIBSON, T. G. Major, W. Yorks. Regt. (W.) *M.*   1905
GIDLOW-JACKSON, C. W. Capt., R.E. (W.) *M. Order*   1908
  of St Anne, 3rd Class, with swords (Russia)
✠GIELGUD, H. L. F. A. Lieut.-Col., Norfolk Regt. (W.)   1900
  M.C.
  Killed in action 30 Nov. 1917
GILDEA, Sir J., K.C.V.O., C.B. Hon. Colonel, R. Warwick-   1855
  shire Regt. *G.B.E.*
✠GILES, E. Capt. and Adjt., London Regt. (R. Fus.)   1912
  Died 16 July 1916 of wounds received in action
GILLAN, G. V. B. Major, 9th Gurkha Rifles, Indian   1909
  Army. *Brevet Major. M.*
✠GILLIES, C. P. Lieut., Loyal N. Lancs. Regt.; Capt.,   1911
  M.G.C. *M.C.*
  Died 5 May 1916 of wounds received in action 25 April
  1916
GILLIGAN, A. E. R. Capt., Lancs. Fus. and Gen. List   1914
  (P. and B.T. Staff)
GISBORNE, L. G. Lieut.-Col., R.F.A.(T.F.) *C.M.G.*   1885
  M 2.
GODLEE, S. Capt., R.G.A. (W 2.)   1902
GODSON, F. P. Lieut., E. Yorks. Regt.; Capt., Spec.   1906
  List (cmdg. Tunnelling Coy., R.E.) *M.C.*
GOLDING, H. C. Capt., D. of Wellington's (W. Riding   1911
  Regt., T.F.); attd. T.M.B.; Capt., Spec. List
  (cmdg. Sound-ranging Section, R.E.) (W.) *M.C.*
  M 3.
GOLDSCHMIDT, W. N. Lieut., R.A.M.C.   1912
GOLDSMITH, E. O. Capt., R.A.M.C.   1910
GOOCH, C. T. 2nd Lieut., R.E.   1907
GOOCH, K. T. Staff Capt.; Major, R.F.A. *M.C.*   1912
GOODALL, H. M. Lieut., Worcestershire Regt.   1915
GOODMAN, B. M. 2nd Lieut., S. African Force   1911
✠GORDON, A. J. M. Capt., London Regt. (Queen's West-   1914
  minster Rifles)
  Killed in action 27 Nov. 1917
GORDON, A. S. Capt., R.A.S.C.(M.T.) *M* 2.   1907
GORDON, R. E. C. Lieut., Gordon Hdrs.; attd. Cameron   1908
  Hdrs. (W.)
GORDON, S. Capt., I.M.S. *M.C. M.*   1903

✠GORELL-BARNES, C. R. Capt. and Adjt., Rifle Brigade; [1914]
G.S.O. 3. *D.S.O. M.C. M* 2.
Died 21 *April* 1918 *of wounds received in action* 5 *April*
1918
GOULD, H. F. Lieut., R.F.A. 1906
GOULD, K. L. Capt., R.A.S.C. 1896
GOULD BUTSON, H. S. Capt., R.A.S.C. 1902
GOVER, Rev. C. E. J. C.F. 4th Class, R.A.C.D. 1909
GOW, L. H. Capt., R. Glasgow Yeo.; A.D.C.; Staff 1910
Lieut. *M.*
✠GRAHAM, M. H. Lieut., Yorkshire Regt. 1913
Killed in action at Givenchy 15 *June* 1915
GRAHAM, W. J. Capt., Gordon Hdrs.; Staff Capt.; 1909
Deputy Asst. Controller of Salvage. (W.) *M.C. M* 2.
Chevalier, Ordre de la Couronne (Belgium)
GRANT, G. N. Lieut., R.A.S.C. 1915
GRANT, R. M. 2nd Lieut., R.F.A. 1908
✠GRANT, W. ST C. Capt., Cameron Hdrs. (W.) *M.C.* 1913
Belgian Croix de Guerre
Killed in action 26 *Sept.* 1918
GRAY, R. E. G. Capt., R.A.M.C. *Greek Medal for* 1897
Military Merit, 4th Class
GRAY, W. S. Capt., R.F.A.(T.F.) *M.* 1910
GRAYSON, D. H. H. Lieut., Irish Gds. and Gds. M.G. 1912
Regt.
✠GREENHILL,T.W. Lieut., 4th (R. Irish) Dragoon Gds. *M.* 1911
Killed in action 11 *Feb.* 1916
GREER, H. Lieut., R.A.S.C. 1901
GREGSON, P. Lieut., R.G.A. *M.* 1910
GRENSIDE, C. F. Capt., R.A.S.C. 1903
GRIER, S. M. Lieut., Nigerian Land Contingent 1897
GRIERSON, H. Capt., Northamptonshire Regt. (W.) 1910
GRIFFIN, Rev. T. N. R. C.F. 4th Class, R.A.C.D. 1894
✠GROSE-HODGE, D. E. 2nd Lieut., Suffolk Regt. 1911
Killed in action near Ypres 24 *April* 1915
GROSE-HODGE, H. Lieut., I.A.R.O., attd. Cavalry 1910
GUGGENHEIM, H. F. Lieut., United States Naval Res. 1911
✠GUILLEBAUD, E. C. 2nd Lieut., Worcestershire Regt. 1912
Died 1915 *of illness contracted on active service*
GUNN, J. D. Major, R.A.M.C. 1902
GUNNING, C. S. 2nd Lieut., I.A.R.O. 1908

HACKING, E. M. Capt., Sherwood Foresters (Notts. and 1901
Derby Regt.); attd. Rifle Brigade (T.F.) (W.)

✠HADLEY, P. S.   Capt., Northamptonshire Regt.   (W 2.) [1914]
   M.C.
   Died 25 Oct. 1918 of septic pneumonia following influenza
✠HAIG-BROWN, A. R.   Lieut.-Col., Middlesex Regt. (W 2.)   1896
   D.S.O.   M 2.
   Killed in action 25 March 1918
HALE, E. N.   Capt., Black Watch (T.F.); G.S.O. 3. (W.)   1889
   M. French Croix de Guerre
HALES, H. W.   Surgeon Lieut., R.N.   1909
HALL, G. E.   Capt., R. Scots; Major, G.S.O. 2.   *M.C.*   1909
   Brevet Major.   M 4.   Greek Medal for Military
   Merit, 3rd Class
✠HALL, H. S.   Lieut., R.A.M.C.   1899
   Died 14 March 1915 of pneumonia
HALL, J. B.   Capt., R.A.M.C.(T.F.)   1884
HALL, R.   Capt., 11th Bn., Australian Infy.; Staff Capt.   1896
   M.C.   M 2.
HALL-SMITH, P.   Capt., R.A.M.C.   1899
HAMMICK, H. A.   Capt., Manchester Regt.(T.F.); Major,   1900
   Spec. List. (W.)   *M.C.   M 2.*
HAMPSHIRE, C. D.   Capt., R. Berkshire Regt.(T.F.) (W.)   1896
   M.C.
HANHART, A. A.   Capt., R.G.A.   1898
HANKEY, Rev. B.   C.F. 4th Class, R.A.C.D.   1896
HANNINGTON, Rev. J. E. M.   C.F. 4th Class, R.A.C.D.   1896
HARGREAVES, Rev. H. C.   C.F. 4th Class, R.A.C.D.   *M.*   1899
HARGREAVES, Rev. H. P.   C.F. 4th Class, R.A.C.D.   (W.)   1909
   M.C.
HARGREAVES, Rev. W. F.   C.F. 4th Class, R.A.C.D.   1902
HARKE, S. L.   Surgeon Lieut., R.N.   1895
✠HARKER, G. C. W.   Capt., London Regt. (Rangers). (W.)   1910
   M.C.
   Died 1 Dec. 1917 of wounds received in action 27 Nov.
   1917
HARKNESS, H. L.   Capt., S. and T. Corps, Indian Army;   1897
   attd. R.F.C.
HARLING, R. W.   Capt., Oxford and Bucks. L.I. (T.F.);   1890
   G.S.O. 3.
HARPER, K. J.   Lieut., I.A.R.O., attd. 12th Cavalry   1900
HARRIS, C. R.   Lieut., Middlesex Regt.(T.F.)   1911
HARRIS, J. C. N.   Capt., R.A.M.C.   1910
HARRIS, W. B.   Lieut., Gen. List, attd. R.E. (Signals)   1908
HARRIS, W. E.   Lieut., Northumberland Fus.(T.F.)   1909
   (W 2.)

HARRISON, G. R. D. Major, Montgomeryshire Yeo. 1896
HARTCUP, J. A. Capt. and Adjt., E. Yorks. Regt.; Major, 1908
S.O. 2, R.A.F. (W.)
HARVEY, G. H. Lieut.-Col., R.A.S.C. *D.S.O. M* 5. 1896
French Croix de Guerre
HARVEY, N. R. Capt., Rifle Brigade 1914
HASLAM, W. A. 2nd Lieut. (T.), R.A.F. 1899
HASLUCK, R. FF. Capt., I.A.R.O., attd. Sappers and 1910
Miners. *M.*
✠HATCH, L. C. Lieut., Durham L.I. 1912
Killed in action 27 Sept. 1915
HATT-COOK, G. Major, Cheshire Regt.(T.F.) 1901
HAVELL, C. C. W. Lieut., Suffolk Regt.(T.F.); Capt., [1914]
Spec. List (cmdg. T.M.B.) *M.C. M* 2.
✠HAYWARD, C. O. Lieut., Lincolnshire Regt.; attd. R.F.C. 1912
Killed in action near Ledeghem 17 Jan. 1916
HEALING, J. A. Lieut., R. Warwickshire Regt.; Major, 1892
Manchester Regt. (W.) *M.C.*
HEARD, N. Major, R.E. 1903
HEARFIELD, T. Pte., King's Own (R. Lancaster Regt.) 1899
HEATH, A. F. Lieut., Sherwood Foresters (Notts. and 1912
Derby Regt.) (W 2.)
HEATH, R. J. Lieut., R.A.S.C. *M.B.E.* 1911
✠HEATHCOCK, T. Capt., E. Yorks. Regt. 1912
Killed in action 10 July 1916
HEESOM, K. E. 2nd Lieut., R.E. (W.) 1916
✠HEMMANT, M. Capt., Rifle Brigade 1906
Killed in action 14 Aug. 1917
HEMUS, W. L. Capt., R. Warwickshire Regt. and Wor- 1913
cestershire Regt. (W 2.)
HENKEL, W. E. G. Capt., Middlesex Regt. (W.) 1910
HERDMAN-NEWTON, C. Capt., R.A.M.C. 1909
HERDMAN-NEWTON, R. H. Surgeon Lieut., R.N. *M.* 1905
✠HERIZ-SMITH, A. J. C. Lieut., Devon Regt.(T.F.) 1897
Killed in action in Mesopotamia 8 March 1916
HERIZ-SMITH, Rev. E. E. A. C.F. 4th Class, R.A.C.D. 1907
✠HERVEY, D. F. Lieut., Norfolk Regt.(T.F.) 1914
Died 17 May 1917 *of wounds received in action 19 April*
1917
✠HERVEY, G. A. Lieut., R.G.A.(T.F.) 1900
Killed in action 8 Aug. 1917
HESKETH, G. E. Lieut., R.G.A. 1900
HEYCOCK, M. S. Capt., Rifle Brigade and R.E. (Signals). 1903
(W 2.) *M.C.*

HEYLAND, H. M. Major, King's Royal Rifle Corps; 1909
Lieut.-Col., M.G.C. (W 2.) *D.S.O. M* 2.
HEYN, R. G. Major (A.), R.A.F. *O.B.E. m.* 1907
✠HEYWOOD, L. J. 2nd Lieut., R. Fusiliers 1906
Killed in action 20 *July* 1916
HIGGINS, C. A. Lieut., Rifle Brigade; Capt. (T.), R.A.F. 1905
(Aircraft Production Dept.) (W.)
HILES, M. Capt., Wiltshire Regt.(T.F.) and Spec. List. 1902
O.B.E. m 2.
HILL, G. Lieut., R.F.A. (W.) 1909
HILL, G. B. Major, R.A.S.C.(M.T.) *O.B.E. M* 2. 1893
HILL, R. N. 2nd Lieut., R.F.A. (W.) 1916
HILLS, W. H. Capt., R.A.M.C. 1896
✠HIND, C. R. Lieut., S. Staffs. Regt. *M.* 1912
Killed in action 30 *May* 1916
HINDE, Rev. H. W. C.F. 4th Class, R.A.C.D. (W.) 1896
HINMERS, J. R. Major, King's (Shropshire L.I.) (W 3.) [1914]
M.C. French Croix de Guerre
✠HINNELL, T. S. 2nd Lieut., Suffolk Regt.(T.F.) 1912
Killed in action 12 *Aug.* 1915
HIRD, F. L. Lieut., E. Surrey Regt.(T.F.); Lieut. (A.), 1915
R.A.F. *M.C.*
HISCOTT, G. S. Lieut., R.G.A. (W.) 1915
HISCOTT, L. S. Pte., H.A.C.; Lieut., R.G.A.; Lieut.(Ad.), 1912
R.A.F. (W.)
HITCHCOCK, W. H. L. Lieut., S. Wales Borderers (T.F.) 1904
✠HOARE, A. B. Capt., Loyal N. Lancs. Regt.(T.F.) (W.) 1901
Killed in action near Poelcapelle 26 *Oct.* 1917
HOBBS, E. N. B. Lieut., R.A.S.C. 1903
HODGE, J. D. V. Bengal Light Horse, Indian Defence 1906
Force
HODSON, G. S. Lieut., R.E. (Signals, T.F.) 1914
HODSON, R. Capt., R.A.M.C. *M.C.* 1905
HOLBERTON, T. E. Lieut., R.H.A.(T.F.) *M.C. and Bar.* 1901
M.
HOLDER, N. F. Lieut., R. Warwickshire Regt. and Tank 1903
Corps. (W.)
HOLMAN, Rev. J. H. T. Pte., Canadian A.M.C.; Chaplain, 1896
Canadian Force. *M.M.*
HOME, C. F. M. Capt., Welsh Regt. 1910
HOOPER, R. G., D.S.O. Major, E. Riding of Yorkshire Yeo. 1892
HOPLEY, F. J. V. Capt., Grenadier Gds.; empld. R.M.C., 1902
Sandhurst. (W.) *D.S.O. M.*
HORNE, J. W. Lieut., R.F.A. 1899

HORNER, M. S. Pte., R.A.S.C.(M.T.)   1913
HORNIDGE, D. G. P. Capt., R.A.S.C.   1900
HOTBLACK, G. F. 2nd Lieut., R.G.A. *M.*   1901
HOTHAM, J. C. Major, 4th Cavalry, Indian Army; Supt.   1900
  of Remounts
HOUSLEY, C. 2nd Lieut., R. Defence Corps   1890
✠HOWARD, C. R. Capt., R.A.M.C. *O.B.E.* *M* 2.   1893
  Killed in action in E. Africa 6 Sept. 1918
HOWE, J. C. Lieut., R.G.A.; empld. War Office   1902
✠HOYLE, H. K. 2nd Lieut., Lancs Fus.(T.F.)   [1914]
  Killed in action in Gallipoli 1 May 1915
✠HOYLE, J. B. Lieut., S. Lancs. Regt. *M.C.*   1911
  Killed in action 1 July 1916
HUBBUCK, R.E. Lieut., R.F.A.; empld. Ministry of Muni-   1906
  tions
HUDSON, L. C. A. Lieut., E. Surrey Regt. and Gen. List   1898
HUDSON, Rev. R. C.F. 2nd Class, R.A.C.D.(T.F.)   1882
HUDSON-KINAHAN, G. F. Lieut.-Col., Durham L.I.;   1898
  attd. Egyptian Army. *C.B.E.* *M* 2.
HUGGAN, G. H. Capt., Queen's Own (R.W. Kent Regt.) [1914]
HUGHES, M. B. Paymaster Sub-Lieut., R.N.V.R.   1904
HUGHES, N. W. Lieut., Rifle Brigade and R.F.A. (W.)   1912
HUGHES, T. W. G. J. Capt., N. Irish Horse. *M.*   1908
HULBERT, C. G. K. Capt., R.E.; R.T.O.   1906
HUME, W. E. Colonel, A.M.S. *C.M.G.* *M* 2.   1897
✠HUMPHREYS, D. F. Pte., London Regt. (Artists Rifles);   1909
  2nd Lieut., The Queen's (R. W. Surrey Regt.)
  Died 16 May 1915 of wounds received in action near
  Ypres
HUNTER, J. DE G. Trooper, United Provinces Horse,   1900
  Indian Defence Force; Capt., Mesopotamia Survey
  Party
HUTCHINSON, E. H. P. Capt., R. Guernsey Militia   1890
✠HUTCHISON, D. H. 2nd Lieut., London Regt. (Queen's [1914]
  Westminster Rifles)
  Killed in action 9-10 Aug. 1915

IBBOTSON, A. W. Capt., I.A.R.O., attd. Indian Defence   1905
  Force; Staff Capt. *M.C.* *M.B.E.*
IGGLESDEN, R. S. Capt. and Adjt., The Buffs (E. Kent   1908
  Regt.); Capt., Labour Corps
INGPEN, W. F. Lieut., R.F.A. (R. of O.)   1896
INNES, W. K. Capt., King's Own Scottish Borderers;   1912
  Brigade Major. (W 2.) *D.S.O.* *M.*

IRONSIDE, R. W. Capt., R.A.M.C. 1898

✠ISAAC, D. C. Lieut., N. Staffs. Regt.; Capt., M.G.C. 1912
(W.) *M.*
Killed in action 10 *April* 1917

IZARD, K. H. 2nd Lieut., R. Sussex Regt. and Norfolk 1906
Regt.

JACKSON, C. B. A. Capt., Suffolk Yeo.; A.D.C.; Staff 1900
Capt. *M.C. M.*

JACKSON, I. Capt. and Adjt., E. Yorks. Regt.; Staff 1904
Capt. (W 2.) *M.C.*

JACKSON, W. Capt., Sherwood Foresters (Notts. and 1889
Derby Regt.)

JAMES, J. N. A. Capt., S. Wales Borderers and Gen. List 1910
(R.T.O.)

JAMESON, G. D. Capt., R.A.M.C. 1907

✠JAQUES, A. Capt., W. Yorks. Regt. 1907
Killed in action 27 *Sept.* 1915

JENKINSON, C. H. Capt., R.G.A. 1901

JENNINGS, C. Capt., Leicestershire Regt. and Gen. List. 1900
(P.)

JEPHSON, P. H. R. Capt., E. Surrey Regt.; Major, 1906
M.G.C. and Gen. Staff. (W.) *O.B.E. m.*

JEPSON, A. C. Capt., R.A.M.C. 1904

JOHNSON, G. S. Capt., 61st Pioneers, Indian Army. 1910
M.C. M.

✠JOHNSON, M. R. W. Lieut., I.A.R.O., attd. R.G.A. 1907
Killed in action in Mesopotamia 28 *June* 1918

JOHNSON, W. L. Major, R.A.M.C. 1905

✠JOHNSTON, B. 2nd Lieut., Rifle Brigade 1898
Killed in action 3 *Sept.* 1916

JOHNSTONE, C. P. Lieut., Highland L.I. (W.) [1914]

JOHNSTONE, R. O. S. Pte., H.A.C.; Lieut., R.G.A. (W.) 1913

JONES, C. R. SELOUS. Corpl., R.E.; Lieut., R.G.A. 1913

JONES, H. K. Gnr., R.G.A. 1902

JONES, J. S. Trooper, Strathcona's Horse, Canadian Force 1907

JORDAN, H. R. Major, Devon Regt.; attd. King's Own 1902
(Yorkshire L.I.) *M.*

JUCKES, R. Capt., R.E. (W.) *M.C. M.* 1911

KANN, P. W. G. Lieut., The Buffs (E. Kent Regt.); 1913
Capt., Tank Corps. (W.)

✠KEATS, F. T. Lieut., Suffolk Regt. 1911
Killed in action 25 *May* 1916

KELSEY, L. R. Capt., S. African Horse Artillery   1894
KEMBLE, H. M. Major, R.G.A. *D.S.O. M.*   1896
KENDALL, H. B. Capt. and Adjt., R.F.A.(T.F.) *M.*   1904
KENDALL, Rev. H. E. Chaplain, R.N. *O.B.E.*   1907
KENNEDY, G. H. Sergt., Signal Corps, United States 1913
Army
KENSINGTON, H. LE G. Lieut., Rifle Brigade. (W.)   1905
KENYON, H. G. Major, R.F.A. (W 2.) *M.*   1899
KEOWN, R. W. Capt. and Adjt., The Buffs (E. Kent 1912
Regt.) and Gen. List (Staff Capt.) *M.C. and Bar. M.*
KERR, P. W. Capt. and Adjt., R.F.A. (W.)   1904
✠KEWNEY, Rev. G. S. Chaplain and Instructor, R.N.   1892
Killed in action in the Battle of Jutland 31 *May* 1916
KEYMER, Rev. B. N. C.F. 3rd Class, R.A.C.D. *M* 2. 1890
KEYMER, Rev. B. W. C.F. 4th Class, R.A.C.D. *O.B.E.* 1894
M.
KEYNES, G. L. Major, R.A.M.C. *M.*   1906
KIDD, E. L. Capt., R.F.A.   1908
KIDD, L. S. Lieut., R.E.   1912
KIDSTON, R. A. P. R. Capt., R.F.A. *M.*   1912
KING, H. H. Lieut., R.N.V.R.; attd. R.N.A.S.   1898
KING, R. H. Gnr., H.A.C.; Capt. and Adjt., R.F.A. *M.* 1911
KINLOCH, Rev. M. W. C.F. 3rd Class, R.A.C.D. *O.B.E.* 1884
M. m.
✠KINNACH, S. J. 2nd Lieut., Yorkshire Regt. (W.)   1913
Killed in action 15 *July* 1916
KIRBY, H. R. Lieut., M.G.C.   1908
KIRKBY, N.W. Lieut.,Yorkshire Regt.(T.F.); Lieut.(O.), 1908
R.A.F.
KNIGHT, C. M. 2nd Lieut., The Buffs (E. Kent Regt.); 1913
Capt., M.G.C. and Tank Corps. (W.) *M.C.*
KNIGHT, P. D. Capt., Spec. List (Asst. Supt., Remount 1899
Sqdns.)
✠KNIGHTON, G. G. Major, Oxford and Bucks. L.I. *M.* 1906
Died 30 *April* 1917 *of wounds received in action near
Arras* 28 *April* 1917
KNOWLES, F. Capt., R.F.A. *M.C. M. Cavalier,* 1910
Order of the Crown of Italy

LAGDEN, L. A. Lieut., Rifle Brigade   [1914]
LAGDEN, R. B. Major, Rifle Brigade. (W.) *M.C.*   1911
LAHORE, Bishop of. Chaplains' Dept., Indian Army. 1890
C.B.E. M 2.
LAKIN, E. L. Lieut., R.G.A.   1898

LAMBERT, J. E. H. Capt., King's African Rifles. *M.C.* 1909
LAMBERTON, A. R. Lieut., Highland L.I. (W.) *M.C.* 1914
LANCASTER, H. Lieut., London Regt. (Finsbury Rifles) 1898
LANCHESTER, Rev. H. C. O. C.F. 4th Class, R.A.C.D. 1896
LANE, S. F. B. Lieut., R.A.S.C. 1902
LANE-CLAYPON, J. C. 2nd Lieut., Lincolnshire Regt.; 1900
Lieut., Gen. List. (W.)
LANGTON, Rev. H. B. C.F. 4th Class, R.A.C.D. 1895
LARNER, Rev. H. M. C.F. 4th Class, R.A.C.D. 1885
LARPENT, J. P. G. DE H. Capt. and Adjt., R. Fusiliers; 1906
Capt., Gen. List
LATHAM, P.H. Major, Haileybury College O.T.C. *Brevet* 1891
Major. m.
LA TOUCHE, W. F. D. Capt. and Adjt., Border Regt.(T.F.) [1914]
(W.) *m.*
LATTEY, H. P. T. Lieut., I.A.R.O., attd. 7th Gurkha 1902
Rifles. (W 2.)
LAURANCE, J. B. Capt., Huntingdonshire Cyclist Bn. 1908
LAW, C. Lieut., Devon Regt.; attd. Worcestershire Regt. 1909
✠LAW, H. 2nd Lieut., Rifle Brigade; Lieut., R. Welsh 1911
Fus. *M* 2.
Died 21 *July* 1915 *of wounds received in action* 10 *June*
1915
LAWRENCE, H. R. Major, 84th Punjabis and Super- 1897
numerary List, Indian Army. *M.*
✠LAWRENCE, J. R. M. Pte., R. Fusiliers (P. S. Bn.); 2nd 1913
Lieut., E. Surrey Regt.
Killed in action 16 *Aug.* 1916
LAWRENCE, T. Capt., R.A.S.C. *M.* 1903
LAWSON, C. G. Lieut., R.N.V.R. *M.* 1904
LAWSON, J. C. Lieut.-Cdr., R.N.V.R. *O.B.E.* *M.* 1893
Cavalier, Order of the Redeemer, Greece. Greek Medal
for Military Merit, 3rd Class
LAWSON-WALTON, A. 2nd Lieut., Rifle Brigade. (W.) 1913
LEA, E. I. Major, R. Warwickshire Regt. (T.F.); Lieut.- 1897
Col., A.Q.M.G. *M.C.* *T.D.* *M* 3. *Chevalier,*
Legion of Honour (France)
LEACH, C. DE L. Capt., Rifle Brigade; A.D.C. *M.* 1914
Order of the Redeemer, 5th Class (Greece)
LEACH LEWIS, A. F. Major, R. East Kent Yeo.; D.A.A.G. 1901
LEACROFT, J. Capt. (A.), R.A.F. *M.C. and Bar* 1907
LE BRASSEUR, J. H. Capt., R.F.A. (W.) 1910
LE BROCQ, C. N. Surgeon Capt., R. Jersey Med. Corps; 1897
attd. R.A.M.C.

LEDWARD, C. H. Lieut., R.G.A. 1908
LEDWARD, E. F. Capt., Suffolk Regt.; Major, Tank Corps. 1910
  (W 2.)
LEE, H. F. Capt., Epsom College O.T.C. 1892
LEE-NORMAN, F. T. Capt. and Adjt., R.E. *M.C. M.* 1905
LEES, A. Lieut., Queen's Own (R. W. Kent Regt.); [1914]
  Lieut. (O.), R.A.F. (W.) (P.) *M.*
✠LEGGETT, H. A. Major, Sherwood Foresters (Notts. and 1892
  Derby Regt.) and Gen. List. (W.)
  Died 3 March 1920 of the effects of trench fever
✠LEIGH, E. H. Lieut., Rifle Brigade. *M.* 1907
  Killed in action at Fromelles 9 May 1915
LESLIE, L. D. A. Cadet, O.C.B. 1918
LETCHWORTH, G. H. S. Capt., R.A.M.C. 1904
✠LEVINSTEIN, G. E. Lieut., Manchester Regt. 1905
  Killed in action 12 Oct. 1916
LEVY, L. Lieut., R.N.V.R. 1899
✠LEY, C. F. A. Capt., S. Notts. Hussars; attd. R.F.C. (W.) 1912
  Killed in flying accident 10 March 1918
LEY, R. L. Capt., R.A.M.C. 1901
LIGHT, D. O. Capt., R.A.S.C. (W.) (P.) *M.* 1908
LING, H. W. Lieut., R. Fusiliers. (W.) *M.B.E.* 1908
LINSLEY, A. R. Lieut., R.A.S.C.(M.T.) 1915
LISTER, A. V. Lieut., London Regt. (R. Fus.); attd. Wilt- 1910
  shire Regt. (W.)
LISTER, W. K. Capt., R.G.A.(T.F.) (W.) 1897
LITCHFIELD, Rev. W. G. Chaplain and Instructor Cdr., 1891
  R.N.
LITTLEJOHN, H. A. Major, R.F.A.; attd. Egyptian Army. 1912
  (W.) *M.C. Order of the Nile, 4th Class (Egypt)*
✠LIVESEY, A. G. H. Lieut., Loyal N. Lancs. Regt. 1908
  Killed in action 25 Sept. 1915
LLOYD, M. A. Lieut., R.N.V.R. 1906
✠LOCK, W. A. Lieut., Wiltshire Regt. [1914
  Killed in action in the Battle of Loos 25 Sept. 1915
✠LONGMAN, F. Lieut., R. Fusiliers. (W.) 1909
  Killed in action 18 Oct. 1914
LONGRIDGE, R. B. Lieut., 16th Lancers; A.P.M.; Capt., 1905
  S.O. 3, R.A.F.
LONGRIGG, G. E. Capt., N. Somerset Yeo. (W.) 1896
LOVELESS, M. L. Capt., R.A.M.C. 1908
LOVELESS, W. B. Capt., R.A.M.C. (W 2.) *M.C.* 1907
LOWE, C. N. Capt., R.A.S.C.; Capt. (A.), R.A.F. (W.) 1911
  M.C. D.F.C.

LOWE, W. D.   Major, W. Yorks. Regt.; Lieut.-Col.,   1898
E. Lancs. Regt. and Durham L.I. *D.S.O. M.C.*
M 4.

LOWE, W. W   Lieut., Malvern College O.T.C.   1893

LOWNDES, W. P.   Lieut., Loyal N. Lancs. Regt.; Lce.-   1910
Corpl., H.A.C. (W 2.)

✠LOWRY, S. H.   Capt., Hertfordshire Regt. *M.C.*   1907
Killed in action 31 *July* 1917

LUCAS, G. F.   Capt., Yorkshire Regt.; Hon. Capt. (T.),   1897
R.A.F. *M.*

LUCAS, R. B.   Lieut., Res. Regt. of Cavalry; A.D.C.; Staff   1893
Capt. *M.*

LUKER, R.   Lieut.-Col., Lancs. Fus.; A.A.G. *C.M.G.*   1897
M.C. Brevet Lieut.-Colonel. M 6.

LUKER, S. G.   Major, R.A.M.C. *M.*   1900

LUMSDEN, H. B.   Lieut., R. Scots; Capt., Spec. List.   1903
· *M.C.*

LUMSDEN, R.   Capt., Gordon Hdrs. (W.) *M.C. French*   1912
Croix de Guerre

✠LYLE, T. B.   2nd Lieut., Black Watch   [1914]
Killed in action 9 *May* 1915

LYSTER, A. ST G.   Lieut., I.A.R.O., attd. Sappers and   1906
Miners; Cmdt., Labour Corps. *M.*

✠McAFEE, L. A.   Capt., Rifle Brigade. (W.)   1907
Killed in action at Hooge 30 *July* 1915

MACARTNEY, M. H. H.   Lieut., Spec. List (R.T.O.)   1899

MACBRAYNE, L.   Cdr., R.N.V.R. *O.B.E.*   1885

McCLELAND, N. P. K. J. O'N.   Capt., Queen's Own   1906
(R.W. Kent Regt.); Chemical Adviser. (W.) *M.*

MACDONALD, G. K.   Lieut., Sherwood Foresters (Notts.   1908
and Derby Regt.); Capt. (A.), R.A.F.; Major, S.O. 2.
(W.)

MACDONALD, N. J.   Surgeon Sub-Lieut., R.N.V.R.   1913

MACDONALD, S. H.   Capt., Cameron Hdrs. (W.)   1911

✠McDOUGALL, R.   Lieut., The Buffs (E. Kent Regt.)   1908
Killed in action 20 *Oct.* 1914

McGRIGOR, A. M.   Capt., Gloucestershire Yeo.; A.D.C.   1906
O.B.E. M 2. *Chevalier, Military Order of Avis*
(Portugal)

MACILWAINE, G. W.   Lieut., Res. Regt. of Cavalry. (W.)   1913

✠MACKENZIE, G. M.   Capt., Seaforth Hdrs. (W.)   1908
Killed in action 21 *April* 1916

MACKENZIE, Sir J. K. D., Bart.   Lieut., R.N.V.R   1877

MACKENZIE, R. S. Capt., R. Warwickshire Regt.(T.F.) 19(
m.

MACKENZIE, R. T. H. Capt., Bombay Bn., Indian De- 19(
fence Force

MACKERN, G. T. G. Capt., R. Irish Fus.; empld. War 19
Office

M'LACHLAN, T. K. Capt., Argyll and Sutherland Hdrs. [191
(T.F.) (W.)

MACLAREN, J. F. P. Lieut., Ayrshire Yeo.; attd. R. Scots 19:
Fus.; Lieut., (A.), R.A.F. *M.*

MACLEOD, K. G. Capt., Gordon Hdrs. (W.) *m.* 19(

McNAUGHTON, H. L. Lieut., R. Scots Fus.; Capt. (Ad.), 19(
R.A.F. *m.*

McNEILE, Rev. A. H. C.F. 4th Class, R.A.C.D. 18{

McQUADE, W. F. Gnr., R.G.A. 19(

MADDEN, J. G. Capt., Manchester Regt. (W.) *D.S.O.* 19(
M. m.

MAGNAY, Sir C. B. W., Bart. Capt., 2nd Dragoon Gds. 19(
(Queen's Bays). *M.C.*

MAILE, W. C. D. Capt., R.A.M.C.(T.F.) (W.) 19(

MAKEIG-JONES, T. G. R. 2nd Lieut., Oxford and Bucks. [191
L.I.; Lieut., R.E. *M.C.*

✠MALCOMSON, H. Lieut. and Adjt., R. Irish Regt. (W.) *M.* 19(
Died 16 *Sept.* 1916 *of wounds received in action*

MALCOMSON, W. D. Corpl., London Regt. (London 19:
Scottish). (W.)

✠MANFIELD, N. P. Lieut., Northamptonshire Regt.(T.F.); 19:
attd. R.F.C.
Killed in action 9 *Sept.* 1916

✠MANN, C. J. Lieut., 20th Hussars. (W.) 19:
Killed in action 3 *Oct.* 1918

MANN, E. J. Capt., Norfolk Regt.(T.F.) (W.) 19(

MANN, F. T. Capt., Scots Gds. (W 3.) 19(

MANNERING, Rev. L. G. C.F. 4th Class, R.A.C.D. *M.C.* *19:

MANSFIELD, J. H. Capt., Coldstream Gds. 19:

MARBURG, C. L. H. Capt., R. Scots. (W.) 19(

¹MARSH, B. C. Capt., Cheshire Regt.; attd. 69th Punjabis, 19(
Indian Army

MARSH, O. DE B. Capt., R.A.M.C. *O.B.E. M. French* 19(
Médaille des Epidémies

✠MARSHALL, R. C. Lieut., R.F.A.(T.F.) (W.) 19(
Died 7 *Jan.* 1918 *of wounds received in action*

¹ Killed in action in Waziristan after the armistice.

✠MARSHALL, W.   Lieut., Durham L.I.   1907
   Accidentally killed 27 April 1915
MARSHALL, W. H.   Capt., R.A.M.C.   1907
MARTIN, C. F.   Lieut., R.G.A.   1905
MARTIN, Rev. E. W.   C.F. 3rd Class, R.A.C.D.   *m.*   1908
✠MARTIN, F. H.   2nd Lieut., R.E.   1907
   Killed in action 24 Nov. 1917
MARTIN, J. A.   Lieut., R.A.M.C.   1906
MARTINDALE, J. R.   Lieut., R.G.A.(T.F.)   (W.)   *M.*   1914
MARTYN, R. V.   Capt., Coldstream Gds.   (W.)   *M.*   1912
MARTYN-LINNINGTON, A. L.   Capt., Suffolk Yeo. and   1911
   Suffolk Regt.   (W.)
MARZETTI, C.   Lieut., The Queen's (R. W. Surrey Regt.);   1908
   empld. War Office
MARZETTI, L.   Lieut., The Queen's (R. W. Surrey Regt.)   1910
MATHER, E. L.   Sub-Lieut., R.N.V.R.   1909
MATHER, G. R.   Lieut., King's (Shropshire L.I.)   (W.)   1908
   (P.)
MATHEWS, A. G.   Major, R.G.A.   1892
MATTHEWS, C.   Capt., London Regt. (Queen's)   1904
MATTHEWS, M. C.   Major, Spec. List; Hon. Lieut.-Col.,   1881
   attd. Gen. Staff
MATTHEWS, M. H.   Lieut., Nigeria Regt., W. African   1909
   Frontier Force
MATTHEY, G. A.   Trooper, Strathcona's Horse, Canadian   1906
   Force
MAW, F. G.   Cadet, O.C.B.   1918
✠MAW, G. O.   Capt., R.A.M.C.   1906
   Died 10 July 1916 *of wounds received in action on the*
   Somme
MAXWELL, Rev. M. L.   C.F. 4th Class, R.A.C.D.   1906
✠MAYER, G. M.   Capt., London Regt.   *M* 2.   1911
   Died 16 Feb. 1917 *of wounds received in action 1 Jan.*
   1917
MEAD, G. C. F.   Capt., Aldenham School O.T.C.   1910
MEADE-KING, W. T. P.   Major, R.A.M.C.(T.F.)   (P.)   *M.*   1895
MEERS, R. H.   Capt. (T.), R.A.F.   1898
MELHUISH, T. W.   Capt., R.A.M.C.   1907
MELLERSH, F. G.   2nd Lieut., London Regt. (Surrey   1914
   Rifles); Capt., T.M.B.
MELLOR, P. H. L.   Capt., W. Yorks. Regt.; P. and B.T.   1906
   Staff.   *m.*
METCALFE, C. H. F.   Major, Bedfordshire Regt. (T.F.);   1906
   G.S.O. 2.   *D.S.O.*   *M* 2.

METCALFE, P. K. Capt., R.A.S.C.   189(
METCALFE-GIBSON, A. 2nd Lieut., R.A.S.C.   190'
MIDDLEMAS, P. Lieut., E. Lancs. Regt.; attd. M.G.C.;   191:
   Capt. (T.), R.A.F. *M.B.E. M.*
MILES, B. L. Capt., London Regt. (Queen's West-   190:
   minster Rifles). *M.C. M.*
✠MILES, C. V. 2nd Lieut., S. Wales Borderers; Capt.,   191
   Welsh Regt.
   Killed in action in the Battle of Loos 25 Sept. 1915
✠MILES, H. R. Pte., R. Fusiliers (Sportsman's Bn.); 2nd   188
   Lieut., Connaught Rangers
   Killed in action 18 *July* 1916
MILES, W. H. Capt. and Adjt., Somerset L.I. (W.) *M.*   190'
✠MILLAR, G. H. Lieut., R.N.V.R. (R.N.D.); Capt. (A.),   190
   R.A.F. (P. *Escaped from Germany*)
   Killed in flying accident 29 *April* 1918
✠MILLER, H. T. Lieut., E. Yorks. Regt.; attd. D. of Well-   191
   ington's (W. Riding Regt.) (W.)
   Died 6 *May* 1915 *of gas poisoning*
MILLER, P. T. Capt., R. Welsh Fus. (W.)   190
MILLER, W. M. Capt., London Yeo. (Rough Riders); Hon.   191
   Capt. (A.), R.A.F. (W.)
MILLIGAN, W. Capt., R.F.A.(T.F.); attd. R.G.A.; Staff   191
   Capt. *M.*
MILLIKEN, H. E. Capt., King's Royal Rifle Corps. (W 2.)   190
MILLS, A. E. 2nd Lieut. (T.), R.A.F.   191
MILLS, T. G. Capt. and Adjt., R.G.A.(T.F.)   190
MILLS, W. G. Capt., D. of Cornwall's L.I. (W 3.)   189
MILN, C. J. Capt. (T.), R.A.F. *M. Greek Military Cross*   190
MILNE HOME, A. C. Capt., Northumberland Fus. and   190
   Nigeria Regt., W. African Frontier Force; Brigade
   Major. *M.C. M.*
MILNER-WHITE, R. 2nd Lieut., I.A.R.O.   190
MOLONY, A. W. Lieut., King's Royal Rifle Corps   191
✠MOLSON, E. E. Lieut., R. Scots   191
   Killed in action 2 *April* 1915
MOLSON, H. E. Capt., King's Royal Rifle Corps. (W.)   191
MONKS, F. R. Major, S. Lancs. Regt.(T.F.)   190
MONTAGU, G. W. Lieut., R.A.S.C.   191
MONTEITH, H. G. Lieut.-Col., R.A.M.C. *D.S.O.*   190
   O.B.E. M 2.
✠MONTFORD, D. R. Capt., 98th Infy., Indian Army;   190
   A.D.C. (W 2.) *M.*
   Missing, presumed killed in action (12 *April* 1918)

✠Moon, L. J. Lieut., Devon Regt. 1906
Died 23 Nov. 1916 of wounds received in action
✠Moor, C. 2nd Lieut., Hampshire Regt. (W.) 1910
Killed in action in Gallipoli 6 Aug. 1915
Moore, C. A. St G. Lieut., R.E.(T.F.) M.B.E. 1900
Moore, J. W. Lieut., R.A.S.C.(M.T.) M. 1914
✠Morgan, Rev. G. W. F. Chaplain, R.N. 1900
Killed in action in the Battle of Jutland 31 May 1916
Morley, B. C. Lieut., R.N.V.R. 1911
Morley, C. Major, Manchester Regt. (W.) (P.) 1897
Morrice, W. Capt., R. Glasgow Yeo.; A.D.C.; Hon. 1912
Capt. (A.), R.A.F.
✠Morris, C. A. S. Major, Bedfordshire Regt.; attd. R. 1913
Irish Fus. (W 2.)
Died in German hands 7 May 1917 of wounds received
in action in the Battle of Arras 28 April 1917
Morris, F. B. Major, S. Staffs. Regt. M. 1899
✠Morse, C. Lieut., The Buffs (E. Kent Regt.) and R.E. 1912
(Tunnelling Coy.)
Killed in action 7 Dec. 1917
✠Morse, E. V. Capt., The Buffs (E. Kent Regt.) M.C. 1910
Killed in action 23 Oct. 1918
Morton, Rev. C. J. C.F. 4th Class, R.A.C.D. 1904
Morton, H. J. S. Capt., R.A.M.C. 1905
✠Morum, J. P. 2nd Lieut., Rifle Brigade 1914
Killed in action 1 July 1916
Moss, H. K. Staff Sergt.-Major, R.A.S.C.; Lieut., 1894
Labour Corps (Cmdt., P. of W. Camp)
Mosseri, F. N. 35° Regt. Fanteria, Italian Army 1912
Mossop, A. G. Capt., R.A.M.C. 1904
Mountain, S. W. Capt., R. Fusiliers. *Cavalier, Order* 1911
of the Redeemer (Greece)
Moxey, E. R. Corpl., R.E.; Capt. (T.), R.A.F. M. 1910
Moxey, J. L. Capt., R. Fusiliers. (W 2.) 1908
Muggeridge, G. D. Instructor Lieut., R.N. 1896
Mugliston, F. H. Lieut., D. of Cornwall's L.I.; empld. 1904
Home Office. (W.) O.B.E. *Chevalier, Ordre de la*
Couronne (Belgium)
Muirhead, M. Major, D.A.A.G.; Lieut.-Col., R.F.A. 1897
D.S.O. and Bar. Brevet Lieut.-Colonel. M 5. Cheva-
lier, Legion of Honour (France). Belgian Croix de
Guerre
✠Murly-Gotto, J. Lieut., R.E. M. 1908
Died 20 Aug. 1916 of wounds received in action

Murray, A. R.   Capt., Seaforth Hdrs.; Staff Capt.   1910
Murray, C. M.   Lieut.-Col., S. African Med. Corps.   1895
  D.S.O. M 2.

✠Nadin, T.   Capt. and Adjt., Sherwood Foresters (Notts   1896
  and Derby Regt., T.F.)
  Died 8 June 1918 *of pneumonia following wounds
  received in action*
✠Napier, G. G.   Capt., 35th Sikhs, Indian Army   1903
  Died 25 Sept. 1915 *of wounds received in action*
Narayan, Maharaj K. H.   Hon. Lieut., Indian Army. *M.*   1908
Nash-Wortham, F. L. D.   Capt., R.A.M.C. *M.*   1901
Naylor, P. A. E.   Capt., Rifle Brigade; A.D.C.; Hon.   1913
  Capt. (A.), R.A.F. (W.)
✠Neate, N. R.   Capt., R. Fusiliers; attd. H.A.C. (W2.)   [1914]
  M.C.
  Killed in action 3 *May* 1917
New, T. G.   Sergt., R.E. *M.S.M.*   1900
Newmarch, J. G.   Surgeon Lieut., R.N.   1904
Newton, C. H.   *See* Herdman-Newton, C.
Newton, R. H. H.   *See* Herdman-Newton, R. H.
Nicholl, V.   Lieut.-Col. (A. and S.), R.A.F. *D.S.O.*   1911
  D.S.C.
Nicolls, Rev. G. E.   C.F. 4th Class, R.A.C.D.   1881
✠Niven, E. O.   Lce.-Sergt., Bedfordshire Regt.   1909
  Died 19 *April* 1917 *of wounds received in action*
✠Nix, P. K.   Fleet Surgeon, R.N.   1888
  Killed in explosion on H.M.S. Bulwark 26 *Nov.* 1914

Ogilvie, P. G.   Capt., I.A.R.O.; Inspector of Munitions   1908
Oglethorpe, H. C.   Capt., King's College School,   1904
  Wimbledon, O.T.C.
Oldfield, G. E. B.   Major, 74th Punjabis, Indian Army;   1893
  Lieut.-Col., 89th Punjabis
Oldfield, R. W.   Capt., R.F.A.; Major, D.A.A.G. (W 2.)   1910
  *D.S.O. M.C. and two Bars.   Brevet Lieut.-Colonel
  on promotion to substantive Major.   Brevet Major.
  M* 6.   *Italian Bronze Medal for Military Valour.
  Italian Croce di Guerra*
✠Oliver, R. E. C.   2nd Lieut., Rifle Brigade   1912
  Missing, presumed killed in action, 25 *Aug.* 1916
Oliver-Jones, W. S.   Lieut., Bedfordshire Regt. (W 3.)   1913
  M.C.

ORDE, S. E. H. Capt. (T.), R.A.F. *M.* 1912
ORLEBAR, R. A. B. Capt., Bedfordshire Regt. and R. Irish 1913
Fus.; attd. King's Own (R. Lancaster Regt.); empld.
War Office; S.O. 3, R.A.F. (W 2.)
ORMOND, W. P. S. Cadet, R.F.A. 1917
ORPEN, H. F. Lieut., The Queen's (R. W. Surrey Regt.) 1908
(W.)
ORPEN-PALMER, H. B. H. Lieut.-Col., R. Irish Fus.; 1895
Brig.-Gen. *C.M.G. D.S.O. Brevet Lieut.-Colonel.*
M 5. *Order of St Stanislas, 3rd Class, with swords*
(Russia)
✠ORR, E. F. B. Corpl., R.E. (Signals); Lieut., R.F.A. 1913
Killed in action 23 *March* 1918
ORR-EWING, A. Surgeon Lieut. R.N. 1910
OWEN, S. H. E. G. Lieut., Pembroke Yeo. (W.) 1898

¹PAGE, C. F. G. Lieut.-Col., R.G.A. *C.M.G. D.S.O.* 1898
M 3. *m. Italian Croce di Guerra. Italian Silver*
Medal for Military Valour
PAGET, C. W. Lieut.-Col., R.E.; D.A.D. R.T. *C.M.G.* 1901
D.S.O. M 4. *Officer, Legion of Honour (France).*
Officer, Ordre de la Couronne (Belgium)
✠PAIN, E. D. Pte., R. Fusiliers; Capt., Somerset L.I. 1898
Killed in action 18 *Oct.* 1916
PAIN, J. W. Capt., Suffolk Regt.; Capt. (A.), R.A.F. (W.) 1905
PALMER, B. H. Capt., R.A.M.C. 1900
✠PARADISE, J. R. T. 2nd Lieut., R. Warwickshire Regt. 1913
Missing, presumed killed in action, 30 *Oct.* 1917
PARKER, C. L. Y. Capt., R.E.; Staff Capt., War Office. 1910
(W.)
PARKER, H. E. Capt. (Airship), R.A.F. 1909
PARKER, J. D. Lieut., R.N.V.R. (Coastal Motor-boat 1906
Service)
PARMITER, C. L. Major, The Buffs (E. Kent Regt.) and 1886
King's (Liverpool Regt., R. of O.). *O.B.E.*
PARRY-JONES, P. E. H. Capt., S. Wales Borderers; empld. 1911
O.C.B. (W.)
PARSONS, F. P. N. Surgeon Lieut., R.N. 1913
✠PARTINGTON, J. B. Capt., Devon Regt.(T.F.) 1903
Killed in action 3 *Feb.* 1917
✠PARTRIDGE, R. H. Capt., Norfolk Regt.(T.F.) 1909
Accidentally killed on active service 4 *Sept.* 1917

¹ Died since the armistice of injuries received on service.

PATERSON, G. McL.   Lieut.-Cdr. (Asst. Constructor),   1909
Naval Construction Dept., Admiralty
PATON, E. R.   Lieut., Gen. List (T.F. Res.), empld. Min-   1907
istry of National Service
PATON, F. A. R.   Capt., King's (Liverpool Regt.); Lieut.,   1914
Gen. List. (W.)
✠PATON, J. E.   2nd Lieut., Monmouthshire Regt.   M.   [1914]
Killed in action 31 *Dec.* 1914
PATTESON, C.   Lieut., Marlborough College O.T.C.   1911
✠PAUL, J. W. E.   2nd Lieut., King's Royal Rifle Corps. (W.)   1914
Killed in action 27 *July* 1916
PEAD, J. H.   Surgeon Cdr., R.N.   M.   *Chevalier, Legion*   1887
of Honour (France). Order of St Stanislas, 2nd Class,
with swords (Russia)
PEARSON, C. McM.   Lieut., I.A.R.O., attd. S. and T. Corps   1901
PEARSON, D. G.   Capt., R.A.M.C.   1900
✠PEED, S. W.   N. Zealand Force   1886
Died in Egypt 22 *March* 1916 *of pneumonia*
PELLY, E.   Lieut., R.A.S.C.   *M.B.E.*   1903
PEMBERTON, W. H.   Capt., R.A.S.C.   *M.*   1908
PENDLEBURY, H. S.   Capt., R.A.M.C.(T.F.)   1890
PENNELL, V. C.   Capt., R.A.M.C.   1908
PEPIN, A. R.   Sub-Lieut., R.N.V.R.   1912
PERKINS, Rev. F. L.   C.F. 4th Class, R.A.C.D.(T.F.)   1884
¹PERRIN, M. N.   Major, R.A.M.C.; attd. R.A.F.   1906
PESHALL, Rev. C. J. E.   Chaplain, R.N.   *D.S.O.*   *M.*   1901
PETERS, A. N. G.   2nd Lieut., Yorkshire Regt.(T.F.);   1915
attd. Manchester Regt.
PHILLIPS, D. M. P.   *See* SCOTT-PHILLIPS, D. M. P.
✠PHILLIPS, E. S.   Lieut., Monmouthshire Regt. (W.)   1901
Killed in action 8 *May* 1915
PHILLIPS, P. R. O'R.   Capt., R.A.M.C.   1910
PHILLIPS, T.   Capt., Cambridge Univ. O.T.C.   1894
✠PIGGOT, A. A.   Lieut., Northumberland Fus.   1910
Killed in action in the Battle of Loos 26 *Sept.* 1915
PIGGOTT, J. I.   Capt., Gen. List; A.D.C.; G.S.O. 3   1907
(Intelligence).   *M.C.*   *M.*
PIGOU, H. LA T.   Lieut., Herefordshire Regt.; Draft   1890
Conducting Officer
PILCHER, W. H.   Lieut., Black Watch; Capt., Cameron   1904
Hdrs. (W.)
PILDITCH, P. H.   Major, R.F.A.(T.F.)   *M.*   1909

---

¹ Killed in flying accident after the armistice.

PILKINGTON, D. H.   2nd Lieut., Suffolk Regt.(T.F.) (W.)   1912
PIPER, J. H.   Lieut.-Col., Northamptonshire Regt.; Capt.,   1900
 Gen. Staff (O.C.B.) (W.) *M.C. and Bar. m.*
PIRKIS, G. C. L. M.   Capt., York and Lancaster Regt.   1896
 and M.G.C. (W.)
PLAYNE, B. A.   Surgeon Lieut., R.N.; Major (Med.), R.A.F.   1904
 D.S.O.
PLAYNE, H. F.   2nd Lieut., Upper Burma Bn., Indian   1904
 Defence Force; Major, I.A.R.O., attd. Military
 Accounts Dept. *M.*
PLUMPTRE, E. A. W.   Lieut., Northumberland Fus.; attd.   1907
 R.E. (W 2.) *French Croix de Guerre*
POCOCK, W. A.   Surgeon Lieut., R.N.   1907
✠PONSONBY, C. T.   Lieut., King's Royal Rifle Corps   1912
 Killed in action 23 Aug. 1916
✠POOLE, R. E. S.   Lieut., King's Royal Rifle Corps   [1914]
 Killed in action 4 Nov. 1918
POOLEY, E. H.   Capt., R.G.A.(T.F.)   1895
✠PORTER, A. G.   Capt., R. Irish Fus. *M.C.*   [1914]
 Died 29 Oct. 1918 *of wounds received in action* 25 *Oct.*
 1918
POTTER, Rev. W. N.   C.F. 4th Class, R.A.C.D.   1903
✠POUND, M. S.   2nd Lieut., The Queen's (R. W. Surrey   1910
 Regt.)
 Died 7 Nov. 1914 *of wounds received in action*
POWELL, M. B.   H.A.C.   1909
PREST, H. E. W.   Capt., R. Berkshire Regt. and Spec.   1908
 List (Chief Instructor, School of Instruction). *M.*
 French Croix de Guerre
PRESTON, E. W.   Lieut., The Queen's (R. W. Surrey   1905
 Regt., T.F.); Capt., Spec. List
PRIESTLEY, D. R. O.   Capt., R.E. (Signals). *M.C.*   1912
PRIOR, A. V.   Paymaster Lieut.-Cdr., R.N.V.R. (R.N.D.)   1912
PRIOR, Rev. C. E.   C.F. 4th Class, R.A.C.D.   1899
PRITCHARD, F. C.   Capt., R.F.A.(T.F.) *M.C. Italian*   1913
 Bronze Medal for Military Valour
PROCTER, R. F.   Pte., R.A.M.C.   1898
PRYOR, G. D.   Major, Cambridgeshire Regt. and R.A.F.;   1901
 S.O. 2, Air Ministry
PUSINELLI, S. J.   Capt., R.F.A.   1908
PYNE, F. S.   Major, R.F.A. (W 2.) *D.S.O. M.*   1904

✠QUINCEY, T. E. DE Q.   2nd Lieut., Rifle Brigade   1912
 Killed in action 9 *May* 1915

✠RAMSAY, A. H. Pte., Foreign Legion, French Army; 2nd   1904
Lieut., Oxford and Bucks. L.I.
Killed in action 13 *Oct.* 1915
RANGER, Rev. A. S. B. Chaplain, R.N.   1898
RANKING, G. L. Lieut., R.A.M.C.   1896
RANKING, R. M. Major, R.A.M.C. (R. of O.)   1895
RANSOM, J. Capt., R. Berkshire Regt.; empld. Records.   1911
(W.) *M.C. French Médaille d'Honneur*
RANSOM, P. W. Capt., R.A.M.C. (W.)   1906
RATTRAY, R. C. Capt., R.E. (Signals). *M.*   1908
RAWLINSON, A. R. Lieut., York and Lancaster Regt.   1912
and M.G.C.; empld. War Office. *M.B.E. m.*
✠RAYNER, E. Surgeon Lieut., R.N.   1905
Killed in explosion on H.M.S. Vanguard 9 *July* 1917
READMAN, C. H. B. Lieut., Durham L.I.; Capt. (A.),   1913
R.A.F. (W.)
READMAN, J. F. A. Major, R.E. (W.) *M.C.*   1906
REDMAN, C. E. Capt., R.A.M.C. (P.) *m.*   1900
✠REID, G. M. Capt., London Regt. (Finsbury Rifles)   1905
Killed in action 9 *May* 1918
REID, M. B. Major, R.E. (W 2.) *M.C. M.*   [1914]
REINER, N. A. Lieut., I.A.R.O., attd. 6th Gurkha Rifles   1910
RENSHAW, H. W. Pte., Middlesex Regt.; Lieut., Hamp-   1907
shire Regt. (W.) (P.)
✠RENWICK, H. A. Capt., S. Wales Borderers; Capt. (A.),   1909
R.A.F. (W.)
Killed in flying accident 10 *Aug.* 1918
RHYS JONES, I. Lieut., Suffolk Regt.   1915
RICHARD, W. R. Capt., R. Scots (T.F.) (W 2.)   1914
✠RICHARDSON, R. S. Pte., Middlesex Regt. (P. S. Bn.);   1911
2nd Lieut., Cameronians (Scottish Rifles); Lieut.,
M.G.C. *M.C.*
Died 1 *Sept.* 1916 *of wounds received in action* 31 *Aug.*
1916
✠RICKERBY, J. H. E. Capt., Gloucestershire Regt.(T.F.)   [1914]
M.C. Italian Silver Medal for Military Valour
Killed in action near St Quentin 22 *March* 1918
RILEY, C. J. M. Capt., Coldstream Gds. (W.) *M.C. M.*   1912
RILEY, H. C. C. 2nd Lieut., Coldstream Gds.   1916
✠RILEY, Rev. T. Capt., R.F.A.   1903
Died 5 *Aug.* 1916 *of wounds received in action* 3 *Aug.*
1916
✠RITCHIE, T. P. A. 2nd Lieut., Rifle Brigade   1913
Killed in action 15 *March* 1915

ROBBINS, F. H. Major, R.A.M.C.(T.F.) *M.C.* *M.*   1906
ROBERTS, Rev. B. C. C.F. 4th Class, R.A.C.D.   1906
ROBERTS, F. W. Capt., Northamptonshire Regt.; Major,   1904
   Gen. List (O.C.B.) *m.*
ROBERTS, H. E. F. Lieut., Imperial Service College,   1902
   Windsor, O.T.C. *m.*
✠ROBERTS, J. R. B. 2nd Lieut., Northumberland Fus.   1910
   Killed in action near Hill 60 1 *Feb.* 1916
ROBERTS, S. C. Lieut., Suffolk Regt. (T.F.); empld.   1906
   O.C.B. (W.)
ROBERTS, S. R. P. Lieut., R. Sussex Regt.; Interpreter; 1913
   R.T.O. (W.)
ROBINSON, Rev. E. V. C.F. 4th Class, R.A.C.D. *M.C.*   1903
ROBINSON, G. 2nd Lieut., R.F.A.(T.F.); Lieut., R.H.A., [1914]
   Indian Army. (W.)
✠ROBINSON, Rev. G. B. Chaplain, R.N.   1890
   Drowned on H.M.S. Formidable 1 *Jan.* 1915
ROBINSON, H. M. Capt. and Adjt., N. Staffs. Regt.   1908
   (W 2.) *M.*
ROCKE, E. M. Gnr., R.G.A.   1902
ROE, S. V. Lieut., R.A.M.C.   1891
ROPNER, W. G. Capt., R.G.A.(T.F.); Instructor in   [1914]
   Gunnery. (W.)
ROSHER, Rev. H. G. C.F. 4th Class, R.A.C.D. *Order of* 1890
   St Sava, 5*th Class* (*Serbia*)
✠ROSS, W. M. Lieut., Gordon Hdrs.   1911
   Killed in action 11 *March* 1915
ROWE, B. W. Capt., Cambridgeshire Regt.; attd. R.E.   1913
   (Signals). *M.C.* *M.*
✠ROYLE, A. L. Pte., R. Fusiliers   1894
   Killed in action 3 *Aug.* 1916
RUSSELL, P. Major, R.F.A. *M.C. and Bar*   1903
RUSSELL, W. S. K. Capt., R. Sussex Regt. and Gen. Staff. [1914]
   O.B.E. *M.*
RUST, N. A. Lieut., I.A.R.O.   1899
RUST, P. J. 2nd Lieut., I.A.R.O.   1901
RUSTON, V. F. M. Capt., R.G.A.   1916

SALT, C. E. F. Lieut., R.A.M.C.   1899
SALUSBURY, J. T. Lieut., R.G.A. *M.*   1900
✠SANDERSON, A. K. Pte., R. Fusiliers (P.S. Bn.); 2nd Lieut., 1913
   Middlesex Regt.; attd. London Regt.
   Killed in action 25 *Sept.* 1915
SATTERTHWAITE, M. E. Sergt.-Major, Remount Service   1900

SCHOLES, W. N. Lieut., Manchester Regt.; Staff Capt.; 1908
    Capt., R.E. (Spec. Bde.) *O.B.E.* *M* 2.

✠SCHOOLING, Rev. C. H. C.F. 4th Class, R.A.C.D. *M.* 1903
    Died 21 June 1917 of wounds received in action

✠SCHWALM, C. E. Lieut., Gloucestershire Regt.(T.F.) 1911
    Accidentally killed on active service 22 Nov. 1917

✠SCOTT, J. G. 2nd Lieut., Black Watch 1910
    Killed in action at Rue du Bois 9 May 1915

SCOTT, J. G. C. Trooper, Indore Mtd. Infy., Indian 1907
    Defence Force

SCOTT-PHILLIPS, D. M. P. Lieut., Middlesex Regt. 1910

✠SEALY, C. F. N. P. Pte., London Regt. (Kensington Bn.); 1912
    2nd Lieut., R. Fusiliers
    Killed in action near Ypres 24 May 1915

SEARLE, C. F. Major, R.A.M.C. (W.) *M.C.* *M* 2. 1901

SEARLE, W. C. Capt., Bedfordshire Regt.; attd. R. Innis- 1908
    killing Fus.; empld. O.C.B.

✠SEATON, A. A. Capt., Cambridgeshire Regt. 1903
    Died 4 Sept. 1915 of wounds received in action

SEBAG-MONTEFIORE, J. Pte., R. Fusiliers (P.S. Bn.); 2nd 1910
    Lieut., R.F.A. (W.)

SETH-SMITH, G. Lieut., R.A.S.C. 1906

SETH-SMITH, L. M. Lieut., E. African Transport Corps. 1898
    M.C.

SEWELL, A. P. Capt. and Adjt., R.G.A. *M.* 1898

SEWELL, E. P. Colonel, R.A.M.C.; D.D.M.S. *C.M.G.* 1892
    D.S.O. *M* 3.

SEYMOUR-BROWNE, R. C. Lieut., R. Fusiliers. *M.* [1914]

SHARP, H. W. Capt., Leicestershire Regt. 1907

✠SHARP, S. O. Lieut., York and Lancaster Regt. 1909
    Killed in action 1 July 1916

SHARPE, H. Major, R.A.M.C.(T.F.) *Brevet Major* 1902

SHEEPSHANKS, E. Lieut., I.A.R.O. (Cavalry) 1903

SHEPPARD, J. H. D. Major, R.A.O.C.; D.A.D.O.S. *M* 2. 1907

SHERSTON, W. M., D.S.O. Hon. Colonel, N. Somerset 1877
    Yeo.; Lieut.-Col., Gen. List (T.F. Res.); Camp
    Cmdt.

SHUTER, L. R. W. A. Capt., R.E. (Fortress, T.F.) 1906

SIMCOX, J. L. Capt., R. Warwickshire Regt.(T.F.) (W.) 1906

SIMCOX, W. M. 2nd Lieut., R. Warwickshire Regt. 1907

SIMPSON, J. H. 2nd Lieut., Grenadier Gds. 1902

SING, L. M. Major, R.F.A.(T.F.) (W 2.) 1906

✠SINGH, K. I. Capt., I.M.S. *M.C.* 1902
    Killed in action 1 Dec. 1914

SINGH, K. S. Major, I.M.S.   1897
SINGLETON, J. E. Capt. and Adjt., R.F.A. *M.*   1902
SLACK, E. Capt., R.A.M.C.   1893
SLINGSBY, W. E. Capt. (T.), R.A.F.   1904
SMALE, G. F. P. Lieut., Lancs. Fus.; attd. Gloucester-   1913
shire Regt. (W 3.)
SMEDLEY, R. D. Capt., R.A.M.C.   1895
SMITH, A. K. 2nd Lieut., Bombay Light Horse, Indian   1897
Defence Force; Lieut., I.A.R.O., attd. 12th Cavalry;
A.D.C.
SMITH, H. H. M. Capt., Loyal N. Lancs. Regt. (W.)   1910
M.C.
✠SMITH, J. A. H. 2nd Lieut., R. Scots   1909
Killed in action 14 *Aug.* 1915
SMITH, Rev. N. C. C.F. 4th Class, R.A.C.D.   1906
✠SMITH, W. A. Major, King's (Liverpool Regt.); Lieut.-   1899
Col., Manchester Regt. *M.*
Died 9 *July* 1916 *of wounds received in action*
SMYLY, A. F. Capt., S. Staffs. Regt. (W.)   1905
SMYTH, W. J. D. Capt., R.A.M.C. *M.*   1903
SMYTH, W. R. B. Lieut., R.A.S.C.   1912
SNEATH, R. E. F. Lieut.-Col., London Regt. (R. Fus.);   1911
Capt., M.G.C. *M.C.* *M.*
SOLOMON, B. A. Pte., S. African Force   1904
SOMERS, J. P. Major, Gen. List (Instructor, School of   1892
Musketry). *O.B.E.* *Brevet Major.* *m.*
✠SOMERS-COCKS, R. Capt., Somerset L.I. *M.C.* *M.*   1912
Killed in action 24 *April* 1918
✠SOUTHERN, H. 2nd Lieut., I.A.R.O., attd. Infy.   1905
Missing, presumed killed in action, 18 *April* 1916
SPEIR, G. T. Lieut.-Col., S. Staffs. Regt. and Northern   1893
Cyclist Bn.
SPEIR, K. R. N. Lieut.-Col., R.E. *D.S.O.* *M* 2. *Chev-*   1902
alier, Legion of Honour (France)
✠SPENCE, C. B. Lieut. (A.), R.F.C. *M.*   1907
Killed in action 9 *May* 1915
✠SPIELMANN, H. L. I. Capt., Manchester Regt.(T.F.)   1911
Killed in action in Gallipoli 13 *Aug.* 1915
SPITTLE, J. T. Major (T.), R.A.F. *O.B.E.* *m.*   1905
STACK, E. H. E. Capt., R.A.M.C. (2nd S. Gen. Hospital,   1884
T.F.)
STALLARD, Rev. H. K. Chaplain, R.N.   1894
STAPLETON, E. P. Lieut., R. Fusiliers; Major, S.O. 2,   1908
R.A.F. (W.) *O.B.E.*

STEAVENSON, A. G. Lieut., R.A.S.C.; empld. Records   1905
STEDMAN, J. A. 2nd Lieut., E. Surrey Regt. and   [1914]
Connaught Rangers; Lieut. (A. and S.), R.A.F.
STENHOUSE, R. H. R.N.V.R. (R.N.D.)   1905
STEPHEN, J. G. Capt., Highland L.I. (W.) *M.C.*   1913
STEPHENS, Rev. J. F. D. C.F. 4th Class, R.A.C.D.   1885
STEVENSON, R. W. Capt., Worcestershire Regt. (T.F.); 1912
Major, D.A.A.G. *M.C. M.*
STEWART, N. B. Lieut., R.N.V.R. (Coastal Motor-boat   1910
Service). *M.*
STICKLAND, J. R. Capt., Cambridgeshire Regt. and   1906
R.G.A. (W.) *M.*
STIDSTON, Rev. P. H. C.F. 4th Class, R.A.C.D. (W.)   1905
✠STILEMAN, C. H. 2nd Lieut., R. Fusiliers; attd. London 1912
Regt. (Civil Service Rifles); attd. R.F.C.
Killed in action 2 Feb. 1916
✠STILEMAN, F. W. C. Pte., H.A.C.; Capt., Gloucester- 1905
shire Regt.
Killed in action 23 July 1916
STILEMAN, G. R. 2nd Lieut., Devon Regt. (T.F.) and   1917
Labour Corps
✠STOBART, J. G. 2nd Lieut., Rifle Brigade   1910
Killed in action 15 March 1915
✠STONE, W. N. Capt., R. Fusiliers   1910
V.C. "For most conspicuous bravery when in com-
mand of a company in an isolated position 1000 yards
in front of the main line and overlooking the enemy's
position. He observed the enemy massing for an attack,
and afforded invaluable information to Battalion Headquarters. He was ordered to withdraw his company,
leaving a rearguard to cover the withdrawal. The attack
developing with unexpected speed, Capt. Stone sent three
platoons back and remained with the rearguard himself.
He stood on the parapet with the telephone under a
tremendous bombardment, observing the enemy, and
continued to send back valuable information until the
wire was cut by his orders. The rearguard was eventu-
ally surrounded and cut to pieces, and Capt. Stone was
seen fighting to the last, till he was shot through the
head. The extraordinary coolness of this heroic officer
and the accuracy of his information enabled dispositions
to be made just in time to save the line and avert
disaster."—Supplement to *The London Gazette*, 13 Feb.
1918.
Killed in action 30 Nov. 1917

✠STONEY, T. R. 2nd Lieut., King's Own Scottish Borderers   1901
  Killed in action 10 *April* 1918
STORR, Rev. E. C. C.F. 4th Class, R.A.C.D.; attd. R.A.F.   1899
STORRS, Rev. C. E. C.F. 4th Class, R.A.C.D.   1907
STORRS, R. H. A.   Brig.-Gen., attd. Egyptian Army.   1900
  C.M.G. C.B.E. M 2. *Commander, Order of the
  Crown of Italy. Commander, Order of the Redeemer
  (Greece)*
STRAKER, H. G. Major, R.F.A. (W.) *M* 2. *m.*   1908
STRANGE, H. St J. B. Lieut., Black Watch. (W.)   1910
STREATFEILD, A. H. O. Capt., R. Sussex Regt.   1897
STREET, H. Capt., 20th Hussars (R. of O.); Staff Capt.   1889
✠STURDY, A. C. Capt., R.A.M.C. *M.C.*   1902
  Died 1 *May* 1919 *of dysentery contracted on active
  service*
STURDY, E. C. 2nd Lieut., I.A.R.O., attd. 28th Light   1903
  Cavalry
STURT, Rev. H. C.F. 4th Class, R.A.C.D.   1888
✠SUGDEN, G. H. Lieut., D. of Wellington's (W. Riding   1907
  Regt.)
  Killed in action 12 *Oct.* 1916
SURRAGE, H. J. R. Surgeon Lieut., R.N.   1912
SURRAGE, J. L. Lieut., Hampshire Regt.   1915
SUSSKIND, M. J. Lieut., Transvaal Scottish, S. African   1909
  Force; 2nd Lieut., R.G.A. (W.)
SUTTON, K. H. M. Lieut., Grenadier Gds. and Gds.   1910
  M.G. Regt. (W.)
✠SUTTON, W. M. Lieut., York and Lancaster Regt.   1914
  Died 17 *Sept.* 1916 *of wounds received in action* 16 *Sept.*
  . 1916
SWAN, F. G. Capt., Tonbridge School O.T.C.   1906
SWAN, H. N. Capt., R.A.S.C.   1908
SWEET, R. McM. Cadet, O.C.B. (R.E.)   1918
SYMONDS, S. L. Capt. and Adjt., Oxford and Bucks. L.I.   1914
  (W.) *M.C.*

TAIT, M. W. Capt., London Regt. (London Scottish);   1913
  Major, M.G.C. (W.) *M.C. M. Belgian Croix de
  Guerre*
TALBOT, Rev. A. T. S. C.F. 4th Class, R.A.C.D.(T.F.)   1897
TANNER, L. E. Hon. Lieut., Spec. List (Navy and Army   1909
  Canteen Board)
TATE, J. F. F.   Major, King's Royal Rifle Corps;   1895
  Colonel, A.A.G., War Office. *m.*

TAYLOR, F. C. Lieut., R.N.V.R.; empld. British Military 1895
Mission

TAYLOR, G. P. B. *See* BROOKE TAYLOR, G. P.

✠TAYLOR, H. H. Capt., R.A.M.C. 1900
Died 3 April 1918 *of wounds received in action*

TAYLOR, J. HOLMAN. *See* HOLMAN, Rev. J. H. T.

TAYLOR, Rev. J. R. S. C.F. 4th Class, R.A.C.D. 1903

TAYLOR, L. M. Major, King's Own (Yorkshire L.I., 1901
T.F.); G.S.O. 2. *D.S.O. M.C. M* 5. *French
Croix de Guerre*

✠TAYLOR, M. L. 2nd Lieut., Rifle Brigade 1897
Killed in action 26 *Aug.* 1916

TAYLOR, R. E. Lieut., Middlesex Regt.; Staff Capt. 1899
M.C. M.

✠TAYLOR, R. F. 2nd Lieut., King's (Shropshire L.I.) 1907
Killed in action 8 *Aug.* 1915

TAYLOR, S. S. Lieut.-Col., S. African F.A. *C.M.G.* 1894
D.S.O. M 3. *Order of St Stanislas, 3rd Class, with
swords (Russia). French Croix de Guerre*

TEMPLER, W. F. Lieut.-Col., Army Pay Dept.; Com- 1883
mand Paymaster. *C.B.E. M.*

TENNANT, B. V. A. Lieut., Hertfordshire Regt. 1909

TENNANT, N. R. D. Capt., London Regt. (St Pancras 1902
Bn.) (W.)

TETLEY, R. F. Capt., W. Yorks. Regt. (T.F.); empld. 1907
War Office

THACKERAY, J. M. Capt., Suffolk Regt. and Labour 1907
Corps. *O.B.E. M.*

✠THICKNESSE, R. S. 2nd Lieut., Lancs. Fus. 1902
Killed in action 10 *Oct.* 1917

THOMAS, A. G. I. Capt., The Queen's (R. W. Surrey [1914]
Regt., T.F.) (W.)

THOMAS, B. H. Major, R.A.S.C. *O.B.E. M* 2. 1902

THOMAS, E. M. *See* ROCKE, E. M.

THOM-POSTLETHWAITE, A. C. S. 2nd Lieut., Bedford- 1902
shire Regt.

THOMPSON, A. G. G. Major, R.A.M.C. (Sanitary Service, 1908
T.F.) *M.*

THOMPSON, A. H. J. Major, Spec. List empld. War Office. 1898
O.B.E.

THOMPSON, B. C. Major, Lincolnshire Regt.(T.F.Res.) 1895
T.D.

THOMPSON, E. Lieut.-Col., R.E. *O.B.E. M.* 1899

THOMPSON, J. B. London Regt. (W.) 1901

✠THOMPSON, J. C. C. 2nd Lieut., Scots Gds. 1900
Killed in action 25 Jan. 1915
THOMPSON, N. F. P.O., Calcutta Port Artillery, Indian 1902
Defence Force
THOMPSON, R. G. Major, The Queen's (R. W. Surrey 1910
Regt.) (W.)
THOMPSON, W. F. Major, R.A.M.C. 1905
THOMSON, D. G. Capt., R.E. (Fortress, T.F.) 1908
✠THOMSON, S. P. D. Lieut., Leicestershire Yeo. 1907
Killed in action near Ypres 13 May 1915
THOMSON, W. L. H. Lieut., Highland L.I. 1916
THORBURN, M. M. Capt., Black Watch. (W.) *M.C.* 1907
THORMAN, J. L. Lieut., Durham L.I. and R.E.; empld. 1911
British Military Mission
THORNEYCROFT, T. H. Capt., Argyll and Sutherland [1914]
Hdrs.(T.F.) (W.)
THORNTON, A. R. Lieut., R.G.A. *M.* 1895
THYNNE, G. A. C. Major, R. North Devon Yeo.; A.D.C.; 1888
Capt., Labour Corps
TILLARD, E. R. Major, Suffolk Regt.(T.F.) 1892
TILLARD, P. S. Capt., R.F.A.(T.F.) 1894
✠TILLY, J. Capt., Yorkshire Regt. (W 2.) *M.C.* 1905
Died 6 June 1918 of wounds received in action
TINDALL, C. G. Capt., Queen's Own (R.W. Kent Regt.) 1912
(W.) *M.C.*
✠TINDALL, H. S. Lieut., R. Berkshire Regt. 1905
Killed in action 31 July 1917
✠TINDALL, R. F. 2nd Lieut., Lincolnshire Regt. 1909
Killed in action 25 Sept. 1915
TITLEY, Rev. L. G. C.F. 4th Class, R.A.C.D. 1895
TOD, A. K. Pte., R. Scots; Capt., Cameron Hdrs.; attd. 1909
Bedfordshire Regt.
TONGE, R. D. Capt., Cheshire Regt. (W 2.) *M.C.* 1910
TONKIN, R. S. Lieut., E. Yorks. Regt. and 111th Ma- 1911
hars, Indian Army
TOPPING, A. R. Gnr., R.G.A. 1911
TOWNSEND, Rev. J. H. C.F. 4th Class, R.A.C.D. 1898
TOWNSEND, J. M. Midshipman, R.N.V.R. 1917
✠TREE, C. J. Lieut., Worcestershire Regt. 1909
*Died 20 July 1915 of wounds received in action in
Gallipoli*
TRENCH, M. C. Lieut., R.E.; Hon. Lieut. (O.), R.A.F. [1914]
✠TREVOR, F. P. 2nd Lieut., D. of Cornwall's L.I. 1900
Killed in action near Ypres 8 May 1915

TREW, M. F. Capt., Coldstream Gds.   1911
✠TREWBY, A. Lieut., R.E.   1899
   Died 17 May 1915 of wounds received in action
TREWHELLA, C. B. Capt., R.G.A.(T.F.) (W.)   1913
✠TRYON, G. A. Lieut.-Col., King's Royal Rifle Corps.   1905
   (W.) *M.C. M.*
   Killed in action 7 Nov. 1918
✠TUCK, G. B. O. Lieut., Australian Force   1900
   Killed in action 1917
TUNNICLIFFE, G. H. Hon. Major, N. Staffs. Regt. *m.*   1878
TURNER, D. P. R. Fusiliers; 2nd Lieut., Spec. List   1895
TURNLY, J. E. A. L. Capt., R.A.M.C.   1889
TWISLETON-WYKEHAM-FIENNES, N. I. E. Major, R.F.A.   1894
   (W.) *D.S.O. M* 2.
TYERS, F. G. Capt., S. African Infy. (W.)   1899
TYLOR, G. C. Lieut., R.F.A.; Staff Capt. *O.B.E.*   1908
   M.
TYRWHITT-DRAKE, Rev. B. H. C.F. 4th Class, R.A.C.D.   1901

ULOTH, A. W. Major, R.A.M.C. *M.C.*   1908
URE, C. McG. Capt., R.E. (P.)   1911
URQUHART, W. L. A. W. Capt., Black Watch   1893

VALLANCE, H. I. A. Capt., R. East Kent Yeo.   [1914]
VAN DER BYL, A. H. Imperial Light Horse, S. African   1905
   Force
VAN DER BYL, A. M. Capt., H.A.C.; Capt. (K.B. and A.),   1900
   R.A.F.
VAN DER BYL, P. B. Capt., R.H.A. (T.F. Res.)   1886
VAN DER BYL, P. V. G. Capt., S. African Defence Force;   1907
   G.S.O. 3; Capt., S.O. 3, R.A.F. *M.C. M* 2. *Che-*
   valier, Legion of Honour (France)
VAN SOMEREN, H. A. A. Capt., R.F.A. (W.)   1903
✠VARDY, A. T. Pte., Middlesex Regt. (P. S. Bn.); 2nd   1907
   Lieut., R. Warwickshire Regt.
   Killed in action 4 July 1916
VIGO, J. D. Capt., Rifle Brigade and Spec. List (cmdg.   1912
   T.M.B.)
✠VILLAR, R. P. Major, King's (Liverpool Regt.)   1904
   Killed in action 22 March 1918
✠VINCENT, C. A. 2nd Lieut., Rifle Brigade   1913
   Killed in action 13 April 1915
✠VIPOND, H. J. Pte., Coldstream Gds.   1904
   Killed in action Feb. 1917

Vyvyan, E. C. F. Capt., King's Royal Rifle Corps. (W.)   1905

✠Wace, H. E. Capt., King's (Shropshire L.I., T.F.)   1908
Killed in action 14 April 1918
✠Waddy, J. R. Lieut., R.A.M.C. (W.) *M.C. M.*   1906
Killed in action 17 March 1915
Wade, H. B. Capt., W. Somerset Yeo. *M.*   1902
Wadham, W. F. A., v.d. Lieut.-Col., King's Own (R.   1883
Lancaster Regt., T.F. Res.) *m.*
Waggett, E. B. Major, R.A.M.C.(T.F.) *D.S.O. V.D.*   1884
M 3.
Wakelam, H. B. T. Capt., R.F.A. (W.) *M.*   1911
✠Walden-Vincent, A. C. Capt., Dorset Regt.   1908
Killed in action 26 Sept. 1916
Walker, A. Capt., R.A.M.C.   1883
✠Walker, D. Pte., H.A.C.; 2nd Lieut., E. Lancs. Regt.   1907
(T.F.); attd. M.G.C.
Died 19 Sept. 1916 of wounds received in action
✠Walker, M. J. L. 2nd Lieut., Queen's Own (R. W. Kent   1911
Regt.)
Killed in action 3 May 1917
✠Wallis, D. B. Lieut., Connaught Rangers; attd. R. Mun-   1910
ster Fus.
Died 23 July 1917 of wounds received in action
Wallis, G. D. 2nd Lieut., Scots Gds.   1901
Wallis, P. B. Surgeon Lieut.-Cdr., R.N.   1903
✠Wanklyn, K. Lieut., R.F.A.   1911
*Died 15 Nov. 1918 of pneumonia contracted on active
service*
Ward, O. W. Lieut., R. Sussex Regt. and Gen. Staff   1901
Ward, Rev. R. S. C.F. 4th Class, R.A.C.D.   1899
Warden, H. F. W. Capt., R.A.M.C.   1906
Warner, C. Surgeon Lieut., R.N.   1906
Warren, G. M. Capt., Wiltshire Regt.(T.F.)   1911
Warry, H. E. Capt., Devon Regt.; Lieut., 109th Infy.,   [1914]
Indian Army. *M.*
Waters, J. B. Capt., King's Own Scottish Borderers;   1901
Major, Spec. List (School of Instruction)
Watson, A. H. Lieut., Remount Service and Border   1911
Regt. (W.)
Watson, Rev. T. H. C.F. 4th Class, R.A.C.D.   1900
Watson-Scott, C. H. Capt., R.A.S.C. *M.*   1909
✠Waugh, A. J. Capt., R.A.M.C.   1905
Killed in action 17 Aug. 1916

WEBB, J. H. J.   Capt., R.A.S.C.   1892
WEBB, M. E.   Major, R.E. (Signals).   *D.S.O.   M.C.*   1898
   M 3.
WEBB-PEPLOE, Rev. H. M.   C.F. 2nd Class, R.A.C.D.   1889
   O.B.E. M 3.   *Order of St Sava, 4th Class (Serbia)*
WEBER, R. E.   Major, R.F.A.(T.F.)   (W 2.)   *M.C.*   1902
WEDDERBURN, C. C.   Cadet, O.C.B.   1900
WELLS, Rev. E.   C.F. 4th Class, R.A.C.D.   1899
WELLS, J. P.   2nd Lieut., London Univ. O.T.C.   1913
✠WENDEN, G.   Lieut., Border Regt.; Capt. (A.), R.F.C.   1911
   Killed in action 16 *March* 1917
✠WHALE, A.   Lce.-Corpl., R. Fusiliers   1907
   Killed in action 3 *Aug.* 1916
WHALE, G.   Major, S.O. 2, R.A.F.   *m.*   1905
WHEELER, F. O.   Lieut., R.F.A.(T.F.)   1914
WHELPTON, M.   Lieut., Cheshire Regt. and Gen. List,   1912
   attd. R.E., Signals
WHITAKER, F.   Capt., The Buffs (E. Kent Regt.); Major,   1911
   D.A.A.G.   (W.)   *M.C.   M.   French Croix de Guerre*
WHITE, A. E.   Lieut., R.E.   .   [1914]
WHITE, B.   Capt., Highland L.I.; attd. R.F.C. (Balloon   1907
   Officer).   (W.)
WHITE, Rev. R. A. R.   C.F. 3rd Class, R.A.C.D.(T.F.)   1872
WHITELEGGE, M. H.   Capt. (K.B.), R.A.F.   1908
WHITFIELD, Rev. J. O.   Capt., Shrewsbury School O.T.C.   1904
WILKIN, W. H.   Capt., Sherwood Foresters (Notts. and   1895
   Derby Regt.)   (P.)
WILKINSON, H. A.   Lieut., Dorset Yeo.   1910
WILKINSON, K.   Capt. and Adjt., Middlesex Regt.   (W.)   1910
WILLIAMS, E. A.   Capt. and Adjt., E. Surrey Regt.   [1914]
   (T.F.)   (W.)
WILLIAMS, R. B.   Capt., London Regt.   (W.)   1906
WILLIAMS, T. R.   Capt., R. Welsh Fus.   *M.C.   M.*   1909
WILLIAMS, W. C. B.   Major, R. Welsh Fus.   *M.C.   M.*   1904
WILLIAMS, W. E.   Cadet, O.C.B.   1918
✠WILLIAMSON, A. J. N.   2nd Lieut., Seaforth Hdrs.   1907
   Killed in action 14 *Sept.* 1914
WILLIAMSON, J. N.   2nd Lieut., Life Gds.; Lieut., Gds.   1915
   M.G. Regt.
WILLINK, A. H.   Capt., Border Regt. (T.F. Res.)   1878
✠WILSON, A. H.   2nd Lieut., Rifle Brigade   1911
   Killed in action 17 *March* 1915
WILSON, A. L.   Pte., R. Sussex Regt.   1899
WILSON, A. P.   Capt., Border Regt.(T.F.)   (W.)   1908

✠Wilson, E. Sergt., Rand Rifles; Lieut., S. African Infy. 1894
Killed in action 3 *May* 1916
Wilson, G. H. B. Capt., R.A.S.C.; Capt. (A.), R.A.F. 1914
M.C. A.F.C.
Wilson, Rev. G. M. C.F. 4th Class, R.A.C.D. 1899
Wilson, H. B. Major, R.A.M.C. *O.B.E. M* 2. 1902
Wilson, H. W. Lieut., R.N.V.R. 1896
Wilson, J. P. Major (S.), R.A.F. *D.S.C. A.F.C.* 1902
Chevalier, Ordre de la Couronne (Belgium)
Wilson, J. R. M. Capt., R.E. *O.B.E. m.* 1910
Wilson, P. M. Pte., London Regt. (Artists Rifles); 2nd 1909
Lieut., R.G.A. (W.)
Wilson, R. N. P. Lieut., W. Yorks. Regt. (W 2.) 1913
Wilson, R. S. Capt., London Regt. (Surrey Rifles). [1914]
(W 2.)
✠Wilson, T. B. Pte., Middlesex Regt. (P. S. Bn.); 2nd 1911
Lieut., Irish Gds.
Killed in action 18 *July* 1917
Wilson, W. A. Capt., Rifle Brigade; empld. O.C.B. (W.) 1912
Wilson, W. E. Pte., R. Fusiliers 1901
Wimbush, H. G. Lieut., Devon Regt.; Major, M.G.C. 1912
M 2.
✠Winch, E. M. 2nd Lieut., Rifle Brigade 1913
Died 25 *March* 1915 *of wounds received in action*
7 *March* 1915
Wingate-Gray, W.S. Major, R.H.A. (W 3.) *M.C. M* 2. 1909
✠Wink, J. E. 2nd Lieut., Seaforth Hdrs. 1915
Died 21 *Sept.* 1916 *of appendicitis*
Wolffsohn, A. W. Capt., R. Welsh Fus. [1914]
Wood, G. E. C. Capt., Gloucestershire Regt.; Staff Capt. 1912
(W.) *M.C. M.*
Wood, R. McK. Sapper, R.E.; 2nd Lieut., R.A.F. (Tech- 1911
nical Res.)
✠Woodroffe, K. H. C. Lieut., Rifle Brigade. *M.* 1912
Killed in action 9 *May* 1915
✠Woodroffe, W. G. Capt., Middlesex Regt. (T.F.) *French* 1912
Croix de Guerre
Killed in action 16 *Sept.* 1916
Woods, G. C. Lieut., R.G.A. 1904
Woods, Rev. S. C. C.F. 4th Class, R.A.C.D. 1886
✠Woolston, J. H. Lce.-Corpl., S. African Infy. 1893
Died 28 *Oct.* 1918 *of wounds received in action* 10 *Oct.*
1918
Worthington, G. V. Lieut., R.A.M.C. 1887

✠WREFORD, B. W. H.   Capt., Devon Regt.   (W.)   1913
  Killed in action 23 April 1917
WRIGHT, A. G.   Lieut., R.A.S.C.   1913
WRIGHT, A. G. W.   Lieut.-Col., R.F.A.(T.F.)   *T.D.*   1897
WRIGHT, C. C. G.   Capt. and Adjt., Durham L.I.   1906
WRIGHT, J. M. M.   Surgeon Sub-Lieut., R.N.V.R.   1912
✠WRIGHT, W. E. B.   Lieut., King's Own (Yorkshire L.I.)   1913
  Killed in action 22 Sept. 1915
✠WRIGHT-INGLE, C. H.   2nd Lieut., R. Fusiliers; attd.   1903
  Leinster Regt.
  Killed in action 30 April 1916
WROTH, E. C.   Lieut., R. Warwickshire Regt.   (W.)   1902
WYLIE, A.   Capt., R.A.M.C.   (W.)   1895
✠WYLIE, H. M.   Pte., London Regt. (London Scottish);   1913
  2nd Lieut., Seaforth Hdrs.
  Killed in action on the Tigris 7 Jan. 1916
WYNDHAM, J.   Capt., Welsh Regt. (R. of O.); attd. W.   1898
  African Frontier Force

YEATMAN, H. M.   Capt., Wiltshire Regt.; Capt. (A.),   [1914]
  R.A.F.   (W 2.)
YELD, G. G.   2nd Lieut., Labour Corps   1897
YETTS, L. M.   Capt., The Queen's (R.W. Surrey Regt.,   1905
  T.F.); A.P.M.   *M.C.   M.*
YOUNG, G. P.   Lieut., Loyal N. Lancs. Regt.   1916
YOUNG, J. D.   Lieut., R.G.A.(T.F.)   *m.*   1902
✠YOUNG, M. H.   Lieut., Lancs. Fus.(T.F.)   1913
  *Died in German hands 29 June 1916 of wounds received
  in action*
YOUNGHUSBAND, L. N.   Major, R.F.A.   *M.C.   M.*   1912

ZAIMAN, B. A.   Lieut., I.A.R.O., attd. 70th Burma Rifles   1911

PETERHOUSE

ABRAHAM, L. A. Lieut., Gen. List (T.F. Res.); empld. 1913
Ministry of National Service
✠ABRAMS, L. G. Lieut., R.A.S.C. 1902
Died 3 Nov. 1918 of pneumonia
✠ADAMS, E. G. Pte., Cambridgeshire Regt.; 2nd Lieut., 1915
Norfolk Regt. (W.)
Died 26 June 1918 of wounds received in action
ADCOCK, W. R. C. 2nd Lieut., R.E. (Signals); Lieut., 1902
Nigeria Regt., W. African Frontier Force. *m.*
ADSHEAD, A. R. Sergt., Manchester Regt.(T.F.) 1911
ALCOCK, J. H. Lieut., Lincolnshire Regt. (P.) 1913
ALDERSON, M. J. G. Major, R.A.S.C.(T.F.) 1886
ANDREWS, E. A. Trooper, Assam Valley Light Horse, 1908
Indian Defence Force
ANDREWS, J. L. Capt., Hampshire Regt.(T.F.) (W.) 1912
ANSELL, E. 2nd Lieut., King's (Liverpool Regt.) (W.) 1916
ASHTON, A. A. G. Transport Officer, E. African Force 1909
✠ATKINSON, G. H. Lieut. and Adjt., Rattray's Sikhs, Ind- 1909
ian Army. *M.*
Died 1 Feb. 1917 of wounds received in action
AUSTIN, Rev. T. Chaplain, R.N. *1878

BAKER, F. B. Capt., York and Lancaster Regt.; Asst. 1911
Officer i/c R.E. Records. (W.) *M.B.E. m.*
BALES, P. G. Capt., D. of Wellington's (W. Riding Regt., 1906
T.F.) *M.C. M.*
BARKER, Rev. G. D. C.F. 4th Class, R.A.C.D.(T.F.) *1903
✠BEALE, E. Sergt., R. Fusiliers (P. S. Bn.) 1911
Killed in action 2 Jan. 1916
BELL, R. L. Capt., R.A.M.C. *M.* 1890

BELL, Rev. W. G.　C.F. 4th Class, R.A.C.D.(T.F.)　　　*1902
BELL, W. S.　Capt., Lancs. Fus.　　　　　　　　　　1903
BERRY, Rev. B. A.　C.F. 3rd Class, R.A.C.D.(T.F.)　　1889
BEST, R. W. G.　Pte., Army Cyclist Corps; 2nd Lieut.,　1911
　　R.G.A.
BHATIA, S. L.　Lieut., I.M.S.　*M.C.*　　　　　　　　1910
BIRDWOOD, G. T.　Lieut.-Col., I.M.S.　　　　　　　1886
BIRDWOOD, H. B.　Colonel, 27th Light Cavalry, Indian　1889
　　Army; Brig.-Gen.
✠BIRDWOOD, H. F.　2nd Lieut., London Regt. (Blackheath　1913
　　and Woolwich Bn.); Lieut. (A.), R.F.C.
　　Killed in action 2 March 1916
BISHOP, G. S.　2nd Lieut., R.G.A.　　　　　　　　　1898
BLACKIE, A.　Pte., London Regt. (Artists Rifles); Capt.,　1901
　　R.E. (London Electrical Engineers, T.F.)
BLAKENEY, J. E. C.　Major, Essex Regt.; Lieut.-Col.,　1885
　　Gen. Staff.
✠BOARDMAN, T. H.　Major, R. Fusiliers; Lieut.-Col., R.　*1896
　　Inniskilling Fus.　*D.S.O.　M.*
　　Died 5 Aug. 1917 *of wounds received in action*
✠BODINGTON, C. H.　Capt., R. Horse Gds. and Household　1899
　　Bn.
　　Killed in action 11 *April* 1917
BOYLE, G. L.　Capt., Welsh Regt.　(W.)　　　　　　[1914]
BRICKWOOD, H.　Lieut., R.N.V.R.　*m.*　　　　　　　1895
BURNE, S. A. H.　Lieut., King's (Shropshire L.I., T.F.)　1898
BUTTERWORTH, A. B.　Major, R.A.S.C.　*O.B.E.　M.*　1906
　　Greek Medal for Military Merit

CALLIS, M. C.　Capt., R.E.(T.F.)　(W.)　　　　　　1912
CAMP, J.　Instructor Cdr., R.N.　　　　　　　　　　1895
CHAFFER, C.　Instructor Lieut., R.N.　　　　　　　1903
✠CHALMERS, R.　Lieut., London Regt.(Civil Service Rifles).　1911
　　M.
　　Died 25 May 1915 *of wounds received in action*
CLARK, Rev. P. N.　Capt., Spec. List　　　　　　　1888
CLARKE, Rev. F. W.　C.F. 4th Class, R.A.C.D.　　　1896
CLAYTON, Rev. G. H.　C.F. 4th Class, R.A.C.D.　*M.*　*1908
CLEMMOW, C. A.　Lieut., R.G.A.; empld. Ministry of　1907
　　Munitions
CLEMMOW, E. P.　Lieut., R.G.A.; empld. R.E.　　　1908
COLLINS, E. R., D.S.O.　Major, E. Lancs. Regt.　(W.)　1889
　　(P.)
COLMAN, C. J.　Capt., King's (Liverpool Regt.)　(W.)　1911

✠COLSON, A. F. D. Lieut., R.F.A. *M.C.*   1911
   Killed in action 10 *Nov.* 1917
COLVILLE, R. N. K. Lieut., N. Staffs. Regt.; empld. Com- 1901
   mand Depôt
COOPER, L. G. 2nd Lieut., R.A.S.C.(M.T.)   1897
COSGROVE, W. O. Lieut., R.F.A.(T.F.)   1914
COSTELLO, L. W. J. Capt., R.A.S.C.   *1900
CRAIG, N. C., M.P. Lieut.-Cdr., R.N.V.R.   1887
CRANSTON, H. N. Lieut., R.N.V.R. *M.*   1905
CROCOMBE, F. R. Lieut., 76th Punjabis, Indian Army   *1912
CRUICKSHANK, R. S. Capt., R.A.S.C. *O.B.E. M* 3.   1898
CURTIS, I. Instructor Capt., R.N.; empld. R.A.F.   1893

DARBYSHIRE, Rev. H. S. C.F. 4th Class, R.A.C.D. *m.*   1895
DAVIES, V. P. Capt., M.G.C. (W.)   [1914]
✠DAWKINS, C. J. R. 2nd Lieut., Welsh Regt.   1910
   Killed in action 25 *Sept.* 1915
✠DAY, G. R. Lieut., Bedfordshire Regt.(T.F.); Capt. R.   1907
   Warwickshire Regt. (W.)
   Killed in action on the Somme 27 *Aug.* 1916
DE HAHN, C. P. Lieut., Imperial Russian Mtd. Grenadier   1912
   Gds. (W.) *Order of St Anne, with swords* (*Russia*).
   Cross of St Stanislas (*Russia*)
DEIGHTON, F. Lieut.-Col., R.A.M.C.(T.F.)   1873
DENT, G. J. C. Pte., H.A.C.   1897
DREW, Rev. J. A. Lieut., Black Watch (T.F.)   1899
DRY, E. F. K. Lieut., R.N.V.R. (R.N.D.)   1901
DRYSDALE, J. M. Capt. (A.), R.A.F. (W.) *m* 2.   1905
✠DRYSDALE, R. G. 2nd Lieut., R. Warwickshire Regt.   1908
   Died 15 *April* 1915
DU VALLON, G. C. D. DE J. Lieut., R.F.A. (W.)   1897
DYMOND, G. W. Lieut., Cheshire Regt. *M.C.*   1913

EDGINGTON, H. Major, R.A.S.C. *O.B.E. M* 2.   1891
EDWARDS, H. J., C.B., T.D. Hon. Colonel, Unattd. List, *1899
   T.F.; cmdg. O.C.B. *C.B.E. O.B.E. m* 3.
✠ELKINGTON, T. G. Pte., R. Fusiliers (P. S. Bn.); 2nd   1912
   Lieut., Suffolk Regt.
   Died 4 *March* 1916 *of wounds received in action* 3
   March 1916
✠ELLIS, E. W. Pte., R. Fusiliers (P. S. Bn.); Lieut.,   1911
   R.N.V.R. (R.N.D.)
   Killed in action 4 *Feb.* 1917

English, D. A. Capt., London Regt. (Surrey Rifles); 1890
Capt. (T.), R.A.F.
Evans, F. H. F., d.s.o. Major, King's Own (R. Lancaster 1886
Regt.); Adjt., Loyal N. Lancs. Regt. Depôt; empld.
Board of Trade. *O.B.E.*
Evans, T. M. Lieut., R. Defence Corps. (W.) 1898
Exham, R. K. S. Lieut., King's (Shropshire L.I., T.F.) 1913
(W.)

Falkner, A. H. Major, R.A.M.C.(T.F.) (W 2.) *M* 2. 1894
Fisher, A. R. C. Lieut., R.G.A. 1910
Fleming, N. Capt., King's (Liverpool Regt.); attd. E. 1907
Surrey Regt. *M.*
Fletcher, P. Pte., Canadian A.M.C. *1887
✠Formby, T. H. Capt., Cambridgeshire Regt. (W.) 1909
Killed in action 13 Oct. 1916
Franklin, W. Lieut., Dorset Regt.; Lieut. (A.), R.A.F. [1914]
(W 2.)
French, C. H. A. Capt., Lincolnshire Regt.; Major, [1914]
Gen. List (R.E., Signals). (W.) *M.C. M* 2.
Frink, F. C. B. Capt., S. Staffs. Regt. and Labour Corps 1887

Gaskin, E. A. L. Lieut., Spec. List (R.T.O.) [1914]
Gavin, A. G. D. 2nd Lieut., Black Watch; attd. R.F.C. 1911
(Balloon Section). *M.C.*
Gibb, J. H. O. Lieut., attd. 4th (R. Irish) Dragoon Gds. 1910
(W.)
Giles, L. T. Capt., R.A.M.C. 1887
Gilham, C. W. Corpl., R.E.; 2nd Lieut., R.G.A. (W 2.) 1910
Green, J. E. S. Capt., Rifle Brigade. (W 2.) 1905
Green, R. G. 2nd Lieut., M.G.C. 1917
Greenwood, J. Lieut., S. Lancs. Regt. and Spec. List 1905
(Loyal N. Lancs. Regt. Depôt). (W 2.)
Greenwood, O. Lieut., Yorkshire Regt. (W.) (P.) 1908
Griffin, E. H. Capt., R.A.M.C. (W 4.) (P.) *D.S.O.* 1895
M.C. and Bar. M 3.
Gundry, Rev. R. H. C.F. 3rd Class, R.A.C.D.(T.F.) *1887
Gurney, J. C. Capt., Northamptonshire Regt.; G.S.O. 3. 1912
O.B.E. M 2. *Belgian Croix de Guerre*
Guy, P. C. Lieut., Worcestershire Regt.; Capt., Spec. 1899
List, empld. Ministry of National Service

✠Hamilton, C. F. P. Capt., Scots Gds. *M.* 1898
Died 27 Oct. 1914 of wounds received in action

HAPPOLD, F. C. Lieut., Loyal N. Lancs. Regt.; Capt., 1912
 Gen. List (School of Instruction). (W.) *D.S.O. M.*
HARGROVE, C. R. Capt., R.A.S.C. 1900
HART, Rev. P. H. Sergt., R.G.A. *1908
✠HARTLEY, W. J. Capt., R. Irish Fus. 1907
 Killed in action in Gallipoli 16 *Aug.* 1915
✠HEATLEY, L. Capt., King's (Liverpool Regt.) (W.) 1911
 Died 17 *Aug.* 1917 *of wounds received in action*
✠HENDERSON, W. L. 2nd Lieut., Northumberland Fus.; 1902
 Capt., W. Yorks. Regt. (W.) *M.*
 Died 3 *May* 1916 *of wounds received in action* 3 *April*
 1916
HENMAN, W. W. Lce.-Corpl., Military Police 1898
HILL, V. ST C. Capt., M.G.C. *M.C. M.* 1913
HODGETTS, W. J. Driver, H.A.C. 1917
HOLMAN, B. W. Trooper, Otago Mtd. Rifles, N. Zealand 1895
 Force; Pte., N. Zealand Ordnance Corps; Capt.,
 Labour Corps; attd. R.A.O.C.
HONEYBURNE, W. R. Capt., R.A.M.C. 1896
HOUSDEN, E. F. Major, R.F.A. (W.) *M.C.* 1911
HOUSDEN, E. J. T. Major, R.F.A. (W 2.) *M.C. M* 4. 1907
HUGHES, H. C. Lieut., R.F.A.(T.F.) (W.) 1911
HURST, E. E. 2nd Lieut., Northamptonshire Regt. *M.* 1908
HYDE, G. A. 2nd Lieut., King's Royal Rifle Corps; Capt. 1913
 (A.), R.A.F. *M.C.*
HYLTON STEWART, B. D. Lieut., Haileybury College 1910
 O.T.C.

JEFFCOCK, W. P. Capt., Yorkshire Dragoons (T.F. Res.) 1887
JERVOIS, R. C. W. 2nd Lieut., R.G.A.; Lieut. (O.), 1915
 R.A.F.
JONES, W. H. *See* MACNAUGHTEN-JONES, Rev. W. H.

KAUFMANN, H. P. Lieut., Norfolk Regt.(T.F.); attd. 1911
 Gloucestershire Regt. (W.)
KEIGWIN, A. L. Capt., Lancs. Fus. (W.) 1908
✠KEIGWIN, H. D. 2nd Lieut., Lancs. Fus. 1900
 Killed in action 20 *Sept.* 1916
KEIGWIN, R. P. Lieut., R.N.V.R. *Chevalier, Order of* 1902
 Leopold (*Belgium*)
KENRICK, C. H. W. 2nd Lieut., The Buffs (E. Kent Regt.) 1914
✠KERSHAW, M. 2nd Lieut., Gloucestershire Regt. 1905
 Killed in action 7 *Nov.* 1914
KITSON, Rev. B. M. C.F. 4th Class, R.A.C.D. 1905

LAURIE, M., M.V.O. Capt., R.G.A.(T.F.); empld. War 1887
Office

✠LAWSON, H. S. Lieut., R.F.A.(T.F.) 1895
Killed in action 5 Feb. 1918

✠LEIGH, B. H. 2nd Lieut., R. Berkshire Regt. 1908
Killed in action 18 Aug. 1917

LEWIS, V. Lieut , R.F.A. 1913

LIAS, E. T. M. Sapper, R.E. 1911

LIDDLE, G. E. Capt., K. Alfred's School, Wantage, 1904
O.T.C.

LIGHTFOOT, B. Major, R.E. *M.C. M.* 1906

LILLIE, W. H. 2nd Lieut., United States Air Service 1913

LINDSAY, R. L. G. Lieut., R.E. (Signals) 1913

✠LIVINGSTONE, F. D. Capt., R.A.S.C. 1904
Died 22 March 1918 *of wounds received in action*

LLOYD, G. W. D. B. Major, R. Welsh Fus.; empld. 1885
Ministry of National Service. *O.B.E.*

LLOYD, K. Capt., London Regt. (Q.V.R.); empld. O.C.B. 1913
(W.)

✠LLOYD, R. A. 2nd Lieut., King's (Liverpool Regt.) 1913
Killed in action near Ypres 27 April 1915

LLOYD, Rev. W. R. Lieut., Haileybury College O.T.C. *1907

LONG, F. W. C. Sapper, R.E. (Signals). (W.) 1914

✠LORD, C. E. Major, S. Staffs. Regt. 1887
Died 23 June 1915 *of wounds received in action*

LÖWY, A. E. Flt. Sub-Lieut., R.N.A.S. 1907

LUTTMAN, R. L. Sub-Lieut., R.N.V.R. 1894

McBAIN, W. R. B. Lieut., R.F.A.(T.F.); Major (A.), 1910
R.A.F. *M.C. A.F.C. M* 3. *French Croix de Guerre*

McCARTHY, Rev. J. D. Chaplain, R.N. 1894

McCARTHY, J. M. Lieut.-Col., R.A.M.C. 1891

McKEOWN, W. W. Lieut., R.F.A. *M.C.* 1914

MACLEAN, J. E. B. B. Major (S.), R.A.F. (W.) *D.S.C.* 1913
M 2.

MACNAMARA, E. D. Capt., R.A.M.C. 1887

MACNAUGHTEN-JONES, Rev. W. H. C.F. 4th Class, 1888
R.A.C.D.(T.F.)

MANSER, F. B. Major, R.A.M.C. 1894

MARCHANT, T. H. S. Major, 13th Hussars; Brig.-Gen. 1893
D.S.O. M 3.

MARILLIER, H. C. Lieut., R.N.V.R. 1884

MARLEY, A. E. Lieut., Spec. List (Interpreter) *1914

MARRIOTT, G. E. J. Capt., Lancs. Fus.(T.F.) 1907

MARSHALL, F. W. D. Pte., R.A.M.C. 1908
MARSHALL, P. T. Capt., R.A.S.C. 1898
✠MARTIN, T. 2nd Lieut., The Queen's(R.W.Surrey Regt.) 1904
Killed in action 7 June 1917
MARTYN, R. F. Lieut., R.A.S.C. *M.* 1912
MASON, A. S. Major, Devon Regt.(T.F.); D.A.Q.M.G. [1914]
(W.)
MASON,R. F. Capt., R.F.A.; Staff Capt. (W.) *M.C. M.* 1913
MAY, Rev. C. J. C.F. 4th Class, R.A.C.D. 1906
MAYNARD, C. B. Lieut., S. Lancs. Regt. (W.) 1910
MEADOWS, R. Capt., R. Warwickshire Regt.; attd. King's 1914
Own (Yorkshire L.I.) (W.)
MIDDLETON, H. S. Lieut., Suffolk Regt.(T.F.) 1913
MILLER, A. G. S. Capt. and Adjt., Fife and Forfar Yeo. 1909
MILNER, P. R. Capt., Leicestershire Regt. (W 2.) *M.C.* 1911
and Bar
✠MOND, F. L. Lieut., R.F.A.(T.F.); Staff Lieut.; Lieut. *1914
(A.), R.A.F.
Killed in action at Bouzencourt 15 *May* 1918
MORGANS, G. E. Lieut.-Col., R.E. *O.B.E. m.* 1901
MORRIS, P. E. 2nd Lieut., R.A.S.C. 1899
MURRAY, E. Lieut.-Col., King's Royal Rifle Corps and 1904
Gen. List (Staff Lieut.) (W.)

NEVILLE, M. R. Lieut., R.G.A. *M.C.* 1913
NORTH, J. B. 2nd Lieut., 2nd Dragoons (R. Scots Greys) 1915
and Labour Corps
NORTHFIELD, H. D. Pte., R. Scots 1915
NORTON, L. M. Capt., R.G.A.(T.F.) *1908

OAKDEN, W. M. Capt., R.A.M.C. 1906
¹OON ISRASENA, M. L. Interpreter, Siamese Exp. Force 1914

PACKARD, H. N. Capt., Spec. List (O.C.B.) 1914
PARISH, A. J., C.B. Instructor Cdr., R.N.; Dep. Adviser 1881
on Education. *C.B.E.*
PARISH, Rev. W. O., T.D. C.F. 1st Class, R.A.C.D.(T.F.) 1878
PARKINSON, W. Lieut., R.E. (Signals). *M.C. M.* 1906
PAYNE, F. R. Lieut., R.A.S.C. *M.* 1899
PEARCE, Ven. E. H., T.D. C.F. 1st Class, R.A.C.D.; 1884
A.C.G. *C.B.E.*
PERRIN, E. C. Capt., Cheshire Regt.(T.F.); Major, 1905
S.O. 2, R.A.F. *O.B.E.*

---

¹ Accidentally killed on service after the armistice.

PHILLIPSON, E. Sergt., R.A.M.C.; 2nd Lieut., Lancs. 1911
Fus.(T.F.)
PINFOLD, E. S. Pte., Upper Burma Bn., Indian Defence 1907
Force
PLASKITT, G. M. Lieut., Middlesex Regt. 1913
✠PUCKLE, J., D.S.O. Lieut.-Col., R.A.S.C. *M.* 1889
Drowned on H.M. transport 15 *April* 1917

RAWLINS, F. H. Major, R.E. 1880
READ, E. Capt., R.F.A.(T.F.) *Belgian Croix de Guerre* [1914]
REYNOLDS, H. E. K. 2nd Lieut., York and Lancaster 1913
Regt.
RHODES, W. E. Lieut., R.E. (W.) 1912
RITCHIE, A. G. Capt., R.E. (Signals). *M* 2. 1911
✠ROBINSON, J. C. C. H. Capt., E. Lancs. Regt.(T.F.) 1906
Killed in action 3 *June* 1917
✠ROBINSON, W. DE H. Pte., R. Fusiliers (P.S. Bn.); Capt., 1907
Border Regt. (W 2.) *M.C.*
Killed in action 27 *Jan.* 1917
ROTTNER-SMITH, R. Cadet, O.C.B. 1917
ROUTH, A. L. Major, R.G.A. 1896
ROUTH, H. V. Capt., R.F.A. *M.* 1897
RYFFEL, J. H. Capt., R.A.M.C.(T.F.) 1896

✠SANDERSON, C. O. ST J. Lieut., R.E. (Signals). *M.C.* 1910
Killed in action 27 *April* 1918
SCOTT, G. M. Capt., R.A.M.C.; Lieut.-Col., N. Zealand *1884
Med. Service
✠SCRACE, J. Lieut., The Buffs (E. Kent Regt.); Lieut. (A.), 1911
R.A.F.
Killed in flying accident 24 *Aug.* 1918
SEALY, P. T. Major, R.A.S.C. *O.B.E.* *M.* 1907
SEALY, W. H. Capt., R.A.S.C. *M.* 1912
✠SEWELL, H. V. 2nd Lieut., R.F.A. 1907
Killed in action 13 *Nov.* 1916
✠SHIPLEY, A. H. B. Pte., R. Fusiliers (P. S. Bn.); 2nd [1914]
Lieut., Yorkshire Regt.
Killed in action 27 *Sept.* 1916
SMITH, Rev. E. F. H. Chaplain and Instructor Cdr., 1894
R.N.
SMITH, J. Y. Pte., R.A.S.C.(M.T.) 1913
SPRING, A. Lieut. (T.), R.A.F. (Aircraft Production 1906
Dept.)
SPRINGFIELD, C. O. Capt., R.E. 1888

✠SPROTT, M. W. C. Capt. and Adjt., Norfolk Regt. (W.) 1906
 M.C. M.
 Killed in action 21 *March* 1918
✠SPROXTON, C. Capt., Yorkshire Regt.(T.F.) (W 2.) 1909
 M.C. M.
 Killed in action 19 *July* 1917
STACKHOUSE, J. H. Lieut., Sherwood Foresters (Notts. 1908
 and Derby Regt.); Capt., R.A.S.C. (W.)
STEPHEN, L. P. Lieut., R.A.S.C. 1890
STEWART, A. C. Capt., Welsh Regt. and R.E. (Field 1911
 Survey Coy.)
STIMSON, J. P. Sub-Lieut., R.N.V.R.(R.N.D.) (W.) 1909
STONEHAM, R. T. Corpl., Rangoon Bn., Indian Defence 1906
 Force

TAIT, J. G. Lieut.-Col., Bangalore Rifle Vols. 1880
✠TAYLOR, C. T. Lieut., 18th Hussars 1909
 Killed in action 24 *Aug.* 1914
✠TAYLOR, F. Major, York and Lancaster Regt. 1874
 Killed in action 13 *March* 1916
TEBB, B. M. 2nd Lieut., Suffolk Regt. 1917
TEBB, R. N. S. Capt., Spec. List (O.C.B.) and Hamp- 1913
 shire Regt.
TEMPERLEY, H.W.V. Capt., Fife and Forfar Yeo.; Major, *1904
 G.S.O. 2; Asst. Military Attaché, Belgrade. O.B.E.
 m 2. *Officer, Order of the Crown of Roumania, with*
 swords. Order of the White Eagle, 5th Class, with
 swords (Serbia)
TEMPLE, R. J. G. Trooper, Dorset Yeo.; Lieut., R.G.A.; 1913
 Capt. (T.), R.A.F.; Instructor, School of Aeronautics,
 Toronto
THOMAS, K. G. Capt., E. Lancs. Regt.(T.F.); attd. Man- 1907
 chester Regt. M.
✠TINDALL, J. H. Gnr., R.G.A. 1908
 Died 15 *Feb.* 1917 *of malaria*
✠TISDALL, J. T. ST C. 2nd Lieut., King's (Liverpool 1913
 Regt.) (W.)
 Killed in action 8 *Aug.* 1916
TOMSON, D.V. Lieut., R.F.A.(T.F.) (W.) M.C. and Bar 1902

UTTING, H. A. Lieut., R.F.A.(T.F.) 1914

VELLACOTT, P. C. Major, S. Lancs. Regt. and Gen. List 1910
 (Brigade Major). (W.) (P.) D.S.O. M 2.

✠WAKERLEY, A. J. Capt., Leicestershire Regt.(T.F.)   1914
　Killed in action 8 June 1917
WALKER, E. M. Lieut., I.A.R.O., attd. S. and T. Corps. 1912
WALTER, H. C. A.B., R.N.V.R.   1911
WATSON, G. T. Lieut., R.A.M.C.   1890
WATTS, N. H. Major, Sherwood Foresters (Notts. and 1904
　Derby Regt.); empld. O.C.B.
WEIR, N. Lieut., Gloucestershire Regt. (W.)   1908
WHITEHEAD, E. T. Capt., Yorkshire Hussars; G.S.O. 3, 1892
　War Office
WHITEHOUSE, H. E. Lieut., R.G.A. *M.C.*   1915
WHITTAKER, Rev. G. Chaplain, R.N.   1908
WILLEY, B. Lieut., W. Yorks. Regt. (P.)   1916
WILLIAMS, Rev. A. J. C.F. 4th Class, R.A.C.D.   1893
WILLIAMS, G. V. Capt., Loyal N. Lancs. Regt.(T.F.)   1912
WILLIAMS, Rev. R. C. L. C.F. 1st Class, R.A.C.D.; 1900
　A.C.G. *D.S.O. M* 2.
WILLIAMS, T. Capt., Welsh Regt.; Major, D.A.D. Docks *1905
WILLIS, R. E. B. Lieut., R. Warwickshire Regt.   [1914]
WILSON, T. M. Capt. (T.), R.A.F.   1912
WISEMAN, C. L. Instructor Lieut., R.N.   1912
✠WOOD, H. G. W. Capt., Worcestershire Regt.(T.F.)   1909
　(W.) *D.S.O. M* 2.
　Killed in action 3 Aug. 1918
✠WOOD, T. P. Lieut., I.A.R.O., attd. Gurkha Rifles   1901
　Killed in action 25 Sept. 1915

YELD, P. H. Capt., Spec. List (R.T.O.)   1903

QUEENS' COLLEGE

✠ADAM, H. W. Lieut. (A.), R.A.F.   1915
  Killed in flying accident 4 July 1918
✠ADAMS, L. H. Lieut., Rifle Brigade   1906
  Killed in action 22 April 1918
AITCHISON, G. C. Lieut.-Col., Sherwood Foresters   1881
  (Notts. and Derby Regt.) *m.*
AMBROSE, W. J. L. Lieut., Res. Regt. of Cavalry and   1897
  Nigeria Regt.,W.African Frontier Force. (W.) *Chev-*
  alier, Ordre de l'Etoile Noire (France)
ANDREWS, Rev. L. M. C.F. 4th Class, R.A.C.D. (W.)   1906
  M.C.
ANTHONY, H. D. Lieut., Loyal N. Lancs. Regt. and   1911
  R.E. (Sound-ranging Section)
✠ARDEN, H. W. 2nd Lieut., R.G.A.   1911
  Died 6 June 1917 of wounds received in action
ATKINSON, R. H. Lieut., Durham L.I.; Capt., R.E.   1909
  (Spec. Bde.); empld. Ministry of Munitions. (W.) *m.*
AUSTIN, Rev. H. W. C.F. 4th Class, R.A.C.D. *M.*   1910

✠BAILEY, W. G. W. Capt., Hampshire Regt.   1914
  Killed in action 15 Sept. 1916
BALL, A. E. Lieut., Middlesex Regt.(T.F.) (W.)   1909
✠BARKER, Rev. E. W. C.F. 4th Class, R.A.C.D.   1907
  Died 18 March 1918 of wounds received in action 9
  March 1918
BARKER, H. A. K. Capt., Loyal N. Lancs. Regt. (W.)   1911
✠BARLTROP, E. A. Lieut., R.E.(T.F.); attd. R.F.C.   1909
  Killed in action 23 April 1917
BARLTROP, I. C. Major, R.E.(T.F.)   1911
BARTON, J. F. Trooper, Calcutta Light Horse, Indian   1904
  Defence Force

BENTLEY, R. C.   Lieut., Yorkshire Regt.   (W 2.) (P.)   1910
BENTLEY, W. W.   Major, R.G.A.(T.F.) (W.)   1903
BEST, Rev. J. K.   C.F. 4th Class, R.A.C.D.(T.F.) *M.C.*   1907
M.
BEST, O. H.   Lieut., R.E. (Signals)   1912
BEVERLEY, R.   Capt. and Adjt., R.F.A.(T.F.)   1908
BIGGER ,W. G.   Surgeon Lieut., R.N.   *D.S.C.   Order*   1907
of St Anne, 3rd Class (Russia). Belgian Croix de Guerre
✠BINKS, B. H.   2nd Lieut., King's Own (R. Lancaster Regt.)   1906
Killed in action 23 Oct. 1916
BLACK, L. L. D.   Lieut., R.G.A.   1896
BLACKDEN, S. C.   2nd Lieut., Oxfordshire Yeo.   1910
BLACKER, H. A. C.   Capt., I.A.R.O., attd. 3rd Punjab   1908
Rifles; Asst. Recruiting Officer
BLACKWALL, Rev. W. A.   C.F. 4th Class, R.A.C.D.   1899
BLEE, E. L.   Lieut., York and Lancaster Regt.; attd.   1914
Manchester Regt.; empld. Ministry of Munitions.
(W.)
✠BONE, H.   Corpl., R.E. (Spec. Bde.) *D.C.M.*   1915
Died 30 Aug. 1917 of gas poisoning caused by an ex-
plosion
BOSWELL, P. R.   Capt., R.A.M.C. (W.) *M.C.*   1908
✠BOTWOOD, Rev. E. K.   C.F. 4th Class, R.A.C.D.(T.F.)   *1892
Died 28 July 1916 of illness contracted on active service
BOUMPHREY, D.   Lieut., King's (Shropshire L.I.); Major,   1912
M.G.C. *M.C. M.*
BOURCHIER, Rev. B. G.   C.F. 4th Class, R.A.C.D.(T.F.)   1890
BRAILEY, W. H.   Major, R.A.M.C. (2nd E. Gen. Hos-   1893
pital, T.F.)
BRISCOE, F. E.   Major, Yorkshire Regt.; attd. Norfolk   1912
Regt.(T.F.) *D.S.O. M.*
BROADBENT, H. G.   2nd Lieut., St Bees School O.T.C.   1911
✠BRODIE, M. M.   2nd Lieut., London Regt. (London   [1914
Scottish); attd. Seaforth Hdrs.
Killed in action 7 Jan. 1916
BROWNE, A. D.   Capt., R.G.A.   1908
✠BUCKLEY, E. J. K.   Flt. Sub-Lieut., R.N.A.S. *Belgian*   1912
Croix de Guerre
Killed in flying accident 28 Sept. 1917
BUDGETT, S. G.   Lieut., King's (Shropshire L.I.); Lieut.   [1914
(A.), R.A.F. (W.)
BULL, G. G. C.   2nd Lieut., R.E.(T.F.); Lieut., Bedford-   [1914
shire Regt.; attd. 98th Infy., Indian Army
BULLARD, R. W.   Capt., Spec. List. *C.I.E.*   1901

QUEENS' COLLEGE 293

Burton, G. D. Capt., R.E. *M* 2. 1912
Bussey, A. Corpl., Suffolk Yeo. 1913
Butcher, T. A. 2nd Lieut., King's Royal Rifle Corps; 1912
Capt., R.A.M.C. (W 2.) *O.B.E. M.*
Butler, W. G. 2nd Lieut., Christ's Hospital O.T.C. 1905

✠Callinan, T. W. 2nd Lieut., Durham L.I.(T.F.) 1902
Killed in action near Ypres 25 April 1915
Carnley, W. B. 2nd Lieut., R.A.O.C.; Capt. (T.), 1903
R.A.F. *M.C.*
✠Carr, D. N. 2nd Lieut., R. Fusiliers; Capt., S. Persian 1913
Rifles
*Died 26 Nov. 1918 of pneumonia contracted on active
service*
Case, H. A. Lieut.-Col., Dorset Regt. (W.) *C.M.G.* 1898
D.S.O. Brevet Lieut.-Colonel. M 3.
Cassels, W. C. Capt., Worcestershire Regt. (W2.) *M.C.* 1913
✠Catmur, H. A. F. V. Pte., R. Fusiliers (P. S. Bn.); Lieut., 1911
R. Sussex Regt.; attd. M.G.C. *M.*
Killed in action 1 July 1916
Challenor, B. H. Capt., Lincolnshire Regt.(T.F.) (P.) 1913
Champion, Rev. A. C. C.F. 4th Class, R.A.C.D. 1908
Chandler, H. E. Capt., The Queen's (R. W. Surrey 1912
Regt.); Staff Capt., War Office. (W.) *M.B.E. m* 2.
Chevalier, Ordre de la Couronne (Belgium)
Channing, C. E. Lieut., R.A.S.C.(T.F.); Lieut. (O.), 1914
R.A.F. *A.F.C.*
Chase, Rev. G. A. C.F. 4th Class, R.A.C.D. *M.C.* 1905
Clarke, C. M. S. Corpl., R.A.M.C. 1914
Clayton, N. W. Capt., M.G.C. and Gen. List, attd. 1897
Indian Political Dept. *M.C. M.B.E. M* 2.
Clear-Davidson, F. R. 2nd Lieut., R.G.A. 1911
Cleworth, Rev. T. H. C.F. 4th Class, R.A.C.D. *M.C.* 1906
Coast, J. P. C. Lieut., R. Warwickshire Regt.; Capt., 1901
The Queen's (R. W. Surrey Regt.)
✠Coates, B. M. 2nd Lieut., Rifle Brigade 1912
Killed in action 7 Sept. 1915
✠Cohen, E. 2nd Lieut., R. Fusiliers. *M.C.* 1914
Killed in action 31 July 1917
✠Cohen, J. I. Lieut., E. Lancs. Regt.; Capt., Labour Corps 1911
Died 24 Aug. 1917 of wounds received in action
Colchester, G. V. Capt., R.E. (W.) *M.C.* *1908
Colenutt, F. A. Lieut., Spec. List (Interpreter) 1906
Collins, B. S. 2nd Lieut., Herefordshire Regt. [1914]

COLLIS, F. S. 2nd Lieut., W. Kent Yeo.; attd. Corps of   1914
Guides, Indian Army
CONDER, A. C. Lieut., Black Watch (T.F.) (W.)   1911
COOKE, Rev. H. R. C.F. 4th Class, R.A.C.D. (W.)   1904
M.C. M 2.
COOKSON, R. T. C. Pte., London Regt. (Artists Rifles);   1894
Lieut., R.F.A.(T.F.)
COPE, H. E. Cadet, O.C.B.   1913
CORTAZZI, F. E. M. Major, R. Scots. (W.)   1909
COTTON, H. W. S. Capt., Cheshire Regt. (W.) *M.*   1913
COUCH, C. J. 2nd Lieut., M.G.C. and Tank Corps; Capt.,   1912
Cheshire Regt
COUCHMAN, Rev. M. L. C.F. 4th Class, R.A.C.D.   1910
✠COULTAS, T. B. Lieut., E. Yorks. Regt. (W.)   1912
Killed in action on the Somme 26 *Sept.* 1916
COWELL, S. J. Capt., R.A.M.C. (W.)   1909
CRAIGS, W. N. Capt., Northumberland Fus.(T.F.) (W2.)   1910
M.C.
CROW, A. D. Capt., E. Surrey Regt.; Director of Ball-   1913
istics, Woolwich Arsenal. (W.) *m.*
CROZIER, Rev. P. H. C.F. 3rd Class, R.A.C.D. *M.*   1892
CRUMP, G. H. Capt. and Adjt., Essex Regt.   1909
CULLEN, Rev. A. H. C.F. 4th Class, R.A.C.D.   1912
CULVERWELL, C. T. Lieut., R.A.S.C.(M.T.)   1913
CURRYER, W. H. S. Lieut., R.F.A.(T.F.) (W.)   1913
CURTOIS, P. A. Lieut., Suffolk Regt.; attd. The Queen's   1911
(R.W. Surrey Regt.) (W 2.)

✠DALLEY, J. P. 2nd Lieut., I.A.R.O.; attd. R.F.C.   1911
Killed in action 9 *Nov.* 1917
DALTROFF, E. M. 2nd Lieut., R. Fusiliers; empld. War   1909
Office
DAVIDSON, G. S. Lieut., I.A.R.O., attd. S. and T. Corps   1901
DAVIES, D. H. S. 2nd Lieut., S. Wales Borderers; Lieut.,   1914
R. Warwickshire Regt.; Capt. (A.), R.A.F. (W.)
DENYER, S. E., C.M.G. Capt., R.A.M.C. *m* 2.   1891
DEVEY, J. H. J. C. Lieut., Monmouthshire Regt.; Capt.,   1914
Tank Corps. (W.)
DEWÉ, C. D. E. Lieut., Gloucestershire Regt. (W.)   1898
✠DICK, J. McN. Pte., Cameron Hdrs. and M.G.C.   1915
Died 2 *Oct.* 1918 *of wounds received in action* 1 *Oct.* 1918
DICKSON, Rev. R. J. C.F. 4th Class, R.A.C.D.   1896
DIXON, H. J. Capt. and Adjt., R. Warwickshire Regt.   1914
M.C

DODSON, C. S.   Capt., R.A.M.C.   *M.*   1908
✠DOGGETT, G. P.   Corpl., Cambridgeshire Regt.; 2nd [1914]
    Lieut., D. of Wellington's (W. Riding Regt.); attd.
    T.M.B. *M.*
    Died 4 July 1917 of wounds received in action 7 June
    1917
DOWN, R. A.   Capt., E. Surrey Regt.   1914
DREYFUS, B. E.   Lieut., I.A.R.O., attd. 32nd Lancers   1911
DUFFIELD, C. A. W.   Lieut., Queen's Own (R. W. Kent   1906
    Regt.) *M.C.*
DUKE-BAKER, C. A.   Lieut., R.G.A.(T.F.); Staff Capt. *M.*   1911
✠DUNCAN, J. F.   Capt. and Adjt., Cameronians (Scottish   1913
    Rifles). *M.*
    Killed in action 25 Sept. 1915
DURRANT, C. E.   Capt., Norfolk Regt.(T.F.)   1907
DYSON, W. L.   Capt. and Adjt., Border Regt.   1911

✠EADIE, R. A.   2nd Lieut., Lincolnshire Regt.   1912
    Killed in action 6 Aug. 1916
✠EAGLE, G. C.   2nd Lieut., Suffolk Regt. (W.)   [1914]
    Killed in action 12 Oct. 1916
EATHERLEY, W.   Capt., R.G.A.   *O.B.E.* *M.* *Italian*   1900
    Croce di Guerra
EDWARDS, F.M.   Lieut., Egyptian Camel Transport Corps   1904
EDWARDS, Rev. J. L. A.   C.F. 4th Class, R.A.C.D. (W.)   1908
    (P.)
EDWARDS, R. G.   2nd Lieut., Somerset L.I.; Major, Re-   1910
    mount Service
ELEY, H. J.   Lieut., Sherwood Foresters (Notts.and Derby   1913
    Regt.) (W.)
ELLISON, A. D.   Trooper, K. Edward's Horse; Capt.,   1912
    R.F.A. (W.) *M.C.*
ELLISON, H. S.   Trooper, K. Edward's Horse; Major,   1914
    R.F.A. (W 3.) *M.C.* *M.* *French Croix de Guerre*
EMTAGE, W. L.   2nd Lieut., Middlesex Regt.; Lieut.,   1911
    British W. Indies Regt.
EVANS, A. LL.   Capt., Monmouthshire Regt.; Lieut., 9th   1910
    Bhopal Infy., Indian Army. (W 2.) *M.*
EVANS, G. S. W.   Lieut., S. Wales Borderers. *M.*   1915
EVANS, H. G. Lieut., R.A.S.C.; attd. Rifle Brigade. (W.)   1912
EVELYN-WHITE, Rev. K. V.   C.F. 4th Class, R.A.C.D.   1905
EWBANK, A. L. J.   Capt., R. Dublin Fus. and Gen. Staff   1910
    (O.C.B.)
EWING, A. G.   2nd Lieut., K. Edward's Horse   1912

FAILES, Rev. B. J. Chaplain, R.N. *M* 2. 1906
FALLOON, Rev. W. M. C.F. 4th Class, R.A.C.D. *M.* 1891
FARNFIELD, A. J. Capt., King's Royal Rifle Corps 1900
FARNFIELD, Rev. H. V. C.F. 4th Class, R.A.C.D. 1904
FARNFIELD, P. H. Lieut., Sidcup Hall School O.T.C. 1908
✠FARRAR, H. R. 2nd Lieut., Leicestershire Regt.; attd. 1906
Manchester Regt.
Killed in action 24 Dec. 1914
FAWKES, R. B. Capt., Northamptonshire Regt. (W 2.) 1913
D.S.O. M.C. M.
✠FEARNLEY-WHITTINGSTALL, G. H. 2nd Lieut., R.A.S.C.; 1910
Lieut., Northumberland Fus. (W.)
Killed in action 3 Aug. 1916
FENTON, V. N. Pte., R.A.M.C.(1st E. Gen. Hospital, T.F.) 1914
✠FENWICK, M. E. E. 2nd Lieut., Devon Regt. 1913
Killed in action 2 April 1917
FERGUSON, M. G. Lieut., R.G.A. 1907
FERGUSON, W. H. Major, R.A.M.C. (W.) *M.C. and* 1909
Bar. M.
FIELD, H. T. C. Capt., Oxford and Bucks. L.I. (W.) *M.* 1909
FINCH, E. G. Major, King's (Liverpool Regt., T.F. Res.); 1889
empld. Records
FISON, C. H. Lieut., The Queen's (R.W. Surrey Regt.) [1914]
(W.)
FORD, J. C. Pte., H.A.C. 1914
FRY, D. G. Pte., London Regt.; Lieut., Gloucestershire 1898
Regt.; Capt., Spec. List (Education Officer). *M.B.E.*

GALLOWAY, W. Lieut., King's Own Scottish Borderers 1904
(T.F.) (W.)
GARDNER, F. W. Major (T.), R.A.F. 1909
GARDNER, H. W. Q.M.S., Suffolk Regt. 1912
GARDNER, Rev. R. L. C.F. 4th Class, R.A.C.D. 1904
✠GARRETT, H. F. Lieut. and Adjt., E. Yorks. Regt. 1913
Killed in action 4 June 1915
GARROD, W. E. E. Capt., Yorkshire Regt.(T.F.); attd. 1912
King's Own (Yorkshire L.I.) (W.) *M.C. and Bar*
✠GEARE, Rev. W. D. C.F. 4th Class, R.A.C.D. 1909
Killed in action in the Third Battle of Ypres 31 July
1917
GENTLE, F. W. Lieut., Life Gds. and Gds. M.G. Regt. 1912
GIBBS, W. J. R. Capt. and Adjt., R.A.S.C. *M.* *1904
GIBSON, S. R. Pte., London Regt. (Artists Rifles); ·1909
Lieut., R.G.A. (W.)

GLOVER, J. G.   Lieut., King's (Liverpool Regt.); attd.   1911
Cheshire Regt. (W.)

GODDARD, E. T.   Capt., R.E. (Signals).   *M.C.*   1914

GOOD, C. W.   Capt. and Adjt., Sherwood Foresters   1911
(Notts. and Derby Regt.)   *M.*

GOODWYN, P. W.   Pte., Cameronians (Scottish Rifles).   1911
(W.) (P.)

✠GRACE, H. C.   Pte., R. Fusiliers (P. S. Bn.); Capt., Nor-   1910
thamptonshire Regt.
*Died in German hands 2 Sept. 1917 of wounds received
in action*

GRACE, Rev. H. M.   Chaplain, E. African Force   1907

✠GRANT, G. L.   Pte., London Regt. (London Scottish);   1908
Capt., R.A.M.C.   *m.*
Killed in action 11 Oct. 1915

GRAY, E. C. G.   Pte., Middlesex Regt.; Capt. and Adjt.,   1895
R.A.S.C.   *M.B.E.*   *m.*

GRAY, G.   Capt., Lancs. Fus. (W 2.) (P.)   1901

GREEN, Rev. J.   Senior Chaplain, Australian Force   1907

GREEN, Rev. H. T.   Pte., R.A.M.C. (W.)   1905

GREEN, R. J.   Lieut., Norfolk Regt.   1910

GREENWOOD, A. W.   Pte., R.A.M.C.   1898

GREGORY, A. I.   2nd Lieut., Labour Corps   1915

GROVES, J. P. K.   Lieut., Cameronians (Scottish Rifles)   1908
and Gen. List. (W.)

GUILDFORD, Rev. E. M.   C.F. 3rd Class, R.A.C.D.   *M.C.*   1914

GURNEY, P. S.   Lieut., R.G.A. (P.)   1914

HAKE, H. D.   Capt., Hampshire Regt.(T.F.)   *M.*   [1914]

HALLETT, H. J.   Capt., King's (Liverpool Regt., T.F.);   1911
attd. Manchester Regt.

✠HALSE, L. W.   2nd Lieut., Gloucestershire Regt.   1912
*Died 17 Oct. 1918 of wounds received in action 21 Aug.
1918*

✠HAMER, A. D.   Capt., Northern Cyclist Bn.; attd. Man-   1913
chester Regt.
Killed in action 6 Nov. 1918

HAMPSON, S. H.   Capt. and Adjt., Lancs. Fus.   (W.)   1912
M.C.

HANDFORD, J. R.   Lieut., York and Lancaster Regt.(T.F.)   1911

HARGREAVES, R.   Capt., S. Lancs. Regt.(T.F.)   *M.C.*   1914

HARRISON, G. B.   Capt., The Queen's (R. W. Surrey   1913
Regt., T.F.); Staff Capt.

HARRISON, G. L.   Major, Middlesex Regt.; Lieut.-Col.,   1903
   The Queen's (R.W. Surrey Regt.)   *M.C.*
✠HARVEY, S.   Pte., Devon Regt.   1913
   Killed in action 25 Sept. 1915
✠HAUGHTON, A. J.   Lieut., Durham L.I.(T.F.)   1900
   Killed in action 23 June 1915
HAYWARD, A. D.   Pte., London Regt. (Artists Rifles);   1910
   Lieut., W. Yorks. Regt.
HEATH, W. E.   Surgeon Lieut., R.N.   *Order of St Stanislas,*   1912
   3rd Class, with swords (Russia)
HEMSWORTH, E. P. D.   Capt., Norfolk Regt.   [1914]
HERAPATH, C. A.   2nd Lieut., King's (Shropshire L.I.)   1909
✠HERAPATH, N. F.   2nd Lieut., Somerset L.I.   [1914]
   Killed in action 11 April 1917
✠HERIZ-SMITH, D. M.   2nd Lieut., Northamptonshire Regt. [1914]
   Died 17 Feb. 1917 of wounds received in action
HEWITT, L. McN.   *See* McNEILL-HEWITT, L.
HITCHCOCK, Rev. A. E. N.   C.F. 4th Class, R.A.C.D.   *M.*   1906
HOARE, F. O.   Lieut., R.F.A.(T.F.); Staff Lieut. (W.)   1913
   M.C.
HOBSON, C. M.   Lieut., S. Lancs. Regt. and M.G.C.   1912
HODGES, A. N.   Capt., R.A.M.C.   *M.*   1902
HOLBECH, L.   Capt., Grenadier Gds.; A.D.C. (W.)   1907
   D.S.O. M.C.
✠HOLCROFT, G. C.   2nd Lieut., Durham L.I.   1913
   Killed in action 9 Aug. 1915
HOLDEN, A.   Lieut., Sheffield Univ. O.T.C.   1900
HOLLIS, D.   Pte., Nigeria Land Contingent and Somerset   1897
   L.I.; Lieut., R.F.A.(T.F.)
✠HOLME, B. L.   Lieut., R. Welsh Fus.; Staff Capt.   1906
   Died 25 April 1916 of wounds received in action 10
   April 1916
HOOLE, B.   2nd Lieut., Bloxham School O.T.C.   1911
HOOLE, Rev. D.   Lieut., R. Fusiliers; C.F. 4th Class,   1908
   R.A.C.D.
HOOPER, K. A.   Lieut., R.G.A.   1907
✠HOPE, R. A.   Lieut., N. Staffs. Regt. (W.)   1913
   Killed in action 31 July 1917
HOPEWELL, A. F. J.   Lieut., D. of Wellington's (W. Rid-   1911
   ing Regt.) (W.)
HOUSEMAN, Rev. F. O.   C.F. 4th Class, R.A.C.D.   1895
HUBBARD, J. W.   2nd Lieut., Gloucestershire Regt.;   1913
   Lieut., R.A.S.C.(M.T.) *M.*
HUGHES, H. H.   R.N.   1906

HUGHES, Rev. L. A.   C.F. 3rd Class, R.A.C.D.   1900
✠HUGHES-GAMES, J. B. Major, Durham L.I. (W2.) *M.C.*   1907
   Died 17 *Oct.* 1918 *of wounds received in action*
HUMBY, S. R.   Capt., R.E. (T.F.) (W.) *M.C.*   1910
HUNT, F. R. W.   Capt., The Queen's (R.W. Surrey Regt.) 1910
   (W.)
HUTCHINSON, L. C.   Major, E. Yorks. Regt.; attd. R.   1914
   Inniskilling Fus.; empld. O.C.B. (W 2.)

✠INGLE, R. G.   2nd Lieut., Lincolnshire Regt.   1905
   Killed in action 1 *July* 1916
INGLESON, P. Lieut., R. Fusiliers (P.S. Bn.); Capt., Gen. 1911
   List (Staff Capt.) *M.*
INGLIS, W. M. Lieut., Sherwood Foresters (Notts. and   1912
   Derby Regt.) (W.)
ISAACSON, Rev. C. H.   C.F. 4th Class, N. Zealand Chap-   1890
   lain's Dept.

JAMES, J. H.   Lieut., E. Surrey Regt.   1902
JAMESON, T. B.   Major, Durham L.I.(T.F.) (W 3.)   1913
   M.C. M.
✠JOHNSON, T. P.   Lieut.-Col., R.A.S.C. *D.S.O. M* 3.   1890
   Died 12 *June* 1918
JOHNSTON, C. McA. Lieut., Seaforth Hdrs.; attd. London 1899
   Regt.
✠JOYCE, G. E.   Lieut., Leicestershire Regt.   *1907
   Killed in action 20 *Sept.* 1916

KAFKA, E. J.   Pte., Middlesex Regt.   1901
KEANE, R. D.   Lieut., R.E. *M.*   1914
KELLY, I. G.   Capt. (K.B.), R.A.F. *A.F.C.*   1904
KELLY, P. J.   Gnr., R.G.A.   1900
KELTON, P. ST G.   Capt., The Buffs (E. Kent Regt.);   1905
   Major, Gold Coast Regt., W. African Frontier Force;
   attd. Gen. Staff. (W 2.) *M.C. M* 2. *Officer, Mili-*
   tary Order of Avis (*Portugal*)
KENNEDY, F. R.   Pte., Middlesex Regt.; Lieut., M.G.C.   1913
   (W.) *M.*
KENNETT, B. L. A.   Lieut., Border Regt. and Gen. List, 1910
   empld. Egyptian Govt. (W.)
KENNETT, Rev. E. J. B. M.   C.F. 4th Class, R.A.C.D.   1909
KHAN, T. H. Interpreter, Indian Army   1913
✠KIDSON, C. W.   Lieut., R. Dublin Fus. (W.)   1913
   Killed in action 17 *Oct.* 1918

KIDSON, N. S. Capt., London Regt. (Rifles). (W.) *M.C.* 1913
✠KING, E. H. 2nd Lieut., R. Sussex Regt. 1910
Killed in action July 1917
KINGDON, G. H. Capt., Sherwood Foresters (Notts. and 1912
Derby Regt.) (W.)
KIRKLAND, W. N. Capt., London Regt. (Post Office 1912
Rifles); Lieut., R.A.S.C.
KNIGHT, F. H. Lieut., The Queen's (R.W. Surrey Regt.) 1900

LAFFAN, Rev. R. G. D. C.F. 4th Class, R.A.C.D. *Order* *1912
of St Sava, 5th Class (Serbia)
LAMBERT, H. E. Lieut., Gloucestershire Regt. and King's 1912
African Rifles. (W.)
✠LAMBERT, M. B. Lieut., Yorkshire Regt. 1913
Killed in action in Gallipoli 7 Aug. 1915
LANCASTER, E. T. 2nd Lieut., St Paul's School O.T.C. 1906
LANGLEY-SMITH, N.H. Lieut., Gloucestershire Regt. (W.) 1911
LEIGH-CLARE, H. J. L. Lieut., I.A.R.O., attd. 34th 1910
Poona Horse and 6th Cavalry. *M.C.*
LEWIS, M. B. Lieut., Tank Corps 1910
LHOYD-OWEN, E. E. 2nd Lieut., Loyal N. Lancs. Regt. 1916
LILLEY, T. G. Lieut., D. of Cornwall's L.I. 1914
LOCKE, C. E. L. Capt., R. Welsh Fus. 1903
LOEWE, H. M. J. 2nd Lieut., Lincolnshire Regt.; Lieut., 1901
Gen. List
✠LOMAX, E. H. Capt., S. Lancs. Regt. 1914
Killed in action 13 Aug. 1917
LUNN, H. F. Lieut., R.G.A. 1894
LYON, A. J. Hon. Colonel, Cambridgeshire Regt. and *1879
Spec. List (cmdg. School of Instruction)

MACDONALD, R. Lieut., King's (Liverpool Regt., T.F.); 1914
Lieut. (Ad.), R.A.F. (W.) *M.B.E.*
MACGREGOR, A. M. Lieut., R.G.A. (W.) 1907
✠MCKENZIE, K. N. 2nd Lieut., E. Yorks. Regt. 1913
Killed in action 4 June 1915
MCNEILL-HEWITT, L. Capt. and Adjt., R.A.S.C. 1909
MALDEN, H. R. Lieut., Rifle Brigade; empld. Intelli- 1903
gence Staff
MANSELL, R. Lieut., R.F.A.; Major, Tank Corps. (W.) 1912
MARLEY, F. L. Lieut., R. Warwickshire Regt.(T.F.) (W.) 1903
MASTER, Rev. C. H. C.F. 4th Class, R.A.C.D. *M.* *1886
MAXWELL, E. W. Lieut., London Regt. (Civil Service 1915
Rifles). (W.)

MAYNARD, Rev. A. C. M. C.F. 4th Class, R.A.C.D. *1904
(W.)
MOLESWORTH, G. E. N. Capt., Devon Regt.; attd. 69th 1913
Punjabis, Indian Army. (W.)
MOORE-ANDERSON, M. E. 2nd Lieut., R.A.S.C. 1899
MOYLE, T. Lieut., R. Fusiliers; attd. Gloucestershire [1914]
Regt. (W.)

✠NASON, J. W. W. Capt., R. Sussex Regt. and R.F.C. 1908
Killed in action 26 Dec. 1916
NIBBS, Rev. C. A. J. Chaplain, R.N. 1889
NICHOLL, Rev. E. McK. C.F. 4th Class, R.A.C.D. (W 2.) 1910
M.C.
NICHOLL, J. W. McK. Surgeon Lieut., R.N. 1912
NICHOLLS, G. B. Capt., Middlesex Regt. (W.) 1913
NIGHTINGALE, C. L. Lieut. (S.), R.A.F. 1910
NOBLE, A. H. Capt., R.A.S.C. *M.* 1905
NOBLE, Rev. R. H. C.F. 4th Class, R.A.C.D. 1914
NORDEN, F. L. 2nd Lieut., R. Scots; 2nd Lieut. (O.), 1913
R.A.F. (W 4.)
NORTH, J. Capt., Worcestershire Regt. 1913
✠NOSWORTHY, P. C. 2nd Lieut., Cheshire Regt. [1914]
Killed in action 11 May 1915
NUNN, V. W. H. 2nd Lieut., The Queen's (R.W. Surrey 1917
Regt.); attd. Middlesex Regt.

O'FLYNN, D. R. C. D. Major, King's (Liverpool Regt.); 1899
attd. W. African Regt.; empld. O.C.B.
OLIPHANT, G. R. Capt., S. Lancs. Regt.; empld. War 1908
Office. (W.)
ORME, E. S. Surgeon Lieut., R.N. 1911

PAGE, Rev. C. A. C.F. 4th Class, R.A.C.D. 1907
PAGE, Rev. F. A. C.F. 4th Class, R.A.C.D. 1910
PAIN, K. W. Lieut., R.F.A.; Asst. Officer i/c R.A.M.C. 1910
Records. (W.) *M.*
PARKER, P. H. Lieut., King's (Liverpool Regt., T.F.) (W 2.) 1911
PARKER, T. W. L. Lieut., King's (Liverpool Regt., T.F.); 1911
attd. Middlesex Regt.
PARNELL, H. 2nd Lieut., Tank Corps 1914
PARTRIDGE, G. J. Capt., Sherwood Foresters (Notts. and 1912
Derby Regt.) and Gen. Staff
PARTRIDGE, Rev. J. W. C.F. 4th Class, R.A.C.D. 1909
PARTRIDGE, Rev. W. W. C.F. 4th Class, R.A.C.D. 1901

PATERSON, A. G. Hon. Major, R.A.M.C. *M.*   1881
PEACE, L. R. Lieut., R.F.A.(T.F.)   1908
PEARSON, A. H. Capt., Loyal N. Lancs. Regt.; Major,   1904
    M.G.C. *M.C.*
PEARSON, C. H. M. Capt. and Adjt., R.F.A. *M.*   1906
PERRY, G. A. Lieut., R.A.S.C.   1910
PERRY, Rev. H. C. C.F. 4th Class, R.A.C.D.   1905
PERRY, L. B. Capt., R.A.M.C.   1903
PETTMAN, H. C.F. 4th Class, R.A.C.D.   1893
PHILLP, J. DE R. Capt., R. Warwickshire Regt.(T.F.)   1907
    (W 2.)
PICKARD, W. B. Corpl., London Yeo. (Middlesex   1908
    Hussars); attd. T.M.B. (W.) (P.)
✠PINDER, A. H. Lieut., Leicestershire Regt. *M.*   1906
    Killed in action 15 *Sept.* 1916
POOLE, E. F. Lieut., Northamptonshire Regt. and Spec. [1914]
    List (R.T.O.)
PRICE, Rev. C. L., T.D. C.F. 1st Class, R.A.C.D.(T.F.)   1889
    m.
✠PRICHARD, A. I. Pte., London Regt. (Civil Service Rifles)   1899
    Killed in action at Vimy Ridge 23 *May* 1916
PROCTOR, S. H. A. R. *See* RATHBONE-PROCTOR, S. H.
PUGH, C. D. O. Capt., R.G.A. *M.*   [1914]
PYE, A. N. W. Sub-Lieut., R.N.V.R.   1916

RANKIN, J. K. 2nd Lieut., Rifle Brigade   1905
RATHBONE-PROCTOR, S. H. Capt., R.E. (W.)   1913
RAYNER, E. B. A. 2nd Lieut., The Buffs (E. Kent Regt.);   1913
    Capt., S.O. 3, R.A.F. (W.) *M.*
REDWOOD, Rev. F. A. C.F. 4th Class, R.A.C.D.; 2nd   1909
    Lieut., King's (Shropshire L.I.)
RIDDELL, G. B. Capt., Northumberland Fus. (W 2.) *M.C.*   1910
ROBBINS, C. Paymaster Sub-Lieut., R.N.V.R.   1909
✠ROBINSON, J. H. 2nd Lieut., Somerset L.I.(T.F.); attd.   1907
    N. Staffs. Regt.(T.F.)
    Killed in action 30 *Nov.* 1917
ROCHE, A. R Capt., R.A.M.C. (W.) *M.C. M.*   1894
RODWAY, A. R. 2nd Lieut., E. Surrey Regt.; Capt.,   1913
    M.G.C. (W 2.)
ROGERS, Rev. T. G. C.F. 4th Class, R.A.C.D.   1905
ROGERS, W. D. Capt. and Adjt., S. Lancs. Regt.   1908
RUSHMER, H. F. Lieut., Norfolk Regt. (W 2.)   1913
✠RUTHERFURD, H. G. G. Pte., R. Fusiliers.   1905
    Killed in action near Pozières (15 *July* 1916)

SAMSON, Rev. A. M. C.F. 4th Class, R.A.C.D.   *1911
SANDBERG, Rev. W. B. C.F. 4th Class, R.A.C.D.(T.F.)   1893
✠SANDERSON, R. B. 2nd Lieut., R.G.A.   1908
   Died 17 April 1918 of wounds received in action
SAVAGE, K. Sapper, R.E.   1911
SAVILL, S. C. Capt. and Adjt., W. Yorks. Regt.(T.F.);   1913
   Hon. Capt. (A.), R.A.F. (W 2.)
✠SAXON, H. Lieut., King's Own (R. Lancaster Regt.) *M.*   1913
   Killed in action 30 Nov. 1916
SCOTT, J. T. 2nd Lieut., R. Berkshire Regt.   1909
SCOTT, M. H. B. Lieut., R.N.V.R.   1910
SELBY-LOWNDES, Rev. G. N. C.F. 4th Class, R.A.C.D.   1905
SHELTON, A. T. Capt., King's Own (Yorkshire L.I.); [1914]
   empld. Ministry of Munitions. (W.)
SIMEY, P. A. T. Rhodesian Volunteers   1911
SIMMONS, C. E. Lieut., I.A.R.O., attd. S. and T. Corps.   1908
M.
✠SIMMS, W. Capt., R. Warwickshire Regt.(T.F.)   1910
   Killed in action 19 July 1917
✠SIMPSON, H. D. Lieut., King's Royal Rifle Corps. (W.)   1914
   Killed in action 24 Aug. 1917
SKELTON, N. A. Lieut., The Queen's (R. W. Surrey   1908
   Regt.) (W.)
SKENE, Rev. A. P. C.F. 4th Class, R.A.C.D.   1901
✠SKEY, C. H. Lieut., R. Fusiliers; Capt., Black Watch.   1909
   (W.) *M.C.*
   Killed in action 18 Aug. 1916
SKEY, C. O. Major, R. Fusiliers. (W.) *D.S.O. M.C. M.*   1911
SLEEMAN, C. M. Lieut., R.N.V.R.   *1912
SLEIGH, G. B. Capt., King's Own (R. Lancaster Regt.)   1908
   (W.)
SLOMAN, A. E. P. 2nd Lieut., R.A.S.C.; Lieut., R.F.A.   1909
SMALES, R. Lieut., Northumberland Fus.   1906
SMELLIE, G. H. Capt., King's Own (R. Lancaster [1914]
   Regt.); attd. Cheshire Regt.
SMITH, Rev. C. M. C.F. 4th Class, R.A.C.D.(T.F.)   1905
SMITH, F. W. Capt., Life Gds.   1912
✠SMITH, H. L. C. Lieut., Sherwood Foresters (Notts. and   1910
   Derby Regt.)
   Killed in action 20 Oct. 1914
SMITH, H. P. Major, R.F.A.(T.F.)   1912
SMITH, Rev. M. C.F. 4th Class, R.A.C.D. (W.) *M.*   1898
SMITH, S. Lieut., Middlesex Regt.; attd. T.M.B. (W 2.)   1908
M.

✠SMITH, W. W. 2nd Lieut., R.A.S.C. (W.) [1914]
Killed in action on the Somme 9 *July* 1916

SNAPE, W. R. C. Lieut., Leicestershire Regt.; attd. 1909
T.M.B. (W.) *M.C.*

SOMERSET, R. H. E. H. Lieut., R.A.S.C.; Capt., Spec. 1904
List, empld. War Office

✠SOWELL, A. D. Lieut., D. of Cornwall's L.I. [1914]
Killed in action 24 *Aug.* 1916

SPACKMAN, E. D. Capt., R.A.M.C. 1912

SPAFFORD, H. H. Pte., Welsh Regt.; 2nd Lieut., R. Welsh 1916
Fus.

SPARLING, H. P. Lieut., R.E. 1908

SPARLING, W. H. Major, Cheshire Regt. (W.) *M.C.* 1910

SPEAR, G. F. Lieut., Spec. List (Recruiting Staff) 1898

SPENCER-SMITH, P. Lieut., London Regt. (Queen's West- 1901
minster Rifles). (W.) (P.)

SPOWART, W. C. Lieut., I.A.R.O., attd. S. and T. Corps. 1908
(W.)

STEARN, Rev. C. H. C.F. 4th Class, R.A.C.D. 1907

STEBBING, T. H. L. Capt., Sherwood Foresters (Notts. 1909
and Derby Regt., T.F.) (W.) *M.C.*

STEPHENS, Rev. E. C. Chaplain, R.N. 1898

STILEMAN, C. E. C. Lieut., E. Surrey Regt.; Capt., Gen. 1911
List, Indian Army, attd. 55th Coke's Rifles. (W.)

STILEMAN, D. C. G. Capt., King's Own (R. Lancaster 1908
Regt.) (W.) *M.*

STILEMAN, D. F. Lieut., R. Berkshire Regt. (W 2.) 1913

STUBBS, Rev. N. H. C.F. 4th Class, R.A.C.D. 1905

✠STUCKEY, R. A. Pte., R. Welsh Fus. 1889
Died 27 *July* 1917 *of heat stroke while on active service*

SWATRIDGE, C. J. Lieut., Sherwood Foresters (Notts. 1914
and Derby Regt.) and M.G.C.; Hon. Lieut. (A.),
R.A.F. (W.) *M.*

SYMONDS, E. T. Corpl., R.E. (Signals); Lieut., Bedford- 1913
shire Regt. (W.)

TAYLOR, A. A. Pte., Queen's Own (R. W. Kent Regt.) 1902

TAYLOR, R. Lieut., R.E.; empld. Ministry of Munitions. 1909
(W.)

TEMPERLEY, A. C. Major, Northumberland Fus.; Lieut.- 1896
Col., Norfolk Regt.; G.S.O. 1. *C.M.G. D.S.O.*
Brevet Lieut.-Colonel. M 8.

THARP, P. A. Capt., Queen's Own (R.W. Kent Regt.) 1909
(W.)

THOMPSON, G. Major, R.A.S.C. 1907
✠THOMPSON, H. B. 2nd Lieut., R. Berkshire Regt. *M.C.* 1909
  Killed in action 24 April 1917
THOMPSON, H. J. Lieut., R. Fusiliers 1910
THOMPSON, M. Capt., R.F.A. (W 3.) 1910
THOMPSON, R. D. 2nd Lieut., Somerset L.I. (W.) 1913
THOMPSON, W. S. Lieut., I.A.R.O., attd. 2nd Gurkha 1910
  Rifles
THORMAN, Rev. F. P. Canadian A.M.C. 1906
THURSBY, W. Capt., R.F.A.; A.D.C. 1909
TINDALL, C. R. W. Lieut., R.A.S.C. 1911
TINSLEY, R. P. Lieut., Middlesex Regt.; attd. T.M.B. 1911
  (W.)
TOWNEND, H. D. Lieut., Bombay Bn., Indian Defence 1910
  Force
TREGLOWN, C. J. H. Lieut., Norfolk Regt.; Capt., 1911
  S. Wales Borderers. (W.) *M.C.*
TULLOCH, H. M. 2nd Lieut., K. Edward's Horse; 1911
  Lieut., 33rd Light Cavalry, Indian Army; Lieut. (A.),
  R.A.F.
TURNBULL, Rev. P. H. C.F. 4th Class, R.A.C.D. 1908
TURNER, Rev. A. Chaplain, R.N. 1906
TURNER, J. W. C. Capt., R.F.A. *M.C.* 1906
✠TURNER, R. Pte., London Regt. (Artists Rifles); 2nd 1904
  Lieut., Essex Regt.(T.F.)
  Killed in action at Suvla Bay 15 *Aug.* 1915

UPWARD, L. V. Capt., R. Fusiliers and Gen. List. (W 2.) 1909

✠VEITCH, A. G. Lieut., R.F.A.(T.F.) 1907
  Killed in action 23 April 1917
VEITCH, J. L. Major, R.H.A.(T.F.) (W.) *Chevalier,* 1914
  Ordre de la Couronne (Belgium). Belgian Croix de
  Guerre

WAGG, F. J. Lieut., Seaforth Hdrs. 1907
WAINWRIGHT, L. A. Lieut., Spec. List (Inland Water- 1909
  ways and Docks)
✠WALKER, A. N. Lieut.-Col., R.A.M.C. 1892
  Killed in action 24 Sept. 1916
✠WARNER, A. 2nd Lieut., London Regt. (R. Fus.) 1902
  Killed in action 1 *July* 1917
WATSON, N. W. Lieut., E. Yorks. Regt.; Hon. Lieut. 1911
  (T.), R.A.F. (W 3.)

✠WATTS, R. W. A.   Pte., Sherwood Foresters (Notts. and   1912
    Derby Regt.); 2nd Lieut., Worcestershire Regt. *M.C.*
    Died 12 *Nov.* 1916 *of wounds received in action* 5 *Nov.*
    1916
✠WELLS, L. H. E.   2nd Lieut., Lancs. Fus.   1904
    Died 4 *May* 1915 *from the effects of gas poisoning at*
    Ypres
WESTALL, B. C.   Capt., Essex Regt.(T.F.)   1912
WESTCOTT, G. F.   2nd Lieut., R.A.S.C.(T.F.); Lieut.   1912
    (A.), R.A.F.   (P.)
✠WHEELER, H. L.   2nd Lieut., The Buffs (E. Kent Regt.);   1914
    attd. Queen's Own (R.W. Kent Regt.)
    Died 26 *Dec.* 1915 *of wounds received in action*
WHEELER, Rev. H. W.   C.F. 4th Class, R.A.C.D.   1906
✠WHITFIELD, J. B.   Lieut., R.E.   1908
    Died 20 *Jan.* 1916 *of wounds received in action*
WHITTY, L. W.   Capt., Lancs. Fus. (W.)   1907
WHYTE VENABLES, H. A.   Capt., R.A.M.C.   1910
WILKINSON, Rev. C. F. W.   Chaplain, R.N.   1904
WILKINSON, Rev. G. A. W.   C.F. 4th Class, R.A.C.D.   1906
    (W.) *M.C.*
WILKINSON, Rev. J. R.   C.F. 4th Class, R.A.C.D.   1912
✠WILKINSON, M. L.   2nd Lieut., Northumberland Fus.   1913
    Died 8 *July* 1917 *of wounds received in action*
WILLIAMS, J. G.   2nd Lieut., King's (Liverpool Regt.)   1914
WILLIAMS, O. H.   2nd Lieut., Army Cyclist Corps   1911
WILLIAMSON, F. A.   Surgeon Lieut., R.N.   1908
WILLIAMSON, T. R.   Lieut., R. Fusiliers. (W.) *M.C.*   1912
WILSON, Rev. B. C.   C.F. 4th Class, Australian Chaplains'   1901
    Dept. *M.*
WISE, Rev. A. T.   C.F. 4th Class, R.A.C.D. *m.*   1902
WRIGHT, E. G. D.   Pte., Rand Rifles, S. Africa Force   1903

YATES, H. G.   Major, R.F.A.(T.F.) *M.C.*   1905

ST CATHARINE'S COLLEGE

ALEXANDER, J. H. R. Lieut., Devon Regt. *1907
ALLEN, Rev. H. C.F. 4th Class, R.A.C.D. *1908
ANABLE, A. Lieut., Norfolk Regt. (W.) 1915
ARMSTRONG, H. R. Major, R.E.(T.F.) *T.D.* 1887
ARMSTRONG, J. L. Lieut., Yorkshire Regt. (W.) 1911
ASHTON, E. G. Leading Telegraphist, R.N.V.R. 1913
ASTLEY, B. A. F. 2nd Lieut., Devon Regt.; Lieut., 1892
Training Res. Bn. and Labour Corps
ATKINS, E. M. Lieut., R.E. (W.) 1909
AUSTIN, Rev. S. Lieut., R.F.A. 1904

BAKER, E. C. Capt., London Regt. (R. Fus.); Major (Ad.), 1911
R.A.F. (W.)
BAKER, Rev. P. C.F. 4th Class, Australian Chaplains' *1909
Dept.
✠BARKER, R. A. Capt., Sherwood Foresters (Notts. and 1914
Derby Regt.); empld. Recruiting Staff. (W.) *M.C.*
Died 13 *Oct.* 1918 *of wounds received in action*
BARTLETT, A. G. Capt., King's (Liverpool Regt., T.F.) 1913
and Labour Corps
✠BARTLETT, L. A. Lieut., Queen's Own (R.W. Kent Regt.) 1903
Killed in action 22 *July* 1916
BARWELL, H. B. 2nd Lieut., W. Yorks. Regt.; Capt., 1912
Gen. List (Recruiting Staff). (W.)
BATES, H. S. Capt., Cambridgeshire Regt.; Lieut. 1912
I.A.R.O., attd. 19th Punjabis. (W 2.)
✠BELCHER, G. Capt., R. Berkshire Regt. *M.C. M.* 1904
Killed in action 15–17 *May* 1915
BENNETT, J. C. S. Sub-Lieut., R.N.V.R. (R.N.D.) (W.) [1914]
M.C.

BENSTEAD, C. R. Lieut., R.G.A. *M.C. M.* 1914
BERWICK, E. B. H., T.D. Major, Rossall School O.T.C. *m.* *1892
BIDGOOD, Rev. G. J. B. C.F. 4th Class, R.A.C.D. 1910
BIRD, M. B. Lieut., Norfolk Regt.(T.F.) 1910
✠BIRD, P. C. H. 2nd Lieut., Norfolk Regt.; attd. Loyal 1911
N. Lancs. Regt. (W.)
Killed in action in Mesopotamia 5 *April* 1916
BIRMINGHAM, Rt. Rev. Bishop of. C.F. 1st Class, 1910
R.A.C.D.(T.F.)
BLACKBURN, Rev. B. R. C.F. 4th Class, R.A.C.D. 1907
M.B.E. m 2.
BLUCKE, R. S. Lieut., Dorset Regt.; Hon. Lieut. (O.), [1914]
R.A.F.
BOOTH, Rev. H. F. C.F. 4th Class, R.A.C.D. 1895
BOOTHMAN, J. H. E. D. 2nd Lieut., The Buffs (E. Kent 1915
Regt.); Pte., R. Fusiliers and M.G.C. (W.)
✠BOULTBEE, A. E. Lieut., Northamptonshire Regt. and 1915
R.F.C.
Killed in action 17 *March* 1917
BOWER, F. Sergt., King's Own (R. Lancaster Regt.); 2nd 1913
Lieut., I.A.R.O., attd. 4th Rajputs. (W.)
BOYCE, A. H. Sergt., E. Surrey Regt.; attd. Middlesex 1914
Regt.
BOYD, C. W. Capt., King's Own Scottish Borderers. 1909
(W.)
BOYD-CARPENTER, Rt. Rev. Bishop, K.C.V.O. Hon. C.F., 1860
R.A.C.D.(T.F.)
BOYD-CARPENTER, J. P. Capt., R. Scots Fus. (W.) 1892
BRACHI, C. C. Capt., King's Own (R. Lancaster Regt.); 1900
attd. Gen. Staff. *M.*
BRAGG, W. H. Capt., R.F.A.(T.F.); Capt. (Ad.), R.A.F. 1913
(W.)
BRAMELD, A. J. M. Capt., R. Warwickshire Regt.(T.F.) 1903
and Labour Corps. (W.)
BRIGLEY, C. G. Lieut., D. of Wellington's (W. Riding 1914
Regt., T.F.); attd. R.E. (W.)
BROWN, C. L. M. Telegraphist, R.N.V.R. 1914
BRUCE, A. A. Capt., R.G.A. (W 2.) *M.C. M.* 1913
✠BUCKLEY, E. Capt., York and Lancaster Regt. (W.) *M.* 1905
Killed in action at Lens 30 *Sept.* 1917
BULL, J. C. Major, D. of Wellington's (W. Riding Regt.) 1900
(W.) *M.C. M* 3.
BULMER, Rev. P. H. C.F. 4th Class, R.A.C.D. 1908
BURDETT, A. F. C.Q.M.S., R.E. *M.* 1913

¹CAIN, R. C. Capt. (A.), R.A.F. (W.) *D.F.C.*   1910
CALTHORPE, Hon. F. S. G. *See* GOUGH CALTHORPE, Hon.
F. S.
✠CARTER, B. 2nd Lieut., Cambridgeshire Regt.   1913
Killed in action 18 Sept. 1918
CARTER, Rev. J. C.F. 4th Class, R.A.C.D. *Order of St*   1911
Sava, 5*th Class (Serbia). M.*
✠CARTWRIGHT, C. 2nd Lieut., Bedfordshire Regt.   1904
Killed in action 19 *April* 1916
CATTLEY, R. Major, W. Yorks. Regt.(T.F.) and Training   1890
Res. Bn. (W 2.)
✠CAYLEY, F. D. E. 2nd Lieut., King's Royal Rifle Corps   1913
Killed in action 29 *Sept.* 1915
CHESTERMAN, H. Capt., R.A.S.C.   1902
CIRCUIT, Rev. E. F. C.F. 4th Class, R.A.C.D.   1908
✠CLARK, G. M. Major, Northamptonshire Regt. *M.*   1899
Killed in action 14 *July* 1916
✠CLARKE, M. T. Pte., 10th Bn., Canadian Infy.   1902
Killed in action (3 *May* 1915)
COCKELL, B. W. Capt., Suffolk Regt.(T.F.); A.D.C.   1913
French Croix de Guerre
COLLINS, Rev. H. E. Chaplain, R.N.   1894
COMPTON, F. 2nd Lieut., Cambridgeshire Regt. (P.)   1915
✠CONAN-DAVIES, B. I. Lieut., Worcestershire Regt.; attd.   *1911
York and Lancaster Regt. (W.)
Died 23 *Nov.* 1918 *of pneumonia contracted on active*
service
COONEY, A. B. Capt., Denbighshire Yeo. and R. Welsh   1910
Fus.
COOPER, Rev. F. T. C.F. 4th Class, R.A.C.D.   *1908
✠CORBETT, H. V. Capt., Cambridgeshire Regt.; attd.   1912
Essex Regt. (W.)
Killed in action 17 *Oct.* 1918
CORFIELD, C. L. Capt., Cambridgeshire Regt.; empld.   1912
O.C.B. (W 2.) *M.C.*
CRISP, Rev. H. Capt., D. of Wellington's (W. Riding   1909
Regt.); empld. Ministry of Pensions. (W.)
CULVERWELL, J. S. Capt., I.A.R.O., attd. 53rd Sikhs.   1908
(W 2.) *M.*
CUMMING, G. E. 2nd Lieut., Gordon Hdrs.; empld.   1911
Command Depôt
CURTIS, S. W. Lieut., R.F.A.   1911

¹ Killed in flying accident after the armistice.

DAVENPORT, S. F. Lieut., R.G.A.   1914
DAVIDSON, M. C. 2nd Lieut., Oxford and Bucks. L.I.; [1914]
    Lieut., M.G.C. (W 3.)
DAVIES, A. L. Seaman, R.N.V.R.   1912
DAVIES, D. LL. E. Capt., W. Yorks. Regt.(T.F.) (W 2.)   1912
DAVIES, J. O. Corpl., Worcestershire Regt.   1917
DAVIES, K. C. J. Capt., R.A.S.C. and 10th Gurkha Rifles,   1912
    Indian Army
DAVIS, J. W. F. McN. *See* McNAUGHT-DAVIS, J. W. F.
DAVISON, G. Lieut., R.A.S.C. *M.*   1912
DAY, Rev. G. P. J. C.F. 4th Class, R.A.C.D.   1907
DELPH, L. W. Lieut., R.E. (W.) *M.C.*   1910
DEMPSEY, G. B. Capt. and Adjt., Manchester Regt. 1912
    M.C. and Bar. M 3.
DIER, C. V. Cadet, O.C.B.   1908
DINGAD-DAVIES, F. LL. Lieut., R.F.A.; Capt., R.A.O.C.   1913
DODD, Rev. J. M. C.F. 4th Class, R.A.C.D.   1906
DRACUP, A. H. 2nd Lieut., I.A.R.O.   *1909
✠DRIFFIELD, H. G. 2nd Lieut., Queen's Own (R. W. Kent   1901
    Regt.)
    Died 1 Aug. 1917 of wounds received in action 22 April
    1917
✠DRIFFIELD, L. T. Capt., St John's School, Leatherhead,   1899
    O.T.C.
    Died 9 Oct. 1917
DUKE, A. C. H. Major, R.G.A. (R. of O.); Lieut.-Col.,   1898
    A.A. and Q.M.G. *C.M.G. D.S.O. M* 4.

EASTER, Rev. A. J. T. 2nd Lieut., R.A.S.C.(T.F.); empld.   1912
    Recruiting Staff
EASTWELL, M. M. Major, Cambridgeshire Regt. and   1908
    Spec. List (Cmdt., Reception Camp)
EDE, E. E. Sub-Lieut., R.N.V.R. (W.)   1911
ELLIS, R. Major, R.A.M.C.(T.F.) *M.*   1903
ELLISTON, G. S. Capt., R.A.M.C. (Sanitary Service,   *1896
    T.F.) *M.C. Order of St John of Jerusalem*
ELWOOD, A. G. F. Capt., Sherwood Foresters (Notts.   1908
    and Derby Regt.) (P.)
EVANS, A. O. Lieut., Sappers and Miners, Indian Army   1906
EVANS, I. Lieut., R.G.A.   1912
EVANS, L. G. Lieut., R. Marines. (W.)   1913
EVERETT, H. F. Major, R.A.M.C.(T.F.) *m* 2.   *1896
EVERINGTON, G. F. Instructor Lieut., R.N.   1910

FARR, H. F.   Instructor Lieut., R.N.   *M.*   1904
FARROW, W. P.   2nd Lieut. (T.), R.A.F.   (W 2.)   1911
✠FLAXMAN, W. J.   2nd Lieut., R.A.S.C.   *1909
   Died on active service in Mesopotamia 27 May 1917
FRANCIS, B. A.   Capt., R.G.A.   (W.)   1897

GARMONSWAY, G. N.   2nd Lieut., R.G.A.   1916
GIBB, Rev, J.   C.F. 4th Class, R.A.C.D.   1905
GIBSON, H. H.   Lieut., Rossall School O.T.C.   1897
GILBERT, Rev. L. A.   Chaplain, R.N.   1903
✠GILL, K. C.   Capt., Cambridgeshire Regt.; Capt. (A.),   1912
   R.A.F.   (W.)   *M.C.*   *M* 2.
   Died 22 Oct. 1918 of wounds received in action
GILL, Rev. W.   Chaplain, R.N.   *1907
GOLDBERG, S. V.   *See* GOLDHURST, S. V.
GOLDHURST, S. V.   Lieut., R.A.M.C.   1910
GOUGH CALTHORPE, Hon. F. S.   Lieut., Staffordshire   *1913
   Yeo; Capt., Spec. List (P. and B.T. Staff)
GRAHAM-BROWN, G. F.   Capt. and Adjt., King's Own   1910
   Scottish Borderers.   (W.)
GRAND, G. C.   Cadet, O.C.B.   1917
✠GRAY, E. T.   2nd Lieut., Durham L.I.   1914
   Killed in action 22 Oct. 1915
GREENHOUGH, H.   2nd Lieut., R. Fusiliers; Lieut., Gen.   1910
   List, attd. R.E. (Signals)
✠GRIFFITHS, C. R.   2nd Lieut., R. Fusiliers   1915
   Died 1 May 1917 of wounds received in action
GRINDON, Rev. A. W. H.   C.F. 4th Class, R.A.C.D.   *1894
GUDGEON, Rev. C. J.   C.F. 4th Class, R.A.C.D.   1905
✠GULLICK, A. L.   Lieut., The Buffs (E. Kent Regt.)   1904
   Killed in action 3 Oct. 1915
GULLICK, L. B.   Lieut., R.A.S.C.   1906
GUY, B. M. E.   2nd Lieut., S. Lancs. Regt.   *M.*   1915

HACKING, Rev. H.   C.F. 4th Class, R.A.C.D.   *1901
HAMILTON, J. W.   Capt., Highland L.I.(T.F.)   1909
HARE, S. G.   Pte., R.A.S.C.(M.T.)   1906
HASLEWOOD, B. T.   Major, R.F.A.   1894
HAYES, J. C.   2nd Lieut., Middlesex Regt.; Capt.,   [1914]
   M.G.C. and Spec. List
HEADLEY, H. H.   Capt., R. Fusiliers   *1906
HELDER, L. B.   Lieut., R. Fusiliers; Lieut. (O.), R.A.F. [1914]
   (P.)
HELLINS, Rev. E. W. J.   C.F. 4th Class, R.A.C.D.(T.F.)   1894

HEPWORTH, L. D.   2nd Lieut., R.G.A.   (W.)   [1914]
HERD, J. G. M.   Lieut., Trinity College, Glenalmond, 1896
  O.T.C.
HITCHCOCK, J. V.   Capt., The Buffs (E. Kent Regt.)   1908
HODDER, H. G.   Lieut., R.E.   (W.) *D.C.M. M.*   1911
HODGSON, F. W.   2nd Lieut., Lancs. Fus. (T.F.); Lieut.,   1915
  R. Warwickshire Regt. (T.F.); empld. O.C.B.
HOFFMEISTER, C. E.   *See* HOUGH, C. E.
HOLLINGWORTH, L.   Pioneer, R.E. (Spec. Bde.)   1913
HOLLIS, A. J.   2nd Lieut., Bedfordshire Regt.(T.F.)   1917
HOPKIN, D.   Capt., E. Yorks. Regt.; Major, R. Fusiliers.   1910
  M.C.
HOSBAND, E. A.   Lieut., S. Staffs. Regt.   (W.)   1915
HOUGH, C. E.   Capt., S. Wales Borderers.   (W 2.)   1905
HOWARD, Rev. G. W. A.   C.F. 4th Class, R.A.C.D.   1909
HOWARD, Rev. P.   C.F. 4th Class, R.A.C.D.   1894
HOWDEN, E. R.   Lieut., R A.S.C.   1914
HOWE, R. G.   Lieut., Sherwood Foresters (Notts. and   1912
  Derby Regt.) and R. Dublin Fus.   (W.) (P.) *m* 2.
HUDSON, G. H.   Capt., York and Lancaster Regt.; attd.   1910
  T.M.B.   (W.) *M.*
✠HUGHES, HAROLD.   2nd Lieut., R.F.A.   1913
  Died 23 April 1917 *of wounds received in action*
HUGHES, HORACE.   Sergt., Welsh Regt.; 2nd Lieut., Nor-   1915
  folk Regt.   (W.) *M.C.*
HUGHES, J. B. W.   Lce.-Corpl., London Regt.; 2nd   1914
  Lieut., Gloucestershire Regt.   (W.) (P.)
HUMPHREYS, G. N.   Hon. Capt. (A.), R.A.F.   (P.) *M.*   1901
HUNT, H. N.   Lieut., D. of Wellington's (W. Riding   1913
  Regt.) and Manchester Regt. (T.F.); Capt., Spec.
  List (Asst. Officer i/c R.E. Records). *m.*
HURST, E. S.   Lieut., R.F.A. (T.F.); attd. T.M.B. (W 2.) 1913

JAY, C. D.   Capt., R. Sussex Regt.; Major, M.G.C.   *1911
  D.S.O. M 3.
JEEVES, Rev. F. W.   C.F. 4th Class, R.A.C.D.   *1911
JOHNSON, Rev. W. H.   C.F. 4th Class, R.A.C.D.   1901
✠JOLLEY, J. A. B.   Sergt., R. Fusiliers (P. S. Bn.); 2nd [1914]
  Lieut., Lincolnshire Regt.
  Killed in action 11 *Oct.* 1915
JONES, A. M.   Lieut., St Paul's School O.T.C.   1899
JONES, W. H. S.   2nd Lieut., Perse School O.T.C.   *1909

KENDALL, Rev. W. A.   C.F. 4th Class, R.A.C.D.   1911

KEY, Rev. S. W. C.F. 4th Class, R.A.C.D.(T.F.)   *1895
KILBURN, D. 2nd Lieut., Durham L.I.   1911
✠KIRKUS, C. H. Capt., R.G.A.   1899
   Killed in action 31 *July* 1917
KNAPP, K. K. Brig.-Gen., R. A. *C.B. C.M.G. D.S.O.*   1885
   *Brevet Colonel. M 7. Order of St Stanislas, 3rd Class
   (Russia). American Distinguished Service Medal*
KNEEN, C. W. Lieut., R. Welsh Fus. and M.G.C.   1912
KNIGHT, J. E. H. Corpl., R.A.V.C.   1907
KÖBLICH, G. R. Lieut., Norfolk Regt.(T.F.); empld. [1914]
Ministry of Munitions

LASBREY, Rev. B. Chaplain, R.N.   1900
✠LEE, H. V. 2nd Lieut., Suffolk Regt.   *1909
   Died 17 *Nov.* 1916 *of wounds received in action*
✠LEMMEY, F. G. Lieut., R. Scots. (W.)   1893
   Killed in action 14 *July* 1916
LEWIS, J. H. Corpl., R. Fusiliers   1908
LEWIS, J. M. C. Lieut., Welsh Regt. (W.)   1913
LLOYD, R. T. Pte., Suffolk Regt. (W.)   1913
LOEWE, H. M. J. 2nd Lieut., Lincolnshire Regt.; Lieut., *1911
Gen. List
LOWNDES, A. G. 2nd Lieut., K. Edward's School, Can-   1910
terbury, O.T.C.
LUSCOMBE, B. P. Lieut., R.F.A.; attd. T.M.B. (P.)   1912
LUTTER, R. B. Lieut., R.G.A. (W 2.)   1916

MCARTHUR, R. Lieut., R.F.A.(T.F.) (P.) *M.C.*   1912
MCGOWAN, Rev. H. C.F. 4th Class, R.A.C.D.   1910
MCMICHAEL, G. W. Pte., Worcestershire Regt.(T.F.);   1910
2nd Corpl., R.E. (Field Survey Coy.)
MCMURTRIE, Rev. S. G. C.F. 4th Class, R.A.C.D.   1896
✠MCNAUGHT-DAVIS, J. W. F. Lieut., S. Wales Borderers   1912
   Killed in action 17 *Jan.* 1915
✠MANN, J. W. 2nd Lieut., The Buffs (E. Kent Regt., T.F.)   1907
   Died 22 *Aug.* 1918 *of wounds received in action*
MARCH, Rev. W. W. C.F. 4th Class, R.A.C.D.   1910
MARSH, A. W. 2nd Lieut., Hampshire Regt.; Lieut., *1914
Gen. List (attd. R.E., Signals)
✠MAYO, W. C. Lieut., Sherwood Foresters (Notts. and   1905
Derby Regt.)
   Killed in action in Gallipoli 7–11 *Aug.* 1915
[1]MILNER, Rev. D. R. Chaplain, R.N.   1909

   [1] Accidentally killed at Archangel after the armistice.

MITCHELL, W. G. Lieut., R.A.S.C.   1913
✠MOORE, G. 2nd Lieut., R. Sussex Regt.   1912
  Killed in action in the First Battle of Ypres 7 Nov. 1914
MORRIS, W. F. Lieut., Norfolk Regt.; Major, Army   1911
  Cyclist Corps. *M.C. M.*
MOUNTFORD, Rev. A. W. C.F. 4th Class, R.A.C.D.   *1910
MOUSLEY, Rev. T. H. C.F. 4th Class, R.A.C.D.   *1908
MULLINS, A. F. Capt., Saskatchewan Regt., Canadian 1909
  Force; Staff Capt. (W.)

NEWELL, A. 2nd Lieut., S. Staffs. Regt.   1892
NICHOLS, F. P. Lieut.-Col., R.A.M.C.   1875
NORBY, Rev. R. H. C.F. 4th Class, R.A.C.D.   1912
NORRIS, C. G. Pte., R. Fusiliers (P.S. Bn.)   1910

O'CONNOR, Rev. J. C.F. 4th Class, R.A.C.D.   *1908
OLIVER, F. J. Capt., Gen. List (T.F. Res.); Instructor *1914
  in Musketry
OTTY, H. R. Lieut., R.E. *M.*   1908

PALMER, E. DE S. Capt., Norfolk Regt.   1907
PARISH, W. O. Lieut., Norfolk Regt.; attd. R. Dublin 1912
  Fus.
PARKER, C. 2nd Lieut., D. of Wellington's (W. Riding 1913
  Regt.) *M.C.*
PARKER, H. N. Lieut., Oxford and Bucks. L.I.; attd.   1909
  Hampshire Regt.(T.F.) (W.)
PARKER SMITH, R. Capt., Perse School O.T.C.   1900
PERKINS, F. H. Lieut., R.A.S.C. (W.)   1915
PHILLIPS, C. K. Lieut., R. Irish Rifles; Major, Gen. List 1899
  (D.A.A.G.) *O.B.E. M.*
PHILLIPS, I. A. Cadet, O.C.B.   1916
POWELL-PRICE, E. Capt., R. Welsh Fus.; A.D.C.; Staff 1912
  Capt. (W.) *M.C. M. Order of the Nile, 4th Class*
  (Egypt)
✠PREDDY, E. F. S. Capt., R.G.A.   1912
  Killed in action 8 Dec. 1917
✠PRITCHARD, R. 2nd Lieut., Devon Regt.; attd. Gloucester- 1904
  shire Regt. (W.)
  Died 22 Aug. 1916 *of wounds received in action*
✠PUDUMJEE, N. S. Pte., R. Fusiliers (P. S. Bn.)   1911
  Drowned on H.M.S. Persia 30 Dec. 1915
PULLIBLANK, Rev. J. C.F. 4th Class, R.A.C.D.   1894
PURVIS, J. S. Lieut., Yorkshire Regt.(T.F.) (W.) *m.* 1909

RAMSEY, H. L. 2nd Lieut., R.A.S.C.   1915
RANKING, G. S. A. Lieut.-Col., R.A.M.C. (3rd S. Gen.   1869
    Hospital, T.F.) *C.M.G.* *m* 2.
✠RAWES, J. H. R. Lieut., Bedfordshire Regt.   [1914]
    Killed in action 1 *July* 1916
RAYNER, C. G. Cadet, R.F.C.; Lce.-Corpl., London   1917
    Regt. (St Pancras Bn.)
✠RIGBY, G. Lieut., York and Lancaster Regt. *M.C.*   1910
    Killed in action 7 *June* 1916
RILEY, W. N. Capt., Leicestershire Regt.(T.F.) (W.)   1911
RIVERS-SMITH, S. Capt., King's African Rifles. *M.*   1898
ROBINSON, Rev. B. C. C.F. 4th Class, R.A.C.D.   1908
ROBINSON, L. R. C. 2nd Lieut., W. Yorks. Regt.; Lieut.,   1909
    I.A.R.O. (Cavalry.) (W.)
ROBINSON, Rev. L. S. C.F. 4th Class, R.A.C.D.   1883
ROGERS, A. D. S. Major, Northumberland Fus. (W.)   1902
ROSE, Rev. C. P. G. Chaplain, R.N.   1905
✠ROSS, W. S. Pte., R. Fusiliers (P.S. Bn.); Lieut., Border   1911
    Regt. (W.)
    Killed in action 23 *July* 1917
ROWLEY, Rev. F. B. Chaplain, R.N.   1893
RUSHMORE, F. M., T.D. Lieut.-Col., Cambridge Univ.   1895
    O.T.C.
✠RYAN, A. C. T. K. Lieut., Middlesex Regt. (W.)   1912
    Killed in action 24 *Oct.* 1918
RYAN, D. P. K. Lieut., King's Royal Rifle Corps   1913

SCOTT, A. D. B. Capt., R. Irish Rifles and Gen. List,   1898
    empld. Ministry of National Service
✠SCOTT, W. F. Pte., London Regt. (Q.V.R.); 2nd Lieut.,   1909
    Somerset L.I.
    Killed in action 1 *July* 1916
SEWELL, F. A. S. Capt., Bedford Grammar School O.T.C.   1899
SHAW, G. E. Flt. Cadet, R.A.F.   1917
SHEPPEY-GREENE, Rev. R. F. Lieut., R.A.S.C.   1905
SKRIMSHIRE, C. V. S. Major, R.G.A.   1897
SLATER, A. Lieut., I.A.R.O., attd. 106th Hazara Pioneers.   1906
    M.
✠SMART, W. E. Sergt., King's Royal Rifle Corps; 2nd   1913
    Lieut., Yorkshire Regt.; attd. W. Yorks. Regt.
    Killed in action near Cambrai 11 *Oct.* 1918
✠SMITH, D. G. Lieut., King's (Shropshire L.I.) (W 2.)   1914
    M.C.
    Died 16 *Aug.* 1917 *of wounds received in action*

SMITH, R. C. S. *See* STANDRING-SMITH, R. C.
SOOLE, Rev. W. B. Gnr., R.G.A.   1898
✠SOUTHWELL, F. E. G. Lieut., E. Yorks. Regt.(T.F.)   1908
    Died 10 *April* 1917 *of wounds received in action*
SQUIRES,A.P.H. Capt.,Lincolnshire Regt.; attd.T.M.B. [1914]
    (W.) *M.C.*
STANDRING-SMITH, R. C. Major, R.A.M.C.(T.F.)   1897
STARLING, G. Flt. Cadet, R.A.F.   *1909
STEARN, G. F. 2nd Lieut., R. Fusiliers. (P.)   1913
STEEL, D. M. Lieut., R.G.A. (W.)   1915
STEERS, J. A. 2nd Lieut., Labour Corps   1916
STEVENSON, W. F. J. F. 2nd Lieut., Seaforth Hdrs.   1913
✠STOKES, R. J. Pte., R. Fusiliers (P.S. Bn.); 2nd Lieut., 1907
    King's Royal Rifle Corps. (W.)
    Killed in action 20 *Aug.* 1916
STUART, J. A. G. Lieut., R.G.A. (W.) (P. *Escaped* 1914
    from Germany)
SWANN-MASON, Rev. R. S. Chaplain, R.N. *O.B.E.*   *1895
✠SWIFT, W. 2nd Lieut., Lincolnshire Regt.   1913
    Killed in action 1–3 *July* 1916

✠TALL, J. J. 2nd Lieut., Devonshire Regt.   1912
    Killed in action 17 *Feb.* 1918
TAVENER, F. E. 2nd Lieut., R.G.A.   1917
TAYLOR, Rev. B. W. C.F. 4th Class, R.A.C.D.   1905
TAYLOR, C. C. Lieut., London Regt. (R. Fus.) (W.)   1909
✠THEOBALD, R. Lieut., Suffolk Regt. (W.) *M.C.*   [1914]
    Killed in action 10 *April* 1918
THOMAS, A. H. Major, Lancs. Fus. *M* 2.   1896
THOMAS, E. A. Capt., R.G.A. (T.F.); Hon. Capt. (A.),   1911
    R.A.F. (W.)
THOMAS, J. O. 2nd Lieut., D. of Wellington's (W. Rid-   1914
    ing Regt.) (W.)
THOMAS, W. E. Leading Telegraphist, R.N.V.R.   1913
THOMPSON, W. B. Seaman, R.N.V.R.   1909
TRIST,L.H. Capt., Lincolnshire Regt.; Major, E. Lancs. 1902
    Regt.; Lieut.-Col., Welsh Regt. (W 2.) *D.S.O.*
    M.C. *M* 2.
TUCK, C. H. Lieut., Lancaster Grammar School   1911
    O.T.C.
TURNER, E. M. Sergt., Gloucestershire Regt. (T.F.)   1908
    M.M.
TURNER, G. McD. Capt., W. Yorks. Regt.(T.F.); Capt.   1909
    (A.), R.A.F.; S.O. 3.

✠UNWIN, E. F. Major (A.), R.F.C. (W.) *M.*   1900
Died 22 March 1916 *of injuries received in flying acci-*
dent 31 *Jan.* 1916

WAKEFIELD, Rev. A. H. C.F. 4th Class, R.A.C.D.   1912
WALBANK, C. F. Writer, R.N.R.   1916
✠WARD-PRICE, L. S. Corpl., K. Edward's Horse; Lieut.,   1912
Life Gds.; Capt. (A.), R.F.C. (W.) *M.*
Killed in action 25 *March* 1917
WATERS, Rev. G. M. Chaplain, R.N.   1889
WATSON, R. E. 2nd Lieut., Seaforth Hdrs.; attd. R.   1916
Scots Fus. (W.)
WATSON, Rev. W. N. C.F. 4th Class, R.A.C.D.   1891
✠WATTS, H. L. Capt., Essex Regt.   1903
Killed in action 20 *Oct.* 1915
WEBSTER, H. Capt., Norfolk Regt.   1912
✠WHITE, F. R. 2nd Lieut., R.E.; attd. R.F.C.   1911
Died 23 *Jan.* 1917 *of wounds received in action*
WHITE, G. E. Lieut., R.G.A. (W.)   1907
WHITHAM, A. 2nd Lieut., The Queen's (R. W. Surrey   1910
Regt.) and Labour Corps
WILKINSON, E. Lieut., R.F.A. (W.)   1912
✠WILLIAMS, H. G. 2nd Lieut., King's Royal Rifle Corps   1913
Died 5 *Jan.* 1917 *of injuries received on active ser-*
vice
WILLIAMS, W. S. 2nd Lieut., Welsh Regt. (W.)   1911
WOLFE, B. T. 2nd Lieut., Cheshire Regt.   1912
WOOD, A. J. 2nd Lieut., Monmouthshire Regt.; Lieut.,   1911
S. Lancs. Regt.
WOOD, E. R. Capt., Cambridgeshire Regt. (W 4.) *M.C.*   1912
and Bar
WOOD, L. S. Capt., R.A.S.C.; Major, D.A.D. S. and T.   1897
M.B.E. M.
WOODCOCK, G. 2nd Lieut., S. Lancs. Regt.; Lieut.,   1912
King's Own (R. Lancaster Regt.); empld. Intelligence
and Education Staff
✠WORMALD, O. E. Capt., Suffolk Regt.(T.F.)   1911
Died 2 *Feb.* 1917 *of appendicitis*
WORMALD, Rev. R. L. C.F. 4th Class, R.A.C.D.; empld. *1908
Indian Army. *M.B.E. M. m.*
WORMELL, R. L. *See* WORMALD, Rev. R. L.
WRIGHT, Rev. A. L. C.F. 4th Class, R.A.C.D.   *1909

ST JOHN'S COLLEGE

ACTON, H. Lieut., S. Staffs. Regt. (W.)   1909
ADAMS, Rev. H. J. C.F. 4th Class, R.A.C.D.   1876
✠ADAMS, J. B. P. Lieut., R. Welsh Fus. (W.)   1909
 Died 27 Feb. 1917 of wounds received in action
✠ADAMSON, F. D. Lieut., Border Regt.   1910
 Killed in action 16 Nov. 1915
ADLER, H. M. Capt. and Adjt., R.A.S.C. *M.B.E. m.*   1894
✠AINLEY, K. E. D. 2nd Lieut., R.E.(T.F.)   1913
 Died 9 June 1915 of wounds received in action in Galli-
 poli 11 May 1915
✠ALEXANDER, Rev. P. G. Chaplain, R.N.   1905
 Drowned on H.M.S. Hampshire 5 June 1916
ALEXANDER, Rev. R. C. Chaplain, R.N.   1905
ALLDRED, R. A. Lieut., Loyal N. Lancs. Regt.; R.T.O.   1915
 (W.)
ALLEN, F. Lieut., I.A.R.O., attd. 28th Punjabis. (W.)   1912
✠ALLEN, G. A. Pte., London Regt. (Artists Rifles); 2nd   1905
 Lieut., Essex Regt.
 Killed in action on the Somme 1 July 1916
ALLOTT, P. B. Capt., Northamptonshire Regt.   1899
ANDERSON, L. R. D. Capt. and Adjt., R.F.A. *M.C.*   1905
ANDREWS, J. A. Capt., R.A.M.C.(T.F.) (W.)   1895
ANDREWS, J. C. Capt. and Adjt., London Regt.(Q.V.R.);   1909
 Staff Capt. *M.C. M 2.*
ANTHONY, A. L. Capt., R.A.M.C. (W.)   1908
ANTROBUS, H. Lieut., R.E.   1910
APPLETON, E. V. Capt., R.E.   1911
ARCHER-HIND, L. 2nd Lieut., Lincolnshire Regt.   1915
ARMITAGE, B. W. F. Lieut., R.A.M.C.   1909

ARNOLD, J. C.   Capt., Northumberland Fus.; empld.   1900
Ministry of Pensions. (W.)
ARNOTT, E. W.   Major, R.F.A.(T.F.)   *O.B.E. M.*   1902
ASHBURNER, W.   Capt., Gloucestershire Regt.(T.F.);   1885
Major, Labour Corps
ASHBY, Rev. N.   Lce.-Corpl., R.A.M.C.   1902
ASKEY, Rev. A. H.   C.F. 4th Class, R.A.C.D.   *1879
ASKEY, S. G.   Capt., R.A.M.C.(T.F.)   1907
ATKINSON, G.   Pioneer, R.E. (Spec. Bde.)   *M.*   1911
✠ATKINSON, H. N.   2nd Lieut., Cheshire Regt. *D.S.O.*   1908
Missing, presumed killed in action, 22 Oct. 1914
ATTLEE, W. H. W.   Major, R.A.M.C.   *M.*   1894
AUBRY, C. P.   Lieut., R.G.A.   1908
AVERILL, T. H.   Lieut., N. Staffs. Regt.   (W.)   1909

✠BADCOCK, A. L.   2nd Lieut., Northamptonshire Regt.   1913
and King's Own (Yorkshire L.I.)
Killed in action 13 Oct. 1915
BAILY, G. G.   Capt., Sherwood Foresters (Notts. and   1892
Derby Regt., T.F.) and Labour Corps
BAKER, M. W.   Capt., R.A.M.C.   1902
BANNERMAN, Rev. W. E.   C.F. 4th Class, R.A.C.D.   1884
BARBOUR, G. B.   Pte., H.A.C.; 2nd Lieut., R.F.A.   1912
BARKER, P. T.   2nd Lieut., R.F.A.   1917
BARLOW, P. S.   Capt., R. Sussex Regt. (T.F.); Capt.   1902
and Adjt., R.E.
BARNES, G. G.   Major, London Regt. (Post Office Rifles).   1905
(W 2.)   *m.*
✠BARNETT, B. L. T.   Capt., R.A.S.C.   1893
Died 18 April 1915
BARRETT, H. S.   Capt., King's (Liverpool Regt., T.F.)   1906
O.B.E. M 2.
BARRETT GREENE, A. H.   Lieut., N. Staffs. Regt.(T.F.)   1913
and Training Res. Bn.
BARRITT, W. V.   Capt., R.A.M.C.(T.F.)   1903
✠BARTLETT,W.H.   Lieut.,Fort Garry Horse, Canadian Force   1896
Killed in action 14 Sept. 1916
BARTON, F. S.   Lieut. (T.), R.A.F.   1914
BEALE, C. E.   Capt., R. Berkshire Regt.; attd. Devon   1907
Regt. (W.)   *m.*
BEARD, A. J.   Capt., Essex Regt.; empld. O.C.B.   (W 2.)   1912
M.C.
✠BEARD, E. C.   Lieut., Essex Regt.(T.F.)   1909
Killed in action at Gaza 26 March 1917

✠Beaumont-Checkland, M. B. Lieut., W. Somerset Yeo.; 1902
attd. Somerset L.I.
Killed in action at Langemarck 17 Aug. 1917
Beckley, V. A. Lieut., R.G.A. *M.C.* 1914
✠Beechey, C. R. Pte., R. Fusiliers 1897
Killed in action in E. Africa 18 Oct. 1917
Beith, I. H. Capt., Argyll and Sutherland Hdrs.; Hon. 1895
Major, M.G.C.; Major, Spec. List, empld. British
Military Mission. *C.B.E. M.C. M.*
Bell, T. O. Capt., Essex Regt. 1905
Bellman, Rev. A. F. C.F. 4th Class, R.A.C.D. 1909
Bennett, C. W. Capt., R.A.S.C. 1898
Bennion, J. M. Lieut., R.A.M.C. 1895
Benoy, Rev. J. C.F. 1st Class, R.A.C.D.; A.C.G. 1882
Benoy, J. F. Lieut., S. Staffs. Regt.; Capt., Spec. List 1913
(Bde. Bombing Officer). (W 2.) *M.*
✠Benson, G. E. Rfn., Rifle Brigade 1913
Killed in action near Fromelles 9 May 1915
Benstead, A. S. Lieut., Lincolnshire Regt.; Major, Gen. 1914
List (Cmdt., Reception Camp)
Bentley, A. J. Capt., Border Regt. (W.) *M.C. and Bar* 1907
Bentley, Rev. J. H. Chaplain, R.A.F. 1903
Beresford, G. A. Lieut., R.F.A. 1907
✠Bernard, H. C. 2nd Lieut., Gloucestershire Regt.; attd. 1912
Worcestershire Regt. (W.)
Killed in action 3 Sept. 1916
Bevan, E. J. 2nd Lieut., King's Own (Yorkshire L.I.) 1914
Bevan, G. T. M. Major, R.E. *M.* 1909
Bevan, Ven. H. E. J. C.F. 3rd Class, R.A.C.D.(T.F.) 1873
✠Billinger, H. F. 2nd Lieut., E. Lancs. Regt. 1911
Killed in action 23 Nov. 1916
Billinghurst, W. B. Capt., Gen. List (T.F. Res.) *m.* 1872
Bilsland, A. S. Capt., Cameronians (Scottish Rifles, 1910
T.F.); Staff Capt. *M.C.*
Bindloss, A. H. Major, R.A.M.C. 1884
Binns, A. L. Capt., Lincolnshire Regt.; empld. R.E. 1911
(W.) *M.C.*
Bisdee, J. S. M. Trooper, K. Edward's Horse; Lieut., 1913
R.F.A.
Black, S. G. Air Mechanic, R.N.A.S. 1910
Bladwell, E. W. Corpl., R.E. 1913
✠Blakeley, F. R. 2nd Lieut., Somerset L.I.; attd. Indian 1914
Army
Killed in action 22 Feb. 1917

BLAXTER, A. P. LL.   Lieut., Northamptonshire Regt.   1910
BLUMHARDT, E. H. F.   *See* MILLS, E. H. F.
✠BODDINGTON, Rev. V. C.   C.F. 4th Class, R.A.C.D.(T.F.)   1905
Died 13 *March* 1917 *of tuberculosis contracted on active*
service
BOND, B. W.   Capt., Connaught Rangers.   (W.)   *M.C.*   1913
✠BONSER, G. A. G.   Capt., R.A.M.C.(T.F.)   (W.)   1907
Killed in action near Armentières 29 *Sept.* 1918
BONSEY, Rev. W. H.   C.F. 4th Class, R.A.C.D.(T.F.)   1892
BOOTH, E.   Lieut., Middlesex Regt. and M.G.C.   1913
BOWDON, Rev. W. S.   C.F. 4th Class, R.A.C.D.   1899
✠BOWEN, L. H.   Corpl., London Regt. (Q.V.R.); Lieut.,   1907
Lincolnshire Regt.
Killed in action 22 *Dec.* 1915
BRACKETT, A. W. K.   Lieut., Queen's Own (R. W. Kent   1913
Regt.)   (W.)
BRASH, E. J. Y.   Major, R.A.M.C.(T.F.)   *Order of St*   1907
Sava, 4*th Class* (*Serbia*)
BRAUNHOLTZ, H. J.   Lce.-Corpl., R.A.M.C.   1908
BRIAN, F. R. H.   Lieut., R.G.A.   1912
BRICE-SMITH, H. F.   Capt., R.A.M.C.   (W 2.)   *M.C.*   1908
M.
✠BRICE-SMITH, J. K.   2nd Lieut., Lincolnshire Regt.   [1914]
Died 11 *Sept.* 1915 *of wounds received in action in the*
Ypres Salient 6 *Sept.* 1915
BRIGGS, G. E.   Sergt.-Instructor, R.E. (Signals)   1912
BRIGGS, Rev. W. A.   Chaplain, R.N.   1900
✠BROCK, E. G.   Capt., King's (Liverpool Regt.,T.F.)   *M.C.* 1911
Killed in action 31 *July* 1917
BROOKE, Z. N.   Capt., E. Surrey Regt. and Gen. List   1902
(Intelligence)
✠BROWN, C. W.   Capt., R. Scots Fus.   (W 2.)   1911
Killed in action 1 *May* 1916
✠BROWN, E. M.   Lieut., Tank Corps.   (W.)   1912
Killed in action 29 *Sept.* 1917
BROWN, S. R.   Lieut., R.F.A.(T.F.)   *M.C.*   1899
BROWN, W. L.   Capt., R.A.M.C. (1st London Gen. Hos-   1889
pital, T.F.)
BROWNE, B.   2nd Lieut., R.A.S.C.   1910
✠BROWNING, Rev. G. A.   Chaplain, R.N.   1896
Killed in action in the Battle of Jutland 31 *May* 1916
BROWNING, H. A.   Surgeon Lieut.-Cdr., R.N.   1898
BROWNING, K. C.   Lieut., R.E.; empld. Ministry of Muni-   1894
tions

✠BROWNSON, R. D. D. D. Capt., R.A.M.C. (W.) 1902
 Died at Peshawar 21 *Oct.* 1918
BUCHANAN, G. B. Major, R.A.M.C.(T.F.) 1887
BUCKLEY, W. H. 2nd Lieut., 6th (Inniskilling) Dragoons. [1914]
 (W.)
BULLEN, F. J. Lieut., R.G.A.; empld. Ministry of Muni- 1911
 tions
BUNT, A. P. Capt. and Adjt., D. of Cornwall's L.I. 1910
BURDON, R., v.D. Hon. Colonel, Durham L.I.(T.F.) 1849
 C.B.E.
BURLING, E. J. P. Capt. (A.), R.A.F. *D.S.C. D.F.C.* 1912
 M. French Croix de Guerre
✠BURR, F. G. Capt., R. Scots Fus. 1908
 Killed in action in the Battle of Loos 26 *Sept.* 1915
BURRELL, J. H. Capt. and Adjt., Durham L.I. (P.) *M.* 1912
BURTON, Rev. H. P. W. C.F. 4th Class, R.A.C.D. 1907
BURTON-FANNING, F. W. Major, R.A.M.C.(T.F. Res.) 1888
BUTLER, A. G. Colonel, Australian A.M.C. *D.S.O.* 1891
 M 2.
BUTTON, A. E. Air Mechanic, R.A.F. 1908

CADLE, H. S. Lieut., E. Surrey Regt.(T.F.); Capt., 1882
 Labour Corps.; empld. Ministry of Labour. *M.*
✠CALLENDER, R. H. 2nd Lieut., Durham L.I. 1913
 Accidentally killed near Armentières 5 *Oct.* 1915
CALVERT, E. Capt., I.M.S. 1907
CAMPBELL, Rev. A. J. C.F. 3rd Class, R.A.C.D.(T.F.) *m.* 1894
CAMPBELL, C. G. H. Capt., R.A.M.C. 1905
CARDWELL, A. G. Lieut. (T.), R.A.F. 1908
CARLILL, H. B. Surgeon Lieut., R.N. *M.* 1900
CARNEGY, Rev. F. W. C.F. 4th Class, R.A.C.D. 1889
CARTER, W. H. Lieut., I.A.R.O., attd. 6th Gurkha 1908
 Rifles and 4th Assam Rifles; Capt., Spec. List. *m.*
✠CASSELS, W. G. Capt., Border Regt. *M.* 1912
 Killed in action near Bouzencourt 13 *July* 1916
CASSON, R. Capt., I.A.R.O. 1897
✠CASTLE, C. W. Lieut., S. Lancs. Regt. 1914
 Killed in action 3 *Aug.* 1917
CHADWICK, B. Ll. 2nd Lieut., R.G.A.; empld. Ministry 1910
 of Labour
CHADWICK, M. Capt., R.A.M.C. 1908
✠CHAPMAN, A. R. B Lieut., Loyal N. Lancs. Regt.(T.F.) 1913
 (W 2.)
 Killed in action 6 *June* 1916

CHAPPLE, A. Lieut. (T.), R.A.F. 1895
CHAPPLE, H. Capt., R.A.M.C. 1901
CHASTENEY, H. E. 2nd Lieut., R.G.A. (W.) 1907
CHECKLAND, M. BEAUMONT. *See* BEAUMONT-CHECKLAND,
M. B.
✠CHEESE, Rev. W. G. C.F. 4th Class, R.A.C.D. 1902
*Died 7 Nov. 1918 of pneumonia contracted on active
service*
CHEESEMAN, A. L. Capt., 9th Infy. Bn., S. African Force 1896
CHEETHAM, E. M. Corpl., R.E. 1912
✠CHELL, H. Lieut., R. Fusiliers 1908
*Died 10 Aug. 1915 of wounds received in action 9 Aug.
1915*
CHESHIRE, F. M. Lieut., 2nd Nagpur Rifles, Indian De- 1906
fence Force
✠CHIDSON, L. D. Capt., King's Royal Rifle Corps. *M.C.* [1914]
M.
Killed in action 24 April 1917
CHURCHWARD, Rev. A. C. Pte., R.A.S.C. *1905
CHURCHWARD, Rev. M. W. C.F. 1st Class, R.A.C.D.; *1879
A.C.G. *C.B.E. m.*
✠CLARK, H. R. E. 2nd Lieut., London Regt. (Civil Ser- 1910
vice Rifles)
*Died 3 June 1915 of wounds received in action 25 May
1915*
✠CLARKE, D. Pte., H.A.C.; 2nd Lieut. (O.), R.F.C. 1913
Killed in action 26 Aug. 1916
CLARKE, J. H. Capt., D. of Cornwall's L.I. (W.) 1912
CLARKE, J. S. Lieut.-Col., Wiltshire Regt.; G.S.O. 2, 1882
War Office. *Brevet Lieut.-Colonel. m.*
✠CLARKE, R. S. Capt., King's (Shropshire L.I.) 1909
Killed in action near Hooge 25 Sept. 1915
CLAY, W. K. 2nd Lieut., R.A.S.C. 1899
CLELAND, J. R. Capt., R.F.A. 1908
CLEMENTS, T. H. 2nd Lieut., R.A.S.C.(M.T.) 1896
CLOUGH, T. Capt., I.A.R.O., attd. 21st Cavalry 1906
COAD, C. N. Capt., R.A.M.C. (W.) *M.C. and Bar. M.* 1902
✠COBBOLD, R. H. W. Lieut., Rifle Brigade 1912
Killed in action 9 Sept. 1915
COLEMAN, Rev. N. D. C.F. 4th Class, R.A.C.D. 1910
CONSTABLE, W. G. Major, Sherwood Foresters (Notts. 1906
and Derby Regt.) and Lancs. Fus. *M.*
COOMBS, A. G. Major, R.G.A. *D.S.O. M. Belgian* 1903
Croix de Guerre

✠Coop, W.   Pte., King's (Liverpool Regt., Liverpool   1902
Scottish, T.F.)
Died 24 June 1915 of wounds received in action in the
Ypres Salient 16 June 1915
Cooper, H.   Capt., Unattd. List T.F. (O.T.C.)   1908
Cooper, M. C.   Lieut., Oxford and Bucks. L.I.; Major,   1898
M.G.C.   *M.C. and Bar.   M* 2.
Cort, J. L. P.   Lieut., R.A.S.C.; Hon. Lieut. (Ad.),   1903
R.A.F.
✠Cotton, Rev. R. H. A.   2nd Lieut., R.A.S.C.   1908
Died at Taranto 12 Oct. 1918 of pneumonia
Cox, H. B.   Lieut.-Col., R.G.A.(T.F.)   *O.B.E.*   1901
Crauford, L. G.   Sapper, R.E. (London Electrical En-   1904
gineers, T.F.)
Crick, L. G. M.   Lieut., Cheshire Regt.(T.F.)   1910
✠Croggon, J. F. S.   Capt., Sherwood Foresters (Notts. and   1899
Derby Regt.)   (W.)
Died 18 Nov. 1918 of influenza contracted on active
service
Crole-Rees, Rev. H. S.   Chaplain, R.N.   1903
Crowther, C. R.   Capt., R.A.M.C.(T.F.)   (P.)   1896
✠Cruickshank, D. E.   Pte., R. Fusiliers (P. S. Bn.); 2nd   1906
Lieut., Border Regt.; attd. Wiltshire Regt.
Killed in action in Mesopotamia 9 April 1916
Cuff, A. W.   Major, R.A.M.C.(T.F. Res.)   *M.*   1888
Cullis, L.   Lieut., I.A.R.O., attd. 23rd Sikh Pioneers   1902
Cummings, R. R.   Instructor Cdr., R.N.   1890
Cummins, F. J.   Capt., Dorset Regt.   (W.)   1914
Curzon-Siggers, W. A.   Air Mechanic, R.F.C.   1913
Cushing, W. E. W.   2nd Lieut., Norfolk Regt.; Lieut.   1909
(Ad.), R.A.F.

Dale, F.   Pte., H.A.C.; 2nd Lieut., King's Own Scottish   1907
Borderers
Darlington, W. A. C.   Capt. and Adjt., Northumber-   1909
land Fus.(T.F.); empld. War Office.   (W.)
✠Davenport, A.   Lieut., Rifle Brigade; attd. Tank Corps.   1915
(W.)
Killed in action near Boyelles 23 Aug. 1918
Davies, E.   Capt., Sherwood Rangers; empld. Egyptian   1908
Govt.   (W.)
Davies, R. M.   Lieut., R.F.A.   (W 2.)   1911
Davis, H.   Lieut., Somerset L.I.(T.F.); attd. 3rd Gurkha   1909
Rifles, Indian Army

DAVIS, H. J. Sergt., R. Welsh Fus   1908
DAVY, C. L. Capt., M.G.C.; attd. Tank Corps. (W 3.) 1914
  M.C.
DAWSON, A. M. Capt., Hampshire Regt.(T.F.) (W.)   1905
  M.C.
DAWSON, R. T. Lieut., Edinburgh Academy O.T.C.   1904
✠DAY, D. I. 2nd Lieut., R.F.A.   1911
  Died 7 Oct. 1915 of wounds received in action at
  Vermelles 25 Sept. 1915
DAY, G. L. Major, Huntingdonshire Cyclist Bn.; attd. 1910
  Gloucestershire Regt. *M.*
DENHAM, H. A. Major, R.G.A.(T.F.) (W.) *D.S.O. M.*   1898
DENHAM, Rev. J. P. C.F. 4th Class, R.A.C.D. *M.*   1908
DESMOND, G. G. Pte., Gloucestershire Regt. (P.)   1890
DIGGES LA TOUCHE, H. N. *See* LA TOUCHE, H. N. D.
DIXON, C. Capt., R. Scots.; empld. O.C.B. (W.)   1906
DODD, Rev. R. P. C.F. 3rd Class, R.A.C.D. (W.)   1905
  M.C. M.
DODD, W. P. Lieut., R. Welsh Fus. (W.) *M.C.*   1908
DONOVAN, E. L. 2nd Lieut., E. Yorks. Regt. (Cyclist 1907
  Bn., T.F.); Lieut., King's African Rifles
DOUGLAS, J. 2nd Lieut., R.E.; Lieut. (A.), R.A.F. (W.) 1913
DOUGLAS, S. M. 2nd Lieut., R. Fusiliers. (W.)   1898
DRUMMOND, J. B. Sapper, R.E.   1914
DRYSDALE, J. H. Lieut.-Col., R.A.M.C. (1st London   1881
  Gen. Hospital, T.F.)
DUFFIELD, H. W. 2nd Lieut., D. of Cornwall's L.I.; [1914]
  Capt., M.G.C. (W.)
DUMAS, A. B. Capt., R. Warwickshire Regt. (W.)   1913
DUNDAS, A. C. Major, Middlesex Regt.; D.A.A.G.   1899
  (W 2.) *O.B.E. M* 2. *m.*
DUNKERLEY, C. L. Capt., Queen's Own (R. W. Kent   1911
  Regt.) (W.) *M.C.*
DUNLOP, J. K. Capt., London Regt. (Rangers); Major, 1910
  M.G.C. and Gen. Staff, empld. British Military
  Mission. (W.) *M.C. M* 2. *m. Order of St Anne,*
  4th Class (*Russia*)
DUTTON, H. Lieut., N. Staffs. Regt. and M.G.C.   1907
DYKE-MARSH, H. ST. G. Sapper, R.E. (Meteorological   1914
  Section)

EARLE, G. F. Lieut., R.A.S.C.   1908
EASTON, J. W. Lieut., R.G.A.   1906
EBERLI, W. F. Surgeon Lieut., R.N.   1910

EDWARDES, F. E. 2nd Lieut., Harrow School O.T.C. 1893
✠EDWARDES, H. F. E. 2nd Lieut., D. of Cornwall's L.I. 1893
    Killed in action 6 Feb. 1917
EDWARDS, A. T. Major, R.A.M.C. 1908
EDWARDS, G. R. Lieut. (A.), R.A.F. (W.) (P.) 1910
EDWARDS, Rev. N. W. A. C.F. 3rd Class, R.A.C.D. 1896
    O.B.E. M.C. M 2.
ELLIS, A. I. Capt., R. Fusiliers 1903
ENGLEDOW, F. L. Lieut.-Col., Queen's Own (R.W. 1910
    Kent Regt. T.F.) *M. French Croix de Guerre*
ENGLEFIELD, F. R. H. Lieut., Hampshire Regt. 1910
ENGLISH, F. H. 2nd Lieut., Aldenham School O.T.C. 1911
EVANS, E. D. Lieut., Middlesex Regt., Labour Corps, 1901
    and R.G.A.
✠EVANS, H. C. Lieut.-Cdr., R.N.V.R. (Nelson Bn., R.N.D.) *1909
    M.
    Killed in action in Gallipoli 5 *June* 1915
EVANS, R. D. 2nd Lieut., King's Royal Rifle Corps. (P.) 1912
EVANS, W. E. Lieut., R.G.A. 1911
✠EVATT, G. R. K. Capt., Middlesex Regt. 1900
    Killed in action near Armentières 14 *Nov.* 1914

FAIRBANK, J. Pte., R.A.S.C.(M.T.) 1914
FAYERMAN, A. P. G. Major, R. Warwickshire Regt.(T.F.) 1904
FERGUSSON, A. Major, Middlesex Regt. (W.) 1900
FERGUSSON, J. N. F. Capt., R.A.M.C. 1900
FERGUSSON, L. R. Lieut., R.F.A.; Capt., Spec. List 1903
✠FERRIS, S. B. C. 2nd Lieut., 10th Hussars 1908
    Accidentally killed 6 *April* 1915
FEWINGS, J. A. 2nd Lieut., R.G.A. 1906
FILMER, W. G. H. Capt. and Adjt., The Buffs (E. Kent 1913
    Regt.) *M.B.E. M.*
FISHER, F. B. Lieut., I.A.R.O., attd. 5th Gurkha Rifles. 1907
    (W.)
FISON, A. K. Capt., Essex Regt. (W 3.) *M.C. Chevalier,* 1910
    Legion of Honour (France). French Croix de Guerre
FLEET, Rev. C. S. C.F. 4th Class, R.A.C.D. *M.C. M.* 1906
✠FLETCHER, J. H. B. Lieut., London Regt. 1899
    Died 13 *May* 1915 *of wounds received in action* 12 *May*
    1915
FODEN, W. B. Gnr., R.G.A. 1911
FORBES, A., D.S.O. Colonel, R.A.O.C.; Major-Gen., 1871
    Principal Ordnance Officer. *C.B. C.M.G. M.*

FORD, F. C. 2nd Lieut., D. of Cornwall's L.I. 1886
FORSTER, M. Pte., R.A.O.C. 1894
FOSTER, Rev. J. R. C.F. 4th Class, R.A.C.D. 1894
✠FOSTER, R. D. Lieut., Lincolnshire Regt. 1910
Wounded and missing, presumed killed in action, in Gallipoli 7 Aug. 1915
FOX, T. S. W. Capt., Oxford and Bucks. L.I.(T.F. Res.) 1897
FRANKLIN, C. S. P. Instructor Cdr., R.N. 1895
FRANKLIN, H. W. Air Mechanic, R.N.A.S. 1915
FRANKLIN, J. H. Lieut., R.N.V.R. *Order of the White* 1898
Eagle (Serbia). French Croix de Guerre
FRANKLIN, T. B. Capt., Fettes College O.T.C. *m* 2. 1901
FRASER, D. S. 2nd Lieut., I.A.R.O. (Cavalry) 1906
FREAN, H. G. Capt., R.A.M.C. 1901
✠FREDERICK, T. Major, Norfolk Regt. (W.) *M.C. M.* 1912
Died 14 Dec. 1917 of wounds received in action near Cambrai 3 Dec. 1917

GALE, C. C. Capt., R.A.S.C. 1908
GALT, R. B. 2nd Lieut., King's (Liverpool Regt.) (W.) 1913
✠GARDINER, K. J. R. Lieut., R.E. (Tunnelling Coy.); 1909
Capt., King's African Rifles
Died on H.M. hospital ship 1 Feb. 1917 of dysentery
GARDNER, J. M. S. Capt., 124th Baluchistan Infy., In- 1913
dian Army
GARNER, H. M. Sub.-Lieut., R.N.V.R. 1911
GARRETT, H. L. O. Capt., I.A.R.O.; Recruiting Officer 1899
GARROOD, J. R. Capt., R.A.M.C.(T.F.) 1892
GAUSSEN, J. M. Major, R. Warwickshire Regt.(T.F.); 1912
empld. O.C.B. (W.) *M.*
✠GAZE, G. A. Capt., London Regt. (Civil Service Rifles) 1900
Killed in action 15 Sept. 1916
GEORGE, J. T. Capt., Monmouthshire Regt.; empld. [1914]
Ministry of Pensions. (W.) *M.C.*
GILL, C. G. HOPE. Capt., R.E. (R. Monmouth) [1914]
GILL, G. A. Lieut., R.G.A. *M.C. and Bar* 1914
GILL, R. G. Sapper, R.E. 1903
GILLESPIE, J. J., T.D. Colonel, Northumberland Fus. 1889
(T.F.) *Brevet Colonel. m.*
GILLESPIE, T. Capt., R.A.M.C. 1894
GILLING, H. T., T.D. Lieut.-Col., R.F.A.(T.F.) *O.B.E.* 1882
GILLSON, A. H. S. Instructor Lieut., R.N. 1908
GLEAVE, Rev. J. W. C.F. 4th Class, R.A.C.D. 1909

✠GLEAVE, T. R. Lieut., S. Lancs. Regt.(T.F.) 1913
   Killed in action 11 *Oct.* 1916
GLEDHILL, W. G. Capt., Norfolk Regt. (T.F.); Capt. 1899
   (T.), R.A.F. (Aircraft Production Dept.) *M.*
GLOVER, J. A. Capt., R.A.M.C. *O.B.E.* 1894
✠GLYN, C. R. 2nd Lieut., Hodson's Horse, Indian Army 1913
   Killed in action in Mesopotamia 17 *Jan.* 1917
GOBBITT, R. H. S. Paymaster Lieut., R.N.R. [1914]
GOLD, E. Lieut.-Col., R.E. (Meteorological Section). 1900
   D.S.O. O.B.E. M 4.
GOLDIE, A. H. R. Major, R.E. (Meteorological Section). 1910
   M 2.
GOLDWATER, H. G. 2nd Lieut., R.G.A. [1914]
GOODE, R. H. Lieut., M.G.C.; empld. Ministry of La- 1908
   bour. (W.)
GOODING, S. Capt., R.A.M.C. 1898
GOOLDEN, H. J. Rfn., King's Royal Rifle Corps. (W.) 1912
GORDON, E. F. S. Surgeon Lieut., R.N. 1912
GOYDER, F. W. Hon. Capt., R.A.M.C. 1896
GRABHAM, G. W. Lieut., R.A.S.C.(M.T.) 1914
✠GRAIL, C. G. Capt., N. Staffs. Regt. *1909
   Died 23 *July* 1915 *of wounds received in action in*
   Gallipoli
GREAR, E. J. L. Lieut., Middlesex Regt. and M.G.C. 1910
   (W 2.)
GREEN, N. Lieut., Sherwood Foresters (Notts. and 1906
   Derby Regt.); Capt., Gen. List. (W.)
GREEN, S. M. Capt., London Regt. (Kensington Bn.) 1907
   (W.) *M.*
GREENLEES, J. R. C. Lieut.-Col., R.A.M.C. *D.S.O. and* 1898
   Bar. M 3. *Chevalier, Legion of Honour (France)*
GREENSTREET, N. B. DE M. 2nd Lieut., Norfolk Regt. 1912
   (T.F.)
GREGORY, A. R. Capt., Border Regt.(T.F.) (W.) 1909
GREGORY, H. L. Major, R.A.M.C.(T.F.) 1891
✠GREGORY, R. P. Capt., Cambridge Univ. O.T.C., empld. 1898
   O.C.B.; 2nd Lieut., Gloucestershire Regt. (W.)
   Died 24 *Nov.* 1918 *of pneumonia following influenza*
   contracted on active service
GRICE, N. Capt., W. Yorks. Regt.(T.F.) (W 3.) 1912
GRIFFITHS, Rev. G. A. M. C.F. 4th Class, R.A.C.D. 1908
GRIGG, P. J. Lieut., R.G.A. 1909
GRIGSON, P. ST J. B. Capt., I.A.R.O., attd. 70th Burma 1901
   Rifles

GUEST-WILLIAMS, W. K. Capt., Spec. List (R.T.O.) 1906
GWATKIN-GRAVES, E. A. Lieut., M.G.C. 1897
✠GWYNNE, H. LL. 2nd Lieut., N. Staffs. Regt. 1911
Killed in action at Grandcourt 18 *Nov.* 1916

HAGGER, N. W. Lieut., R. Sussex Regt.; empld. O.C.B. 1912
HAIGH, P. B. Lieut., I.A.R.O., attd. 114th Mahrattas; 1897
empld. School of Musketry; Major, Poona Bn.,
Indian Defence Force
HALL, Rev. H. A. C.F. 4th Class, R.A.C.D. *M.* 1881
HALL, Rev. S. H. C.F. 1st Class, R.A.C.D.(T.F.) 1869
✠HALLIWELL, W. N. 2nd Lieut., Yorkshire Regt. 1909
Died 21 *Sept.* 1916 *of wounds received in action*
HALSEY, R. T. Lieut., Cheshire Regt. 1907
✠HAMILTON,A.S. Lieut.-Col., Sherwood Foresters (Notts. 1883
and Derby Regt.) and Durham L.I.
Died 13 *Oct.* 1915 *of wounds received in action* 26 *Sept.*
1915
HANSON, J. Lieut., Coldstream Gds. and Gen. Staff 1909
HARDING, Rev. W. H. C.F. 4th Class, R.A.C.D. 1906
HARDMAN, W. H. Major, R.E.(T.F.) (W 2.) *M.C. M.* 1913
HARNETT, W. L. Lieut.-Col., I.M.S. *M.* 1896
HARRIS, H. Pte, R. Fusiliers (P. S. Bn.); Lieut., M.G.C. 1899
M.C.
HARTREE, D. R. Lieut., R.N.V.R. 1915
✠HARVEY, A. W. Capt., R.A.M.C. 1894
Died 7 *Sept.* 1916 *of wounds received in action*
HASLAM, V. K. Lieut., R.G.A. 1906
✠HAWCRIDGE, R. S. Corpl., R. Fusiliers 1905
Killed in action near Delville Wood 28 *July* 1916
HAYES, J. H Capt., Rifle Brigade and Gen. List (O.C.B.) 1894
(W.) *m.*
HAYWARD, A. W. Major, R.A.M.C.(T.F.) 1899
HAZLERIGG, G. 2nd Lieut., Sherwood Foresters (Notts. 1897
and Derby Regt., T.F. Res.)
✠HEALD, W. M. Lieut., R.A.M.C. 1913
Died 8 *Sept.* 1918 *of wounds received in action on the*
Somme 22 *Aug.* 1918
✠HEARN, R. C. Capt., London Regt. (Blackheath and 1911
Woolwich Bn.) *M.C.*
Killed in action near Jerusalem 30 *April* 1918
HEIMANN, H. P. Pte., Essex Regt. 1910
HELLINGS, G. S. Lieut., D. of Cornwall's L.I. 1907
HENDERSON, P. Capt., R.E. 1901

HENRY, W. D. M. Capt., R.A.S.C. *M.* 1909
HEPWORTH, F. A. Major, R.A.M.C.(T.F.) *O.B.E.* 1897
HERZL, H. Pte., Middlesex Regt. 1910
HEWITT, J. T. Major, R.E. and Spec. List, empld. Min- 1887
istry of Munitions)
HIBBERD, A. S. Lieut., Dorset Regt.; Capt. and Adjt., 1912
25th Punjabis, Indian Army
HICKS, Rev. F. W. Chaplain, R.N. 1905
HIGGINS, F. E. Lieut., R.A.M.C. 1909
HIGHFIELD-JONES, P. H. Capt., S. Staffs. Regt. (W.) 1912
M.C.
HIGSON, L. A. Capt., Middlesex Regt. (W 2.) 1912
HILARY, R. J. Lieut., The Buffs (E. Kent Regt.) (W.) 1912
✠HILL, J. R. Pte., W. Yorks. Regt.; 2nd Lieut., R.E. 1902
(Spec. Bde.)
Killed in action 6 May 1917
✠HILLER, A. M. 2nd Lieut., The Queen's (R.W. Surrey 1913
Regt.) *M.*
Killed in action 16 May 1915
HILLIER, T. L. Surgeon Prob., R.N.V.R. 1913
HITCHING, W. W. Lieut., R.G.A.; attd. R.E. 1915
✠HOBBS, A. V. Pte., Queen's Own (R. W. Kent Regt.); 1913
2nd Lieut., R. Sussex Regt. and R.F.C.
Killed in action over Valenciennes 15 Dec. 1915
✠HOBBS, V. W. J. Lieut., The Buffs (E. Kent Regt., T.F.) 1905
Killed in action at Morlancourt 9 Aug. 1918
HOGAN, R. V. J. S. Lieut., E. Lancs. Regt.; Capt., 1904
R.A.F.; S.O. 3, Air Ministry. (W 2.)
HOLDEN, H. F. Lieut., S. Staffs. Regt. (W.) 1914
HOLDEN, J. R. R. Fusiliers (P.S. Bn.); 2nd Lieut., R.E. 1911
(T.F.); Lieut. (A.), R.A.F.
✠HOLDEN, N. V. Lieut., Lancs. Fus.(T.F.) 1909
*Died 4 June 1915 of wounds received in action in Galli-
poli*
HOLTHOUSE, Rev. C. L. C.F. 4th Class, R.A.C.D. 1906
HOLTZAPFFEL, J. G. H. Capt., London Regt. (R. Fus.) 1907
HONEYBOURNE, H. C. Capt. and Adjt., London Regt. 1903
(Blackheath and Woolwich Bn.)
HONEYBOURNE, V. C. Major, R.A.M.C. *M.* 1899
HOOK, C. W. T. Lieut., The Buffs (E. Kent Regt., T.F.); 1911
Capt., Spec. List (T.M.B.)
HORLINGTON, F. Lieut., R.F.A.(T.F.); Staff Lieut. 1913
HORTON-SMITH, L. G. H. Pte., London Regt. (London 1890
Scottish)

HORTON-SMITH-HARTLEY, Sir P., C.V.O. Major, R.A.M.C. 1886
(1st London Gen. Hospital, T.F.)
How, Rev. J. C. H. C.F. 4th Class, R.A.C.D. 1900
HOWE, G. A. Capt., Lancs. Fus. (W.) 1911
✠HOWELL, M. I. B. 2nd Lieut., The Queen's (R. W. [1914]
Surrey Regt.)
Killed in action 25 Sept. 1915
✠HUGHES, J. L. Lieut., Welsh Regt.; attd. R.F.C. 1910
Killed in action 1 Oct. 1917
HUNTER, J. B. Capt., R.A.M.C. M.C. M. 1909
HUNTER, W. Colonel, A.M.S. C.B. *Order of St Sava*, †1887
2nd Class (*Serbia*)
HURRY, A. G. Lieut., Gloucestershire Regt.; attd. R. 1912
Irish Regt. (W.)
HUTCHINSON, R. W. 2nd Lieut., Labour Corps 1914
HYDE, R. W. Capt., Lincolnshire Regt.; attd. Gen. Staff, 1907
Indian Army; A.D.C.

INCHLEY, O. Lieut., R.A.M.C. (1st E. Gen. Hospital, 1892
T.F.)
INGRAM, A. C. Major, I.M.S. 1895
✠IREMONGER, E. V. Pte., R. Fusiliers 1905
Died in German hands at Le Quesnoy 13 *Sept.* 1918
IRVING, J. B. Capt., R.A.M.C. 1896
IRVING, J. C. 2nd Lieut., R.G.A. 1907
IRVING, P. A. Lieut., Bedfordshire Regt.; Capt., R.E. 1906
(Spec. Bde.) (W.)
ISAAC, C. L. Major, R.A.M.C.(T.F.) 1896

JACKLIN, J. V. Capt., Essex Regt. (W 3.) 1911
JACKSON, G. E. Pte., Queen's Own (R. W. Kent Regt.); 1908
2nd Lieut., Northamptonshire Regt.
JACKSON, Rev. J. E. N. C.F. 4th Class, R.A.C.D. 1905
✠JACOB, A. R. 2nd Lieut., Durham L.I. 1912
Died 18 *Sept.* 1916 *of wounds received in action*
17 *Sept.* 1916
JACOBSOHN, A. 2nd Lieut., R.A.S.C. [1914]
✠JACQUEST, S. P. Gnr., Canadian F.A. 1907
Killed in action 18 *Oct.* 1916
✠JAMES, F. A. Capt., Manchester Regt.(T.F.) (W.) 1905
Died 18 *Sept.* 1915 *of wounds received in action in*
Gallipoli
JAMES, G. Capt., R.A.M.C. 1901

† Fellow-Commoner.

JAMES, R. W. Capt., R.E. *M.*   1909
JARCHOW, C. J. F.   2nd Lieut., Sherwood Foresters 1898
   (Notts. and Derby Regt., T.F.)
JEANS, F. A. G. Hon. Major, R.A.M.C.   1896
JOCE, J. B. D. Lieut., R.N.V.R.   1901
JOHNSON, E. F. Lieut., Berkshire Regt. (P.)   1914
JOHNSON, Rev. V. Y. C.F. 4th Class, R.A.C.D.   1910
✠JOHNSTON, F. Major, King's (Shropshire L.I.)   1904
   Died 31 May 1918 of wounds received in action
JOHNSTON, M. C. Capt., R.A.S.C. *M.*   [1914]
JONES, I. E. Major, R. Welsh Fus. (W.)   1913
JONES, R. F. Capt., R.A.M.C.   1904
JONES, R. M. Lieut., Northumberland Fus. (W.)   1905
JOSEPH, F. A. Driver, H.A.C.; attd. R.E.   1914

KEEBLE, C. F. A. Lieut., Border Regt.; attd. R. Scots Fus.   1903
✠KEMP, P. V. Pte., R. Fusiliers (P. S. Bn.); Capt., Dur-   1910
   ham L.I.
   Died 31 May 1918 of gas poisoning
KEMPTHORNE, G. A. Lieut.-Col., R.A.M.C. (W.) (P.)   1895
   D.S.O. M 2.
KENDALL, G. M. Capt., R.A.M.C.   1911
KENNETT, W. H. Major, Rifle Brigade. *M.C. M.*   1899
KENNY, H. T. Colonel, Gen. Staff   1876
KERR, J. Major, R.A.M.C.   1881
KEY, Rev. S. W. C.F. 4th Class, R.A.C.D.(T.F.)   1892
KING, L. A. L. Lieut., R.F.A.(T.F.)   1898
KINGDOM, W. A. Lieut., S. Staffs. Regt. and M.G.C.   1911
   (W.)
KINGSFOLD, Rev. P. A. C.F. 4th Class, R.A.C.D.   1890
KINMAN, G. W. Major, Hertford School O.T.C. *T.D.* 1884
KIRK, J. H. District Officer, Nigeria. (W.)   1909
KIRKNESS, L. H. Lieut.-Col., Spec. List, attd. R.E.;   1901
   A. D. Railways, Salonika Force. *D.S.O. O.B.E.*
   M 4. *Order of the White Eagle, 4th Class (Czecho-*
   Slovakia). Order of the White Eagle, 5th Class (Serbia).
   Greek Medal for Military Merit
KNOWLES, J. A. Capt., Cheshire Regt. (W 2.) *M.C.*   1913
KNOX, R. U. E. Capt., Suffolk Regt.; empld. War Office. 1908
   (W.) *D.S.O. M.*

✠LAIDLAW, C. G. P. Pte., London Regt. (London Scottish) 1907
   Died 2 April 1915 of wounds received in action near
   Neuve Chapelle

✠LAIDLAW, W. S. Lieut., R.E. (W.) 1909
 Killed in action near Ypres 23 Nov. 1917
✠LANE, H. C. H. 2nd Lieut., Border Regt. 1906
 Killed in action 10 July 1917
LASBREY, Rev. P. U. C.F. 4th Class, R.A.C.D. *m.* 1900
LA TOUCHE, H. N. D. Lieut., 63rd Palamcottah L.I., 1910
 Indian Army
LATTEY, H. Capt. Gen. List(T.F. Res.) 1875
✠LAUGHLIN, P. H. Lieut., The Queen's (R. W. Surrey 1914
 Regt.) (W.)
 Died 21 Dec. 1917 of wounds received in action near
 Jerusalem
LAWE, F. W. Capt., E. Yorks. Regt. (W.) (P.) 1913
✠LEAKEY, Rev. H. N. C.F. 4th Class, R.A.C.D. 1909
 Died at Dar-es-Salaam 23 Dec. 1917 of sunstroke
LEDGARD, W. H. Capt., Hampshire Regt.(T.F.) (W.) 1893
 M.C.
✠LEE, E. H. Lieut., King's (Shropshire L.I.) 1914
 Died 19 Sept. 1916 of wounds received in action
LEE, H. Capt., R.A.M.C.(T.F.) 1901
LEE WARNER, R. P. Pte., The Queen's (R. W. Surrey 1911
 Regt.)
LEES, S. Engineer Lieut., R.N. 1906
LEONARD, P. J. Corpl., R.A.S.C.; Lieut., R.G.A. 1905
LEWIS, J. M. Lieut., R.G.A. 1914
LEWIS, P. J. Capt., Herefordshire Regt.; empld. O.C.B. 1903
 (W 2.)
LINCOLN, N. Lieut., I.A.R.O., attd. Mahrattas and Rail- 1904
 way Bn., Indian Defence Force
LINDSELL, J. Capt. and Adjt., Loyal N. Lancs. Regt. 1911
 M.C. M.
LINNELL, J. W. Major, R.A.M.C. (W.) *M.C.* 1899
✠LINNELL, R. McC. Capt., R.A.M.C. 1900
 Died 16 March 1915 of meningitis
LLOYD, E. LL. Capt., S. Wales Borderers. (W 2.) 1912
LLOYD, Rev. W. R. Lieut., Haileybury College O.T.C. 1906
✠LLOYD-JONES, P. A. Major, R.A.M.C.; D.A.D.M.S. 1895
 D.S.O. M 2.
 Died 22 Dec. 1916 of wounds received in action near
 Saulty
LONG, A. E. Pte., Training Res. Bn. 1911
LORD, Rev. A. E. C.F. 4th Class, R.A.C.D. 1892
LORD, G. F. Calcutta Vol. Artillery 1909
LOW, B. B. Gnr., H.A.C.; 2nd Lieut., M.G.C. 1914

LUMB, W. Capt., R.A.S.C. *M.* 1907
LUND, G. S. 2nd Lieut., Manchester Regt.(T.F.) 1913
LUND, W. F. Capt., Gen. List(T.F.) and R. Defence 1880
Corps
✠LUSK, J. Staff Capt.; Capt. and Adjt., Cameronians 1902
(Scottish Rifles, T.F.) *M. Chevalier, Legion of
Honour (France)*
Died 28 *Dec.* 1915 *of wounds received in action* 25 *Dec.*
1915
LYMBERY, A. W. Pte., Canadian Force 1897

MACALISTER, G. H. K. Capt., I.M.S. 1898
✠MCAULAY, F. W. Capt., R.F.A. 1909
Killed in action 21 *May* 1916
MCCORMICK, G. D. Major, 72nd Punjabis, Indian 1897
Army; attd. 112th Infy. *M.*
MCCORMICK, Very Rev. W. P. G. C.F. 1st Class, 1896
R.A.C.D.; D.A.C.G. *D.S.O. M* 4.
MACDONALD, S. G. Capt., R.A.M.C. 1899
MCDONNELL, T. F. R. 2nd Lieut., Rangoon Bn., Indian 1895
Defence Force
MCDOUGALL, W. Major, R.A.M.C. 1890
MCFADYEN, W. A. Capt., The Buffs (E. Kent Regt., 1912
T.F.); empld. Ministry of Munitions. (W.) *M.C.
M.*
MCGRADY, S. H. Bdr., R.G.A. 1904
MCKENZIE, R. P. Lieut.-Col., S. African Med. Corps. 1897
C.M.G.
MACKINLAY, D. M. Capt., King's Royal Rifle Corps. (W.) 1912
✠MACLAY, E. Capt., Cameronians (Scottish Rifles); Lieut., 1909
Scots Gds.
Died 11 *April* 1918 *of wounds received in action*
MACMULLEN, W. A. Lieut., R.A.S.C.(M.T.) *M.B.E.* 1909
MCNEILE, Rev. A. P. C.F. 4th Class, R.A.C.D. *m.* 1892
MANSBRIDGE, E. Capt. (T.), R.A.F. (Aircraft Production 1914
Dept.)
MARCHAND, G. I. C. Capt., R.F.A.(T.F.); Brigade Major. 1907
M.
MARLOW, C. C. 2nd Lieut., R. Warwickshire Regt. 1913
MARR, F. A. Capt., Cambridgeshire Regt.; Brigade 1913
Major. *D.S.O. M.C. M* 2.
MARRACK, J. R. Capt., R.A.M.C. (W.) *D.S.O. M.C.* 1905
M.
MARRS, F. W. 2nd Lieut., Worcestershire Regt. 1899

✠MARSHALL, W. Lieut., Leicestershire Regt. 1912
Killed in action in Gallipoli 4 June 1915
MARSHALL, W. B. Major, R.A.M.C.(T.F.) 1899
MART, W. T. D. Major, R.A.M.C.(T.F.) 1895
MASON, E. W. Capt., Northumberland Fus. (W.) 1909
✠MASON, P. 2nd Lieut., King's Royal Rifle Corps 1915
Killed in action at Miraumont 17 Feb. 1917
✠MAY, F. S. Pte., R. Fusiliers 1895
Killed in action 12 Aug. 1916
MAY, H. R. D. Lieut., Warwickshire Regt.; Capt., Spec. 1897
List. (W.) *M.C.*
✠MAY, P. L. 2nd Lieut., 2nd Dragoons (R. Scots Greys) 1894
Killed in action at Hulluch 13 Feb. 1916
MENENDEZ, F. T. S. Lieut., York and Lancaster Regt.; 1914
Lieut. (A.), R.A.F. (W.) *M.C.*
MERIVALE, B. Capt., London Regt. (Post Office Rifles); 1900
empld. Ministry of Food. *O.B.E.*
METCALF, H. K. 2nd Lieut., R.G.A. 1917
MILLER, F. Major, 108th Infy., Indian Army; attd. 1900
95th Infy.
MILLS, E. H. F. Lieut., Northumberland Fus.(T.F.) 1910
MILLS, E. J. Lieut., Cheshire Regt.(T.F.); Capt. and 1904
Adjt., M.G.C. *O.B.E. M.*
MILLYARD, T. Capt., Herefordshire Regt.; attd. King's 1912
(Shropshire L.I.) (W.)
✠MIRFIN, J. C. 2nd Lieut., York and Lancaster Regt. 1913
Died 17 Aug. 1917 *of wounds received in action 7 Dec.*
1916
MITCHELL, A. H. McN. Lieut.-Col., R.A.M.C. *M.* 1890
MONRO, A. E. Instructor, Cdr., R.N. 1886
MOODY, B. Lieut., I.A.R.O.; Major, D.A.D. Transport- 1908
ation
MOORE, Rev. C. Chaplain and Instructor Cdr., R.N. 1889
MOORE, R. M. Lieut., R.A.M.C. 1902
✠MORLEY, G. H. Lieut., King's (Shropshire L.I., T.F.) 1912
M.
Killed in action 30 Dec. 1917
MORRIS, P. E. Pte., Suffolk Regt. 1914
MORRISON, D. C. A. Major, Wiltshire Regt.(T.F.) 1898
MORTON, F. D. Capt., Highland L.I.; empld. War 1906
Office. *M.C.*
MORTON, W. B. Lieut., Belfast Univ. O.T.C. 1889
MOSELY, F. M. Surgeon Lieut., R.N. 1906
MOWTON, W. E. Pte., Suffolk Regt. 1911

336 ST JOHN'S COLLEGE

MULHOLLAND, W. Lieut., Manchester Regt. (W 2.) 1910
M.C. M.

✠MULLER, Rev. J. S. Pte., Norfolk Regt.(T.F.) 1892
Died 27 June 1918 of illness contracted on active service

MURPHY, W. L. Capt., R.A.M.C.(T.F.) *M. Chevalier,* 1896
Legion of Honour (France). Order of St Sava, 4th Class (Serbia). Cavalier, Order of the Redeemer (Greece). French Croix de Guerre

MURRAY-AYNSLEY, C. M. Lieut., King's Royal Rifle 1913
Corps; attd. Army Cyclist Corps. (W.)

NEED, G. S. Sergt., R.A.M.C.(T.F.) 1912
NEILL, N. C. Sub-Lieut., R.N.R.; Lieut., R.N.V.R.; 1902
empld. Admiralty
NESS WALKER, J. Lieut., R.F.A.(T.F. Res.) 1913
NEWBERY, R. E. Lieut., M.G.C. *M.C.* 1903
NEWLING, S. W. Pioneer, R.E. 1891
✠NEWTON, H. G. T. Capt., 13th Hussars 1904
Drowned 25 April 1917 on active service
NICHOLLS, A. C. Lieut., Leicestershire Regt. and Gen. 1907
List. (W 2.)
NICHOLSON, J. E. Lieut.-Col., R.A.M.C. *m.* 1898
NICKLIN, G. N. Capt., I.A.R.O., attd. 97th Deccan 1908
Infy.
✠NORBURY, F. C. Capt., King's Royal Rifle Corps 1901
Killed in action near Béthune 10 Jan. 1915
NORMAN, A. C. Lieut.-Col., 5th Cavalry, Indian Army 1897
NORMAN-LEE, Rev. F. B. N. C.F. 1st Class, R.A.C.D. 1874
NORREGAARD, Rev. A. H. Chaplain, R.N. 1890
NORTHCOTT, J. F. Surgeon Lieut., R.N. 1892
NORTHORP, Rev. F. C.F. 4th Class, R.A.C.D. *m.* 1906
NOWELL-ROSTRON, Rev. S. C.F. 4th Class, R.A.C.D. 1902
NURSE, H. H. Major, Spec. List. (Recruiting Staff) 1882

ODGERS, L. N. B. Lieut., Middlesex Regt.; Capt., R.E. 1911
(W 3.) *M.C.*
✠ODGERS, R. B. Capt., R.A.S.C.(T.F.) 1908
· *Died 31 Aug. 1917 on active service*
OKELL, C. C. Capt., R.A.M.C. *M.C.* 1908
ORMEROD, G. S. Lieut.-Col., Training Res. Bn.; Major, 1876
Spec. List (Asst. Cmdt., P. of W. Camp). *m.*
OWEN, D. H. Lieut., Welsh Horse and R. Welsh Fus. 1912

OWENS, F. H. Pte., London Regt. (Artists Rifles)   1912

PALMER, T. N. P. 2nd Lieut., Coldstream Gds.   1899
PALMER, W. E. Capt., Dorset Regt. and Training Res.   1912
Bn. *M.*
PARKER, G. Major, R.A.M.C. (2nd S. Gen. Hospital, T.F.)   1873
PARRY, J. H. Capt., I.M.S.   1908
PARSONS, Hon. Sir C. A., K.C.B. Hon. Colonel, North-   1873
umberland Fus.
PASCOE, E. H. Lieut., I.A.R.O., attd. Sikh Pioneers   1897
PASCOE, F. J. Lieut., D. of Cornwall's L.I. and M.G.C.   1912
PASKIN, J. J. Capt., Worcestershire Regt.; Major, M.G.C.   1912
M.C. French Croix de Guerre
PASS, Rev. H. L. C.F. 4th Class, R.A.C.D.   1894
PATERSON, M. W. Major, R.A.M.C.; D.A.D.M.S.   1905
O.B.E. M.C. M 2. French Médaille d'Honneur
PATTERSON, R. F. Lieut., R. Irish Rifles   1907
PAULLEY, H. Capt., Norfolk Regt.   1907
PEARSON, C. E. Lieut., Durham L.I.   1914
PELLOW, J. E. Major, R.A.M.C.   1896
PENFOLD, H. L. Capt., R.E.; empld. Ministry of Labour   1906
PERCY, J. R. Lieut., Border Regt.; attd. R.E.(Signals). (W.) [1914]
PERKINS, A. B. Lieut.-Col., Hampshire Regt. *m.*   1890
PERKINS, J. S. S. *See* STEELE-PERKINS, J. S. S.
PERRY, J. C. Pte., London Regt. (Q.V.R.); Capt. and   1907
Adjt., R.G.A. (W.)
PETERS, A. G. Sergt., Middlesex Regt.   1911
PHILLIPS, H. E. Lieut., Welsh Regt.   1913
PHILLIPS, R. S. Lieut., 39th Garhwal Rifles, Indian Army   1912
PHILLIPS, W. R. Lieut., Lancaster Grammar School   1908
O.T.C.
✠PHILP, C. H. G. Capt., R.A.M.C.   1904
Killed in action 28 March 1918
PHILPOT, F. H. Warrant Schoolmaster, R.N.   1914
PLOWRIGHT, C. T. M. Capt., R.A.M.C.   1897
POLACK, A. I. Lieut., R.E.(T.F.)   1911
✠POLACK, E. E. Lieut., Gloucestershire Regt.(T.F.)   1912
Killed in action 17 July 1916
✠POLLARD, W. M. N. 2nd Lieut., N. Staffs. Regt.(T.F.)   1909
Killed in action 11 April 1917
POOLE, Rev. J. T. Chaplain, R.N.   1900
POTTER, C. G. Bdr., R.F.A.; Lieut., Hampshire Regt.(T.F.) 1895
Killed in action 15 Sept. 1916
POWELL, E. C. Capt., R. Welsh Fus. (W.)   1911

PRALLE, E. L. R.   Capt. (S.), R.A.F.   *A.F.C.*   1914
PRATT, G. W.   Surgeon Lieut., R.N.   1911
PRECIOUS, C. M.   Pte., Middlesex Regt.   (W.)   1915
PRICHARD, R. M.   2nd Lieut., Cheshire Regt.   1913
PRIDEAUX, H. S.   Lieut., D. of Cornwall's L.I.   1901
✠PUDDICOMBE, D. R.   2nd Lieut., E. Yorks. Regt.   1914
  Died 24 July 1916 of wounds received in action on the
  Somme 20 July 1916
✠PULLIN, J. H.   Lieut., Loyal N. Lancs. Regt.   1912
  Died 21 Jan. 1916 of wounds received in action near
  Armentières 19 Jan. 1916
PURSER, Rev. W. C. B.   Pte., Rangoon Bn., Indian De-   1897
  fence Force

QUICK, Rev. E. K.   C.F. 4th Class, R.A.C.D.   *m.*   1907
QUIN, B. G.   Capt., Cambridgeshire Regt. and Suffolk   1914
  Regt.(T.F.)   *M.C.*

RAFFLE, W.   Capt., R.A.M.C.   *M.*   1909
RAVEN, Rev. E. E.   C.F. 4th Class, R.A.C.D.   1909
READ, A. J.   Lieut., D. of Cornwall's L.I.; empld. Min-   1903
  istry of Munitions.   (W.)
READ, G. D.   Capt., R.A.M.C.; D.A.D.M.S.   1908
READE, G. L.   Capt., Rifle Brigade.   *M.C.*   1914
REDLICH, S.   Capt. and Adjt., R.G.A.   *M.B.E.   M.*   1899
✠REES, F. E.   2nd Lieut. (A.), R.A.F.   1914
  Missing, presumed killed in action, 22 Aug. 1918
REEVES, J. H.   Lieut., R.G.A.; empld. Ministry of Labour.   1887
  (W.)   *M.B.E.*
✠RENNIE, D. W.   2nd Lieut., R. Fusiliers; attd. R. War-   1904
  wickshire Regt.
  Killed in action 11 Nov. 1914
REYNOLDS, Rev. W. H. R.   C.F. 4th Class, R.A.C.D.   1910
RICE, Rev. C. M.   C.F. 4th Class, R.A.C.D.   1889
RICE, H. G.   Capt., R.A.M.C.   (W.)   1903
RICE, L. C.   Capt., Loyal N. Lancs. Regt.   (W 3.)   1912
RICHARDSON, A. H.   Surgeon Lieut., R.N.   *O.B.E.*   1903
✠RICHARDSON, R. J. R.   Lieut., S. Staffs. Regt.   (W.)   1913
  Killed in action 25 Sept. 1915
RITCHIE, Rev. C. H.   Chaplain, R.N.   1907
RITCHIE, G. L.   Capt., R. Scots Fus. (W 2.)   *M.C.   M.*   1909
✠RITCHIE, J. N.   2nd Lieut., Seaforth Hdrs.   1899
  Killed in action in Mesopotamia 21 April 1916
RIVERS, W. H. R.   Capt., R.A.M.C.   *1898

ROBB, A. A. Service Sanitaire, French Army. *French* 1894
Croix de Guerre
ROBERTS, Rev. A. C. C.F. 4th Class, R.A.C.D. 1882
ROBINSON, E. H. Major, King's (Shropshire L.I.) (W 3.) *1910
D.S.O. M.C. and Bar. M.
✠ROBINSON, L. F. W. Lieut., R.E. 1912
Killed in action 25 May 1917
✠ROBINSON, M. H. Instructor Lieut., R.N. 1897
Died 15 June 1917
ROLLESTON, Sir H. D., C.B. Surgeon Rear-Admiral, R.N. 1883
K.C.B
RONALDSON, J. B. Surgeon Lieut., R.N.V.R. 1903
ROSE, F. A. Capt., R.A.M.C.(T.F.) 1892
ROSE, H. A. Lieut., R. Scots (Cyclist Bn., T.F.) (W.) 1905
ROSE, H. C. Major, R.A.S.C. *M.* 1902
✠ROSEVEARE, H. W. 2nd Lieut., Wiltshire Regt. [1914]
*Died 20 Sept. 1914 of wounds received in action in the
Battle of the Aisne*
ROSS, Rev. J. E. C. C.F. 4th Class, R.A.C.D. 1905
ROSTRON, S. *See* NOWELL-ROSTRON, Rev. S.
ROWELL, A. H. Corpl., R.E. 1909
ROWETT, F. E. Flt. Lieut., R.N.A.S. 1912
RUDD, W. A. Lieut., R. Berkshire Regt. *m.* 1896
RUSSELL-SMITH, A. Pte., H.A.C. (W.) 1911
✠RUSSELL-SMITH, H. F. Capt., Rifle Brigade 1906
*Died 5 July 1916 of wounds received in action on the
Somme 1 July 1916*
✠RYLEY, D. A. G. B. 2nd Lieut., Manchester Regt.; 1912
Lieut., N. Staffs. Regt.
Killed in action at Hulluch 2 Feb. 1917

SADDLER, W. Lieut., R.G.A. *M.* 1911
SAINT, P. J. Lieut., Pioneers, Indian Army. (W.) 1904
✠SALMOND, W. G. Trooper, 9th Lancers; 2nd Lieut., 1912
N. Somerset Yeo.; Capt. and Adjt., Wellington Regt.,
N. Zealand Force. (W 2.)
Killed in action at Rossignol Wood 9 July 1918
SAMPSON, M. T. Major, King's Royal Rifle Corps. 1914
(W.) *M.C. and Bar*
SANCEAU, R. J. Capt. (A.), R.A.F. *M.* 1910
SANDALL, Rev. H. C. C.F. 4th Class, R.A.C.D. 1899
SANDALL, T. E. Colonel, Lincolnshire Regt.(T.F.) (W.) 1888
C.M.G. M.
SARGENT, E. L. K. Capt., R.A.M.C. 1907

SARGENT, P. W. G.   Lieut.-Col., R.A.M.C.   *C.M.G.*   1891
D.S.O. *M* 2.
SCARBOROUGH, O. L.   Capt., R.A.M.C.(T.F.)   1896
SCARTH, R.E.   2nd Lieut., R.F.A.(T.F.)   1913
✠SCHOLFIELD, R. D.   2nd Lieut., King's Own (R. Lan-   1910
caster Regt.)
Killed in action in Gallipoli 10 *Aug.* 1915
SCHROEDER, A. E.   *See* LONG, A. E.
SCOULAR, A. C.   Major, Border Regt.; attd. Cheshire Regt.   1893
T.D.
SCOULAR, J. G.   Major, R.G.A. (W 2.)   *M.*   1904
SCUTT, J. A. H.   Pte., H.A.C.; Lieut., Hampshire Regt.   1910
(T.F.) *M.C.*
SECCOMBE, P. J. A.   Major, R.A.M.C.   *Order of St Sava,*   1887
5*th Class* (*Serbia*)
SEWELL, S. E.   Capt., Madras Garrison Artillery, Indian   1906
Defence Force; Asst. Proof Officer, Ordnance Inspec-
tion Staff
SHANLY, H.   Capt., London Regt. (St Pancras Bn.);   1912
Major, M.G.C. (W.) *M.*
SHARP, C. G.   2nd Lieut., The Queen's (R. W. Surrey   1903
Regt.) (W.)
SHEPHERD, Rev. E. H.   C.F. 4th Class, R.A.C.D.   1909
SHILLITO, N. W.   Lieut., R.E. *M.C.*   1912
SHIMIELD, W. S.   Lieut., D. of Cornwall's L.I.; Capt.,   1893
Labour Corps
SHORE, L. R.   Capt., R.A.M.C. (W 2.) *M.C. M.*   1908
SHORE, T. H. G.   Capt., R.A.M.C.   1906
SHORT, Rev. J. M.   C.F. 4th Class, R.A.C.D.   1906
SIBLY, T. M.   Capt., Gloucestershire Regt. *M.*   1904
SILK, G. W.   Lieut., E. Yorks. Regt. and Gen. List.   1914
(W.) *M.C.*
SIMPSON, G. C. E.   Lieut.-Col., R.A.M.C.(T.F.) *O.B.E.*   1899
M 2.
SKENE, Rev. C. M. B.   C.F. 4th Class, R.A.C.D.   1903
SKENE, Rev. F. N.   C.F. 4th Class, R.A.C.D.   1896
SLATER, S. B.   Capt., King's Royal Rifle Corps and Spec.   1913
List (T.M.B.) *M.C. M.*
SLEIGHT, A. H.   Pte., R. Fusiliers (P. S. Bn.); Sergt.,   1908
attd. Div. H.Q. (Intelligence Branch)
SMEE, C. W.   Capt., R. Fusiliers   1911
✠SMITH, A. F.   2nd Lieut., Middlesex Regt.; attd. London   1914
Regt. (W.)
Missing, presumed killed in action, 9 *Sept* 1916.

SMITH, Rev. B. T. D.   C.F. 4th Class, R.A.C.D.   *1915
SMITH, O. C.   2nd Lieut., R.G.A.(T.F.)   1906
SMITH, V. S.   Lieut., D. of Wellington's (W. Riding   1913
   Regt.) and I.A.R.O., attd. S. and T. Corps. *M.*
SMITHSON, A. E.   Lieut.-Col., R.A.M.C.   1883
SNOW, Sir T. D'O., K.C.B.   Lieut.-Gen.   *K.C.M.G.*   1877
   M 3. *Commander, Legion of Honour (France). Grand*
   Officer, Order of Leopold (Belgium). Belgian Croix de
   Guerre
SODEN, W. S.   Capt., R.A.M.C.(T.F.) *M.*   1907
SOTHERS, E. D.   2nd Lieut., London Regt. (L.R.B.)   1911
✠SOUPER, N. B.   2nd Lieut., R. Berkshire Regt.   1899
   Killed in action 1 *July* 1916
SOUTHAM, Rev. J. F. S.   C.F. 4th Class, R.A.C.D.   1898
SPACKMAN, H. M.   Capt., R.F.A.; attd. T.M.B. (W.)   1911
SPARGO, F. W.   Lieut., I.A.R.O., attd. 70th Burma Rifles   1907
SPARKS, C. H.   Capt., R.F.A.   1911
SPENCER, G. W.   Capt., R.A.M.C.   1907
STANFORD, H. C.   Capt., Suffolk Regt. and Gen. List   1904
   (Intelligence). *M.C.*
STANHAM, C. T.   Lieut., The Buffs (E. Kent Regt., T.F.)   1910
   and King's African Rifles
STANSFELD, R.   Capt., R.A.M.C.   1907
STEELE-PERKINS, J. S. S.   Capt., R.A.M.C.   1894
STEEN, F. D.   Capt. and Adjt., King's Royal Rifle Corps.   1913
   (W 3.) *M.C.*
STEPHENSON, F.   Lieut., Loyal N. Lancs. Regt.; Capt.,   1915
   Spec. List (Bde. Signal Officer). (W.)
STERNDALE-BENNETT, J.   Major, 107th Pioneers, Indian   1897
   Army; Cmdt., School of Musketry. *O.B.E.*
STERNDALE-BENNETT, J. B.   Pte., H.A.C.; Capt., S. Wales   1907
   Borderers. (P.) *M.C. m.*
STERNDALE-BENNETT, R.   Major, Uppingham School   1901
   O.T.C.
STEVENS, J. K.   2nd Lieut., R. Fusiliers; Lieut., Spec.   1911
   List (R.T.O.) (W.)
STEVENSON, C. M.   Capt., R.A.M.C.   1898
STEWART, D. M.   Lieut., Welsh Regt.   1904
STIMPSON, R.   Pte., London Regt. (Rangers)   [1914]
STOCKWOOD, I. H.   Lieut., S. Wales Borderers; Capt.,   1911
   Tank Corps; Hon. Capt. (O.), R.A.F.
STOKES, J. W. G.   Lieut., R.G.A.   1905
STOPFORD, J.   Lieut., Lancs. Fus.(T.F.) and M.G.C.   1910
STREET, R. O.   2nd Lieut. (T.), R.A.F.   1908

✠STREETEN, Rev. B. R.   C.F. 4th Class, R.A.C.D.   1908
   Died in France 1 *Nov.* 1918 *of pneumonia*
STRONG, S. D.   Lieut., R.F.A.(T.F.)   (W.)   **1914**
STRUTHERS, J. A.   Lieut., Durham L.I.; empld. Ministry   **1914**
   of Labour. (W.)
STUART, C. E.   Lieut., N. Staffs. Regt.; attd. Hampshire   1911
   Regt. (W.)
SWIFT, H. W.   Capt., London Regt. (Q.V.R.) (W.) *M.*   **1914**
SWIFT, Rev. J. M.   C.F. 4th Class, R.A.C.D.   1905
SYKES, M. G.   Lieut. (O.), R.A.F.   1902

TANNER, L. E.   Capt., Gloucestershire Regt.(T.F.);   1910
   empld. Ministry of Munitions. (W.)
TATE, Sir R. W.   Major, Dublin Univ. O.T.C.   *K.B.E.* 1891
   C.B.E.
TAYLOR, E. C.   Major, I.M.S.   1893
TAYLOR, F. L.   Capt., R. Fusiliers.; empld. Ministry   1911
   of Labour. (W.) *M.C.*
✠TAYLOR, H. C. N.   Capt., London Regt. (Blackheath   1911
   and Woolwich Bn.)
   Killed in action on Vimy Ridge 21 *May* 1916
TAYLOR, J. N.   Lieut., Calcutta Light Horse, Indian   1902
   Defence Force
TAYLOR, G. M. C.   Lieut., R. Marines; Capt., R.E.   1904
   M.C. M.
TEAKLE, Rev. S. G.   C.F. 4th Class, R.A.C.D.(T.F.)   1899
TEALL, G. H.   Major, Lincolnshire Regt.; D.A.A.G.   1900
   (W.) *D.S.O. M* 5. *French Croix de Guerre*
TEMPLEMAN, W. H.   Capt., R.A.O.C.   1902
THOMAS, R. B. H.   2nd Lieut., R.G.A.   1913
THOMAS, R. LL.   2nd Lieut., Welsh Regt.   1913
THOMAS, T.   Lieut., Haileybury College O.T.C.   1911
THOMAS, W. W.   Lieut., S. Wales Borderers; Capt.,   1914
   Spec. List (T.M.B.)
THOMPSON, A. R.   Lieut., Berkhamsted School O.T.C.   1906
THOMPSON, C. N.   Capt., Rifle Brigade; empld. O.C.B.   1911
   (W 2.)
✠THOMPSON, E. E.   2nd Lieut., R.G.A.   1903
   Died 16 *Oct.* 1918 *of wounds received in action*
THOMPSON, S. L.   Capt., 113th Infy., Indian Army   1907
✠THOMSON, K. S.   Lieut., 21st Cavalry, Indian Army;   1906
   attd. 16th Cavalry
   Killed in action near the Persian Gulf 3 *March* 1915
THORNE-WAITE, A.   Lieut., King's (Shropshire L.I.)   1905

THURSFIELD, Rev. G. A. R. Junior Chaplain, Indian 1905
Army; C.F. 4th Class, R.A.C.D. *M.*
✠THWAITES, G. Major, R.A.S.C. *D.S.O.* 1897
Accidentally drowned on the White Nile 29 May 1917
TICEHURST, C. B. Capt., R.A.M.C. 1900
TICEHURST, G. A. Capt., R.A.M.C. 1897
TILLARD, L. B. Capt., London Regt. (Rifles) 1906
TODD, Rev. H. W. C.F. 4th Class, R.A.C.D. *M.C. M.* 1908
TOOTH, H. H., c.m.g. Colonel, A.M.S. (T.F. Res.) *C.B.* 1873
M 2. *m.*
TOPLEY, W. W. C. Capt., R.A.M.C. *Order of St Sava,* 1904
4th Class (Serbia)
✠TORRY, A. J. D. Lieut., R.G.A.; attd. R.F.C. (W.) 1905
M.C.
Killed in action 9 *Oct.* 1917
TOWLE, J. H. Lieut., United Provinces Horse, Indian 1897
Defence Force
TOWNSEND, R. W. Capt., Devon Regt. *M.C. M* 2. 1910
TOZER, Rev. E. F. C.F. 4th Class, R.A.C.D 1905
✠TOZER, S. P. Lieut., Devon Regt. 1914
Killed in action near St Quentin 8 *Oct.* 1918
✠TRACHTENBERG, M. I. Lce.-Corpl., R. Fusiliers 1901
Died at Jerusalem 12 *Oct.* 1918 *of malaria*
TRELEAVEN, Rev. W. Corpl., R.A.M.C.; C.F. 4th Class, 1906
R.A.C.D.
TROTMAN, S. R. Capt., Nottingham Univ. College O.T.C. 1890
m.
TROTT, A. C. Lieut., Devon Regt.; Capt., Spec. List. *M.* 1913
TROTT, F. W. Capt., Devon Regt.; Major, S.O. 2, R.A.F. 1912
(W 2.) *O.B.E. M.C. M* 2.
TROUGHT, T. Capt., Queen's Own (R. W. Kent Regt., 1910
T.F.)
TRUMPER, J. H. W. 2nd Lieut., Monmouthshire Regt. 1904
(W.)
TUCKER, D. H. M. Lieut., Manchester Regt. [1914]
TURNER, R. Lieut., York and Lancaster Regt. *M.C.* 1902
✠TWENTYMAN, D. C. T. Capt., York and Lancaster Regt. 1909
(W.)
Killed in action 1 *July* 1916

URIE, R. W. Capt., R.F.A. (W.) *M.* 1913

VALE, H. E. T. Capt., Gen. List, attd. R.E. (Signals) 1909
VAN DRUTEN, H. J. Capt., Middlesex Regt. (W.) 1911

VARWELL, R. P. Capt., R. Irish Rifles; Major, D.A.A.G. 1901
(W.) *M.C. M* 3. *French Croix de Guerre*
✠VAUSE, T. C. 2nd Lieut., W. Yorks. Regt.(T.F.) 1904
Killed in action near Albert 3 *Sept.* 1916
VEEVERS, W. 2nd Lieut., R.G.A. 1905
VERNON, C. H. Lieut., Hampshire Regt. (T.F.); Capt. 1911
(Med.), R.A.F. (W.) *m.*
VINT, J. Lieut., R.G.A. (W.) *M.C.* 1914
VYVYAN, P. H. N. N. Major, R.A.S.C.; D.A.Q.M.G. 1900
O.B.E. M.C. M 2. *m. Italian Croce di Guerra*

WAIT, J. A. Lieut.-Col., R.G.A.(T.F.) *M.* 1883
✠WALES, H. R. 2nd Lieut., E. Yorks. Regt. (W.) 1914
Killed in action 14 *July* 1916
WALKER, J. NESS. *See* NESS WALKER, J.
WALLER, B. P. Lieut., Hertfordshire Regt. 1898
WALMSLEY, Rev. A. M. 2nd Lieut., I.A.R.O., attd. S. *1904
and T. Corps
✠WARREN, J. L. E. Capt., Welsh Regt. (W.) 1913
Killed in action at the Hohenzollern Redoubt 2 *Oct.*
1915
WATERHOUSE, G. Lieut., R.N.V.R. 1907
WATERHOUSE, H. Capt., Lancs. Fus. *M.C.* 1914
✠WATERS, K. S. 2nd Lieut., Garrison Artillery, Indian 1909
Army
Killed in action at Bara Gali 30 *May* 1917
WATSON, B. L. Capt., Gen. List, attd. R.E. (Signals). *M.* 1908
WEATHERHEAD, E. Capt., R.A.M.C. *1894
WELLS, F. A. Capt., Hampshire Regt.(T.F.) 1880
WELLS, W. D. Lieut., Chigwell School O.T.C. 1908
WESTON, E. A. Lieut.-Col., R.E.; A. D. Movement and 1899
Railways, War Office. *C.M.G.*
WESTON, T. A. Capt., R.A.M.C. 1902
WHARTON, J. Capt., R.A.M.C. (2nd W. Gen. Hospital, 1895
T.F.)
WHELDON, W. P. Major, R. Welsh Fus. (W.) *D.S.O.* 1900
M.
WHIDDINGTON, R. Major (T.), R.A.F. *m* 3. 1905
WHITELEY, G. T. Capt., Gen. List (T.F. Res.) and 1892
Cheshire Regt.(T.F.)
✠WHITFIELD, E. H. D. 2nd Lieut., York and Lancaster 1910
Regt.
Killed in action in Gallipoli 7 *Aug.* 1915

WHYE, J. W.   Lieut., Leicestershire Regt.   (W.)   *M.C.*   *1903
✠WICKHAM, B. W. T.   Lieut., S. Staffs. Regt.   (W.)   *M.C.*   1913
   Killed in action near Ypres 14 April 1917
WILLETT, E. W.   2nd Lieut., R.A.S.C.(M.T.)   1905
✠WILLETT, J. A.   Pte., Gloucestershire Regt.; 2nd Lieut.,   1913
   Somerset L.I.; Lieut., R. Fusiliers
   Killed in action in Gallipoli 2 July 1915
WILLIAMS, G. W.   Major, R.E.   *D.S.O.   M.C.   M.*   1898
✠WILLIAMS, H. B.   2nd Lieut., King's (Liverpool Regt.)   1913
   M.C.
   Killed in action in the Battle of Arras 3 May 1917
WILLIAMS, R.   Lieut., R. Warwickshire Regt.; Capt.,   *1899
   Rifle Brigade(T.F.)
WILLIAMS, W. H.   Capt. and Adjt., R.A.S.C.   *M.C.*   1913
WILLIAMSON, H.   Capt., R.A.M.C. (1st London Gen.   1890
   Hospital, T.F.)
WILLIAMSON, K. B.   Capt., R.A.M.C. (Sanitary Service,   1894
   T.F.)   *M* 2.
WILLS, R. G.   Capt., R.A.M.C.(T.F. Res.)   *1898
WILLS, W. K.   Surgeon Lieut.-Cdr., R.N.V.R.   *O.B.E.*   1891
✠WILSON, A. S.   Lieut., S. Lancs. Regt.; attd. M.G.C.   1913
   (W.)
   Killed in action in the Scarpe Valley 23 April 1917
✠WILSON, A. W.   2nd Lieut., Scots Gds.; attd. M.G.C.   1915
   Killed in action 30 July 1917
WILSON, G.   Lieut., Norfolk Regt.   1901
WINDER, R. McD.   Lieut., R. Marines   1908
WINFIELD, P. H.   Lieut., Cambridgeshire Regt.; empld.   1896
   War Office.   (W.)
WOOD, N. W.   Pte., Cheshire Regt.   1915
WOOD, T. A. V.   Capt., D. of Cornwall's L.I.   (W.)   1912
WOODALL, F. E.   Lieut., Gds. M.G. Regt.   1908
WOODMANSEY, Rev. G. E.   C.F. 4th Class, R.A.C.D.   1910
WOODS, B. F.   Capt., R. Fusiliers   1899
✠WOOLER, C. A.   2nd Lieut., W. Yorks. Regt.   (W.)   [1914]
   Died 20 July 1916 *of wounds received in action* 1 *July*
   1916
✠WOOLER, H. S.   2nd Lieut., W. Yorks. Regt.   *M.*   1911
   Died 28 March 1916 *of wounds received in action at*
   St Eloi
WOOLRICH, W. G.   Capt., R.A.M.C.   1912
WORDIE, J. M.   Lieut., R.F.A.(T.F.)   (W.)   1910
✠WORSTENHOLM, J.   2nd Lieut. (O.), R.F.C.   1916
   Killed in action 25 Sept. 1917

WORTHINGTON, F. Lieut.-Col., R.A.M.C. (W.) *D.S.O.* 1898
and Bar. O.B.E. M 2. *French Croix de Guerre*

WREN, T. L. Lieut., R.A.S.C.; empld. Ministry of Muni- 1908
tions

WRIGHT, J. C. Major, R.A.M.C. 1884

WRIGHT, T. 2nd Lieut., King's Own (Yorkshire L.I.) 1912

WYETH, F. J. S. Major, Essex Regt. and Gen. List, 1897
empld. Ministry of Munitions. *M.C. M* 2.

WYNNE-WILLSON, Very Rev. ST J. B. C.F. 4th Class, 1887
R.A.C.D.

YEATS, G. F. W. Pte., Middlesex Regt. 1901

SIDNEY SUSSEX COLLEGE

ABERCROMBIE, D. M. 2nd Lieut., R.A.S.C.   1904
ARMSTRONG, W. E. Pte., R.A.M.C. (W.)   1914
ASTBURY, S. J. 2nd Lieut., Labour Corps and Gen. List,   1916
   empld. Ministry of Munitions
ATKINS, G. R. Lieut., R.E. (T.F.)   1910
ATKINSON, H. G. Lieut.-Cdr., R.N.V.R.; Major (T.),   1906
   R.A.F. (W.) *O.B.E.*
AUSTIN, L. J. Major, R.A.M.C.   1899

BABONEAU, C. A. Lieut., R. Sussex Regt.   1910
BACCHUS, J. G. Gnr., R.F.A.   1913
✠BAILLIE, A. LA T. Capt., Cameronians (Scottish Rifles)   1913
   Killed in action 29 *Oct.* 1915
BAKER, S. E. Capt., D. of Wellington's (W. Riding Regt.);   1909
   Major, Gen. List (O.C.B.) (W 2.)
BALDWIN, C. W. Capt., Durham L.I.; Capt. (A.), R.A.F.   1910
BALL, H. F. Lieut., Gen. List(T.F. Res.) *M.C.*   1909
BALLANCE, G. 2nd Lieut. (A.), R.A.F. (P.)   1917
BARKER, R. A. Capt., Loyal N. Lancs. Regt.; Lieut.,   1910
   3rd Gurkha Rifles, Indian Army. (W 2.)
BARKER, W. B. Corpl., The Buffs (E. Kent Regt.)   1915
BARTLETT, G. B. Capt., R.A.M.C.   1899
BARTON, R. A. E. Lieut., Cambridge Univ. O.T.C.   1913
BATTEN, L. W. Capt., R.A.M.C.   1908
✠BELL, W. A. Corpl., R. Fusiliers (P. S. Bn.); 2nd Lieut.,   1913
   Border Regt.
   Killed in action 14 *June* 1917
BENNETT, G. S. Lieut., Sherwood Foresters (Notts. and   [1914]
   Derby Regt.); Lieut. (O.), R.A.F.
BENNETT, W. E. 2nd Lieut., Norfolk Regt. (W.)   1911
BERENS, H. A. Sapper, R.E.   1908
BINDON, W. F. V. Lieut., R.A.S.C.   1897

BLACKMORE, J. K. Gnr., R.G.A.   1890
✠BLAIR, H. S. P. 2nd Lieut., D. of Cornwall's L.I.   1907
    Died 31 *Oct.* 1916 *of wounds received in action*
BLUMHARDT, R. A. *See* MILLS, R.A.
BORTHWICK, C. H. Capt., R.F.A. (W.) *M.C. m.*   1906
BORTHWICK, L. C. Lieut., E. Yorks. Regt.; Major, M.G.C.   1910
    M.
BOURNE, L. P. S. Lieut., Manchester Regt.   1913
BOWDLER, A. P. Capt., R.A.M.C.   1895
BOYD, E. J. Surgeon Lieut., R.N.; Capt. (Med.), R.A.F.   1907
BRABY, H. W. Pte., R.A.M.C.   1907
BREND, W. A. Major, R.A.M.C.   1892
BRIGGS, M. Pte., R.A.M.C.   1906
✠BROMHEAD, J. P. Pte., R.A.M.C. and R. Fusiliers   1912
    Killed in action 2 *Aug.* 1916
✠BROWN, J. C. B. Lieut., Middlesex Regt.   [1914]
    Killed in action 29 *Sept.* 1918
BRUNDRETT, F. Lieut., R.N.V.R.   1913
BUDDIN, W. Capt., R.A.M.C. (Sanitary Service, T.F.)   1909
✠BURROWS, A. H. Capt., Northamptonshire Regt.   1903
    Killed in action 13 *March* 1916

✠CANE, L. D. Capt. and Adjt., R. Fusiliers   1901
    Killed in action 24 *Jan.* 1916
CARMICHAEL, A. M. Lieut., R.F.A.(T.F.)   1914
CASSIDY, C. Capt., R.A.M.C. and Spec. List, empld.   1899
    Egyptian Army; Major, A.A.G. *M.C. M* 2. *Order
    of the Nile,* 4*th Class (Egypt). Medjidieh,* 4*th Class
    (Egypt)*
CHAPMAN, H. 2nd Lieut., S. Staffs. Regt.   1910
CHAPMAN, P. D. H. Capt., R.A.M.C.   1911
CHASE, C. D. Capt., R. Irish Rifles and Gen. List. *M.C.*   1897
    M.
CLARK-TURNER, F. Lieut., R.A.S.C.(M.T.)   1912
CLARKE, E. R. Capt., Connaught Rangers. *M.C.*   1911
CLARKE, Rev. E. T. C.F. 4th Class, R.A.C.D.   1903
CLARKE, Rev. S. J. C. Chaplain, R.N.   1895
CLAYTON, F. Capt., Cambridgeshire Regt. and Suffolk   1914
    Regt.(T.F.) (W.)
CLEMENT, L. Corpl., R.E.   1903
COLT, G. H. Major, R.A.M.C. *M.*   1897
COOK, S. G. Major, Huntingdonshire Cyclist Bn.;   1891
    G.S.O. 2. *O.B.E.*
COOKE, J. G. Capt., R.A.M.C.(T.F.)   1891
CORNER, E. M. Major, R.A.M.C.(T.F.) *M.*   1891

CORNISH, Rev. A. C.F. 4th Class, R.A.C.D.   1893
COULES, ST V. F. 2nd Lieut., Labour Corps   1914
COYTE, S. E. Lieut., R.E.   1912
CRESWICK, F. N. Capt., R. Defence Corps   1893
CRISP, E. J. Flt. Lieut., R.N.A.S.; Hon. Capt., R.A.F.   1914

DANIELS, M. 2nd Lieut., R.G.A.   1910
✠DANIELS, T. H. R. 2nd Lieut., King's Own (R. Lan-   1914
  caster Regt.)
  Killed in action 9 April 1916
DAVENPORT, A. H. Major, R.E. (W.) *M.C. M.*   1907
DEAN, L. T. Capt., R.A.M.C.   1901
DE LA BERE, I. Capt., Dorset Regt.; attd. Connaught   1911
  Rangers; Capt., Gen. Staff (Intelligence). (W.)
DENTON, H. S. Lieut., Gloucestershire Regt.(T.F.)   1915
DERBYSHIRE, H. Major, R.G.A. *M.C.*   1905
✠DICK, N. B. 2nd Lieut., Middlesex Regt.   1901
  Killed in action 28 April 1917
✠DICKSON, C. G. Lieut., Loyal N. Lancs. Regt.   1909
  Killed in action in E. Africa 4 Nov. 1914
DONALD, A. G. Capt., R.F.A. (W 2.)   1911
DONALDSON, C. E. Cadet, O.C.B.   1917
DONOVAN, S. J. Lieut.-Col., R.A.S.C. *D.S.O. M* 3. *m.*   1898
DOWNING, A. B. Lieut., E. Yorks. Regt.(T.F.)   1899
DRUITT, C. E. H. Capt., The Buffs (E. Kent Regt.) and   1911
  M.G.C. (W.) *M.C.*
DUNLOP, J. B. Lieut., R.A.M.C.   1894

✠EDMONDS, S. F. Trooper, E. African Mtd. Rifles   1898
  Killed in action on the Magadi River 25 Sept. 1914
ELLIOTT, H. D. E. 2nd Lieut., King's (Shropshire L.I.)   1905
✠EMBREY, C. S. 2nd Lieut., S. Staffs. Regt.(T.F.) *M.C.*   1916
  Killed in action 12 Oct. 1918
EUSTACE, E. M. 2nd Lieut., R.G.A.   1899
EVANS, E, T.D. Surgeon Lieut.-Col., Welsh Regt.(T.F.)   1879
EVANS, K. R. Lieut., Lancs. Fus.; attd. King's Own   1913
  (Yorkshire L.I.) (W.)
✠EWEN, G. C. Lieut., Nigeria Regt., W. African Frontier   1908
  Force
  Killed in action 24 Jan. 1917

FAIRCHILD, G. C. Surgeon Lieut., R.N.   1906
FARR, T. H. 2nd Lieut., Res. Regt. of Cavalry   1916
FAWCETT, W. L. Capt., W. Yorks. Regt.(T.F.); Lieut.,   [1914]
  9th Gurkha Rifles, Indian Army. (W.) *M.C.*
FERRAR, H. T. N. Zealand Force   1898

FISHER, Rev. L. N. C.F. 4th Class, R.A.C.D.   1900
FISHER, R. Capt., R.A.M.C.   1903
FISON, W. J. Surgeon Lieut., R.N.   1902
✠FITZHERBERT, G. C. 2nd Lieut., Suffolk Regt.; Lieut.,   [1914]
  York and Lancaster Regt. M.C.
  Killed in action 18 Sept. 1918
✠FLETCHER, R. R. R. Lieut., S. Lancs. Regt. (W.)   1905
  *Died 29 Oct. 1919 of dysentery contracted on active
  service*
FOULDS, J. G. Capt., S. African Military Labour Corps   1909
FOX, C. Gnr., R.G.A.   1915
FOX, J. T. Capt., R.A.M.C.   1903
✠FYSON, G. Lieut., R. Scots. (W.)   1904
  Killed in action in Macedonia 4 Sept. 1918

GAINS, S. G. 2nd Lieut., R.G.A.   1917
✠GARSTIN, D. N. Lieut., 10th Hussars; Capt., M.G.C.   1909
  D.S.O. M.C.
  Killed in action 15 Aug. 1918
GARSTIN, E. J. L. Capt., Middlesex Regt. (W.) M.C.   1911
  M 2.
GATES, C. E. 2nd Lieut., R.G.A. (P.)   1907
GATHERGOOD, G. W. Capt. (A.), R.A.F. A.F.C.   [1914]
GATHERGOOD, L. S. Capt., R.A.M.C.   1911
GAUSSEN, E. A. Capt., Merchiston Castle School O.T.C.   1891
✠GAWAN-TAYLOR, N. 2nd Lieut., York and Lancaster   1913
  Regt.
  Killed in action 24 April 1917
✠GAWAN-TAYLOR, T. F. 2nd Lieut., York and Lancaster   1912
  Regt.
  Killed in action at Hooge 9 Aug. 1915
GLUCKSTEIN, I. M. Capt., London Regt. (Hackney Bn.)   1909
  (W.) M.
GOOCH, G. W. 2nd Lieut., Marlborough College O.T.C.   1911
GOODALL, C. E. G. Capt., Lincolnshire Regt.(T.F.)   [1914]
  (W.) M.C. M.
GOODCHILD, G. F. 2nd Lieut., London Univ. O.T.C.   1895
✠GORDON, W. H. E. Lieut., Gordon Hdrs.   1912
  *Died 30 Sept. 1915 of wounds received in action at
  the Hohenzollern Redoubt*
✠GOUGH, H. P. B. Major, Welsh Regt. M.C. and Bar   1899
  *Died 22 April 1918 of wounds received in action 13 April
  1918*
✠GOULD, W. J. Lieut., Northamptonshire Regt.   1913
  Killed in action near Ypres 23 Aug. 1915

GREEN, H. F.   Capt., N. Staffs. Regt.(T.F.); Major, Asst.   1912
  Chemical Adviser. *M.*
GREEN, R. C.   2nd Lieut., S. Wales Borderers; Lieut.,   1914
  M.G.C.
GREENWOOD, E. T.   Capt., Devon Regt.(T.F.) (W.)   1912
GRIFFITH, A. W.   2nd Lieut., R. Inniskilling Fus.   1912
GRINBERG, S.   Russian Army   1913
GROGAN, J. D.   Lieut., R.E.   1908
GROOM, S. H.   Sergt., Devon Regt.(T.F.); 2nd Lieut.,   1906
  R. Fusiliers; Lieut., Rifle Brigade. (W.)
GROUND, E. G.   Lieut., London Regt. (Finsbury Rifles)   1904

HACKFORTH, R.   Pte., London Regt. (Artists Rifles)   *1912
HAGUE, T. H.   Major, Spec. List, empld. Army Trade   1910
  Test Centre
HAINWORTH, A. D.   2nd Lieut., King's School, Warwick,   1896
  O.T.C.
✠HALL, B.   Lieut., S. Staffs. Regt.   [1914]
  Killed in action in the Battle of Loos 25 Sept. 1915
HALL, J.   Pte., London Regt. (Artists Rifles); Lieut.,   1911
  R.F.A.
✠HALL, J. S.   Lieut., Rifle Brigade. (W.)   1904
  Killed in action 21 March 1918
✠HALL, W.   Lieut., S. Staffs. Regt. (W 2.)   [1914]
  Died 1 July 1916 *of wounds received in action*
HAMILTON, C. J.   Pte., London Regt. (Artists Rifles)   1910
HAMILTON, G. H.   Lieut., R.G.A.(T.F.)   1908
HAMMOND, N. W.   Lieut., St Edward's School, Oxford,   1897
  O.T.C.
HANITSCH, K. V.   Capt., R.F.A. *M.*   1911
✠HARRIS, L. G.   Pte., H.A.C.   1913
  Killed in action near Ypres 28 April 1915
HARRISON, A. M.   2nd Lieut., R.F.A.   1908
HARVEY, R. P.   Lieut., Norfolk Regt.; attd. R.F.C.   [1914]
HASWELL, P.   2nd Lieut., R.G.A.   1907
HATLEY, A. J.   Lieut., R.N.V.R.   1912
HAWORTH, C. W. B.   Lieut., Manchester Regt. (W.)   1911
HAYGARTH, C. H. S.   Lieut., R.E.(T.F.) (P.)   1914
✠HAYTHORNTHWAITE, R. M.   2nd Lieut., The Buffs (E.   1913
  Kent Regt.)
  Killed in action 24 May 1915
HEADS, J. E. B.   Capt., Durham L.I.(T.F.)   1907
HEAP, E. F. G. T.   Capt., R.A.M.C.   1895
HERMAN, W. S.   Lieut., R.A.M.C.   1906
HEWITT, N. S.   Surgeon Lieut., R.N.   1911

HEYER, G. Capt., Spec. List (Directorate of Requisi- 1888
tions and Hirings). *M.B.E. M.*
HOFFMAN, C. D. Corpl., W. Yorks. Regt. 1900
HOLLAND, H. H. Instructor Capt., R.N. 1884
HOLLINGSWORTH, J. H. Capt., R. Marines. *D.S.C.* 1894
Belgian Croix de Guerre
✠HOLMES, B. S. Pte., R.A.S.C.; 2nd Lieut., King's Royal 1903
Rifle Corps and M.G.C.
Accidentally killed 24 Oct. 1916
HOLT, J. L. Instructor Cdr., R.N. 1890
HORAN, A. K. Pte., H.A.C.; Lieut., R.F.A.(T.F.) 1906
HOUSDEN, R. J. Lce.-Corpl., 6th Dragoon Gds. (Cara- 1908
biniers); 2nd Lieut., R. Fusiliers; Lieut., Northamp-
tonshire Regt.; Lieut. (A.), R.A.F.
HUGHES, F. A. 2nd Lieut., Wellington College O.T.C. 1906

JACKSON, A. H. Pte., Foreign Legion, French Army; 1913
Major, R. Fusiliers. (W.)
JACKSON, R. W. Lieut., R.F.A.; Hon. Lieut. (O.), R.A.F. 1912
✠JAMESON, A. B. 2nd Lieut., Cambridgeshire Regt. 1913
Killed in action 21 July 1916
JERWOOD, B. E. Capt., R.A.M.C. 1911
JOBSON, J. S. Surgeon, R.N. 1903
JOHNSON, F. H. Pte., King's Own (R. Lancaster Regt.) 1913
✠JOHNSON, O. B. G. 2nd Lieut., Norfolk Regt. and 1912
Suffolk Regt.
Killed in action 9 April 1917
JONAS, G. J. Lieut., R.G.A.(T.F.) 1912
JONES, E. W. Capt., R. Warwickshire Regt.; attd. Loyal 1913
N. Lancs. Regt. (W 2.) *Belgian Croix de Guerre*
JONES, G. B. H. Lieut., Welsh Horse and M.G.C. *M.C.* 1915
JONES, J. M. *See* MORRIS-JONES, J.
JONES, R. L. Surgeon Cdr., R.N. 1893

KARRAN, T. W. Lieut., R. Welsh Fus. 1908
KERNICK, J. W. Lieut., R.E. 1910
KING, C. B. R. Lieut., Middlesex Regt.; Capt., M.G.C. 1911
(W.) *M.C.*
✠KING, F. C. Rfn., King's Royal Rifle Corps 1915
Killed in action 2 Feb. 1917
KING, H. B. Capt. and Adjt., Northamptonshire Regt.; 1911
Staff Capt. *M.C. M* 2.
KING, N. Major, E. African Force 1900
✠KING, W. O. R. Lieut., Spec. List (Medical Research) 1906
Died 1919 *of illness contracted during the war*

KNIPE, R. C.   Sergt., London Regt. (R. Fus.); Capt.,   1909
R.A.S.C.; attd. Gen. Staff
KNOX-SHAW, P.   Lieut., Sherwood Foresters (Notts. and   1912
Derby Regt.) (P.)
KNOX-SHAW, T.   2nd Lieut., S. Lancs. Regt.; Capt. and   1905
Adjt., York and Lancaster Regt.; Brigade Major.
M.C. *M* 3. *Belgian Croix de Guerre*

LAIRD-CLOWES, G. S.   R.E.; Lieut., Spec. List. *M.*   1902
LANDER, A. J. M.   Capt., Sherwood Foresters (Notts. and 1913
Derby Regt.); empld. O.C.B. (W.) *M.C.*
LANDON, J. W.   Capt., R.E.; Asst. Instructor, School   1898
of Military Engineering. (W.) *M.B.E.*
LANGTON, G. B.   Pte., R. Fusiliers; Capt., S. Staffs. Regt.   1911
✠LAWSON, R. H.   Lieut., Rifle Brigade. (W.) *M.C.* *M.*   1912
Killed in action on the Somme 24 *Aug.* 1916
LEE, N.   Lieut., King's Own Scottish Borderers. (W.)   1912
LEIGH, S. P.   2nd Lieut., Suffolk Regt.(T.F.) (W.)   1913
LINDESAY, J. H. C.   Capt., Army Cyclist Corps. *M.C.*   1912
LINDSAY, W. J.   Lieut., R.A.M.C.   1890
LITTLE, H. L.   Air Mechanic, R.A.F.   1911
LLOYD, J. D.   2nd Lieut., Labour Corps   1903
LOCKSPEISER, B.   Pte., R.A.M.C.; empld. Ministry of   1910
Munitions
✠LONG, L. P.   Lieut., London Regt. (Blackheath and Wool- 1912
wich Bn.)
Killed in action 25 *Sept.* 1915
LONGRIGG, J. H.   Trooper, S. Provinces Mtd. Rifles,   1909
Indian Defence Force
LOW, A. H.   2nd Lieut., R.E. (London Electrical En-   1910
gineers, T.F.)
LUDLOW, F.   Lieut., I.A.R.O., attd. 97th Deccan Infy.   1905

MCARTHUR, G. K.   2nd Lieut., Norfolk Regt.; Lieut.(O.),   1910
R.A.F.
MCFARLAND, J. B.   Capt., R.A.M.C. *M.C.*   *French*   1908
Croix de Guerre
MACKIE, J. B.   Capt., Somerset L.I.(T.F.) *M.*   1913
MCLEOD, E. R.   Capt., Lancs. Fus. (P.)   [1914]
MACRAE, R. D.   Capt., Gen. List (Intelligence)   1907
✠MAIR, E. M.   2nd Lieut., Cameron Hdrs.   1905
Killed in action 3 *Sept.* 1916
MANNERING, Rev. L. G.   C.F. 4th Class, R.A.C.D. *M.C.*   1902
MANNING, C. R. U.   Lieut., Northamptonshire Regt.   1909
(T.F.)

MARSHALL, A. G. Lieut., W. Yorks. Regt.   1914
MARSHALL, Rev. H. C.F. 2nd Class, R.A.C.D. *M* 2.   1903
  Montenegrin Silver Medal for Bravery
MARSHALL, L. P. Capt., W. Yorks. Regt. (W 2.) *M.C.*   1913
✠MARTIN, S. T. Lieut., R. Inniskilling Fus. (W.)   1909
  Killed in action 1 *July* 1916
MARTYN, J. V. 2nd Lieut., R.A.F.   1913
MASON, N. Capt., Punjab Rifles, Indian Defence Force   1908
MATHER, F. H. Lieut., Lincolnshire Regt.; empld. O.C.B.   1914
  (W.)
MATHIESON, W. Major, R.A.M.C. *O.B.E.* *M* 3.   1901
MAY, A. J. Capt R.A.M.C   1902
MAYALL, Rev. J. B. C.F. 4th Class, R.A.C.D. (W 2.)   1910
  M.C. *M.*
MAYALL, R. C. Capt. and Adjt., Northumberland Fus.   1912
  D.S.O. *M.C. and Bar.* *M.* *Italian Bronze Medal for*
  Military Valour
MAYES, Rev. R. M. C.F. 4th Class, R.A.C.D.   1905
MEGSON, M. Lieut.-Cdr., R.N.V.R.   1901
METCALFE, F. W. Capt., Rifle Brigade; empld. Home   1905
  Office
MICHELL, A. H. Lieut., Warwickshire Yeo. and M.G.C.   1901
MILLS, R. A. Lieut., R.A.S.C.(M.T.)   1914
MILMAN, L. C. P. Major, R.F.A.; Brig.-Gen., Asst.   1896
  Director, Ministry of Munitions. *C.M.G.* *M.* *m.*
MITCHELL, A. G. Lieut., Northumberland Fus. and R.E.   1904
MOLONY, A. C. B. Lieut., Border Regt. and M.G.C. (W.)   1911
MOLONY, Rev. J. A. C.F. 4th Class, R.A.C.D.   1909
✠MORRIS, J. W. G. Capt., Welsh Regt.   1913
  Killed in action 1 *April* 1916
MORRIS-JONES, J. 2nd Lieut., Welsh Horse; Lieut., 41st   1915
  Cavalry, Indian Army. *M.*
MOUNTAIN, B. Capt., R.A.M.C.   1902
MULLINS, C. DE C. C. 2nd Lieut., 10th Hussars   1910

NAISH, F. C. P. Capt., R.E. (W.) *M.B.E.*   1900
NEIGHBOUR, P. M. Capt., R.A.M.C.   1912
NOBLE, E. R. Pioneer, R.E. (Spec. Bde.)   1905

OATEN, E. F. Lieut., I.A.R.O., attd. 11th Lancers   1903
OATEN, W. S. Lieut., R.F.A.; Capt., Spec. List (Chemical   1911
  Adviser). (W.) *M.*
O'NEILL, F. R. Capt., R. Inniskilling Fus.; Major,   1898
  R. Sussex Regt.(T.F.) *Brevet Major.* *M.*
OSCROFT, E. P. Lieut., R.E. (Signals)   1914

✠PAINE, W. L.   Pte., Grenadier Gds.; Capt. and Adjt.,   1900
    King's Own (R. Lancaster Regt.); attd. Lancs. Fus.
    Killed in action in Gallipoli 4 June 1915
PAKEMAN, S. A.   Capt., Wiltshire Regt. (W 2.)   *M.C.*   1910
PALMER, W. H.   Lieut., R.A.M.C.   1914
PARGETER, H. A. A.   Surgeon Sub-Lieut., R.N.V.R.   1916
PATERSON, H.   Lieut., R.F.A.   1911
PEAKE, S. C.   2nd Lieut., Norfolk Regt.; Capt., Labour   1914
    Corps. (W.)
PEARSON, A. C.   Major, R.A.M.C.(T.F.)   *M.C.*   1893
PEARSON, B. L.   Capt., R.A.S.C.(M.T.)   *O.B.E. M.*   1911
PECK, S. C.   Lieut.-Col., R.G.A.; G.S.O. 2.   *D.S.O.*   1890
    Brevet Lieut.-Colonel. M 3.
✠PEMBERTON, V. T.   2nd Lieut., R. Munster Fus.; Major,   1913
    R.G.A.   *M.C.*
    Killed in action at Bélicourt 7 Oct. 1918
PINCHES, H. I.   Capt., R.A.M.C.   1897
POINTER, E. H.   Gnr., R.G.A.   1907
POOLE, F. S.   Capt., R.A.M.C.   1901
POOLE, H.   Lieut., The Buffs (E. Kent Regt.) and   1904
    R.G.A.(T.F.)
✠POPE, L. K.   Trooper, Otago Mtd. Rifles, N. Zealand   1907
    Force
    Killed in action in Gallipoli 7 Aug. 1915
PURCHASE, W. B.   Major, R.A.M.C.; D.A.D.M.S. (W.)   1908
    Brevet Major. M.C. M. Order of the White Eagle,
    5th Class (Czecho-Slovakia)

RADFORD, V. N.   Capt. and Adjt., R.A.S.C.   *M 2.*   1913
RADFORD, W. N.   Lieut., R.A.S.C.   1909
RAMSDEN, G. C. F.   Capt., R. Sussex Regt.   1912
✠RAPP, R.   2nd Lieut., D. of Wellington's (W. Riding   1913
    Regt., T.F.)
    Killed in action 18 June 1915
RAPP, T. C.   Capt., D. of Wellington's (W. Riding   1911
    Regt., T.F.); Major (A.), R.A.F. (W.)   *M.C. M.*
✠RATCLIFFE, A. V.   Lieut., W. Yorks. Regt.   1907
    Killed in action 1 July 1916
✠RAYNER, O. C.   Lieut., Manchester Regt.   1911
    Killed in action 18 Nov. 1916
READ, R. S.   2nd Lieut., R.E.   1908
✠REES, A. M.   Lieut., Essex Regt.   1914
    Killed in action at Gueudecourt 18 Oct. 1916
✠REES-MOGG, L. L.   Lieut., R.E.   1908
    Killed in action in Gallipoli 11 Aug. 1915

✠REYNOLDS, J. W. 2nd Lieut., York and Lancaster Regt. *1910
(T.F.)
Killed in action near Ypres 7 Aug. 1915
RICHARDS, C. W. Capt., R.A.S.C.   1912
RICHARDSON, C. A. 2nd Lieut., St Bees School O.T.C. 1910
ROBINSON, J. H. Gnr., R.G.A.   1899
✠ROBINSON, J. S. Instructor Lieut., R.N.   1907
Died on active service 13 *Nov.* 1918 *of meningitis
following influenza*
ROBSON, A. Instructor Lieut., R.N.   1907
ROGERSON, S. Capt., W. Yorks. Regt.   1912
ROPER, H. Capt., Devon Regt. (W.) *M.C.*   1910
✠ROSIER, J. E. R. Lieut., R.F.A.(T.F.)   1912
Died 20 Sept. 1916 *of wounds received in action*
✠ROUQUETTE, D. G. 2nd Lieut., R.A.S.C.; 2nd Lieut. (A), 1910
R.F.C.
Killed in action 26 Sept. 1917
ROY, D. W. Surgeon, R.N.V.R.; Major, R.A.M.C.   1899
RUSSELL, H. B. G. Major, R.A.M.C.; D.A.D.M.S. *M.* 1905
French Croix de Guerre
RUSSELL, Rev. W. B. C.F. 4th Class, R.A.C.D.   1908

SARRA, E. R. Surgeon Sub-Lieut., R.N.V.R.   1913
SAUNDERS, C. Lieut. (A.), R.A.F. (W.)   1914
SCHILLER, L. C. T. Capt., Lincolnshire Regt.(T.F.) [1914]
(W.) *M.C.*
SCHOOLING, A. J. Pte., R.A.M.C.; 2nd Lieut., R.A.S.C. 1900
SCORGIE, N. G. Lieut.-Col., Deputy Director, Army 1903
Printing and Stationery Services. *O.B.E. M*2.
SCOTT, D. A. Lieut., King's Own (Yorkshire L.I.)   1912
SEDGWICK, C. H. Capt. and Q.M., R.A.M.C. (2nd N. 1895
Gen. Hospital, T.F.)
SELLS, A. L. Pte., H.A.C.   1914
✠SHANKSTER, G. Lieut., Northamptonshire Regt. (W 2.) 1912
Killed in action 9 Oct. 1916
SHERWOOD, H. P. Capt., R. Warwickshire Regt.(T.F.); 1912
attd. R.E. (Signals). *M.C. M.*
SHORTER, R. C. 2nd Lieut., R.E.; Capt., Spec. List (Area 1904
Gas Officer)
SILLEY, P. G. Lieut., R.N.V.R.   1892
SIMPSON, S. G. Major, R.A.S.C.; G.S.O. 3 (Education). 1900
*O.B.E. M*2.
SIMS, Rev. F. A. Chaplain, R.N.   1882
SLEIGHT, K. R. Lieut., London Regt. (Blackheath and 1910
Woolwich Bn.)

SMITH, C. W. W. *See* WINWOOD-SMITH, C. W.
SMITH, J. L. Lieut., Denstone College O.T.C.   1908
✠SMITH, W. H. Major, R.F.A. *M* 2.   1904
  Killed in action 12 *April* 1917
SPERO, L. Lieut., King's Royal Rifle Corps. (W.)   1907
✠SPINK, C. C. 2nd Lieut., E. Yorks. Regt.   1910
  Killed in action 4 *June* 1916
SPRING, E. Capt., Somerset L.I.(T.F.) (W.)   1910
STAFFURTH, A. E. Capt., R.A.M.C.   1906
STANHOPE, R. M. 2nd Lieut., R.G.A.   1905
✠STENHOUSE, J. M. Capt., R.A.M.C. *M.C.*   1897
  Died 25 *Aug.* 1916 *of wounds received in action*
STEVENSON, A. W. 2nd Lieut., N. Staffs. Regt. and   1914
  Sherwood Foresters (Notts. and Derby Regt.); Lieut.
  (A.), R.A.F. *D.F.C.*
STEVENSON, F. P. Capt., Radley College O.T.C.   1902
STEWART, E. W. H. Capt., Canadian A.S.C.   1905
STRICKLAND, N. Capt., Repton School O.T.C.   1899
STOKES, F. L. B. 2nd Lieut., Sherwood Foresters (Notts.   1913
  and Derby Regt.)
STUBBS, S. S. Lieut., R.G.A.   1913
SUTCLIFFE, A. L. Surgeon Lieut., R.N. *M.*   1906
SYLVESTER, H. A. Rhodesia Field Force   1911
SYMONS, W. J. F. Capt., R.A.M.C.   1907

✠TAYLOR, G. S. Pte., R.A.M.C.   1911
  Missing, presumed killed in action, 18 *Sept.* 1916
TELFER, L. P. Pte., Bengal Bn., Indian Defence Force   1909
TEMPERLEY, E. E. V. Major, R.E. *M.C. and Bar. Belgian*   1908
  Croix de Guerre
TERRY, H. V. Capt. (Airship), R.A.F. *M.*   1914
THOMAS, D. E. Lieut., R.G.A. (W.) *Italian Bronze*   1904
  Medal for Military Valour
THOMSON, F. G. Capt., R.A.M.C.   1892
TOBIAS, Rev. G. W. R. C.F. 4th Class, R.A.C.D. *M.C.*   1904
TRESAWNA, W. S. Capt., R.A.M.C.(T.F.) *M.*   1898

VOGEL, E. P. *See* OSCROFT, E. P.

WALDRAM, H. G. Capt., Devon Regt.(T.F.) (P.) *M.*   1908
WALES, H. Capt., R.A.M.C. *M.*   1896
WALKER, J. E. Capt., R. Fusiliers and Labour Corps   1896
WALKER, L. H. T. Capt., Welsh Regt. (W.) *M.C.*   1913
WALKER, S. L. Capt., Canadian A.M.C. *M.*   1900
WALLACE, C. R. P. 2nd Lieut., E. Yorks. Regt.   1912

WALLER, F. 2nd Lieut., Border Regt. (W.)   1903
WALTER, C. Lieut., R.G.A.   1896
WARD, Rev. E. H. C.F. 4th Class, R.A.C.D.   1907
✠WARD, W. D. Sergt., London Regt. (Cyclist Bn.); Capt.,   1901
Hampshire Regt. (Cyclist Bn.); attd. Indian Army
Died 4 Sept. 1918 *of injuries accidentally received*
WATKINS, E. V. Lieut., Welsh Regt.   1901
✠WATSON, T. P. Capt. and Adjt., E. Lancs. Regt. (W.)   1910
M.C. M 2.
Killed in action 7 *March* 1917
WEBB, G. C. N. Capt., Dorset Regt. *M.*   [1914]
WEBB-BENTON, J. American Army   1911
WELLER, H. J. 2nd Lieut., Bedfordshire Regt.; Lieut.,   1915
M.G.C. (W 2.)
WESTHEAD, W. H. Lieut., R.G.A. (W.) *M. Chevalier,*   1914
Ordre de la Couronne (*Belgium*). *Belgian Croix de*
Guerre
WHEELER, A. M. Lieut., R.G.A.(T.F.)   1906
WHITE, K. H. Major, R.A.S.C. *M.*   1905
WHITMORE, H. S. 2nd Lieut., King's (Shropshire L.I.)   1909
WILKINSON, C. A. Lieut., Middlesex Regt.(T.F.); Capt.,   1902
Spec. List. *M.B.E. Cavalier, Order of the Crown of*
Italy
WILKINSON, F. Lieut., S. Staffs. Regt.(T.F.); Lieut. (A.)   1913
and Capt. (Ad.), R.A.F. (W 2.) *M.*
WILKINSON, F. C. Hon. Capt., R.A.M.C.   1902
WILLIAMS, C. H. 2nd Lieut., Welsh Regt.   1914
WILLIAMS-ELLIS, R. G. Lieut., R. Welsh Fus.(T.F.);   1896
Capt., R.A.S.C.
WILSON, B. Capt., Manchester Regt.; attd. T.M.B.   1908
WILSON, H. O. S. Lieut., R.A.S.C.   1912
WINWOOD-SMITH, C. W. Lieut., Devon Regt. and Gen.   1912
List (T.M.B.); empld. War Office
WOOD, B. R. Trooper, United Provinces Horse, Indian   1909
Defence Force
WOOD, N. P. 2nd Lieut., Cheshire Regt.   1902
WOOLF, E. S. Capt., R.A.S.C.; Major, D.A.D. Transport   1902
WOOLF, P. S. Lieut., 20th Hussars. (W.) *M.*   1908
WRIGHT, J. ALDREN. Major, R.A.M.C. (1st E. Gen. Hos- *1902
pital, T.F.)
WYCHE, C. K. H. Lieut., Norfolk Regt.   1911
WYNNE-EDWARDS, J. C. Capt., R. Welsh Fus.   1909

YOUNG, J. G. C. Lieut., R.G.A.   1911

TRINITY COLLEGE

ABBOT, H. Capt., R.F.A. (W.) *M.*   1889
ACHESON-GRAY, C. G. A. Lieut., Dorset Regt.(T.F.)   1907
ADAIR, J. V. Capt., N. Irish Horse. *M.C.*   1907
ADAMS, C. W. Lieut., R.G.A.(T.F.) (W.)   1901
ADAMS, E. P. Capt., R.E. *O.B.E. M.*   1902
ADAMS, W. McM. 2nd Lieut., R.E.; Lieut. (K.B.), United   1914
    States Air Service. (W.) *M.C.*
✠ADAMSON, W. Capt., Loyal N. Lancs. Regt.   1904
    Killed in action 24 April 1916
✠ADDY, J. C. Capt., E. Yorks. Regt. *M.C.*   1910
    Killed in action 3 May 1917
ADIE, C. J. M. Lieut., Eton College O.T.C.   1895
ADRIAN, E. D. Capt., R.A.M.C.   1908
AGAR, C. T. Lieut., R.G.A.   1891
AGAR, H. E. T. Major, R.E.(T.F.) *m* 2.   1894
AGIUS, E. E. G. Lieut., London Regt. (R. Fus.); Capt.,   1907
    Spec. List (Adjt., Reception Camp). (W.)
AGNEW, C. G. Capt., Manchester Regt. and Gen. List   1901
    (O.C.B.) *M.*
AGNEW, J. S. Capt., Suffolk Yeo.; D.A.A.G. *M. Cav-*   1898
    alier, Order of the Crown of Italy
AGNEW, V. C. W. Capt., Suffolk Yeo. and Suffolk Regt.   1906
    (T.F.)
AINSWORTH, T. 2nd Lieut., 11th Hussars   1904
AITKEN, D. B. Lieut., Seaforth Hdrs.; Lieut. (A.), R.A.F.   1913
    (W.) *D.F.C.*
✠ALBRIGHT, M. C. Major, Worcestershire Yeo.   1905
    Died 8 Nov. 1917 *of wounds received in action*
✠ALDERSEY, H. Capt., Cheshire Yeo.   1907
    Killed in action 10 March 1918

ALDRIDGE, E. A. Capt., R.A.M.C. (W.) *M.C. Brevet* 1895
Major. M.
ALEXANDER, F. D. Capt., 19th Hussars; Major, D.A.D. 1897
Remounts. (W.) *M* 2. *Belgian Croix de Guerre*
ALEXANDER, J. F. Lieut., R.A.M.C. 1895
ALLAN, A. C. 2nd Lieut., Middlesex Regt. (W.) 1912
ALLCARD, R. Capt., R.E. *O.B.E. M.* 1903
ALLCHIN, G.C. Lieut., Queen's Own (R.W. Kent Regt.); 1914
Capt., R.E. *M.C.*
ALLEN, Rev. G. K. C.F. 4th Class, R.A.C.D. 1901
ALLEN, J. Lieut., R.G.A. 1892
✠ALLEN, J. E. R. Lieut., 16th Lancers. (W.) *M* 2. 1909
Died 8 April 1918 *of wounds received in action*
ALLEN, Rev. L. J. Chaplain, R.N. 1904
✠ALLEN, M. R. H. A. Lieut. (A.), R.F.C. 1910
Killed in flying accident 21 *March* 1917
ALLEN, R. C. Lieut., R.F.A.(T.F.); Lieut. (A. and Ad.), 1914
R.A.F. (W.)
ALLEN, W. H. Hon. Major, R.G.A. 1892
ALLFREY, F. H. Capt., R.A.M.C. *M.* 1891
ALLGOOD,G.H. Capt.,Northumberland Fus. (W.) *M*2. 1911
ALLHUSEN, O. Major, R.F.A.(T.F.) 1907
ALLHUSEN, R. Major, R.F.A. (W.) 1912
ALLIX, C. I. L. Lieut., Coldstream Gds. 1891
✠ALLOM, C. C. G. Capt., R.F.A. 1914
Died 20 *Oct.* 1917 *of wounds received in action* 9 *Oct.*
1917
ALTHORP, Viscount. Capt., Life Guards; A.D.C. (W.) 1910
ANCASTER, Earl of, T.D. Lieut.-Col., Lincolnshire Yeo. 1886
(T.F. Res.) *m.*
ANDERSON, A. E. D. Capt., King's Own Scottish Bor- 1905
derers; Brigade Major; Lieut.-Col., Spec. List
(School of Instruction). (W.) *D.S.O. M.C. M* 3.
ANDERSON, A. P. M. *See* MOORE-ANDERSON, A. P.
ANDERSON, C. A. Surgeon Lieut., R.N. 1895
ANDERSON, G. B. Capt., R.F.A. *M.C.* 1914
ANDERSON, N. L. Capt., S. Staffs. Regt.; empld. O.C.B. 1913
(W 2.)
ANDRAS, J. B. Capt. and Adjt., E. Surrey Regt.(T.F.) 1910
✠ANDREWES, C. N. Lieut., Labour Corps 1895
Died 29 *Nov.* 1918 *of influenza contracted on active*
service
ANDREWS, K. T. Major, R.A.S.C. 1912
ANSBACHER, S. S. *See* ANSLEY, S. S.

ANSDELL, T. A.   Australian A.M.C.   1909
✠ANSELL, A. G.   2nd Lieut., R.E. (Field Survey Coy.)   1912
   Died 25 April 1918 of gas poisoning
ANSLEY, S. S.   Capt., R.H.A.(T.F.) (W.) *M.C.*   1912
ANSON, G. F. V.   Surgeon Lieut., R.N. (W.)   1910
ANSTEY, T. C. R.   Capt., Sherwood Rangers. (W.)   1911
ANTROBUS, M. E.   Capt., King's Royal Rifle Corps. [1914]
   (W 2.)
✠APPERLEY, B. L. M.   2nd Lieut., Queen's Own (R.W.   1911
   Kent Regt.) (W.)
   Died 19 April 1917 of wounds received in action
ARBUTHNOT, L. G.   Capt., Lancs. Fus.; A.D.C. (W.)   1886
   *M.B.E. Order of the White Eagle, 5th Class, with
   swords (Serbia)*
ARBUTHNOT, M. A.   Capt., Seaforth Hdrs.; D.A.M.S.,   1897
   War Office. (W.) *O.B.E. Brevet Major*
ARBUTHNOT, R. W. M.   Capt., R.F.A.; Staff Capt. (W.)   1908
   M.C. French Croix de Guerre
ARCHER, C. W.   Surgeon Lieut., R.N.   1905
ARKWRIGHT, J. A.   Capt., R.A.M.C. *m. Order of the*   1882
   White Eagle, 5th Class, with swords (Serbia)
ARKWRIGHT, R. O. W.   Lieut., 4th Hussars. (W.)   1913
ARMITAGE, N. C.   Lieut., R.G.A.   1896
ARMSTRONG, J. R. B.   Lieut., N. Irish Horse and 8th   1911
   (King's R. Irish) Hussars; Capt., Tank Corps
✠ARMSTRONG, M. R. L.   2nd Lieut., R.F.A. and R.E.   1908
   Killed in action 23 April 1916
ARMSTRONG, R. R.   Capt., R.A.M.C.   1903
ARNALLT-JONES, G. C.   2nd Lieut., Suffolk Regt.   1916
ARNOTT, R. J.   Lieut., King's Royal Rifle Corps   [1914]
ASH, F. H.   Lieut., 4th Hussars. *French Croix de Guerre* 1912
ASH, G. B.   Capt., Spec. List (Dental Surgeon)   1901
ASH, O. A.   Lieut., R.G.A.   1914
ASKEW, E. J. P.   Capt., R.F.A.; empld. Ministry of Labour 1905
ASPINALL, G.   Lieut., Lancs. Hussars   1903
ASSHETON, R. T.   Capt., Cambridgeshire Regt.; Major,   1913
   M.G.C. (W.)
ATHILL, C. R. W.   2nd Lieut., Middlesex Regt.   1915
ATHILL, F. R. I.   Lieut.-Col., Northumberland Fus.;   1899
   D.A.A.G., War Office. (W.) *C.M.G. M 2. m..*
ATKINSON, A. G.   Capt., R.A.M.C. (Sanitary Service,   1900
   T.F.) *M.B.E.*
ATKINSON, H. B.   Capt., E. African Force. *O.B.E. M 2.*   1898
ATKINSON, P. Y.   Lieut., 5th Dragoon Gds. *M.C.*   1905

ATTENBOROUGH, C. R. W.   Capt., London Regt. (R. Fus.)   1906
(W.)
✠AUSTEN-CARTMELL, A. J.   Lieut., King's Royal Rifle Corps   1912
Killed in action 1 *June* 1916
AUSTEN-SMITH, H., C.I.E.   Lieut.-Col., I.M.S.   1884
AYLMER, E. K. G., C.B.   Bt. Colonel, Res. Regt. of Cavalry   1877
AYTON, W. A.   Lieut., R.G.A.   1899

BABER, J. B.   Capt., London Regt. (Queen's Westminster   1911
Rifles) and M.G.C.   *M.C.   M.*
BACK, H. C.   Lieut., Spec. List. (R.T.O.)   1882
✠BACKHOUSE, H. E.   Capt., Sherwood Foresters (Notts.   1901
and Derby Regt.)
Killed in action 15 *Oct.* 1916
✠BACKUS, A. R.   Capt., Rifle Brigade. (W 2.)   *M.C.*   1913
Accidentally killed near Neuve Eglise 22 *Sept.* 1917
BACON, F.   Lieut., R.N.V.R.; empld. Admiralty   1899
BACON, F. R.   Lieut., Cameronians (Scottish Rifles)   1910
BACON, R. C.   Capt., R. Defence Corps   1885
BAERLEIN, H. P. D.   Service Sanitaire, French Army   1893
BAERLEIN, O. F.   Capt., R.A.S.C.   *M.C.*   1911
BAGGALLAY, M. E. C.   Lieut., 11th Hussars; A.D.C.   *M.*   1907
BAHR, P. H.   Capt., R.A.M.C.   *D.S.O.   Brevet Major.*   1900
M.
BAILEY, F. G. G.   Lieut.-Col., R.F.A.   (W.)   *Brevet*   1898
Lieut.-Colonel
BAILEY, W. N.   Instructor Lieut., R.N.   1912
BAINBRIDGE, F. A.   Capt., R.A.M.C.   1893
✠BAINBRIGGE, P. G.   2nd Lieut., Lancs. Fus.; attd. Welsh   1909
Regt.
Killed in action 18 *Sept.* 1918
BAINES, J. T.   Capt., Welsh Regt.; empld. O.C.B.   (W.)   1913
BALFOUR, C. M.   Lieut., R.E.(T.F.); Capt., Tank Corps.   1909
M.
✠BALFOUR, J.   Capt., Scots Gds.; attd. R.E.(Signals).   *M.C.*   1913
M.
Killed in action 21 *March* 1918
BALFOUR, M.   Major, R.F.A.   *M.C.*   1897
BALL, O. J. H.   Hon. Brig.-Gen. (ret.); Staff Lieut.   *m.*   1871
✠BALLAMY, H. W.   Lieut., R.F.A.(T.F.)   (W 2.)   1912
Killed in action 15 *Aug.* 1917
✠BALLANCE, L. A.   2nd Lieut., London Regt. (Civil Service   1907
Rifles); Capt., King's Royal Rifle Corps
Killed in action 28 *Sept.* 1916

BALSTON, F. W.   Capt., R.A.S.C.   1899
BALZAROTTI, G. P.   2nd Lieut., Italian Army.   *m.*   1909
BANBURY, F. E.   2nd Lieut., Coldstream Gds.   1912
BANBURY, R. E.   Capt., R. Fusiliers.   (W.)   1898
BANISTER, C. G.   Lieut., King's (Shropshire L.I.); Capt.,   1908
   R.E.; Hon. Capt. (T.), R.A.F.
BANKS, P.   Capt., R.F.A.   1914
BARBER, J. R.   Capt., Gen. List (T.F. Res.)   *M.C.*   1896
BARBER, T. P.   Major, S. Notts. Hussars. (W.)   *D.S.O.*   1894
   M 3.
BARBER-STARKEY, F. W. G.   Capt., Canadian M.G.C.   1903
   (W.)
BARBER-STARKEY, R. J. K.   2nd Lieut., Shropshire Yeo.   1902
✠BARBER-STARKEY, W. H. J.   Capt., R.F.A.   1898
   Died in German hands 10 *Sept.* 1914 *of wounds received*
   in action at Le Cateau 26 *Aug.* 1914
BARBOUR, R., T.D.   Major, Cheshire Yeo.   1894
BARCLAY, A. V.   Corpl., E. African Mtd. Rifles; Capt.,   1906
   King's African Rifles.   (W 2.)
BARCLAY, C.   Major and Adjt., Res. Regt. of Cavalry;   1885
   attd. 10th Hussars.   *m.*
BARCLAY, Rev. G. A.   C.F. 4th Class, R.A.C.D.   *m.*   1900
BARCLAY, H. G., M.V.O., V.D.   Hon. Colonel, Norfolk   1870
   Regt.(T.F. Res.)
BARCLAY, R. L.   Capt., Norfolk Yeo.; Major, Q.M.G.'s   1886
   Dept., War Office.   *C.B.E.   O.B.E.*
BARCLAY, R. W.   Lieut.-Col., Surrey Yeo.; Capt., 2nd Life   1900
   Gds.
✠BARCLAY, T. H.   Major, Surrey Yeo.   *Silver Medal for*   1902
   gallantry in saving life at sea
   Drowned on H.M. transport Transylvania 4 *May* 1917
BARING, Hon. M.   Major, S.O. 2, R.A.F.   *O.B.E.   M* 2.   1893
   Chevalier, Legion of Honour (France)
BARKER, A.   Capt., R.A.M.C.   1901
BARKER, Rev. A. L.   C.F. 4th Class, R.A.C.D.   1889
BARKER, F. W.   Capt., London Yeo. (Westminster Dra-   1907
   goons).   *M.*
BARKER-HAHLO, H.   Capt., N. Somerset Yeo. and Gen.   1891
   Staff
BARLOW, A. W. L.   2nd Lieut., King's Royal Rifle Corps   1910
BARNARD, Lord.   Major, Westmorland and Cumberland   1907
   Yeo.; attd. Border Regt.   (W 2.)   *M.C.*
BARNES, R. S.   Capt., Suffolk Regt.(T.F.); A.P.M.   *M.*   1898
BARNES, T. H.   Lieut., R.F.A.   (W.)   [1914]

BARNES-GORELL, T. A. R. Lieut., Sherwood Foresters 1911
(Notts. and Derby Regt.) (W.)
BARNETT, B. L. Lieut., R.E.(T.F.) *M.C. M* 2. 1913
BARNINGHAM, E. Capt., Loyal N. Lancs. Regt. 1911
BARNINGHAM, H. Lieut., Loyal N. Lancs. Regt.; Lieut. [1914]
(A.), R.A.F.
BARNSLEY, D. G. Major, Gloucestershire Regt.; Lieut.- 1902
Col., R. Warwickshire Regt. (W.) *M.C. m.*
BARNSLEY, R. E. Major, R.A.M.C.; D.A.D.M.S. (W.) 1905
M.C. Brevet Major
✠BARNSLEY, T. K. Capt., R. Warwickshire Regt. and Cold- 1911
stream Gds. (W.)
Killed in action 31 *July* 1917
BARRACLOUGH, R. F. Lieut., R.A.S.C. *m.* 1903
BARRAN, C. R. Lieut., R.G.A. *M.* 1904
BARRAN, H. V. F. 2nd Lieut., R.F.A. (W.) *M.* 1913
BARRATT, W. D. Capt., King's Own (R. Lancaster Regt., 1902
T.F. Res.)
BARRETT, R. C. Capt., D. of Wellington's (W. Riding 1913
Regt., T.F.); A.D.C. *M.*
BARRON, E. A. W. Lieut., Res. Regt. of Cavalry; attd. 1901
12th Lancers. *M.C.*
BARROW, E. B. P. 2nd Lieut., R.F.C. 1909
BARROWCLOUGH, S. Lieut., R.F.A. 1913
BARRY, E. G. WOLFE. *See* WOLFE BARRY, E. G.
BARRY, K. A. WOLFE. *See* WOLFE BARRY, K. A.
BARRY, T. Lieut., Cameron Hdrs. (W 2.) 1909
✠BARTHROPP, S. A. N. S. 2nd Lieut., R. Sussex Regt. 1910
Killed in action at Cuinchy 29 *Jan.* 1915
BARTLETT, E. G. Lieut., King's Own (Yorkshire L.I.); 1913
Staff Capt. (W.) *O.B.E. M.C. and Bar. M* 2.
BARTRAM, L. H. Surgeon Sub-Lieut., R.N.V.R. 1913
BARWELL, N. F. Major, Oxford and Bucks. L.I.; Lieut.- 1897
Col., Gloucestershire Regt. (W.) *M.C. M.*
BATCHELDER, G. L. Lieut., United States Naval Res. 1914
BATES, F. A. Capt., Denbigh Yeo.; Major (A.), R.A.F. 1903
(W.) *M.C. A.F.C. M* 4. *Greek Military Cross*
BATESON, Hon. E. DE Y. Capt., R.A.S.C.(T.F.) 1903
✠BATLEY, R. C., T.D. Major, Dorset Yeo. 1881
Died 23 *Oct.* 1917
BATTISCOMBE, Rev. G. C. C.F. 4th Class, R.A.C.D.(T.F.) 1879
BAXTER, C. W. Capt., S. Lancs. Regt.(T.F.) (W.) *M.C.* 1913
BAYNES, G. Capt., 3rd Hussars. (W.) 1899
BAYNES, H. G. Capt., R.A.M.C. *M.* 1904

BAYNES, W. E. C.   Capt., Coldstream Gds. and Gen.   1894
Staff. (W 3.) *M.C. M.*
BEALE, H. L.   2nd Lieut., Cambridgeshire Regt.; Capt.,   1897
R.E. (Inland Water Transport). *m.*
✠BEALEY, A. C.   Capt., Somerset L.I. *M.C. M.*   1892
Died 22 *Nov.* 1917 *of wounds received in action in*
Palestine
BEASLEY-ROBINSON, A. C.   Lieut., R.F.A. (W.)   [1914]
BEAUCHAMP, Rev. Sir M. H., Bart.   C.F. 4th Class,   1879
R.A.C.D. *m.*
BEAUFOY, H. M.   Lieut., Spec. List, empld. Ministry of   1906
National Service
BEAUMONT, Hon. W. H. C.   Capt., 2nd Life Gds.; Major,   1909
Gds. M.G. Regt. *M.C.*
✠BEAUMONT-NESBITT, W. H.   Capt., Grenadier Gds. (W.)   1913
M.C.
Killed in action at Bourlon Wood 27 *Nov.* 1917
BEAZLEY, C. M.   Capt., Rifle Brigade. (W 2.)   1909
BECHER, G. G.   Lieut., Marlborough College O.T.C.   1905
✠BECHER, M. A. N.   Capt., King's Own Scottish Borderers   1903
Killed in action in Gallipoli 26 *April* 1915
BEDDINGTON, C.   Lieut.-Col., Westmorland and Cumber-   1885
land Yeo. (T.F. Res.) (W.) *M.*
✠BEDELL-SIVRIGHT, D. R.   Surgeon, R.N.   1899
Died in Gallipoli 5 *Sept.* 1915
BEDFORD, D. J.   Capt., R.A.M.C. *m.*   1888
✠BEER, A. H.   Lieut., R.F.A.(T.F.) *M.C. M.*   1913
Died 21 *April* 1918 *of wounds received in action at*
Béthune 19 *April* 1918
BEETON, A. E.   Capt., R.E. *M.C. M. French Croix*   1898
de Guerre
BELL, C. W. D.   Lieut., 10th Hussars; Capt. (A.), R.A.F.   1911
✠BELL, G. M.   Major, Hampshire Regt. *D.S.O. M.*   1896
Killed in action in the Third Battle of Ypres 31 *July* 1917
✠BELL, J. J.   Major, Ayrshire Yeo.   1891
Died 2 *March* 1915
✠BELL, W. H. D.   Capt., N. Zealand Force and K. Edward's   1902
Horse. *M.*
Killed in action 31 *July* 1917
BELPER, Lord.   Capt., Life Gds.; Major, Tank Corps   1902
BELVILLE, G. E.   Capt., 16th Lancers and Gen. Staff   1897
(O.C.B.) (W.) (P.)
BENJAMIN, C. M.   2nd Lieut., King's Own (Yorkshire   [1914]
L.I.); Lieut. (T.), R.A.F.

BENNETT, E. Capt., R.A.S.C.(M.T.) *M* 2. 1911
BENTINCK, A. W. D. Capt., Coldstream Gds.; attd. 1906
Egyptian Army. (W.)
✠BENTINCK, H. D. A. Major, Coldstream Gds. *Brevet* 1899
Major. M.
Died 2 Oct. 1916 *of wounds received in action* 15 *Sept.*
1916
BENTLIFF, H. D. Lieut., Essex Regt.(T.F.); attd. Middle- 1910
sex Regt.(T.F.) (W.)
BENTWICH, N. DE M. Major, Spec. List, attd. Egyptian 1901
Camel Corps. (W.) *O.B.E. M.C. M* 2.
BERG, A. W. Lieut., Welsh Gds.; Capt., Spec. List 1903
BERGER, S. H. 2nd Lieut., S. Wales Borderers; empld. 1911
Recruiting Staff
BESSBOROUGH, Earl of. Hon. Capt., Suffolk Yeo. (T.F. 1898
Res.); empld. War Office. *C.M.G. m. Chevalier,*
Legion of Honour (France). Cavalier, Order of St
Maurice and St Lazarus (Italy). Officer, Order of
the Redeemer (Greece). Order of St Anne, 3rd Class,
with swords (Russia)
BEST, T. W. Major, Leicestershire Yeo.; Major (Ad.), 1912
R.A.F. (W.)
✠BETHELL, C. Pte., Coldstream Gds.; Capt., King's Own 1904
(Yorkshire L.I.) *M.*
Killed in action 20 *Feb.* 1916
BETHELL, D. J. Lieut., King's Own (Yorkshire L.I.); 1911
Capt., Scots Gds. *M.C. and Bar. M.*
BETHWAY, Rev. W. S. C.F. 4th Class, R.A.C.D. 1910
BEVAN, T. R. Capt., Hertfordshire Regt. (T.F. Res.); 1909
A.D.C.
BEVERIDGE, H. Capt., Dorset Regt. (P.) 1893
BEVES, C. H. Paymaster Lieut., R.N.V.R. *M.* 1905
BEWICKE-COPLEY, R. G. W. Lieut., King's Royal Rifle 1911
Corps; Major, M.G.C. (W.) *M.C. M. Italian*
Bronze Medal for Military Valour
BICKERSTETH, R. A. Major, R.A.M.C. (1st W. Gen. Hos- 1881
pital, T.F.) *m.*
BICKNELL, P. W. Capt., R.A.S.C. 1902
BIDDER, H. F. Major, R. Sussex Regt.; Lieut.-Col., 1894
M.G.C. *D.S.O. M.*
BIDDLE, F. A. Capt., Gen. List (T.F. Res.), empld. School 1896
of Musketry
BIGGE, H. J. Lieut., 19th Hussars 1907
BILNEY, A. A. H. Lieut., R.A.S.C. *M.C.* 1906

✠BINNING, Lord, C.B., M.V.O.   Lieut.-Col., Lothian and   1876
 Border Horse; Brig.-Gen.
 Died 12 Jan. 1917 of pneumonia
BINYON, B. Major (A.), R.A.F. O.B.E.   1904
⁻₁BION, R. E. Lieut., 20th Hussars; Lieut. (A.), R.A.F.   1910
 Killed in action 9 April 1918
BIRCH, A. G. Major, R.E.(T.F.); D. A. D. Light Rail-   1900
 ways. (W.) *D.S.O. and Bar.* O.B.E. M 4.
BIRD, G. F. Major, R.A.M.C.; D.A.D.M.S. M.C. M 3.   1897
BIRD, L. W. Major, R. Berkshire Regt.; empld. School   1901
 of Instruction. (W 2.) *D.S.O.* O.B.E. M 2.
✠BIRKBECK, G. Lieut., Norfolk Yeo.   1913
 Died 19 Feb. 1916
✠BIRKBECK, G. W. Capt., Norfolk Regt.(T.F.) M.   1905
 Killed in action 19 April 1917
BIRKBECK, H. A. Major, Norfolk Yeo. and Norfolk Regt.   1904
 (T.F.) (W.) M.C.
BIRLEY, O. H. J. Capt., R. Fusiliers and Gen. Staff (In-   1898
 telligence). M.C.
BISHOP, J. H. Lieut., R.F.A.   1911
✠BLACK, D. C. 2nd Lieut. (A.), R.A.F.   1916
 Killed in flying accident 23 April 1918
BLACK, J. C. Capt. and Adjt., R.E. M.   1902
BLACK, R. P. Lieut., R.G.A. M.C.   1911
BLACKBURN, A. Capt., Rifle Brigade (T.F.)   1884
BLACKBURN-MAZE, C. I. Lieut., Queen's Own (R.W.   1908
 Kent Regt.)
BLACKETT, B. J. Lieut., N.S.W. Bn., Australian Force   1905
BLACKLOCK, G. H. Lieut., Shropshire Yeo.; Lieut.-Col.,   1896
 A.D. Docks. M.
BLAIR, H. M. Capt., R. Welsh Fus. (W 2.)   1896
✠BLAKE, G. P. Capt. R. Welsh Fus.   1898
 Killed in action 20 July 1916
BLAKENEY, Rev. E. P. C.F. 4th Class, R.A.C.D.   1889
BLANCO-WHITE, G. R. Capt., R.G.A.   1902
BLAND, A. J. T. Lieut., R.F.A. (W.) M.C.   1913
BLOM, A. H. Capt., Irish Gds. (W 2.)   1909
✠BODENHAM, H. E. C. H. 2nd Lieut., Black Watch;   1914
 Lieut., M.G.C.
 Killed in action on the Somme 7 Sept. 1916
✠BOLITHO, G. R. 2nd Lieut., Devon Regt. and R.F.C.   1911
 (W.)
 Died 25 Oct. 1916 of wounds received in action
BOLITHO, T. G. G. Capt. (K.B.), R.A.F. M.C. D.F.C.   1908

BOLTON, D. C.   Capt., Manchester Regt.   1902

✠BOLTON, W. S.   Sergt., R. Fusiliers (Sportsman's Bn.)   1904
(W.)
Died 7 Feb. 1919 of pneumonia contracted on active service

BOND, A. C.   2nd Lieut., King's Own (R. Lancaster Regt.)   1913

✠BOND, C. G.   Capt., Wiltshire Regt.   1900
Killed in action 25 Nov. 1915

BONHAM, E. H., M.V.O.   Major, 2nd Dragoons (R. Scots   1892
Greys). *M. m. Chevalier, Legion of Honour (France)*

✠BONHAM CARTER, A. T.   S. African Defence Force; Capt.,   1887
Hampshire Regt. *m.*
Killed in action 1 July 1916

BONHAM CARTER, F. H.   Capt., R.G.A.   1898

BONVALOT, A. C.   Capt., Coldstream Gds.   [1914]

✠BONVALOT, E. ST L.   2nd Lieut., Coldstream Gds.   1910
Killed in action 9 Oct. 1915

BOOTH, C. Z. M.   A.B., R.N.V.R. (R.N.D.); Lieut., Leic-   1906
estershire Yeo.

BOOTH, T. M.   Major, Gordon Hdrs.; Brigade Major;   1892
Lieut.-Col., Asst. Military Attaché, the Hague. (W.)
D.S.O. and Bar. M 2.

BOSANQUET, A. R.   Capt., King's Own (R. Lancaster   1909
Regt.) (W.) *M.C.*

BOSCAWEN, Hon. M. T.   Major, Rifle Brigade; Lieut.-   1910
Col., London Regt. *D.S.O. M.C. M 2.*

✠BOSCAWEN, Hon. V. D.   2nd Lieut., Coldstream Gds.   1909
Killed in action near Ypres 29 Oct. 1914

BOSTOCK, S. C.   Lieut., Life Gds. (W.)   1912

BOSTOCK-HILL, A. J.   Lieut., R.N.V.R.   1905

BOUGHEY, C. L. F.   Lieut., Grenadier Gds. (W.)   1905

BOUQUET, Rev. A. C.   C.F. 4th Class, R.A.C.D. *m.*   1902

BOURCHIER, Rev. LE G. C.   C.F. 4th Class, R.A.C.D.   1906

BOUWENS, B. G.   Lieut., R.A.S.C.(M.T.) (W.)   1902

BOVILL, E. W.   Lieut., 10th Hussars; attd. Nigeria Regt.,   1911
W. African Frontier Force. (W.)

BOWEN, J. B.   Capt., Pembroke Yeo.; Lieut.-Col. (T.),   1902
R.A.F. *O.B.E. m.*

✠BOWEN COLTHURST, R. M.   Capt., Leinster Regt.   1902
Killed in action 15 March 1915

BOWER, H. M.   Capt., W. Yorks. Regt.(T.F.); empld.   1873
Records

✠BOWES-LYON, G. P.   Lieut., Grenadier Gds.   [1914]
Killed in action 27 Nov. 1917

BOWES-LYON, Hon. P. Major, Essex Regt. 1882
BOWLBY, R. F. Lieut., London Regt. 1909
BOWLE, C. W. Lieut.-Col., R.A.M.C. 1898
BOWMAN, F. Instructor Lieut., R.N. 1911
BOWMAN, G. H. Capt., R. Warwickshire Regt.; Major 1910
(A.), R.A.F. (W.) *D.S.O. M.C. and Bar. D.F.C.
M. Belgian Croix de Guerre*
BOWMAN VAUGHAN, E. W. *See* VAUGHAN, E. W. B.
BOWRING, J. F. E. Capt. and Adjt., Lancs. Fus.; Major, 1885
Labour Corps
✠BOYD, H. A. 2nd Lieut., R. Inniskilling Fus. 1913
Killed in action 7 Sept 1914
BOYD, J. Lieut., United States Ambulance Service 1910
BOYD ROCHFORT, G. A. *See* ROCHFORT, G. A. B.
BOYLE, G. F. Capt., R. Scots Fus. 1912
BOYS, G. V. Corpl., R.E. (Signals). (P.) 1913
BOZMAN, E. F. Capt., Queen's Own (R. W. Kent Regt.); [1914]
attd. The Buffs (E. Kent Regt.) (W.) *M.C.*
BRADFORD, Earl of. Lieut.-Col., R. Scots. *M.* 1893
BRADLEY, M. G. Major, Middlesex Regt. and Labour 1901
Corps
BRADNEY, J. A., C.B., T.D. Hon. Colonel, London Regt. 1877
(Q.V.R., T.F. Res.); Lieut.-Col., Labour Corps. *m.*
✠BRADSHAW, P. C. 2nd Lieut., King's Own Scottish 1914
Borderers
Killed in action 1 May 1916
✠BRADSHAW, R. E. K. Lieut., London Regt. (Rangers) 1914
Killed in action 1 July 1916
✠BRADSHAW, W. D. 2nd Lieut., R.F.A. 1915
Killed in action 31 Oct. 1916
✠BRAGG, R. C. 2nd Lieut., R.F.A. 1912
*Died 2 Sept. 1915 of wounds received in action in
Gallipoli 1 Sept. 1915*
BRAGG, W. L. Major, R.H.A.(T.F.) *O.B.E. M.C. M.* 1909
BRAMWELL, B. S. Capt., R.F.A.(T.F.) 1896
BRAMWELL, J. C. Capt., R.A.M.C. 1907
BRANSON, F. H. E. Lieut., R.A.O.C.; Major, D.A.D. 1896
Equipment and Ordnance Stores, War Office. *O.B.E.
M.B.E. m.*
BRANSON, J. R. B. Major, R.A.O.C.; D.A.D.O.S. 1891
BRANSON, W. P. S. Colonel, A.M.S. *C.B.E. M.* 1893
BRANSTON, C. A. Lieut., R.E. and R.A.S.C.(T.F.) 1904
BRASS, W. Capt., Surrey Yeo.; Capt. (T.), R.A.F. 1904
BRAUN, G. C. P. 2nd Lieut., R.A.S.C. 1908

BRAUNHOLTZ, W. T. K. Sapper, R.E. (Signals)   1913
BRAY, Sir E. H. Brig.-Gen., Q.M.G.'s Dept., Indian   1893
  Army. *C.S.I.*
BRAY, F. E. Major, The Queen's (R. W. Surrey Regt.,   1901
  T.F.) *M.C. M* 2. *Italian Silver Medal for Military*
  Valour
BRAY, J. Capt., Surrey Yeo.(T.F. Res.) and Gds. M.G. 1897
  Regt.
✠BREESE, W. L. 2nd Lieut., R. Horse Gds.   1902
  Killed in action 14 *March* 1915
BREMNER, F. D. H. Capt. (T.), R.A.F.   1911
BRENAN, A. R. M. Capt., R.A.M.C.   1893
BRERETON, J. L. 2nd Lieut., R.G.A.; empld. Ministry 1906
  of Munitions
BRETHERTON, Rev. H. Pte., London Regt. (Artists   1908
  Rifles)
✠BREUL, O. G. F. J. Lieut., R.E. (Signals). *M.C.*   [1914]
  Died on active service 16 *Oct.* 1917
BRIDGEMAN, R. O. Capt., Rifle Brigade; Staff Lieut., 1908
  War Office. (W.) *Brevet Major*
BRIGHTMAN, E. W. Lieut.-Col., R.A.S.C. (Canteens). 1906
  O.B.E. M.
BRINDLE, W. S. Lieut.-Col., Worcestershire Regt. *m.* 1888
✠BROADBENT, C. H. 2nd Lieut., King's Own (Yorkshire 1900
  L.I., T.F.)
  Died 1 *March* 1916 *of injuries received in bombing*
  accident
BROADBENT, W. Major, R.A.M.C.(T.F.)   1886
BROCKLEBANK, J. J., D.S.O. Major, Scottish Horse; attd. 1893
  Northamptonshire Regt.(T.F.) *m.*
✠BRODIE, E. J. Capt., Cameron Hdrs.   1896
  Killed in action 11 *Nov.* 1914
BRODSKY, G. A. 2nd Lieut., 18th Hussars; Capt., Gen. 1906
  List
BROOKE, B. W. D. Hon. Capt., R.H.A.(T.F. Res.)   1897
BROOKE, H. K. Capt., Gen. List, attd. Egyptian Army 1898
BROOKS, H. R. G. Major, R.G.A. (W.) *M.C.*   1912
BROWN, A. O. Lieut., R.E.(T.F.)   1897
BROWN, C. CLIFTON. Lieut., Sussex Yeo. and Grenadier 1906
  Gds.
BROWN, D. CLIFTON. Capt., 1st Dragoon Gds.; attd. 1898
  Army Cyclist Corps; Brigade Major
BROWN, F. C. 2nd Lieut., Sherwood Foresters (Notts. 1900
  and Derby Regt.) (W.)

BROWN, H. C. B.   Capt., Worcestershire Regt.(T.F.) and   1911
Gen. Staff. (W.)

BROWN, H. G.   Capt., London Regt. (Finsbury Rifles).   1894
(W.)

BROWN, J. L. C.   Capt., R.G.A. (W.)   1907

BROWN, J. T.   Trooper, Scottish Horse   1903

BROWN, Rev. R. P.   C.F. 4th Class, R.A.C.D.   1880

BROWN, Rev. T. B.   Pte., London Regt. (Artists Rifles)   1902

BROWN, W. E. L.   Lieut., Cheshire Regt.; empld. Ministry   1912
of Labour. (W 2.) *M.C. M.*

BROWN DOUGLAS, F. C.   Lieut., Rifle Brigade; Capt. (A.),   1912
R.A.F.

✠BROWNE, C. P.   Capt., Corps of Guides, Indian Army   1905
Killed in action 11 *April* 1915

✠BROWNE, M. B.   2nd Lieut., Sherwood Foresters (Notts.   1894
and Derby Regt., T.F.)
Died 30 *April* 1916 *of wounds received in the Irish rebellion*

BROWNE, M. G.   Capt., E. Lancs. Regt. (W 3.) (P.)   1907

BROWNE, O. L.   Lieut., Cheshire Regt.(T.F.); Major,   1913
M.G.C. (W.) *M.*

BROWNING, Rev. P. T.   C.F. 4th Class, R.A.C.D.   1901

BRUCE CLARKE, W. R.   Capt., London Regt. (London   1906
Scottish); Capt. (T.), R.A.F. *M.B.E. M* 2.

✠BRUDENELL-BRUCE, J. E. J.   Lieut., Northamptonshire   1897
Yeo.
Died 11 *April* 1917 *of wounds received in action*

BRUNT, D.   Capt., R.E. (Meteorological Section); attd.   1908
R.A.F. *M.*

✠BRUNTON, E. H. P.   Lieut., R.A.M.C.   1907
Killed in action 8 *Oct.* 1915

BRUNWIN, A. D.   Hon. Capt., R.A.M.C.   1897

BRUTTON, H. L.   Capt., Worcestershire Yeo.; attd. Wor-   1899
cestershire Regt.

BRYCE, W. T. P.   Lieut., R.G.A. *M.*   1910

✠BUCHANAN, A. N.   Lieut. (T.), R.A.F.   1903
Died 14 *Oct.* 1918 *of pneumonia*

BUCHANAN, B. R.   2nd Lieut., Labour Corps   1914

BUCHANAN, J. N.   Capt., Grenadier Gds.; Brigade Major.   1905
D.S.O. M.C. M.

BUCKLAND, D. H.   Lieut., King's Royal Rifle Corps. *M.*   1914

✠BUCKLAND, T. A.   Lieut., Norfolk Regt. *M.*   1911
Died 18 *Oct.* 1915 *of wounds received in action* 13 *Oct.*
1915

BUCKLE, G. W. Lieut., York and Lancaster Regt.; Capt.,   1904
Army Cyclist Corps. *M* 2.
BUCKLEY, J. P. Capt., R.A.M.C.(T.F.)   1901
BUCKLEY, R. M. Capt., King's Royal Rifle Corps;   1913
Major, R.E. *M.C.*
BUCKMASTER, W. S. Service Sanitaire, French Army   1891
BUCKSTON, G. M. Capt., Derbyshire Yeo.   1900
BUDENBERG, C. F. Capt., R.E.(T.F.) *M.C.*   1912
✠BUDENBERG, D. H. Capt., Manchester Regt.   1915
Killed in action near Voormezeele 25 April 1918
BUDGETT, H. M. Lieut., Spec. List   1900
BULL, H. Capt., R.G.A. *M.C.*   1892
BULLER, M. L. Capt., King's Royal Rifle Corps. *M.C.*   1912
✠BULLIVANT, R. P. Capt., London Yeo. (Middlesex Hus-   1902
sars). (W.) *M.C.*
Killed in action 24 *Sept.* 1918
BULLOCK, C. LL. Capt., Rifle Brigade; Capt.(A.), R.A.F.;   1910
Major, S.O. 2, Air Ministry. (W.) *O.B.E. M.*
BULLOCK, H. M. Capt., Scots Gds.; A.D.C. (W.)   1909
M.B.E. Chevalier, Legion of Honour (France)
BULLOUGH, E. Lieut., R.N.V.R., empld. Admiralty   1899
BULSTRODE, C. V. Major, R.F.A. (T.F.); Lieut.-Col.,   1894
R.A.M.C. *D.S.O. M.*
BUNBURY, C. H. N. Lieut., Wiltshire Yeo. and Cold-   1905
stream Gds.
BUNBURY, Hon. T. L. McC. *See* MCCLINTOCK BUNBURY,
Hon. T. L.
BURBIDGE, P. W. Sergt.-Major, N. Zealand Force   1913
BURCHELL, J. M. Capt., London Regt. (Q.V.R.); Staff   1904
Capt. (W.) *O.B.E. M.*
BURDER, G. E. L. Lieut., R.G.A. (W 2.)   1904
BURDETT, Sir F., Bart. Capt., 17th Lancers (R. of O.);   1888
Brigade Major
BURGES, W. E. P. Hon. Colonel, Gloucestershire Regt.;   1879
Lieut.-Col., Spec. List, empld. Ministry of National
Service. *O.B.E. m.*
BURGESS, O. I. 2nd Lieut., Monmouthshire Regt.;   1912
Capt., R.E. (Sound-ranging Section). *M.*
BURGOYNE, L. S. Lieut., King's Royal Rifle Corps. *M.*   1910
BURN, Rev. A. E. C.F. 2nd Class, R.A.C.D.(T.F.)   1882
BURN, J. S. Hon. Capt., R.A.M.C.   1903
BURN-MURDOCH, A. Lieut., R. Scots(T.F.)   1905
BURN-MURDOCH, H. Major, Cameron Hdrs. (R. of O.)   1899
and Argyll and Sutherland Hdrs.

✠Burnaby, G.   Lieut., London Regt. (R. Fus.)   1913
  Died 23 *Oct.* 1916 *of wounds received in action*
Burnaby, Rev. H. B. F.   C.F. 4th Class, R.A.C.D. *M.C.*   1896
Burnaby, J.   Capt., London Regt. (R. Fus.) (W.)   1910
✠Burnand, C. F.   2nd Lieut., Grenadier Gds.   1910
  Killed in action 11 *March* 1915
Burnett, A. E.   Major, King's Own Scottish Borderers.   1900
  (W.) *O.B.E.*
Burns, J. W.   Major, Res. Regt. of Cavalry   1881
Burrell, L. S. T.   Major, R.A.M.C.   1901
✠Burrell, R. F. T.   2nd Lieut., Queen's Own (R.W.   1908
  Kent Regt.)
  Killed in action 26 *Sept.* 1915
Burroughes, H. N.   Lieut.-Col., R.A.M.C.(T.F.)   1896
  D.S.O. M 2. *French Médaille des Epidémies*
Burton, B. L. E.   Capt., R.A.S.C.; Major, D.A.D. Trans-   1909
  port. *M.*
Burton, M. G. W.   Capt., R.A.S.C. (Canteens)   1912
Bury, J.   Lieut., 17th Lancers; A.D.C.   [1914]
Bury, L. E.   Colonel, R.E. *C.B.E. O.B.E. M* 2.   1901
Bury, R. F.   Capt., Essex Regt.; Major, Gen. List   1895
  (D.A.A.G.) (W.) *M.*
Bushby, H. N. G.   Capt., R. Defence Corps   1882
⸬Butcher, W. G. D.   Capt., London Regt. (L.R.B.)   1910
  Killed in action at Glencorse Wood 16 *Aug.* 1917
Butler, Rev. A. J. A.   Capt., Leicestershire Regt.   1894
⸬Butler, G. K. M.   Lieut., Scottish Horse. (W.)   1910
  Died in Egypt 17 *July* 1916
Butler, H. C.   2nd Lieut., R. Inniskilling Fus.; Lieut.,   1910
  R.E. (W.) *M.C.*
Butler, H. G. St P.   Lieut., R.G.A.   1916
Butler, J. R. M.   Capt. and Adjt., Scottish Horse;   1907
  Major, G.S.O. 2 (Intelligence). *O.B.E. M* 2.
Butler, N. M.   2nd Lieut., Scottish Horse and House-   1912
  hold Bn.; Capt., Gen. Staff (Intelligence)
Butler, R. L. G.   Capt., Spec. List; Town Major, Ypres.   1902
  (W.)
Butler, W. M.   Major, R.E.(T.F.)   1901
Butler-Stoney, C. K.   Major, Hampshire Aircraft Parks   1896
  (T.F. Res.); Hon. Major, R.A.F. *m.*
Butlin, Sir H. G. T., Bart.   Capt., Cambridgeshire Regt.   1911
  M.
  Killed in action 16 *Sept.* 1916

¹ Died on service after the armistice.

BUTT, G. M. Capt., R.A.S.C. 1898
BUXTON, ANTHONY. Major, Essex Yeo. (W.) *D.S.O.* 1901
M 2.
BUXTON, Rev. ARTHUR. C.F. 4th Class, R.A.C.D. 1901
BUXTON, ABBOT R. Major, Norfolk Yeo.(T.F. Res.) 1887
✠BUXTON, ANDREW R. Capt., Rifle Brigade 1898
Killed in action 7 June 1917
BUXTON, B. G. Capt., D. of Wellington's (W. Riding 1913
Regt., T.F.) (W.) *M.C. and Bar*
BUXTON, C. E. V. Major, R.F.A.; A.D.C.; G.S.O. 3; 1911
Cmdt., Trench Mortar School. *M.C. M* 4.
BUXTON, E. N. Capt., R.H.A.(T.F.) *M.C. M.* 1912
BUXTON, G. C. Capt., Coldstream Gds.; Major, King's 1897
African Rifles
BUXTON, H. F. Capt., Suffolk Regt.(T.F.) 1894
BUXTON, H. G. Capt., Norfolk Regt. 1889
BUXTON, I. Major, Norfolk Yeo.; Brigade Major. (W.) 1903
D.S.O. M 3.
BUXTON, L. G., M.V.O. Major, R.A. (R. of O.); D.A.A. 1895
and Q.M.G. *M.C. M. Chevalier, Legion of Honour*
(*France*)
BUXTON, M. B. Capt., Norfolk Regt.(T.F.) (W.) *M.C.* 1908
BUXTON, P. A. Capt., R.A.M.C. 1911
BUXTON, R. G. Capt., Norfolk Yeo. 1905
BUXTON, T. F. Lieut., Essex Yeo.; A.D.C. *M.* 1908
BYRNE, L. W. Hon. Lieut.-Cdr., R.N.V.R. 1894

CADBURY, E. Major (A. and S.), R.A.F. *D.S.C.* 1912
D.F.C.
CADMAN, P. S. Major, E. Riding of Yorkshire Yeo.(T.F. 1890
Res.)
CALDWELL SMITH, E. L. Surgeon Lieut., R.N. 1910
CALEDON, Earl of. Capt., 1st Life Gds. and M.G.C. 1905
(W.)
CALLINGHAM, L. F. Lieut., R.N.V.R.(Hood Bn., R.N.D.) 1906
(W.)
CALVERLEY, E. L. Major, Essex Regt.(T.F. Res.) and 1883
Hampshire Regt.; Staff Capt. *O.B.E. M* 2.
CALVERT, H. Lieut., Loyal N. Lancs. Regt.(T.F. Res.) 1895
CALVERT, H. H. Lieut.-Col., Gloucestershire Yeo.(T.F. 1878
Res.)
CALVERT, W. J. R. Capt., Harrow School O.T.C. 1904
CAMDEN, Marquis. Major, W. Kent Yeo.(T.F. Res.) 1892

CAMPBELL, A. D. Lieut., 9th Lancers [1914]

CAMPBELL, A. D. P. Lieut., Denbigh Yeo. and Remount 1899
Service

CAMPBELL, A. Y. G., C.I.E. Major, S. Provinces Mtd. 1891
Rifles, Indian Defence Force. *C.B.E. M.*

CAMPBELL, D. S. Capt., W. Kent Yeo. and The Buffs 1910
(E. Kent Regt., T.F.) *M.C.*

CAMPBELL, E. M. Lieut., R. Scots(T.F. Res.) 1909

CAMPBELL, E. R. Capt., R. Sussex Regt.(T.F.) and Egyp- 1906
tian Camel Corps. (W.) *M. Order of the Nile,
4th Class (Egypt)*

✠CAMPBELL, I. M. Lieut., Sussex Yeo.; attd. R. Sussex [1914]
Regt.
Died 4 April 1918 of wounds received in action

CAMPBELL, Hon. I. M. Major, Lovat's Scouts; Lieut.- 1902
Col., Argyll and Sutherland Hdrs. *D.S.O. M.*

✠CAMPBELL, J. A. Lieut., 6th (Inniskilling) Dragoons 1897
*Died in Germany 2 Dec. 1917 of wounds received in
action*

CAMPBELL, K. A. Lieut., Grenadier Gds. (W 2.) *D.S.O.* 1911
M.

CAMPBELL, R. C. Lieut., Somerset L.I.; Capt. (Ad.), 1914
R.A.F.

CAMPBELL, Sir W., C.B., D.S.O. Major-Gen.; D.Q.M.G. 1882
*K.C.B. K.C.M.G. M 11. Commander, Legion of
Honour (France). Order of the White Eagle, 2nd Class,
with swords (Serbia). Grand Commander, Order of the
Redeemer (Greece). Order of the Nile, 2nd Class
(Egypt). Order of El Nahda, 2nd Class (Hedjaz)*

CAMPBELL, W. G. Lieut., Sussex Yeo.; attd. R. Sussex 1910
Regt.

CAMPBELL-DOUGLAS, Rev. Hon. L. C. H. C.F. 4th Class, 1899
R.A.C.D.

✠CAMPBELL-JOHNSTON, P. S. Lieut., R.F.A.; A.D.C. (W.) 1913
*M.C. Belgian Croix de Guerre
Died 30 Aug. 1919 of wounds received in action 21 May
1918*

CAMPLING, Rev. W. C. C.F. 4th Class, R.A.C.D. 1909

CANTRELL-HUBBERSTY, G. A. J. Major, S. Notts. Hussars 1900
and M.G.C. (W.) *D.S.O. M.*

CAPPEL, N. L. Lieut., R.N.V.R. 1904

CAPSTICK, J. W. Service Sanitaire, French Army 1888

CAREW, P. G. Capt., R. North Devon Yeo. and Remount 1912
Service. (W.)

✠CARLILE, E. H. H.   Capt., Hertfordshire Yeo.; attd. Hert-   1899
fordshire Regt.
Killed in action 22 *March* 1918

CARLISLE, J. C. D.   Capt., London Regt. (Civil Service   1906
Rifles); Major, G.S.O. 2.   *D.S.O.   M.C.   M* 3.

CARMICHAEL, A. D.   Major, Lovat's Scouts and Black   1897
Watch.   *M.*

CARR, A. L.   Lieut., R.E.   *M.*   1911

CARR, C. T.   Capt., Wiltshire Regt.(T.F.); Major,   1897
D.A.A.G.   *M.*

CARR-ELLISON, H. G. C.   Capt., Northumberland Yeo.;   1893
attd. 21st Lancers

CARROLL, H. E.   Lieut., R.E. (Fortress, T.F.)   1902

CARSON, T.   Major, R. Irish Regt.   1884

CARTER, C. N.   Surgeon Lieut., R.N.   1911

CARTER, W. E.   Lieut., R.G.A.; Draft Conducting Officer   1904

CARUS-WILSON, C. C.   Capt., R.M.A.   *M.C.*   1911

CARUS-WILSON, E.   Capt., R.E. (Signals).   *M.C.   M* 2.   1908

CARVER, G. A.   Major, R.F.A.(T.F.)   *M.*   1906

✠CARVER, O. A.   Capt., R.E.(T.F.)   1905
Died 7 *June* 1915 *of wounds received in action in
Gallipoli*

CASEY, R. G.   Major, Gen. List, Australian Force;   1910
G.S.O. 2.   *D.S.O.   M.C.   M* 2.

CASSILLIS, Earl of.   Major, R. Scots Fus. and Gen. Staff   1890
(Town Major of Bailleul).   *M.*

CASTELLAIN, J. G.   Capt., R.A.M.C.   1894

CASTELLAN, V. E.   Major, R.F.A.(T.F.)   *O.B.E.   T.D.*   1891
M.

✠CASTLE, T. R.   Pte., R. Fusiliers (P. S. Bn.); 2nd Lieut.,   1901
The Queen's (R. W. Surrey Regt.)
Killed in action 31 *Aug.* 1916

CASTLE, W. F. R.   Surgeon Lieut., R.N.V.R.   *D.S.C.*   1910

CASTLEMAN, E. W. F.   Major, Dorset Yeo.   (W.)   1889

CASTLEROSSE, Viscount.   Capt., Irish Gds.; G.S.O. 3;   1909
empld. Ministry of Information.   (W.)

CATOR, C. G. L.   Lieut., R.N.V.R.   1891

CATTERALL, E. C.   2nd Lieut., S. Staffs. Regt.; Lieut.,   1913
M.G.C.   (W.)

CAVE, C. J. P.   Capt., R.E. (Meteorological Section).   *m.*   1889

CAVE, L. C. H.   Lieut. (T.), R.A.F.   1914

CAVENDISH, A. E. J.   Colonel, A.A.G.; Brig.-Gen.   *C.M.G.*   1877

✠CAVENDISH, Lord J. S., D.S.O.   Major, 1st Life Gds.   1893
Killed in action 20 *Oct.* 1914

CAVENDISH, Lord R. F. Hon. Colonel, King's Own 1889
(R. Lancaster Regt., T.F.) *C.B. C.M.G. M.*
✠CAY, A. J. Lieut., Worcestershire Yeo. 1898
Killed in action 23 April 1916
CAYLEY, D. C. Capt., King's Own Scottish Borderers; [1914]
Major, M.G.C.
CAZALET, C. H. L., D.S.O. Major, Spec. List 1887
✠CAZALET, E. 2nd Lieut., The Buffs. (E. Kent Regt.) and 1913
Welsh Gds.
Killed in action 10 Sept. 1916
CECIL, A. W. J. Capt., Grenadier Gds. 1895
CECIL, R. E. Major, 21st Lancers; Lieut.-Col., G.S.O. 1. 1897
D.S.O. M.
CHADWICK, H. Capt., R.A.M.C. 1910
CHADWICK, J. Pte., R.A.M.C. 1914
CHADWICK, J. F. Capt., R.E. (Signals). *M.C. M* 2. 1908
✠CHADWICK, J. H. Pte., R. Fusiliers (P. S. Bn.); Lieut.- 1907
Col., Manchester Regt. *D.S.O.*
Killed in action 4 May 1917
CHALLINOR, J. 2nd Lieut., R.G.A. 1913
CHALLINOR, W.F. Hon. Lieut.-Col., R.F.A. *D.S.O. M.* 1900
CHALMERS, I. P. H. Capt., Seaforth Hdrs. (W 2.) 1906
CHALONER, T. W. P. L. Capt., Yorkshire Regt.(T.F.); 1908
Capt. (A.), R.A.F. (P.)
✠CHAMBERLAIN, E. D. 2nd Lieut., Loyal N. Lancs. Regt. 1912
Killed in action 30 Nov. 1917
CHAMBERLAIN, W. B. Lieut., Worcestershire Yeo. (W.) 1901
(P.) *M.C.*
CHAMBERS, B. F. Capt., R.A.S.C. 1905
CHAMBERS, C. E., V.D. Bt. Colonel, R.F.A.(T.F. Res.) *m.* 1881
CHAMBERS, W. F. A. Lieut., King's Royal Rifle Corps. 1913
(W 2.)
✠CHANCE, E. S. Capt., R. Welsh Fus.; Lieut.-Col., 2nd 1900
Dragoon Gds. (Queen's Bays); D.A.A. and Q.M.G.
(W.) *Brevet Major. M* 2.
Killed in action 29 May 1918
CHANCE, R. C. 2nd Lieut., Spec. List 1901
CHANCE, R. J. F. Capt. and Adjt., 4th Dragoon Gds.; 1912
Capt., Rifle Brigade. (W 2.) *M.C. M* 2.
CHANDLESS, C. T. C. Lieut., R.A.S.C.(M.T.) 1906
CHANNELL, H. M. T. 2nd Lieut., R.A.S.C. 1905
CHAPLIN, Rev. A. C.F. 4th Class, R.A.C.D. 1895
CHAPMAN, A. E. Lieut., Gen. List (T.F. Res.); Capt., 1904
Spec. List, empld. Ministry of National Service

Chapman, T. M. G. Lieut., R.A.S.C. 1909
✠Chapman, W. H. Capt., Yorkshire Regt. 1898
 Killed in action in Gallipoli 7 *Aug.* 1915
✠Charles, J. A. M. 2nd Lieut., King's (Shropshire L.I.) 1908
 Died 10 *Feb.* 1915 *of wounds received in action* 23 *Oct.*
 1914
Charles, L. B. Lieut., The Queen's (R. W. Surrey Regt., 1913
 T.F.); Staff Capt. (W.) *M.C. M.*
Chart, H. J. Lieut., R.F.A.(T.F.); empld. Ministry of 1889
 Munitions. *m.*
Cheales, R. D. Major, E. Lancs. Regt.; Lieut.-Col., 1888
 R. Scots and Gen. List. (W.) *O.B.E. M* 2.
Chenevix-Trench, A. S. Major, R.E. (W.) *M.C. M.* 1905
Chepmell, C. H. Major, R.G.A. (R. of O.) 1883
Chester, R. C. Cadet, O.C.B. (Household Bde.) 1914
Chevassut, F. G. 2nd Lieut., R.F.A. (W.) 1909
Cheyne, W. H. W. Surgeon Lieut., R.N. 1907
Chichester, A. O'N. C. Capt. Surrey Yeo.; Major, The 1908
 Queen's (R.W. Surrey Regt.) (W.) *M.C.*
Chichester, Earl of. Major, R. Sussex Regt.(T.F.); 1899
 Lieut.-Col., A.A.G., War Office. *O.B.E. Brevet
 Lieut.-Colonel. Brevet Major. m.*
✠Chichester, W. G. C. Lieut., London Regt. (R. Fus.) 1911
 Killed in action 15 *Sept.* 1916
Chidson, L. H. Lieut., E. Surrey Regt.; Major,M.G.C. [1914]
 M.B.E. M 3.
Child, J. F. 2nd Lieut., Northumberland Fus. 1898
Childers, R. E. Lieut.-Cdr., R.N.V.R.; Major, S.O. 2, 1889
 R.A.F. *D.S.C. M.*
Chisholm, C. J. Major, 9th Lancers. (W 2.) *M.* 1911
Chittock, C. Lieut., Felsted School O.T.C. 1901
Christie, J. Capt., King's Royal Rifle Corps. (W.) 1902
 M.C. M.
Christie, L. D. Capt., R. Sussex Regt.; attd. Gen. Staff 1909
 (Intelligence)
Churchill, A. Lieut., R.N.V.R. (Armoured Car Section) 1903
✠Churchill, W. M. Major, 12th Cavalry, Indian Army. 1901
 (W.) *M. Order of St Anne, 3rd Class (Russia)*
 Died 4 *Nov.* 1918 *of pneumonia*
Clark, A. S. Major, S. and T. Corps, Indian Army 1897
Clark, E. D. Lieut., Yorkshire Regt. (W.) 1906
✠Clark, E. F. Lieut., The Buffs (E. Kent Regt.); attd. [1914]
 R.F.C. (W.)
 Killed in action 1 *Jan.* 1917

CLARK, E. K., T.D. Lieut.-Col., W. Yorks. Regt. (T.F. 1885
Res.)
CLARK, H. D. Capt., Argyll and Sutherland Hdrs.(T.F.) 1906
and M.G.C.; attd. Inland Water Transport. (W.)
CLARK, J. H. M. Lieut., R.N.V.R.   1910
CLARK, S. B. Pioneer, R.E. (Signals)   1896
CLARK, S. H. Major, Worcestershire Regt.(T.F.)   1886
✠CLARK-KENNEDY, A. K. Capt., King's Own Scottish 1902
Borderers (T.F.)
Killed in action 19 *April* 1917
CLARKE, C. S., V.D. Lieut.-Col., R. Sussex Regt.(T.F.) 1892
CLARKE, E. J. Major, W. Yorks. Regt. and Army Cyclist 1897
Corps. *M* 2. *French Croix de Guerre*
CLARKE, E. S. 2nd Lieut., R. Sussex Regt.(T.F.); Lieut., 1912
Scots Gds. (W.) *M.*
CLARKE, H. A. Lieut., R.A.S.C.(M.T.)   1914
CLARKE, H. H. Capt., R.A.M.C.   1894
CLARKE, J. H. P.O., R.N.V.R. (R.N.D.); Capt., R.E. 1909
(Field Survey Coy.)
CLARKE, S. Lieut., Hampshire Regt.   1911
CLARKSON, W. B. Pte., R. Fusiliers (P. S. Bn.); Major, 1909
R.G.A. *D.S.O.* *M.*
CLAY, B. A. Lieut., Res. Regt. of Cavalry; Capt., S.O. 3, 1904
R.A.F. *m.*
CLAY, F. H. Lieut., N. Somerset Yeo. and R.A.S.C.   1895
CLAY, J. H. Lieut., R.A.S.C.   1902
CLAYTON, F. Major, R.A.M.C.(T.F.) *M* 2.   1900
CLEGG, J. A. Lieut., King's (Shropshire L.I., T.F.); 1905
Capt., D. A. D. Labour
CLEGHORN, W. A. Pte., R.A.M.C.; 2nd Lieut., Scottish 1913
Horse
CLIFTON, E. N. Capt., Coldstream Gds.; Major (A.), 1909
R.A.F. (W.)
✠CLIFTON, H. E. 2nd Lieut., Devon Regt. (W.) *M.C.* 1910
Died 4 *Oct.* 1916 *of wounds received in action* 23 *Sept.*
1916
✠CLISSOLD, H. Major, R.E.(T.F.) (W.) *D.S.O.* *M* 2. 1889
Killed in action 28 *Sept.* 1917
✠CLOSE-BROOKS, A. B. Capt., Manchester Regt. *M.C. M.* 1903
Died 10 *Jan.* 1917 *of wounds received in action*
✠CLOSE-BROOKS, J. C. Lieut., Life Gds.   1895
Killed in action 30 *Oct.* 1914
✠CLOUGH, A. Capt., W. Yorks. Regt.   [1914]
Killed in action 1 *July* 1916

CLUTTON, B. Lieut., Bedfordshire Regt. (W.) *m.* 1902
COBBOLD, C. J. F. Lieut.-Col., Suffolk Regt. (Cyclist 1900
Bn., T.F.) *M. m.*
COBBOLD, G. F. Major, York and Lancaster Regt. (W.) 1903
M.C.
COBBOLD, P. W. Capt., Suffolk Regt. 1893
COCHRANE, A. C. Major, R.A.S.C. 1894
COCHRANE, A. K. O. Capt., Yorkshire Regt.; Hon. Capt. 1909
(A.), R.A.F.
COCHRANE, G. D. Lieut., Yorkshire Regt.; empld. W. 1904
African Frontier Force
COCK, T. A. Capt., R.A.S.C. 1896
COCKBURN, A. F. Capt., R.E. (Fortress, T.F.) *M.* 1909
✠COCKERELL, S. P. 2nd Lieut., R.F.C. 1898
Died at Ismailia 20 March 1915 of smallpox
✠COCKS, W. F. Lieut., Lincolnshire Regt. 1911
Died 9 April 1917 of wounds received in action
COCKSHOTT, F. G. Pte., Saskatchewan Regt., Canadian 1899
Force. (W.)
COGGIN, H. F. F. Pte., H.A.C.; Lieut., R. Berkshire 1902
Regt. (W.)
COHEN, C. B. Capt., R.A.M.C. 1913
COHEN, D. H. Capt., Sherwood Foresters (Notts. and 1898
Derby Regt.) and Gen. List, empld. Ministry of
Munitions. (W.)
COHEN, W. S. Lieut., Hertfordshire Yeo.; Capt., Labour 1890
Corps. *M. Order of the Redeemer, 5th Class (Greece).
Greek Medal for Military Merit*
COKE, Hon. RICHARD. Major, Scots Gds. (W 2.) 1895
COLEMAN, C. J. Capt., R.A.M.C.(T.F. Res.) 1893
COLEMAN, P. G. Lieut., N. Staffs. Regt.(T.F.) and Welsh 1914
Gds. (W.) *D.S.O. M.*
COLES, E. J. Major, R.A.O.C. 1906
COLLET, G. G. Lieut.-Col., R.A.M.C. 1901
COLLETT, R. L. Capt., R.A.M.C. (Sanitary Service, 1905
T.F.)
COLLIER-JOHNSTONE, N. S. Lieut., 5th Dragoon Gds. 1910
*Chevalier, Ordre de la Couronne (Belgium). Belgian
Croix de Guerre*
COLLINGWOOD, E. F. Midshipman, R.N. 1918
COLLINS, B. K. T. Capt., R.A.M.C.(T.F.) 1906
COLLINS, D. C. Lieut., Ruahine Regt., N. Zealand Force 1907
COLLINS, R. F. Capt., R. Fusiliers. (W.) *D.S.O. M.C.* 1909
M 2.

COLLINSON, J. W. Major (T.), R.A.F.   1903
COLMAN, J. Capt. and Adjt., London Regt. (Surrey   1905
Rifles). *m.*
COLQUHOUN, G. R. E. Capt., R.A.M.C.   1907
COLTHURST, G. O.   Capt., S. Irish Horse; A.D.C.   1901
French Croix de Guerre
COLTHURST, R. ST J. J. Capt., London Regt. (L.R.B.)   1906
COLTMAN, W. H. Major, Gordon Hdrs.(T.F.) (W.)   1882
T.D. m.
COLVILLE, D. J. Capt., Cameronians (Scottish Rifles,   1912
T.F.) (W 3.)
COLVILLE, Hon. J. G. Lieut., R.N.V.R.   1910
COLVILLE, T. R. Capt., D. of Cornwall's L.I.; empld.   1901
Egyptian Army. *M.*
COLVIN, C. H., D.S.O. Hon. Colonel, Essex Regt. and   1877
Spec. List (Cmdt., P. of W. Camp). *C.B. m.*
COLVIN, R. B., C.B., T.D. Colonel, Spec. List; Brig.-Gen.   1874
m 2.
CONOLLY, C. G. Lieut., R.A.S.C.   1896
COODE, A. P. Major, D. of Cornwall's L.I.(T.F.) *M.*   1890
✠COOK, F. R. Lieut., E. Yorks. Regt. and R.F.C. (W.)   1915
Killed in flying accident 22 Feb. 1918
COOKE, A. Major, R.A.M.C. (1st E. Gen. Hospital, T.F.)   1898
COOKE-HURLE, J. *See* HURLE, J. C.
COOPER, J. G. Capt , R.A.M.C.   1893
COOPER, P. H. Lieut., R. Fusiliers; Capt., M.G.C.   1897
COOPER, W. G. D. Capt., R.A.S.C.   1896
COPE, T. G. Capt., R. Fusiliers; Lieut.-Col., The Buffs   1902
(E. Kent Regt.); Brig.-Gen.   (W 2.)   *C.M.G.*
D.S.O. and Bar. Brevet Lieut.-Colonel. Brevet Major.
M 4. Chevalier, Legion of Honour (France).
COPELAND, W. B. Capt., N. Staffs. Regt.; empld. Min-   1909
istry of Munitions. (W.) *M.*
COPLAND GRIFFITHS, F. A. V. Lieut., Welsh Gds.; Capt.,   1912
O.C.B. (W.) *M.C. M. m*
CORBIN, J. L. Lieut., Northamptonshire Yeo. and Gen.   1901
Staff
CORNFORD, F. M. Capt., Gen. List (School of Musketry)   1893
✠CORNISH, C. L. Lieut., Highland L.I.   1905
Killed in action 13 *Nov.* 1914
CORNISH, H. D. Lieut., R.G.A.   1897
CORNWALL, J. W. Lieut.-Col., I.M.S.   1888
CORRIE, O. C. K.   Lieut., R.F.A.(T.F.); Capt., Spec.   1901
List (T.M.B.) *M.C. M.*

CORRY, F. R. H. L. *See* LOWRY-CORRY, F. R. H.
CORRY, J. P. I. M. Sub-Lieut., R.N.V.R.   1911
CORRY, W. M. F. Lieut., R.F.A.(T.F.) *M.C.*   1912
CORSER, E. E. Lieut., King's (Shropshire L.I.) (W.) [1914]
COTTERILL, G. H. Major, Lancs. Fus.   1896
COTTERILL, H. E. Major, Gen. List (T.F. Res.); Draft   1886
    Conducting Officer
COTTERILL, L. Major, R.A.M.C.   1889
COTTON, B. Major, King's (Shropshire L.I.) and Gen. 1880
    List (Cmdt., Detention Barracks)
COUPER, J. D. C. Lieut.-Col., R.E.; Colonel, D.D. Docks. 1894
    C.B.E. M 2.
COURTAULD, L. Capt., R.A.M.C.(T.F.) (W.) *m.*   1895
COUTTS, H. A. T. Lieut., R.A.S.C.   1912
COVENTON, A. W. D. Capt., R.A.M.C. *French Médaille* 1897
    des Épidémies
COWELL, W. J. R. *See* ROOKE-COWELL, W. J.
COWIE, H. C. Capt., R.E. (W.)   1905
COWLEY, J. N. Capt. and Adjt., R.H.A. *M.*   1904
✠COWPER, G. M. Capt., R.A.M.C. *M.*   1908
    Died 3 Oct. 1918 of wounds received in action
✠COX, D. P. 2nd Lieut., R.F.C.   [1914]
    Killed in action 21 Aug. 1917
COX, W. A. M. Lieut., Black Watch; Lieut. (A. and [1914]
    Ad.), R.A.F. (W.)
COXON, A. W. Major, Army Pay Dept.; Staff Pay- 1890
    master. *O.B.E. m.*
CRACKANTHORPE, O. M. Capt., R. Scots and Border Regt. 1894
    M.
CRADOCK, N. Capt., R.F.A.(T.F.)   1900
CRANE, L. F. N. Capt., Loyal N. Lancs. Regt. and Gen. 1898
    List. *O.B.E. M. m.*
CRANMER BYNG, L. A. Capt., Gen. List (T.F. Res.); Cmdt., 1891
    P. of W. Camp
CRANWORTH, Lord. 2nd Lieut., Norfolk Yeo.; Capt., 1896
    R.F.A. (R. of O.) *M.C. M* 2. *French Croix de*
    Guerre
CRAWFORD, D. Sqdn. Sergt.-Major, K. Edward's Horse; 1909
    Lieut., R.F.A. (W.)
CRAWFORD, K. A. Lieut., R.G.A.   1916
CRAWHALL, Rev. T. E. C.F. 2nd Class, R.A.C.D.(T.F.) 1886
    D.S.O. T.D. M 2.
✠CRAWLEY, E. Major, 12th Lancers. *M.*   1886
    Killed in action 2 Nov. 1914

CRAWSHAY, J. W. L. 2nd Lieut., Scottish Horse; Capt., [1914]
  Welsh Gds. *M.C.*
CREED, P. R. Capt., Rifle Brigade and Gen. List   1892
✠CREWDSON, T. W. Capt., Manchester Regt.; A.D.C.   1914
  Died 6 Nov. 1916 of wounds received in action 28 Oct.
  1916
CREWDSON, W. D. Lieut.-Col., Border Regt.   1898
CRIPPS, W. L. Surgeon, R.N.   1896
✠CRISPIN, H. T. Lieut.-Col., Northumberland Fus. and   1887
  R. Sussex Regt. *M.*
  Killed in action 30 Oct. 1914
CROCKER, J. A. Capt., London Yeo. (Sharpshooters);   1893
  Capt. and Adjt., Tank Corps
✠CROFT, J. A. C. 2nd Lieut., R. Warwickshire Regt.;   1907
  attd. D. of Wellington's (W. Riding Regt.)
  Killed in action at Hill 60 18 April 1915
✠CROPPER, JOHN. Lieut., R.A.M.C.   1883
  Drowned on H.M.S. Britannic 21 Nov. 1916
CROPPER, J. W. Major, Westmorland and Cumberland   1898
  Yeo. (T.F. Res.); empld. War Office
CROSS, E. K. 2nd Lieut., Rifle Brigade. (W.)   1916
✠CROSSLEY, B. Lieut., Highland L.I. *M.*   1904
  Killed in action 18 May 1915
CROSSLEY, E. Major, 11th Hussars. *O.B.E. m.*   1897
CROW, C. A. Capt. (T.), R.A.F. (Aircraft Production   1914
  Dept.)
CROWDER, W. I. R. Capt., Border Regt.(T.F.) *m.*   1904
✠CROWE, H. B. Lieut., R. Fusiliers   1912
  Drowned on H.M. transport off Gallipoli 28 Oct. 1915
CUNDELL, J. Capt., R.A.S.C.   1900
CUNLIFFE, N. Capt., Spec. List (Inspection Staff, Wool- 1908
  wich Arsenal). *M.B.E. m.*
CUNNINGHAM, A. J. W. Capt., R.A.M.C. *M.*   1901
CUNNINGHAM, Rev. B. K. C.F. 4th Class, R.A.C.D.   1889
  O.B.E. M.
✠CUNNINGHAM, J. M. Capt., Suffolk Regt.   1897
  Died 28 March 1918 of wounds received in action
✠CUNNINGHAM, J. S. Sergt., R. Highlanders, Canadian   1904
  Force
  Killed in action 31 Oct. 1916
CUNNINGHAM, T. E. Capt., King's (Liverpool Regt.,   1905
  T.F.)
CUNNINGHAM, W. A. Capt., R. Welsh Fus.; attd. The   1901
  Queen's (R.W. Surrey Regt.) (W.)

✠Currie, R. F. I. Lce.-Corpl., R. Fusiliers 1899
 Killed in action 15 *July* 1916
Curry, P. A. Capt., Gen. List, attd. R.E.; Major, Asst. 1902
 Embarkation S.O. *O.B.E.* *M* 2. *American Dis-*
 tinguished Service Medal
Curtis, A. R. W. Capt., 11th Hussars; attd. R.F.C. (W.) 1908
 M.C. *M.*
Curtis, T. L. C. Capt., Coldstream Gds.; Major, Gds. 1907
 M.G. Regt.
Curtis-Bennett, H. H. Lieut., R.N.V.R. 1897
Cuthbert, C. A. Capt. (T.), R.A.F. 1910

✠Daffarn, M. 2nd Lieut., N. Rhodesian Police 1906
 Killed in action in Rhodesia 24 *April* 1915
Dale, F. R. Capt., R. Welsh Fus. and Welsh Regt. 1902
 D.S.O. *M.C.* *M.*
Dalton, J. O. C. 2nd Lieut., R.F.A. 1917
Dalton, T. E. Canadian A.M.C. *M.M.* 1892
Daniell, H. E. B. Capt., Durham L.I.(T.F.); attd. R.E. 1903
 (W 2.) *M.C.*
Darby, W. S. Lieut., R.A.M.C. 1892
Darley, H. R., d.s.o. Major, 4th Dragoon Gds. (R. of 1884
 O.); Staff Capt. *O.B.E.* *m* 2.
Darmady, E. S. Hon. Capt. and Q.M., R.A.M.C.(T.F.) 1886
Darnton, R. E. Capt. (A.), R.A.F. *D.F.C.* 1913
Darroch, A. R. Hon. Capt., Spec. List (Navy and Army 1899
 Canteen Board)
✠Dart, H. Pte., Middlesex Regt. (P.S. Bn.); Capt. and 1900
 Adjt., York and Lancaster Regt.
 Died 2 *July* 1916 *of wounds received in action*
Darwin, B. R. M. Major, R.A.O.C.; D.A.D.O.S. *M.* 1894
Darwin, C. G. Capt., R.E. (Field Survey Bn.); attd. 1906
 R.A.F. *M.C.*
✠Darwin, E. 2nd Lieut., Yorkshire Regt.(T.F.) 1901
 Killed in action 25 *April* 1915
Darwin, W. R. Capt., R.E. (W.) 1913
Daukes, A. H. Capt., King's Royal Rifle Corps; Staff 1908
 Capt., War Office. *Brevet Major.* *m.*
Daun, E. 2nd Lieut., Devon Regt. 1904
David, W. T. Major, Spec. List, empld. Ministry of 1910
 Munitions. *m.*
Davidson, D. F. Lieut.-Col., cmdg. Depôt, Cameron 1879
 Hdrs.
Davidson, L. S. P. Capt., Gordon Hdrs.(T.F.) (W.) 1913

DAVIDSON, M. G. Capt., Cameron Hdrs. (W.) 1912
✠DAVIDSON, N. R. Lieut.-Col., R.H.A.; G.S.O. (W.) 1897
   D.S.O. and Bar. Brevet Lieut.-Colonel. M 3.
   Died 5 Oct. 1917 of wounds received in action
✠DAVIES, A. C. Capt., R. Welsh Fus. 1896
   Killed in action 10 Aug. 1915
DAVIES, Rev. A. R. C.F. 4th Class, R.A.C.D. (W.) 1908
✠DAVIES, G. LL. 2nd Lieut., King's Royal Rifle Corps; 1912
   attd. Rifle Brigade.
   Killed in action 15 March 1915
DAVIES, H. M. Capt., R.A.M.C. 1897
DAVIES, H. R. Section Sanitaire, French Army 1881
DAVIES, L. G. Capt., R.A.M.C. 1898
DAVIES, P. LL. *See* LLEWELYN-DAVIES, P.
DAVIES, R. A. LL. *See* LLEWELYN-DAVIES, R. A.
DAVIES, R. R. Capt. and Adjt., 16th Lancers; A.D.C.; 1910
   Staff Capt. (W.) *M.*
DAVIES-COLLEY, H. Capt., R.A.M.C. 1894
DAVIES-COLLEY, T. H. Lieut.-Col., Manchester Regt. 1885
   (T.F. Res.)
DAVIS, J. R. A. Major, Spec. List 1880
DAVIS, R. G. Lieut., Buckinghamshire Yeo. 1911
DAVISON, J. F. Capt., Spec. List, empld. Records; Hon. 1901
   Capt. (O.), R.A.F. *M.C.*
DAWNAY, C. H. Capt. and Adjt., Yorkshire Regt. *M.C.* 1910
DAWSON, J. Capt., R.E. (Fortress, T.F.) *M.C. M.* 1904
✠DAY, M. C. Lieut., 13th Rajputs, Indian Army 1910
   Killed in action in E. Africa 4 Nov. 1914
DEAKIN, H. V. Surgeon, R.N.; Capt., R.A.M.C. 1907
DEANE, A. P. W. Pte., R.A.S.C.(M.T.) 1907
DEANE, C. H. Major, R.A.O.C.; D.A.D.O.S. *M.C. m.* 1902
DEANE, R. W. Bt. Colonel, Lancs. Fus., empld. Gen. 1878
   Staff. *C.B.E. m 2.*
DEBENHAM, F. J. Section Sanitaire, French Army 1888
DE CANDOLLE, R. Major-Gen., Director-General of 1883
   Transportation, Mesopotamia. *C.B. M. Grand*
   Officer, Order of the Crown of Roumania
DE CERJAT, C. S. Lieut., Grenadier Gds. 1913
DEEPING, G. W. Major, R.A.M.C.(T.F.) *M.* 1895
DEERHURST, Viscount. Lieut.-Col., Gen. List, T.F. *m.* 1884
DE GEIJER, E. N. Lieut., Grenadier Gds. (W 2.) *M.C.* 1912
DE GEIJER, W. A. W. G. Capt., Hampshire Regt. 1907
DEIGHTON, F. M. Lieut., R.F.A.; attd. R.E. (W 2.) 1905
   M.C.

✠DEIGHTON, J. Capt., R.A.M.C. 1906
Died 20 Sept. 1916 of wounds received in action
DE JANASZ, G. K. A. Lieut., R.A.S.C. 1909
DE LA PRYME, Ven. A. G. Pte., N. Rhodesian Rifles, 1889
S. African Force; C.F. 4th Class, R.A.C.D.
DE NAVARRO, J. M. United States Army 1915
DENIS DE VITRÉ, D. F. *See* DE VITRÉ, D. F. D.
✠DENMAN, R. C. Pte., H.A.C.; Lieut., Grenadier Gds. 1914
Killed in action 1 *Dec.* 1917
DENMAN, R. P. G. Lieut., R.E. (Signals). *M.* 1913
DENNING, W. F. Capt., D. of Wellington's (W. Riding 1899
Regt., T.F.); empld. O.C.B.
✠DENNISTOUN, J. R. Lieut., Fort Garry Horse, Canadian 1913
Force; attd. R.F.C. *M.*
Killed in action 4 *May* 1916
DENT, G. Lieut., 4th (R. Irish) Dragoon Gds.; Major, 1910
M.G.C. (Cavalry). *M.C.*
DENT, L. M. E. Capt., Oxford and Bucks. L.I.; Major, 1907
G.S.O. 2. (W.) *D.S.O. M* 3. *Chevalier, Legion
of Honour (France)*
DENT, R. A. W. Lieut., King's Royal Rifle Corps; A.D.C. 1913
(W.) *M.*
DENT, W. E. Lieut., 8th (King's R. Irish) Hussars; 1913
empld. Foreign Office
DENT-BROCKLEHURST, G. E. Lieut., Warwickshire Yeo. 1904
DERHAM, J. A. T. 2nd Lieut., London Regt. (L.R.B.) 1905
(W.) (P.)
D'ERLANGER, H. R. C. A.D.C.; Lieut., M.G.C. 1914
DE ROTHSCHILD, A. G. Capt., Buckinghamshire Yeo.; 1906
empld. War Office. (W.) *M.*
✠DE ROTHSCHILD, E. A. Major, Buckinghamshire Yeo. *M.* 1904
Died 17 Nov. 1917 of wounds received in action
DE ROTHSCHILD, J. E. A. Lieut., R. Canadian Dragoons; 1897
Major, R. Fusiliers
DE ROTHSCHILD, L. N. Major, Buckinghamshire Yeo. 1900
(T.F. Res.); empld. Recruiting Staff. *O.B.E. m.*
DESBOROUGH, G. Lieut., Bedfordshire Regt. 1904
DE SIBOUR, Vicomte L. Lieut., 94me Regt., French Army. 1912
(P.) *French Médaille Militaire. French Croix de
Guerre*
DETERDING, H. Lieut., Montgomeryshire Yeo. 1915
DE TRAFFORD, R. E. F. Capt., Spec. List (G.S.O. 3). 1912
O.B.E. M 2. *Chevalier, Order of the Crown of
Roumania, with swords*

DE VITRÉ, D. F. D.   Capt., Spec. List (Recruiting Staff).   1886
m.

DEVONSHIRE, Duke of, K.G.   Hon. Colonel, Sherwood   1887
Foresters (Notts. and Derby Regt., T.F.); Commander-in-Chief, Dominion of Canada

DEWAR, M. B. U.   Lieut., R.E. (Fortress, T.F.); Major,   1905
Spec. List, empld. Ministry of Munitions. *O.B.E.*
m 2.

DEWHURST, C.   Major, Lancs. Hussars; empld. Navy and   1892
Army Canteen Board. (W.)

DEWHURST, C.   Sergt., N. Rhodesian Rifles, S. African   1907
Force

⊁DEWHURST, G. C. L.   Lieut., Rifle Brigade. (W.)   1910
Killed in action 1 *July* 1916

DEWHURST, G. P.   Hon. Capt., Cheshire Yeo. (T.F. Res.)   1890
m.

DE ZOETE, H. W.   Capt., Essex Yeo.   1895

DIAMOND, A. S.   Driver, R.H.A. (W.) *M.M.*   1916

DICK, H. P.   Capt., R.G.A.; attd. T.M.B. (W 2.) *M* 2.   1910

DICKEY, E. M. O'R.   Pte., The Queen's (R.W. Surrey   1911
Regt.); 2nd Lieut., R.G.A.

DICKINSON, A. H.   Capt., Coldstream Gds. (W.) *M.C.*   1890
M.

DICKINSON, G. N.   2nd Lieut., R. Marines   1892

⊁DICKINSON, R. S.   Capt., London Regt. (Queen's West-   1912
minster Rifles)
Killed in action 2 *Oct.* 1915

DICKINSON, W. H.   Capt., R.A.M.C.(T.F.)   1893

DICKSON, E. C. S.   Lieut., Highland L.I.(T.F.)   1909

DICKSON, J. W. E.   Capt., Seaforth Hdrs. (W 3.) *M.C.*   1908

DICKSON, K. B.   Lieut.-Col., R.A.M.C. (W.)   1906

DIGGES LA TOUCHE, G. G.   Lieut., R.F.A.(T.F.) (W 3.)   1907

DILL, J. M. GORDON.   Capt., 5th (R. Irish) Lancers and   1908
M.G.C.; empld. O.C.B. (W.)

DILLON, T. A.   Capt., Connaught Rangers. *M.*   1913

DINGWALL, C. F.   Capt., E. Surrey Regt.; Major, M.G.C.   1911
(W.)

DIXON, E. T.   Major, R.F.A.; empld. Ministry of Muni-   1899
tions. *O.B.E. m.*

DIXON, G.   Lieut.-Col., Border Regt.(T.F. Res.) and   1890
King's Own (R. Lancaster Regt.); Courts-Martial
Officer. *T.D.*

DIXON, H.   Capt., D. of Wellington's (W. Riding Regt.);   1893
Major, Essex Regt. *M* 2.

✠DIXON, J. E. B. Capt., R. Warwickshire Regt.(T.F.) 1913
Killed in action 1 *July* 1916
DIXON, O. Capt., Lincolnshire Regt.(T.F.) (W.) 1901
DIXSON, H. F. Lieut., 7th Hussars; attd. R.E. (Signals) 1910
DOBBS, F. W. Lieut., Eton College O.T.C. 1895
✠DOBBS, W. C. Capt., Middlesex Regt.; attd. R. Fusiliers. (W 2.) 1889
Killed in action 31 *July* 1917
DOBBS, W. E. J. Lieut., I.A.R.O.; Major, D.A.A.G. 1899
DOBSON, J. F. 2nd Lieut., Bristol Univ. O.T.C. 1894
DOCKRAY, J. V. 2nd Lieut., The Buffs (E. Kent Regt.) 1917
✠DODGSHON, A. J. C. Lieut., Gloucestershire Regt.(T.F.) [1914]
Killed in action 10 *Nov.* 1917
✠DODGSON, F. Capt., Yorkshire Regt. 1908
Killed in action 10 *July* 1916
DODGSON, P. H. Capt., R.F.A.(T.F.) (W.) *M.C.* 1910
DOLL, M. H. C. Lieut., 13th Hussars; Staff Capt. (W.) *M.* 1907
✠DON, A. W. R. Lieut., Black Watch 1909
Died in Macedonia 11 *Sept.* 1916 *of dysentery*
DON, F. P. Capt., Scottish Horse; Capt. (A.), R.A.F.; Major, S.O. 2. (W.) (P.) *m.* 1904
DONALD, M. H. 2nd Lieut., Border Regt.; Lieut., R.G.A. 1913
DONALD, W. G. C. 2nd Lieut., Norfolk Regt. 1915
DONALDSON, E. Capt., R.A.M.C.(T.F.) 1907
✠DONALDSON, Sir H. F., K.C.B. Brig.-Gen., empld. Ministry of Munitions 1877
Drowned on H.M.S. Hampshire 6 *June* 1916
DONALDSON, M. Capt., R.A.M.C. (P.) *M.* 1902
✠DONALDSON, N. Lieut., R.F.A. *M.* 1897
Killed in action 10 *March* 1915
DONALDSON, S. H. M. Lieut., King's Royal Rifle Corps; Capt., Spec. List; Hon. Capt. (Ad.), R.A.F. 1905
DONNER, J. D. 2nd Lieut., R.F.A. 1906
DORMAN, Sir A. J. Hon. Major, Yorkshire Regt.(T.F. Res.) *M.* 1900
DORMAN, B. L. Capt., R.A.O.C. and Spec. List (Staff Capt., War Office). *O.B.E.* *m.* 1897
DOUGLAS, F. C. B. *See* BROWN DOUGLAS, F. C.
DOUNE, Lord. Capt., Scottish Horse; Capt. (A.), R.A.F.; S.O. 3. (W.) *M.C.* 1911
DOVE, Rev. F. J. C.F. 4th Class, R.A.C.D. 1910
✠DOWLING, G. C. W. Capt., King's Royal Rifle Corps 1910
Killed in action at Hooge 30 *July* 1915

DOWSON, E. M. 2nd Lieut., Labour Corps   1899
DRAKE, C. W. T. *See* TYRWHITT DRAKE, C. W.
DRAKE, H. R. O. Lieut., R.E. (Signals). *M.*   1912
DREW, A. L. Capt., R.A.S.C. *m.*   1905
✠DREWE, A. Capt., R.G.A. *M.*   1910
  Killed in action 12 *July* 1917
DREWE, C. Lieut., R.F.A. (W.)   1914
DRINKWATER, R. C. Lieut., Cambridge Univ. O.T.C.;   1912
  empld. O.C.B.
DROOP, A. H. 2nd Lieut., Northamptonshire Regt. and   1899
  Gen. List, empld. Ministry of National Service
DROOP, C. E. Capt., R.A.M.C.   1896
DRUCE, V. P. Lieut.-Col., Bedfordshire Regt.; empld.   1897
  P. of W. Camp
DRUCE, W. G. Capt., Dorset Yeo.   1891
DRUMMOND, G. H. Lieut., R.H.A.(T.F.) and Res. Regt.   1901
  of Life Gds. (W.)
✠DRYSDALE, D. R. Lieut., Dorset Regt. (W.)   1913
  Died 25 *Sept.* 1916 *of wounds received in action*
DUBS, C. I. A. Capt. and Adjt., Ayrshire Yeo. and R.   1909
  Scots Fus.
DUCANE, C. G. Lieut.-Col., R.E. *O.B.E.* *M* 3.   1897
DUCKWORTH, A. C. Major, 2nd Dragoons (R. Scots   1889
  Greys, R. of O.); D.A.Q.M.G. *Brevet Major.* *M* 2.
DUDFIELD, S. R. O. Capt., R.A.M.C. (Sanitary Service,   1879
  T.F.); empld. War Office. *O.B.E.* *M.*
DUFF, A. G. Lieut., R.A.O.C.   1902
✠DUFF, B. P. 2nd Lieut., Cameron Hdrs.   1911
  Killed in action 25 *Sept.* 1915
DUFF, D. G. Capt., R.A.M.C. *M.C.* *M.*   1906
DUFFIELD, K. L. 2nd Lieut., R. North Devon Yeo.;   1903
  Lieut., R. Warwickshire Regt.(T.F.)
DUFFIELD, W. G. Lieut. (T.), R.A.F.   1901
DUFFIN, C. G. Major, R.F.A. (W.) *M.C.* *M.*   1908
DUFTON, A. F. Lieut., R.F.A.(T.F.); attd. Gen. Staff.   1913
  (W.)
DUFTON, J. T. Capt., W. Yorks. Regt.   1911
DUKE, D. ST J. Lieut., R.N.V.R.   1895
DUKE, R. E. Lieut. (A.), R.A.F. (P.)   1913
DUKES, E. H. Lieut., Lincolnshire Regt. (W.)   1911
DUNCAN, Rev. G. S. C.F. 4th Class, R.A.C.D. *O.B.E.*   1906
  M 2.
DUNCAN-HUGHES, J. G. Capt., R.F.A. *M.C.* *Belgian*   1902
  Croix de Guerre

DUNCANNON, Viscount. *See* BESSBOROUGH, Earl of
DUNKELS, E. Lieut., R.A.S.C. *M.* 1898
DUNKELS, W. Capt., King's Royal Rifle Corps and Gen. 1904
   Staff. (W.)
DUNLOP, J. S. Major, R.A.S.C. *M* 3. 1896
DUNNING, G. K. Capt., Hampshire Regt.(T.F.) 1913
DUNVILLE, J. Lieut.-Col. (K.B.), R.A.F. *C.B.E.* 1885
✠DUNVILLE, J. S. 2nd Lieut., 1st Dragoons [1914]

𝖁.𝕮. "For most conspicuous bravery. When in charge
of a party consisting of scouts and Royal Engineers engaged in the demolition of the enemy's wire, this officer
displayed great gallantry and disregard of all personal
danger. In order to ensure the absolute success of the
work entrusted to him, 2nd Lt. Dunville placed himself
between an N.C.O. of the Royal Engineers and the
enemy's fire, and, thus protected, the N.C.O. was enabled
to complete a work of great importance. 2nd Lt. Dunville,
although severely wounded, continued to direct his men
in the wire-cutting and general operations until the raid
was successfully completed, thereby setting a magnificent
example of courage, determination and devotion to duty
to all ranks under his command. This gallant officer has
since succumbed to his wounds."—Supplement to *The
London Gazette*, 2 Aug. 1917.

Died 26 *June* 1917 *of wounds received in action* 25 *June*
1917

DUPREE, E. Capt., Hampshire Regt. *M.* [1914]
DUPUIS, C. E. Lieut.-Col., R.E. 1882
DURACK, J. J. E. Lieut., I.A.R.O., attd. 34th Poona Horse; 1900
   Capt., R.E. (attd.)
DUTHIE, W. L. Capt., R.F.A. (T.F.); empld. Ministry 1911
   of Munitions. (W.) *M.*
DYSON, C. B. Capt., R.A.M.C. 1908
DYSON, W. Major, R.A.M.C.(T.F.) *O.B.E. M.* 1895

✠EADE, A. 2nd Lieut., Yorkshire Regt. 1910
   Killed in action 9 *Oct.* 1917
EADEN, J. Lieut., R.F.A. *M.* 1900
EADIE, P. Lieut., R.E. (Fortress, T.F.); Hon. Lieut. (T.), 1914
   R.A.F.
EAMES, E. J. H. Capt., R.A.S.C.(T.F.) *M* 2. 1907
EARLE, L. M. Lieut., R.A.S.C. 1900
EASTERLING, H. G. Air Mechanic, R.A.F. 1906
EASTON, G. L. E. Major, R.F.A. *M.C. and Bar* 1910

EASTWOOD, H. E.   Major, R.A.O.C.   *M.C.   Chevalier,*   1907
Legion of Honour (France)
EASTWOOD, J. F.   Lieut., Grenadier Gds.; Capt., Spec.   1906
List (Courts-Martial Officer).   *m.*
EASTWOOD, N. W.   Lieut., 3rd Hussars; attd. Egyptian   1909
Army. (W.)
EATON, Hon. F. O. H.   Capt., Grenadier Gds.; Major   1913
(Ad.), R.A.F.   *D.S.O.   M.*
EBDEN, C. H. M.   Lieut., R.N.V.R.   1899
ECCLES, W. E. L.   Lieut., Res. Regt. of Cavalry and Spec.   1898
List; A.D.C.   *M.*
ECKERSLEY, T. L.   Lieut., R.E. (Signals)   *M* 2.   1909
EDDISON, Rev. F. W.   C.F. 4th Class, R.A.C.D.(T.F.)   *M.*   1894
EDGE PARTINGTON, Rev. E. F.   *See* PARTINGTON, Rev.
E. F. E.
EDWARDS, G. B.   Capt., King's (Liverpool Regt., T.F.)   1910
and R.E. (Signals). (P.)   *M.C.   M.*
EDWARDS, H. J., C.B., T.D.   Hon. Colonel, Unattd. List,   1888
T.F.; cmdg. O.C.B.   *C.B.E.   O.B.E.   m* 3.
EDWARDS, H. V.   Surgeon Lieut., R.N.   1914
EDWARDS, L. P. L.   *See* FIRMAN-EDWARDS, L. P. L.
EDWARDS-MOSS, J.   Capt., R.G.A.(T.F.)   1901
✠EGERTON, P. DE M. W.   Capt., 19th Hussars   1913
Killed in action 8 *Oct.* 1918
EGGAR, A. T. E.   Lieut., R.G.A.; Capt., S.O. 3, R.A.F.   1895
M.
EGGAR, J.   Sub-Lieut., R.N.V.R.   *C.B.E.   O.B.E.*   1899
✠EILOART, H. A.   Major, London Regt. (R. Fus.) (W 2.)   1908
D.S.O.   M.C. and Bar.   M 3.
Died June 1920 *from the effect of wounds received in*
action 28 *May* 1918
ELBORNE, J.   2nd Lieut., Huntingdonshire Cyclist Bn.   1912
and R.G.A.
ELIOT, Rev. E. F. W.   C.F. 4th Class, R.A.C.D.(T.F.)   1882
ELLICE-CLARK, S. T.   Capt., Suffolk Regt. and Tank   1905
Corps; empld. Ministry of Munitions. (W.)
✠ELLICOTT, F. A. J.   2nd Lieut., King's Own Scottish   1911
Borderers
Killed in action 8 *July* 1916
✠ELLIOT, Hon. G. W. E.   Lieut., Scots Gds.   [1914]
Died 6 *Aug.* 1917 *of wounds received in action*
ELLIOT, H. W. A.   Capt., Wiltshire Regt.(T.F.)   1909
✠ELLIOT, W. E.   2nd Lieut., Dorset Regt.   1912
Killed in action 26 *Sept.* 1916

ELLIOTT, E. C. B. Capt., R.H.A.(T.F.)   1912
ELLIOTT, G. L. L. Lieut., R.F.A. (W 2.)   1912
ELLIOTT, T. C. J. Lieut., R.A.O.C. (W.)   1895
ELLIOTT, T. R. Colonel, A.M.S. *C.B.E. D.S.O. M* 3.   1896
ELLIS, J. W. H. Capt., Canadian Infy. (W.) (P.)   1897
ELLIS, Rev. W. F. P. Chaplain, R.N.   1907
ELLISON, A. J. Capt., York and Lancaster Regt. (W.)   1914
ELPHICK, H. C. Lieut., R. Berkshire Regt.; Capt., 15th   1912
    Sikhs, Indian Army; attd. 47th and 54th Sikhs
ELPHINSTONE, K. V. Lieut., W. African Frontier Force   1897
ELPHINSTONE, L. H. Major, Inns of Court O.T.C. and   1898
    British Honduras Defence Force
ELVEDEN, Viscount, C.B., C.M.G. Capt., R.N.V.R.   1896
ELWELL, R. G. Surgeon Lieut., R.N. *D.S.C. M.*   1895
EMMETT, R. H. Capt., R.E. (Fortress, T.F.)   1912
ENGLAND, E. T. Capt., Exeter School O.T.C.   1896
ENGLAND, F. DE F. Lieut., 16th Lancers   1907
ESHER, Viscount, G.C.B., G.C.V.O. Colonel, empld. War   1870
    Office
ESTRIDGE, C. L. Capt., E. Yorks. Regt. (R. of O.);   1896
    Major, Spec. List (Chief Instructor, School of In-
    struction). (W.) *D.S.O. M* 3.
EVANS, A. G. Surgeon Lieut., R.N.   1905
✠EVANS, B. Lieut., Middlesex Regt. and R.F.C. *M.*   1906
    Died 8 April 1917
EVANS, E. W. Lieut., Welsh Regt.   1902
EVANS, F. D. Sergt., R. Fusiliers   1896
EVANS, H. S. Trooper, London Yeo.; Capt., R.A.M.C.   1909
    (W.)
EVANS, J. H. Lieut., R. Welsh Fus. (W 3.)   1899
EVANS, J. W. D. Capt., 21st Lancers. (W.) *M.*   1903
✠EVANS, R. A. Sergt., H.A.C.; 2nd Lieut., W. Yorks.   1909
    Regt.
    Accidentally killed 25 Jan. 1916
EVANS, R. C. A.B., R.N.V.R. (Anti-Aircraft)   1893
EVANS, V. L. Lieut., R.A.S.C.   1905
EVANS-LOMBE, E. H. Capt., R. Defence Corps; Major,   1880
    Labour Corps
EVERARD, W. L. Lieut., 1st Life Gds. and Gds. M.G. Regt.   1908
EVERY, Sir E. O., Bart. Capt., Norfolk Yeo.; Major, R.E.   1905
    (Signals). *Brevet Major. M.*
✠EWING, A. H. Capt., E. Yorks. Regt. (W.) *M.C. and*   [1914]
    Bar. M.
    Died 8 Sept. 1918 *of wounds received in action*

TRINITY COLLEGE 393

EXMOUTH, Viscount. Lieut., R.A.F. 1909
✠EZRA, D. Lieut., R.G.A. 1902
Killed in action 6 Aug. 1918

FALMOUTH, Viscount. Capt., Coldstream Gds. 1905
FANE, W. V. R. Colonel, Lincolnshire Regt. *Brevet* 1886
Colonel. m.
FARLEY, C. F. Capt., 4th (R. Irish) Dragoon Gds. *M.C.* 1911
FARLEY, R. L. Major (K.B.), R.A.F. (W.) *O.B.E.* 1909
✠FARMER, H. C. M. 2nd Lieut., King's Royal Rifle Corps 1911
Killed in action 10 May 1915
✠FARQUHAR, H. B. Capt., London Regt. (Civil Service 1892
Rifles)
Killed in action near Vimy Ridge 21 May 1916
FARRANT, M. Major, R.F.A. 1903
FARREN, W. S. Capt. (T.), R.A.F. *M.B.E. m.* 1911
FARROW, E. P. Lieut., Manchester Regt. 1911
FAULKNER, R. Capt., S. Lancs. Regt. and Gen. List, 1911
empld. Ministry of Munitions. *M.*
FAWCETT, H. H. J. Lieut.-Col., R.A.M.C. *D.S.O. M.* 1897
FAWCUS, J. G. Pte., R. Defence Corps 1867
FAWCUS, L. R. Lieut., I.A.R.O. (Cavalry) 1906
FAWKES, Rev. W. H. C.F. 4th Class, R.A.C.D. *M.C.* 1894
FAYRER, F. D. S. Lieut.-Col., I.M.S. 1888
FEATHERSTONE, H. W. Capt., R.A.M.C. 1911
FEETHAM, Rev. F. G. C.F. 4th Class, R.A.C.D. 1905
FEILDING, Hon. F. E. H. J. Lieut., R.N.V.R. *O.B.E.* 1887
Order of the Nile, 4th Class (Egypt). Order of El Nahda (Hedjaz)
✠FEILDING, Hon. H. S. Lieut., K. Edward's Horse; 1912
A.D.C.; Capt., Coldstream Gds.
Died 9 Oct. 1917 of wounds received in action
FELTON, L. B. Lieut., Somerset L.I. and Gen. List 1911
✠FENWICK, A. L. Capt., Lincolnshire Regt. (W.) *M.* 1913
Killed in action 16 Feb. 1918
FENWICK, B. A. Capt., E. Surrey Regt. (W.) (P.) *m.* 1908
FENWICK, J. C. Lieut., Northumberland Yeo. 1892
FENWICK, M. C. Capt., Suffolk Regt.(T.F.); attd. Man- 1908
chester Regt.
FERGUSON, C. L. Lieut., King's Royal Rifle Corps; Capt., 1914
O.C.B. (W.)
FERGUSON, D. F. 2nd Lieut., R.M.A. 1907
✠FERGUSON, H. M. Capt., S. Staffs. Regt. 1910
Killed in action 11 June 1917

FERGUSSON, N. M. Lieut., Scots Gds. (W.) 1901
FERMOR-HESKETH, T. Major, Lancs. Hussars 1904
FERRERS GUY, A. W. Pte., R. Fusiliers (P. S. Bn.); 2nd 1891
Lieut., R.G.A.
FEWTRELL, A. H. H. Lieut., R. Sussex Regt.; Capt. and 1913
Adjt., 27th Light Cavalry, Indian Army. (W.)
FIELD, M. Lieut., United States F.A. 1912
FILDES, F. L. V. Lieut., Coldstream Gds.; Major, P. and 1897
B.T. Staff
FILDES, G. P. A. Lieut., Coldstream Gds. 1906
FILDES, P. G. Hon. Surgeon Lieut.-Cdr., R.N.V.R. 1900
✠FINCH, H. A. I. Pte., 2nd Bn., Canadian Infy.; attd. 1897
T.M.B.
Died 28 April 1916 of wounds received in action
FINNIS, C. R. Lieut., Scots Gds. (W.) *Belgian Croix* 1891
de Guerre
FIRMAN-EDWARDS, L. P. L. Surgeon Lieut., R.N 1912
✠FIRTH, ARNOLD. 2nd Lieut., R.F.A.(T.F.) 1901
Killed in action 15 *April* 1917
FIRTH, A. C. D. Capt., R.A.M.C. 1898
FIRTH, A. M. B. Capt., York and Lancaster Regt. 1908
FIRTH, L. G. Capt., R.F.A. (W.) 1906
✠FIRTH, R. C. D. Lieut., S. Lancs. Regt. 1897
Died 21 Dec. 1914
✠FISHER, J. W. Capt., Sherwood Foresters (Notts. and 1910
Derby Regt.) (W 3.) *D.S.O. M.*
Died 8 July 1916 *of wounds received in action*
✠FISKE, C.H. 2nd Lieut., 111th Regt., United States Army 1914
Killed in action near Fismes (Aisne) 12 *Aug.* 1918
FITZGERALD, D. Lieut., Remount Service and Spec. List 1910
FITZGERALD, E. A. Major, 6th (Inniskilling) Dragoons; 1890
empld. War Office
FITZGERALD, G. M. Capt., London Yeo. (Sharpshooters) 1902
and M.G.C. (W.)
FITZGERALD, J. F. Staff Sergt.-Major, R.A.S.C. 1891
FITZGERALD, M. P. Capt. and Adjt., R.F.A. (W 2.) *M.* 1906
FITZHERBERT, J. A. Lieut., R.G.A.; Lieut. (O.), R.A.F. 1913
(W.) *M.C.*
FITZPATRICK, E. R. Lieut.-Col., Loyal N. Lancs. Regt.; 1896
Brig.-Gen., D.A.G. *C.B.E. D.S.O. Brevet Lieut.-*
Colonel. Brevet Major. M 3. Chevalier, Legion of
Honour (France)
FITZWILLIAM, Earl, K.C.V.O., D.S.O. Major, Oxford and 1891
Bucks. L.I.; Lieut.-Col., R.H.A.(T.F.) *C.B.E. M.*

TRINITY COLLEGE   395

FLETCHER, F. C. Hon. Capt. and Q.M., R.A.M.C.(T.F.)   1908
FLETCHER, HERBERT M. Major, R.A.M.C. (1st London   1884
   Gen. Hospital, T.F.)
FLEURET, F. S. Capt., The Buffs (E. Kent Regt., T.F.)   1904
   (W.)
FLINT, A. H. Capt., R.G.A. (W.) (P.)   1901
FLOOK, H. S. Major, S. African Med. Corps   1899
FLOWER, N. A. C. Lieut., Grenadier Gds. (W.)   1902
FLYNN, A. J. Capt., R.A.S.C. and Gen. Staff   1911
FORBES, Rev. E. A. C.F. 4th Class, R.A.C.D.   1888
FORBES-TWEEDIE, D. Capt., London Yeo. (Rough   [1914]
   Riders); A.D.C. (W.)
FORDHAM, E. K. Lieut., R.A.S.C.   1899
FORDHAM, H. A. Lieut., Northumberland Fus.; Capt. 1911
   (A.), R.A.F.; Major, S.O. 2. (W.)
FORDHAM, O. 2nd Lieut., Oxford and Bucks. L.I.(T.F.) 1907
FORDYCE, A. DINGWALL. Major, R.A.M.C.   1893
FORDYCE, R. DINGWALL. Major, 2nd Dragoons (R. Scots 1894
   Greys)
FORESTER, Lord. Capt., R. Horse Gds.(R. of O.); Lieut.- 1887
   Col., Shropshire Yeo.
FORESTER, O. ST M. W. See WELD-FORESTER, Rev. O. ST M.
FORREST, H. Capt., S. Staffs. Regt.; attd. T.M.B. (W.) 1913
   M.C.
✠FORREST, J. W. 2nd Lieut., Seaforth Hdrs.   1912
   Killed in action 27 Sept. 1915
FORSHAW, J. H. Capt., R. Berkshire Regt.; Major, attd. 1893
   R.E. (Signals). M.
✠FORSTER, F. A. Capt., R. Fusiliers   1898
   Died 23 Sept. 1914 of wounds received in action at Mons
FORSTER, T. Lieut., R.E.(T.F.) (W 2.) M.C.   1910
✠FORSTER, W. Pte., R. Fusiliers   1910
   Killed in action 7 Oct. 1916
FORTESCUE, Earl, K.C.B., T.D. Hon. Colonel, R. North 1872
   Devon Yeo.; A.D.C. to the King
FORWOOD, P. L. Lieut., R.E. (W.)   1909
✠FOSTER, B. LA T. Lieut., Manchester Regt.   1912
   Killed in action 24 July 1916
FOSTER, H. E. Pte., R.A.S.C.   1907
FOSTER, Rev. K. G. Chaplain, Indian Army   1886
FOSTER, M. G. Major, R.A.M.C.(T.F.) O.B.E. M 2.   1881
FOSTER, M. R. Capt., I.A.R.O.   1911
FOSTER, M. R. W. Major, Hampshire Regt. (T.F.);   1888
   G.S.O. 2, E. Command. m.

FOSTER, O. B. Major, Northumberland Fus.; D.A.Q.M.G.   1899
   M.C. M 5. *Chevalier, Ordre du Mérite Agricole*
   (*France*)
FOSTER, P. LA T. Lieut., Manchester Regt.; Lieut. (A.),   1910
   R.A.F. (P.)
FOWLE, T. E. Colonel, A. A. and Q. M. G., S. Africa.   1881
   C.B.E.
FOWLER, C. H. Lieut., R.F.A.(T.F.); Staff Capt., Min-   1905
   istry of Munitions. *M.B.E.*
✠FOWLER, D. D. 2nd Lieut. (A.), R.F.C. (W.)   1915
   Killed in action 16 *March* 1917
✠FOWLER, J. D. Lieut., 5th (R. Irish) Lancers   1910
   Killed in action 30 *Nov.* 1914
FOWLER, R. H. Capt., R.M.A.; empld. Ministry of Muni-   1908
   tions. (W.) *O.B.E.*
Fox, Rev. H. W. C.F. 3rd Class, R.A.C.D. *D.S.O. M* 2.   1891
Fox, J. C. Capt., R.A.M.C.   1900
Fox, W. S. Capt., R.A.M.C.   1893
✠FOYSTER, P. T. Capt., R.E.   1906
   Died 11 *Dec.* 1916 *of wounds received in action* 6 *Dec.*
   1916
FRANCIS, E. G. 2nd Lieut., Cambridgeshire Regt. (W.)   1903
FRANKLIN, W. B. 2nd Lieut., King's Royal Rifle Corps;   1910
   Capt., Spec. List, empld. Ministry of National Service
FRANKLIN-SMITH, N. C. Lieut., Res. Regt. of Cavalry,   1903
   attd. 7th Hussars
FRANKLYN, A. H. Lieut., Res. Regt. of Cavalry; Traffic   1905
   Control Officer
FRASER, C. S. Lieut., R. Fusiliers; Capt., Gen. List   1907
   (Staff). (W.)
FRASER, G. T. Lieut., R.E.   1900
FRASER-MACKENZIE, E. R. L. Major, R.H.A.(T.F.) (W.)   1911
   D.S.O. M.C. M.
FRASER-MACKENZIE, J. A. O. 2nd Lieut., Lovat's Scouts;   1909
   Lieut., E. African Force (M.T.)
FREEMAN, P. B. 2nd Lieut., Worcestershire Regt.   1906
FREEMAN MITFORD, Hon. C. B. O. *See* MITFORD, Hon.
   C. B. O. F.
FREER, G. H. Lieut., Res. Regt. of Cavalry, attd. 12th   1905
   Lancers
FREESTON, B. D. Lieut., R.H.A.(T.F.)   1913
✠FRENCH, Hon. E. A. Capt., S. Wales Borderers   1913
   Died 16 *Aug.* 1917 *of wounds received in action*
FREND, Rev. J. P. C.F. 4th Class, R.A.C.D.   1887

✠FREND, W. R. Capt., Sherwood Foresters (Notts. and 1893
Derby Regt.)
Killed in action 20 Sept. 1914
FRERE, J. G. Capt., Norfolk Yeo.; attd. Norfolk Regt. [1914]
FREWEN, H. M. Lieut., R.N.V.R. (W.) 1904
FREWEN, S. Lieut.-Col., A.A. and Q.M.G. 1875
FREYER, D. J. Major, London Regt. (London Irish 1901
Rifles); cmdg. Depôt
✠FROST, E. L. Lieut., S. Lancs. Regt.(T.F.) 1909
Killed in action 16 *June* 1915
FRY, C. R. Lieut. (T.), R.A.F. 1907
FRY, F. McG. Lieut., R.F.A. (W 2.) 1912
FRY, J. A.B., R.N.V.R. (Anti-Aircraft) 1896
FURLONGER, R. C. Capt., R.A.S.C.(T.F.) 1899
FURSDON, G. E. S. Lieut., London Regt. and Spec. List 1912
(Recruiting Staff). (W.)

✠GADDUM, R. C. S. 2nd Lieut., R. Fusiliers 1899
Killed in action 10 *Sept.* 1916
GADDUM, W. F. Capt., Westmorland and Cumberland 1907
Yeo. and Border Regt. (W.)
✠GALBRAITH, A. N. Capt., Ceylon Rifles 1896
Accidentally killed in Egypt (20 *Feb.* 1916)
GAME, H. A. A.B., R.N.V.R. (Anti-Aircraft) 1892
GARDINER, J. Capt. (T.), R.A.F. 1905
GARDNER, H. D. Capt., R.A.M.C. 1911
GARDNER, J. C. Lieut., R. Marines and Gen. List, empld. 1901
Ministry of Munitions. *O.B.E. M.*
GARDNER, R. G. Capt., 25th Punjabis, Indian Army 1904
GARDNER-MEDWIN, F. M. Capt., R.A.M.C. 1896
✠GARFIT, T. N. C. Lieut., Durham L.I. 1910
Killed in action in Gallipoli 30 *April* 1915
✠GARNETT, K. G. Seaman, R.N.R.; Lieut., R.F.A. *M.C.* 1911
French Croix de Guerre
Died 22 *Aug.* 1917 *of wounds received in action* 21 *Aug.*
1916
✠GARNETT, W. H. S. Lieut.-Cdr., R.N.R.; Lieut., R.F.C. 1900
Killed in flying accident 21 *Sept.* 1916
✠GARNETT-BOTFIELD, A. C. F. 2nd Lieut., Rifle Brigade; 1912
Lieut., S. Wales Borderers
Killed in action 9 *May* 1915
GARNETT-BOTFIELD, W. McL. Lieut., R.A.S.C. 1901
GARRATT, G. H. Major, Border Regt. and R. Sussex Regt. 1895
GARRETT, L. C. 2nd Lieut., R.G.A. 1906

✠GARRETT, S. Capt., Suffolk Regt.(T.F.)   1897
    Killed in action 12 *March* 1915
GARRICK, G. C. Major, Surrey Yeo.   1897
GARSIDE, G. C. Pte., R.A.S.C.   1915
GAVIN, W. Lieut., R.N.V.R.   1907
GAY, C. D. Capt., E. Lancs. Regt. (W 2.) *M.C.*   1913
GAYE, A. S. Major, R.A.S.C.; Lieut.-Col., empld. Min-   1900
    istry of Munitions. *O.B.E. M* 2. *m.*
GEARD, D. A. A. Lieut., Life Gds. and Gds. M.G. Regt.   1912
✠GEDGE, C. B. 2nd Lieut., London Regt. (R. Fus.)   1885
    Killed in action 25 *Sept.* 1915
✠GEE, R. F. McL. 2nd Lieut., Wiltshire Regt.   [1914]
    Died 27 *Oct.* 1914 *of wounds received in action*
GELDARD, N. Capt., D. of Wellington's (W. Riding Regt.,   1908
    T.F.) and Tank Corps. (W 6.) *D.S.O. M.C. M.*
✠GELDERD-SOMERVELL, R. F. C. 2nd Lieut., Grenadier   1904
    Gds.
    Died 13 *March* 1915 *of wounds received in action*
GERARD, Lord. Capt., R. Horse Gds. (W 2.) *M.C.*   1902
GERVIS, H. Capt., R.A.M.C.(T.F.)   1881
✠GETHING, H. B. 2nd Lieut., Gloucestershire Yeo.   1902
    Killed in action in Gallipoli 21 *Aug.* 1915
GIBBON, E. L. L. Lieut., R.F.A.   1898
GIBBON, J. H. Major, R.F.A. (W.) *D.S.O. Brevet*   1897
    Lieut.-Colonel. M 3. *m.*
✠GIBBONS, E. I. Pte., R. Fusiliers; Lieut., Lancs. Fus.   1911
    Killed in action 29 *April* 1917
GIBBS, W. D. Capt., Hertfordshire Yeo. *M* 2.   1907
GIBSON, C. M. Lieut., E. Surrey Regt.   1913
GIBSON, G. M. Capt., R.A.S.C.(M.T.)   1897
✠GIBSON-CRAIG, Sir A. C., Bart. Lieut., Highland L.I. *M.*   1902
    Killed in action 13–17 *Sept.* 1914
GIBSON-WATT, J. M. Major, S. Wales Borderers   1895
GIDLOW-JACKSON, G. H. Lieut., R.A.M.C.   1911
GILES, E. Capt., King's Own Scottish Borderers; attd.   1913
    W. Yorks. Regt.; empld. O.C.B. (W 5.) *M.C.*
GILLILAND, G. F. Lieut., R.N.V.R.   1902
✠GILLILAND, V. K. Capt., R. Irish Rifles. (W.)   1907
    Killed in action 8 *May* 1915
✠GILMOUR, A. S. 2nd Lieut., Argyll and Sutherland Hdrs.   1906
    Killed in action 15 *Sept.* 1916
✠GILSON, R. Q. Lieut., Suffolk Regt.   1912
    Killed in action 1 *July* 1916
GIRDLESTONE, C. M. Sergt., Norfolk Regt.   1915

ʒERS, L. Capt., Seaforth Hdrs.   1912
Killed in action 4 *Oct.* 1917
ʒLAZEBROOK, A. R. Capt., W. Yorks. Regt.(T.F.); empld.   1910
Ministry of Munitions. (W.) *M.C. M.*
ʒLEED, R. W. A. Lieut., S. Staffs. Regt. (W 2.) *M.C.*   1908
ʒLEN, R. R. Lieut., R. Glasgow Yeo.   1911
ʒODBER, H. T. Lieut., Connaught Rangers; Capt., Spec.   1909
List (Cmdt., Bde. Signal School)
ʒODDARD, A. S. Capt., Canadian Infy.   1905
Killed in action 26 *Sept.* 1916
ʒODDARD-JACKSON, N. W. 2nd Lieut., Northampton-   1914
shire Regt.
Killed in action at High Wood 9 *Sept.* 1916
ʒODSAL, HERBERT. Capt., Hampshire Yeo.   1886
ʒODSAL, HUGH. Capt., R.F.A. (W.) *M.*   1912
ʒODSELL, R. T. Lieut., R.A.S.C.   1899
ʒOFF, Sir H. W. D. Hon. Capt., R.A.S.C.   1890
ʒOLDIE, C. J. D. Capt., R.F.A.; Staff Capt. *M.C. M.*   1896
ʒOLDIE, N. B. Lieut., R.G.A.; Staff Capt. *M.*   1901
ʒOLDNEY, H. H. Lieut., R.E. *M.C.*   1905
ʒOLDSCHMIDT, J. P. Capt., Manchester Regt.   1912
ʒOMME, A. W. Pte., R.A.S.C.; Lieut., Spec. List   1905
ʒOMME, G. J. L. 2nd Lieut., Cheshire Regt.; Lieut.,   1910
R.G.A.
ʒOODHART, G. W. Capt., R.A.M.C. (2nd London Gen.   1899
Hospital, T.F.) *m.*
ʒOODHART-RENDEL, H. S. Lieut., Grenadier Gds.   1905
ʒOODWIN, A. D. Lieut. (T.), R.A.F. (Aircraft Production   1904
Dept.)
ʒOODWIN, H. D. Lieut., Middlesex Regt.   1908
Killed in action 1 *July* 1916
ʒOOLDEN, A. W. Lieut., E. Surrey Regt.; empld. O.C.B.   1908
(W.)
ʒORDON, A. R. Lieut., Northamptonshire Regt. (W.)   1912
ʒORDON, C. T. Hon. Lieut.-Col., R. Scots (T.F. Res.)   1877
ʒORDON, Rev. J. G. C.F. 2nd Class, R.A.C.D.; D.A.C.G.   1900
M. Italian Bronze Medal ' della Salute Publica'
ʒORDON CUMMING, A. P. Capt., Cameron Hdrs.; Brigade 1912
Major. (W 2.) *M.C. M.*
ʒORE BROWNE, H. T. T. Pte., Canadian Mtd. Rifles;   1904
2nd Lieut., King's Royal Rifle Corps
Died 23 *Aug.* 1916 *of wounds received in action* 19 *Aug.*
1916

¹ Killed in action in Afghanistan after the armistice.

GORRINGE, W. H. Major, R. Sussex Regt.(T.F.) 1886
GORST, G. T. Capt., E. Lancs. Regt. (W.) 1913
GOSLING, T. S. Lieut., R.G.A. 1897
GOSNELL, R. P. Capt., H.A.C. 1899
GOSSAGE, A. F. W. Lieut., 17th Lancers. *M.C.* 1909
GOSSAGE, E. L. 2nd Lieut., R.F.A.; Lieut.-Col. (A.), 1909
  R.A.F. *D.S.O. M.C. M* 4.
GOTCH, M. S. Capt., Northamptonshire Regt. (W.) 1910
GOURLAY, W. B. Capt., R.A.M.C. *M.C.* 1899
Gow, A. S. F. 2nd Lieut., Eton College O.T.C. 1905
Gow, I. B. 2nd Lieut., Black Watch [1914]
GRACE, C. L. P. Lieut., Highland Cyclist Bn. 1910
✠GRACEY, H. C. Capt., Rifle Brigade. (W.) 1911
  Killed in action at Le Transloy 18 *Oct.* 1916
GRACEY, R. L. Major, R.E.(T.F.) *D.S.O. M* 2. *Order* 1910
  of the White Eagle, 5th Class, with swords (Serbia)
GRAHAM, G. Capt., R.A.M.C. *M.* 1901
GRAHAM, H. A. R. Capt., Grenadier Gds.; A.D.C.; 1911
  Capt., Spec. List (School of Instruction). (W.)
GRAHAM, H. H. C. Sub-Lieut., R.N.V.R. 1914
GRAHAM, J. C. W. Capt., R.A.M.C. (1st E. Gen. Hos- 1890
  pital, T.F.)
GRAHAM, J. R. N. Capt., Argyll and Sutherland Hdrs.; 1911
  Major, M.G.C. (W.)

V.C. "For most conspicuous bravery, coolness and resource when in command of a Machine Gun Section. Lt. Graham accompanied the guns across open ground, under very heavy rifle and machine gun fire, and when his men became casualties, he assisted in carrying the ammunition. Although twice wounded, he continued during the advance to control his guns and was able, with one gun, to open an accurate fire on the enemy, who were massing for a counter-attack. This gun was put out of action by the enemy's rifle fire, and he was again wounded. The advancing enemy forced him to retire, but before doing so he further disabled his gun, rendering it useless. He then brought a Lewis gun into action with excellent effect till all the ammunition was expended. He was again severely wounded, and forced through loss of blood to retire. His valour and skilful handling of his guns held up a strong counter-attack which threatened to roll up the left flank of the Brigade, and thus averted what might have been a very critical situation."—Supplement to *The London Gazette*, 14 Sept. 1917.

GRAHAM, M. W. A. P. Lieut., Life Gds.; Capt. and 1913
Adjt., Gds. M.G. Regt. (W 2.) *M.C. M* 2.

GRAHAM, R. P. Lieut., King's Royal Rifle Corps. (W.) 1914
(P.) *M.C.*

GRAHAM CAMPBELL, J. Lieut., Argyll and Sutherland 1906
Hdrs. (W.)

✠GRANT, A. F. M. 2nd Lieut., The Queen's (R. W. Surrey 1911
Regt.)
Died 18 *June* 1916 *of gas poisoning*

GRANT, B. D. 2nd Lieut., King's Own Scottish Borderers 1910
GRANT, Rev. H. S. C.F. 4th Class, R.A.C.D. 1895
GRANT, M. F. Lieut.-Col., R.A.M.C. 1896
GRANT-WATSON, E. L. 2nd Lieut., Hampshire Yeo. 1906
(T.F. Res.)

✠GRANTHAM, E. R. H. 2nd Lieut., Northumberland Fus. 1914
Died 31 *March* 1917 *of wounds received in action*

✠GRANTHAM, F. W. Capt., R. Munster Fus. 1889
Killed in action 9 *May* 1915

GRANTHAM, W. W., V.D. Major, R. Sussex Regt.(T.F.) 1886
GRASEMANN, C. Capt., R.E. 1908

✠GRATTAN-BELLEW,W. A. 2nd Lieut., Connaught Rangers; 1913
Major, R.F.C. *M.*
Died 24 *March* 1917 *of wounds received in action*

GRAY, F. L. Capt., R.A.S.C. 1905

✠GRAY, M. Lieut., 2nd Dragoon Gds. (Queen's Bays); 1908
Capt., M.G.C.
Killed in action 8 *Aug.* 1918

GREAVES, G. M. Lieut., Leicestershire Yeo.; Capt., 1907
R. Horse Gds.; Major, Gds. M.G. Regt.

GREAVES, L. B. Pte., R. Fusiliers (P. S. Bn.); Lieut., [1914]
S. Wales Borderers. (W.) *M.C. Order of the White
Eagle, 5th Class, with swords (Serbia)*

GREAVES, R. C. J. Lieut., R. Welsh Fus. 1908
GREEN, B. Capt., Oxford and Bucks. L.I.(T.F.); Major, 1907
M.G.C. (W 2.) *M.C. M.*

GREEN, D. Lieut., Suffolk Regt. *M.C.* 1912
GREEN, H. Pte., London Regt. (Artists Rifles) 1903

✠GREEN, H. S. Major, London Regt. *M.* 1902
Killed in action 20 *Sept.* 1917

GREEN, R. D. Capt., Durham L.I.; attd. T.M.B.; empld. 1914
British Military Mission. *M.C.*

GREENE, W. P. C. Capt., 13th Hussars 1903
GREENWELL, B. E. Major, Hampshire Yeo.(T.F. Res.) 1893
M.B.E.

GREENWOOD, J. A. Section Sanitaire, French Army   1883
GREG, A. H. Capt., R.A.M.C. *O.B.E.* *M* 2. *French* 1891
Médaille des Épidémies
GREGORY, G. M. Capt., I.A.R.O., attd. Sappers and 1908
Miners; Recruiting Officer. *M.*
✠GREGORY, J. S. Capt., R.A.S.C. and R.F.C. *M.*   1908
Killed in action 19 *Feb.* 1918
GREGSON, H. G. Lieut., R. Wiltshire Yeo.; attd. Wilt- 1912
shire Regt. (W.)
GRENVILLE-GREY, G. Cdr.,R.N.V.R.(Anti-Aircraft). *m.* 1878
GREVILLE SMITH, S. H. Lieut., Middlesex Regt. (T.F. 1906
Res.) and Northamptonshire Regt.
GREY, Earl. Major, Northumberland Fus.; G.S.O. 2. 1898
M 2.
✠GRIBBLE, C. H. Lieut., The Buffs (E. Kent Regt., T.F.) 1907
Killed in action 30 *Nov.* 1917
GRICE-HUTCHINSON, Rev. R. E. C.F. 4th Class, R.A.C.D. 1904
M.C. M.
GRIEVE, F. C. L. Major, R.F.A.   1898
GRIEVE, W. R. Capt., R.F.A.   1896
GRIFFIN, A. W. M. S. Capt., N. Rhodesian Rifles. *M.C.* 1906
GRIFFIN, H. J. S. Major, R.F.A. (W.)   1903
✠GRIFFITH, G. F. Capt., London Regt. (Q.V.R.) *M.* 1910
Killed in action 26 *Sept.* 1917
GRIFFITH, H. K. Capt., R.A.M.C.(T.F.)   1904
GRIFFITH, H. L. W. 2nd Lieut., R.H.A.; Capt., Spec. 1909
List, empld. Directorate of Requisitions and Hirings.
Chevalier, Ordre du Mérite Agricole (France)
GRIFFITH, J. Major, N. Staffs. Regt.(T.F.) *T.D.* 1899
GRIFFITHS, Rev. C. C. C.F. 4th Class, R.A.C.D. *M.C.* 1910
✠GRIFFITHS, R. E. Pte., Australian Force   1907
Killed in action in Gallipoli 1915
GRINLING, A. G. Capt., Hertfordshire Regt.; attd. Bed- [1914]
fordshire Regt. (W.) *M.C.*
GRISSELL, T. DE LA G. Major, Suffolk Yeo.; Lieut.-Col., 1897
Suffolk Regt. (W.) *M.C. M.*
GRONER, R. E. E. Lieut., Sherwood Foresters (Notts. 1903
and Derby Regt.) (W 2.) (P.)
GROVES, K. G. Capt., London Regt. (Poplar and Stepney 1906
Rifles). *M.*
GUEST, Hon. L. G. W. Major, R.A.F.; S.O. 2, Air Min- 1899
istry. *O.B.E. M.*
GUEST, Hon. O. M. Major (A.), R.A.F.; S.O. 2. (W.) 1906
GUINNESS, Hon. R. *See* ELVEDEN, Viscount   1896

GUINNESS, R. S. Lieut., R.N.V.R. (W.) 1907
GUNSTON, D. W. Capt., Irish Gds. *M.C.* 1910
GURNEY, C. R. Capt., R.E. *M.* 1903
GURNEY, E. H. Capt., Suffolk Yeo.(T.F. Res.) 1885
GURNEY, Q. E. Major, Norfolk Yeo. 1901
GURNEY-DIXON, S. Capt., R.A.M.C. *M* 2. 1897
GUETERBOCK, P. G. J. Capt., Gloucestershire Regt.(T.F.); 1905
Brigade Major. (W.) *D.S.O. M.C. M* 3.
GUTHRIE, P. S. Lieut., Life Gds.; A.D.C. 1913
✠GWYNNE, R. T. S. 2nd Lieut., King's Own (Yorkshire 1912
L.I., T.F.)
Died 23 May 1915 of wounds received in action
GWYTHER, G. H. Lieut.-Col., R. Welsh Fus.; empld. 1890
War Office. (W.) *D.S.O. M.*

✠HABERSHON, L. O. Capt., E. Yorks. Regt. 1912
Killed in action 13 Nov. 1916
HACKFORTH, R. Pte., London Regt. (Artists Rifles) 1905
HADRILL, E. W. 2nd Lieut., Queen's Own (R.W. Kent 1910
Regt.); Lieut. (A. and Ad.), R.A.F. (W.)
HAHLO, H. B. *See* BARKER-HAHLO, H.
HAKE, H. M. Lieut., Cambridgeshire Regt. and Gen. 1910
Staff. *French Croix de Guerre*
HALE, D. B. Major, R.F.A. *M.* 1896
HALES, J. B. Lieut., Oxford and Bucks. L.I.(T.F.); Capt., 1907
G.S.O. 3. *M.C. M* 2.
HALL, A. A. Lieut., R.E. (Signals) 1913
HALL, A. C. Major, Suffolk Regt. 1888
✠HALL, F. G. Capt., Cheshire Regt. 1909
Killed in action 7 July 1916
HALL, R. S. Lieut., R.N.V.R. 1904
✠HALLAM, H. G. S. Lieut., R.A.S.C.(T.F.); attd.Egyptian [1914]
Camel Corps
Killed in action near Jaffa 1 Dec. 1917
HALLER, B. C. Capt., R.A.M.C. 1901
HALLETT, H. G. Capt., R. Fusiliers 1895
HALLEY, K. B. Lieut., Middlesex Regt. (W.) 1914
HALLIDAY, D. R. J. Lieut., 11th Hussars and R.E. (Sig- 1907
nals)
✠HALLIDAY, J. A. Capt., 11th Hussars 1894
*Died 13 Nov. 1914 of wounds received in action at
Messines 31 Oct. 1914*
HALLIDAY, M. A. C. Lieut., Bedfordshire Yeo. and 1905
M.G.C. (Cavalry)

HALNAN, E. T. Capt., R.G.A. (W.) *M.*   1908
HAMBRO, R. O. Capt., Coldstream Gds.; G.S.O. 3. *M.*   1905
Belgian Croix de Guerre
HAMILL, J. M. Major, R.A.M.C.(T.F.); D.A.D.M.S.   1898
O.B.E. M 2.
HAMILL, P. Major, R.A.M.C.   1902
HAMILTON, E. R. Instructor Lieut., R.N.   1913
HAMILTON, E. W. Capt., London Regt.; empld. Ministry   1912
of Munitions. (W.)
HAMILTON, G. Capt., Scottish Horse and Black Watch   1911
(T.F.) *M.C.*
✠HAMILTON, H. O. Lieut., Northumberland Fus.   1911
Killed in action in the Battle of Loos 25 Sept. 1915
✠HAMILTON, K. Lieut., W. African Frontier Force   1905
Died in Nigeria 15 *Nov.* 1918 *of influenza contracted*
on active service
HAMMOND, C. E. Lieut., Irish Gds. *M.C.*   1908
HAMOND-GRAEME, E. H. M. Major, Hampshire Yeo.   1895
HAMPDEN, Viscount. Major, 10th Hussars (R. of O.);   1887
Colonel, Hertfordshire Regt.; Brig.-Gen. *C.B.*
C.M.G. M 7. *Officer, Legion of Honour (France)*
✠HANDFORD, E. F. S. 2nd Lieut., Sherwood Foresters [1914]
(Notts. and Derby Regt., T.F.)
Killed in action 15 *Oct.* 1915
✠HANDFORD, H. B. S. Capt., Sherwood Foresters (Notts.   1912
and Derby Regt., T.F.)
Killed in action 15 *Oct.* 1915
HANNA, W. B. Lieut., 92nd Infy. Bn.; Capt., Gen. List,   1911
Canadian Force
HANNEN, L. G. 2nd Lieut., R.F.A. (W.)   1916
HANSON, H. J. Lieut., R.N.V.R. *O.B.E.*   1893
✠HANSON, O. H. Lieut.-Cdr., R.N.V.R.   1891
Killed while prisoner in German hands 5 *Nov.* 1914
HANSON, R. J. E. Surgeon Cdr., R.N.V.R. *O.B.E.*   1888
HARCOURT, R. V., M.P. Lieut., R.N.A.S. (Anti-Aircraft)   1897
HARDIE, M. Capt., Spec. List (Censor's Staff). *M.*   1895
HARDING, E. Capt., R.A.M.C. *M.C. M.*   1910
HARDINGE, Hon. A. H. L. Capt., Grenadier Gds. (W.)   1911
M.C.
HARDY, C. Capt., London Regt. (Rangers); Major,   1906
King's (Liverpool Regt.) (W.) *D.S.O. M* 2.
HARE, F. Capt., Northumberland Fus.(T.F.) and R.E.   1912
(Field Survey Bn.)
HARFORD, C. F. Capt., R.A.M.C.   1883

TRINITY COLLEGE 405

HARGREAVES, A. R. Capt., R.A.M.C. (W.) 1903
HARGREAVES, J. A. Lieut., King's (Liverpool Regt., T.F.) 1898
(W.)
HARMENS, W. Capt., R.A.M.C. (W.) 1901
✠HARMSWORTH, Hon. V. S. T. Lieut., R.N.V.R.(R.N.D.) [1914]
Killed in action 13 *Nov.* 1916
HARRATON, J. R. Lieut., Durham L.I. 1909
HARRILD, W. C. Major, Yorkshire Regt. 1889
HARRIS, E. R. Lieut., Wiltshire Regt.(T.F.) and M.G.C. [1914]
M.C.
HARRIS, H. B. Capt., Essex Regt. 1890
HARRISON, A. P. B. Capt., Rifle Brigade; Lieut.-Col., 1893
Spec. List
HARRISON, ERNEST. Lieut., R.N.V.R. 1896
✠HARRISON, EVERARD. Capt., R.A.M.C.(T.F.) 1901
Killed in action 18 *April* 1917
HARRISON, E. F. Lieut.-Col., Gen. List, Australian Force; 1898
G.S.O. 1. *m. Officer, Legion of Honour (France).
Order of St Maurice and St Lazarus (Italy)*
HARRISON, F. E. H. Major, R.F.A.(T.F.) 1896
HARRISON, H. E. Capt., The Queen's (R.W. Surrey Regt.) 1898
M.C.
HARRISON, T. E., D.S.O., T.D. Lieut.-Col., Hertfordshire 1881
Yeo. (T.F. Res.) and Gen. Staff. *m.*
✠HARROWING, J. S. Capt., R.A.S.C. and R. Warwickshire 1907
Regt. *M.C. Chevalier, Legion of Honour (France)*
Killed in action at Bullecourt 4 *May* 1917
HART, R. J. D'A. Pte., H.A.C.; Lieut., R.G.A. 1913
HARTINGTON, Marquis of. Hon. Colonel, Sherwood 1913
Foresters (Notts. and Derby Regt.); Capt., Derby-
shire Yeo. *M.B.E. M. m. Chevalier, Legion of
Honour (France)*
HARTLEY, C. R. Capt., D. of Lancaster's Own Yeo. *M.* 1905
✠HARTLEY, W. E. Instructor, R.N. 1896
Accidentally killed on H.M.S. Vanguard 9 *July* 1917
HARVEY, Rev. C. Pte., R.A.M.C.; C.F. 4th Class, 1903
R.A.C.D. (W.)
HARVEY, Rev. E. J. W. C.F. 4th Class, R.A.C.D. 1908
✠HARVEY, D. L. 2nd Lieut., 9th Lancers 1911
Killed in action 2 *Nov.* 1914
✠HARVEY, F. L. Lieut., 9th Lancers 1909
Killed in action 30 *Oct.* 1914
HARVEY, G. R. M. Pte., R. Fusiliers (Sportsman's Bn.) 1890
and Middlesex Regt.

HARVEY, J. E. Capt., Irish Gds.   1912
HARVEY, O. C. Capt., Norfolk Regt. and Gen. List (In-   1912
   telligence). *M.*
✠HASKINS, F. W. Pte., Cheshire Regt.   1908
   Died July 1916
✠HASLAM, W. K. S. Capt., R.F.A.(T.F.)   1911
   Killed in action 27 *April* 1917
HASTINGS, W. H. Surgeon Lieut.-Cdr., R.N.   1897
HATHORN, K. H. Lieut., 8th S. African Horse   1897
HAUSBURG, E. F. Major, Suffolk Regt.; G.S.O. 3, War   1896
   Office. *M. m.*
HAVELOCK-ALLAN, Sir H. S. M., Bart. Major, Lancs.   1891
   Fus. and Gen. List. (W.)
HAWKER, C. A. S. Capt., Somerset L.I. (W 2.)   1913
HAWKES, C. P. Major, Northumberland Fus.   1894
HAWKINS, H. D. Major, R.G.A. (W.) *D.S.O. M* 2.   1901
HAWKINS, H. H. B. Capt., R.G.A. *M.*   1895
HAZLEHURST, C. A. C. Capt., Westmorland and Cum-   1906
   berland Yeo.; attd. Border Regt. and Durham L.I.
   (W.)
HAZLERIGG, Sir A. G., Bart. Capt., Spec. List; Hon.   1898
   Capt. (Ad.), R.A.F.
HEAD, H. Capt., R.A.M.C. (2nd London Gen. Hospital,   1880
   T.F.)
HEADLAM, T. A. Lieut.-Col., E. Yorks. Regt.; attd. Welsh 1894
   Regt.(T.F.) *M.*
HEALD, W. H. A. Lieut., R. Fusiliers; empld. War Office   1912
HEALE,. R J. W Major, Indian Army, empld. Political   1896
   Dept. *O.B.E. M.*
HEAP, J. M. Capt. (A.), R.A.F.   1907
✠HEAPE, B. R. Capt., R.F.A.   1911
   Killed in action 16 *May* 1917
HEARN, Rev. E. H. C.F. 4th Class, R.A.C.D.   1896
HEATH, J. R. Capt., R.A.M.C.   1905
HEATH, L. C. Capt., Surrey Yeo.   1912
HEATH, O. Capt., R.A.M.C.   1896
HEATHCOTE, E. H. Major, Sherwood Foresters (Notts.   1900
   and Derby Regt., T.F.)
HEATHCOTE-DRUMMOND-WILLOUGHBY, Hon. C. S. Major,   1888
   Scots Gds. (R. of O.); Colonel, T.F.; Brig.-Gen.
   C.B. C.M.G. M 5.
HEATON, D. R. Capt., The Queen's (R.W. Surrey Regt.);   1912
   Staff Capt. (W 2.) *D.S.O. M.*
HEATON, J. B. Lieut., King's Royal Rifle Corps. (W 2.) 1914

HEATON-ARMSTRONG, W. D. F. Major, Lancs. Fus. and 1904
Labour Corps. *M.*
HEATON-ELLIS, C. H. B. Major, Bedfordshire Regt.; 1882
Lieut.-Col., Spec. List. *C.B.E.*
✠HEBBLETHWAITE, C. J. Lieut., Nigeria Regt., W. African 1903
Frontier Force
Killed in action near the Nigerian frontier 7 April 1915
HEDGES, K. M. F. Capt., R.A.S.C.; Major, D.A.D. 1908
Transport. *D.S.O. M* 3.
HEDLEY, O. W. E. Lieut., R.E. (Tyne Electrical Engin- 1902
eers, T.F.)
✠HEDLEY, W. A. C. Lieut., The Buffs (E. Kent Regt.) [1914]
M.
Died 19 *July* 1918 *of wounds received in action*
HEINEMANN, A. B. Lieut., R.F.A.(T.F.) 1889
HELLABY, F. A. Lieut., N. Zealand Force; Major, [1914]
M.G.C. *M.C. M.*
HELLYER, F. E. Capt., Hampshire Regt.; S.O. 3 and 1907
Major (Ad.), R.A.F. (W 2.) *O.B.E. M.*
✠HELM, H. P. D. Capt., Border Regt.; Capt. (O. and Ad.), 1912
R.A.F. *M.*
Died 6 *Nov.* 1918
HELME, J. Lieut., R.A.O.C. 1902
HELME, J. M. Capt., King's Own (R. Lancaster Regt.) 1907
(W.)
HELME, R. E. Capt., R.F.A.; empld. War Office 1910
HELME, R. M., V.D. Hon. Lieut.-Col., R. Sussex Regt. 1881
(T.F. Res.)
HELME, T. W. Lieut., R.A.O.C. 1899
HELPS, Rev. A. L. C.F. 4th Class, R.A.C.D. (W.) *M* 2. 1890
HENDERSON, A. I. Capt., Highland L.I.(T.F.) (W.) 1912
✠HENDERSON, A. S. Capt., London Regt. (R. Fus.) 1905
Died 25 *April* 1915 *of wounds received in action*
HENDERSON, J. K. 2nd Lieut. (Ad.), R.A.F. 1902
HENEAGE, Hon. G. E. Lieut.-Col., Lincolnshire Regt. 1885
(R. of O.); empld. Ministry of National Service.
O.B.E.
✠HENN, E. H. L. 2nd Lieut., Rifle Brigade; attd. King's 1910
Royal Rifle Corps
Killed in action 25 *Sept.* 1915
✠HENRI, F. Capt., Northumberland Fus. (W.) 1912
Killed in action 15 *June* 1918
HENRY, C. J. Capt., Leicestershire Yeo. *M.* [1914]
HENRY, D. C. Capt., R.E. (Signals). (W.) *M.C.* 1912

HENRY, S. A. Hon. Capt., R.A.M.C. (W.) *Chevalier,* 1898
  Ordre de la Couronne (Belgium)
HEPBURNE-SCOTT, Hon. C. F. Lieut., Scottish Horse 1902
HEPBURNE-SCOTT, Hon. W. G. *See* POLWARTH, Lord
HEPBURNE-SCOTT, Hon. W. T. Capt., Lothian and Border 1909
  Horse
HERBERT, A. G. Lieut., The Buffs (E. Kent Regt.) 1897
HERBERT, E. Capt., The Queen's (R.W. Surrey Regt., 1913
  T.F.) *M.C. M.*
HERBERT, E. A. F. W., T.D. Major, Yorkshire Hussars 1889
HERBERT-SMITH, G. M. Lieut., R. Welsh Fus.; Major, 1910
  M.G.C.; empld. British Military Mission. *m.*
HERCUS, E. O. Lieut., R.N.V.R. 1914
✠HERDMAN, G. A. 2nd Lieut., King's (Liverpool Regt.) 1914
  Killed in action 1 *July* 1916
✠HERMAN, G. A. Lieut., Cambridgeshire Regt. 1911
  Killed in action near Givenchy 20 *July* 1916
HERON-MAXWELL, Sir I. W., Bart. Capt., Spec. List, 1890
  empld. British Mission to Russia
✠HERRIES, A. D. Y. Capt., King's Own Scottish Borderers 1911
  Killed in action on the Somme 23 *July* 1916
HERVEY, D. E. F. C. 2nd Lieut., Seaforth Hdrs. 1914
HERVEY, E. S. Lieut., Surrey Yeo.; Capt., D.A.P.M. *m.* 1898
HERZOG, F. J. Major, R.F.A. *M.C.* 1908
HESELTINE, N. E. Lieut., Essex Regt.(T.F.) 1904
HESKETH, W. Capt., D. of Lancaster's Own Yeo.; attd. 1898
  King's Own (R. Lancaster Regt.)
✠HESLOP, G. H. Capt., Middlesex Regt. (W.) [1914]
  Killed in action 1 *July* 1916
✠HESS, H. Pte., R. Fusiliers (P. S. Bn.); 2nd Lieut., [1914]
  Middlesex Regt. *M.*
  Died 28 *Oct.* 1916 *of wounds received in action*
HETHERINGTON, A. L. 2nd Lieut., Spec. List, empld. 1900
  War Office
HETHERINGTON, R. G. Lieut., R.E. (Inspection Staff). 1894
  O.B.E. m.
HETHERINGTON, T. R. Lieut., R.F.A.(T.F.) *M.C.* [1914]
✠HETHERINGTON, T. W. Lieut., Durham L.I. 1911
  Killed in action 17 *July* 1916
HETT, H. A. Capt., R.A.S.C. 1901
HEWLETT, J. H. Instructor Cdr., R.N. 1894
✠HEXT, T. M. 2nd Lieut., King's Royal Rifle Corps 1915
  Killed in action 29 *April* 1917
HEYCOCK, J. H. Major, Labour Corps 1880

✠Heywood, A. G. P. Major, Manchester Regt.; G.S.O. 3. 1904
(W.)
*Died 12 Sept. 1918 of wounds received in action 28
Aug. 1918*
✠Heywood, B. C. P., t.d. Colonel, Manchester Regt. 1882
(T.F. Res.)
Died 28 Oct. 1914
Heywood, C. C. Lieut.-Col., Manchester Regt.(T.F. 1883
Res.); Major, R.A.M.C. *m.*
Heywood, Sir G. P., Bart. Lieut.-Col., Staffordshire Yeo. 1897
(W.) *D.S.O. T.D. M* 2.
Heyworth, G. A. F. Capt., R.A.M.C. 1900
✠Heyworth, H. P. L. Capt. and Adjt., N. Staffs. Regt. 1896
Killed in action in Gallipoli 6 Aug. 1915
Hickman, C. E. Major, R.F.A.(T.F.) (W.) *M.* 1909
✠Hicks, B. P. Lieut., R. Berkshire Regt. 1911
Killed in action 25 Sept. 1915
Hicks, E. P. Surgeon Prob., R.N.V.R.; Capt. (A.), R.A.F. 1910
M 2.
Hicks, R. S. Hon. Capt., Suffolk Yeo.(T.F. Res.) 1890
Hicks, W. F. Pte., R.A.O.C.; Lce.-Corpl., Wiltshire Regt. 1914
Higham, C. S. S. Capt., Manchester Regt. 1909
✠Hilary, H. J. 2nd Lieut., R.F.A. 1897
Died 3 June 1917 of wounds received in action
Hill, A. G. E. Capt., Cameron Hdrs.(T.F.) (W.) 1912
Hill, A. V. Capt., Cambridgeshire Regt.; empld. 1905
Ministry of Munitions. *O.B.E. Brevet Major. m* 2.
✠Hill, C. E. C. Lieut. and Adjt., Highland L.I. *M.* 1913
Killed in action in Mesopotamia 17 April 1916
Hill, C. L. Capt., Sherwood Foresters (Notts. and [1914]
Derby Regt., T.F.) *M.*
Hill, H. O. Engineer Lieut.-Cdr., R.N. 1906
Hill, R. G. Lieut., R.F.A.(T.F.) 1910
Hill, T. A. M. Capt. and Adjt., R.E. (Signals). *M. m.* 1908
Hill, W. J. M. Major, Scots Gds. (R. of O.) and Loyal 1895
N. Lancs. Regt.; Lieut.-Col., London Regt. (Hackney
Bn.) *D.S.O. M* 2. *French Croix de Guerre*
Hilleary, E. L. Major, Lovat's Scouts. *O.B.E. M* 2. 1890
*m. Order of the White Eagle, 4th Class, with swords
(Serbia). Greek Medal for Military Merit, 3rd Class*
✠Hills, W. F. W. Lieut., R.F.A. and R.F.C. 1912
Killed in action 6 March 1917
✠Hilton, H. D. 2nd Lieut., Middlesex Regt. 1902
Killed in action 19 Dec. 1914

✠HILTON, M. V. Colonel, E. Lancs. Regt. 1875
  Killed in action 20 *Oct.* 1915
HINDLIP, Lord. Capt., Spec. List. *O.B.E.* *M* 2. 1895
HINGSTON, A. A. Major, R.A.M.C.(T.F.) 1890
HIPPISLEY, E. T. Sergt., R.E.; Lieut., R.G.A.; Capt., 1912
  R.E. (Field Survey Coy.)
HIRST, G. S. Lieut., R.A.S.C.(T.F.) 1906
HIRST, J. Hon. Major and Q.M., I.M.S. *m.* 1903
HISSEY, J. B. R.N.A.S. (Anti-Aircraft) 1903
HOARE, Rev. A. R. C.F. 4th Class, R.A.C.D. *M.* 1890
HOARE, B. S. Lieut., Grenadier Gds. 1910
HOARE, E. G. Capt., King's Own (Yorkshire L.I.); 1898
  Lieut.-Col., King's Own (R. Lancaster Regt.)
  D.S.O. M 2.
HOARE, E. R. D. Lieut., Grenadier Gds. (W.) 1912
HOARE, F. R. G. Major, R.A.O.C.; Lieut.-Col. (T.), 1898
  R.A.F. *C.B.E. M. m.*
HOARE, G. DE M. G. Capt. and Adjt., London Regt. 1889
  (Post Office Rifles). *T.D. m.*
HOARE, H. Hon. Major, Suffolk Yeo.(T.F. Res.) *m.* 1884
✠HOARE, H. C. A. Capt., Dorset Yeo. (W.) 1907
  Died 19 *Dec.* 1917 *of wounds received in action Nov.*
  1917
HOARE, J. E. A. Capt. (S.), R.A.F. *D.S.C.* [1914]
HOARE, R. B. Capt., Northumberland Yeo. 1889
HOARE, W. R. Capt., Hampshire Regt.(T.F.) and R.F.C. 1887
HOBHOUSE, A. L. Capt., Spec. List 1904
HOBSON, A. C. 2nd Lieut., R. Fusiliers 1891
HODGE, H. S. VERE. Capt., Tonbridge School O.T.C. 1900
  Brevet Major. m 2.
HODGES, Rev. E. C. C.F. 4th Class, R.A.C.D. 1903
HODGES, W. V. A. Lieut., R.G.A. *M.C.* 1915
HODGSON, B. T., V.D. Lieut.-Col., R. Sussex Regt.(T.F.) 1882
  C.M.G. m 2.
✠HODGSON, C. A. G. Capt., R. North Devon Yeo. 1902
  Died 20 *March* 1918 *of pneumonia following malaria*
  contracted on active service
HODGSON, F. W. K. Capt., Spec. List 1896
✠HODGSON, G. W. H. Lieut., Border Regt. 1907
  Died 6 *Nov.* 1914 *of wounds received in action* 2 *Nov.*
  1914
HODGSON, H. E. A. Lieut., The Queen's (R.W. Surrey 1904
  Regt.); empld. O.C.B.; Capt., Norfolk Regt.

HODSON, E. A. Capt., Rifle Brigade; Major, M.G.C.; 1912
empld. British Military Mission. *D.S.O. M* 2. *m.*

HOFFMANN, G. S. Capt., R.A.M.C. (Sanitary Service, 1894
T.F.)

HOLDGATE, W.W. Lieut., Sutton Valence School O.T.C. 1891
m.

HOLDSWORTH, G. L. Bt. Colonel, 7th Hussars (R. of O.); 1882
Brig.-Gen., Director of Remounts. *C.B. C.M.G.
m* 3. *Order of the White Eagle, 3rd Class (Serbia)*

HOLLAND-HIBBERT, T. 2nd Lieut., Hertfordshire Yeo.; 1907
Lieut., 2nd Dragoons (R. Scots Greys)

HOLLAND-HIBBERT, W. Capt., Hertfordshire Yeo.; A.D.C. 1914

HOLLOND, E. R. Capt., R.A.S.C. 1895

HOLLOND, G. E. Lieut., Suffolk Regt.; A.D.C. *M.* 1914

HOLLOND, H. A. Lieut., R.G.A.; Major, D.A.A.G. 1903
D.S.O. O.B.E. M 3.

HOLLOND, S. E. Colonel, Rifle Brigade; Brig.-Gen. 1892
*C.B. C.M.G. D.S.O. Brevet Colonel. Brevet
Lieut.-Colonel. M* 7. *Chevalier, Legion of Honour
(France)*

HOLMAN, A. McA. Lieut., 6th Dragoon Gds. (Carabin- 1908
iers). (W.)

✠HOLMAN, D. Lieut., Middlesex Regt.; attd. The Queen's [1914]
(R. W. Surrey Regt.)
Killed in action 8 *Aug.* 1918

HOLROYDE, D. Capt., R.A.M.C. 1895

HOMIAKOFF, A. N. Russian Army 1913

HONY, H. C. Capt., Spec. List (Interpreter). *M.B.E.* 1907
M.

HOPE, J. H. 2nd Lieut., R.E. 1910

✠HOPGOOD, J. L. Pte., Middlesex Regt. (P. S. Bn.); 2nd [1914]
Lieut., The Queen's (R.W. Surrey Regt.)
Died 17 *Aug.* 1916 *of wounds received in action* 13 *Aug.*
1916

✠HOPKINSON, B., F.R.S. Major, Unattd. List, T.F.; Colonel, 1892
D.A.D., Air Ministry. *C.M.G. m* 2.
Killed in flying accident 26 *Aug.* 1918

✠HOPKINSON, E. H. Lieut., Cambridgeshire Regt. *M.C.* 1913
M 2.
Died in German hands 2 *June* 1915 *of wounds received
in action*

✠HOPKINSON, R. C. Lieut., R.E. (Signals). *M.* 1909
Died 9 *Feb.* 1917 *of wounds received in action* 24 *Nov.*
1915

✠Hopley, G. W. V. 2nd Lieut., Grenadier Gds. 1910
Died 12 *May* 1915 *of wounds received in action Feb.*
1915
Horne, M. Capt., R.A.M.C. (2nd London Gen. Hos- 1889
pital, T.F.)
✠Hornsby, R. L. W. 2nd Lieut., Lincolnshire Regt. 1911
Killed in action 9 *Oct.* 1915
Hornung, G. Capt., R.F.A. (W.) 1908
✠Hornung, J. P. 2nd Lieut., R.F.A. (W.) *M.C.* 1913
Died 20 *Feb.* 1916 *of wounds received in action*
Horsfield, R. B. Capt., Worcestershire Regt.; D.A.A. 1905
and Q.M.G. (W.) *M.*
Horton, C. E. Sub-Lieut., R.N.V.R. 1915
Horton, Le G. G. W. Capt. and Adjt., King's Royal 1912
Rifle Corps; Major, R.A.F.
Hoskin, T. J. H. Capt., R.A.M.C. *M.* 1907
Houghton, R. L. Lieut., R.F.A.; empld. Ministry of 1911
Labour
Hoult, J. M. Major, R.F.A. 1908
Houstoun-Boswall, T. R. Capt., R. Scots 1900
How, Rev. J. C. H. C.F. 4th Class, R.A.C.D. *1907
Howard, Hon. B. E. Capt., Lovat's Scouts 1903
Howard, B. H. E. Lieut., Manchester Regt.; Capt. (A.), 1900
R.A.F. *M.C.*
Howard, C. F. Pte., London Regt. (Artists Rifles) 1910
Howard, Hon. D. S. P. Capt., 3rd Hussars. *Belgian* 1910
Croix de Guerre
Howard, Hon. G., M.P. Capt., R.N.V.R. (R.N.D.) *M.* 1895
Howard, G. W. Capt. and Adjt., King's Royal Rifle 1911
Corps. *M.C.*
Howard, H. S. Lieut., R. Warwickshire Regt.(T.F. Res.) 1899
✠Howard, J. B. Capt., R. Welsh Fus.(T.F.) (W.) [1914]
Died 6 *Sept.* 1918 *of wounds received in action*
Howard, J. P. 2nd Lieut., Hampshire Regt. 1907
Howard, Hon. M. F. S. Lieut., 18th Hussars. *M.* 1897
Howard, N. M. C. Capt., R.F.A. (W.) *M.C. M.* 1908
Howard, Rev. R. W. C.F. 4th Class, R.A.C.D. 1906
Howard, W. S. Pte., Army Pay Corps 1906
Howard-McLean, J. R. Hon. Colonel, King's (Shrop- 1879
shire L.I., T.F. Res.) and Gen. Staff. *m.*
✠Howard Smith, G. Lieut., S. Staffs. Regt.(T.F.) *M.C.* 1899
M.
Killed in action 29 *March* 1916
Howden, P. F. 2nd Lieut., R.F.A.(T.F. Res.) 1906

HOWICK, Viscount. *See* GREY, Earl
HOWITT, F. D. Lieut., R.A.S.C.; Hon. Lieut., R.A.F. 1913
(W.)
✠HOWKINS, G. A. 2nd Lieut., Northumberland Fus. 1913
Killed in action 25–27 Sept. 1915
HOWORTH, H. Major, Sherwood Foresters (Notts. and 1893
Derby Regt.); R.T.O.
HOWSON, Rev. J. F. C.F. 3rd Class, R.A.C.D. *m.* 1875
HOWSON, R. S. Sergt., 107th Infy. Bn., United States 1901
Army
HOYLAND, C. E. Capt., Gen. List (T.F. Res.) 1888
HOYLE, L. R. 2nd Lieut., E. Lancs. Regt.(T.F.); Lieut., [1914]
R.G.A.
✠HUBBACK, F. W. 2nd Lieut., London Regt. (Rifles) 1903
Died 12 *Feb.* 1917 *of wounds received in action*
HUBBARD, L. E. Lieut., R.A.S.C. 1900
HUBBARD, M. E. Cadet, R.F.A. 1918
HUBBARD, P. W. Capt., E. Surrey Regt. (W 3.) 1911
HUBBUCK, G. M. Capt., Hampshire Regt. *M* 3. 1909
✠HUDSON, A. C. Major, R. Fusiliers 1895
Died 2 *Oct.* 1916 *of wounds received in action*
HUDSON, Rev. E. C. C.F. 4th Class, R.A.C.D. 1902
HUDSON, F. A. 2nd Lieut., R.E.(T.F.) 1908
✠HUDSON, R. P. M. Capt., D. of Wellington's (W. Riding 1910
Regt.)
Died 25 *March* 1920 *from the effect of wounds received
in action*
HUGGINS, H. W. Major, R.H.A. (W.) *D.S.O. M.C.* 1910
Brevet Major. M 6.
HUGHES, A. W. Lieut., R.F.A.; Lieut. (T.), R.A.F. (W.) 1913
HUGHES, G. E. Lieut., E. Surrey Regt.(T.F.); empld. 1903
Inland Water Transport
HUGHES, G. R. Lieut., Dorset Regt.; Capt., Gen. List, 1906
empld. War Office
✠HUGHES, N. A. Pte., R. Fusiliers (P. S. Bn.); Capt., Welsh 1907
Regt.
Killed in action 18 *Sept.* 1918
HUGHES, R. Major, Berkshire Yeo. (T.F. Res.) 1885
HUGHES, R. J. Capt., R. Warwickshire Regt.(T.F.) 1901
HUGHES, T. G. Lieut., Gen. Staff (Intelligence) 1905
✠HUGHES, T. McK. Pte., London Regt. (Artists Rifles); 1902
Lieut., King's Royal Rifle Corps and Gen. Staff (In-
telligence), attd. R.F.C. *M.*
Killed in action near Polderhoek 5 *Feb.* 1918

✠HUGHES-GIBB, H. F. Lieut., R.F.A.   1910
  Killed in action 18 *April* 1917
HULBERT, H. L. P. Capt., R.A.M.C.   1891
HULBERT, J. G. Lieut.-Col., I.M.S.   1885
HULL, Sir C. P. A. Colonel, Middlesex Regt.; Major-   1883
  Gen. *K.C.B.* *C.B.* *Brevet Colonel.* *M* 8. *Order
  of St Vladimir, 4th Class, with swords (Russia).
  French Croix de Guerre*
HULTON, A. H. Capt., R.F.A.(T.F.); Capt.(Ad.), R.A.F.   1892
✠HULTON-SAMS, Rev. F. E. B. Lce.-Corpl., Bedfordshire   1900
  Regt.; Lieut., D. of Cornwall's L.I.
  Killed in action at Hooge 30 *July* 1915
HUMPHERY, H. M. Major, Hampshire Regt. (W.)   1894
HUMPHREYS, W. A. Lieut., 2nd Dragoon Gds. (Queen's   1905
  Bays)
HUMPHREYS-OWEN, A. E. O. Major, R. Welsh Fus.; attd.   1898
  Dorset Regt. (W.)
HUMPHRY, A. M. Major, R.A.M.C. *m.*   1907
HUMPHRY, L. Lieut.-Col., R.A.M.C.(T.F.)   1873
HUNT, C. A. 2nd Lieut., Labour Corps; attd. R. Sussex 1895
  Regt.
HUNT, E. R. Lieut.-Col., R.A.M.C. *M.*   1891
HUNTER, W. E. Lieut., R.A.S.C. and R.F.A. (P.)   1913
HUNTINGTON, L. W. Lieut., R.N.V.R. (W.)   1903
✠HUNTSMAN, B. C. Capt., Sherwood Foresters (Notts.   [1914]
  and Derby Regt., T.F.)
  Killed in action 7 *April* 1917
HURFORD, C. C. Capt., R.E.   1896
HURLE, J. C. Capt., W. Somerset Yeo.   1879
HURRELL, J. N. Lieut., Devon Regt.; attd. Worcester-   1902
  shire Regt. and T.M.B. (P.)
HUTCHINSON, F. A. J. Capt., R.A.M.C.(T.F.)   1888
HUTCHINSON, L. T. R. Lieut.-Col., I.M.S.   1889
HUXLEY, G. A. Capt., R.E.   1906
HUXLEY, M. H. 2nd Lieut., Grenadier Gds.   1916

INGLEBY, R. A. O. Hon. Capt., Army Pay Corps   1897
INGRAM, H. F. 2nd Lieut., R.G.A.   1899
INGRAM, R. S. S. Capt. (A.), R.A.F. (P.)   [1914]
✠INGRAM, T. L. Capt., R.A.M.C. *D.S.O.* *M.C.* *M* 2. 1894
  Killed in action 16 *Sept.* 1916
INMAN, R. T. Paymaster Sub-Lieut., R.N.V.R.   1902
INNES, A. C. W. Capt., Irish Gds. and R. Irish Fus.   1906
  (W.) *M.C.* *M.*

INSOLE, A. V. Lieut., R.F.A. (W.) 1913
INSOLE, E. R. Lieut., Gen. List (T.F. Res.) *m.* 1908
✠INSOLE, G. C. L. Capt., Welsh Gds. (W.) *M.C.* 1907
 Killed in action 12 April 1918
✠IPSWICH, Viscount. Lieut., Coldstream Gds.; Lieut. (A.), 1903
 R.A.F.
 Killed in flying accident 23 April 1918
IRELAND, J. F. Capt., R.F.A. (W.) *M.C. M.* 1907
IRWIN, C. Major, Cheshire Regt.(T.F.) *M.C. M 2.* 1907

✠JACKSON, B. R. Capt., Coldstream Gds. 1906
 Killed in action 15 Sept. 1916
✠JACKSON, E. P. 2nd Lieut., R. Warwickshire Regt.; attd. 1912
 S. Wales Borderers
 Killed in action 9 May 1915
JACKSON, Hon. F. S., M.P. Major, R.F.A.(T.F.); Lieut.- 1889
 Col., W. Yorks. Regt.(T.F. Res.); empld. Ministry
 of Munitions
JACKSON, G. C. Lieut., Warwickshire Yeo. and 2nd Life 1912
 Gds.; Capt., Gds. M.G. Regt.
JACKSON, H. A. Capt. and Adjt., King's Royal Rifle 1904
 Corps. (W 2.) (P.)
JACKSON, H. C. Lieut.-Col., Bedfordshire Regt.; Major- 1897
 Gen. (W 2.) *C.B. C.M.G. D.S.O. Brevet*
 Colonel. Brevet Lieut.-Colonel. M 8. Officer, Legion
 of Honour (France)
JACKSON, J. 2nd Lieut., Rifle Brigade 1909
JACKSON, R. W. *See* WARD-JACKSON, R.
JACKSON, W. E. Pte., Northumberland Fus., Yorkshire 1900
 Regt., and York and Lancaster Regt.
JAMES, A. I. Capt., R.F.A. (W.) *M.C. French Croix* 1909
 de Guerre
JAMES, A. L. Capt., R.E. *M.C.* 1908
JAMES, A. W. H. Lieut., 3rd Hussars; Major (A.), R.A.F.; 1912
 Lieut.-Col., Dep. Inspector of Training. *M.C. M.*
JAMES, Rev. S. R., V.D. C.F. 1st Class, R.A.C.D.(T.F.) 1874
 C.B.E. m.
JAMES, T. C. Lieut., Aberystwith Univ. College O.T.C. 1899
JAMESON, G. J. Capt., S. Irish Horse 1907
JAMIESON,E.A.O.A. Lieut.-Col.(K.B.),R.A.F. *A.F.C.* 1899
 M 2.
JANASZ, G. K. A. *See* DE JANASZ, G. K. A.
JÁRMAY, I. B. Capt., Cheshire Yeo.; A.D.C. *M.* 1903
JARVIS, L. K. Major, London Yeo.(T.F. Res.) *T.D.* 1876

416   TRINITY COLLEGE

JAY, C. D.   Capt., R. Sussex Regt.; Major, M.G.C.   1908
    D.S.O. M 3.
✠JEAKES, J. W. Lieut., R. Berkshire Regt. (W.)   1899
    Died 12 Oct. 1917 of wounds received in action
JEFFREYS, H. G. G. Capt., R.A.M.C.   1904
JEFFREYS, J. G.   Capt., Welsh Regt. and Spec. List   1901
    (A.M.L.O.)
JEFFREYS, W. M. Capt., R.A.M.C.   1897
JEFFRIES, W. F. C. Capt., R. Dublin Fus.; Major, Spec.   1909
    List (Chief Instructor, Reinforcement Camp). (W 2.)
    D.S.O. M 2.
JEMMETT, F. R.   Capt., R.E. (Fortress, T.F.)   1904
✠JENKIN, L. F. 2nd Lieut., Loyal N. Lancs. Regt.; Capt., [1914]
    R.F.C. (W.) *M.C. and Bar*
    Killed in action 11 Sept. 1917
JENKYN, Rev. C. W. O.   C.F. 3rd Class, R.A.C.D.   1892
    M.C. M.
JEWELL, B. S.   Capt., Spec. List (Graves Registration   1899
    Commission). *M.*
JEWELL, C. J. S. Capt., R.F.A.(T.F.)   1910
✠JOHN, H. G.   2nd Lieut., York and Lancaster Regt.;   1914
    attd. Northumberland Fus.(T.F.)
    *Wounded and missing, presumed killed in action, at
    Hooge 16 June 1915*
JOHNSON, Rev. A. D. C.F. 4th Class, R.A.C.D. M.C.   1903
JOHNSON, E. S. *See* DARMADY, E. S.
✠JOHNSON, G. A. M. T.   2nd Lieut., London Regt. (St [1914]
    Pancras Bn.)
    Killed in action 21 May 1917
JOHNSON, P. R. Major, Devon Regt.(T.F.); empld. War   1898
    Office. (W.) *Brevet Major. m.*
✠JOHNSON, R. T. Capt., N. Staffs. Regt.(T.F.)   1898
    Killed in action near Hulluch 13 Oct. 1915
✠JOHNSON, W. M. Capt., Manchester Regt.   1900
    Killed in action at Montauban 2 July 1916
JOHNSON-FERGUSON, E. A. J.   Major, Lanarkshire Yeo.   1893
    and M.G.C. (W.) T.D. M.
JOHNSTON, Rev. H. L. C.F. 4th Class, R.A.C.D.   1893
JOHNSTONE, G. H. Capt., R. 1st Devon Yeo. and Devon   1900
    Regt. (T.F.); Staff Capt. *M.*
JOHNSTONE, J. J. Capt. and Adjt., D. of Cornwall's L.I.   1908
    (W.)
JOICEY, E.   Hon. Colonel, Northumberland Fus. (T.F.   1884
    Res.) *m.*

✠JOICEY, Hon. S. J. D.   Capt. and Adjt., Northumberland   1903
Fus.
Killed in action 20 *March* 1916
JOLLEY, L. B. W.   Capt. (T.), R.A.F. (Aircraft Produc-   1904
tion Dept.)
JOLLY, H. L. P.   Lieut., R.E.   1906
JOLOWICZ, H. F.   Lieut., Bedfordshire Regt. and Gen.   1909
List, empld. War Office
JONES, Rev. BERTRAM.   C.F. 4th Class, R.A.C.D.   1901
✠JONES, C. H.   Capt., R. Welsh Fus. (W 2.)   1906
Killed in action 18 *Sept.* 1918
JONES, C. W.   Capt., R. Welsh Fus.; G.S.O. 2, War Office.   1899
C.B.
✠JONES, E. D.   2nd Lieut., R. Fusiliers; Lieut. (A.), R.A.F.   1911
Killed in action 2 *April* 1918
✠JONES, F. J. J. R.   Trooper, 27th Regt. of Dragoons, French   1913
Army
Died 23 *Feb.* 1915 *of wounds received in action*
JONES, Ven. H. G.   C.F. 4th Class, R.A.C.D.   1899
JONES, Rev. I. K.   C.F. 4th Class, R.A.C.D.   1909
JONES, O. T.   Hon. Lieut., Spec. List   1900
JONES, T. B.   Lieut., R. Fusiliers. (W.) (P.)   1907
JONES, W. D.   Lieut.-Col., Spec. List   1873
JONES, W. P. M.   Capt., D. of Lancaster's Own Yeo.   1901
JOSEPH, H. M.   Capt., R.A.M.C. (W.) *M.C.*   1897
JOWETT, A. C.   Capt. (A.), R.A.F.   1911
✠JOWETT, E. C.   Lieut., Northumberland Fus.; Lieut.   [1914]
(A.), R.F.C.
Died in German hands 9 *July* 1916 *of wounds received
in action* 8 *July* 1916
JOY, N. H.   Capt., E. Yorks. Regt.(T.F.) and Spec. List   1908
(Officer i/c Anti-Gas Schools). (W.)
JULER, F. A.   Capt., R.A.M.C.   1898
JUMP, H.   Capt., 1st Dragoons. (P.)   1901
JUMP, R. L.   Air Mechanic, R.A.F.   1907
JUST, T. H.   Capt., R.A.M.C. *M.*   1905

KARNEY, Rev. A. B.   Chaplain, R.N.; C.F. 4th Class,   1893
R.A.C.D. (P.)
KAYE, G. W. C.   Capt., R.E. (London Electrical En-   1905
gineers, T.F.); Major (T.), R.A.F. (Aircraft Produc-
tion Dept.) *O.B.E. T.D. M. m.*
KEELING, B. F. E.   Lieut.-Col., R.E. (W.) *O.B.E. M.C.*   1898
M 2.

✠KEELING, F. H. C.S.M., D. of Cornwall's L.I. (W.)   1904
  Killed in action 18 *Aug.* 1916
KEELING, O. H. Capt., R.E.(T.F.) (W.) *M. m.*   1904
✠KEEN, A. W. Major (A.), R.A.F. *M.C.*   1913
  Died 2 *Sept.* 1918 *of wounds received in action* 15 *Aug.*
  1918
KEENAN, J. B. Capt. and Adjt., Irish Gds. (W 2.)   1914
✠KELSEY, A. E. Fleet-Surgeon, R.N.; Capt., R.A.M.C.   1883
  Drowned on H.M. hospital ship Glenart Castle 26 *Feb.*
  1918
KEMP-WELCH, H. A. Lieut., Hampshire Regt.(T.F.) and   1906
  M.G.C.
KEMPE, Rev. E. C. C.F. 3rd Class, R.A.C.D.   1899
KEMPSON, E. W. E. Major, R.E. and R.A.S.C. *M.C.*   1899
  M 2.
KENDALL, F. R. N. 2nd Lieut., R.F.A.   1910
KENNEDY, Rev. E. H. C.F. 4th Class, R.A.C.D.   1891
KENNEDY, Lord H. Lieut., Coldstream Gds. (W 2.) [1914]
  M.C. M.
✠KENNEDY, H. T. 2nd Lieut., N. Staffs. Regt.; Lieut.,   1908
  R. Scots Fus.; attd. R.E. (Field Survey Coy.) (W.)
  Killed in action 6 *June* 1917
✠KENNEDY, J. M. S. Lieut., Seaforth Hdrs.   1912
  Killed in action 10 *Aug.* 1915
KENNEDY, M. S. N. Capt., Border Regt.; empld. Infy.   1908
  Base Depôt. (W.) *M.*
KENNEDY, S. D. 2nd Lieut., Spec. List   1900
KENNEDY, W. T. Capt., Rifle Brigade and King's Liver-   1902
  pool Regt.)
KENNEDY-COCHRAN-PATRICK, N. J. Capt., R. Scots Fus.;   1884
  empld. Ministry of National Service. *M.B.E.*
KENNEDY-COCHRAN-PATRICK, W. J. C. Capt., Rifle Bri- [1914]
  gade; Major (A.), R.A.F.; S.O. 2, Air Ministry.
  D.S.O. M.C. and Bar. M.
KENYON, M. N. Lieut., D. of Lancaster's Own Yeo.;   1905
  attd. S. Lancs. Regt.
KERBY, C. C. Capt., R.A.M.C.   1904
KERR, W. H. Lieut., Cheshire Yeo. and 11th Hussars   1913
✠KERRISON, R. O. Lieut.-Col., Res. Regt. of Cavalry; attd.   1891
  Australian F.A.
  Died 18 *Sept.* 1917 *of dysentery contracted on active
  service*
KERSEY, R. H. Capt., R.A.S.C.   1909
KERSHAW, J. 2nd Lieut., R.G.A.   1912

KESWICK, H. Capt., King's Own Scottish Borderers   1889
KESWICK, H. G. 2nd Lieut., 13th Hussars   1906
KIDD, C. B. Lieut., Surrey Yeo. and The Queen's   1898
(R.W. Surrey Regt.)
KIDD, F. S. Capt., R.A.M.C.   1896
KIDD, H. L. Lieut., R.A.S.C. (Camel Corps)   1898
KIDD, R. H. 2nd Lieut., R.E. (Signals)   1915
KILLICK, C. Major, R.A.M.C.(T.F. Res.)   1893
KINAHAN, A. E. Lieut., R.F.A.; Supt., Remount Depôt   1890
KINDERSLEY, Rev. C. E. C.F. 3rd Class, R.A.C.D.(T.F.)   1884
KINDERSLEY, H. R. Major, Dorset Yeo. and Labour Corps   1882
KINDERSLEY-PORCHER, C. P. W. Capt., Coldstream Gds.   1875
(R. of O.), empld. Irish Gds.; Lieut.-Col., King's
Royal Rifle Corps
✠KING, A. M. Major, Rifle Brigade   1888
Killed in action 15 March 1915
KING, B. N. 2nd Lieut., R.A.S.C.(M.T.)   1904
KING, C. Capt., R.A.M.C. *O.B.E.*   1897
KING, C. M. Capt., Coldstream Gds.; empld. Gds. Depôt   1896
KING-WEBSTER, H. C. R. Fusiliers   1897
KINGHAM, W. R. Gnr., H.A.C.   1906
KINLOCH, Sir G., Bart. Lieut., Gen. List (T.F. Res.);   1898
empld. Ministry of National Service
✠KINNAIRD, Hon. D. A. Capt., Scots Gds.   1898
Killed in action 24 Oct. 1914
KINNAIRD, Hon. K. F. Capt., Scottish Horse. *M.*   1899
KIRKE SMITH, A. Lieut., I.A.R.O., attd. 11th Bengal   1896
Lancers and 12th Cavalry
KIRKPATRICK, Rev. A. P. Chaplain, R.N.   1904
KITSON, Hon. R. D. Capt., W. Yorks. Regt.; Brigade   1901
Major. *D.S.O. M.C. M* 2.
KITSON, S. D. Capt., Yorkshire Hussars; Major, A.P.M.   1889
m.
KNEESE, Rev. R. H. W. Capt., King's School, Rochester,   1907
O.T.C.; C.F. 4th Class, R.A.C.D.
✠KNIGHT, J. O. C. 2nd Lieut., The Queen's (R.W.   1916
Surrey Regt.)
Killed in action 30 Nov. 1917
✠KNIGHT, P. C. Pte., H.A.C.; 2nd Lieut., Somerset L.I.   1911
(W.)
Killed in action 1 July 1916
KNIGHT BRUCE, R. E. C. Capt., R. 1st Devon Yeo.;   1909
Major (Ad.), R.A.F.
KNOBEL, W. B. Capt., R.A.M.C.   1893

KNOWLES, A. J.   Major, London Regt. (Queen's West-   1882
minster Rifles)

KNOWLES, D.   Capt. (Airship), R.A.F.   *D.S.C.*   1914

KNOWLES, G. J. F.   Capt., R.G.A.   *M* 2.   *French Croix*   1898
de Guerre.   Greek Military Cross

KNOWLES, Sir L., Bart., C.V.O.   Lieut.-Col., Lancs. Fus.   1875
O.B.E.   T.D.

KNOWLES, R. K.   Capt., Manchester Regt.   *M.*   1908

KNOX, Rev. C. W.   Pte., R.A.M.C. (Sanitary Service,   1884
T.F.)

KNOX, G. G.   Lieut., R.N.V.R. and Spec. List (Intelli-   1906
gence)

KOHAN, C. M.   Capt., R.F.A.(T.F.)   *O.B.E.*   1903

LACE, L. E. C. D.   2nd Lieut., 11th Hussars; A.D.C.   [1914]

LACEY, F. A.   Capt., I.A.R.O., attd. 53rd Silladar Camel   1906
Corps

LACY THOMPSON, T. A.   Lieut., Northumberland Fus.   1913
(W.)   *D.S.O.   M.C.   M* 2.

✠LAFONE, E. W.   Capt., Durham L.I. (W.)   *M.C.   M.* [1914]
French Croix de Guerre
Killed in action 15 *June* 1918

LAIDLAW, F. F.   Capt., R.A.M.C.   1895

LAING, B.   Capt., Sherwood Rangers; empld. Admiralty   1896

LAING, C. M.   Capt., Northumberland Yeo.; A.D.C.   1904
(W 2.)   *M.C.   M* 2.   *Belgian Croix de Guerre*

LAING, J. C.   Lieut., Black Watch; empld. Ministry of [1914]
Munitions

LAMB, C. H.   Major, 44th (W. Australia) Bn., Australian   1906
Infy.   *M.C.*

LAMB, G. J.   Lieut., Cranleigh School O.T.C.   1909

LAMB, R. E.   Capt., R.A.S.C.   *M.*   1898

LAMB, R. P.   Lieut. (K.B.) and Capt. (Ad.), R.A.F.   (W.)   1900

LAMBERT, E. T.   Major, Bombay Vol. Artillery   1897

LAMBERT, H.   Lieut., Bengal Nagpur Railway Bn., Indian   1899
Defence Force

✠LAMBERT, H. M.   Capt., 1st Dragoons   1897
Killed in action near Ypres 13 *May* 1915

LAMBERT, R. E.   Lieut., R.H.A.(T.F.); Asst. Inspector,   1901
Woolwich Arsenal

LAMBERT, ST J. M.   Capt., R.H.A.(T.F.)   *M.*   1903

LANCASTER, S.   Capt., Dorset Regt.; empld. O.C.B.   (W.)   1911

✠LANDALE, D. B.   Lieut., Rifle Brigade.   *M.*   1909
Killed in action 23 *Oct.* 1914

LANDER, T. E. Capt., Highland L.I.; Hon. Capt. (A.), 1913
R.A.F. (W.) (P.) *M.C.*

✠LANG, A. H. 2nd Lieut., Grenadier Gds. 1909
Killed in action at Cuinchy 25–26 Jan. 1915

LANG, B. T. Capt., R.A.M.C. 1899

LANG, Rev. L. H. C.F. 4th Class, R.A.C.D. 1909

LANGLANDS, N. M. S. Instructor Lieut., R.N. 1912

LARMOUR, Rev. A. C. Capt., Wellington College O.T.C. 1905

LA TOUCHE, G. G. D. *See* DIGGES LA TOUCHE, G. G.

LAURENCE, C. Capt., London Yeo. (Rough Riders); attd. 1900
London Regt. (St Pancras Bn.) (W.)

LAURENCE, C. H. Gnr., R.F.A.; attd. Gen. Staff (Intelli- 1899
gence)

LAW, R. A. Lieut., Yorkshire Regt.; empld. War Office. 1911
(W.)

LAWLEY, Sir A., G.C.S.I., G.C.I.E., K.C.M.G. Colonel, Spec. 1879
List. *m* 4. *Chevalier, Order of Leopold (Belgium)*

LAWRENCE, A. C. C. Capt., R.A.M.C.(T.F.) 1901

LAWRENCE, B. L. Lieut., Grenadier Gds. (W.) 1909

✠LAWRENCE, C. H. 2nd Lieut., King's Royal Rifle Corps 1913
Killed in action 13 Oct. 1914

✠LAWRENCE, M. C. Capt., Coldstream Gds. (W.) 1913
*Died 16 Sept. 1916 of wounds received in action 15
Sept. 1916*

✠LAWRENCE, O. J. 2nd Lieut., London Regt. (Post Office 1912
Rifles). *M.*
Killed in action at Festubert 26 May 1915

LAWRENCE, W. H. A. Lieut., Essex Regt.; attd. Rifle 1912
Brigade (T.F.)

LAWRIE, C. V. E., C.B., D.S.O. Hon. Colonel, King's Own 1874
Scottish Borderers (T.F. Res.)

LAWRIE, J. M. 2nd Lieut., Spec. List (Intelligence) 1913

LAWSON, G. Major, Westmorland and Cumberland Yeo. 1899

LAWSON, R. C. Capt., Saskatchewan Regt., Canadian Force 1893

✠LAWSON-JOHNSTON, A. McW. Lieut., Buckinghamshire 1904
Yeo. and Grenadier Gds. *M.C.*
Died 22 Feb. 1917 of wounds received in action

✠LAYMAN, F. H. Major, R. Defence Corps 1876
Died 3 Oct. 1917

LEA WILSON, B. H. C. Major, R.A.M.C.(T.F.); empld. 1904
Egyptian Army

✠LEADER, B. E. Capt., The Queen's (R.W. Surrey Regt.) 1896
Killed in action 12 Oct. 1916

LEADER, E. E. Lieut., R.N.V.R. 1901

LEAF, C. S. Lieut., The Buffs (E. Kent Regt.) and [1914]
M.G.C.
LEAF, E. H. Lieut.-Col., R.E.(T.F.) 1886
LEAF, F. A. Lieut., R.E. (Signals); empld. War Office 1909
LEAF, H. M. Lieut.-Col., R.E. (London Electrical En- 1881
gineers, T.F.) (W.) *D.S.O. M.*
LEAK, E. A. Surgeon Sub-Lieut., R.N.V.R.; Lieut., 1909
R.A.M.C.
LEAK, W. N. Lieut., R.A.M.C. 1909
LEATHAM, C. B. Major, King's Own (Yorkshire L.I.); 1912
attd. London Regt. (W 2.) *M.C. and Bar. M.*
LEATHAM, H. W. Capt., R.A.M.C. 1910
LEATHER, K. J.W. Lieut.-Col., Durham L.I. (W.) *C.B.E.* 1896
✠LE BLANC SMITH, C. R. P.O., R.N.R.; Lieut., Rifle Bri- 1909
gade. (W.)
Killed in action in the Ypres Salient 27 Nov. 1915
LE BLANC SMITH, T. E. Major, R.F.A. (W 2.) *M.C.* 1913
✠LE BLOND, R. C. G. DU P. Capt., Rifle Brigade 1906
Died 16 *May* 1915
LEDWARD, H. D. Capt., R.A.M.C. 1896
LEE, A. N. Major, Sherwood Foresters (Notts. and 1896
Derby Regt., T.F.); Lieut.-Col., G.S.O. 1. *D.S.O.*
O.B.E. T.D. M 3. *Officer, Ordre de la Couronne*
(Belgium). Belgian Croix de Guerre. Order of the
Sacred Treasure, 4th *Class (Japan). Order of the*
Crown of Siam, 3rd *Class. Order of the White Eagle,*
4th *Class, with swords (Czecho-Slovakia)*
LEE, C. B. Major, R.F.A.(T.F.) 1903
LEE, W. E. Major, R.A.M.C. 1894
✠LEEKE, CHARLES. Lieut., Grenadier Gds. 1906
Died 11 *April* 1916 *of wounds received in action*
LEEKE, Rev. CHRISTOPHER. C.F. 4th Class, R.A.C.D. 1901
LEEKE, Rev. E. J. C.F. 4th Class, R.A.C.D. 1903
LEEKE, J. A. Capt., Norfolk Regt. (W.) *M.C.* 1904
LEFROY, E. J. Capt., Wiltshire Regt. and R.E.; empld. 1911
War Office. (W.)
✠LEFROY, F. P. 2nd Lieut., R.E. [1914]
Killed in action 28 *April* 1916
LEGG, Sir G. E. W., M.V.O. Capt., S. Staffs. Regt. (R. of 1887
O.) *K.B.E. Chevalier, Legion of Honour (France)*
LEHMANN, F. H. *See* LAYMAN, F. H.
LEITH, H. G. Colonel, Northumberland Yeo.; Dep. 1898
Controller of Salvage, War Office. *C.B. C.B.E.*
M 2. *Officer, Order of the Crown of Italy*

Le Lacheur, W. J. Lieut., R.N.V.R. 1895
Le Ray, H. G. 2nd Lieut., Worcestershire Regt.; Lieut., 1914
R.F.A. (P.)
Le Roy-Lewis, H., c.b., d.s.o., t.d. Colonel, General 1879
Staff; Military Attaché, Paris. *C.M.G.* *M.* *Com-*
mander, Legion of Honour (France). *French Croix de*
Guerre. *Order of St Stanislas, 1st Class (Russia).*
Order of St Anne, 3rd Class (Russia). *Order of Danilo,*
2nd Class (Montenegro). *Order of the Black Star of*
Benin, 1st Class. *Order of the Crown of Roumania,*
3rd Class. *Order of the White Eagle, 4th Class (Serbia)*
Leslie, A. Lieut., R.F.A.; empld. Ministry of Muni- 1908
tions; Capt., Spec. List (Courts-Martial Officer). (W.)
Leslie-Melville, A. B. Capt. and Adjt., Sherwood 1881
Foresters (Notts. and Derby Regt., T.F.) (W.) *M.*
Lever, D. Instructor Lieut., R.N. 1906
Levett, A. R. 2nd Lieut., King's Royal Rifle Corps and 1914
Suffolk Regt.
Levett, E. C. Capt., R.E. (Fortress, T.F.) 1907
Levi, W. H. Lce.-Corpl., Essex Regt. 1914
✠Levinge, H. G. Lieut.-Col., Norfolk Regt. and Loyal 1883
N. Lancs. Regt. *M.*
Killed in action in Gallipoli 10 Aug. 1915
Levita, C. E. Capt., Spec. List (A.P.M.) *M.* 1886
Levita, H. P. Hon. Lieut.-Col., Spec. List; Draft Con- 1879
ducting Officer; Cmdt., Command Depôt. *m.* *Order*
of St Stanislas, 2nd Class (Russia)
✠Lewin, K. R. Lieut., D. of Cornwall's L.I. 1906
Killed in action 9 March 1916
✠Lewthwaite, C. G. Lieut., R.F.A.(T.F.) (W.) *M.C.* 1903
M.
Killed in action 29 July 1917
Lewthwaite, W. 2nd Lieut., R.F.A. 1901
✠Lias, R. J. M. Pte., Middlesex Regt. (P.S. Bn.); Lieut., 1909
R. Sussex Regt.
Killed in action 23 Feb. 1916
Lichfield, Earl of. Capt., London Regt. (L.R.B.); A.D.C. 1902
M.
Lichtenberg, W. A. Lieut., R.G.A. 1911
Liddell, C. F. J. Lieut., King's Royal Rifle Corps; 1908
Capt., Spec. List (cmdg. T.M.B.) *M.C.* *Chevalier,*
Ordre de la Couronne (Belgium). *Belgian Croix de*
Guerre
Lidderdale, F. J. Capt., R.A.M.C. *M.C.* *M.* 1888

✠LIGHTBODY, W. P. Lieut., Norfolk Regt. 1911
  Killed in action 26 Sept. 1915
LINDEMERE, V. Capt., R.A.S.C. *M.* 1900
LINDLEY, W. M. Capt., R.E. (Signals). *M.C. M. Che-* 1910
  valier, Legion of Honour (France)
LINDSAY, J. H. Lieut.-Col., London Regt. (London 1889
  Scottish). (W.) *D.S.O. M* 2.
LINDSAY, Hon. L. Pte., R. Fusiliers (P.S. Bn.); Capt., 1897
  King's Royal Rifle Corps; empld. O.C.B. and
  Foreign Office. *M.C. Chevalier, Legion of Honour*
  (France)
✠LINGARD, J. R. Lieut., Manchester Regt.; attd. Lancs. 1903
  Fus.
  Killed in action in Gallipoli 21 Aug. 1915
✠LISTER, A. H. Lieut.-Col., R.A.M.C.(T.F.) *C.M.G.* 1883
  M.
  Died 17 July 1916 of tuberculosis
LISTER, A. R. Capt., R.F.A.; Staff Capt. *M.C. M.* 1913
LISTER, Sir W. T. Colonel, A.M.S. *K.C.M.G. C.M.G.* 1886
  M 5. *m.*
LITTLEBOY, C. N. Capt., Durham L.I.(T.F.) and Sher- 1913
  wood Foresters (Notts. and Derby Regt., T.F.) (W 2.)
  M.C. and Bar
LITTLEWOOD, J. E. 2nd Lieut., R.G.A.(T.F.); empld. 1903
  Ministry of Munitions
LLEWELYN-DAVIES, P. Lieut., King's Royal Rifle Corps. [1914]
  M.C.
✠LLEWELYN-DAVIES, R. A. Lieut., R. Fusiliers. *Serbian* 1911
  Distinguished Service Medal
  Killed in action 4 Oct. 1918
✠LLOYD, A. S. Lieut., R.F.A. *M.C.* 1907
  Killed in action 4 Aug. 1916
LLOYD, C. G. Capt., E. Riding of Yorkshire Yeo. *M.* 1905
LLOYD, E. A. Lieut., London Regt. (R. Fus.); Major, 1904
  D.A.D. Docks. (W.) *M.*
LLOYD, E. I. Surgeon Lieut., R.N. 1911
LLOYD, Sir G. A., M.P. Capt., Warwickshire Yeo. and 1898
  Gen. Staff. *G.C.I.E. C.I.E. D.S.O. M* 3. *Order*
  of St Anne, 3rd Class, with swords (Russia)
LLOYD, H. C. Capt., Yorkshire Regt. 1909
LLOYD, H. G. Lieut., D. of Cornwall's L.I. and Gen. 1912
  Staff. (W.) *M.C.*
✠LLOYD, J. F. S. Major, N. Staffs. Regt.(T.F.) 1900
  Killed in action 18 June 1915

LLOYD, L. S. Capt., R.F.A.(T.F.) 1908
LLOYD, R. LL. 2nd Lieut., R.F.A. 1913
LLOYD GREAME, Y. Lieut., R.F.A. 1890
LLOYD-JONES, I. G. Hon. Major, Gen. List (T.F. Res.) 1888
T.D.
LLOYD-WILLIAMS, A. R. C. Lieut., Lancs. Fus. 1899
LOCKER-LAMPSON, G. L. T. 2nd Lieut., Wiltshire Yeo. 1894
(T.F. Res.)
LOCKER-LAMPSON, O. S. Lieut.-Cdr., R.N.V.R. (Arm- 1900
oured Car Section). *C.M.G. D.S.O. Officer, Order
of Leopold (Belgium). Order of St Vladimir, 3rd Class,
with swords (Russia)*
LOCKETT, J. Lieut., Lancs. Hussars; attd. King's (Liver- 1900
pool Regt.)
LOCKETT, V. N. Capt., 17th Lancers; Major, 19th Hussars 1899
LOCKYER, W. J. S. Major (T.), R.A.F. 1887
LODER, J. DE V. Capt., R. Sussex Regt.(T.F.) and Gen. [1914]
Staff (Intelligence). *M.*
LODER, N. W. Lieut., R.A.S.C. 1905
✠LODER, R. E. Lieut., R. Sussex Regt.(T.F.); Staff Capt. 1906
M 2.
Killed in action 29 March 1917
LONG, W. G. 2nd Lieut., Tank Corps 1916
✠LONGBOTTOM, H. 2nd Lieut., S. Lancs. Regt. 1913
Killed in action in Gallipoli 9 *Aug.* 1915
LONGHURST, A. L. Lieut.-Col., 7th Gurkha Rifles, Indian 1891
Army. (W 2.) *Brevet Lieut.-Colonel. M* 4.
LONGHURST, H. B. 2nd Lieut., London Regt. (Rangers) 1909
LONGMAN, H. K. Capt., Gordon Hdrs. (R. of O.); Major, 1900
D.A.Q.M.G. *D.S.O. M.C. M* 3.
LONGMAN, R. G. Capt., Gordon Hdrs.; empld. O.C.B. 1902
(W.) *m.*
✠LONGRIDGE, Rev. A. O. C. C.F. 4th Class, R.A.C.D. 1902
(W.)
Died 12 *Oct.* 1918 *of pneumonia following influenza
and gas-poisoning*
LONGRIDGE, Rev. M. Chaplain, R.N. 1891
LONGSTAFF, C. C. Lieut., Durham L.I. (W.) 1914
✠LONSDALE, A. C. G. Lieut., King's Royal Rifle Corps; 1910
attd. R. Scots Fus.
Killed in action 10 *March* 1915
✠LOVETT, Rev. R. D. Pte., Middlesex Regt. 1890
Killed in action July 1916
LOWE, H. ST A. Capt., Radley College O.T.C. 1894

✠LOWRY CORRY, F. R. H.   Lieut., R.F.A.   1908
  Died 30 *Sept.* 1915 *of wounds received in action* 25 *Sept.*
  1915
  LOWTHER, C. W.   Capt., Westmorland and Cumberland   1905
  Yeo.; Major, A.P.M. (W.) *M.*
  LOYD, E. N. F.   Capt., Warwickshire Yeo.; Lieut., La-   1899
  bour Corps
✠LOYD, L. F. I.   Capt., Lovat's Scouts; Major, Worcester-   1898
  shire Yeo.
  Died 21 *Sept.* 1918 *of pneumonia*
  LOYD, R. A.   Capt., Remount Service   1904
  LOYD, W. H.   Lieut., R.E. and Spec. List (R.T.O.)   1913
✠LUBBOCK, Hon. H. F. P.   Lieut. and Adjt., W. Kent   1906
  Yeo.; Lieut., Grenadier Gds.
  Killed in action 4 *April* 1918
  LUCAS, A. R. F.   Major, R.F.A. (W.) *M.C.* *M.*   1912
  LUCAS, C. E.   Capt., R. Fusiliers; Staff Capt. *m* 2.   1904
  LUCAS, D.   Pte., H.A.C.; Lieut., Spec. List. *m.*   1906
  LUCAS, E. M.   Major, Remount Service   1879
  LUCAS, F. L.   Lieut., Queen's Own (R.W. Kent Regt.)   1913
  and Gen. Staff (Intelligence). (W 2.) *M.*
  LUCAS, G. M. E.   Pte., R. Fusiliers (P. S. Bn.); Capt., R.   1906
  Inniskilling Fus. *M* 2.
  LUCAS, H. A.   Major, R.A.M.C.(T.F.) *M* 2.   1904
✠LUCAS, K.   Capt., R.F.C. (Hampshire Aircraft Parks,   1898
  T.F.)
  Killed in flying accident 5 *Oct.* 1916
  LUCAS, W.G.   Major, R. Fusiliers; attd. R.N.A.S.; Lieut.-   1900
  Col., R.G.A.
  LUCAS, W. L.   Major, R.F.A. (W.)   1885
  LUCKOCK, E. H. M.   Capt., S. Wales Borderers (T.F.);   1890
  empld. Musketry Staff. *m* 2.
  LUCKOCK, R. M.   Lieut.-Col., King's Own (R. Lancaster   1896
  Regt.); G.S.O. 1. *C.M.G.* *D.S.O.* *Brevet Lieut.-
  Colonel.* *M* 8. *Officer, Legion of Honour (France).
  French Croix de Guerre*
  LUMLEY, C. H.   Capt., S. Lancs. Regt.; empld. Ministry   1898
  of Munitions. (W.) *M.B.E.* *m.* *Chevalier, Legion
  of Honour (France)*
  LUMLEY-SMITH, T. G.   Capt., 21st Lancers; Major,   1898
  A.P.M. *D.S.O.* *M* 2.
  LUMSDEN, J. A.   2nd Lieut., R.G.A.   1897
  LUMSDEN, W. F.   Major, R.G.A.; Lieut.-Col., A.Q.M.G.   1898
  D.S.O. *M* 2.

LUND, H. Capt., R.A.M.C. (2nd W. Gen. Hospital, T.F.) 1878
LUPTON, A. C. Capt., Yorkshire Hussars and Remount 1893
Service
LUPTON, B. C. Capt., D. of Wellington's (W. Riding 1913
Regt., T.F.) (W 2.) *M.C. and Bar*
✠LUPTON, F. A. Major, W. Yorks. Regt.(T.F.) 1904
Killed in action 19 *Feb.* 1917
LUPTON, H. R. Capt., W. Yorks. Regt.; attd. North- 1912
umberland Fus. (W 4.) *M.C. M.*
✠LUPTON, L. M. Lieut., R.F.A.(T.F.) (W.) *M* 2. 1910
Killed in action 16 *July* 1916
✠LUPTON, M. Capt., W. Yorks. Regt. 1906
Killed in action 19 *June* 1915
LUPTON, N. D. Major, W. Yorks. Regt.(T.F.) and 1894
London Regt. (Rifles); Major, Spec. List (Cmdt.,
Reception Camp)
LYCETT, C. V. L. Capt., R.E. (Signals). (W.) *M.* 1912
LYELL, G. D. Lieut., I.A.R.O., attd. 7th Hariana Lancers 1905
LYMAN, T. Major, Engineers, United States Army 1901
✠LYON, E. L. Major, 18th Hussars; attd. Somerset L.I. 1896
(W 2.) *M.*
Died 17 *Sept.* 1916 *of wounds received in action*
LYON, R. E., V.D. Hon. Colonel, R.F.A.(T.F. Res.) *C.B.* 1884
LYSTER, L. F. Lieut., R.A.O.C. 1909
LYTHGOE, R. J. 2nd Lieut., R.G.A. 1915
LYTTELTON, A. G. Major, Welsh Regt.; Lieut.-Col., 1903
M.G.C. *D.S.O. Brevet Major. M* 4.
LYTTELTON, Rev. Hon. C. F. C.F. 4th Class, R.A.C.D. 1905
M.C.
LYTTELTON, Hon. G. W. Lieut., Eton College O.T.C. 1902
LYTTELTON, O. Capt., Grenadier Gds.; Brigade Major. 1912
(W.) *D.S.O. M.C. M* 2.
LYTTELTON, Hon. R. G. Major, R.F.A.(T.F.) (W.) 1913
French Croix de Guerre

MACANDREW, C. G. Capt., Ayrshire Yeo.; Major, M.G.C. 1906
(Cavalry)
MACARTHUR-ONSLOW, J. W. Colonel, Australian Oversea 1887
Transport Service
MACARTNEY, C. A. 2nd Lieut., Hampshire Regt.; Lieut., 1914
R.F.A.; attd. T.M.B. (W.)
✠MACARTNEY, H. B. G. Capt., R. Fusiliers 1893
Killed in action 24 *June* 1915

MACBETH, A. H. Capt., D. of Cornwall's L.I.   1903
MCCALL, H. W. Lieut.-Col., Yorkshire Regt.; A.A. and   1897
    Q.M.G. (W.) *C.M.G. D.S.O. Brevet Lieut.-*
    Colonel. M 2. Chevalier, Legion of Honour (France).
    Order of the Nile, 4th Class (Egypt)
MCCALL, H. W. L. Capt., R.A.S.C. *M.*   1900
MCCALMAN, J. A. C. Capt., E. Surrey Regt.   1893
MCCANDLISH, P. D. Major, Argyll and Sutherland   1889
    Hdrs. (R. of O.); Lieut.-Col., A.Q.M.G. *C.B.E.*
    D.S.O. Brevet Lieut.-Colonel. Brevet Major. M 3.
    Order of the White Eagle, 5th Class (Serbia).
MCCLINTOCK, Rev. E. L. L. C.F. 4th Class, R.A.C.D.   1905
MCCLINTOCK BUNBURY, Hon. T. L. Lieut., Spec. List.   1898
    M.B.E. M. Cavalier, Order of the Crown of Italy.
    Italian Croce di Guerra
MCCLURE, K. A. J. Capt., Middlesex Regt. and Spec.   1911
    List, empld. British Military Mission
MCCORMICK, E. H. Lieut., United States Naval Air   1908
    Service
MCCORMICK, L. J. Capt., 343rd Infy. Bn., United States   1907
    Army
MCCOSH, R. Capt., Lanarkshire Yeo.; Major, D.A.Q.M.G.   1904
    O.B.E. M.C. M 2. Order of the Nile, 4th Class
    (Egypt)
MCCRAITH, K. Y. Capt., Sherwood Foresters (Notts.   1909
    and Derby Regt., T.F.) and Gen. Staff. (W.)
MACDONA, C. L. Major, Spec. List (D.A.D.R.T.) *O.B.E.* 1906
    M.
MACDONALD, A. D. Capt., R.F.A.   1893
MACDONALD, Rev. A. J. M. C.F. 4th Class, R.A.C.D.   1906
MCDOUGAL, E. T. M. Lieut., Scots Gds. *M.C. M.*   1912
MACEWEN, D. L., C.B. Lieut.-Col., Cameron Hdrs.;   1886
    Brig.-Gen.; D.Q.M.G., E. Command. *C.M.G. M.*
    Commander, Legion of Honour (France)
MCEWEN, J. H. F. Capt., Cameron Hdrs.; Hon. Capt.   1912
    (O.), R.A.F. (P.)
✠MCEWEN, J. R. D. Lieut., R. Scots Fus.; A.D.C.   [1914]
    Killed in action 12 Oct. 1916
MACGREGOR, D. H. Lieut., R.E. (Signals, T.F.); Capt.,   1898
    G.S.O. 3. *M.C. M.*
MACGREGOR, M. E. Capt., Spec. List   1909
MCINTYRE, E. Capt., Cameron Hdrs. and Labour Corps   1904
MCINTYRE, N. Capt., R.A.S.C.   1902
MACIVER, C. R. Capt., R.E. (Light Railways). (W.)   1910

✠MACKAY, E. R.   Capt., Argyll and Sutherland Hdrs.   1903
  Killed in action in Gallipoli 13 *June* 1915
MACKAY, G. R.   Pte., H.A.C.; Lieut., London Regt.   1911
  (Q.V.R.)
MACKAY, Hon. K.   Capt., 12th Lancers   1906
MACKAY, R. D.   Lieut., London Regt. (Rangers)   1908
MACKENNALL, Rev. W. L.   C.F. 4th Class, R.A.C.D.   1903
✠MACKENZIE, C. R.   Flt.-Cdr., R.N.A.S.   *D.S.O.   M.*   1910
  French Croix de Guerre
  Killed in action 24 *Jan.* 1917
✠MCKENZIE, J.   2nd Lieut., Seaforth Hdrs.   1914
  Killed in action 30 *Oct.* 1915
MACKENZIE, L. H. L.   Major, I.M.S.   (W.)   *Brevet*   1899
  Major. M.
MACKENZIE, S. M.   Capt., R.A.M.C.   1898
MCKERRELL BROWN, J.   Capt., Seaforth Hdrs.; Capt. and   1907
  Adjt., Highland L.I.; attd. Gen. Staff.   *m.*
MACKINLAY, A. B.   Pte., R. Fusiliers   1911
MACKWORTH-PRAED, C. W.   Lieut., Scots Gds.   1911
MACLAREN, D.   Lieut., King's Own Scottish Borderers   1896
MCLAREN, D. B.   Lieut., Canadian F.A.   1892
MACLAREN, N.   Major, R.A.M.C.(T.F.)   *T.D.*   1894
✠MCLAREN, S. B.   Lieut., R.E. (Signals)   1897
  Died 13 *Aug.* 1916 *of wounds received in action*
MCLEAN, A.   Major and Adjt., Inns of Court O.T.C.   1895
  M.B.E. Brevet Major. m 2.
MCLEAN, C.   Capt., R.G.A.   (W.)   1900
✠MACMASTER, D. C. D.   Lieut., Cameron Hdrs.   1913
  Killed in action 26 *Sept.* 1915
✠MACMICHAEL, M. W. A.   2nd Lieut., Devon Regt.; Capt.,   1913
  Essex Regt.
  Died 16 *Sept.* 1916 *of wounds received in action*
✠MACMICKING, G. T. G.   2nd Lieut., Cambridgeshire Regt.   1913
  Died in Holland 11 *Nov.* 1918
MACMILLAN, D.   2nd Lieut., S. Notts. Hussars   1909
MACMILLAN, J. M.   Capt., R. Defence Corps   1896
✠MACMULLEN, E. R.   Capt., E. African Force; A.D.C.   *M.*   1903
  Killed in action 30 *June* 1916
✠MACNAGHTEN, A. C. R. S.   Lieut., Black Watch   1906
  Killed in action 29 *Oct.* 1914
✠MACNAGHTEN, Sir A. D., Bart.   2nd Lieut., Rifle Brigade   1914
  Killed in action 15 *Sept.* 1916
MACNAGHTEN, C. M.   Lieut.-Col., 4th (N.S.W.) Bn.,   1898
  Australian Force.   (W 2.)   *C.M.G.   M.*

✠McNeile, J. Lieut.-Col., King's Own Scottish Borderers   1881
  Wounded and prisoner, presumed killed in action, 12 *July* 1915
McNeile, J. H. Lieut., Coldstream Gds. (W.) (P.)   1911
✠MacNeill, A. D. Capt., R.G.A.   1900
  Killed in action 29 *July* 1917
Macnutt, Rev. F. B. C.F. 4th Class, R.A.C.D.(T.F.)   1894
MacRobert, T. M. 2nd Lieut., R.G.A.   1906
Madan, A. G. Lieut., R. Fusiliers. (W.)   1912
✠Maddox, J. M. 2nd Lieut., Lancs. Fus.   1915
  Killed in action 12 *Aug.* 1916
Maillet, A. L. Battery Cdr., Belgian Artillery   1913
Mainprize, S. L. 2nd Lieut., Army Cyclist Corps;   1913
  Lieut., Tank Corps and R.E. (Signals)
Mair, R. P. Capt., Sussex Yeo.   1904
✠Maitland, Hon. A. H. Major, Cameron Hdrs.   1890
  Killed in action 19 *Sept.* 1914
[1]Maitland, E. M. Lieut.-Col., Essex Regt.; Wing Cdr.,   1898
  R.N.A.S.; Brig.-Gen., R.A.F. *C.M.G. D.S.O.*
  A.F.C. American Distinguished Service Medal
✠Maitland, G. McD. 2nd Lieut., Irish Gds.   1897
  Killed in action at Klein Zillebeke 1 *Nov.* 1914
Maitland, J. Lieut., R.G.A. *M* 2.   1898
✠Maitland-Makgill-Crichton, C. J. Lieut., Seaforth   1899
  Hdrs.; Major, Gordon Hdrs.
  Killed in action 25 *Sept.* 1915
Makins, F. K. Trooper, Chota Nagpur Light Horse,   1908
  Indian Defence Force
Makins, Sir P. A., Bart. Major, Remount Service   1890
Makower, W. Lieut., R.N.V.R.   1902
Malcolm-Dickinson, W. 2nd Lieut., R. Scots Fus.;   1911
  Capt., Highland L.I.; empld. O.C.B. (W 2.)
✠Malden, W. Capt., R.A.M.C.(1st E. Gen. Hospital,T.F.)   1877
  Died Nov. 1918
Malim, F. B. Capt., Haileybury College O.T.C.   1891
Mallaby-Deeley, G. M. Lieut., 5th Dragoon Gds.   1915
Mallalieu, W. Capt., R.F.A. (W.)   1912
Mallison, H. V. Pte., Durham L.I.   1915
Manchester, Duke of. Lieut., R.N.V.R.   1894
Mander, C. A. Major, Staffordshire Yeo. (W.) *T.D.*   1903
✠Mander, D'A. W. Major, Durham L.I.   1888
  Killed in action 20 *Sept.* 1914
Mander, F. W. 2nd Lieut., R.A.S.C.   1891

[1] Killed in the wreck of airship 'R. 38,' Sept. 1921

MANDER, G. LE M. Lieut., Spec. List, empld. Ministry 1900
of National Service; Hon. Lieut. (T.), R.A.F.
MANDLEBERG, J. H. 2nd Lieut., S. Lancs. Regt. (T.F. 1904
Res.); attd. R.N.A.S.
MANDLEBERG, L. C. Major, Lancs. Fus. (W.) *D.S.O.* 1911
M.C. and Bar. M 2.
MANLEY, R. S. Capt., Staffordshire Yeo. 1911
MANN, E.W. Gnr., R.F.A.; attd. British Embassy, Copen- 1901
hagen
✠MANN, I. A. Lieut., Cameronians (Scottish Rifles, T.F.); 1913
attd. R.F.C. *M.C.*
Killed in action 9 *Aug.* 1916
MANNERS, Hon. F. H. Lieut., Grenadier Gds. (W.) 1914
M.C.
MANNERS, Sir G. Major, A.P.M., London District; attd. 1879
Cyclist Bde. *M.*
✠MANSEL-PLEYDELL, J. M. 2nd Lieut., R.F.A.; A.D.C. 1903
Died 22 *Sept.* 1916 *of wounds received in action*
MANSFIELD, R. S. Capt., R.E. (Signals); Staff Capt. 1910
O.B.E. M.
MANSON, C. M. Capt., The Queen's (R. W. Surrey [1914]
Regt., T.F.); Hon. Capt. (O.), R.A.F.
✠MAPPLEBECK, G. W. Capt., N. Staffs. Regt. *M.* 1898
Died 30 *July* 1917 *of wounds received in action*
MARC, G. J. A. Lieut., R.F.A.(T.F.); Staff Capt. *M.* 1908
MARDON, H. A. Pte., R. Fusiliers 1911
✠MARGERISON, C. W. Lieut., Border Regt. *M.* [1914]
Died 6 *July* 1916 *of wounds received in action* 1 *July*
1916
MARIGOLD, J. E. 2nd Lieut., R. Warwickshire Regt. 1912
MARKS, J. D. 2nd Lieut., 5th Dragoon Gds.; Lieut., 1907
R.F.A.
MARLBOROUGH, Duke of, T.D. Hon. Colonel, Oxford and 1890
Bucks. L.I. and Gen. Staff
MARLING, W. J. P. Major, Gloucestershire Regt. 1884
MARSDEN, C. A. Instructor Lieut., R.N. 1913
MARSDEN, Rev. E. McL. Pte., R.A.M.C. 1888
✠MARSH, A. S. Capt., Somerset L.I. 1909
Killed in action 6 *Jan.* 1916
MARSH, F. D. Major, R.A.M.C.(T.F.) *M.C.* 1907
MARSHALL, A. P. Lieut., Cameron Hdrs.(T.F.); Capt., 1895
O.C.B.
✠MARSHALL, A. S. F. Section Sanitaire, French Army 1897
Died 25 *July* 1918 *from the effects of war service*

MARSHALL, W. S. D. Lieut., R.F.A.(T.F.) 1893
MARSHAM, Rev. A. F. C.F. 4th Class, R.A.C.D. 1904
MARSON, A. A. Major, R.F.A. *M.C. M.* 1909
MARTEN, A. J. Major, R.F.A.; empld. Ministry of Muni- 1892
  tions
MARTIN, S. P. Capt. (Motor-boat), R.A.F. 1913
MARTIN, T. L. Indian Defence Force 1903
✠MARTIN, W. F. Major, Leicestershire Yeo. *M.* 1894
  Killed in action 13 *May* 1915
MARTIN, W. M. Corpl., Scots Gds. (W.) 1904
MARTIN-TOMSON, W. J. Lieut. (A.), R.A.F. (P.) 1907
MARTINET, M. Trooper, 29th Dragoons, French Army 1911
MARYON WILSON, A. G. *See* WILSON, A. G. MARYON
MASSINGBERD, S. Major, Lincolnshire Regt. and Gen. 1888
  Staff. *M.*
✠MASTER, G. G. O. Lieut., Gloucestershire Regt.(T.F.) 1913
  Killed in action 25 *July* 1916
MASTER, L. C. H. Lieut., R.F.A.; A.D.C. (W.) 1909
MASTERTON, H. W. Instructor Lieut., R.N. 1907
MATHER, A. Lieut., Highland L.I. (T.F.) 1904
✠MATHER, A. L. 2nd Lieut., York and Lancaster Regt. 1904
  Killed in action 7 *Jan.* 1917
MATHER, E. G. Capt., King's (Liverpool Regt.) *M.* 1901
MATHER, Rev. H. Section Sanitaire, French Army 1893
MATHER, L. E. Capt., R.E.(T.F.) 1905
MATHESON, I. McL. A. Capt., Lothians and Border [1914]
  Horse. *O.B.E. French Croix de Guerre. Order of
  the White Eagle, 5th Class (Serbia)*
MATHEW, F. A. H. Capt., R.E. (W.) *O.B.E. M.C.* 1911
  M 2. *French Croix de Guerre*
MATHIAS, C. D. Capt., R.A.M.C.(T.F.) 1895
MATTHEWS, E. A. C. Major, I.M.S. *D.S.O. M.* 1891
MATTHEWS, E. C. Lieut., Middlesex Regt.; Capt. Gen. 1911
  List (P. and B.T. Staff)
MAUDE, E. A. W. Capt., N. Irish Horse; A.D.C.; Capt., 1913
  Tank Corps
MAUNSELL, S. A. W. Capt., R.A.S.C. 1909
MAXWELL, I. CONSTABLE. Capt., Cameron Hdrs. (W.) 1910
MAXWELL, M. T. Lieut., R.F.A. (W.) *M.C.* 1907
MAXWELL, R. CONSTABLE. Major, Spec. List, attd. 1910
  Egyptian Army and R.N.A.S. *M.*
✠MAXWELL, W. F. J. Lieut., King's Own Scottish Bor- 1905
  derers (T.F.)
  Killed in action in Gallipoli 13 *Aug.* 1915

MAXWELL, W. H. Major, King's (Liverpool Regt., T.F.) 1893
T.D.
MAY, G. H. Capt., Canadian A.S.C. 1905
✠MAYBROOK, W. R. Pte., London Regt. (Artists Rifles); 1913
2nd Lieut., Wiltshire Regt.
Killed in action 24 April 1916
MAYER, P. G. Capt., Rifle Brigade. (W 2.) 1912
MAYHEWE, K. G. 2nd Lieut., Grenadier Gds. 1903
MAYNE, Rev. W. C. C.F. 3rd Class, R.A.C.D. 1896
MEAKIN, B. Capt., R.A.S.C. 1903
MEAKIN, L. Major, R.A.M.C.; D.A.D.M.S. (W.) *M.* 1901
MEAKIN, W. Lieut., N. Staffs. Regt.(T.F.) 1895
MEDCALF, H. Capt., Hampshire Aircraft Parks (T.F.) 1905
MEDLYCOTT, H. M. Major, Dorset Yeo.(T.F. Res.) 1893
MEEK, J. 2nd Lieut., Unattd. List, T.F. 1906
MEIER, F. A. Capt., Rugby School O.T.C. 1907
MELLER, R. W. Surgeon Lieut., R.N.; attd. R.A.F. 1905
MELLER, S. A. Capt. (K.B.), R.A.F. *M.* 1904
✠MELVILLE, H. C. 2nd Lieut., Sherwood Foresters (Notts. 1905
and Derby Regt.)
Killed in action in the Ypres Salient 14 Feb. 1916
MELVILLE-SMITH, H. McL. 2nd Lieut., R.E. (Fortress, 1912
T.F. Res.)
✠MERCER, E. D. 2nd Lieut., Lancs. Fus. 1913
Died 2 May 1917 *of wounds received in action*
MERCER, H. Bt. Colonel, 3rd Dragoon Gds. (R. of O.); 1880
cmdg. Res. Regt. of Cavalry
MERCER, J. Instructor Cdr., R.N. 1903
✠MERRYWEATHER, C. W. Major, Lancs. Fus. (W.) *M.* 1900
Killed in action 23 Nov. 1916
MERTON, G. Major (A.), R.A.F. (W.) *M.C. M* 2. 1911
METHUEN, A. P. Lieut., Bedfordshire Regt. (W 2.) 1903
✠MEWS, J. K. Capt., London Regt. (R. Fus.) (W.) [1914]
Died 24 Aug. 1918 *of wounds received in action*
✠MEYRICK, E. E. Lce.-Sergt., Cambridgeshire Regt. 1912
Died 30 July 1916 *of sickness contracted on active
service*
MEYSEY-THOMPSON, A. DE C. C. Lieut., R.F.A.; empld. 1905
Ministry of Munitions
MEYSEY-THOMPSON, E. C., M.P. Lieut.-Col., R.F.A. *m.* 1877
MEYSEY-THOMPSON, H. C. Capt., King's Royal Rifle 1902
Corps. (W.)
✠MICHELL, N. B. Capt., R. Fusiliers. (W.) *M.* 1905
Killed in action 22 March 1918

MIDDLETON, R. C. G. Capt. and Adjt., R. Sussex Regt. 1909
(W.) *M.C. M* 2. *French Croix de Guerre. Belgian
Croix de Guerre*

MIDGLEY, E. C. Capt., Spec. List (Asst. Area Gas Officer) 1900

MILBURN, A. Lieut., 20th Hussars; attd. Staffordshire 1910
Yeo.

MILBURN, A. W. Capt., Northumberland Yeo. *M.* 1905

MILBURN, J. D. Lieut., Black Watch 1904

MILBURN, Sir L. J., Bart. Lieut., Res. Regt. of R. Horse 1902
Gds.; A.P.M. (W.)

✠MILBURN, R. G. 2nd Lieut., E. Surrey Regt. 1912
Killed in action 9 *Feb.* 1915

MILDMAY, Rt. Hon. F. B. Hon. Lieut.-Col., W. Kent 1879
Yeo.; A.D.C.; attd. Gen. Staff. *T.D. M* 4.

✠MILEY, M. Lieut., R.F.A.(T.F.) 1908
Died 30 *Dec.* 1915 *of wounds received in action*

MILLAIS, J. G. Lt.-Cdr., R.N.V.R. (Intelligence) 1883

MILLER, C. D. Capt., Sherwood Foresters (Notts. and 1887
Derby Regt., T.F. Res.)

MILLER, C. H. Colonel, A.M.S. *C.B.E. M. m. Jap-* 1894
anese Order of Merit

✠MILLER, E. C. Capt., Loyal N. Lancs. Regt. 1897
Killed in action 23 *Oct.* 1914

MILLER, E. D., D.S.O. Capt., 17th Lancers (R. of O.); 1883
Lieut.-Col., Pembroke Yeo.; *C.B.E. M* 2.

MILLER, G. W. M. Capt., R. Scots (T.F.); Major, [1914]
Durham L.I. *M.C. M.*

MILLER, R. B. Major, R.F.A 1905

MILLER, R. W. R. Lieut., R.E.; empld. Ministry of Muni- 1910
tions

MILLS, F. R. Lieut., R. Fusiliers; attd. R.E. (W.) 1897

✠MILLS, T. R. Lieut., Manchester Regt.(T.F.) 1906
Killed in action in Gallipoli 4 *June* 1915

MILNE, A. A. Lieut., R. Warwickshire Regt.; empld. 1900
War Office. (W.)

✠MILNE, A. R. Capt. and Adjt., Hertfordshire Regt. [1914]
Killed in action 31 *July* 1917

MILNE, E. A. Lieut., R.N.V.R.; empld. Ministry of 1914
Munitions. *M.B.E.*

MILNE, E. O. Capt., Somerset L.I.(T.F.) (W.) 1913

MILNER, M. H., M.V.O., D.S.O. Major, Remount Service 1883
and Spec. List; A.D.C. *M. Belgian Croix de Guerre*

MILNES-GASKELL, E. Major, Yorkshire Dragoons; Asst. 1896
Special Salvage Officer. *M* 2.

MILSOM, C. F. Major, R.A.S.C. *D.S.O.* *M* 3. 1901
MILSOM, H. L. Capt., Somerset L.I. (W.) 1907
MIRRLEES, A. J. Major, Sherwood Rangers. *O.B.E.* *M*. 1895
MITCHELL, E. S. Capt., Worcestershire Regt. (W.) 1913
  M.C.
MITCHELL, Rev. P. R. C.F. 2nd Class, R.A.C.D. *O.B.E.* 1895
  m.
✠MITFORD, Hon. C. B. O. F. Major, 10th Hussars. (W.) 1896
  D.S.O.
  Killed in action 13 *May* 1915
MOLONY, B. C. Capt., Hertfordshire Regt.; Staff Capt. 1911
  (W 2.) *O.B.E.* *M*.
MOLTENO, D. J. Cadet, R.M.C., Sandhurst 1913
MOMBER, R. M. S. T. Capt., R.A.S.C. 1906
MONCKTON, T. A. Lieut.-Col. (T.), R.A.F. *O.B.E.* *M*. 1905
MONCRIEFF, D. C. Capt., R.F.A.(T.F.) (W 2.) *M.C.* 1909
MONKSWELL, Lord. 2nd Lieut., Spec. List (Interpreter) 1894
  and R.F.A.
MONTAGU, J. G. E. Major, R.F.A. (W 2.) 1911
MOOR, F. Lieut., R. Berkshire Regt. (W.) *M.C.* 1911
MOORE, A. H. Surgeon Lieut., R.N. 1900
MOORE, A. H.-G. C. Lieut., Sherwood Foresters (Notts. 1914
  and Derby Regt., T.F.)
MOORE, E. S. Capt., R.F.A.(T.F.) (W.) 1901
✠MOORE, G. A. C. Lieut., Cameronians (Scottish Rifles) 1910
  Died 11 *July* 1915 *of wounds received in action in*
  Gallipoli 28 *June* 1915
MOORE-ANDERSON, A. P. Capt., S. African Med. Corps. 1892
  M 2.
MOORE-BRABAZON, J. T. C. Lieut.-Col., R.A.F.; S.O. 1, 1901
  Air Ministry. *M.C.* *M* 2. *Chevalier, Legion of*
  Honour (*France*)
✠MOORSOM, A. E. Pte., R.A.M.C.(T.F.); Lieut., Suffolk 1912
  Regt.(T.F.)
  Died 3 *Aug.* 1916 *of wounds received in action* 15 *July*
  1916
MOORSOM, C. W. M. Capt., Harrow School O.T.C. 1893
MORCOM, R. K. Lieut.-Col., R.E. *C.B.E.* *M.B.E.* 1896
  M 2.
MOREING, A. C. Capt., London Regt. (R. Fus.) 1909
MOREING, A. H., M.P. Capt., R.F.A.(T.F.) *M*. 1907
✠MORGAN, A. C. O. Lieut., R.F.A.(T.F.) *M*. 1903
  Killed in action at the Hohenzollern Redoubt 13 *Oct.*
  1915

MORGAN, S. C.   Major, S. Wales Borderers and Gen.   1906
Staff (O.C.B.) (W.) *M.B.E.* *m* 2.

MORISON, Sir T., K.C.I.E. Lieut., Cambridgeshire Regt.;   1882
Lieut.-Col., G.S.O. 1, War Office. *K.C.S.I. C.B.E.*
M. Officer, Order of Leopold (Belgium)

MORLEY, C., jun. Lieut., R.F.A.   1903

MORLEY, C. C. Lieut., R.N.V.R. *O.B.E.*   1896

MORLEY, Hon. C. H. Capt., Grenadier Gds. (W.) *M.*   1906

MORLEY, F. W.   Lieut., Somerset L.I.(T.F.); empld.   1900
Ministry of National Service

MORRICE, G. W. Capt., R.A.S.C. *M.*   1902

MORRIS, G. G. 2nd Lieut., Sherborne School O.T.C.   1907

MORRIS, T. S.   Capt., Rifle Brigade; Major, M.G.C.   1914
M.C. M.

MORRIS-EYTON, R. E. Lieut., R.F.A.(T.F.) (W.)   1911

MORRISON, H. N. Instructor Lieut., R.N.   1913

MORRISON, J. S. F. Major (A. and S.), R.A.F. *D.F.C.*   1911
*and Bar. M. Italian Silver Medal for Military
Valour. Italian Bronze Medal for Military Valour*

MORRISON, R. G.   Lieut., 3rd Hussars; Hon. Lieut. (T.),   1913
R.A.F.

MORSE, G. G. Capt., E. Surrey Regt. (W.) *M.C.*   1914

MORSHEAD, R. S. Capt., R.A.M.C. *M.C. M.*   1905

MORTON, R. F. S. Major (A.), R.A.F. (W.) *M.*   1905

MOSS-BLUNDELL, F. B.   Colonel, R.F.A.(T.F.)   (P.)   1891
C.M.G. D.S.O. T.D. M 5.

MUGGERIDGE, C. E.   Major, King's African Rifles;   1894
G.S.O. 2. *M.C.*

✠MUIR, B. L. Capt., R.A.S.C. and Spec. List (Courts-   1909
Martial Officer)
Died 4 Nov. 1918 of pneumonia following influenza

MUIR, D. M. Surgeon Lieut., R.N.   1907

MUIR, J. Capt., R.A.M.C.(T.F.) *O.B.E.*   1897

MUIR, J. B. Major, Black Watch   1897

MUIR, M. W. Capt., Gloucestershire Yeo.; Bde. M.G.   1897
Officer

MULES, F. J.   Capt., Wellingborough Grammar School   1892
O.T.C. *T.D.*

MULHOLLAND, Hon. G. J. A. M. L.   Capt. and Adjt.,   1911
R.A.S.C. *M.C. M.*

MULHOLLAND, Hon. H. G. H. 2nd Lieut., Res. Regt.   1909
of Cavalry; Lieut. (T.), R.A.F.

✠MULLENS, C. J. A. Flt. Sub-Lieut., R.N.A.S.   1915
Drowned in action off the coast of Flanders 5 May 1916

MUNTZ, A. I. Capt., W. Somerset Yeo.; empld. Ministry   1888
    of Food
¹MURRAY, A. G. W. Capt., Spec. List (Adjt., Staff School).   1903
    M.B.E.
MURRAY, C. W. Sub-Lieut., R.N.V.R.   1913
✠MURRAY, G. A. Major, R.F.A. *M.C.*   1912
    Died 4 April 1918 of wounds received in action
MURRAY, G. R. Colonel, A.M.S.   1883
MURRAY, J. C. Lieut., 1st Life Gds.   1912
MURRAY, J. S. Australian Force   1905
✠MURRAY, M. G. D. Australian Force   1907
    Died 16 Nov. 1918 from the effects of war service
MURRAY, P. J. Capt., Wiltshire Regt. and Gen. List.   1900
    M.
MURRAY, R. B. Capt., London Regt. (Q.V.R.) and R.E.   1909
    M.
MURRAY, T. H. E. Trooper, Natal Light Horse; Lieut.,   1910
    R.F.A.
MURRAY-JOHNSON, F. K. Lieut., 1st Dragoon Gds.; Staff   1902
    Capt. (W.)
✠MURRAY SMITH, A. G. Lieut., 2nd Life Gds.   1905
    Died 2 Nov. 1914 of wounds received in action
MURTON, E. Lieut., R.N.V.R.   1885

NAISH, A. E. Major, R.A.M.C.(T.F.)   1890
NAPIER-CLAVERING, Rev. H. P. C.F. 4th Class, R.A.C.D.   1879
NASH, J. V. Lieut. (E.O.), R.F.C.   1911
NATHAN, S. H. Capt., R.A.M.C.   1890
NAWANAGAR, Jam of. Lieut.-Col., Spec. List; A.D.C.   1889
    K.C.S.I. M.
NAYLER, W. A. 2nd Lieut., Charterhouse School O.T.C.   1904
NAYLOR, J. M. Capt., London Regt.(L.R.B.) (W.)   1907
NAYLOR, T. H. Capt., Montgomeryshire Yeo.; attd. R.   1909
    Welsh Fus. *M.*
NEALE, A. K. H. Capt., King's (Liverpool Regt.); empld. 1911
    Ministry of Munitions
✠NEGROPONTE, J. J. 2nd Lieut., S. Lancs. Regt. *M.*   1912
    Died 29 Oct. 1916 of wounds received in action
NEILSON, D. F. A. Capt., R.A.M.C.   1909
NEILSON, G. E. Capt., W. Somerset Yeo. and Spec. List   1905
    (Bde. Signal Officer)

¹ Died after the armistice of influenza contracted on military service.

NEILSON, H. J. T. 2nd Lieut., Life Gds.; Lieut., 1911
R.A.M.C. and R.A.S.C.(T.F.)

NESHAM, R. A. Surgeon-Major, R.F.A.(T.F.) 1887

NETTLEFOLD, E. J. Capt., 5th Dragoon Gds.; Major, 1904
Spec. List. (W.) M.

NETTLEFOLD, J. H. Lieut., 5th Dragoon Gds.; empld. 1909
Ministry of Munitions. (W 2.)

✠NEVILE, B. P. Capt., Lincolnshire Regt. 1910
Killed in action 11 *Feb.* 1916

✠NEVILE, H. G. Lieut., S. Wales Borderers (W.) 1898
Killed in action 21 *Aug.* 1915

NEVILLE, R. A.B., R.N.V.R. (Anti-Aircraft) 1891

✠NEWALL, J. H. M. Sub-Lieut., R.N.V.R. (R.N.D.) 1914
Killed in action 13 *Nov.* 1916

NEWCOMB, W. D. Capt., R.A.M.C. 1908

NEWCOMBE, H. W. Sapper, R.E.; 2nd Lieut., R.G.A.; 1910
empld. Admiralty. (W.)

NEWCOMBE, W. A. Lieut., D. of Cornwall's L.I. 1892

NEWMAN, J. B. Lieut., Middlesex Regt.(T.F.); empld. 1907
Ministry of Munitions. (W.)

NEWMAN, J. C. Capt., R.A.M.C.(T.F.) *O.B.E.* M 2. 1891

NEWMAN, J. R. B. Major, Middlesex Regt. 1890

NEWPORT, Viscount. Major, R. Scots 1893

✠NEWSON, W. A. Major, London Regt. 1882
Died 15 *April* 1917

✠NICHOLAS, H. C. Lce.-Corpl., Australian Light Horse 1900
Killed in action 4–6 *Aug.* 1916

NICHOLAS, T. C. Major, R.E. *O.B.E.* *M.C.* M 2. 1907

NICHOLSON, A. F. Lieut., Shropshire Yeo.; attd. R.E. 1899

NICHOLSON, B. D. Lieut., R.N.V.R. 1912

NICHOLSON, C. O. E. Capt., Scottish Horse. *Brevet* 1893
Major. M 2. *Order of the Redeemer, 4th Class
(Greece)*

NICHOLSON, H. J. Lieut., 6th Dragoon Gds. (Carabiniers). 1912
M.C.

NICHOLSON, P. C. Staff-Sergt., R.F.A. 1908

NICHOLSON, R., T.D. Major, Hampshire Yeo. 1886

NICHOLSON, W. N. Lieut.-Col., Suffolk Regt.; A.Q.M.G. 1896
C.M.G. *D.S.O.* *Brevet Lieut.-Colonel.* M 7.

NICOL, J. Capt., R.A.M.C.(T.F.) 1900

NIGHTINGALE, A. D. Major, Oundle School O.T.C. 1891

NIGHTINGALE, D. A. 2nd Lieut., R. Defence Corps 1899

NIX, C. G. A. Hon. Major, Gen. List (T.F. Res.); In- 1892
spector, Woolwich Arsenal. *O.B.E.*

TRINITY COLLEGE 439

NIXON, B. H. Lieut., Devon Regt. and Gen. List 1903
✠NOEL, Hon. R. E. T. M. Capt., R. Fusiliers, attd. Nigeria 1906
Regt., W. African Frontier Force
Died in E. Africa 2 Feb. 1918 of dysentery and malaria
NORBURY, C. G. Capt., Rifle Brigade; empld. War [1914]
Office. (W.) *M. m.*
NORMAN, C. L. Capt., Queen's Own (R.W. Kent Regt., 1890
T.F.)
NORMAN, C. W. Capt., 9th Lancers. (W.) (P.) *M.* 1910
✠NORRIS, W. F. Lieut., Norfolk Regt.(T.F.); attd. Div. 1912
Cyclist Coy.
Killed in action in Gallipoli 25 Aug. 1915
NORTHCOTE, D. S. Lieut., Oxford and Bucks. L.I. (W.) 1909
NORTHCOTT, W. W. Capt., Spec. List (Recruiting Staff); 1877
Major, S. Staffs. Regt. and Labour Corps
NORTHEN, E. Major, 19th Hussars; Brigade Major. 1897
(W.)
NORTHEN, F. Capt., R. Defence Corps. *O.B.E. m.* 1894
NORTON, H. E. Major, S. Irish Horse; Brigade Major; 1895
Lieut.-Col., R. Irish Regt. and Tank Corps. (W.)

OAKEY, J. M. Pte., London Regt. (Artists Rifles); 2nd 1907
Lieut., Rifle Brigade; Major, R.E. (Spec. Bde.) *M.C.*
M.
OAKSHOTT, T. A. Capt., Northumberland Fus. (W.) 1914
OATES, B. W. G. Lieut., R.N.V.R. 1901
OATES, J. S. C. Capt., Sherwood Foresters (Notts. and 1913
Derby Regt.) (W.) *D.S.O. M.C. ˙ M* 3.
OATS, G. Major, R.G.A.(T.F.) *T.D.* 1903
✠O'CONNOR, A. C. Capt., Norfolk Regt. (W.) *M.C.* 1910
Killed in action 27 July 1916
ODGERS, F. W. Lieut., Rugby School O.T.C. 1898
O'DRISCOLL, P. F. Lieut., Irish Gds. (W 2.) 1914
O'FERRALL, C. L. Capt., Sherwood Foresters (Notts. 1910
and Derby Regt.); Lieut., R.E. (Signals)
OGILVIE, A. Lieut.-Col. (T.), R.A.F. (Aircraft Produc- 1901
tion Dept.) (W.) *C.B.E. O.B.E. M* 2.
OGILVIE, G. L. Lieut., Quebec Regt., Canadian Force 1901
O'HAGAN, Lord. Major, R.F.A.(T.F.) 1900
OLIVER, M. W. B. Major, R.A.M.C. *O.B.E. M.* 1900
✠OLIVER, T. F. 2nd Lieut., Sherwood Foresters (Notts. 1905
and Derby Regt.) (W.)
Died 26 Oct. 1918 of heart failure following pneumonia

OLLIVANT, R. C. Lieut., R.F.A.(T.F.); Staff Capt. 1901
O.B.E. M 2. *French Croix de Guerre*
ONSLOW, J. W. M. *See* MACARTHUR-ONSLOW, J. W.
OPENSHAW, C. G. Capt., The Buffs (E. Kent Regt.) and 1901
Gen. List (Transport Officer)
OPPENHEIM, L. C. F. Major, Highland L.I.; Lieut.-Col., 1889
Military Attaché, the Hague. *C.M.G. Brevet Lieut.-*
Colonel. Brevet Major. m 2.
✠ORDE-POWLETT, W. P. 2nd Lieut., Yorkshire Regt. 1913
Killed in action 17 *May* 1915
ORGILL, T. C. Lieut., I.A.R.O., attd. 125th Napier's 1903
Rifles
ORIEL, T. H. B. Major, R.G.A. *M.C.* 1911
ORMROD, L. A. Lieut., 13th Hussars 1913
ORR, G. P. L. Capt., Bedfordshire Regt.; attd. Rifle 1902
Brigade (T.F.)
ORR-EWING, A. I. Lieut., Berkshire Yeo.; Lieut. (A.), 1902
R.A.F. (P.)
OSBORN, A. P. Colonel, United States Infy. 1905
OTTER, A. Lieut., R.N.V.R. [1914]
OVERTON, I. G. Cadet, O.C.B. 1888
OWEN, A. R. B. Lieut., E. Surrey Regt. and Spec. List 1912
(Recruiting Staff). (W.)
OWEN, D. C. Lieut.-Col., Middlesex Regt. *D.S.O. M* 3. 1899
OWEN, H. Capt., R.F.A. *M.C.* 1902
OWEN, S. A. Capt., R.A.M.C. 1898
OXLEY, A. E. Major (T.), R.A.F. 1908

PAGET, J. B. Major, W. Yorks. Regt. (R. of O.); R.T.O. 1888
PAINE, H. H. Capt., R. Welsh Fus. and R.E. *M.C.* 1905
PAINE, W. A. Capt., R. Welsh Fus. (W 3.) *M.C.* 1909
PALLIS, A. A. Lieut., Spec. List (Interpreter). *O.B.E.* 1907
M.
PALMER, G. F. N. Capt., Coldstream Gds. (W.) 1912
PALMER, H. G. Lieut., R.E.; empld. Admiralty (W.) 1906
PALMER, K. R. Lieut., Life Gds. (P.) 1909
PARBURY, F. C. S. Lieut., Surrey Yeo. 1901
PARKER, F. A. Lieut., King's (Shropshire L.I.) (W.) 1913
¹PARKER, F. B. Capt., Yorkshire Regt. (W 2.) [1914]
PARKER, G. D. S. Capt., Rifle Brigade. (W.) 1913
PARKER, G. W. T. Lieut., R.G.A. 1890
PARKER, H. E. Pte., 1st Rhodesia Regt., S. African Force; 1909
Lieut., R.G.A.

¹ Killed in action in N. Russia after the armistice.

PARKER, Hon. J. H. 2nd Lieut., R.E. 1904
PARKER, R. H. Capt. and Adjt., 5th Dragoon Gds. (W.) 1908
M.C.
PARKER, W. H. Lieut., Suffolk Regt. and Gen. List. *M.* 1908
PARKIN, J. Major, Border Regt.(T.F.) 1891
PARKINS, F. D. Pte., United States Army [1914]
✠PARRY, F. A. Major, R. Warwickshire Regt. (W.) *M.C.* 1901
Killed in action 27 Sept. 1918
✠PARRY, N. C. Lieut., York and Lancaster Regt. (W.) 1905
Killed in action 27 July 1915
PARRY, N. E. Lieut., I.A.R.O., attd. 7th Gurkha Rifles 1906
PARRY-JONES, M. M. Capt., R. Fusiliers; A.D.C.; Major, 1907
G.S.O. 2. *M.C. M* 2.
✠PARSONS, D. C. Capt., Irish Gds. (W.) *M.* 1909
Killed in action 15 Sept. 1916
PARSONS, J. R. Lieut., R.N.V.R. 1904
PARSONS, R. E. Lieut.-Col., R.E.(T.F.) *m.* 1907
PART, G. M. Capt., R.A.F.; S.O. 3, Air Ministry. *m.* 1911
PARTINGTON, Rev. E. F. E. C.F. 3rd Class, R.A.C.D. 1904
M.C. and Bar
PASCHKOFF, A. A. Chevaliers-Gardes, Russian Army 1908
PASCHKOFF, A. B. Chevaliers-Gardes, Russian Army 1908
PASTEUR, F. M. Capt., King's Royal Rifle Corps; Major, [1914]
M.G.C. *M.C. and Bar. M.*
PATERSON, J. J. Lieut., Lanarkshire Yeo. *M.* 1901
PATERSON, R. J. Lieut., London Yeo. (Westminster Dra- 1896
goons), Coldstream Gds., and Gds. M.G. Regt. *M.*
PATON, J. D. Lieut., 8th (King's R. Irish) Hussars. *M.* 1910
PATON, R. Y. Surgeon Sub-Lieut., R.N.V.R. 1915
PATON SMITH, E. A. Pte., 9th Kieff Hussars, Russian 1909
Army
PATRON, J. A. Capt., London Yeo. (Rough Riders); [1914]
Major, M.G.C. (W.) *M.C.*
PATTERSON, Rev. L. C.F. 4th Class, R.A.C.D. 1903
✠PATTESON, J. D. 2nd Lieut., 5th Dragoon Gds 1907
Killed in action 13 Oct. 1914
PAUL, Sir R. J. Capt. (A.), R.A.F. (P.) *M. French* 1902
Croix de Guerre
PAUNCEFORT DUNCOMBE, Sir E. P. D. Major, Bucking- 1904
hamshire Yeo.; Brigade Major. *D.S.O. M* 3.
French Croix de Guerre
PAWLE, J. Capt., Hertfordshire Regt. (W.) 1903
PAYNE, M. W. Lieut., R. Fusiliers; Staff Capt.; attd. 1903
Egyptian Army

PAYNE GALLWEY, L. P. Lieut., 7th Hussars; attd. Life   1910
Gds.; Capt., Spec. List. *M.C.*
PAYTON, W. H. Capt., I.A.R.O., attd. 6th Gurkha Rifles   1911
PEABODY, Rev. M. E. Chaplain, United States Army   1910
PEACHE, R. C. Capt., R.E. (W.)   1908
PEACOCK, J. Pte., Princess Patricia's Canadian L.I.   1903
PEACOCK, Rev. M. R. Major, Suffolk Regt.(T.F.); attd.   1906
London Regt.
✠PEARCE, R. S. 2nd Lieut., Rifle Brigade   1913
Killed in action 9 *May* 1915
PEARCE-SEROCOLD, O., v.d. Lieut.-Col., R. Berkshire   1883
Regt.(T.F. Res.) *C.M.G. M. m.*
PEARSON, A. G. Capt., R. Berkshire Regt.; G.S.O. 3;   1907
Major, Tank Corps. *D.S.O. M.*
PEARSON, Hon. B. C. Capt., Sussex Yeo.   1905
PEARSON, J. S. Major and Adjt., D. of Wellington's   1895
(W. Riding Regt.)
PEARSON, R. S. Major, Yorkshire Hussars; Brigade   1892
Major. *O.B.E. m.*
PEARSON, T. A. Lieut., M.G.C.   1907
PEASE, C. E. Lieut., Yorkshire Regt.(T.F. Res.)   1893
PEASE, E. 2nd Lieut., Spec. List (Interpreter). (W.)   1901
PEASE, N. A. Capt., E. Surrey Regt. (W.) *M.C. and*   [1914]
Bar
PEASE, R. A. Capt., Northumberland Yeo.; empld. War   1909
Office. (W 2.) *M.*
PECKHAM, W. D. Lieut., Spec. List (Interpreter). *M.*   1906
PEEK, Sir W., Bart. Capt., R. 1st Devon Yeo.; Camp   1903
Cmdt., Indian Army. *D.S.O. M* 4.
PEEL, W. R. Lieut.-Col., Yorkshire Regt.; attd. Man-   1905
chester Regt.(T.F.) (W 3.) *D.S.O. and two Bars.*
M 5.
PELHAM, Hon. M. H. Lieut., Life Gds. and Gds. M.G.   1912
Regt.
PELHAM, Hon. S. G. Capt., 11th Hussars. (W.) *M.C.*   1908
PELHAM, Rev. W. H. C.F. 4th Class, R.A.C.D.   1905
PELHAM-CLINTON, G. E. Capt., R.E. *M.C.*   1912
PELLY, A. R. Capt., Norfolk Regt.(T.F.) and Spec. List.   1914
(W.)
PELLY, E. G. Lieut.-Col., R.A.S.C. *D.S.O. M.C.*   1908
M 5.
PELLY, E. P. L. 2nd Lieut., Essex Yeo. (W.)   1913
PELLY, F. B. Lieut. (O.), R.A.F. *A.F.C.*   1908
PELLY, Rev. R. A. C.F. 1st Class, R.A.C.D.(T.F.) *T.D.*   1877

✠PEMBERTON, F. P. C. Capt., Life Gds.   1903
  Killed in action near Roulers 19 *Oct.* 1914
PENN, A. H. Capt., Grenadier Gds. (W.) *M.C. M.* 1905ˈ
  French Croix de Guerre
✠PENN, E. F. 2nd Lieut., Norfolk Yeo.; Capt., Grenadier 1897
  Gds. *M.*
  Killed in action 18 *Oct.* 1915
✠PENN, G. M. 2nd Lieut., Rifle Brigade; attd. Somerset L.I. 1905
  Killed in action 11 *Feb.* 1915
PENNELL, V. H. Capt., R.A.S.C.   1894
PENNYMAN, J. B. W. Capt., King's Own Scottish Bor- 1902
  derers; Major, M.G.C. (W.)
✠PENROSE, E. J. McN. Capt., R. Irish Fus. (W.) *M.* 1907ˈ
  Killed in action near St Julien 25 *April* 1915
✠PENROSE FITZGERALD, M. J. Lieut., The Queen's (R.W. 1913
  Surrey Regt.)
  Died 26 *July* 1916 *of wounds received in action*
PENTON, C. F. Capt., Queen's Own (R.W. Kent Regt.) 1905
  and Gen. List. (W.)
✠PEPLOE, K. Capt., Oxford and Bucks. L.I.   1913
  Killed in action 9 *Nov.* 1916
PERCIVAL, H. F. Surgeon Lieut., R.N. *O.B.E.*   1901
PERKINS, C. H. Lieut., Buckinghamshire Yeo. *M.C.* [1914]
PERRENS, C. N. T. Capt., R.A.S.C.   1907
PERRINS, M. D. Lieut., Lincolnshire Regt.   1910
✠PERRY, E. W. C. 2nd Lieut., R.F.C.   1908
  Killed in flying accident 16 *Aug.* 1914
PERRY, W. A. C. Capt., R.E.; Staff Capt. *M* 2.   1906
✠PERSSE, C. DE B. G. 2nd Lieut., 7th Dragoon Gds.; attd. 1895
  Irish Gds.
  Died 19 *July* 1915 *of wounds received in action*
PETERS, A. Capt., Leicestershire Regt. *M.C. M.* 1912
PETERS, W. J. Lieut., Devon Regt. and Spec. List 1903
  (T.M.B.) *M.C.*
✠PETERSEN, W. S. 2nd Lieut., Life Gds.   1910
  Killed in action 6 *Nov.* 1914
PETHERICK, G. G. 2nd Lieut., Life Gds.; Capt., R. 1st 1905
  Devon Yeo.; empld. Admiralty
PETHERICK, J. C. Capt., 3rd Hussars; Major, M.G.C. 1908
  (Cavalry). (W.) *M.C. M. Italian Silver Medal for*
  Military Valour
PETHERICK, M. 2nd Lieut., 2nd Dragoons (R. Scots 1912
  Greys)
PETRIE, A. Capt., R. Scots Fus. (W.) *M.C.*   1903

PHARAZYN, H. H.   Capt., Worcestershire Regt.   1896
PHEAR, A. G.   Colonel, A.M.S.   *C.B.*   *M* 2.   1885
PHELPS, H. M. P.   2nd Lieut., R. Fusiliers.   (W.) (P.)   1916
PHELPS, T. T.   Capt., London Yeo. (Middlesex Hussars)   1891
PHILIPSON, R.   Capt., Coldstream Gds.   1914
PHILIPSON-STOW, R. M. P.   Lieut., King's Own   (R.   1913
  Lancaster Regt.); attd. King's African Rifles
PHILLIPPS, F. A.   Lieut., Seaforth Hdrs.   (W.)   1910
PHILLIPS, G. W.   Major, R.E.; D.A.D. Light Railways.   1909
  M.
PHILLIPS, L. C. W.   Capt., Surrey Yeo.(T.F. Res.)   1886
✠PHILLIPS, R. N.   Capt., R. Welsh Fus.   1896
  Died 27 Dec. 1914 of wounds received in action
PHILPOT, W.   Lieut., R.F.A.(T.F.)   1898
PICKLES, A.   Capt., Suffolk Regt.; Staff Capt.   1903
PICKTHORN, K. W. M.   Capt., London Regt. (Civil Ser-   1911
  vice Rifles); empld. War Office; Capt. (O.), R.A.F.
  (W 2.)
PIGEON, H. R.   Lieut., R.A.S.C.   1902
PIGGOTT, J. C. C.   Lieut., D. of Cornwall's L.I.; Lieut.   [1914]
  (A.), R.A.F.   (W.)
PIKE, G.   Capt., R.A.S.C.   *M.*   1905
PIKE, S. A.   Lieut.-Col., R. Berkshire Regt.   *M.C.*   *M* 2.   1908
  Order of the White Eagle, 5th Class (Serbia)
PILCHER, G. ST C.   Lieut., Spec. List (Intelligence).   1909
  M.C. *M.*
PILKINGTON, D. F.   Lieut., R.A.S.C.(M.T.)   *M.B.E.* *M.*   1912
PILKINGTON, E. F.   Major, Manchester Regt.(T.F. Res.)   1904
PILKINGTON, F. M. F.   Capt., R.A.S.C.   1906
PILKINGTON, G. R.   Major, S. Lancs. Regt.(T.F.)   (W 2.)   1900
  D.S.O. *M.*
✠PILKINGTON, H. B.   Capt., Manchester Regt.(T.F.)   *M.*   1905
  Killed in action in Gallipoli 4 June 1915
PILKINGTON, W. N.   Major, S. Lancs. Regt.(T.F.)   *D.S.O.*   1896
  and Bar. *M* 3.
PINSENT, G. H. S.   Lieut., R.G.A.   *M.*   1907
PITE, A. G.   Capt. and Adjt., R.F.A.   *M.C.*   1914
PITE, I. B.   Capt., R.E.   1909
PITT, P. S.   Capt., R.A.S.C.(M.T.)   1900
PITTS-TUCKER, G. S.   Lieut., Cheshire Regt. and King's   1905
  African Rifles.   (W 2.)
PLAISTER, A. J.   Lieut., R.F.A.   [1914]
PLATT, E. A.   Lieut., Army Printing and Stationery   1907
  Services

✠PLATT, M. C. Sub-Lieut., R.N.V.R. (R.N.D.) *m.*   1912
  *Died 26 Nov. 1918 of illness contracted during intern-
  ment*
PLATT, R. C. Capt., E. Surrey Regt. (R. of O.)   1896
PLATT HIGGINS, F. M. Capt., Cambridgeshire Regt. and 1893
  Remount Service. *M.C. M.*
POCHIN, V. R. 2nd Lieut., Res. Regt. of Life Gds. and 1898
  Gds. M.G. Regt.
POLHILL, C. C. Lieut., Dorset Yeo.   1908
POLLARD, A. R. Lieut., I.A.R.O., attd. 1st Sappers and 1900
  Miners. (W.) *M.B.E. M 2.*
POLLARD, S. 2nd Lieut., R.F.A.; empld. Ministry of 1912
  Munitions
POLLITT, H. C. Lce.-Corpl., R.A.M.C.   1889
✠POLLOCK, C. T. A. Capt., Inns of Court O.T.C.; attd. 1906
  E. Yorks. Regt. *M 2.*
  Killed in action 31 March 1918
POLLOCK, H. H. Major, R.F.A.(T.F.) *M.C. M 2.*   1895
POLLOCK, HAMILTON R. Cadet, R.A.F.   1903
POLLOCK, HUMPHREY R. Capt., R.A.M.C.   1908
POLLOCK, H. W. Lieut. (T.), R.A.F.   1896
✠POLLOCK, M. V. Lieut., S. Wales Borderers   1906
  Killed in action 9 May 1915
POLLOCK, R.C.G. Major, Corps of Guides, Indian Army; 1900
  attd. 51st Sikhs. (W.)
POLWARTH, Lord. Hon. Colonel, R. Scots and Gen. Staff. 1882
  C.B.E. m 2.
PONSONBY, Hon. B. B. Lieut., Grenadier Gds.; empld. 1904
  War Office. (W.)
PONSONBY, Rev. S. G., V.D. C.F. 1st Class, R.A.C.D. 1876
  (T.F.)
POOLEY, J. S. Capt., R.A.M.C.   1908
POORE, W. G. Major, R.F.A.(T.F.) (W 2.) *M.C.*   1909
POPE, A. R., T.D. Major, Dorset Regt.   1890
POPE, C. Capt., Bedfordshire Regt. (P.)   1909
✠POPE, C. A. W. Capt., R.A.M.C.   1896
  Drowned on H.M. transport Transylvania 4 May 1917
PORTER, A. R. Z. Lieut., R.E. (London Electrical En- 1899
  gineers, T.F.)
✠PORTER, E. J. Lieut., London Regt. (Queen's)   1909
  *Died in German hands 22 Sept. 1916 of wounds received
  in action*
POWELL, A. T., T.D. Lieut.-Col., R.F.A.(T.F.); attd. 1902
  R.G.A. *M. Order of the Nile, 3rd Class (Egypt)*

POWELL, E. W. Lieut.-Col. (A.), R.A.F. *O.B.E. M* 4. 1905
✠POWELL, R. C. FF. 2nd Lieut., Highland L.I. 1910
    Killed in action at Verneuil 13 *Sept.* 1914
✠POWELL, R. H. 2nd Lieut., R. Sussex Regt.(T.F.) 1902
    Killed in action at Richebourg l'Avoué 9 *May* 1915
POWELL, R. V. Lieut., Scots Gds. (W 3.) *M.C.* 1903
POWELL, T. F. Capt., Coldstream Gds. *French Croix* 1905
    de Guerre
POWELL, Rev. V. P. C.F. 3rd Class, R.A.C.D. *M.* 1899
✠POWER, J. W. 2nd Lieut., Somerset L.I.; attd. D. of 1912
    Cornwall's L.I.; Lieut., Welsh Gds.
    Killed in action 10 *Sept.* 1916
POWERS, C. Capt., St Edmund's School, Canterbury, 1903
    O.T.C.
POWNALL, J. C. G. Lieut., R.F.A.(T.F.) 1909
POWNEY, C. DU P. P. Lieut.-Col., Hampshire Regt. 1880
    M.B.E. m.
PREECE, C. T. Lieut., R.G.A. *M.C.* 1898
PREECE, P. J., T.D. Lieut.-Col., London Regt. (Post 1889
    Office Rifles, T.F. Res.); empld. Ministry of Labour
✠PRETOR-PINNEY, C. F., D.S.O. Lieut.-Col., Rifle Brigade. 1883
    (W.) *M.*
    Died 28 *April* 1917 *of wounds received in action* 24
    April 1917
PRICE, J. D. 2nd Lieut., King's (Liverpool Regt.); 1900
    Lieut., Training Res. Bn.
PRICE, Rt. Rev. McC. E. C.F. 1st Class, R.A.C.D. 1882
    M. Order of the White Eagle, 2*nd Class (Serbia).*
PRICE, W. R. Gnr., R.F.A. 1905
PRICHARD, W. A. Capt., R.F.A. *M.C.* 1914
PRIESTLEY, H. W. Major, London Regt. (Post Office 1906
    Rifles). (W.) *M.C.*
✠PRING, B. C. Pte., Middlesex Regt.; Lieut., Worcester- 1906
    shire Regt. and M.G.C.
    Killed in action 1 *July* 1916
✠PRINGLE, A. S. Capt., Cameronians (Scottish Rifles) 1896
    Killed in action in the Battle of Loos 25 *Sept.* 1915
PRINSEP, A. L. Lieut., R.N.V.R. 1907
PRIOR-WANDESFORDE, R. H. Capt., R.F.A. 1888
PRITCHARD, J. E. M. Major, S.O. 2., R.A.F. *O.B.E.* 1909
    A.F.C.
PRITCHARD, N. P. Capt., R.A.M.C. *M.C.* 1903
PRITTIE, Hon. H. C. O'C. Major, Rifle Brigade. (W.) 1896
    D.S.O.

PROCTER, R. Lieut., R.N.V.R. *D.S.C. M* 2. 1897
PROCTER, R. G. Capt., K. Edward VII School, Sheffield, 1897
O.T.C.
PRYCE-JONES, H. M. Major, Coldstream Gds.; Lieut.- 1897
Col., A.A.G. *M.V.O. D.S.O. M.C. Brevet*
Lieut.-Colonel. M 7. *Chevalier, Legion of Honour*
(France). Chevalier, Ordre du Mérite Agricole (France)
PRYOR, N. S. Capt. and Adjt., R.F.A.(T.F.) *M.* 1914
✠PRYOR, R. S. 2nd Lieut., King's Own (R. Lancaster 1913
Regt.)
Killed in action at Ypres 1 *May* 1915
PRYOR, W. M. Capt., Hertfordshire Regt.; Lieut.-Col., 1898
R. Warwickshire Regt. *D.S.O. and Bar. Brevet*
Major. M 4. *Italian Bronze Medal for Military Valour*
PUGH, F. H. Lieut., R.A.S.C.; empld. British Military 1913
Mission
PUGHE, E. B. Capt., Rifle Brigade; empld. O.C.B. *M.* 1911
PULLING, C. R. D. Lieut., King's Royal Rifle Corps 1912
PULLINGER, A. F. 2nd Lieut., Essex Regt.; Lieut., 1914
Suffolk Regt.; empld. Ministry of Munitions. (W.)
✠PURSER, F. D. Lieut., R.N.V.R. (R.N.D.) 1906
Killed in action 27 *Dec.* 1917
PYE, D. R. Capt. (T.), R.A.F. 1905
PYE, E. W. Pte., Nagpur Rifles, Indian Defence Force 1907
✠PYM, C. J. Pte., Canadian Force; Lieut., Irish Gds. 1911
Died 27 *March* 1917 *of injuries accidentally received*
24 *March* 1917
PYM, R. M. Sub-Lieut., R.N.V.R. (Hood Bn., R.N.D.) 1911
(W.)
PYM, Rev. T. W. C.F. 1st Class, R.A.C.D.; A.C.G. 1905
D.S.O. M 3.
PYM, W. ST J. Lieut., R.G.A.(T.F.); empld. War Cab- 1908
inet

QUILTER, Sir W. E. C., Bart., M.P. Capt., Suffolk Yeo. 1892
(T.F. Res.); R.T.O. *m.*

RADCLYFFE, E. J. D. 2nd Lieut., Huntingdonshire Cyclist 1902
Bn.
RADNOR, Earl of. Bt. Colonel, Wiltshire Regt.(T.F. Res.); 1886
Brig.-Gen., Director of Agricultural Production.
C.I.E. C.B.E. M 2. *Officer, Legion of Honour (France)*
✠RAIKES, F. S. W. 2nd Lieut., Rifle Brigade 1912
Killed in action 9 *May* 1915

RAMSAY, J. D. Capt., Scottish Horse; attd. Argyll and 1896
Sutherland Hdrs. *M.C.*
RAMSDEN, Sir J. F. Capt., Norfolk Yeo.(T.F. Res.) 1895
RANDALL, B. E. Capt. and Adjt., R.A.S.C.(T.F.) 1906
RANDALL, G. F. Lieut., Hampshire Regt.(T.F.); Lieut. 1911
(Ad.), R.A.F.
RANKIN, G. C. Lieut., R.G.A. 1897
RANKIN, R. Capt., Irish Gds. (W.) 1901
RATHBONE, C. G. Pte., R. Fusiliers (P. S. Bn.); Major, 1910
R.E. (Spec. Bde.) *M.C. M.*
RATHBONE, M. P. Major, S. Lancs. Regt. 1884
RATHBONE, R. R. Capt., King's (Liverpool Regt.) (W 2.) 1910
M.C. and Bar
✠RATTIGAN, C. S. Capt., R. Fusiliers 1904
Killed in action 13 Nov. 1916
✠RAW, R. 2nd Lieut., Lancs. Fus. 1903
Killed in action 7 Aug. 1915
[1]RAWLINGS, P. T. Capt. (T.), R.A.F. *D.S.C. M.* 1906
RAWLINS, F. McC. Lieut., Gloucestershire Regt. (W.) 1911
RAWLINS, H. G. Lieut., R.N.V.R. 1908
RAWLINS, J. D. Capt., R.E. *M.C. M.* 1913
RAWSON, H. F. R. Instructor Lieut., R.N. 1910
RAWSON, R. R. Capt., R.E. *M.C. and two Bars. M.* 1912
RAYMENT, G. V. Instructor Cdr., R.N. *C.B.E. Order* 1897
*of the Sacred Treasure, 3rd Class (Japan). Order of
the White Elephant, 3rd Class (Siam). Order of the
Striped Tiger, 4th Class (China)*
REARDEN, T. R. Capt., I.A.R.O.; R.T.O. 1902
REDFERN, A. S. Capt., The Queen's (R. W. Surrey 1914
Regt., T.F.); Major (A.), R.A.F.
REDFERN, W. A. K. Capt., R.F.A. and Spec. List (Adjt., 1900
Graves Registration Units); Staff Capt.
REDMAYNE, T. Capt., R.A.M.C. 1881
✠REED, Rev. C. H. C.F. 4th Class, R.A.C.D. *M.C.* 1907
Killed in action at Messines 7 June 1917
REED, H. S. Capt. and Adjt., Devon Regt.(T.F.); Staff 1905
Capt.
✠REED, H. W. T. 2nd Lieut., Monmouthshire Regt. 1905
Killed in action 2 May 1915
REED, J. Lieut., R.N.V.R. 1909
✠REID, J. Capt., Highland L.I. *M.* 1909
Killed in action 25 Sept. 1915
REID, J. S. Trooper, K. Edward's Horse; Capt., R.F.A. 1907

_____
[1] Killed in flying accident after the armistice.

REID, P. J. Lce.-Corpl., 19th Hussars; Lieut., Leicester- 1885
shire Yeo.; empld. Traffic Control

RENDALL, F. G. Pte., London Regt. (Artists Rifles); 1909
Staff Lieut.; Lieut., R. Fusiliers; Capt., Spec. List
(cmdg. T.M.B.) (W.)

RENDALL, P. S. Lieut., King's (Shropshire L.I.) and [1914]
Gen. List (Draft Conducting Officer); empld. Air
Ministry

RENNOLDSON, H. F. Capt., R.F.A.(T.F.) (W.) *M.* 1906

RENSHAW, A. H. Lieut., Lanarkshire Yeo. and R. Scots 1907
Fus.; Capt., Spec. List (cmdg. T.M.B.)

RENSHAW, J. A. K. Capt., Manchester Regt. (T.F. Res.) 1889

RENSHAW, Sir S. C. B., Bart. Capt., Ayrshire Yeo. 1903

REUNERT, C. Gnr., S. African Force (Armoured Train) 1906

REVILLON, A. J. Pte., Middlesex Regt. (P. S. Bn.); 2nd 1907
Lieut., King's Royal Rifle Corps

REYNARD, C. E. Major, E. Riding of Yorkshire Yeo. *M.* 1899

REYNOLDS, C. H. Capt., R.G.A.(T.F.) *Belgian Croix de* 1904
Guerre

REYNOLDS, G. W. M. 2nd Lieut., Malvern College 1913
O.T.C.

✠REYNOLDS, J. W. 2nd Lieut., York and Lancaster Regt. 1905
(T.F.)
Killed in action near Ypres 7 Aug. 1915

REYNOLDS, L. Major, I.M.S. 1893

REYNOLDS, N. C. W. Capt., Irish Gds. (W.) *O.B.E. m.* 1908

RHODES, E. C. Instructor Lieut., R.N. 1911

RICARDO, F. Lieut., Gloucestershire Regt. and M.G.C. 1906
(W.)

RICE, G. C. D. Major, R. Fusiliers and Rifle Brigade; 1889
Courts-Martial Officer. *T.D.*

RICE, G. E. Capt., R. Wiltshire Yeo.; empld. War Office. 1891
m.

RICH, N. J. 2nd Lieut., R.E.; Lieut. (K.B.), R.A.F. 1911

RICHARDS, R. C. Lieut., R.E. 1899

RICHARDSON, C. L. Capt., R.A.S.C. *M.* 1906

✠RICHARDSON, D. S. Lieut., Border Regt. 1910
Killed in action 16 May 1915

RICHARDSON, J. P. A. Lieut., R.N.V.R. *D.S.C. Italian* 1904
Silver Medal for Military Valour

✠RICHARDSON, J. S. 2nd Lieut., Northumberland Fus. 1895
Killed in action 9 April 1917

✠RICHARDSON, J. W. Major, York and Lancaster Regt. 1900
Killed in action 3 May 1917

RICHARDSON, M. E.   Lieut.-Col., 20th Hussars and   1897
  Northumberland Fus.; Brig.-Gen. (W.) *D.S.O.*
  M 3. *Chevalier, Legion of Honour (France)*
RIDDELL, J. R.   2nd Lieut., Unattd. List, T.F.   1903
✠RIDLEY, H. L.   Capt., R. Dublin Fus. (W.) *M.C.*   1913
  Killed in action 15 *July* 1917
✠RIDLEY, H. Q.   Lieut., Australian Infy.   1901
  Killed in action 12 *Oct.* 1917
RIGDEN, C.   Major, R. East Kent Yeo.   1908
✠RILEY, A. C.   Capt., London Regt. (St Pancras Bn.)   1901
  Killed in action 25 *Sept.* 1915
RILEY-SMITH, W.   2nd Lieut., 1st Dragoon Gds.; Lieut.,   1909
  13th Hussars
RIPLEY, H. W. G.   Lieut., King's (Shropshire L.I.) (W.)   1905
RITCHIE, Rev. C. S.   Chaplain, R.N.   1901
✠RITCHIE, R. B.   Capt., Cameronians (Scottish Rifles).   1912
  M.C.
  Killed in action 20 *July* 1916
✠RITSON, A. S.   Gnr., R.F.A.; 2nd Lieut., Durham L.I.   1910
  Killed in action 5 *Nov.* 1916
✠RITSON, J. A.   Capt., S. Lancs. Regt.   1911
  Killed in action 23 *July* 1916
RITSON, R.   Capt., N. Staffs Regt. and King's African   1906
  Rifles. (W.)
RITTNER, G. H.   Capt. and Adjt., N. Staffs. Regt.(T.F.)   1894
RIVINGTON, R. T.   2nd Lieut., R.A.S.C.   1900
✠RIX, J. C.   Capt., R.A.M.C.   1895
  Killed in action 6 *July* 1916
ROBERTS, C. C. G.   Capt., London Regt. (Queen's West-   1899
  minster Rifles); Major, Camp Cmdt. *O.B.E. M* 2.
ROBERTS, P. M.   Pte., R. Fusiliers; Capt., Spec. List   1914
  (R.T.O., attd. H.Q., D.G.T.)
ROBERTS BUCHANAN, B.   *See* BUCHANAN, B. R.
ROBERTSON, D. H.   Lieut., London Regt. (Finsbury   1908
  Rifles). *M.C.*
ROBERTSON, D. S.   Major, R.A.S.C. *M* 2.   1904
ROBERTSON, H. J.   Capt., R.A.S.C.(M.T.) *M.C.*   1904
✠ROBERTSON, K. F.   Capt. and Adjt., Durban L.I., S.   1908
  African Force, and Rifle Brigade. *M.*
  Killed in action 27 *Aug.* 1916
ROBERTSON, M. K.   Capt., R.A.M.C.(T.F.)   1910
✠ROBERTSON, R.   Capt., Highland L.I.   1905
  Died 13 *Sept.* 1917
ROBINSON, Rev. F. T.   Chaplain, R.N.   1899

ROBINSON, H. Capt., R.A.M.C. (W.) 1896
ROBINSON, J. B. Lieut. (A.), R.A.F. 1908
ROBINSON, J. G. Capt., London Regt. (L.R.B.); Capt. 1906
(Ad.), R.A.F.
✠ROBINSON, R. F. 2nd Lieut., King's Royal Rifle Corps 1898
Killed in action at Hooge 30 July 1915
ROBINSON, W. H. Capt., R.F.A. 1909
ROBSON, E. Lieut., Durham L.I.(T.F.) and North- 1912
umberland Fus.; attd. 2nd Rajput L.I., Indian Army
✠ROBSON, G. D. Lieut., King's Royal Rifle Corps. (W.) 1912
Killed in action 24 Aug. 1917
ROCHDALE, Lord. Lieut.-Col., Lancs. Fus.(T.F. Res.) 1884
ROCHFORT, G. A. BOYD. Lieut., Scots Gds. 1898
V.C. "For most conspicuous bravery in the trenches
between Cambrai and La Bassée on 3rd August, 1915.
At 2 a.m. a German trench mortar bomb landed on the
side of the parapet of the communication trench in which
he stood, close to a small working party of his Battalion.
He might easily have stepped back a few yards round the
corner into perfect safety, but, shouting to his men to
look out, he rushed at the bomb, seized it and hurled it
over the parapet, where it at once exploded. There is no
doubt that his splendid combination of presence of mind
and courage saved the lives of many of the working
party."—Supplement to *The London Gazette*, 1 Sept. 1915.
ROGET, S. R. Lieut., R.N.V.R. 1894
ROLLO, W. H. Lieut., 2nd Dragoons (R. Scots Greys). 1908
M.C.
ROMANIS, W. H. C. Lieut., R.A.M.C. 1908
RONALDSHAY, Earl of. Major, Yorkshire Regt. G.C.I.E. 1894
ROOKE-COWELL, W. J. Capt., London Yeo. (Rough 1887
Riders); empld. Ministry of Munitions
ROPER, F. A. Major, R.A.M.C.(T.F.) *M.* 1902
✠ROSE, Sir F. S., Bart. Capt., 10th Hussars 1896
Killed in action 26 Oct. 1914
ROSE, Sir H. A. Lieut.-Col., R. Scots. D.S.O. M. 1894
ROSE, L. Capt., S. Wales Borderers. (W 2.) M.C. 1913
ROSHER, J. B. Major, Durham L.I.; Lieut.-Col., M.G.C. 1907
(W 2.) D.S.O. and Bar. M.C. M 4.
ROSS, R. D. Major, N. Irish Horse; Brigade Major. 1907
M.C. French Croix de Guerre
ROSS, W. G. 2nd Lieut., R.F.A.; Lieut., R.A.S.C.(M.T.) 1907
✠ROSSI, R. 2nd Lieut., Engineers, Italian Army 1912
*Died 19 March 1920 from the effects of active service
during the war*

ROTHBAND, P. L.   Capt., S. Lancs. Regt. *M.*   1902
ROUSE, P. G.   Lieut., R.F.A.; Lieut.-Cdr., R.N.V.R. *M.*   1902
ROWLANDS, R. B. J.   2nd Lieut., R. Welsh Fus.; In-   1913
structor Lieut., R.N.
ROWLEY, C. S.   Capt., Grenadier Gds. (W.) (P.)   1910
ROWLEY, G. R. F.   Lieut., R. Horse Gds. (W.)   1907
ROXBURGH, A. C.   Surgeon Lieut., R.N.   1905
ROXBURGH, J. F.   Lieut., R.E. (Signals). *M.*   1907
ROYCE, F. C.   Capt., King's Own Scottish Borderers   1912
and R.E. (Sound-ranging Section). (W.) *M.*
ROYSTON-PIGOTT, W. M.   Major, R.A.S.C.; D.A.D.S.   1899
and T., N. Command. *D.S.O. M. Chevalier,
Legion of Honour* (*France*)
RÜCKER, A. N.   Lieut., Suffolk Regt. (W 3.)   [1914]
RUFFHEAD, A. C.   Pte., Northamptonshire Regt.   1914
RUGGLES-BRISE, E. A.   Major, Essex Yeo. (W.) *M.C. M.*   1901
RUSHTON, H. L.   Capt., D. of Lancaster's Own Yeo.;   1901
attd. S. Lancs. Regt.
RUSHWORTH, A. N.   Surgeon Lieut., R.N.   1906
RUSSELL, E. N.   Capt., R.A.M.C.   1903
RUSSELL, J. D.   Capt., R.E. (Fortress, T.F.)   1909
RUSTON, W.   Capt., R. North Devon Yeo. and Lincoln-   1893
shire Regt.
RUTHVEN-STUART, A. W.   Capt., Gordon Hdrs.(T.F.) and   1902
R.A.S.C.(T.F.)
RUTTER, H. F. P.   Lieut., Cheshire Regt.   1913
RYCROFT, Sir R. N., Bart.   Major, London Regt. (Cyclist   1878
Bn., T.F. Res.)
RYDER, A. F. R. D.   Capt., R.F.A.(T.F.) (W 4.) *M.C.*   1910
and Bar
RYDER, F. J.   Bt. Colonel, Gen. List; Officer i/c Cavalry   1885
Records. *C.M.G. M 2.*

SAGAR-MUSGRAVE, C. L.   Capt., W. Yorks. Regt.(T.F.)   1914
(W.) *M.C.*
ST AUBYN, E. G.   Lieut.-Col., King's Royal Rifle Corps;   1899
Brig.-Gen. (W 2.) *D.S.O. M. French Croix de
Guerre*
ST AUBYN, Hon. L. M.   Capt., King's Royal Rifle Corps   1897
and Gen. Staff. *M.*
✠ST AUBYN, M. J.   Major, King's Royal Rifle Corps.   1910
(W 2.) *M.C. M.*
Killed in action near St Quentin 22 *March* 1918

St Clair, A. H. Lieut., Argyll and Sutherland Hdrs.; 1913
Lieut. (K.B.), R.A.F. (W.) *M.C.*
St Johnston, A. Capt., R.A.M.C. 1906
St Levan, Lord, c.b., c.v.o. Colonel, Grenadier Gds.; 1876
Brig.-Gen. *M.*
✠Salaman, L. H. Seaman, R.N.V.R.(R.N.D.) 1901
Killed in action in Gallipoli (Dec. 1915)
Salisbury, T. H. L. Lieut. (T.), R.A.F. (Aircraft Pro- 1902
duction Dept.)
Salter, F. R. Lieut., Rifle Brigade; Capt., G.S.O. 3, 1905
Irish Command. (W.)
Sampson, F. A. Capt., R. Fusiliers. (W.) (P.) 1909
Sampson, N. C. Lieut., 2nd Dragoon Gds. (Queen's 1902
Bays); Major (A. and Ad.), R.A.F.
Sampson, R. H. Capt., London Regt. (Q.V.R.) and [1914]
M.G.C.
Sampson, S. J. M. Major, London Regt. (Q.V.R.) (W.) 1902
M.C. T.D. M.
Samuelson, F. H. B. Capt., Yorkshire Hussars 1908
Sandars, E. T. Major, R.A.S.C. and Spec. List 1895
(D.A.D.R.T.) *O.B.E. M. Chevalier, Military Order
of Avis (Portugal)*
✠Sanders, L. Y. 2nd Lieut., R.G.A. (W.) 1912
Killed in action 10 *March* 1917
Sanderson, Rev. C. P. C.F. 4th Class, R.A.C.D. 1872
Sanderson, Rev. G. P. M. C.F. 4th Class, R.A.C.D. 1897
Sanderson, I. C. Capt. and Adjt., Black Watch; Major, 1905
Argyll and Sutherland Hdrs. *M.C. M* 2. *French
Croix de Guerre. Greek Military Cross*
Sanderson, J. R. Lieut., Spec. List (Staff Lieut.) *M.* 1907
✠Sanderson, R. H. Lieut.-Col., R.F.A. *M. Chevalier,* 1895
Legion of Honour (France).
Killed in action 17 *April* 1918
Sanderson, T. S. 2nd Lieut., Life Gds.; Lieut., 12th 1909
Lancers and Gds. M.G. Regt.
Sandilands, H. R. Major, Northumberland Fus.; 1894
Lieut.-Col., G.S.O. 1. (W 2.) *C.M.G. D.S.O.
Brevet Lieut.-Colonel. M* 5. *Officer, Legion of Hon-
our (France)*
Sandilands, J. E. Capt., R.A.M.C. *M.C. M* 2 1890
Sandison, A. Capt., R.A.M.C. *French Médaille d'Honneur* 1904
Sanger, P. M. Lieut., R. Marines. (W.) 1903
Sanger-Davies, F. M. Lieut., R. Sussex Regt.(T.F.) [1914]
(W.) *M.*

✠SANGER-DAVIES, Ll. H. Capt., Durham L.I. 1912
   Killed in action 1 *July* 1916
SANKEY, H. B. Lieut., R.F.A.(T.F.) *M.C.* [1914]
SASSOON, E. V. Capt. (Ad.), R.A.F. 1900
SASSOON, H. W. Lieut., Grenadier Gds. and Gds. M.G. 1906
   Regt.
SAUMAREZ, Hon. J. ST V. B. Capt., Scots Gds. (W.) 1908
✠SAUNDER, G. B. 2nd Lieut., The Buffs (E. Kent Regt.) 1912
   Killed in action 15 *April* 1917
SAVILLE, S. H. Capt., Essex Regt. 1910
SAVORY, C. H. Surgeon Lieut., R.N. 1908
SAYER, H. Capt., Sussex Yeo.; Brigade Major. *D.S.O.* 1907
   M.C. M 2.
SCARLETT, J. A. Lieut.-Col., R.F.A. *D.S.O. Brevet* 1896
   Lieut.-Colonel. M 3.
SCHACHT, A. G. Pte., London Regt. [1914]
SCHLOSS, W. F. R. *See* CASTLE, W. F. R.
SCHOLFIELD, C. N. Lieut., R.G.A. 1906
SCHOLFIELD, E. P. Lieut., E. Riding of Yorkshire Yeo. 1895
   and R.G.A.
SCHON, B. C.S.M. (Instructor), School of Musketry 1901
SCHREINER, O. D. Capt., Northamptonshire Regt. and 1911
   S. Wales Borderers. (W.) *M.C.*
SCHUSTER, L. F. Capt. and Adjt., R.G.A.(T.F.) (W.) *M.* 1907
SCHWANN, F. H. *See* SWANN, F. H.
SCORGIE, N. G. Lieut.-Col., Deputy Director, Army *1906
   Printing and Stationery Services. *O.B.E. M* 2.
SCOTT, Hon. C. F. H. *See* HEPBURNE-SCOTT, Hon. C. F.
SCOTT, E. Sergt.-Major, R.E. 1910
SCOTT, G. E. 2nd Lieut., R.A.S.C. [1914]
SCOTT, Rev. R. B. C.F. 3rd Class, R.A.C.D.(T.F.) 1892
SCOTT, Hon. W. G. H. *See* POLWARTH, Lord
SCOTT, W. L. Lieut., S. Staffs. Regt. (W.) 1903
SCOTT, Hon. W. T. H. *See* HEPBURNE-SCOTT, Hon. W. T.
SCOTT-DAVIDSON, W. W. Capt. (T.), R.A.F. *M.* 1909
SCOTT-ELLIOT, G. F. Capt., King's Own Scottish Bor- 1879
   derers (T.F. Res.) *Order of the Nile, 4th Class (Egypt)*
SCOTT-KERR, R., C.B., M.V.O., D.S.O. Brig.-Gen. (W.) 1877
   C.M.G. M 2.
SCOTT-MURRAY, A. E. Capt., Norfolk Regt.; Staff Capt. 1900
   M.C. M 2.
SCOTT-MURRAY, R. C. Capt., R. Warwickshire Regt.; 1897
   Major, Spec. List (Chief Instructor, School of In-
   struction). *M.*

SEALY, H. N. Capt., R.A.M.C. 1905
SEARIGHT, T. P. Capt., R.A.S.C.; Major, S.O. 2, R.A.F. 1900
M. m.
SEARLES, P. A. Capt., The Queen's (R.W. Surrey Regt.); 1881
Major, R.F.A.(T.F.)
✠SEELY, C. G. Capt. and Adjt., Hampshire Regt.(T.F.) 1913
M.
Killed in action in the Second Battle of Gaza 19 *April*
1917
SEELY, F. E., T.D. Lieut.-Col., S. Notts. Hussars (T.F. 1883
Res.); A.D.C.
SEELY, Rt. Hon. J. E. B., D.S.O., T.D. Lieut.-Col., Hamp- 1887
shire Yeo.; Major-Gen. *C.B. C.M.G. M* 4.
Commander, Legion of Honour (France). Commander,
Ordre de la Couronne (Belgium). Belgian Croix de Guerre
✠SEGNITZ, H. F. Corpl., H.A.C.; 2nd Lieut., London 1911
Regt. (St Pancras Bn.)
Accidentally killed 25 *Sept.* 1915
SEVERNE, E. C. W. Capt., Warwickshire Yeo.; attd. 9th 1906
Lancers; A.D.C.; Lieut., Spec. List. (W.) *M.*
SEVESTRE, R. Major, R.A.M.C. (5th N. Gen. Hospital, 1886
T.F.)
SEWELL, H. S. Lieut.-Col., 4th (R. Irish) Dragoon Gds.; 1899
Brig.-Gen. (W.) *C.M.G. D.S.O. and Bar. Brevet*
Lieut.-Colonel. M 4. *Chevalier, Legion of Honour*
(France)
SEWELL, J. P. C. Major (A.), R.A.F. *O.B.E. M. Che-* 1907
valier, Legion of Honour (France)
✠SEYMOUR, F. Lieut., King's Royal Rifle Corps 1904
Killed in action at Hooge 30 *July* 1915
SEYMOUR TAYLOR, E. M. Capt., R.F.A. *M.C. M.* 1914
SEYS-PHILLIPS, H. Capt., Bedfordshire Regt. *French* 1911
Croix de Guerre
SHACKEL, G. M. Capt., R. Sussex Regt. (W 2.) *M.C.* 1912
M.
SHACKLE, R. J. Lieut., R.A.S.C. 1914
SHAKESPEAR, G. A. Capt., R.A.S.C. 1897
SHANKS, E. B. 2nd Lieut., S. Lancs. Regt.; empld. War 1910
Office
SHARP, H. Pte., R.A.M.C. and London Regt. (Queen's) 1914
SHARP, L. E. S. Capt., Spec. List (Uganda Med. Service) 1908
SHARPE, Rev. C. C. C.F. 4th Class, R.A.C.D. 1888
SHARPE, G. W. Lieut.-Col., King's Own (R. Lancaster 1897
Regt.) (W.) *O.B.E. M.*

✠SHAW, A. 2nd Lieut., Northamptonshire Regt. and Nor- 1910
folk Regt.
Killed in action 12 Oct. 1916
SHAW, E. B. Lieut., London Regt. (London Irish Rifles) 1910
SHAW, G. S. 2nd Lieut., R.F.A.(T.F.) 1905
SHAW, J. A. P. Surgeon Sub-Lieut., R.N.V.R. 1914
✠SHAW, R. P. Capt., R. Fusiliers 1905
Killed in action in Gallipoli 28 *Nov.* 1915
SHEARME, J. S. Capt., Repton School O.T.C. 1892
SHEBBEARE, H. V. Lieut., R.G.A. and Labour Corps; 1895
Draft Conducting Officer
SHEEPSHANKS, A. C. Major, Rifle Brigade; Lieut.-Col., 1903
King's Royal Rifle Corps; empld. School of Instruc-
tion. (W 2.) *D.S.O. M* 2.
✠SHEEPSHANKS, C. J. H. Capt., Devon Regt. 1904
Killed in action 17 March 1916
SHEEPSHANKS, R. H. Capt., 12th Cavalry, Indian Army. 1903
D.S.O. M.
SHELDON, Rev. F. H. C.F. 4th Class, R.A.C.D. 1905
SHELDON, Rev. L. G. M. C.F. 4th Class, R.A.C.D. 1911
SHELLEY, G. E. Capt. and Adjt., Grenadier Gds. (W.) 1909
SHELLEY, J. F. Capt., R. 1st Devon Yeo. and Devon 1905
Regt.
✠SHENNAN, D. F. F. Lieut., King's Royal Rifle Corps 1911
Killed in action near Ypres 8 May 1915
SHEPHERD, F. McA. Capt., Surrey Yeo. 1910
SHEPHERD, J. C. Lieut., R.F.A. (W 3.) *M.C.* 1914
✠SHEPHERD, J. M. E. 2nd Lieut., Rifle Brigade; Capt., 1914
R.F.C.
Killed in action 15 Feb. 1917
SHEPPARD, B. F. Sapper, R.E. (W.) 1914
SHEPPARD, G. A. Sub-Lieut., R.N.R.; Lieut., Hertford- 1886
shire Yeo.
SHERRIFF, C. B. 2nd Lieut., Argyll and Sutherland 1914
Hdrs.; Capt., R.A.S.C.
SHEWELL, H. W. B. Surgeon Cdr., R.N. *O.B.E. M.* 1891
SHIPMAN, G. A. C. Major, R.A.M.C. (4th N. Gen. Hos- 1894
pital, T.F.) *m.*
SHIRREFF, C. R. Capt., Durham L.I. 1896
SHORT, H. S. Lieut., R.G.A.(T.F.); empld. Admiralty. 1907
(W.)
SHORT, P. S. Lieut., R.G.A.(T.F.) 1910
SHOVE, R. S. Major, R.F.A. (W.) *m.* 1908
SHUTT, J. E. Air Mechanic, R.A.F. 1914

✠Silvertop, F. S. J. Lieut., Oxfordshire Yeo. 1901
Killed in action 20 *May* 1917
Simeon, L. S. B. Lieut., R. Fusiliers and Gen. Staff. 1909
(W.) *M.C.*
✠Simpson, C. S. Capt. and Adjt., Yorkshire Regt. 1910
Killed in action 10 *July* 1916
Simpson, Rev. F. A. C.F. 4th Class, R.A.C.D. *m.* 1910
Simpson, L. S. Colonel, R.E.; Chief Mechanical En- 1892
gineer. *C.B.E. D.S.O. M* 4.
Simpson, N. D. 2nd Lieut., R.A.S.C.(M.T.) 1908
¹Simpson, R. C. Major, W. Kent Yeo. 1902
Simpson, R. G. L. G. Lieut., R.A.F. 1914
Simson, C. C. Major, Australian A.M.C. *M.C.* 1889
Sinclair, D. J. O. Lieut., R. Irish Fus. and Tank Corps 1911
Singer, C. M. Lieut., Devon Regt. and M.G.C. (Motor). 1908
M.C.
Sington, A. J. C. Capt. and Adjt., Manchester Regt. 1905
(T.F.)
Sington, E. C. Capt. and Adjt., Lancs. Fus.(T.F.) 1911
Skipwith, Sir G. H. D'E., Bart. Capt., London Regt. 1903
(T.F. Res.)
Slade, G. O. Lieut., Essex Regt. (W.) 1909
Slater, B. H. Major, R.A.M.C. 1897
Smart, W. M. Instructor Lieut., R.N. 1911
Smiley, H. S. Capt., R. Fusiliers, attd. Egyptian Army 1901
Smith, A. C. S. Lieut., R.A.M.C. *M.C. M* 2. 1908
Smith, A. J. H. Capt., Coldstream Gds.; Major, G.S.O. 2. 1899
M.C. M. French Croix de Guerre
Smith, B. A. Lieut., R.G.A.; attd. R.E. 1907
Smith, B. Abel. Major, S. Notts. Hussars; Lieut.-Col., 1897
Middlesex Regt.
Smith, C. H. C. Major (S.), R.A.F. *D.S.C.* 1907
✠Smith, C. J. Dudley. 2nd Lieut., Grenadier Gds. [1914]
Killed in action 16 *June* 1915
Smith, D. Abel. Lieut., Grenadier Gds.; Capt. and 1911
Adjt., Gds. M.G. Regt. (W 2.) *M.C. M.*
Smith, G. Gnr., R.G.A. 1916
Smith, G. Dudley. Capt., Remount Service 1885
Smith, G. M. Herbert. *See* Herbert Smith, G. M.
Smith, H. Capt., Hampshire Regt.(T.F. Res.) 1885
Smith, H. Austen. *See* Austen-Smith, H.
Smith, H. V. Sergt., R.A.M.C. 1899

---

¹ Died of pneumonia shortly after the armistice.

✠Smith, J. H. Martin. 2nd Lieut., Spec. List (Intelligence) 1906
  Died 10 *Sept.* 1914
✠Smith, J. H. Michael. 2nd Lieut., Manchester Regt. 1908
  Died 17 *Sept.* 1914 *of wounds received in action*
Smith, N. B. Capt., R.F.A. (T.F.); empld. War Office. 1884
  (W.)
Smith, O. Martin. Capt., Grenadier Gds. (W.) 1904
✠Smith, Peter. Lieut., R.E.; attd. R.F.C. *M.* 1912
  Killed in action 28 *April* 1917
Smith, Prince. 2nd Lieut., R.F.A. (W.) *M.C.* 1916
Smith, R. Lce.-Corpl., Mtd. Infy., Indian Defence Force 1900
Smith, R. A. Lieut., R.F.A.(T.F.) 1906
Smith, R. Abel. Capt., Hertfordshire Yeo. *M.C. M.* 1908
Smith, R. S. S. Surgeon Sub-Lieut., R.N.V.R. *Albert* 1909
  Medal, 2nd Class
Smith, R. W. Lieut., R.A.S.C. (W.) 1902
Smith, S. B. 2nd Lieut., S. Staffs. Regt.; Capt. (A.), 1909
  R.A.F. *M.C.*
✠Smith, S. H. 2nd Lieut., S. Staffs. Regt. 1910
  Killed in action 24 *Nov.* 1915
Smith, W. O. Major, Lancs. Fus. 1906
Smith-Barry, R. R. Colonel (A.), R.A.F. *A.F.C.* 1904
  Brevet Major. Officer, Order of Leopold (Belgium)
Smyth, H. W. Lieut., R.N.V.R. *C.M.G. M.* 1886
✠Snelgrove, S. H. Lieut., King's Royal Rifle Corps 1910
  Killed in action at Hooge 30 *July* 1915
Soames, A. L. Lieut., R.A.S.C. 1896
Soames, J. B. 2nd Lieut., Res. Regt. of Cavalry; Lieut.- 1902
  Cdr., R.N.A.S. *Order of St Anne (Russia). Order*
  of St Vladimir, with swords (Russia)
Soames, M. H. Major, London Regt. (L.R.B.) 1897
Soames, R. M. Capt., R.A.M.C. (P.) 1901
✠Soole, S. W. Gnr., R.F.A. 1895
  Died 3 *Feb.* 1917 *of cerebro-spinal meningitis*
Soper, R. G. Lieut., Northumberland Fus.(T.F.) (W.) 1906
Sotham, F. A. Lieut., Cheshire Regt. (W.) *M.* 1914
Southey, E. Capt., S. Wales Borderers (R. of O.); 1894
  Major, R. Welsh Fus.; Supt., Military Detention
  Barracks. *m.*
Southwell, R. V. Lieut., R.A.S.C.(M.T.); Lieut.-Cdr., 1907
  R.N.V.R.; Major (T.), R.A.F. (Aircraft Production
  Dept.)
Sparkes, W. L. Capt., Devon Regt.(T.F.) 1913
Sparrow, E. C. Capt., R.A.M.C. 1897

✠SPARTALI, C. 2nd Lieut., R. Berkshire Regt.   1907
Killed in action at Loos 13 *Oct.* 1915

SPEDDING, J. A. Lieut., London Regt. (Queen's, Cadet 1897
Bn.)

✠SPEER, A. H. T. L. Pte., R. Fusiliers (P.S. Bn.); Lieut., 1913
R.F.A.(T.F.); attd. R.F.C.
Killed in action 9 *July* 1916

SPEER, F. A. Major, Herefordshire Regt. and Gen. Staff 1888
(Area Cmdt.)

SPENCER, G. T. L. Capt., R. Warwickshire Regt. *M.B.E.* 1902

SPENCER, H. V. Lieut., Bedfordshire Yeo.; Capt., Tank 1897
Corps

SPENCER, T. D. Capt., Coldstream Gds.   1909

✠SPENS, A. W. Lce.-Corpl., Essex Regt.   1890
Died 7 *Aug.* 1917

SPENS, T. P. Lieut., Cameronians (Scottish Rifles, T.F.) 1913
and Gen. Staff. (W.) *M.C. m.*

✠SPICER, E. E. Capt., London Regt. (R. Fus.)   1912
Killed in action at Oppy Wood 28 *March* 1918

SPICER, G. E. Capt., R.A.M.C. (W.) *M.C. M.* 1909

SPICER, L. D. Capt. and Adjt., King's Own (Yorkshire 1912
L.I.); Brigade Major. (W.) *D.S.O. M.C. and Bar.*
M 3.

SPICER, R. Capt., H.A.C. (W.) *M.C.*   1904

✠SPIERS, A. L. C. Lieut., King's (Shropshire L.I.) 1903
Killed in action 26 *Sept.* 1917

✠SPRAGG, C. E. W. Capt., E. Yorks. Regt.(T.F.) (W.) 1911
Killed in action 10 *Sept.* 1918

SPRAGGE, F. B. B. Capt., R.F.A. (W.) *M.C. M* 2. 1911

SPRANGER, J. A. Lieut., R.E.; Capt., Spec. List. *m.* 1908

✠SPRIGG, H. A. G. Pte., Middlesex Regt. (P. S. Bn.); Capt., 1901
Hampshire Regt.(T.F.) (W.)
Killed in action in Palestine 9 *April* 1918

SPRINGMAN, J. B. Capt., Denbigh Yeo. and R. Welsh 1910
Fus. *M.C.*

SPRING RICE, C. Capt., R.A.S.C.   1906

SPROT, Sir A., Bart., M.P. Bt. Colonel, Gen. Staff (Ad- 1871
ministrative Cmdt.) *C.M.G. M* 2. *French Croix*
de Guerre

SQUIRE, C. E. Major, Rifle Brigade. (W 2.) *M.C.* 1908

STANBURY TAYLOR, G. R. M. *See* TAYLOR, G. R. M. S.

STANCLIFFE, R. S. Lieut., Life Gds.; Capt., R.E. (Sig- 1914
nals). *M* 3.

STANLEY, A. S. W. Lieut.-Col., Suffolk Regt. *M.* 1880

STANLEY, A. W. W. Lieut., R. Horse Gds.; Capt., Gds. 1909
M.G. Regt. *M.C.*
STANLEY, C. S. B. W. Lieut., W. Kent Yeo.; Capt. and 1910
Adjt., The Buffs (E. Kent Regt.)
STANLEY, C. W. Hon. Major, Cambridgeshire Regt. 1879
STANNING, J. Lieut., D. of Lancaster's Own Yeo. and 1896
Manchester Regt.
STARKIE, R. P. A. Capt., R.A.M.C. *M.* 1908
STATHERS, G. N. Surgeon Lieut., R.N. 1904
STEANE, S. W. 2nd Lieut., R.F.A.; A.D.C.; Capt., 1904
I.A.R.O.
STEDMAN, G. F. Capt. and Adjt., York and Lancaster 1913
Regt. *M.C. M* 2.
STEEL, S. S. Major, Lothians and Border Horse 1900
STEINTHAL, R. E. Lieut., King's Own (R. Lancaster [1914]
Regt.)
✠STEPHENSON, D. G. Pte., H.A.C.; Lieut., Scots Gds. 1901
Killed in action 16 *May* 1915
STEVENS, A. L. W. Capt., Middlesex Regt. and Spec. [1914]
List, empld. Ministry of Munitions
STEVENS, C. J. DUFF. 2nd Lieut., Somerset L.I. 1911
STEVENSON, S. D. Major, Black Watch 1905
STEWART, C. A. Lieut., R.E. 1909
STEWART, C. T. Lieut., S. Irish Horse and R. Irish Regt. 1896
STEWART, F. W. Lieut., I.A.R.O., attd. 19th Punjabis. 1904
(W.) *M.C.*
STEWART, H. Colonel, Canterbury Regt., N. Zealand 1904
Force. (W.) *C.M.G. D.S.O. and Bar. M.C. M* 5.
French Croix de Guerre
✠STEWART, J. A. L. Lieut., Rifle Brigade 1911
Killed in action at Wieltje 13 *May* 1915
✠STEWART, R. J. Lieut., Seaforth Hdrs. *M.C. M.* 1911
Died 28 *Jan.* 1916 *of wounds received in action in*
Mesopotamia 13 *Jan.* 1916
STEWART-BROWN, R. Capt. and Adjt., D. of Lancaster's 1891
Own Yeo.
✠STEWART-JONES, T. A. Capt., R. Sussex Regt.(T.F.) 1892
Killed in action 9 *May* 1915
STIGAND, I. A. Lieut., Queen's Own (R.W. Kent Regt., 1899
T.F.)
STIRLING, A. Lieut.-Col., Lovat's Scouts (T.F. Res.); 1885
Brig.-Gen. *M. m.*
STIRLING-MAXWELL, Sir J. Hon. Colonel, Cameronians 1884
(Scottish Rifles, T.F.)

STIVEN, H. E. S. Capt., R.A.M.C. *M.*   1902
STOCKER, A. H. Capt., Hampshire Yeo.   1894
STOCKER, C. J. Major, I.M.S. *M.C.* *M* 2. *Order of* 1904
the Lion and Sun, 3rd Class (Persia)
STOGDON, J. H. Air Mechanic, R.A.F.   1895
STOKES, F. F. Pte., Hampshire Regt.; Lieut., Cambridge- 1899
shire Regt.
STOREY, K. L. Lieut., 20th Hussars; Capt., Res. Regt. 1905
of Cavalry
STOREY, R. A. Capt., R.A.S.C. *M.*   1907
STOTT, A. W. Major, R.A.M.C.(T.F.)   1904
STOTT, M. D. Capt., Border Regt. *M.C.*   1905
STOTT, R. Lieut., Lancs. Fus.   1908
STRACHAN CARNEGIE, A. B. Capt., R.G.A.   1893
STRADBROKE, Earl of, C.B., C.V.O., V.D. Hon. Colonel, 1880
R.F.A.(T.F.); A.D.C. to the King. *C.B.E.*
✠STRAIN, J. L. Capt., R.G.A. *M.*   1915
Killed in action 31 *July* 1917
STRAKER, I. A. Capt., 9th Lancers. (W.)   1908
STREET, H. B. Lieut., R.G.A.   1887
STUART, Viscount. 2nd Lieut., R. Berkshire Regt.; Capt., 1908
Gen. List; Major, M.G.C. and Spec. List (Cmdt.,
School of Instruction). *M.C.*
✠STUART, C. E. Capt., Suffolk Regt. (Cyclist Bn., T.F.); 1902
attd. York and Lancaster Regt.
Died 15 *March* 1917 *of wounds received in action*
12 *March* 1917
STUART, W. R. Capt., Gordon Hdrs.(T.F.) (W.)   1902
STUDD, H. W., D.S.O. Colonel, Coldstream Gds.; Brig.- 1889
Gen. (W.) *C.B.* *C.M.G.* *Brevet Colonel.* *M* 5.
Commander, Legion of Honour (France). Commander,
Order of the Crown of Italy. Italian Croce di Guerra.
Officer, Order of Leopold (Belgium). Grand Officer,
Military Order of Avis (Portugal). American Dis-
tinguished Service Medal
✠STUDD, Rev. L. F. Capt., London Regt. (Rangers)   1909
Killed in action 14 *Feb.* 1915
STUDD, V. M. Lieut., Rifle Brigade; attd. Sierra Leone 1909
Bn., W. African Frontier Force
✠SULIVAN, E. G. Capt., E. Surrey Regt.   1911
Killed in action 8 *May* 1917
✠SUMMERS, A. S. M. Capt., 19th Hussars; attd. R.F.C. 1905
M.
Killed in action 15 *Sept.* 1916

SURTEES, A. A. Capt., Northumberland Fus. and Gen. 1884
List (Army Canteen Committee)

✠SUTHERLAND, A. G. Pte., Gordon Hdrs. 1907
Missing, presumed killed in action, 23 March 1916

✠SUTTON, H. J. Lieut., Welsh Gds. 1905
Killed in action 27 Sept. 1915

SUTTON, L. N. Capt., Berkshire Yeo. 1912

SWAINE, J. K. Capt., R.A.S.C. 1903

SWANN, F. H. Lieut.-Cdr., R.N.V.R.; Major (O.), R.A.F. 1892
M.

SWANSTON, C. B. Lieut., King's Own Scottish Border- 1901
ers. (W.)

SWANWICK, F. B. Capt., Derbyshire Yeo. 1905

✠SWANWICK, R. K. Lieut., Gloucestershire Regt. 1903
Killed in action 15 Sept. 1914

SYDNEY, H. Major, R.A.S.C. *M* 2. 1906

SYMES, Rev. R. C.F. 4th Class, R.A.C.D. 1889

SYMONS, Rev. C. D. Gnr., R.F.A.(T.F.); C.F. 4th Class, 1905
R.A.C.D. *M.C.*

SYMPSON, T. M. Lieut., E. Riding of Yorkshire Yeo. 1908

TABOR, J. C. Colonel, Essex Regt.; attd. Queen's Own 1896
(R. W. Kent Regt.) (W.)

TACON, R. C. Lieut., R.A.S.C. 1901

TAGART, Sir H. A. L., C.B., D.S.O. Colonel, 15th Hussars; 1888
Major-Gen., D.A. and Q.M.G. *K.C.M.G. M* 4.
Commander, Legion of Honour (France)

TALBOT, J. Major, Newcastle-on-Tyne Grammar School 1895
O.T.C.

TANGYE, R. T. G. Major, Gen. List. *O.B.E. M* 2. 1894
*Chevalier, Order of Leopold (Belgium). French Croix
de Guerre*

TANSLEY, L. B. Capt., R.F.A.(T.F.); Staff Capt. (W.) 1912
M.C.

TATCHELL, E., D.S.O. Lieut.-Col., Lincolnshire Regt. *m.* 1888

TATE, A. W. 2nd Lieut., Cameronians (Scottish Rifles); 1906
Capt., Black Watch; Lieut.-Col., M.G.C. (W.)
D.S.O. M 2.

TATHAM, C. K. Major, London Regt. (R. Fus.); empld. 1900
O.C.B.

✠TATHAM, G. B. Capt., Rifle Brigade; Brigade Major. *M.C.* 1902
Killed in action 30 March 1918

✠TATHAM, L. C. S. 2nd Lieut., Devon Regt. and R.F.C. 1913
Killed in action 10 Jan. 1918

TAYLOR, A. L. Capt., Norfolk Regt.(T.F.) 1900
TAYLOR, C. W. H. Major, Queen's Own (R. W. Kent 1899
Regt.); A.P.M. *D.S.O.* *Brevet Major.* *M* 4.
Officer, Order of the Redeemer (Greece). Order of the
White Eagle, 4th Class, with swords (Serbia)
TAYLOR, E. M.ʾ S. *See* SEYMOUR TAYLOR, E. M.
TAYLOR, G. I. Major, Spec. List (Meteorological Service); 1905
attd. R.A.F. *m.*
✠TAYLOR, G. R. M. S. Lieut., R.F.A.(T.F.) 1914
Died 30 *Sept.* 1917 *of wounds received in action*
✠TAYLOR, G. W. Lieut., R.F.A. (W.) 1910
Died 9 *Nov.* 1917 *of gas poisoning*
TAYLOR, H. D. 2nd Lieut., R.G.A. 1899
TAYLOR, H. G. Surgeon Lieut., R.N. 1913
TAYLOR, H. M. Capt., Norfolk Regt.(T.F.); Major, 1913
M.G:C. *M.C. M.*
TAYLOR, Rev. H. M. S. C.F. 4th Class, R.A.C.D. *O.B.E.* 1909
M.
✠TAYLOR, L. E. Capt., Madras Gds., Indian Defence Force 1901
Died 3 *Dec.* 1917 *of enteric fever*
TAYLOR, Rev. S. C.F. 4th Class, R.A.C.D. (W.) 1903
TEMPERLEY, C. E. Capt. and Adjt., Rifle Brigade. (W.) 1912
O.B.E. M.C.
TEMPLE, M. Lieut., R.A.S.C. *m.* 1901
TEMPLER, J. F. H. Major, R. Fusiliers. *M.* 1904
✠TENNANT, C. G. 2nd Lieut., Seaforth Hdrs.(T.F.) 1901
Killed in action 9 *May* 1915
TENNANT, H. V. Lieut., R.E. 1910
✠TENNANT, W. G. Lieut., Strathcona's Horse, Canadian 1897
Force
Killed in action 25 *May* 1915
✠TENNYSON, Hon. A. A. Capt., Rifle Brigade; G.S.O. 3. 1910
Killed in action 21 *March* 1918
TENNYSON, Hon. L. H. Major, Rifle Brigade. (W 3.) 1908
M 2.
✠TERRY, R. J. A., M.V.O. Major, R. Sussex Regt.; Brigade 1888
Major. *D.S.O. M.*
Killed in action 3 *Oct.* 1915
TETLEY, C. H. Lieut.-Col., W. Yorks. Regt.(T.F.) *D.S.O.* 1895
T.D. M 3.
TETLEY, M. H. Lieut., W. Yorks. Regt.(T.F.) (W.) 1906
THEOBALD, A. C. L. Major, R.F.A.; attd. R.M.A., Wool- 1896
wich. *D.S.O. M.*
THEOBALD, W. G. 2nd Lieut., R.G.A.; attd. R.A.F. 1898

THODAY, D. Lieut., Manchester Univ. O.T.C. 1902
THOMAS, J. 2nd Lieut., R. Scots Fus.(T.F.) (W 2.) 1908
   M.C.
THOMAS, O. V. Major (A.), R.A.F. *O.B.E. M* 2. 1908
THOMAS, W. E. Capt., Labour Corps 1909
THOMPSON, C. H. F. Major, London Regt. *(L.R.B.); 1901
   D.A.Q.M.G. *D.S.O. O.B.E. M* 3. *French Croix
de Guerre*
✠THOMPSON, F. C. Lieut., R.F.A. 1907
   Died 3 *Oct.* 1917 *of wounds received in action* 2 *Oct.*
   1917
THOMPSON, H. S. Lieut., R.F.A.(T.F.) (W.) (P.) *M.* 1903
THOMPSON, J. D. Capt. and Adjt., Loyal N. Lancs. Regt. 1902
THOMPSON, T. A. L. *See* LACEY THOMPSON, T. A.
THOMPSON, W. J. Major, Worcestershire Regt. 1904
THOMPSON, W. W. Hon. Capt. and Q.M., Lancs. Fus. 1876
   O.B.E.
THOMSON, G. P. Capt., The Queen's (R. W. Surrey 1910
   Regt.); empld. British Military Mission; attd. R.A.F.
   m.
THOMSON, J. B. Capt., R.A.S.C. *M.* 1907
THOMSON, J. O. Capt., King's Own (Yorkshire L.I.) 1911
   and Gen. Staff (Intelligence). *O.B.E.*
THORESBY, M. (*late* THORESBY-JONES). Pte., London 1909
   Regt. (Artists Rifles); Lieut., R.F.A. (W.)
✠THORNHILL, G. R. Lieut., The Buffs (E. Kent Regt.) 1910
   Killed in action 22 *Oct.* 1914
THORNTON, Rev. C. C. Sergt., R.A.S.C.(M.T.) 1897
THORNTON, E. 2nd Lieut., R. Fusiliers 1912
THORNTON, F. Capt., 16th Lancers. (W.) *M.* 1912
THORNTON, F. R. Lieut.-Col., R.A.M.C. (W.) *M.C.* 1902
   and Bar. M 2.
THORNTON, G. L. Capt., R.A.M.C. *M.C. and Bar* 1890
THORNTON, Rev. G. R. C.F. 4th Class, R.A.C.D. 1901
THORNTON, Rev. J. G. C.F. 4th Class, R.A.C.D. *M.* 1904
✠THORNTON, N. S. Sergt., R. Fusiliers (P.S. Bn.); Major, 1902
   Rifle Brigade. *D.S.O. M.C. M* 2.
   Died 10 *April* 1918 *of wounds received in action* 3
   April 1918
THORP, B. L. Capt., R.A.S.C. and Tank Corps. *M.C.* 1900
   M.
THORP, E. B. 2nd Lieut., N. Staffs. Regt. (W.) 1904
TIARKS, J. G. E. Lieut., 1st Dragoon Gds. [1914]
TICKELL, E. J., D.S.O. Lieut., 14th Hussars (R. of O.) *m.* 1880

✠TILLARD, T. A. Lieut., Norfolk Yeo.; Capt. (A.), R.F.C. 1902
(W.)
Killed in action 6 Dec. 1916
TIMES, W. O. Major, Bedfordshire Regt.; D.A.A.G. 1907
(W.) *M.C. M* 2.
TIMMIS, R. B. Capt., R.G.A. (W 2.) *M* 2. 1899
TINKER, H. W. C. Lieut., R.N.V.R. *O.B.E.* 1903
TINSLEY, R. L. Capt., W. Yorks. Regt.; A.D.C. 1912
TIRARD, N. S. Capt., R.A.M.C. 1909
✠TISDALL, A. W. ST C. Sub-Lieut., R.N.V.R. (Anson Bn., 1909
R.N.D.)

𝔙.𝔠. "During the landing from the S.S. "River Clyde"
at V Beach in the Gallipoli Peninsula on the 25th April,
1915, Sub-Lieutenant Tisdall, hearing wounded men on
the beach calling for assistance, jumped into the water
and, pushing a boat in front of him, went to their rescue.
He was, however, obliged to obtain help, and took with
him on two trips Leading Seaman Malia and on other
trips Chief Petty Officer Perring and Leading Seamen
Curtiss and Parkinson. In all Sub-Lieutenant Tisdall
made four or five trips between the ship and the shore,
and was thus responsible for rescuing several wounded
men under heavy and accurate fire."—Supplement to
The London Gazette, 31 March, 1916.

Killed in action in Gallipoli 6 May 1915

TODD, E. W. Surgeon Lieut., R.N. 1908
TODD, J. Lieut., R.F.A. (P.) 1910
TODHUNTER, H. W. Lieut.-Col., King's Own Scottish 1892
Borderers; Experimental Officer, School of Musketry;
empld. Ministry of Munitions. *C.M.G. Brevet
Lieut.-Colonel. m* 3.
✠TOLLEMACHE, A. H. W. 2nd Lieut., R.E.; attd. R.F.C. 1912
Killed in action 19 *July* 1916
TOLLEMACHE, Hon. M. G. Capt., Suffolk Regt. (T.F. 1890
Res.); empld. O.C.B. *M.*
✠TOLLER, G. R. Lieut., Lincolnshire Regt. 1890
Died 27 *July* 1917
✠TOMLINSON, F. R. J. 2nd Lieut., S. Staffs. Regt. 1910
Killed in action near Ypres 26 *Oct.* 1914
TOMLINSON, T. S. Capt., R. Munster Fus.; attd. Lein- 1896
ster Regt.
✠TOMPSON, A. H. 2nd Lieut., E. African Mtd. Rifles and 1899
Grenadier Gds.
Killed in action 27 *Sept.* 1915
TOMSON, W. J. M. *See* MARTIN-TOMSON, W. J.

TOPLIS, J. Hon. Colonel, Spec. List (Financial Adviser). 1895
M 2.
TORR, H. J. Capt., R. Defence Corps 1883
TORR, J. H. G. Capt., Lincolnshire Regt. (W.) 1911
TORREY, C. E. Capt., King's (Liverpool Regt.) (W 2.) 1908
M.
TORREY, G. E. F. Capt., King's (Liverpool Regt.); 1902
D.A.Q.M.G., E. Command. (W.) *M.C.*
TOSSWILL, C. G. Major, R. Defence Corps; attd. 1894
R.A.F. *m.*
TOWER, F. F. Lieut.-Cdr., R.N.R.; Cdr., R.N.V.R. 1878
O.B.E. Italian Bronze Medal for Military Valour
TOWER, G. E. Capt., R.F.A. *M.C.* 1910
TOWNLEY, C. E. Capt., Suffolk Regt. and Gen. List 1906
(Intelligence). *M* 2.
TOWNLEY, M. G. Major, Remount Service 1882
TOWNSEND, J. S. E. A.B., R.N.V.R.; Major, Spec. List. 1895
Chevalier, Legion of Honour (France)
TOWNSHEND, H. Lieut., R.E. (Sound-ranging Section). 1909
(W.)
TOWSE, H. B. Lieut.-Col., E. African Force. *M* 2. 1885
TOYE, J. F. Lieut., R.N.V.R. 1904
TRAFFORD, C. E. J. Lieut., Scots Gds.; S.O. 4, R.A.F. 1901
M.C. M.
TRAILL, R. R Capt., R.A.M.C. 1911
TRASENSTER, W. A. Major, R. Fusiliers. *M.C. M* 2. 1909
TREDCROFT, J. L. Capt., R.A.S.C. 1908
TREEBY, F. W. 2nd Lieut., R.F.A. 1914
TREGONING, E. A. Capt., Northumberland Fus.; Staff 1902
Capt., E. Indies
TREGONING, G. N. Capt., Welsh Regt. and Spec. List, 1900
empld. Ministry of National Service. *m.*
TRENCH, F. C. Lieut., R.G.A. 1896
TRENCH, R. H. Major, Garrison Artillery, Indian 1899
Defence Force
TRENCH, W. L. Major, W. Yorks. Regt. *M.C.* 1899
TRITTON, H. L. M. Major, Essex Yeo. 1888
✠TROTTER, C. L. Lieut., King's African Rifles 1909
Died 22 Jan. 1918
TROTTER, C. W., T.D. Hon. Colonel, S. Notts: Hussars 1883
(T.F. Res.) and Gen. Staff. *C.B. M* 2. *m.*
✠TROTTER, K. S. 2nd Lieut., Rifle Brigade 1911
Killed in action 26 April 1915
TROTTER, R. D. Capt., Rifle Brigade 1905

✠Trouton, E. A. Lieut., R. Inniskilling Fus. 1910
Killed in action 1 *July* 1916
✠Trouton, F. T. Capt., Cameronians (Scottish Rifles) 1910
Killed in action 25 *Sept.* 1915
✠Truscott, F. G. Lieut., Suffolk Regt. (Cyclist Bn., 1912
T.F.); attd. R.F.C. *M.C. M.*
Killed in action 6 *April* 1917
Tuck, N. J. Capt., Norfolk Regt. (W 2.) 1911
Tufnell, N. C. Capt., Grenadier Gds. 1907
✠Tuke, Rev. F. H. C.F. 4th Class, R.A.C.D. 1886
Killed in action 20 *July* 1916
Turnbull, R. W. Lieut., R.F.A.(T.F.); Staff Capt. 1901
M.C. M 2.
✠Turner, A. C. Pte., R. Fusiliers; 2nd Lieut., Rifle Brigade 1900
Killed in action 16 *Jan.* 1918
Turner, A. W. Capt., D. of Cornwall's L.I. (W 3.) 1908
M.C.
Turner, F. G. Capt., Gen. List (Brigade Major). *O.B.E.* 1908
M.C. M.
Turner, H. E. M. Major, Norfolk Regt. (W.) 1893
Turner, H. H. Lieut.-Col., R.E. 1891
Turner, W. A. S. Major, R.F.A. *M.C. M.* 1908
Tweedie, H.A. Capt.(A.),R.A.F.; Major,S.O.2. *A.F.C.* 1907
Tweedy,W.R. Q.M.S.,Canadian Hdrs.; Major,R.A.S.C. 1907
(W.) *M.*
Twomey, R. A. Instructor Lieut., R.N. 1913
Twopeny, R. E. N. Lieut., K. Edward's Horse. (W.) 1913
M.C. and Bar
Tyrwhitt Drake, C. W. Lieut., R. Defence Corps. (W.) 1898

Ullman, R. B. Capt., R.F.A.(T.F.) (W 3.) *M.C.* 1913
Ulyat, Rev. E. S. Chaplain, R.N. 1906
Ungoed, G. T. 2nd Lieut., Middlesex Regt.(T.F.); 1900
empld. War Office
Unna, P. J. H. Lieut.-Cdr., R.N.V.R. 1896
✠Upjohn, W. M. Capt., Welsh Gds. 1903
Killed in action 24 *Aug.* 1918
Urwick, R. H. Capt., R.A.M.C. 1894
Usher, T. C. Capt., R.F.A.; Staff Capt. *M* 2. 1898
Uthwatt, Ven. W. A. C.F. 4th Class, R.A.C.D. 1900
Uzielli, C. F. Lieut., King's Own (R. Lancaster Regt.) 1902
and Tank Corps. (W 2.) *M.C.*

Valentine, Rev. H. T. C.F. 4th Class, R.A.C.D. 1875

Van Duzer, F. C. Lieut., R.F.A.(T.F.) *French Croix* [1914]
de Guerre
Van Duzer, S. R. Capt., York and Lancaster Regt.; 1899
empld. War Office
✠Van Praagh, R. B. 2nd Lieut., King's Royal Rifle [1914]
Corps. (W.)
Killed in action 9 *April* 1917
Van Raalte, N. M. Lieut., R.N.V.R. 1907
Vane, Hon. C. W. *See* Barnard, Lord
Vane, Hon. R. F. Capt., Durham L.I. 1909
Vane-Tempest, E. C. W. Lieut., R.N.V.R. (W.) *D.S.C.* 1912
M.
✠Varley, L. Lieut., D. of Wellington's (W. Riding Regt., 1911
T.F.)
Killed in action 12 *Nov.* 1915
Vaughan, E. W. B. Lieut., E. Surrey Regt.; empld. 1907
O.C.B.
Vaughan, R. B. 2nd Lieut., R.A.S.C. 1904
Vaughan-Williams, R. 2nd Lieut., R.G.A. 1892
Veater, A. W. Instructor Cdr., R.N.; empld. Admiralty. 1894
Chevalier, Legion of Honour (France)
Venn, J. A. Capt., Cambridgeshire Regt. 1902
Venning, J. A. Capt., R.A.M.C. 1899
Vere Hodge, H. S. *See* Hodge, H. S. Vere
Vereker, G. G. M. Capt., Grenadier Gds. *M.C. M.* 1907
Vereker, Hon. S. R. Lieut., R.H.A.(T.F.) (W.) *M.C.* 1907
M.
Verey, H. E. Lieut.-Col., Spec. List (A.D.G.T.) *D.S.O.* 1896
M.
Vernon, J. C. Sergt., H.A.C. (W.) 1904
✠Vernon, W. H. Lieut., London Regt. (R. Fus.) 1914
Killed in action near Les Bœufs 7 *Oct.* 1916
✠Verrall, C. F. Lieut., R. Sussex Regt. *M.* 1907
Killed in action 22 *Dec.* 1914
Verrall, P. J. Capt., R.A.M.C. 1902
✠Vickers, R. 2nd Lieut., R.F.A.(T.F.) 1912
Died 10 *Dec.* 1917 *of wounds received in action*
Vincent, R. B. Capt., Gordon Hdrs.(T.F.); Major, 1906
D.A.D.R.T. *Brevet Major*
Vinter, P. J. Lieut., Devon Regt.(T.F.); Major, A.P.M. 1889
Vivian, Hon. O. R., t.d. Major, Glamorgan Yeo.; 1893
Lieut.-Col., Cameron Hdrs. *M.V.O. D.S.O. M.*
Vizard, W. G. Lieut., Dorset Regt.(T.F.); Staff Capt. [1914]
M.

TRINITY COLLEGE 469

VON SCHRÖDER, Baron W. H. Capt., Remount Service 1886
VOS, S. Lieut., Devon Regt.(T.F.) 1907

WADE, E. B. H. Lieut., R.N.V.R. 1891
WADE, H. O. Lieut.-Col., W. Yorks. Regt.(T.F.) and 1887
Gen. Staff. (W.) *D.S.O. M* 2.
WADSWORTH, J. Corpl., R.E. (Meteorological Section) 1913
WAECHTER, Sir H., Bart. Hon. Colonel, R.F.A.(T.F.) 1889
and Gen. Staff. *C.M.G. Italian Croce di Guerra*
WAGGETT, Rev. P. N. C.F. 4th Class, R.A.C.D. *M* 2. *1910
WAINWRIGHT, B. M. Lieut. (A.), R.A.F. (P.) [1914]
WAINWRIGHT, Rev. R. C. C.F. 4th Class, R.A.C.D. 1908
M.
WAKEFIELD, A. W. Lieut. (M.O.), Newfoundland Regt.; 1895
Lieut., R.A.M.C.; Capt., Canadian A.M.C. *M.*
WAKEFIELD, E. W. Capt., Cheshire Regt.; Major, Border 1880
Regt. (T.F.); Capt., Labour Corps
WAKEFIELD, J. H. Lieut., W. Somerset Yeo. 1905
✠WAKEFORD, E. K. Lieut., Leicestershire Regt. (W.) 1912
Killed in action 16 *July* 1916
WALE, E. H. Capt., R.E. *M.C. M.* 1910
WALKER, E. E. Lieut., R.E. (London Electrical En- 1902
gineers, T.F.); empld. Ministry of Munitions
WALKER, F. G. Major, R.A.S.C. *M* 3. 1901
✠WALKER, G. F. Pte., R. Fusiliers (P.S. Bn.); 2nd Lieut., 1895
York and Lancaster Regt.(T.F.)
Killed in action 7 *Dec.* 1916
WALKER, J. P. E. Lieut., 2nd Dragoons (R. Scots Greys). 1911
(W 2.) *M. French Croix de Guerre*
WALKER, K. P. Capt., York and Lancaster Regt.; Major, 1905
W. Yorks. Regt. (W.) *M.C. M.*
WALKER, M. A. Lieut., Madras and S. Mahratta Railway 1903
Rifles, Indian Defence Force
WALKER, N. O. Hon. Major, Spec. List. *O.B.E.* 1895
WALKER, Sir R. J. M., Bart. Capt., Coldstream Gds.; 1908
empld. Gen. Staff, N. Zealand Force
WALKER, R. W. S. Lieut., R.A.M.C. 1901
WALKER, T. A. Lieut., R.N.V.R. 1896
WALKER, W. E. Major, Durham L.I.(T.F.) 1896
WALL, A. H. Lieut.-Col., Marlborough College O.T.C. 1892
m.
WALL, T. Capt., R.G.A. (W.) *M.C.* 1914
WALLACE, Rev. A. W. W. C.F. 4th Class, R.A.C.D. 1907
WALLACE, G. L'E. Major, Dorset Regt. 1914

WALLACE, J. Capt., R.A.M.C.(T.F.)   *O.B.E.*   1880
WALLACE, J. A. V. 2nd Lieut., R.F.A.   1910
✠WALLACE, W. E. Lieut., R. Scots (T.F.)   1907
  Killed in action 17 April 1917
WALLER, H. K. Capt., R.A.M.C.   1900
✠WALROND, V. Major, R.F.A. (W.) *M* 2.   1908
  Killed in action 26 April 1917
WALSH, A. D. Pte., London Regt. (Artists Rifles); 2nd   1909
  Lieut., Loyal N. Lancs. Regt.
✠WALSH, P. Lieut., Loyal N. Lancs. Regt. (W.) *M.*   1914
  Died 8 July 1916 *of wounds received in action*
WALTERS, A. M. Lieut., Res. Regt. of Cavalry   [1914]
✠WALTERS, G. Y. L. Lieut., Irish Gds.   1913
  Died 15 Sept. 1916 *of wounds received in action*
WALTERS, W. L. 2nd Lieut., R.F.A.   1907
WANLISS, D. S. Lieut.-Col., 5th Infy. Bn. and Gen. List,   1884
  Australian Force. *C.M.G. M.*
WARBURG, O.E. Capt., R.G.A.and Gen.Staff. *O.B.E. m.*   1895
WARD, C. B. Capt., R.F.A.(T.F. Res.)   1893
✠WARD, R. O. C. Capt., The Buffs (E. Kent Regt.);   1900
  Major, Tank Corps. (W 2.) *M* 2.
  Killed in action 20 Nov. 1917
WARD, W. DUDLEY, M.P. Lieut.-Cdr., R.N.V.R. *M.*   1896
WARD, W. J. Lieut., I.A.R.O., attd. Rangoon Bn., Indian   1906
  Defence Force
WARD-JACKSON, R. Capt., Leicestershire Regt.(T.F.)   1910
  (W.)
WARDE-ALDAM, W. ST A. Capt., Coldstream Gds.;   1900
  Lieut.-Col., London Regt. (Blackheath and Woolwich
  Bn.) (W.) *D.S.O. Brevet Major. Brevet Lieut.-
  Colonel. M* 4. *Chevalier, Legion of Honour (France)*
WARDELL, J. M. Lieut., S. Irish Horse; Capt., R. Irish   1904
  Regt. (W.) (P.) *M.*
WARDELL-YERBURGH, G. B. Flt. Sub-Lieut., R.N.A.S.   1912
✠WARDLEY, G. C. N. Lieut., R.G.A.   1910
  Died 24 July 1916 *of wounds received in action*
✠WARE, F. H. Capt., London Regt. (Kensington Bn.)   1891
  Killed in action 1 July 1916
WARE, J. G. W. Capt., R.G.A.(T.F.) (W.)   1902
WARE, Rev. M. S. C.F. 4th Class, R.A.C.D.   1891
WARINGTON SMYTH, H. *See* SMYTH, H. W.
WARMINGTON, E. S. Capt., Labour Corps   1900
WARRE DYMOND, G. W. Capt., E. Surrey Regt. (P.)   1907
  M.C. M.

TRINITY COLLEGE

TRINITY COLLEGE 471

WARRINGTON, J. C. Capt., R.E. *M* 2. *French Croix de* 1905
Guerre
WARRINGTON, T. Capt., R.A.M.C. 1907
WARWICK, H. B. Lieut.-Col., Northumberland Fus. 1894
(R. of O.) (W.) *M.*
✠WASBROUGH, W. L. 2nd Lieut., Loyal N. Lancs. Regt. 1910
Killed in action 25 Sept. 1915
WATERLOW, G. W. Lieut., R.A.S.C.; Capt., Spec. List 1902
(R.T.O.) *M.*
✠WATKYN-THOMAS, A. Capt., Highland L.I. 1910
Missing, presumed killed in action, 13 *Nov.* 1916
WATKYN-THOMAS, F. W. Capt., R.A.M.C. 1906
WATNEY, C. N., T.D. Lieut.-Col., Queen's Own (R.W. 1887
Kent Regt., T.F.)
WATNEY, G. N. Capt., King's Own (Yorkshire L.I.) 1897
WATNEY, M. H. Capt., R.A.M.C. 1906
✠WATNEY, W. H. Lieut., Rifle Brigade 1898
Killed in action 10 May 1915
WATSON, B. B. Lieut., Irish Gds. *O.B.E.* 1896
WATSON, D. P. Lieut.-Col., R.A.M.C. *D.S.O. M.* 1893
WATSON, F. B. Capt., London Regt. (R. Fus.) 1898
WATSON, H. Sapper, R.E. (Meteorological Section) 1907
WATSON, J. B. Capt., R.F.A.(T.F.) and Gen. Staff 1891
WATSON, R. A. Lieut., Border Regt. and M.G.C. (W.) 1911
WATSON, Hon. R. B. W. Lieut., R. Scots (T.F.) (W.) 1901
WATSON, R. H. LINDSAY. Lieut., Gordon Hdrs. 1905
WATSON-ARMSTRONG, Hon. W. J. M. Capt., Northum- 1911
berland Fus.(T.F.) (W.) *M.*
✠WATSON-TAYLOR, A. S. 2nd Lieut., London Regt. 1902
Killed in action 14 Sept. 1917
WATSON-TAYLOR, C. A. Lieut., R.N.V.R. 1904
WATT, W. O. Capt. (Aviation), Foreign Legion, French 1896
Army; Lieut.-Col. (A.), Australian Flying Corps.
O.B.E. M 4. *m. Chevalier, Legion of Honour (France).*
French Croix de Guerre
WATTS, A. E. Lce.-Corpl., Middlesex Regt.; 2nd Lieut., 1907
Indian Army
WAUTON, E. A. Capt., R.A.S.C. *M.* 1910
WEATHERHEAD, E. Capt., R.A.M.C. 1892
WEAVER, A. B. Lieut., E. Yorks. Regt.(T.F.); attd. Rifle 1893
Brigade (T.F.)
✠WEBB, J. B. Lieut., N. Staffs. Regt.; attd. Bedfordshire 1913
Regt.
Killed in action near Ypres 21 April 1915

WEBB-PEPLOE, M. H. Capt., R.G.A. *M.C. M.*   1915
✠WEBSTER, J. F. 2nd Lieut., Black Watch; attd. Gordon   1912
Hdrs. *M.*
Killed in action 30 *Oct.* 1914
WEBSTER, R. G. Capt., Spec. List (Recruiting Staff) and   1864
R.F.A.
✠WEDGWOOD, A. F. Capt., N. Staffs. Regt.(T.F.) (W.)   1895
Killed in action 14 *March* 1917
WEDGWOOD, F. H. Capt., Spec. List (Recruiting Staff).   1886
m.
WEDGWOOD, R. L. Lieut.-Col., R.E.; Brig.-Gen., Di-   1892
rector of Docks. *C.B. C.M.G. M* 4. *Officer,
Legion of Honour (France). French Croix de Guerre.
Commander, Ordre de la Couronne (Belgium). Officer,
Order of St Maurice and St Lazarus (Italy)*
WEEKES, C. R. H. Lieut., R. Sussex Regt. (W.)   1912
✠WEGG-PROSSER, C. F. 2nd Lieut., R. Sussex Regt. and   1911
Rifle Brigade
Killed in action 3 *Sept.* 1916
WEGUELIN, T. N. Capt., Hampshire Regt.; Capt. (T.),   1906
R.A.F.
WEIR, G. A. Colonel, 3rd Dragoon Gds.; Brig.-Gen.   1895
(W.) *C.M.G. D.S.O. Brevet Colonel. Brevet
Lieut.-Colonel. M* 4. *Officer, Order of St Maurice and
St Lazarus (Italy). French Croix de Guerre .*
WEIR, H. B. Capt., R.A.M.C. (5th London Gen. Hos-   1899
pital, T.F.)
WEIR, H. H. Capt., R.A.M.C.   1894
WELCH, J. Capt., King's Own (R. Lancaster Regt., T.F.)   1903
and R.E. (Sound-ranging Section). (W.)
WELCH, J. J. Lieut., R.G.A.   1907
WELD-FORESTER, Hon. G. C. B. *See* FORESTER, Lord   1887
WELD-FORESTER, Rev. O. St M. C.F. 4th Class, R.A.C.D.   1896
✠WELDON, Sir A. A., Bart., C.V.O., D.S.O. Colonel, Leinster   1881
Regt. *Brevet Colonel
Died* 28 *June* 1917
✠WELSH, A. R. Lieut., Yorkshire Regt.(T.F.) (W 2.) *M.*   1902
Died 19 *Feb.* 1916 *of wounds received in action*
WENDELL, J. 2nd Lieut., United States F.A.   1915
WENHAM, C. H. Capt., Rifle Brigade. *M.*   1910
WENHAM, E. H. Capt., R.F.A. (W 2.)   1912
WENHAM, J. H. Lieut., Suffolk Yeo.   1909
WENTWORTH-FITZWILLIAM, G. J. C. 2nd Lieut., North-   1907
amptonshire Yeo.

✠WEST, C. S.   Cdr., R.N.V.R.(R.N.D.) (W.) *D.S.O.* *M*3.   1908
Killed in action 30 *Dec.* 1917
WEST, E. B.   Lieut., Shropshire Yeo. and R.E. (Field   1911
Survey Coy.)
WEST, E. E.   Capt., 5th Lancers (R. of O.); Major, cmdg.   1886
Cavalry Depôt
✠WESTBY, P. ST G. C.   Capt., R.F.A.(T.F.)   1908
Killed in action 23 *Sept.* 1917
WESTERN, O.   Sergt., H.A.C.; Lieut., R.G.A.   (W.)   1907
WESTMACOTT, P. G.   Capt., 31st Punjabis, Indian Army   1913
WESTOLL, J.   Capt., Durham L.I.(T.F.) and Spec. List   1908
(Asst. Instructor in Musketry)
WETHERED, H. E.   Capt., Welsh Gds.; G.S.O. 3. *M.*   1907
WHADCOAT, W. H.   Capt., Spec. List, empld. Ministry   1889
of National Service
WHARTON, J. R.   Capt., R. Warwickshire Regt.(T.F.)   1900
(W.)
✠WHATFORD, G. L.   Capt., 66th Punjabis, Indian Army   1896
Killed in action at the Persian Gulf 22 *Nov.* 1915
WHATLEY, W. H.   Major, R.A.S.C. *M.*   1894
WHATMAN, W. D.   Bt. Colonel, Remount Service; Cmdt.,   1878
Remount Depôt. *C.M.G. M* 3.
WHATTON, Rev. A. B. W.   C.F. 4th Class, R.A.C.D.   1881
✠WHEATCROFT, G. H.   2nd Lieut., R.G.A.   1907
Killed in action 13 *Aug.* 1915
WHEELER, E. V. V., V.D.   Hon. Colonel, Worcestershire   1877
Regt.(T.F.) *O.B.E.*
WHEELER, W. R.   Capt., London Regt. (Queen's). *M.C.* [1914]
WHIDBORNE, B. S.   Lieut., R.F.A.(T.F.)   *M.C. French*   1912
Croix de Guerre
✠WHIDBORNE, G. F.   Lieut., Coldstream Gds. (W.) *M.C.*   1909
M.
Died 24 *Oct.* 1915 *of wounds received in action*
✠WHITAKER, F.   Lieut., R.A.M.C.   1893
Died 28 *Oct.* 1916
WHITAKER, V.   Lieut., R.F.A.   (W.)   *M.C. M.*   1905
WHITE, Sir A. W., Bart.   Lieut.-Col., R.H.A.   1896
WHITE, C. F. O.   Capt., R.A.M.C.   1896
WHITE, E. A. S.   Lieut., Bedfordshire Regt.; empld. [1914]
O.C.B.   (W.)
WHITE, F. B. HOWARD.   Capt., R.E. *M.C. M* 3.   1914
WHITE, H. E.   Trooper, Calcutta Light Horse, Indian   1904
Defence Force. (W.)
WHITE, J. D. C.   Capt., R.A.M.C.   (W.)   1890

✠White, L. W.   Lieut., 1st Dragoon Gds.; attd. 2nd   1905
Dragoon Gds. (Queen's Bays)
*Died 4 Sept. 1914 of wounds received in action at Nery
1 Sept. 1914*
White, R. D.   Major, Hampshire Yeo. and Hampshire   1906
Regt.(T.F.)
✠White, R. E.   2nd Lieut., R.E.(T.F.)   1909
*Died 5 March 1915 of wounds received in action at
Ypres 4 March 1915*
Whitehead, F.   Lieut., D. of Lancaster's Own Yeo.;   1908
attd. R.F.C. (W.)
✠Whitehead, J. R. G.   2nd Lieut., R.F.C.   1908
Killed in flying accident 3 Aug. 1916
Whitehead, R. W.   Lieut., R.F.A.(T.F.) (W.) *M.C.*   1907
Whitehead, T. N.   Capt., R.A.S.C.(M.T.); empld. Min-   1910
istry of Munitions
Whitehorn, R. D.   Lieut., Calcutta Bn., Indian Defence   1910
Force. *M.B.E. M.*
Whitelaw, J. B.   Capt., R. Defence Corps. *m.*   1889
Whitfield, S. P.   Trooper, London Yeo.; Air Mechanic,   1909
R.A.F.
Whitham, J. W.   Lieut., Worcestershire Regt.; R.T.O.   1910
Whitlark, J. H.   Major, R.A.S.C. *Brevet Major. M.*   1908
Whitley, E. N.   Lieut.-Col., R.F.A.(T.F.); Brig.-Gen.   1892
C.B. C.M.G. D.S.O. T.D. M 7.
Whittington, T.   Capt., R.A.S.C.   1909
Whittle, D.   Lieut., S. Staffs. Regt. (W 2.) *M.C.*   1908
Whitworth, E. E. A.   Capt., S. Wales Borderers. (W.)   1908
M.C. M 2. *French Croix de Guerre*
Whitworth, Rev. G. E. A.   2nd Lieut., R.G.A.   1906
Whitworth, W. H. A.   Lieut., Dorset Regt. (T.F.);   1905
Capt. (A.), R.F.C. (W.) *M.C.*
Widdowson, F. J.   Capt., Durham L.I. (W.)   1888
Wiggin, Sir C. R. H., Bart.   Major, Staffordshire Yeo. *M.*   1903
✠Wiggin, G. R.   Lieut., Worcestershire Yeo.   1907
Killed in action in Egypt 23 April 1916
Wiggin, W. H.   Major, Worcestershire Yeo.; Lieut.-Col.,   1906
Sherwood Rangers. (W 2.) *D.S.O. and Bar. M* 4.
Wigram, C. K.   2nd Lieut., R.A.S.C.(M.T.)   1908
Wigram, Rev. H. F. E.   C.F. 4th Class, R.A.C.D.   1892
Wilde, R. W.   Capt., Manchester Regt.; empld. Command   1880
Depôt
✠Wilding, A. F.   Capt., R. Marines   1902
Killed in action in Gallipoli 9 May 1915

WILENKIN, C. Lieut., R.F.A. (W.)   1914
WILKES, J. F. Capt., R.A.S.C.(T.F.)   1898
WILKIN, W. R. Lieut., London Regt. (L.R.B.); attd.   1905
  Lancs. Fus. (W.)
WILKINSON, Rev. G. R. C.F. 4th Class, R.A.C.D. *M.*   1894
WILKINSON, Rev. H. R. Chaplain, R.N. *O.B.E.*   1891
WILKINSON, R. J., C.M.G. Commander-in-Chief, Sierra   1886
  Leone
✠WILLANS, R. ST J. Lieut., Northumberland Fus.   1896
  Killed in action 9 *Nov.* 1914
WILLETT, W. L. Lieut., London Regt.(L.R.B.) (W 2.) *M.* 1909
WILLIAMS, A. K. 2nd Lieut., R. Welsh Fus.   1913
WILLIAMS, C. Lieut., R.N.V.R.   1905
✠WILLIAMS, C. E. 2nd Lieut., R.A.S.C.   1900
  Killed in action 17 *Oct.* 1917
WILLIAMS, E. Capt., Yorkshire Regt.(T.F.); attd.   1909
  R.A.O.C. (W.)
✠WILLIAMS, E. G. Lieut., Grenadier Gds.   1907
  Killed in action 12 *Aug.* 1915
✠WILLIAMS, G. Capt., Welsh Regt. (W.) *M.*   1908
  Died 15 *Nov.* 1918 *of pneumonia following influenza
  contracted on active service*
WILLIAMS, G. H. 2nd Lieut., R.A.S.C.   1910
✠WILLIAMS, G. T. Lieut., R.F.A.   1911
  Died 19 *April* 1918 *of injuries accidentally received*
✠WILLIAMS, N. D. Lieut., S. Lancs. Regt. and Gen. Staff 1910
  (Intelligence). *M.*
  Killed in action 22 *Oct.* 1918
WILLIAMS, P. Lieut., R.E. (W.)   1903
✠WILLIAMS, R. D. GARNONS. Lieut.-Col., R. Fusiliers   1874
  Killed in action 25 *Sept.* 1915
WILLIAMS, S. C. Capt., Leicestershire Regt. and S.   1897
  and T. Corps, Indian Army; Major, D.A.Q.M.G.
WILLIAMS-ELLIS, B. C. Capt., Welsh Gds. and Gen.   1902
  Staff. *M.C. M.*
WILLIAMS-FREEMAN, A. P. Major, D. of Cornwall's L.I.;   1884
  Lieut.-Col., R.A.O.C.; Ordnance Officer, 2nd Class;
  A.D.O.S. *D.S.O. O.B.E. M* 5.
WILLIAMS-GREEN, W. T. Capt., Manchester Regt. (W 2.)   1911
  M.C.
WILLIAMS-THOMAS, F. S. Major, Worcestershire Yeo.   1897
  (P.) *D.S.O. M.*
WILLIAMS WYNN, W. Lieut., 1st Dragoons. (W.)   1909
WILLIAMSON, D. A. Lieut., 11th Hussars   1912

WILLIAMSON, G. E. Capt., E. Surrey Regt.(T.F. Res.) 1905
WILLIAMSON, J. B. Capt., R.A.M.C. *M.* 1911
WILLIAMSON, S. K. G. Capt., London Yeo. (West- 1906
minster Dragoons); Major, M.G.C. *M.*
WILLINK, H. U. Major, R.F.A.(T.F.) *M.C. M.* 1912
French Croix de Guerre
WILLOUGHBY, Hon. C. S. H. D. *See* HEATHCOTE- 1888
DRUMMOND-WILLOUGHBY, Hon. C. S.
✠WILLOUGHBY, F. G. G. Capt., Rifle Brigade 1908
Killed in action 9 Aug. 1915
✠WILLOUGHBY, Sir J. C., Bart. Major, R.A.S.C. *D.S.O.* 1884
M 2.
Died 16 *April* 1918 *of illness contracted on active ser-*
vice in E. Africa
✠WILLS, O. B. W. Lieut. (A.), R.A.F. *M.C.* 1911
Died 10 *Nov.* 1918 *of wounds received in action*
✠WILLS, R. B. M. Capt., R.E.(T.F.) *M.* 1908
Killed in action 15 *Feb.* 1915
WILLS, R. D. Capt., Somerset L.I.(T.F.); Hon. Capt. 1910
(T.), R.A.F.
WILLS, S. W. Capt., E. Surrey Regt.; empld. O.C.B. 1907
WILLS, W. D. M. Capt., N. Somerset Yeo. *Chevalier,* 1906
Ordre du Mérite Agricole (France)
WILSON, A. C. Lieut., 12th Lancers; Major (A.), R.A.F. 1913
✠WILSON, A. G. MARYON. Trooper, Australian Light 1900
Horse
Killed in action 15 *May* 1915
WILSON, A. H. R. Lieut., Black Watch (T.F.) (W.) 1908
WILSON, B. FITZG. Capt., King's Royal Rifle Corps and 1907
Gen. List (Staff Capt.) *M.C.*
WILSON, C. Capt., Lincolnshire Yeo. and M.G.C. *M.* [1914]
WILSON, C. E. Lieut., 1st Dragoon Gds. 1911
WILSON, C. T. Lieut., R.F.A.(T.F.) 1907
WILSON, E. R. Lieut., Rifle Brigade; Staff Lieut. (In- 1898
telligence)
WILSON, F. B. Lieut., R. Fusiliers. (W.) 1900
WILSON, G. Lieut., R.M.A. *M.* 1914
WILSON, G. B. 2nd Lieut., I.A.R.O., attd. 45th Rattray's 1906
Sikhs
WILSON, H. N. S. Major, Worcestershire Yeo. 1903
WILSON, J. C. Lieut., Worcestershire Regt. (W.) *M.* 1910
✠WILSON, J. S. Lieut., S. Staffs. Regt. (W.) *M.* 1914
Died 12 *Oct.* 1917 *of wounds received in action*
WILSON, K. H. Lieut., R.E. *M.C.* 1903

✠WILSON, L. C. 2nd Lieut., Norfolk Regt.   1914
   Died 12 Aug. 1915 of wounds received in action 7 July 1915

WILSON, L. G. Capt., Gen. List (R.T.O.)   1895

✠WILSON, R. E. Lieut., R. Scots. (W.)   1911
   Died 28 Sept. 1915 of wounds received in action 25 Sept. 1915

WIMBORNE, Rt. Hon. Lord. Lieut.-Gen., Lord Lieu-   1890
   tenant of Ireland

WINBY, I. S. Lieut., R.E.   1897

WINBY, L. P. Major, London Yeo. (Westminster   1894
   Dragoons); Lieut.-Col., Labour Corps. *M* 2. *Belgian
   Croix de Guerre*

WINCH, A. B. Capt., Queen's Own (R. W. Kent Regt.);   1893
   attd. R.E. *M.B.E.*

WINCH, GEORGE B. Hon. Lieut.-Col., R. East Kent Yeo.   1886
   (T.F. Res.) *m* 2.

✠WINCH, GORDON B. Major, R.F.A.(T.F.) *D.S.O. M.*   1895
   *Died 10 April 1918 of wounds received in action 9
   April 1918*

✠WINCH, R. B. 2nd Lieut., R. East Kent Yeo.   [1914]
   Accidentally killed 16 April 1915

WINCH, S. B. Major, R.A.O.C.; D.A.D.O.S. O.B.E.   1903
   M 2.

WINDSOR, Viscount. Capt., Worcestershire Yeo. and Gen.   1907
   Staff (Intelligence). *M.*

✠WINDSOR-CLIVE, Hon. A. Lieut., Coldstream Gds.   1909
   Killed in action 25 Aug. 1914

WINGATE, R. C. Lieut., R.A.O.C.   1904

WINGFIELD, C. T. 2nd Lieut., Bedfordshire Regt.;   1907
   Lieut., R. Dublin Fus.

WINGFIELD, J. M., D.S.O. Major, Coldstream Gds. (R. of   1881
   O.); Lieut.-Col., Spec. List (R.T.O.) O.B.E. M.

WINKWORTH, H. S. Lieut., 2nd Dragoon Gds. (Queen's   [1914]
   Bays); Hon. Lieut. (O.), R.A.F.

WINTER, CECIL E. 2nd Lieut. (Ad.), R.A.F.   1898

WINTER, CLAUD E. Pte., R.A.O.C and Queen's Own   1901
   (R. W. Kent Regt.); 2nd Lieut., E. Surrey Regt.

WINTER, Rev. E. E. C.F. 4th Class, R.A.C.D.   1903

WINTER, W. DE L. Capt., Cambridge Univ. O.T.C.;   1889
   empld. O.C.B.

WINTERBOTHAM, E. M. Lieut., R.G.A. M.C.   1901

✠WINTHROP-SMITH, B. R. Lieut., Scots Gds.   1900
   Died 15 Nov. 1914 of wounds received in action

WOLFE BARRY, E. G.   Lieut., R.N.V.R.(R.N.D.)   (W 2.)   1904
WOLFE BARRY, K. A.   Capt., R.G.A. and Spec. List,   1897
  empld. Ministry of Munitions.   *O.B.E.*   *m 2.*
WOLLASTON, G. W., M.V.O.   A.B., R.N.V.R.   1893
WOLLASTON, H. C.   Capt., Sherwood Foresters (Notts.   1908
  and Derby Regt., T.F.) and M.G.C.
WOLRYCHE-WHITMORE, J. E. A.   Lieut., King's (Shrop-   1902
  shire L.I.); empld. Directorate of Docks.   (W.)
WOOD, A. R.   Capt., Lancs. Hussars.   *M.C.*   1908
WOOD, Rev. C. T. T.   C.F. 4th Class, R.A.C.D.(T.F.)   1903
  M.C.
WOOD, E. R.   Lieut., W. Kent Yeo. and Spec. List (In-   1904
  telligence)
WOOD, F.   Capt. and Adjt., Lancs. Fus.(T.F.); Major,   1908
  E. Lancs. Regt.(T.F.)   (P.)   *M.C.*
WOOD, J. L.   Major, R.A.M.C.   *O.B.E.*   *M* 3.   *Chevalier,*   1899
  Military Order of Avis (Portugal)
WOOD, T. L. C.   Lieut., London Regt. (L.R.B.) and   1898
  Labour Corps
WOODALL, J. C.   Lieut., Surrey Yeo.   *M.*   1902
✠WOODHOUSE, E. J.   Lieut., I.A.R.O., attd. Cavalry   1903
  Died 18 *Dec.* 1917 *of wounds received in action* 1 *Dec.*
  1917
WOODHOUSE, R.   Major, Essex Yeo.(T.F. Res.)   1872
✠WOODLAND, C. A.   Asst. Paymaster, R.N.V.R.; Lieut.,   1903
  N. Staffs. Regt.; attd. King's Own (Yorkshire L.I.)
  (W.)
  Died 1 *April* 1918 *of cerebro-spinal meningitis*
✠WOODROFFE, N. L.   Lieut., Irish Gds.   *M.*   1911
  Killed in action 6 *Nov.* 1914
WOODS, Rev. E. S.   C.F. 4th Class, R.A.C.D.   1896
WOODS, Rt. Rev. F. T.   C.F. 4th Class, R.A.C.D.(T.F.)   1892
WOODS, J. M.   Lieut., Loyal N. Lancs. Regt.   1906
WOODSEND, H. D.   Capt., R.F.A.; Staff Capt.   (W.)   1914
  Italian Silver Medal for Military Valour
✠WOOLF, C. N. S.   2nd Lieut., 20th Hussars   1907
  Died 30 *Nov.* 1917 *of wounds received in action* 27 *Nov.*
  1917
WOOLLEY, E. C.   2nd Lieut., Loyal N. Lancs. Regt.   1907
  (W.)
WOOSNAM, Ven. C. M.   C.F. 4th Class, R.A.C.D.(T.F.)   1875
WOOSNAM, M.   Lieut., Montgomeryshire Yeo.   1911
✠WOOTTON, J. W.   Capt., Suffolk Regt.   (W.)   *m.*   1910
  Died 11 *Oct.* 1917 *of wounds received in action*

✠WORDSWORTH, O. B. 2nd Lieut., Oxford and Bucks. 1906
L.I.; Lieut., M.G.C.
Killed in action 2 April 1917
✠WORKMAN, E. Lieut., R. Irish Rifles. *M.C. M.* 1905
Died 26 Jan. 1916 of wounds received in action
WORKMAN, E. W. Intelligence Section, French Army 1908
✠WORMALD, D. F. P. Capt., R.G.A.(T.F.) and Gen. Staff 1904
Died 4 Nov. 1918 of septic pneumonia
WORMALD, F. W., D.S.O. Lieut.-Col., 1st Dragoons. *M* 2. 1888
✠WORMALD, G. Capt., Lancs. Fus. 1902
Killed in action 14 Sept. 1916
WORMALD, H. Lieut., King's (Liverpool Regt.) and 1903
S. Lancs. Regt.
WORRALL, P. Lieut., R.A.S.C.(T.F.) 1899
WORSDELL, G. B. Major, Yorkshire Regt. *Brevet Major.* 1900
O.B.E. M.
WORTHINGTON, R. T. Major, R.A.M.C. (W.) 1893
WRAITH, H. D. Lieut., D. of Wellington's (W. Riding 1890
Regt., T.F.)
WRIGHT, Rev. A. B. C.F. 3rd Class, R.A.C.D. (W 2.) 1899
M.C. M.
WRIGHT, Sir A. E. Colonel, A.M.S. *K.B.E. C.B. M* 3. 1886
Officer, Ordre de la Couronne (Belgium)
WRIGHT, H. FITZH. Capt., R.F.A.(T.F. Res.) 1889
WRIGHT, H. G. 2nd Lieut., R.F.A. 1914
WRIGHT, R. M. Capt., Coldstream Gds.; Major, Gds. 1909
M.G. Regt. (W 3.) *M.C. and Bar. M.*
WRIGHTSON, R. G. Major, London Regt. (Post Office 1888
Rifles). *m.*
WRIGHTSON, T. G. Major, Durham L.I.(T.F.) *m.* 1889
WRIGHTSON, W. I. Lieut., Durham L.I.(T.F.) 1894
✠WRIGLEY, C. J. O. Trooper, K. Edward's Horse 1913
Killed in action 26 May 1915
WYKEHAM, P. H. Capt., R.F.A.(T.F.); Staff Capt. *M.C.* 1899
M 2.
WYNNE, A. M. Capt. (A.), R.A.F. (W.) *A.F.C.* 1910
WYNNE, J. B. Lieut., Hampshire Regt. 1895
✠WYNNE-JONES, M. Lieut., R.E. 1905
Killed in action 29 Oct. 1914
WYNYARD WRIGHT, A. T. 2nd Lieut., E. Surrey Regt.; 1913
Lieut. (A.) and Capt. (T.), R.A.F.

✠YARROW, E. F. 2nd Lieut., Argyll and Sutherland Hdrs. *M.* 1913
Killed in action near Ypres 8 May 1915

YATES, J. M. ST J. Lieut., R.N.V.R. 1897
YEO, H. E. Capt., King's Own (Yorkshire L.I.); 1913
Major,D.A.Q.M.G. (W.) *M.C. Brevet Major. M*2.
✠YEO, L. F. Lieut., S. Staffs. Regt. 1911
Died 10 *March* 1915 *of wounds received in action*
YOOL, G. A. Major, S. Staffs. Regt.; Lieut.-Col., 1895
Lincolnshire Regt.(T.F.) (W 2.) *D.S.O. M* 2.
YOUNG, C. F. Pte., R.A.S.C. 1883
YOUNG, E. HILTON, M.P. Lieut.-Cdr., R.N.V.R. (W.) 1897
D.S.O. D.S.C. M. Order of Karageorge, 4th Class
(Serbia). Serbian Medal for Valour. French Croix de
Guerre
YOUNG, F. H. Capt., R.A.M.C. *O.B.E. M.* 1910
YOUNG,H.A. Lieut.,Cameron Hdrs.and Gen.List. (W.) 1900
YOUNG, H. T. L. Capt., R.A.S.C. 1899
YOUNG, T. Lieut., King's (Liverpool Regt.) and Tank 1913
Corps
YOUNG, W. A. Capt., R.E. *O.B.E. M* 2. 1913
YOUNGER, W. J. Lieut.-Col., R. Scots. *m.* 1886

ZABRISKIE, G. G. Lieut., United States Naval Air Service 1910
ZAMBRA, N. Capt., R.F.A. *M.C.* 1900

TRINITY HALL

ABDY, J. R. Capt., Sherwood Rangers. (W.) *M* 2. 1913
French Croix de Guerre. Italian Silver Medal for
Military Valour

ACLAND TROYTE, G. J. Major, King's Royal Rifle Corps.; 1895
Lieut.-Col., A.A. and Q.M.G. *C.M.G. C.B.E.*
D.S.O. M 5. *m. French Croix de Guerre*

ADAMS, N. P. Capt., K. Edward's Horse 1901

✠ADAMS, R. S. Capt., R.F.A. *M* 2. 1908
Killed in action 5 *Oct.* 1917

✠ADAMSON, W. C. Capt. (A.), R.F.C. *M.* 1905
Killed in action 5 *Sept.* 1915

AGNEW, A. G. Major, R.F.A.(T.F.) *M.* 1906

AKROYD, R. Lieut., 9th Lancers 1905

✠ALBU, W. G. Capt. (A.), R.A.F. *Order of St Stanislas,* 1910
2nd Class, with swords (Russia). French Croix de
Guerre
Died 29 *May* 1920 *from illness contracted on active*
service

ALCOCK, W. B. Capt., R.A.M.C. *M.* 1906

ALFORD, C. E. Capt., London Regt. (Finsbury Rifles) 1904

ALLEN, H. C. G. Capt., R.E. 1896

ALLEN, J. W., C.M.G. Lieut.-Col., King's (Liverpool 1883
Regt.) *M.*

ALLEN, S. E. Major, R.A.O.C. *M.* 1903

ANDERSON, J. Major, Canterbury Regt., N. Zealand Force. 1901
M.

✠ANNESLEY, Earl. Sub-Lieut., R.N.V.R. 1904
Killed in action 5 *Nov.* 1914

ANSDELL, R. C. Capt., 7th Dragoon Gds. (W.) 1907

✠Arbuthnot, W. J. 2nd Lieut., I.A.R.O., attd. Infy.　　1904
　Killed in action 9 *Jan.* 1917
✠Arnott, J. Capt., 15th Hussars. *M.C.* M 2.　　　　1904
　Killed in action 30 *March* 1918
Ashby, M. W. Lieut., R.G.A.(T.F.)　　　　　　　　1900
Aspinall, J. R. Major, Lancs. Hussars (T.F. Res.)　　1896
Atkey, S. C. Capt., Hampshire Regt.(T.F.)　　　　1892
Atkinson, G. B. 2nd Lieut., Durham L.I.　　　　　1908
Aubry, J. F. A. Asst. Paymaster, French Navy　　[1914]
Austin, Sir W. M. B., Bart. Capt., R.A.M.C.　　　1892
Avory, D. H. Major, R. Berkshire Regt. (W.) *M.*　1905
Ayliff, J. Cadet, R.A.F.　　　　　　　　　　　1909

Back, I. G. Capt., R.A.M.C.(T.F.)　　　　　　　1898
Backhouse, M. R. C. Major, Northumberland Yeo.;　1897
　Lieut.-Col., Yorkshire Regt. *D.S.O. and Bar.* M 3.
Bailey, P. J., d.s.o. Major, 12th Lancers　　　　1892
Bailey-Hawkins, A. G. Major, Durham L.I. *m* 2.　1907
Baines, M. T. Capt., R. Wiltshire Yeo.; Capt. (A. and　1912
　Ad.), R.A.F. (W.)
✠Baker, A. F. W. Lieut., D. of Cornwall's L.I.; Capt. (A.),　1909
　R.F.C. *M.*
　Killed in action 11 *April* 1917
Baker, R. L. Capt., R.F.A.; empld. Ministry of Muni-　1897
　tions. (W.) *O.B.E. m.*
Balfour, A. M. Lieut.-Col., R.F.A.(T.F. Res.) *D.S.O.*　1889
　M 2.
✠Barclay, G. W. Major, Rifle Brigade. (W.) *M.C. M.*　1910
　Killed in action 28 *July* 1916
Barclay, H. F. Lieut.-Col., Bedfordshire Regt.;　　1888
　D.A.A.G. *m* 2.
Barclay, Rev. H. G. C.F. 4th Class, R.A.C.D. *M.C.*　1900
　M.
Barclay, M. E. Major, Norfolk Yeo. and Norfolk Regt.　1905
　(T.F.) (W 2.) *M* 2. *Order of the Nile, 4th Class*
　(*Egypt*)
Barclay-Milne, J. Major, R.F.A. (W.) *M.C. M.*　1904
　French Croix de Guerre
✠Barnato, J. H. W. Pte., R. Fusiliers (P. S. Bn.); Capt.　1912
　(A.), R.A.F. *M.*
　Died 26 *Oct.* 1918 *of pneumonia*
Barnato, W. J. Capt., R.F.A.　　　　　　　　1913
Barnsdale, J. D. Major, Lancs. Fus.(T.F.) (W.)　　1897
Barr, A. G. 2nd Lieut., Spec. List (Interpreter)　　1898

BARRETT, J. H. Lieut., King's Own (R. Lancaster Regt.) 1910
and Gold Coast Regt., W. African Frontier Force
BARRINGER, R. E. Lieut., Sherwood Foresters (Notts. 1911
and Derby Regt.) and Labour Corps.
BARRINGTON, W. R. S. Capt., Oxford and Bucks. L.I. 1892
✠BARTON, B. B. Lieut., King's Royal Rifle Corps 1905
Killed in action 30 *Nov.* 1917
✠BARTON, G. R. Capt., Cheshire Regt. (W.) 1893
Killed in action 9 *April* 1918
✠BARTON, T. E. 2nd Lieut., R. Irish Rifles 1906
Killed in action 16 *July* 1916
BARTRAM, H. Lieut., Gen. List, Australian Force 1903
BASSETT, H. LL. Lieut., Welsh Regt.; Capt., R.E. (Spec. 1908
Bde.); Chemical Adviser. *M. French Croix de Guerre*
BATES, Rev. G. L. C.F. 4th Class, R.A.C.D. 1890
BATLEY, J. Lieut., Worcestershire Yeo. (W.) 1911
BATTEN, H. C. C. Major, Dorset Regt.; D.A.A.G. (W.) 1903
D.S.O. M 5. *Chevalier, Ordre du Mérite Agricole*
(*France*)
BATTEN, H. C. G. Hon. Colonel, Dorset Regt. *m.* 1866
✠BATTEN, J. H. S. Capt., King's (Liverpool Regt.) 1894
Killed in action 25 *Oct.* 1914
BELL, A. S. Capt., Derbyshire Yeo. 1893
BELL, W. A. J. Lieut., London Yeo.(T.F. Res.); Major, 1902
R.A.S.C.
BELLEW, B. B. Lieut., S. Irish Horse and R. Irish Regt.; 1909
attd. T.M.B.; A.D.C. (W.) *M.C. M* 2.
BELLEW, E. H. Capt. (Ad.), R.A.F. *M.B.E.* 1908
BENNETT, D. Pte., H.A.C. 1905
BENNETT, G. M. Lieut.-Col., S. African H.A. *D.S.O.* 1896
BENNETT, G. N. Lieut., R.A.S.C. 1908
BENNETT, R. Lieut., Hertfordshire Regt. 1901
BENYON, H. A. Capt., Berkshire Yeo. and Remount 1903
Service
BERESFORD, C. V. Major, Worcestershire Regt.; Major 1898
(Ad.), R.A.F.
✠BERESFORD, C. W. Major, R. Defence Corps 1895
Died 9 *Oct.* 1917
BERESFORD, M. DE LA P. 2nd Lieut., R.F.A. 1899
BERESFORD, T. DE LA P. Capt. (T.), R.A.F. 1906
BERNEY, R. G. G. Air Mechanic, R.A.F. 1915
BERNEY, Sir T. R., Bart. Major, Norfolk Regt.(T.F.) 1912
M.C.
BESWICK, W. T. Surgeon Lieut., R.N. 1911

BEWES, C. T. A. Capt., Devon Regt.(T.F.)   1905
BICKERTON, H. R. Surgeon Lieut., R.N.   1913
BINNEY, J. Capt., Gen. List (T.F. Res.)   1887
BIRCHENOUGH, R. P. Major, Derbyshire Yeo. *M. Greek*   1904
    Military Cross
BIRKBECK, J. Lieut.-Col., D. of Wellington's (W. Riding   1890
    Regt., T.F. Res.) and Gen. Staff
BIRKETT,G.E. Surgeon-Prob.,R.N.V.R.;Capt.,R.A.M.C.   1912
    (W.) *M.C.*
BISPHAM, C. Lieut., R.E. (W.)   1908
BLACK, L. P. Lieut., R.A.M.C.   1890
✠BLACKBURN, G. G. Capt., W. Yorks. Regt.   1907
    Killed in action 1 *July* 1916
BLACKBURN, L. O. G. Major, R.A.S.C. *O.B.E. M.*   1904
BLAINE, F. H. Lieut., Manchester Regt.; Capt., R.E.   1892
BLAKE, F. E. C. Capt., Northumberland Yeo.   1913
BLAND, J. C. *See* COOPER BLAND, J.
BLOOMFIELD, E. A. R. R. 2nd Lieut., Hauraki Regt.,   1889
    N. Zealand Force
BONHAM-CHRISTIE, R. A. Capt., N. Somerset Yeo.;   1911
    Lieut., R.A.S.C.
BONOMI, J. I. Colonel, King's Own (R. Lancaster Regt.)   1874
    C.B.E. Brevet Colonel. m.
BOOKLESS, J. S. Capt., R.A.M.C.   1897
✠BOTT, J. A. Capt., R. Fusiliers. (W.)   1893
    Died 5 *Aug.* 1917 *of heart-failure*
BOULTER, C. S. C. Capt., R.F.A.   1899
BOVEY, F. H. W. Major, Quebec Regt., Canadian Force;   1903
    D.A.A.G. *O.B.E. Médaille de la Reconnaissance*
    Francaise, 3rd Class
BOWES LYON, Hon. M. Capt., Life Gds. (R. of O.) and   1893
    M.G.C.; A.D.C. (W.) *M.*
✠BOYD, G. J. 2nd Lieut., Rifle Brigade   1917
    Died 3 *Nov.* 1918 *of pneumonia*
✠BOYLE, Hon. J. Capt., R. Scots Fus.; A.D.C. *M.*   1898
    Killed in action near La Bassée 18 *Oct.* 1914
BOYLE, R. F. R. P. Capt., Oxford and Bucks. L.I.(T.F.)   1906
BRABAZON, Hon. C. M. P. Major, Irish Gds.; Lieut.-   1894
    Col. (Airship), R.A.F. *O.B.E.*
✠BRAIN, F. S. Lieut., R. Berkshire Regt.; Capt., Dorset   1912
    Regt. *M.*
    Killed in action 3 *Oct.* 1918
BRANDON, A. DE B. Major (A.), R.A.F. *D.S.O. M.C.*   1902
    M.

BRIDGE, E. A. Capt., Gen. List (T.F. Res.) 1890
BRIDGWATER, H. N. Major, Norfolk Regt.(T.F.); 1896
D.A.A.G. *D.S.O. O.B.E. M* 3.
BROCKLEHURST, E. H. Capt., R.A.S.C. *M.* 1895
BROCKLEHURST, Sir P. L., Bart. Major, Derbyshire Yeo. 1904
and Spec. List, empld. Egyptian Army. (W.)
✠BROCKLEHURST, T. P. Capt., The Queen's (R.W. Surrey 1905
Regt.)
Killed in action 1 *July* 1916
BROMLEY-DAVENPORT, H. R. Lieut., Spec. List (Inland 1890
Waterways and Docks); Capt., P. and B.T. Staff.
O.B.E. M.
✠BROOKSBANK, S. Lieut., Yorkshire Regt. 1905
Killed in action 26 *Sept.* 1915
BROOMAN-WHITE, C. J. Major, Rifle Brigade and Gen. 1904
List. *C.B.E.*
BROWN, A. Lieut., R.A.S.C. *M.* 1911
BROWN, H. F. Capt., R.A.S.C. *M.* 1911
BROWN, H. N. Capt., Yorkshire Regt. (W.) 1912
BROWN, N. A. S. Lieut., Hampshire Regt.(T.F.); In- 1913
structor, School of Musketry
BROWNE, A. W. Capt., W. Yorks. Regt. (W.) 1895
BRUCE, S. M. Capt., Worcestershire Regt. and R. 1903
Fusiliers. (W 2.) *M.C. M. French Croix de*
Guerre
BRUCE-KERR, J. 2nd Lieut., Argyll and Sutherland Hdrs. 1900
BUCHANAN, H. 2nd Lieut., Cameron Hdrs. (W.) 1910
BUCKLER, F. W. Lieut., I.A.R.O., attd. 37th Lancers 1910
and 23rd Cavalry
BUCKLEY, C. M. Staff Capt., Australian Force 1889
BUCKLEY, P. N. Major, R.E.; attd. Staff of High Com- 1887
missioner for Australia
BUCKNALL, L. C. Major, Northamptonshire Yeo.; A.P.M. 1892
D.S.O. M 2. *Italian Croce di Guerra*
BULLARD, F. R. Lieut., Derbyshire Yeo.; attd. R.E. 1900
BULLARD, G. T. Lieut.-Col., Norfolk Yeo. *m.* 1894
BUNBURY, H. W. Capt., Suffolk Regt. and Labour 1907
Corps; Capt. (Ad.), R.A.F.
BURDON, W. W. Capt., Northumberland Yeo. (W.) 1909
BURRELL, R. E. Capt., Army Cyclist Corps 1908
✠BURY, E. W. Capt., King's Royal Rifle Corps 1904
Killed in action 5 *Dec.* 1915
BUSH, J. R. 2nd Lieut., The Buffs (E. Kent Regt.); [1914]
Lieut., M.G.C.

BUSK, E. W. Major, R.F.A.(T.F.) *M.C. M* 2. *French* 1911
Croix de Guerre

CAFFIN, E. G. Lieut.-Col., Yorkshire Regt.; attd. North- 1889
umberland Fus.; cmdg. Depôt. *M.*

CAHUSAC, S. D. N. Capt., 10th Lancers (Hodson's 1905
Horse), Indian Army. *M.*

CAIN, E. Lieut., R.A.S.C. 1911

✠CAIRNES, A. B. Major, R. Irish Rifles 1894
Killed in action 9 *Sept.* 1916

CAITHNESS, Earl of. Capt., Gordon Hdrs.(T.F.); Lieut.- 1881
Col., Inspector of Q.M.G.'s Services, N. Command.
m.

CALDWELL, K. F. T. Capt. and Adjt., R.F.A. (W.) *m.* 1906
Italian Silver Medal for Military Valour

CAMPBELL, B. A. Capt. and Adjt., Scottish Horse; 1908
Brigade Major. *m.*

CAMPBELL, D. N. Lieut., R.A.S.C. 1904

CAMPBELL, J. A. Major, Argyll and Sutherland Hdrs. 1868
M.

✠CAMPBELL, K. G. Lieut. and Adjt., Highland L.I. [1914]
Killed in action in the Battle of Loos 25 *Sept.* 1915

CAMPBELL-MUIR, D. E. Capt., Res. Regt. of Cavalry 1895
and Remount Service

✠CANTLE, L. H. Lieut., Surrey Yeo.; attd. R.F.C. 1914
Killed in action 8 *April* 1917

CAPORN, A. C. Capt., R.F.A.(T.F.) and Gen. Staff 1903

CAPRON, G. Capt., York and Lancaster Regt. (R. of O.); 1885
Major, N. Staffs. Regt.(T.F.); Lieut.-Col., Cheshire
Regt.

CARDIFF, R. H. W. Colonel, Durham L.I. *Brevet Col-* 1890
onel. m.

CAREY, Rev. D. F. C.F. 1st Class, R.A.C.D.; A.C.G. 1895
D.S.O. M 2.

CARPMAEL, E. V. 2nd Lieut., King's Royal Rifle Corps 1900

CASLAW, J. M. Lce.-Sergt., London Regt. (W.) *M.M.* 1911

CAVE, A. L. Capt. and Adjt., Welsh Horse and Res. 1892
Regt. of Cavalry; Capt., Tank Corps

CHANDLER, W. K. Lieut.-Col., Manitoba Regt., Canadian 1902
Force. *D.S.O. French Croix de Guerre*

CHARLESWORTH, C. B. Lieut.-Col., King's Own (York- 1896
shire L.I.) (W.)

CHASE, Rev. G. A. C.F. 4th Class, R.A.C.D. *M.C.* *1913

TRINITY HALL 487

CHASEMORE, P. A. Capt., 18th Hussars. (W.) *M.* 1903
CHIRNSIDE, R. G. Capt., Gen. List, Australian Force; 1902
A.D.C. (W.) *O.B.E. M. Chevalier, Legion of Honour (France). Chevalier, Military Order of Avis (Portugal)*
CHOLMLEY, H. A. Lieut., Yorkshire Hussars 1896
CHRISTIE, H. A. H. Capt., W. Kent Yeo.; Major, M.G.C. 1903
(W.)
CHRISTIE, R. A. B. *See* BONHAM-CHRISTIE, R. A.
CLARK, R. Lieut., R.A.S.C.(T.F.) 1913
CLARKE, E. P. Lieut., R.N.V.R. 1890
CLARKE, W. G. Lieut., Life Gds.; Capt., Gds. M.G. 1912
Regt.
CLARKE-WILLIAMS, A. R. Lieut., R.F.A.; attd. R.H.A. 1913
(W.)
✠CLAYHILLS, G., D.S.O. Capt., E. Lancs. Regt. 1895
Killed in action 2 Nov. 1914
✠CLEGG, J. Capt., King's Own (Yorkshire L.I.) 1898
Killed in action 16 Sept. 1916
CLIFFORD, A. W. Capt., Gloucestershire Regt. and Gen. 1897
List (O.C.B.)
COATES, C. A. Pte., R. Fusiliers 1913
COHAM-FLEMING, B. B. Pte., London Regt.; 2nd Lieut., 1903
R.G.A.
COKE, Hon. REGINALD. Major, Scots Gds.; Courts- 1882
Martial Officer
COLE, T. G. O. Capt., Denbigh Yeo.; A.P.M. *M.* 1897
COLLINGS-WELLS, L. C. Lieut., King's African Rifles. 1907
(W.)
COMBE, H. A. B. 2nd Lieut., Res. Regt. of Cavalry; 1903
Capt., Spec. List (A.P.M.) *M.B.E. M* 2. *French Croix de Guerre*
COMPSTON, G. D. Capt., R.A.M.C. 1906
✠COOKE, C. P. 2nd Lieut., King's (Shropshire L.I.) 1907
Killed in action 22 Aug. 1917
✠COOPER, H. A. Sergt., Canadian Infy. 1890
Killed in action 19 Aug. 1916
COOPER, J. R. Capt. and Adjt., R.F.A.(T.F.) (W.) *M.* 1910
COOPER, P. A. Capt., R.F.A.(T.F.); empld. Ministry 1906
of Munitions. (W.) *m* 2.
COOPER BLAND, J. Lieut., 20th Hussars [1914]
COPEMAN, G. W. B. Capt., R.E. 1893
✠CORRIE, L. Paymaster Sub-Lieut., R.N.R. 1893
Died 23 Oct. 1918 *of pneumonia following influenza*

✠Cotton, B. G. H.　Capt., London Regt. (Poplar and Step-　1908
  ney Rifles)
  Died 8 Nov. 1917 of wounds received in action
Courthope-Munroe, C. H.　Capt., I.A.R.O., attd. 32nd　1908
  Lancers; attd. R.F.C. (P.)
✠Courthope-Munroe, J.W.　2nd Lieut., R.A.S.C.(M.T.)　1911
  Died at Alexandria 24 Jan. 1916 of enteric
Cousins, N. A. C.　Capt., London Regt. (Queen's). (W.)　1910
Cox, B. C.　Lieut., R.N.V.R.　　　　　　　　　　　　1896
Cox, E. H. M.　Lieut., R. Marines　　　　　　　　　　1912
Cox, H. P.　Lieut., R.N.V.R.　　　　　　　　　　　　1892
Craig, A. D. E.　Capt., London Regt. (Queen's)　　　1904
Crawford, C. G.　Capt., I.A.R.O., attd. 30th Punjabis　1909
Crawley, W. H. T. E.　Capt., R. Warwickshire Regt.　1910
  and Gen. Staff. *M.*
Crocker, R. W.　Capt., R.A.S.C.　　　　　　　　　　1906
Croft, H. P., m.p.　Lieut.-Col., Hertfordshire Regt.;　1899
  Brig.-Gen. *C.M.G. T.D. M* 2.
Croft, R. P.　Lieut.-Col., Bedfordshire Regt. *m.*　　1891
Custance, C. V. H.　Lieut., R.G.A.　　　　　　　　　1914
Custance, E. C. N.　Lieut., Norfolk Regt.; Capt., Tank　1913
  Corps

Darwin, G. A. M.　Capt., W. Yorks. Regt.　　　　　[1914]
Davidson, H. G. L.　Hon. Major, King's Own R. Lan-　1890
  caster Regt. (R. of O.)
d'Avigdor-Goldsmid, O. E.　Lieut.-Col., R.A.S.C. *M.*　1895
Davy, P. L.　Lieut., R.G.A. (W.)　　　　　　　　　1901
✠Davy, W. J.　Pte., Ceylon Planters Rifle Corps; 2nd　1907
  Lieut., Somerset L.I.
  Killed in action 18 Aug. 1916
de la Rue, R. W.　Capt., R.A.S.C.　　　　　　　　　1904
✠Denham-Cookes, A. B.　Capt., London Regt. (Queen's)　1910
  Died 5 Nov. 1918
✠de Pass, C. A.　2nd Lieut., Res. Regt. of Cavalry; attd.　1912
  Tank Corps
  Killed in action 22 March 1918
De Villiers, D. I.　Lieut., M.G.C.　　　　　　　　　1913
De Waal, D.　Lieut.-Col., S. African Force. *D.S.O. M.*　1894
✠Dick, C. W.　Lieut., R.N.V.R.　　　　　　　　　　1913
  Died 7 Nov. 1918
✠Dickens, C. C.　Major, London Regt. (Kensington Bn.)　1907
  (W.) *M.*
  Killed in action 10 Sept. 1916

DICKENS, P. C. Lieut., Welsh Gds. (W 2.)   1906
DIGBY, T. H. Lieut., 4th (R. Irish) Dragoon Gds. and   1910
  M.G.C. (Motor). *M.*
DILKE, Sir F. W., Bart. Capt. and Adjt., R. Berkshire   1895
  Regt. (T.F.); empld. War Office
DOHERTY, H. L. 2nd Lieut. (T.), R.A.F.   1896
DOLBEY, R. C. Lieut., King's Own Scottish Borderers.   1907
  (W 2.) *M.*
DOLL, W. A. M. B.S.M., R.G.A.   1904
DONISTHORPE, E. R. Capt., R. Defence Corps   1884
DOURO, Marquis of. 2nd Lieut., Grenadier Gds.; Lieut., 1895
  Spec. List, empld. Inland Waterways and Docks
DOVE, G. V. Capt., Lincolnshire Regt.; empld. Ministry 1897
  of National Service
✠DRAKE, G. E. 2nd Lieut., Worcestershire Regt.   1900
  Died 28 *Jan.* 1918 *of wounds received in action*
DRYSDALE, M. B. Lieut., Sherwood Foresters (Notts.   1911
  and Derby Regt., T.F.) (W.) *M.C.*
DRYSDALE, S. A. Lieut., Dorset Regt. and Gen. List   1895
  (T.M.B.)
DUBERLY, E. H. J. Lieut., Grenadier Gds.; Capt.,   1905
  G.S.O. 3, N. Command. *M.C. m.*
DUFF, I. A. J. Capt., Dorset Regt.(T.F.); Capt. (A.), [1914]
  R.A.F. (W 2.) *M.C. M.*
DUFF, K. D. J. 2nd Lieut., R.G.A.   1908
DUFF, W. S. B. Capt., R.N.V.R.   1896
DUMARESQ, R. G. F. 2nd Lieut., Rifle Brigade; Major,   1899
  M.G.C. (P.) *M.C. M.*
DUNBAR, A. R. Air Mechanic, R.A.F.   1914
DUNCAN, H. A. Lieut.-Col., Argyll and Sutherland Hdrs. 1893
  D.S.O. M.
DUNLOP, F. L. A.B., R.N.V.R.; 2nd Lieut., R.G.A.;   1895
  Capt., Tank Corps

EDGAR, W. H. A. Capt., Labour Corps   1906
✠EDWARDS, W. A. Lieut., Glamorgan Yeo.; attd. Welsh   1909
  Regt. (W.)
  Died 1 *Nov.* 1917 *of wounds received in action*
EGERTON, Hon. F. W. G. Capt., D. of Lancaster's Own   1894
  Yeo. *m.*
ELLIS, W. H. M. Lieut., R.N.V.R.   1893
ELTON, W. *See* MARWOOD-ELTON, W.
ELWORTHY, P. A. Lieut., Life Gds.   1900

ESCOMBE, F. J. Sub-Lieut., R.N.V.R.   1897
EVANS, E. Capt., R.A.S.C.   1905
EVANS, Rev. H. R. Pte., R.A.M.C.; Lieut., King's Own   1908
    (R. Lancaster Regt.) (W.) *M.C.*
EVANS, W. V. E. Gnr., R.G.A.   1907

✠FARMILOE, G. F. 2nd Lieut., H.A.C. *M.C.*   1905
    Killed in action 26 June 1917
FARMILOE, T. H. Capt., London Regt. (Q.V.R.) *M.*   1908
FARQUHARSON, H. F. W. Lieut. (Ad.), R.A.F.   1898
FAWKES, F. H. Major, Yorkshire Hussars (T.F. Res.)   1890
FEARNSIDES, E. G. Hon. Major (Med.), R.A.F.   1902
FENWICK, G. Lieut.-Col., R.F.A.(T.F.); Area Cmdt.   1888
FERNIE, W. J. Lieut.-Col. (T.), R.A.F. *O.B.E.*   1892
FETHERSTONHAUGH, R. G. Capt., 4th (R. Irish) Dragoon   1908
    Gds. (W.) *M.*
FIREBRACE, R. C. 2nd Lieut., R.F.A.   1917
FIRTH, E. L. Capt., S. Irish Horse and R. Irish Regt.   1905
    (W 2.)
FISHER, O. Capt., Glamorgan Yeo. and Welsh Regt.   1904
    (W.) *M. French Croix de Guerre*
FITZHUGH, A. E. L. Lieut., R. Sussex Regt.   1889
FITZROY, Rev. H. S. Instructor, R.N.   1889
FLANNERY, H. FORTESCUE. Capt., R.H.A.(T.F.); empld.   1907
    Ministry of Munitions. *M.B.E.*
FLAWN, N. G. 2nd Lieut., R.G.A.   1899
FOGG-ELLIOT, C. T. Capt., Durham L.I.   1890
FOLEY, C. P. Lieut.-Col., E. Lancs. Regt. and Spec.   1887
    List. *M.*
FORD, R. M. Lieut., S. Wales Borderers. (W.) *French*   1902
    Croix de Guerre
FORDHAM, H. J. Lieut., Hertfordshire Yeo., Res. Regt.   1900
    of R. Horse Gds., and Gds. M.G. Regt.
FORSHAW, H. P. Capt., King's Own (R. Lancaster Regt.)   1895
    M.C. and Bar
FOSTER, C. W. Capt., R. Marines   1905
FOSTER, F. E. Lieut., R.N.V.R.   1896
FOSTER, W. M. Major, Dorset Regt.(T.F.) (W.) *T.D.*   1905
FOWKE, G. H. S. Capt., Gordon Hdrs. (W.) (P.)   1899
FOX, J. ST V. Major, Lincolnshire Regt.   1898
FOX-ANDREWS, N. R. Lieut., D. of Cornwall's L.I. and   1912
    M.G.C.
FRAENKL, E. G. H. *See* FREMANTLE, E. G. H.
FRANCIS, W. H. Major, R. Defence Corps   1876

FRASER, M. H. Capt., Seaforth Hdrs. and King's 1908
African Rifles
FRASER-TYTLER, W. T. Major, Lovat's Scouts 1881
✠FREAM, W. Lieut., Gloucestershire Regt.(T.F.) (W.) 1911
Killed in action 21 *July* 1916
FREMANTLE, E. G. H. Capt., R.A.S.C. 1899

GABRIEL, A. Pte., R. Fusiliers (Sportsman's Bn.) 1891
GARRETT, N. L. Major, King's Royal Rifle Corps 1884
GERARD, Lord. Capt., R. Horse Gds. (W 2.) *M.C.* *1904
GIBBONS, S. A. 2nd Lieut., London Regt. (W.) 1909
GIBBS, A. H., T.D. Lieut.-Col., N. Somerset Yeo.; In- 1894
spector, Q.M.G.'s Services, S. Command
GILBERT, R. T. E. Capt., Norfolk Regt. (T.F. Res.) 1890
GILBERT, T. 2nd Lieut., I.A.R.O.; Lieut. (A.), R.A.F. 1907
GILES, H. O'H. Major, R.F.A. *M. French Croix de* 1908
Guerre
GILMOUR, H. Lieut., 16th Lancers (R. of O.) 1898
GILMOUR, J., M.P., T.D. Lieut.-Col., Fife and Forfar 1895
Yeo.; attd. Black Watch. (W.) *D.S.O. and Bar. M* 2.
GINN, D. B. Capt., Suffolk Yeo. and Suffolk Regt.(T.F.) 1898
GLADSTONE, H. S. Capt., King's Own Scottish Borderers 1896
(T.F. Res.); empld. War Office
GLADSTONE, K. S. M. Capt., Rifle Brigade; Staff Capt. 1913
M.C. M 2.
GOLDBLATT, D. Lieut., King's Own (Yorkshire L.I., T.F.) 1914
GOLDSWORTHY, E. W. Capt., London Yeo. (Rough 1913
Riders); Hon. Capt. (A.), R.A.F. (W.)
✠GOMME, E. E. C. Pte., R. Fusiliers (P. S. Bn.); Capt., 1904
Suffolk Regt. (W 2.)
Killed in action 18 *June* 1917
GORDON, A. F. L. Lieut.-Col., Irish Gds. (W.) *D.S.O.* 1911
M.C. M.
GOSLING, W. S. Major, Scots Gds. (R. of O.) *m.* 1889
GOTT, W. W. M. Capt., Rifle Brigade; attd. King's 1893
Royal Rifle Corps. *m.*
GOTTO, H. S. Air Mechanic, R.N.A.S. 1902
GOULDSMITH, C. C. Major, R.F.A.(T.F.) 1894
GOWER, J. R. Capt., 6th Dragoon Gds. (Carabiniers). 1909
(W.)
GRAHAM, J. D. Lieut., R. Warwickshire Regt. 1891
GRANBY, Marquis of. Capt., Leicestershire Regt.(T.F.); 1906
A.D.C.

✠GRAY-CHEAPE, H. A. Lieut.-Col., Worcestershire Yeo. 1897
D.S.O. and Bar. M 2.
Drowned on H.M. transport Leasowe Castle 27 April
1918
GREEN, J. E. S. Capt., Rifle Brigade. (W 2.) *1912
GREER, T. M. Major, Manchester Regt.(T.F.) 1888
GREGORY, G. M. A. Lieut.-Col., R.F.A. *Brevet Lieut.-* 1896
Colonel. M 3.
GRIFFITH-JONES, J. S. Capt., S. Wales Borderers and 1898
Gen. List
GRIFFITH-JONES, M. P. Major, Gen. List (Staff Capt., 1895
War Office). *O.B.E. m.*
GUINNESS, K. E. L. Lieut., R.N.V.R. 1906
GUNNING, J. E. Major, R. Irish Rifles 1899
✠GUNTHER, C. E. Lieut., Life Gds.; attd. Gds. M.G. 1910
Regt. *M.*
Killed in action 24 Sept. 1918
GWYNNE, R. V. Capt., Sussex Yeo.; Lieut.-Col., The 1900
Queen's (R.W. Surrey Regt.) (W 2.) *D.S.O.*

✠HAGGARD, M. Capt., Welsh Regt. 1894
Died 15 Sept. 1914 *of wounds received in action*
HAGGARD, T. B. A. Capt., R.A.M.C. 1893
HAGGIE, F. R. Lieut., Life Gds. 1912
HAGON, A. C. 2nd Lieut., R. Warwickshire Regt.; 1910
Major (A.), R.A.F.
HAIG, O. Hon. Lieut.-Col., London Yeo.(T.F. Res.) 1894
✠HAINES, W. R. Sub-Lieut., R.N.V.R. (R.N.D.) 1903
Killed in action 17 Feb. 1917
HALL, A. H. Capt., Essex Regt.(T.F.) 1892
HALL, G. D. Capt., Queen's Own (R. W. Kent Regt.); 1896
empld. Ministry of Munitions
HALL, R. H. E. Capt., Oxfordshire Yeo.(T.F. Res.) 1901
HAMPSON, O. D. Capt., E. Lancs. Regt. (W.) 1897
HANNEN, L. C. D. Capt., R.E. (Signals). *M.* 1913
HANNEN, N. M. B. 2nd Lieut., R.F.A. 1917
HARBAUGH, G. W. F. Pte., London Regt. (Artists Rifles) 1915
HARBER, E. W. Lieut. (K.B.), R.A.F. 1905
HARGREAVES, H. Major, Cheshire Regt. 1899
HARMSWORTH, V. G. Capt. and Adjt., R.A.S.C. 1899
HARRIS, H. S. Lieut.-Col., Kimberley Regt., S. African 1902
Defence Force; Capt., R. Fusiliers; attd. Gold Coast
Regt., W. African Frontier Force. (W.) *O.B.E.*
M.

HARRISON, E. J. Lieut.-Col., King's (Liverpool Regt., 1895
T.F.) (W.) *T.D. M.*
HASELDEN, R. B. Capt., Lancs. Fus.; Lieut., Nigeria 1899
Regt., W. African Frontier Force
HATTON-HALL, H. C. Lieut., King's Own Scottish Bor- 1911
derers; Capt., Tank Corps. (W.) *M.C.*
✠HAVILAND, J. D. Lieut., R. Fusiliers. (W.) 1901
Died 16 *July* 1916 *of wounds received in action* 15 *July*
1916
HEATON-ARMSTRONG, J. D. 2nd Lieut., Spec. List (In- 1907
terpreter); Capt., I.A.R.O., attd. 20th Deccan Horse.
(W.)
HELM, J. H. Capt., Manchester Regt.(T.F.) (W.) 1899
HENN-GENNYS, E. C. Lieut., Remount Service 1899
HERMON, J. V. Capt., Cheshire Yeo.; attd. 6th Dragoon 1893
Gds. (Carabiniers). (W 3.) *D.S.O. M.*
HESELTINE, C. Major, R. Fusiliers; Lieut.-Col., Gen. 1890
Staff. *O.B.E. M* 2.
HESELTINE, G. Capt., 6th Dragoon Gds. (Carabiniers) 1889
HICKLING, A. R. Lieut., W. Yorks. Regt. and R.E. 1906
HICKMAN, J. O. Lieut., Bedfordshire Regt. and Gen. 1888
Staff
HILTON-GREEN, C. C. H. Lieut., 1st Dragoons. (W.) [1914]
✠HIND, L. A. Lieut.-Col., Sherwood Foresters (Notts. 1896
and Derby Regt., T.F.) (W.) *M.C. M* 2.
Killed in action 1 *July* 1916
HIND, O. W. Capt., Sherwood Foresters (Notts. and 1891
Derby Regt., T.F. Res.)
✠HISSEY, T. B. Lieut., R.A.S.C. 1914
Died July 1919 *from the effects of active service during*
the war
HODGES, W. C. Major, R.A.M.C.(T.F.) *M.* 1902
HODGKINSON, G. A. 2nd Lieut., Rifle Brigade; Capt., 1898
M.G.C.
HODSON, J. Capt. (S.), R.A.F. 1911
HOLDEN, H. C. Capt., Lancs. Fus.(T.F.); empld. Re- 1895
cruiting Staff
HOLDEN, N. E. Major, Gen. List. *O.B.E. m.* 1897
✠HOLDSWORTH, A. M. Lieut.-Col., R. Berkshire Regt. 1894
M.
Died 7 *July* 1916 *of wounds received in action*
HOLE, C. H. Lieut., R.A.S.C. 1896
✠HOLLAND, J. D. C. 2nd Lieut., Oxford and Bucks. L.I. 1911
Killed in action 13 *Nov.* 1916

HOLLAND, S. C., D.S.O. Major, 1st Dragoon Gds. (R. 1897
of O.); empld. War Office. *Brevet Major. Chevalier,
Legion of Honour (France)*
HOLLAND, V. B. Lieut., R.F.A.; Staff Capt. *O.B.E. M* 3. 1905
HOLLAND, W. G. C. 2nd Lieut., Gordon Hdrs. 1909
HOLLINS, P. L. Lieut., R.A.S.C.(M.T.) 1899
✠HOLLIST, A. M. C. Capt., The Buffs (E. Kent Regt.) 1891
Killed in action in the Battle of Loos 25–27 Sept. 1915
HOLMES, T. V. Air Mechanic, R.N.A.S. 1911
HOLMES-TARN, H. Major, King's Royal Rifle Corps 1892
HOPE, A. T. 2nd Lieut., Suffolk Regt.; Capt. (A.), 1913
R.A.F.
HOPE, L. N. Capt., R. North Devon Yeo. and Devon 1901
Regt.(T.F.); attd. R.E.
✠HOPE-WALLACE, J. Lieut., Northumberland Fus.(T.F.) 1894
M.
Killed in action 15 Sept. 1916
HOPKINS, W. D. Lieut., R.A.M.C. 1901
HORAN, Rev. F. S. C.F. 4th Class, R.A.C.D.(T.F.) *m.* 1892
HORN, D'A. Capt., R.A.S.C. *O.B.E. M.* 1900
HORNIDGE, E. S. Capt., R.A.S.C. *O.B.E. M.* 1906
HOWETT, F. Lieut., R.A.S.C.(M.T.) *Serbian Gold Medal* 1903
✠HUDSON, G. Lieut., Queen's Own (R. W. Kent Regt.); 1912
Major, M.G.C. (W.) *M.C. M.*
Killed in action 12 April 1918
✠HUDSON, R. B. 2nd Lieut., Oxford and Bucks. L.I.(T.F.) 1910
Killed in action 19 July 1916
HUGHES, D. 2nd Lieut., S. Wales Borderers; Lieut., 1906
M.G.C.
✠HULTON-HARROP, H. DE L. Lieut., Life Gds. (W.) 1899
Killed in action 12 May 1915
HUME, A. Hon. Colonel, King's Own Scottish Borderers 1863
HUME-KELLY, F. V. Major, N. Staffs. Regt. *M.* 1896
HUME-WILLIAMS, R. E. Capt., R.A.S.C. 1907
HUMPHRIES, G. N. P. Lieut., Somerset L.I.; attd. R.E. 1915
(Spec. Bde.)
HUMPHRIES, R. P. 2nd Lieut., Somerset L.I., attd. 1912
Devon Regt.
✠HUNTER, G. J. 2nd Lieut., 5th (R. Irish) Lancers 1907
Killed in the Irish rebellion 26 April 1916
HUNTRISS, C. G. 2nd Lieut., 21st Lancers; Lieut., Res. 1899
Regt. of Cavalry
HUNTRISS, E. M. Lieut.-Col., D. of Wellington's (W. 1899
Riding Regt.) (W.) *M.C. M*

HURRELL, H. W. Major, Gen. List (T.F. Res.) 1882
HURRELL, W. C. Capt., Spec. List 1881
✠HUTCHINSON, A. C. C. Capt., R. Fusiliers; Major, M.G.C. 1902
 *Died 18 Nov. 1918 of pneumonia contracted on active
 service*
HUTCHINSON, G. C. Lieut., R.F.A. 1903

INGPEN, D. L. Capt., W. Yorks. Regt. and Gen. Staff 1903

JACKSON, E. W. 2nd Lieut., Labour Corps 1899
✠JAFFRAY, Sir J. H., Bart. 2nd Lieut., Worcestershire Yeo. 1913
 Killed in action 23 April 1916
JEFFCOCK, W. P. Lieut., S .Notts. Hussars and Res. Regt. 1911
 of Life Gds.
✠JENNINGS, G. M. Pte., Australian Infy. 1896
 *Died Aug. 1916 of wounds received in action on the
 Somme*
JEPPE, O. R. Lieut., Cape Corps, S. African Force. (W.) 1905
JESSE, W. J. Lieut., R.G.A.(T.F.) 1902
JESSELL, R. P. Hon. Major, Spec. List (Recruiting Staff) 1886
JOEL, W. S. Lieut. (A.), R.A.F. 1911
JOHNS, N. S. C. 2nd Lieut., Yorkshire Regt. 1914
JOHNSON, H. A. Colonel, Manchester Regt. (W.) *M* 2. 1884
JOHNSON, J. G. T. Major, Derbyshire Yeo. *D.S.O.* 1904
 M 2.
JOHNSON, G. B. B. Capt., Army Printing and Stationery 1906
 Services. *M.*
✠JOICEY, C. M. Capt., Northumberland Fus.(T.F.) (W 2.) 1911
 Killed in action 5 June 1917
JOICEY, E. R. 2nd Lieut., Northumberland Yeo.; Lieut., 1910
 9th Lancers. (P.) *M.C.*
JONES, T. C. Lieut., Pembroke Yeo. and R.F.A.(T.F.) 1893

KAPLAN, I. 2nd Lieut., York and Lancaster Regt.; 1907
 Lieut., M.G.C.
KEIGWIN, C. H. S. 2nd Lieut., R.F.A. 1909
KEMP, W. R. Capt., R.A.M.C.; Capt. (Med.), R.A.F. · 1890
✠KENDALL, P. D. 2nd Lieut., King's Liverpool Regt. 1896
 (Liverpool Scottish, T.F.)
 Killed in action near Ypres 25 Jan. 1915
KERR, J. BRUCE. *See* BRUCE-KERR, J.
✠KERRICH, H. L. Lieut., Sherwood Foresters (Notts. and [1914]
 Derby Regt.)
 Died 27 Sept. 1917 of wounds received in action

KERR-SMILEY, P. K., M.P. Lieut., 21st Lancers (R. of O.); 1899
A.D.C.; Major, R. Irish Rifles

✠KILLEN, E. O. B. Lieut., R.E. 1913
Killed in action in Mesopotamia 15 Jan. 1917

KING, H. R. Capt., Durham L.I.; Hon. Capt. (Ad.), 1907
R.A.F.

KING, P. B. Lieut., R.A.S.C.; attd. S. Wales Borderers. 1911
(W.)

KIPPING, C. H. S. Lieut., London Regt. (Q.V.R.) 1910

KITCHING, H. E. Capt., Durham L.I.(T.F.) *M.B.E. M.* 1904

KNOWLES, E. A. Pte., R. Fusiliers 1900

KNOWLES, R. M. Capt., Norfolk Regt.; Hon. Capt. (T.), 1913
R.A.F. (W.) *M.C.*

KNOX, P. F. Lieut., R. Fusiliers. (W.) 1894

KNOX, W. D. C. Lieut., R. Scots and M.G.C. 1886

LAIDLAY, J. C. 2nd Lieut., Black Watch; Lieut., Seaforth 1908
Hdrs.

✠LANDALE, C. Capt., King's Royal Rifle Corps. (W.) *M.* 1899
Killed in action 21 Aug. 1918

LANDALE, D. G. Lieut., Rifle Brigade; Capt., Spec. 1903
List (P. and B. T. Staff) and Gen. Staff, empld.
British Military Mission

✠LANGHAM, C. R. Capt., R. Sussex Regt.(T.F.) 1910
Killed in action 16 Aug. 1917

LANGHAM, F. G., C.M.G., V.D. Lieut.-Col., R. Sussex 1882
Regt. (T.F.) and Labour Corps. *M.*

LANGTON, S. J. Capt., London Regt. (Post Office Rifles, 1889
T.F. Res.)

LARMAN, G. E. 2nd Lieut., R. Fusiliers 1914

LAWSON, Sir D., Bart. Capt., Yorkshire Hussars; attd. 1898
19th Hussars; Capt., W. Yorks. Regt. *M.*

LAWSON, D. A. Capt., R.F.A. *M.* 1898

LAYE, P. A. W. Major, King's Royal Rifle Corps; attd. 1908
Gen. Staff. (W 2.)

✠LEA, M. B. 2nd Lieut., Northamptonshire Regt. 1913
Killed in action 18 Aug. 1916

LEAKE, C. F. Capt., King's (Shropshire L.I., T.F.) 1902

LEATHAM, C. G. Lieut., King's Royal Rifle Corps; 1905
Capt., The Queen's (R. W. Surrey Regt.) (W 2.)
M.C. and Bar

✠LEE, J. M. 2nd Lieut., Border Regt. 1908
Killed in action 27 Sept. 1915

LEE-BOOKER, R. Lieut., S. Lancs. Regt. (W.) 1909

LEICESTER, C. B. W. Lieut., 1st Dragoon Gds.; attd. [1914]
  Cheshire Yeo.
✠LEIGH, C., D.S.O. Major, King's Own Scottish Borderers 1891
  Died 29 *Aug.* 1918 *of wounds received in action at Mons*
LEIGHTON, F. M. 2nd Lieut., Bedfordshire Regt.; Capt. 1914
  and Adjt., Welsh Regt. *M.C.*
LETTS, E. M. Capt., Oxford and Bucks. L.I.(T.F.); 1910
  Lieut. (Ad.), R.A.F. (Aircraft Production Dept.) (W.)
LEWES, W. Lieut., Welsh Regt.(T.F.) and Gen. List 1898
  (T.F. Res.), empld. Ministry of National Service
LEWEY, A. W. Capt., Middlesex Regt.(T.F.) (W 2.) 1913
LEWIN, A. C., D.S.O. Hon. Colonel, Connaught Rangers; 1893
  Lieut.-Col., Wiltshire Regt.; Brig.-Gen.; A.D.C. to
  the King. *C.B. C.M.G. Brevet Colonel. M* 6.
  Order of St Anne, 2nd *Class, with swords* (*Russia*)
✠LEWIS, B. R. Major, R.F.A. 1909
  Killed in action 2 *April* 1917
LEWIS, F. G., C.M.G., T.D. Lieut.-Col., London Regt. 1892
  (Kensington Bn.); Brig.-Gen. (W.) *C.B. M* 3.
  Belgian Croix de Guerre
LINDLEY, Hon. J. E. Colonel, 1st Dragoons; Major-Gen. 1878
  m.
LITTLE, T. H. Capt., Worcestershire Regt. (W.) 1885
LITTON, W. R. U. Capt., Spec. List (Adjt., P. of W. 1905
  Camp)
LIVINGSTON, C. P. 2nd Lieut., King's Royal Rifle Corps. 1911
  (W.)
LLEWELLYN, O. J. Capt., R.A.S.C. 1888
LOCKWOOD, E. M. Lieut.-Cdr., R.N.V.R. (Hawke Bn., 1909
  R.N.D.) (W 3.) *D.S.O. M* 2.
✠LOGAN, H. Lieut., Leicestershire Yeo.; attd. R.E. 1903
  Died Nov. 1918 *of pneumonia*
LOGAN, J. M. Capt., Leicestershire Yeo.; empld. War 1902
  Office
LONG, J. A. E. Capt., Hampshire Yeo.; attd. Hampshire 1908
  Regt.
LONG, W. E. Capt., 4th Hussars (R. of O.); Major, Re- 1890
  mount Service. *O.B.E.*
LONGSTAFFE, V. C. H. Lieut.-Cdr., R.N.V.R.; Major 1904
  (Ad.), R.A.F.
LORD, H. D. Capt., Hampshire Regt. 1910
✠LORING, W. L. Lieut.-Col., R. Warwickshire Regt. 1886
  (W.) *M.*
  Killed in action 23 *Oct.* 1914

Love, E. W. P. Major, 20th Hussars; Adjt., D. of Lan- 1897
caster's Own Yeo.
Low, H. F. Capt., Durham L.I. and Labour Corps 1894
Lucas, L. W. Lieut.-Col., The Buffs (E. Kent Regt.) 1897
and Spec. List. *D.S.O. M.C. M* 2.
Lyon, C. G. Major, E. Riding of Yorkshire Yeo. and 1900
M.G.C. (W.) *M.*
Lyon, W. A. Lieut., Cambridgeshire Regt. 1910
Lysley, W. L. Hon. Major, R. Wiltshire Yeo.(T.F. Res.) 1894

McCleary, G. F. Capt., R.A.M.C.(T.F.) 1890
McKelvie, J. Lieut., R.E.(T.F.); Major (A.), R.A.F. 1899
A.F.C. Belgian Croix de Guerre
MacLaren, T. G. Lieut.-Col., Seaforth Hdrs.(T.F. 1880
Res.) *m.*
Macnamara, C. R. Capt., R. Dublin Fus. 1913
Madden, J. C. W. Lieut.-Col., R. Irish Fus. *m.* 1889
✠Maddison, G. Lce.-Corpl., Essex Regt.; 2nd Lieut., 1905
Norfolk Regt.
Killed in action 28 *Aug.* 1918
Maine, H. C. S. Lieut., Grenadier Gds.; empld. War 1903
Office. (W.)
Mainwaring, C. F. K. Capt., King's (Shropshire L.I.) 1891
and Tank Corps
Malden, Rev. E. E. C.F. 4th Class, N. Zealand Chap- 1898
lains' Dept. *M.B.E.*
Manisty, E. A. Major, Lincolnshire Yeo.(T.F. Res.) 1892
Margetts, F. B. H. Capt., Hampshire Regt.; Lieut., 1899
Spec. List (Recruiting Staff)
Marrow, E. A. Capt. and Adjt., King's Own Scottish 1871
Borderers
Marshall, W. S. Capt., Sherwood Foresters (Notts. 1895
and Derby Regt., T.F.)
Martineau, B. G. Capt., R. Warwickshire Regt.(T.F.) [1914]
(W 2.)
Martineau, E., c.m.g., v.d. Hon. Colonel, R. Warwick- 1879
shire Regt.(T.F.) *M. m.*
Martineau, W. Capt., R. Warwickshire Regt.(T.F.); 1908
Major, R.E. (Signals). *M.C. M.*
Marwood-Elton, W. Lieut.-Col., Welsh Regt. 1885
Mason, A. D. C. Lieut., Cheshire Regt.(T.F.) and 1908
R.F.A.
Mason, G. H. Capt., W. Yorks. Regt.; Major, Middlesex 1897
Regt. (W 2.)

MATHESON, I. M.   Capt., Seaforth Hdrs.; Capt. (A.),   1912
  R.A.F. (W.)
MAXWELL, S. W.   Air Mechanic, R.A.F.   1913
MAYER, A.   Capt., London Regt. (Queen's)   1890
MEIGGS, J. C.   Capt., R.A.S.C.   1889
✠MELLES, G. F.   Lieut., R.F.A.(T.F.)   1903
  Died at Alexandria 6 Nov. 1915 *of septic poisoning*
MELLOR, A.   2nd Lieut., Durham L.I.; Lieut., Labour   1908
  Corps. (W.)
MELLOR, J. E. P.   Capt., Hampshire Regt.(T.F.) *M.*   1900
MELLOR, J. F. S.   Capt. and Adjt., The Queen's (R.W. 1897
  Surrey Regt.) and R.A.S.C.
MELLOR, J. G. S.   Brig.-Gen., R. of O.; Dep. Judge-   1890
  Advocate-General. *C.B.* *M* 2. *Chevalier, Legion*
  of Honour (France)
MENZIES,V. M. G.   2nd Lieut., R. Scots; Capt., Scots Gds.   1912
✠MERRIMAN, G.   Pte., Nyasaland Vol. Res.   1903
  Died 9 *Sept.* 1914 *of wounds received in action in*
  Nyasaland
✠METCALFE-SMITH, B. C.   Pte., London Regt. (Queen's   1913
  Westminster Rifles); Lieut., W. Yorks. Regt.
  Died 22 *April* 1918 *of wounds received in action* 18
  April 1918
MEYRICK, F. C., C.B.   Colonel, Res. Regt. of Cavalry;   1880
  Brig.-Gen.; Colonel, Remount Service; D. D. Re-
  mounts. *C.M.G.* *M* 2. *m.*
MILLER, D. O. DE E.   Lieut., R.F.A.; Staff Capt. *M.C.*   1910
  M.
✠MILLER, J. H.   Capt., Loyal N. Lancs. Regt.; attd. Egyptian   1902
  Army
  Died 25 *Aug.* 1917 *of blackwater fever*
MILNER-GIBSON, W. A.   Major, R.A.S.C.; A.D.C. *m.*   1897
MILTON, H. A.   Major, London Regt. *M.C. M. French*   1900
  Croix de Guerre
✠MILVAIN, Sir T., C.B., K.C.   Judge Advocate-General, War   1863
  Office
  Died 1916
MITCHELL, G. D.   Sapper, R.E.   1906
MOFFATT, C. H.   Lieut., King's (Shropshire L.I.)   1902
MONTAGU, J. F.   Lieut., 15th Hussars; A.D.C.   1906
MONTAGU DOUGLAS SCOTT, Lord H. A., D.S.O.   Major,   1892
  Irish Gds. (R. of O.); Lieut.-Col. London Regt.
  (T.F. Res.); D.A.M.S. *C.M.G. Officer, Legion of*
  Honour (France)

MONTEUUIS, L. E. Lieut., Berkshire Yeo. and M.G.C. 1901
✠MONTGOMERY, H. 2nd Lieut., 12th Lancers (R. of O.); 1899
Lieut., Irish Gds.
Killed in action 13 *Sept.* 1916
MOORE, C. D. H. Colonel, R. Warwickshire Regt.; Brig.- 1895
Gen. *C.M.G. D.S.O. Brevet Colonel. M* 5.
*Chevalier, Legion of Honour (France). Order of the
Nile, 3rd Class (Egypt)*
MOORHOUSE, E. R. Bdr., R.F.A. 1913
MOORHOUSE, W. B. R. *See* RHODES-MOORHOUSE, W. B.
MORGAN, H. R., V.D. Major, Norfolk Regt.(T.F. Res.) 1882
✠MORGAN, W. W. Lieut., R.N.V.R. (Hawke Bn., R.N.D.) 1905
Killed in action in Gallipoli 19 *June* 1915
MORLEY, Earl of. Capt., R. 1st Devon Yeo.(T.F. Res.) 1896
and Gen. Staff
MORRIS, J. W. Capt., R. Welsh Fus. *M.C.* 1914
MORRISON, R. J. A. Pte., London Regt. 1886
MORTIMER, F. G. C. Major, R.A.O.C.; D.A.D.O.S. 1901
O.B.E. M.
MOSTYN-OWEN, G. C. Lieut., Shropshire Yeo. and 12th 1910
Lancers; attd. Egyptian Army. *M.*
MOY, E. T. 2nd Lieut., Suffolk Regt. 1914
MUNCEY, R. W. L. Pte., Norfolk Regt. 1911
✠MURRAY SMITH, G. Lieut., R. Fusiliers [1914]
Killed in action 29 *Sept.* 1915

NAINBY-LUXMORE, C. C. 2nd Lieut., R.F.A.; Lieut., 1910
Scots Gds. (W.)
NAIRN, R. S. Major, Fife and Forfar Yeo.; Staff Capt., 1900
Scottish Command. *T.D. m.*
✠NATHAN, L. C. 2nd Lieut., D. of Wellington's (W. Riding 1913
Regt.)
Killed in action 14 *Sept.* 1916
NEAVE, Sir T. L. H., Bart. Major, Gen. List (T.F. Res.) 1893
and R. Defence Corps. *m.*
✠NESHAM, C. F. Major, H.A.C. 1892
Died 24 *April* 1919 *of illness contracted on active service*
NEWBERRY, E. E. Corpl., R.E. (Signals) 1903
✠NEWBOROUGH, Lord. Lieut., Denbigh Yeo., Durham 1893
L.I., and Welsh Gds.
Died 19 *July* 1916 *of illness contracted on active service*
✠NEWMAN, C. C. Capt., Hampshire Regt.; attd. Hamp- 1913
shire Yeo. (W.) *M.C.*
Killed in action 4 *Sept.* 1918

NEWMAN, E. D. Major, Lincolnshire Yeo. and M.G.C. 1906
(W.)
NICHOLSON, M. 2nd Lieut., Army Cyclist Corps; Capt., 1907
R.F.A.; Lieut.-Col., S.O. 1, R.A.F. *M.B.E.*
NUTTING, A. R. S. Capt., Irish Gds. (W.) *M.C.* 1907

OLIVER, L. G. Bt. Colonel, Middlesex Regt. and North- 1877
umberland Fus.(T.F.) *C.M.G. M.*
OLIVIER, E. Capt., S. African Defence Force 1907
O'NEAL, T. W. B. Pte., The Queen's (R. W. Surrey 1886
Regt.); 2nd Lieut., R. Defence Corps and Spec. List
(Interpreter)
ORMROD, J. Capt., R. Welsh Fus. 1903
OSBORN, Sir A. K. B., Bart. Capt., Bedfordshire Regt. 1891
and Labour Corps
OWEN, G. C. Lieut., R. Scots Fus.; Capt., Gen. List 1900

PAGE, C. G. Major, Border Regt. (W.) *M.C.* 1904
PAGE CROFT, H. *See* CROFT, H. P.
PAGE CROFT, R. *See* CROFT, R. P.
PAGET, G. N. Lieut., Norfolk Regt. (P.) 1908
PAGET TOMLINSON, T. R. Major, Westmorland and 1894
Cumberland Yeo.(T.F. Res.) and Labour Corps. *m.*
PAGET TOMLINSON, W. G. Major, 7th Hussars. (W.) 1896
D.S.O. M 3. *Officer, Order of the Star of Roumania*
PARHAM, H. J. Capt., R.E.(T.F.) *M.* 1911
PARKER, H. C. T. Capt., R.F.A. 1892
PARKER, L. H. Capt., R.E.; empld. Ministry of Munitions 1909
✠PARRY, D. G. DE C. Major, R.F.A. [1914]
Killed in action 5 April 1918
PARRY, R. B. Lieut., Army Cyclist Corps and S. Wales 1912
Borderers. (W.)
PATERSON, E. W. Capt., Berkshire Yeo. (W.) 1907
✠PAYNE, J. H. A. Lieut., S. African Force *1896
Died 29 July 1917 *of malaria*
✠PEAKE, C. G. W. Capt., Lincolnshire Regt. *M.* 1910
Killed in action at Neuve Chapelle 10 *March* 1915
PEAKE, G. H. Major, Sherwood Rangers (T.F. Res.) 1880
✠PEARSON, Hon. F. G. Warrant Officer, R.A.S.C.(M.T.) 1909
Killed in action 6 Sept. 1914
PEASE, E. H. Capt., Yorkshire Regt.(T.F.) and Spec. 1890
List (School of Instruction). *O.B.E. m.*
PEASE, R. 2nd Lieut., W. Yorks. Regt.(T.F.); Lieut., 1916
Tank Corps

PENNY, A. O. V., T.D. Capt., Kelly College, Tavistock, 1879
O.T.C.
PENROSE, J. D. Capt., R.A.S.C.(T.F.) *M.* 1903
PERKIN, A. L. D. Lieut., Middlesex Regt.; Capt., R. 1911
Marines
PERSHOUSE, F. S. Major, R.F.A. 1893
PHILIPPS, G. W. F. Capt., Welsh Gds. (W.) 1897
PHILIPPS, H. E. E. Capt., Spec. List (A.D.C.) 1890
PHILLIPS, N. McG. Lieut., London Regt. (Q.V.R.) and 1901
R.E. (Signals, T.F.)
PHILLIPS, W. M. Capt., Lincolnshire Regt.(T.F.); Major, 1903
Loyal N. Lancs. Regt.(T.F.) (W.)
PHIPPS, C. B. H. 2nd Lieut., King's (Shropshire L.I.); 1909
Lieut., Res. Regt. of Life Gds. (W.)
PIGOTT, G. G. C. 2nd Lieut., R. Berkshire Regt. and 1908
R.A.F.
PILKINGTON, F. C., D.S.O. Lieut.-Col., 15th Hussars. *M* 2. 1890
✠PILLEAU, A. L. Major, Hampshire Regt. 1881
Killed in action in Gallipoli 10 *Aug.* 1915
PINE-COFFIN, J. E., D.S.O. Major, Loyal N. Lancs. Regt. 1887
(R. of O.) and Sherwood Foresters (Notts. and Derby
Regt.)
POTTS, F. A. Lieut., D. of Wellington's (W. Riding 1901
Regt.); Capt., R.E. (Spec. Bde.)
✠POULETT, Earl. Capt., R.H.A.(T.F.) 1902
Died 11 *July* 1918 *of pneumonia following influenza*
PRATT, G. C. Lieut., W. Yorks. Regt. (W.) 1908
PRINCE, G. W. Lieut., R. Sussex Regt. (W.) *M.C.* 1909
PROTHEROE, A. H. Major, R.A.S.C. *O.B.E. M.C. M* 3. 1901

✠QUILTER, J. A. C. Lieut.-Cdr., R.N.V.R. (Hood Bn., 1894
R.N.D.) *M.*
Killed in action in Gallipoli (12 *May* 1915)
QUITZOW, A. Lieut., R. Fusiliers 1890

✠RAM, G. E. Capt., N. Staffs. Regt.; attd. S. Staffs. Regt. 1900
Died 25 *March* 1916 *of pneumonia*
RAMSDEN, G. T. Lieut., R.F.A.(T.F.) 1897
RAMSEY, W. J. Capt., R.A.S.C.(T.F.) and King's African 1903
Rifles
RAPHAEL, Sir H. H., Bart., M.P. Major, King's Royal 1877
Rifle Corps and Gen. List (A.P.M.)
RAWDON, C. H. Capt., King's Own (Yorkshire L.I.) (P.) 1900

RAWLINS, Rev. G. C. Lieut., R.N.V.R. 1913
RAWNSLEY, G. T. 2nd Lieut., Rifle Brigade 1903
REDMAN, G. A. Capt., London Regt. (L.R.B., T.F. Res.) 1900
RENDELL, W. R. Capt., Cambridge Univ. O.T.C., attd. *1904
Gen. Staff, War Office
✠REYNARD, C. F. P. Capt., E. Yorks. Regt. 1907
Died 16 *June* 1918
✠RHODES MOORHOUSE, W. B. 2nd Lieut. (A.), R.F.C. *M.* 1908
V.C. "For most conspicuous bravery on 26 April, 1915,
in flying to Courtrai and dropping bombs on the railway
line near that station. On starting the return journey
he was mortally wounded, but succeeded in flying for
35 miles to his destination, at a very low altitude, and
reported the successful accomplishment of his object.
He has since died of his wounds."—Supplement to *The
London Gazette*, 21 May 1915.
Died 26 *April* 1915 *of wounds received in action*
RICHARDSON, C.W. Lieut.-Col., R.G.A. (R. of O.); Cmdt., 1891
L. of C. *O.B.E. M.*
✠RICHARDSON, J. M. Hon. Lieut.-Col., R.G.A. (T.F.) and 1869
Gen. Staff (Agriculture)
Died 30 *March* 1918 *of wounds received in action*
21 *March* 1918
RICHARDSON, T. D. Lieut., R.A.S.C. 1905
RIDEAL, E.K. Lieut., R.A.M.C.; Capt., R.E. *M.B.E. M.* 1908
RIESLE, W. B. Lieut., S. African Garrison Artillery 1905
RIX, A. H. Lieut., E. Riding of Yorkshire Yeo.; attd. 1900
E. Yorks. Regt.
ROBB, Sir F. S., K.C.B., K.C.V.O. Major-Gen., Military 1876
Secretary, War Office; Major-Gen. i/c Administra-
tion, E. Command. *K.C.M.G. M.*
ROBERTS, C. H. Lieut.-Cdr., R.N.A.S. *D.S.C. French* 1912
Croix de Guerre
ROBERTS, J. C. Lieut., S. Wales Borderers. (W.) 1913
ROBERTSON, H. G. Capt., Connaught Rangers 1892
ROBERTSON, W. P. Capt., Hertfordshire Yeo. and R.F.A.; 1898
Staff Capt.
RODNEY, Hon. J. H. B. Capt., Rifle Brigade; Capt. (A.), 1911
R.A.F.; Major, S.O. 2. (W 3.) *M.C. M.*
RODOCANACHI, P. Sub-Lieut., R.N.A.S. 1909
✠ROGERSON, W. E. Capt. and Adjt., Durham L.I. 1891
Died 13 *Nov.* 1914 *of heart failure*
✠ROMER, M. L. R. Capt., King's Royal Rifle Corps 1913
Died 20 *Sept.* 1916 *of wounds received in action*

ROSKILL, W. G. Pte., R. Fusiliers (P.S. Bn.); 2nd Lieut., 1908
R.A.S.C.; Lieut., Gen. Staff (Intelligence)
ROSSDALE, S. J. Lieut., R.F.A. 1916
ROTCH, C. D. Capt., R.A.S.C. 1898
✠ROWLANDSON, T. S. Capt., Yorkshire Regt.(T.F.) *M.C.* 1901
M.
Killed in action 15 Sept. 1916
ROWLATT, J. F. C.P.O., R.N.V.R. 1888
✠RUSSELL, J. 2nd Lieut., The Buffs (E. Kent Regt.) 1904
Killed in action 9 Aug. 1917
✠RUTTER, E. F. Major, E. Lancs. Regt. *M.* 1889
Killed in action 13 May 1915

SALAMAN, R. N. Capt., R.A.M.C. *M.* 1893
SANDEMAN, B. S. Capt., R.G.A. 1911
SANDERS, H. R. Lieut., London Regt. (Cyclist Bn.) 1902
SAURIN, W. M. Major, W. Yorks. Regt.; R.T.O. (W.) 1896
Officer, Order of Leopold (Belgium)
SAVORY, K. S. Major (A.), R.A.F. *D.S.O. and Bar* [1914]
SCOTT, B. G. A. Lieut.-Cdr., R.N.V.R. 1901
SCOTT, Lord H. A. M. D. *See* MONTAGU DOUGLAS SCOTT,
Lord H. A.
SCRATTON, E. W. H. B. Capt., R. 1st Devon Yeo.; Major, 1902
R.A.O.C. *O.B.E. m.*
SELIGMAN, G. A. Lieut., R.A.O.C. 1905
✠SHARP, J. S. Pte., R. Fusiliers (P. S. Bn.); Major, R. 1911
Berkshire Regt. *M.*
Killed in action 17 March 1917
SHAW, E. H. Capt., R.A.M.C. *Chevalier, Ordre de la* 1913
Couronne (Belgium)
SHAW, S. Lieut., R.A.M.C. (Sanitary Service, T.F.) 1911
✠SHAW-HELLIER, A. J. B. Lieut., S. Staffs. Regt. 1905
Killed in action in Gallipoli 9 Aug. 1915
SHEPPARD, G. A. Capt., Worcestershire Regt.; empld. 1910
O.C.B. (W 2.)
SHEPPARD, Rev. H. R. L. C.F. 4th Class, R.A.C.D. 1901
SHERBURN, J. C. Capt., E. Yorks. Regt. and Gen. List 1906
(A.D.C.)
SHILLINGTON, J. M. Lieut., R.N.V.R. 1896
SHIMWELL, H. Capt., London Regt. (R. Fus.) *m.* 1903
SHIMWELL, O. Capt., London Regt. (R. Fus.) 1904
SHRAGER, E. H. Lieut., Middlesex Regt. (W.) *M.C.* 1912
SILLEM, C. F. Hon. Lieut., Spec. List., empld. British 1885
Red Cross

✠SIMPSON, G. B. Capt., York and Lancaster Regt. 1909
Died 12 *Nov.* 1915 *of wounds received in action*
SIMPSON, G. H. Sub-Lieut., R.N.V.R.; Capt. (Ad.), 1912
R.A.F.
✠SIMPSON, W. A. Trooper, Canadian Mtd. Rifles 1904
Killed in action 1 *Dec.* 1915
SINCLAIR, R. C. H. Lieut., R.F.A.; A.D.C. 1897
SKENE, Rev. R. E. C.F. 4th Class, R.A.C.D. *1901
SLAUGHTER, A. Capt., Manchester Regt.; empld. P. of W. 1904
Camp
SLOLEY, R. Lieut., R.A.S.C. 1912
SMITH, A. W. E. Lieut., R. Sussex Regt.(T.F.) 1898
SMITH, E. S. Lieut., Labour Corps 1917
SMITH, F. A. Pte., Black Watch 1907
SMITH, J. T. *See* TILDEN SMITH, J.
SMITH, M. V. Capt., Herefordshire Regt. and Labour 1900
Corps
SMITH, R. Lieut., R.F.A. *M.* 1910
SMITH, W. F. Lieut., Cambridge Univ. O.T.C. 1905
SMITH-SLIGO, R. W. M. G. J. Capt., Highland L.I.; 1911
attd. Egyptian Army
✠SOAMES, W. N. Lieut., Cheshire Yeo. 1907
Died 19 *May* 1916 *of heart failure*
SOLOMON, C. G. R. Lieut., S. African H.A. 1904
SPENCER, L. D. Major, King's Own Scottish Borderers; 1894
Lieut.-Col., Spec. List (Military Governor). (W 2.)
m 2. *Medjidieh, 3rd Class. Osmanieh, 4th Class (Egypt)*
SPICER, M. Colonel, R.A.F.; S.O. (Equipment). *M.* 1902
SPICER, N. 2nd Lieut., Bedfordshire Regt. 1899
✠SPRINGFIELD, G. P. O. Capt., 2nd Dragoon Gds. (Queen's 1891
Bays)
Killed in action 12 *Sept.* 1914
SPURRELL, R. J. Lieut.-Col., R. Sussex Regt.; Cmdt., 1874
L. of C. *M.*
✠STATHAM, N. H. Lieut., E. Surrey Regt.(T.F.); attd. 1912
Devon Regt.
Killed in action 3 *Feb.* 1917
STEELE, A. R. Major, 4th Hussars. (W.) 1895
STEELE, C. M. Capt., R.G.A.(T.F.) 1896
STENHAM, B. B. Chief Yeoman, Mine Force, United 1910
States Navy
✠STERNBERG, E. A. J. 2nd Lieut., King's Own (R. Lan- 1908
caster Regt.)
Killed in action 16 *Oct.* 1916

STEWARD, R. D. Capt. and Adjt., R.F.A. *M.C.* *M* 2. 1899
STEWART, F. C. Capt., R.A.O.C. *m.* 1891
STEWART, F. D. L. 2nd Lieut., R.G.A. 1914
STEWART, J. C. Major, Scottish Horse (T.F. Res.); Bri- 1876
gade Major
✠STIEBEL, C. Lieut., I.M.S. 1894
Killed in action in Mesopotamia 3 *Feb.* 1917
STRINGER, H. W. Pte., R. Fusiliers (Sportsman's Bn.) 1885
STUART, C. M. Lieut., R.N.V.R. 1908
STUART, D. C. R. Lieut., Border Regt.; Capt., Spec. List 1905
(Courts-Martial Officer). (W.) *M.*
STUBBER, R. H. Major, S. Irish Horse; attd. Life Gds. 1897
D.S.O.
SWANN, A. Lieut., R.N.V.R. (Coastal Motor-boat Ser- 1911
vice). *D.S.C.*
SWANN, L. H. 2nd Lieut., Suffolk Yeo. 1893
SWANN, Rev. S. E. C.F. 4th Class, R.A.C.D. (W.) 1909
✠SWEET, J. L. L. Pte., Canadian Hdrs.; 2nd Lieut., R. 1906
Scots Fus. *M.*
Killed in action near Givenchy 16 *June* 1915
SWEETING, H. C. Capt., King's Royal Rifle Corps; empld. 1904
Ministry of National Service. (W.) *O.B.E.* *m.*
SYME, H. R. Lieut., R.A.S.C. (W.) 1914
✠SYMONDS-TAYLER, F. K. Capt., King's (Shropshire L.I.) 1913
(W 2.)
Died 17 *April* 1917 *of wounds received in action*
SYMONDS-TAYLER, R. H. Hon. Lieut.-Col., Hereford- 1886
shire Regt. (T.F. Res.)
SYMINGTON, R. E. Lieut., S. Lancs. Regt.; attd. T.M.B. [1914]
(W.)

TACON, D. G. T. Capt., R.F.A. *M.* 1907
TAYLEUR, W. Capt., Shropshire Yeo.(T.F. Res.); Lieut.- 1890
Col., Labour Corps. *O.B.E.* *T.D.* *M* 2.
✠TAYLOR, W. E. Lieut., R.A.S.C. 1899
Drowned 2 *June* 1917
THOMAS, J. C. C. Major, N. Staffs. Regt. 1891
THOMAS, K. D. P. 2nd Lieut., R.E. (Signals) 1917
THOMAS, L. D. C. 2nd Lieut., Worcestershire Regt. 1898
✠THOMAS, O. C. Lieut., Grenadier Gds.; attd. Gds. M.G. 1907
Regt.
Killed in action 1 *Dec.* 1917
THOMAS, Rev. R. A. Capt., Cheshire Regt.(T.F. Res.); 1892
C.F. 3rd Class, R.A.C.D.

THOMPSON, A. C. Capt., Middlesex Regt.; attd. Oxford   1914
and Bucks. L.I. (W 2.) *M.C.*
THOMPSON, H. C. S. Capt., S. Lancs. Regt.   1879
THOMSON, G. L. Lieut.-Col. (A. and S.), R.A.F. *D.S.C.* 1906
D.F.C. M 2.
THOMSON, J. Lieut., London Regt. (Rifles)   1905
THOMSON, J. G. O. Capt., Ayrshire Yeo.; A.D.C.   1900
THORNELY, R. R. Sub-Lieut., R.N.V.R. (Armoured Car   1908
Section); Capt. (A.), R.A.F. (W.) *D.S.C. M.*
THORNEWILL, C. C. Capt., Lincolnshire Yeo. and M.G.C.   1904
THORP, D. B. Lieut. (T.), R.A.F.   1898
THYNNE, L. W. Lieut., Rifle Brigade   1904
TILDEN SMITH, J. 2nd Lieut., R. Fusiliers   1914
TILL, W. S. Capt., R. Sussex Regt.; empld. O.C.B. (W.) 1912
TINGEY, W. R. H. Capt., R.E. *M.*   1913
TINLINE, G. C. M. 2nd Lieut., Cameron Hdrs.; Lieut.,   1913
Highland L.I.
TOLER-AYLWARD, H. J. Trooper, Res. Regt. of Cavalry   1914
TOULMIN, H. W. Lieut., Suffolk Yeo.   1889
TRACY, G. C. Major, D. of Cornwall's L.I.; Lieut.-Col., 1895
Spec. List (Cmdt., School of Instruction). (W.)
D.S.O. M 2.
✠TRAILL, J. M. Major, Bedfordshire Regt.   1884
Killed in action 30 *Oct.* 1914
TRAILL, J. W. Major, S. Lancs. Regt. and Spec. List   1875
TREDENNICK, J. N. E. Lieut., R. Warwickshire Regt. and 1911
Gen. List, empld. Ministry of National Service. (W.)
✠TRENCHARD, F. A. Lieut., R.F.A. (W.) *M.*   1906
Killed in action 24 *May* 1915
TRISTRAM, U. H. Major, S. Notts. Hussars (T.F. Res.)   1892
and Remount Service; Lieut.-Col., Res. Regt. of
Cavalry
TROLLOPE, T. C. S. Pte., London Regt. (Artists Rifles); 1912
2nd Lieut., Labour Corps
TROTTER, J. F. A. Major, R.F.A. *O.B.E. M.*   1906
TROYTE, G. J. ACLAND. *See* ACLAND TROYTE, G. J.
TRUSTED, H. H. Lieut., D. of Cornwall's L.I.; Staff Capt., 1909
E. Indies
TUDOR OWEN, F. H. G. Lieut., Rifle Brigade; Staff Capt., 1904
S. Command. (W.) *m.*
TURRALL, R. G. Capt., R.E. *M* 2.   1912
TYLDEN-WRIGHT, W. R. Capt., 3rd Hussars; Major,   1899
D.A.A. and Q.M.G. *D.S.O. M* 3.
TYTLER, W. T. F. *See* FRASER-TYTLER, W. T.

USHER, H. B. Capt., Middlesex Regt.; attd. E. Surrey 1912
Regt.; empld. War Office. (W.)
USHER, T. Capt., Suffolk Regt. *M.* 1902
UTLEY, B. T. Lieut., Connaught Rangers. (W.) 1913

VACHELL, F. T. Trooper, K. Edward's Horse; Major, 1908
R.F.A. *M.C.*
✠VAULKHARD, J. V. 2nd Lieut., Bedfordshire Regt. 1914
Killed in action 15 *Sept.* 1916

WALKER, C. C. Capt., Argyll and Sutherland Hdrs. 1894
✠WALKER, J. A. Capt., R. Welsh Fus. 1911
Killed in action 19 *Feb.* 1916
✠WALKER, O. R. Capt., Worcestershire Regt.; attd. R. 1902
Fusiliers
Killed in action in Gallipoli 4 *June* 1915
WALLER, Rev. W. H. Chaplain, R.N. 1887
WALSH, A. ST G. Capt. and Adjt., Manchester Regt. *M.* 1912
WALTER, C. E. H. L. Lieut., R.A.S.C. 1907
WARD, H. L. 2nd Lieut., R.A.S.C. 1900
WARD, J. S. M. 2nd Lieut., Rangoon Bn., Indian Defence 1905
Force
WARD, Hon. R. A. Capt., Spec. List. *M* 2. 1890
WARE, B. G. Lieut., Spec. List 1899
WASBROUGH, H. C. S. Lieut., Oxford and Bucks. L.I. 1897
WATERHOUSE, C. Lieut., Life Gds.; Capt., Tank Corps. 1913
(W.) *M.C.*
WATSON, A. B. 2nd Lieut., Scottish Horse; Lieut., Black 1890
Watch
✠WATSON, A. T. Capt., Remount Service; D.A.D. Re- *1890
mounts; Major, King's Royal Rifle Corps. (W.)
Died 5 *Aug.* 1917 *of wounds received in action*
WATSON, H. N. Lieut.-Cdr., R.N.V.R. 1907
WATSON, T. H. Capt., R.A.S.C.(M.T.) 1900
WAUCHOPE, D. A., D.S.O., T.D. Major, Lothians and 1889
Border Horse; attd. Staffordshire Yeo.
WEBSTER, R. B. Capt., Northumberland Fus.(T.F.) 1908
WEBSTER, S. W. Lieut.-Col., 6th Dragoon Gds. (Cara- 1893
biniers). *m.*
WEBSTER, W. G. Trooper, K. Edward's Horse; Lieut., 1909
R.F.A.
✠WELSBY, S. W. H. Pte., R. Fusiliers (P. S. Bn.); Lieut., 1910
Cheshire Regt. (W.)
Killed in action 30 *April* 1917

WESSELS, C. H. Staff Lieut., S. African Force   1903
✠WHARTON, F. H. Lieut., Loyal N. Lancs. Regt.   1909
  Killed in action 25 Sept. 1915
WHATMAN, A. D. Major, The Buffs (E. Kent Regt.,   1892
  T.F.)
WHEELER, M. Capt., R. Berkshire Regt.(T.F.)   1895
WHIFFEN, T. W. Capt., Recruiting Staff, London District 1900
WHITAKER, J. L. Lieut. (A.), R.A.F.   1915
WHITE, R. J. Capt. and Adjt., R. Warwickshire Regt.;   1898
  A.P.M. *M. Chevalier, Military Order of Avis*
  (*Portugal*)
WHITEHEAD, J., T.D. Major, Lancs. Fus.(T.F.) *M.*   1892
✠WHITFELD, N. B. Lieut., R. North Devon Yeo.; attd.   1909
  Devon Regt.; Lieut. (A.), R.A.F.
  Killed in flying accident 7 July 1918
✠WICKHAM, W. J. Capt., Scots Gds.   1893
  Killed in action 31 Oct. 1914
WILKINSON, H. E. T. 2nd Lieut., Yorkshire Hussars   1893
WILLIAMS, F. J. Capt., R. Inniskilling Fus. (W.)   1890
WILLS-SANDFORD, T. G. Lieut., Remount Service   1899
WILSON, E. R. Capt., R. Irish Fus.; attd. Tank Corps; 1907
  empld. War Office. (W 2.)
WILSON, H. M. Capt., N. Zealand Med. Corps   1895
WILSON, R. K. 2nd Lieut., R.F.A. (W 2.)   1917
WILSON-TODD, J. H. Lieut., Scots Gds.   1911
WINGFIELD, C. R. B. Major, King's (Shropshire L.I.)   1894
WINGFIELD DIGBY, F. J. B. Major, Dorset Yeo. *D.S.O.* 1905
  M.
✠WINTERBOTTOM, D. D. Capt., Manchester Regt.(T.F.)   1910
  Killed in action 7 Aug. 1915
WINTERBOTTOM, O. D. Capt., Cameron Hdrs. and R.E.   1909
  M.
WODEHOUSE, Lord. Lieut., 16th Lancers; A.D.C. (W.)   1902
  M.C. M 2.
WODEHOUSE, Hon. P. Lieut., Spec. List   1905
WOOD, E. B. Capt., R.A.S.C.; Inspector of M.T. *M.*   1902
WOOD, J. C. Capt., Rifle Brigade   1896
WOODHEAD, Sir G. S., V.D. Colonel, R.A.M.C. (Sani-   *1899
  tary Service, T.F.) *K.B.E. O.B.E. Brevet Colonel.*
  m 2.
WOODHOUSE, G. H. Major, E. Riding of Yorkshire Yeo.;   1908
  Staff Capt.
WOODRUFF, J. S. Pte., Australian Force   1906
WOOLF, H. G. Major, S. Staffs. Regt. *m.*   1885

WRIGHT, A. Capt., Cheshire Regt. and R. Welsh Fus. 1879
WRIGHT, H. T. Lieut., Scots Gds.; Staff Capt., London 1896
District
WYNN, Rev. H. E. C.F. 3rd Class, R.A.C.D. *M.* 1907
Italian Croce di Guerra

YARROW, K. G. 2nd Lieut., Black Watch (T.F.); Lieut., 1905
R.A.S.C.
YOUNG-HERRIES, W. D. Lieut.-Col., King's Own Scottish 1885
Borderers. *m.*

SELWYN COLLEGE

✠ADAM, A. G. A. Capt., The Buffs (E. Kent Regt.) *M.* 1904
Killed in action in Mesopotamia 21 Jan. 1916

ADAMS, J. K. Lieut., Devon Regt.(T.F.); attd. Rifle 1911
Brigade

ADAMS, Rev. W. S. C.F. 4th Class, R.A.C.D. 1896

✠ADAMSON, H. B. 2nd Lieut., Suffolk Regt.; Capt., W. 1901
Yorks. Regt.
Died 30 Oct. 1916 *of wounds received in action 22 Oct.*
1916

ALDERSON, J. H. Trooper, United Provinces Horse, 1893
Indian Defence Force

✠ALDERSON, R. Capt., Lancs. Fus. (W.) *M.C. M.* 1913
Died 25 March 1918 *of wounds received in action*

✠ALDERTON, C. F. Pte., H.A.C.; 2nd Lieut., Manchester 1908
Regt.
Killed in action 7 July 1916

✠ALSTON, G. K. 2nd Lieut., Suffolk Regt.(T.F.) 1912
Killed in action in Gallipoli 31 Aug. 1915

ARCHER, Rev. G. D. C.F. 4th Class, R.A.C.D. 1907

✠AVERNS, R. F. J. Pte., Queen's Own (R. W. Kent Regt.) 1914
Died in German hands Oct. 1918

BACON, J. N. H. Sergt., The Queen's (R. W. Surrey Regt.) 1914
BARKER, F. Sapper, R.E. (Signals) 1912
BARKER, Rev. T. W. C.F. 4th Class, R.A.C.D. 1910
BARNES, F. Capt. and Adjt., Rifle Brigade. (W.) *m.* 1905
BARNICOAT, Rev. G. H. C.F. 4th Class, R.A.C.D. 1906
BARR, L. B. Lieut., R.G.A.(T.F.); empld. Ministry of 1914
Labour. (W.)
BARRETT, Rev. C. B. G. C.F. 4th Class, R.A.C.D. 1905

BAXANDALL, A. Pte., R.A.M.C. 1912
BEAMENT, W. O. 2nd Lieut., Dorchester School O.T.C.; 1912
attd. Highland L.I.
BEAN, J. W. B. Major, Australian A.M.C. (W.) 1898
✠BEANLAND, J. W. Lieut., R. Welsh Fus. 1913
Killed in action in Gallipoli 28 *Aug.* 1915
BEAVEN, V. Pte., London Regt. 1909
BELL, J. H. Pte., E. Surrey Regt.; Capt. and Adjt., 1889
R. Defence Corps
BELL, L. B. Pte., H.A.C.; Capt., London Regt. (Fins- 1913
bury Rifles)
BENDALL, F. W. D. Lieut.-Col., London Regt. (R. Fus.) 1901
and Middlesex Regt. (W.) *C.M.G. M* 2.
BENGOUGH, G. D. Capt., R.G.A.(T.F.) 1895
BENNETT, T. C. 2nd Lieut., Somerset L.I.; Lieut., 1911
M.G.C. (W.) *M.*
BETHUNE, Rev. F. P. Capt., Australian M.G.C. *M.C.* 1901
BETHUNE, Rev. J. W. C.F. 4th Class, R.A.C.D. 1901
BETTON, H. R. B. 2nd Lieut., Norfolk Regt. (W.) 1911
BILSBOROUGH, J. H. 2nd Lieut., Exeter School O.T.C. 1907
BIRKS, C. T. E. Pte., E. Surrey Regt.; 2nd Lieut., Nor- 1915
thamptonshire Regt.
BLACKWALL, J. E., T.D. Lieut.-Col., Sherwood Foresters 1892
(Notts. and Derby Regt., T.F.) *D.S.O. M.*
Chevalier, Legion of Honour (France)
✠BLAKESTON, B. M. 2nd Lieut., I.A.R.O., attd. Infy. 1910
Killed in action 25 *March* 1917
✠BLAXLAND, J. B. Capt., S. Wales Borderers 1910
Killed in action 24 *Jan.* 1917
BLEASDELL, J. T. Capt., R.A.M.C. *M* 2. 1908
BLUNDELL, Rev. E. K. C.F. 4th Class, R.A.C.D. 1905
BLYTH, M. M. Pte., R. Fusiliers (P. S. Bn.) 1894
BODE, Rev. J. E. V. Chaplain, R.N. 1907
✠BORTON, C. E. Major, Malay States Guides. *M.* 1898
Killed in action 2 *Aug.* 1917
✠BOTT, W. E. Capt., R. Fusiliers 1912
Killed in action 18 *Sept.* 1918
BOURDILLON, Rev. G. L. Chaplain, R.N. 1905
✠BOURNE, A. S. Pte., R. Fusiliers (P.S. Bn.); 2nd Lieut., 1910
S. Staffs. Regt. (W.)
Died 25 *April* 1917 *of wounds received in action*
✠BOURNE, C. 2nd Lieut., The Queen's (R. W. Surrey 1907
Regt.)
Died 11 *April* 1917 *of wounds received in action*

BOYCOTT, A. G. Lieut., R.A.S.C.; empld. War Office 1907
BOYLE, Rev. G. E. C.F. 4th Class, R.A.C.D. 1903
BREE, Rev. H. R. S. C.F. 4th Class, R.A.C.D. 1904
BRIDGES, L. W. 2nd Lieut., Queen's Own (R.W. Kent 1909
Regt.)
BRISCOE, J. R. Capt., R.A.M.C. 1896
BRISCOE, W. T. Capt., R.A.M.C.(T.F.) 1897
BROWN, G. Lieut., R.G.A. (W.) 1895
BROWN, R. C. Capt., R.A.M.C. 1884
BROWN, W. R. R. Lieut., E. Yorks. Regt.(T.F.) (W.) 1910
BROWNING, H. Lieut., Hampshire Regt. and R.E. 1913
(Signals). *M.B.E. M* 2. *French Croix de Guerre*
BROWNING, Rev. W. F. Pte., R.A.M.C. 1908
BUNN, F. A. Pte., R.A.M.C. 1910
BURFIELD, S. T. Lieut., King's (Liverpool Regt.) (W.) 1908
BURROWES, R. V. Capt., Suffolk Regt. (W 3.) *M.C.* 1912
BUTLER, E. H. Lieut., Wiltshire Regt. (W.) 1911
BUTLER, F. H. C. Lieut., Hampshire Regt.; Capt., Gen. 1913
Staff (A.P.M.) *M.*

CALDERBANK, Rev. J. C.F. 4th Class, R.A.C.D. 1910
CAMERON, Rev. C. C.F. 4th Class, R.A.C.D. 1906
CANDLER, G. Capt., R.A.M.C.(T.F.) 1888
✠CARR, B. A. 2nd Lieut., R.G.A. *M.* 1898
Killed in action 25 July 1917
CARVER, Rev. B. N. Chaplain, R.N. 1908
CASTLEHOW, Rev. J. A. S. C.F. 4th Class, R.A.C.D. 1909
✠CHARLEWOOD, W. H. Capt., Northumberland Fus. 1912
Died 22 July 1916 of wounds received in action
CHARLTON, G. D. Capt., N. Staffs. Regt.(T.F.) 1909
CHEW, Rev. J. E. C.F. 4th Class, R.A.C.D. 1905
CHUBB, R. N. Capt., Army Cyclist Corps. *M.* 1910
CIVIL, H. G. V. Major, Wellington College O.T.C. 1906
CLARK-KENNEDY, Rev. A. C. C.F. 4th Class, R.A.C.D. 1899
CLARKSON, Rev. E. R. T. Major, R.A.M.C. 1889
CLEMO, F. A. Capt. and Adjt., D. of Cornwall's L.I.; 1910
Staff Capt. *M.C. M* 2.
CLOSE, A. V. Pte., R. Fusiliers (P. S. Bn.); Lieut., Tank 1911
Corps. (W 2.)
✠CLOSE, R. W. M. Lieut., Yorkshire Regt. 1907
Killed in action 27 May 1918
COLLIER, Rev. G. H. Chaplain, R.N.; attd. R.A.F. *m.* 1907
COLLIS, A. J. Lieut.-Col., R.A.M.C.(T.F.) 1887
COMYN, K. Capt., I.M.S. (W.) 1902

CONRAN, Rev. M. W. T.   C.F.   4th   Class,   R.A.C.D.   *1885
M.C. M.
COPEMAN, C. E. F.,   Lieut.-Col.,   Cambridgeshire Regt.   1886
and   Northamptonshire   Regt.(T.F.)   C.M.G.   T.D.
m 3.
COUPE, Rev. T. O.   2nd Lieut., R.A.S.C.   1905
COWHAM, A. G.   Pte., London Regt.; 2nd Lieut., W.   1914
Yorks. Regt. (W.)
CRAWLEY, Rev. J. L.   C.F. 3rd Class, R.A.C.D.   (W.)   1910
O.B.E. M.
CROCOMBE, F. R.   Lieut., 76th Punjabis, Indian Army   1911
CROSTHWAITE, W. H.   Capt., Spec. List (Map Section).   1902
O.B.E. M 2.
CURREY, R. G. T.   Major, Leinster Regt.; Lieut.-Col.,   1894
Lancs. Fus. (W.)

DANVERS, Rev. G. C.   C.F. 4th Class, R.A.C.D.   (W.)   1900
M.C.
✠DAUBENEY, G. R.   Lieut., Queen's Own (R. W. Kent   1913
Regt.)
Killed in action near Ypres 23 April 1915
DAVIES, C.   2nd Lieut., Essex Regt.   1908
✠DAVIES, G. B.   Capt., Essex Regt.   1912
Killed in action 26 Sept. 1915
DAVIS, E. B.   Lieut., W. Yorks. Regt.   [1914]
DAVIS, Rev. F. B.   C.F. 4th Class, R.A.C.D.   M.   1907
DAWSON, S.   Pte., R.A.M.C.   1913
DEALTRY, F. H. B.   Lieut., empld. with Cadet unit   1897
DE CHAUMONT, Rev. T. S. B. F.   C.F. 4th Class, R.A.C.D.   1903
DE COETLOGON, Rev. C. E. C.   Lieut., Spec. List (Re-   1885
cruiting Staff)
DE MOWBRAY, L. ST J.   Capt., R. Berkshire Regt.   [1914]
DE RIDDER, L. E.   Lieut., Gloucestershire Regt.(T.F.)   1914
DEVEREUX, N.   Capt., R.A.M.C.   1885
DEVEREUX, W. C   Major, R.A.M.C.   1883
✠DICKENSON, L. A. F. W.   2nd Lieut., Bedfordshire Regt.;   1912
attd. R. Irish Rifles
Died 10 May 1915 of wounds received in action at Ypres
DICKENSON, Rev. L. G.   C.F. 3rd Class, R.A.C.D.   1888
D.S.O. m.
DOUGLAS, H. A.   Capt., R.A.M.C.   1905
DOUGLAS, J.   Lieut., Middlesex Regt.   1891
DOWELL LEE, R. W.   Capt., Dorset Regt.; empld. O.C.B.   1910
(W.) M 2. Order of the White Eagle, 5th Class (Serbia)

DOWNES, G. S. J. Lieut., W. Yorks. Regt.; Major, M.G.C. 1914
(W.) *M.C. M.*
✠DUCKWORTH, W. C. 2nd Lieut., Welsh Regt.; attd. King's 1909
(Shropshire L.I.)
Killed in action 8 Oct. 1918
✠DUNWELL, F. L. 2nd Lieut., R. Fusiliers 1907
Killed in action 6 Jan. 1916
DUTTON, P. E. Pte., Grenadier Gds. 1894
✠DUVALL, Rev. J. R. C.F. 4th Class, R.A.C.D. *M.* 1908
Died 6 Oct. 1917 *of wounds received in action in
Macedonia*
DYER, Rev. B. S. Junior Chaplain, Indian Army 1898

✠EDMUNDS, C. V. Capt. and Adjt., Essex Regt.(T.F.) 1902
Killed in action 26 March 1917
EDWARDS, E. D. Lieut., Lancs. Fus.; Hon. Lieut. (Ad.), 1913
R.A.F. (W.)
EDWARDS, H. J., C.B., T.D. Hon. Colonel, Unattd. List, *1895
T.F.; cmdg. O.C.B.; *C.B.E. O.B.E. m* 3.
EHLVERS, F. W. V. Lieut., R.F.A. 1909
ELLIOTT, Rev. J. S. C.F. 4th Class, R.A.C.D. 1901
ELLIS, J. 2nd Lieut., E. Yorks. Regt. 1909
ELSEY, J. W. R.N. 1915
ETHERIDGE, F. Major, 7th Rajputs, Indian Army; 1899
D.A.A.G. *D.S.O. M* 3.
EVANS, A. G. Capt., Devon Regt. 1890

FABER, V. V. Lieut., R.F.A. 1913
FAGAN, Rev. H. W. F. Senior Chaplain, Indian Army 1890
FISHER, C. E. (*formerly* FISCHER). Sergt.-Major, R.A.F. 1912
(W 2.)
FITZMAURICE, Rev. G. L. C.F. 4th Class, R.A.C.D. 1895
FITZMAURICE, W. H. Lieut., Gloucestershire Regt. (W.) 1905
FLETCHER, Rev. B. F. C.F. 4th Class, R.A.C.D. 1885
✠FLETCHER, M. Pte., R. Fusiliers (P. S. Bn.); Capt., R. 1904
Munster Fus. *M.C.*
Killed in action 9 Sept. 1916
FLETCHER, P. Pte., Canadian A.M.C. 1885
FLETCHER, W. T. Capt., 97th Deccan Infy., Indian *1904
Army. (P.)
FORBES, Rev. A. G. C.F. 4th Class, R.A.C.D. 1889
FORD, Rev. F. T. C.F. 4th Class, R.A.C.D. *M.* 1906
✠FORD, F. W. Capt., Cambridgeshire Regt. *M.C. M.* 1912
Killed in action 26 Sept. 1917

FOSTER, Rev. D. B. L. C.F. 4th Class, R.A.C.D. 1908
FOWLER, H. R. R. Major, R.A.M.C.(T.F.) 1886
FRANCIS, E. C. Lieut. and Adjt., Norfolk Regt. 1905
FREND, E. C. Pte., Queen's Own (R.W. Kent Regt.) 1889
✠FURZE, A. Capt. and Adjt., King's Own (Yorkshire L.I.) 1911
  Killed in action 16 *Sept.* 1916

GALE, A. J. V. Corpl., R.E. (Spec. Bde.); Cadet, R.G.A. 1913
GALL, A. Pte., London Regt. (Artists Rifles) 1909
GARDNER, Rev. J. L. C.F. 4th Class, R.A.C.D. 1899
GARRETT, A. H. Lieut., R.E. *M.* 1913
GAWNE, H. D. 2nd Lieut., Worcestershire Regt. 1910
✠GEDGE, Rev. B. J. C.F. 4th Class, R.A.C.D. *M.* 1901
  Died 25 *April* 1917 *of wounds received in action*
✠GEDGE, P. Lieut., Suffolk Regt. 1909
  Killed in action 13 *Oct.* 1915
✠GIBSON, P. C. F. Capt., R. Fusiliers 1898
  Killed in action 10 *April* 1917
GIBSON, T. B. Lieut., Calcutta Bn., Indian Defence Force 1907
GIDNEY, F. Capt., Rifle Brigade; attd. R.E. (Signals); 1912
  G.S.O. 3.
GILBERT, G. G. T. 2nd Lieut., Devon Regt. 1899
GILROY, P. K. Capt., I.M.S. *M.C. M* 2. 1903
GIRLING, E. A. Capt., Hampshire Regt. (W.) *M.C.* 1907
✠GOATCHER, F. Lieut., Suffolk Regt. (W.) 1908
  Died 31 *Oct.* 1917 *of wounds received in action* 20 *Oct.*
  1917
GOLDING, R. H. C. 2nd Lieut., R.G.A. 1914
GOLDSMITH, Rev. S. W. C.F. 4th Class, R.A.C.D. 1889
GOSLING, W. R. Major, S. Wales Borderers and Welsh 1910
  Regt. *O.B.E. M* 2.
GRANT, D. P. Lieut., King's Own (Yorkshire L.I., T.F.); 1914
  Capt. and Adjt., York and Lancaster Regt.(T.F.) (W.)
  M.C.
GRAY, Rev. F. H. A. Major, King's Own Scottish Bor- 1896
  derers and R. Scots Fus. *M.C.*
✠GREGSON, A. H. 2nd Lieut., Queen's Own (R. W. Kent [1914]
  Regt.)
  Killed in action 19 *April* 1917

✠HAILSTONE, G. R. Capt., R. Welsh Fus.(T.F.) 1912
  Killed in action in Palestine 6 *Nov.* 1917
HALL, A. F. W. Lieut., Essex Regt. and Nigeria Regt., 1914
  W. African Frontier Force

HALL, C. S. Lieut., Dorset Regt. (W.)   1904
HAMMOND, Rev. J. V. C.F. 4th Class, R.A.C.D.   1889
HANSON, Rev. E. C. C.F. 4th Class, R.A.C.D.   1912
HARDING, Rev. C. R. C.F. 4th Class, R.A.C.D.   1889
HARDY, T. L. Capt., R.A.M.C. M.   1905
HARGREAVES, C. R. Pte., R. Fusiliers; 2nd Lieut., King's   1915
Own (R. Lancaster Regt.)
HARPER, Rev. W. E. C.F. 4th Class, R.A.C.D.   1907
HARRIS, J. B. Capt., S. Wales Borderers. M.C. M.   1910
HATTEN, Rev. J. C. LE P. C.F. 4th Class, R.A.C.D.   1896
✠HEALEY, R. E. H. Lieut., Queen's Own (R.W. Kent Regt.)   1904
Killed in action on the Somme 23 July 1916
✠HEATON-ELLIS, C. E. R. Lieut., King's Own (Yorkshire   1912
L.I.)
Killed in action 19 March 1916
HEDGES, Rev. P. D. C.F. 4th Class, R.A.C.D.   1890
HEMSWORTH, N. E. C. 2nd Lieut., Norfolk Regt.; attd.   1913
Worcestershire Regt.; Lieut., 29th Punjabis, Indian
Army
HENDRIE, H. A. Capt., Manchester Regt.; attd. T.M.B.   1910
(P.)
HENSLOW, T. G. W. Lieut., Argyll and Sutherland Hdrs.   1897
HILL, W. A. Major, Indian Army   1886
HODGES, Rev. R. A. C.F. 4th Class, R.A.C.D.   1911
HODGSON, Rev. A. D. C.F. 4th Class, R.A.C.D.   1908
HOGBEN, E. O'N. 2nd Lieut., N. Staffs. Regt.; Capt.,   1912
Army Cyclist Corps. (W 2.) M.C.
HOLMES, Rev. A. Lieut., Sherwood Foresters (Notts.   1891
and Derby Regt.)
HONEYBALL, F. R. 2nd Lieut., R. Fusiliers; attd. London   1910
Regt.; Capt., 124th Baluchistan Infy., Indian Army.
(W.)
✠HOOD, J. W. Lieut., R.G.A. M 2.   1909
Died at Valenciennes 15 Nov. 1918 of influenza
HORNE, Rev. C. W. E. Chaplain, Canadian Force   1896
HOUGHTON, Rev. J. C. C.F. 4th Class, R.A.C.D.   1898
HOWARD, W. E. W. Major, R.A.S.C.   1906
HOWLETT, Rev. C. E. C.F. 4th Class, R.A.C.D.   1907
✠HUBBLE, H. R. 2nd Lieut., King's (Liverpool Regt.)   1911
Killed in action 20 May 1917
HUCK, J. Major, Border Regt.(T.F.) O.B.E. M 2.   1901
HUDSON, Rev. R. C.F. 2nd Class, R.A.C.D.(T.F.)   *1889
✠HUDSON, T. H. Capt., R. Berkshire Regt.   1908
Killed in action 13 Oct. 1915

518 SELWYN COLLEGE

HUGHES, B. Major, R.A.M.C.(T.F.) *D.S.O.* M 2. 1898
  Order of St Sava, 4th Class (Serbia).
HUGHES, Rev. S. J. C.F. 4th Class, R.A.C.D. 1903
HUNTER, L. A. W. Lieut., Seaforth Hdrs. 1915
HURLY, M. R. Lieut.-Col., Indian Army *1883
HYBART, Rev. A. J. F. Pte., R. Welsh Fus. 1905
✠HYDE, J. C. Pte., London Regt. (London Scottish); [1914]
  2nd Lieut., Sherwood Foresters (Notts. and Derby
  Regt.)
  Killed in action 1 July 1916

ICELY, Rev. F. Chaplain, R.N. 1887
INGHAM, W. Pte., R.A.S.C. (British E. Africa) and Tank 1908
  Corps
✠IRVING, T. H. 2nd Lieut., King's (Liverpool Regt.) 1913
  Killed in action 19 Aug. 1916
IRVING, W. R. Lieut., King's (Liverpool Regt.) (W.) 1911
IRWIN, H. M. Lieut., Nigeria Regt., W. African Frontier 1904
  Force

JAGG, Rev. V. T. S. C.F. 4th Class, R.A.C.D. (W.) 1906
JAMES, H. M. 2nd Lieut., R.F.A.(T.F.) 1914
JEFFERY, E. J. B. Lieut., Devon Regt. 1911
✠JERVIS, A. C. 2nd Lieut., King's (Liverpool Regt.); 1906
  Capt., King's African Rifles
  Killed in action in Portuguese E. Africa 3 July 1918
JERVIS, Rev. E. O. C.F. 2nd Class, R.A.C.D. *M.* 1892
JESSE, W. Lieut., I.A.R.O., attd. S. and T. Corps 1888
JEUDWINE, W. W. Major, I.M.S. *C.M.G.* *M.* 1895
JOBLING, J. S. Lieut., R. Fusiliers; empld. Admiralty [1914]
JOELS, W. A. Lieut., E. Surrey Regt. *M.* 1914
JOHNSON, J. B. Lieut., Uppingham School O.T.C. 1909
JONES, J. D. Capt., R.A.M.C. *M.* 1906
JONES, W. H. S. 2nd Lieut., Perse School O.T.C. 1894
JONES-BATEMAN, Ven. W. Chaplain, Canadian Force 1883
JOSCELYNE, C. H. 2nd Lieut., Leicestershire Regt. 1910

KEATCH, F. H. Lieut., R.F.A.; A.D.C.; Staff Capt. 1913
  (W.) *M.C. Belgian Croix de Guerre.*
KENNEDY, D. D. A.B., R.N.V.R. (Anti-Aircraft); Lieut., 1913
  E. Surrey Regt.
KER, R. A. Lieut., Malvern College O.T.C. 1900
✠KESTEVEN BALSHAW, N. Capt., King's Royal Rifle Corps 1911
  Killed in action 13 April 1918

KETTLEWELL, Rev. H. H.   C.F. 4th Class, R.A.C.D.   1907
KETTLEWELL, L.   Major, Wiltshire Regt.   (W.)   *D.S.O. M.*   1912
✠KEWLEY, W. C.   Pte., Canadian Infy.   1910
Killed in action at St Eloi 13 *April* 1916
KEYWORTH, W. D.   Capt., I.M.S.   *M.*   1899
KING, P. E.   Pte., R.A.S.C.; Lieut., R.F.A.; attd. R.G.A.   1909
KIRBY, Rev. J. B.   C.F. 4th Class, R.A.C.D.   1885
KIRTLAND, J.   Lieut., R.F.A.; Capt., Spec. List (School   1907
of Instruction). (W.)

LABEY, T. H.   2nd Lieut., R.G.A.   1912
✠LANGDON, Rev. C.   C.F. 4th Class, R.A.C.D.   1901
Killed in action 31 *Oct.* 1917
LANGDON, Rev. C. G.   C.F. 4th Class, R.A.C.D.   1895
✠LANGDON, L.   Lieut., Hampshire Regt.   1893
Died 14 *March* 1916 *of wounds received in action*
LARNER, Rev. H. M.   C.F. 4th Class, R.A.C.D.   *1894
✠LAWRENCE, T. E.   Pte., R.A.S.C.   1914
Died 6 *Nov.* 1916 *of fever*
LAWSON, Rev. W. R.   C.F. 4th Class, R.A.C.D.   *M.*   1902
LEWARNE, Rev. F. T.   C.F. 4th Class, R.A.C.D.   1888
LIGHTBURNE, Rev. H. R. H.   Chaplain, R.N.   1904
✠LINE, E. A. T.   2nd Lieut., R.A.S.C.   1914
Died in Macedonia 16 *Dec.* 1916
LISTER, J. B.   2nd Lieut., E. Yorks. Regt.   1914
LITTLE, Rev. C. S.   C.F. 4th Class, R.A.C.D.   1908
LOUND, Rev. R.S.   C.F. 4th Class, R.A.C.D.   1901
LOWNDES, Rev. J.   C.F. 4th Class, R.A.C.D.   1908
✠LUCAS, A.   2nd Lieut., K. Edward's Horse.   (W.)   1899
Killed in the Irish rebellion 28 *April* 1916
LUMLEY, D. O.   Capt., Wiltshire Regt. and Gen. List   1913
(Recruiting Staff). (W.)   *O.B.E. M.B.E. m.*
LUSH, E. J.   Capt., King's (Liverpool Regt.)   1907
LUSH, Rev. J. A.   C.F. 4th Class, N. Zealand Chaplains'   1900
Dept. *M.*
LYDEKKER, Rev. N. W.   C.F. 4th Class, R.A.C.D.   1906

McCALL, T. H.   Capt., W. Yorks. Regt.; empld. Ministry   1912
of Labour. (W 2.)
✠McCOLL, W. L.   Sergt., London Regt.; 2nd Lieut.,   1912
Northamptonshire Regt.
Died 18 *July* 1916 *of wounds received in action*
✠McKIEVER, V. C.   2nd Lieut., Manchester Regt.   1908
Died 18 *May* 1915 *of wounds received in action*

✠MACKWORTH, F. J. A. Major, R.F.A.; Brigade Major   1895
    Killed in action 1 *Nov.* 1914
MACLEOD, Rev. W. A. C.F. 4th Class, R.A.C.D.   1888
McMICHAEL, J. F. Capt., Indian Army   1905
McMULLAN, H. Lieut., Lancs. Fus.; Capt., King's   1913
    (Liverpool Regt.) (W.)
MACPHERSON, C. E. H. C. Lieut., R. Dublin Fus.;   1909
    Major (A.), R.A.F.
MACSWINEY, Rev. A. J. E. Chaplain, R.N.   1900
MADGE, R.E. Capt., Lincolnshire Regt. *M.*   1911
✠MAITLAND, H. M. Capt., Spec. List (Intelligence). *M.C.*   1907
    M 2.
    Died 10 *Nov.* 1918 *of pneumonia*
MALDEN, Rev. R. H. Chaplain, R.N.   *1907
MAPLES, A. C. Capt., R. Sussex Regt.; Major, Cheshire   1897
    Regt. *m* 2.
MAPLES, E. W. Major, R. Welsh Fus. and Gen. List   1889
    (Staff Capt.) *O.B.E. m.*
MARRIOTT, A. E. C. 2nd Lieut., Sherwood Foresters   1914
    (Notts. and Derby Regt.)
MARSH, Rev. F. S. C.F. 4th Class, R.A.C.D.   1903
MARSHALL, G. J. P. 2nd Lieut., W. Yorks. Regt.   1914
MARTIN, F. J. 2nd Lieut., Leicestershire Regt.; Capt.   1910
    (A.), R.A.F.
MASTERS, P. G. Pte., R.A S.C.(T.F.); Corpl., R.E.;   1904
    2nd Lieut., London Regt. (R. Fus.)
✠MATTHEWS, N. A. 2nd Lieut., London Regt. (Finsbury   1911
    Rifles)
    Killed in action 15 *Sept.* 1916
MAY, C. A. C. Capt., Cheshire Regt.; Brigade Major.   1911
    (W 2.) *M.C. M. Greek Military Cross*
MEADE, Rev. L. G. C.F. 4th Class, R.A.C.D.   1902
MELLERSH, E. L. Capt. and Adjt., R.G.A. *M.*   1909
MELVILLE, Rev. W. G. C.F. 2nd Class, R.A.C.D.   1885
    (T.F.)
MERCER, Rev. G. H. Cadet, O.C.B.   1910
MEYLER, Rev. E. M. Junior Chaplain, Indian Army   1895
MILLER, H. C. Gnr., R.F.A.; Cadet, O.C.B. (W.)   1913
MILLES, G. H. Pte., S. African Force.   1896
✠MILSOM, S. 2nd Lieut., Rifle Brigade.   1905
    Killed in action at Hooge 30 *July* 1915
MITCHELL, J. C. Sqdn. Sergt.-Major, R. North Devon   1911
    Yeo.; Lieut., Devon Regt. *M.C.*
MONTAGUE, W. J. Lieut., R.G.A.   1914

SELWYN COLLEGE 521

MONTGOMERY, D. S. Capt., British Columbia Regt., 1905
Canadian Force; Staff Capt.
MONTGOMERY, J. C. 2nd Lieut., Cameronians (Scottish 1914
Rifles).
✠MONTGOMERY, N. Lieut., British Columbia Regt., Cana- 1905
dian Force
Killed in action 21 Aug. 1917
MOORE, Rev. C. A. G. 2nd Lieut., R.A.S.C. 1904
MOORE, G. G. 2nd Lieut., R.F.A. 1907
MOORE, Rev. J. W. B. Chaplain, R.N. 1905
MORRISON, H. H. Lieut., R.N.V.R. 1902
MOTT, C. C. Major, Spec. List 1884
✠MURRAY, R. H. Capt., Yorkshire Regt. *M.* 1913
Killed in action 7 July 1916

NASH, Rev. W. W. H. C.F. 4th Class, R.A.C.D. 1903
NEWCOMBE, W. L. Major, Worcestershire Regt.; Brigade 1896
Major
NEWMAN, J. C. F. Lieut., R. Sussex Regt. (W 2.) 1913
NEWPORT, Rev. H. C.F. 4th Class, R.A.C.D. (W.) 1908
NICHOLSON, H. H. Pte., R. Fusiliers (P. S. Bn.); Capt., 1911
Durham L.I. (W 2.)
NORRIS, Rev. E. W. M. C.F. 1st Class, R.A.C.D. 1887
NORTON, L. M. Capt., R.G.A.(T.F.) 1906
NOSWORTHY, J. L. Lieut., R.F.A.(T.F.) 1912

OGLE, K. W. S. 2nd Lieut., King's Own (R. Lancaster [1914]
Regt.)
OLIVER, L. W. Lieut., R.A.M.C. 1885
ORME, B. C. Lieut., King's Own (Yorkshire L.I.) and 1911
M.G.C. (W 2.)
✠ORPEN,W.S. 2nd Lieut.,N.Staffs.Regt.; attd.Lancs.Fus. 1912
Killed in action on the Somme 6 July 1916

PAINTER, H. S. 2nd Lieut., Northamptonshire Regt.; 1911
Lieut., Manchester Regt. (W.) *M.C.*
PARSONS SMITH, S. H. Major, S. and T. Corps, Indian 1896
Army
PAYNE, Rev. M. G. J. C.F. 4th Class, R.A.C.D. 1906
✠PEAK, N. 2nd Lieut., Manchester Regt. 1908
Killed in action 1 July 1916
✠PERKS, W. L. Pte., H.A.C.; 2nd Lieut., Worcestershire 1913
Regt.
Killed in action 24 Aug. 1916

PERROTT, G. F. D. Cadet, R.A.F.   1917
PESKETT, J. C. Lieut., R. Sussex Regt. *M.C.*   [1914]
✠PETTINGER, J. W. Capt., R.A.M.C.   1892
    Died 6 Oct. 1917 of pneumonia
PIERCY, Rev. H. M. M. Pte., R.A.M.C.   1906
✠PINCHES, E. L. Lieut., Loyal N. Lancs. Regt.   1915
    Died 28 Nov. 1917 of wounds received in action
✠PLOWMAN, C. H. Lieut., Wiltshire Regt.   [1914]
    Killed in action 24 April 1917
POCHIN, H. Capt., S. Staffs. Regt. and M.G.C. (W.)   1902
    M.C.
POOLE, A. L. Lieut., Gloucestershire Regt. (W.)   *1912
POOLE, C. A. Lieut., R.F.A.(T.F.)   1913
POWELL, A. G. C. Corpl., R.G.A.   1914
POWELL PRICE, J. C. Major, I.A.R.O. *M.*   1907
PRANKERD, Rev. J. C.F. 4th Class, R.A.C.D.   1898
PRENTICE, Rev. T. N. R. C.F. 4th Class, R.A.C.D.   1907
PRIESTLAND, J. F. E. Lieut., Sherwood Foresters (Notts. 1904
    and Derby Regt.) and M.G.C.
PRISSICK, C. Lieut.-Col., 56th Punjabi Rifles, Indian   1890
    Army. *M* 2. *Order of the Nile, 3rd Class (Egypt).*
✠PRYNNE, E. G. F. Capt., R. Fusiliers; attd. London Regt. 1910
    Killed in action on the Somme 16 Sept. 1916
✠PRYNNE, N. F. 2nd Lieut., Devon Regt.   1915
    Killed in action 24–5 April 1917

RAINE, R. T. Capt., R.A.M.C. (W.) *M.C. and Bar. M.* 1909
RATCLIFFE, C. ST A. 2nd Lieut., London Regt. (Surrey   1910
    Rifles); attd. Durham L.I.
RAWCLIFFE, W. B. 2nd Lieut., Hampshire Regt.; attd.   1910
    R.F.C.
✠REAY, T. S. Pte., R. Fusiliers (P.S. Bn.); Lieut., D. of 1913
    Cornwall's L.I.
    Died 1 March 1918 of wounds received in action
    28 Feb. 1918
REED, L. H. B. 2nd Lieut., R.F.A.; Lieut., T.M.B. (W.) 1911
REEVE, Rev. F. P. Pte., R.A.M.C.   1911
REEVES, Rev. R. F. Pte., R.A.M.C.   1898
REYNOLDS, Rev. J. W. V. Chaplain, R.N.   1904
RHODES, E. L. N. Capt., R.A.M.C. *M.*   1901
RHODES, W. F. Capt., R.A.M.C.   1902
RICE, Rev. M. N. C.F. 4th Class, R.A.C.D.   1892
RICHARDS, E. I. G. Capt. and Adjt., Welsh Regt. (W.)   1908
RIDLEY, D. F. Capt., Border Regt. (W 2.) *M.C. M.*   1912

RICKETTS, G. D. *See* BENGOUGH, G. D.
ROBBS, F. W. Lieut., W. African Frontier Force; R.T.O.   1893
ROE, R. G. Pte., Canadian Scottish; Lieut., Gordon   1907
   Hdrs.; Major, R.E. (Signals). (W.)
ROGERSON, Rev. T. S. C.F. 4th Class, R.A.C.D.   1905
✠ROPER, O. S. Capt., King's Own (Yorkshire L.I.)   1913
   Killed in action 27 *Nov.* 1917
ROSE, Rev. A. L. Capt., Sherwood Foresters (Notts. and   1908
   Derby Regt., T.F.)
ROSS, R. W. Capt., Seaforth Hdrs. (W 2.) *M.C. m.*   1899
ROWLAND, E. W. S. Capt., R.A.M.C.(T.F.) *m.*   1890
RUBIE, Rev. G. O. Pte., London Regt. (Artists Rifles)   1906

SADGROVE, K. H. O'R. Lieut., S. Lancs. Regt. (W 2.) (P.)   1912
SAMSON, Rev. A. M. C.F. 4th Class, R.A.C.D.   1910
SANDERSON, P. M. Capt., Worcestershire Regt.; empld.   1904
   War Office
SCOBIE, J. Capt., Loyal N. Lancs. Regt.   [1914]
SCOTT, Rev. C. W. 2nd Lieut., Labour Corps   1898
SCRUBY, F. S. Capt., Cambridgeshire Regt.; attd. R.E.   1899
   O.B.E. M.
SEAMAN, Rev. A. J. C.F. 4th Class, R.A.C.D.   1906
SELLWOOD, H. E. Air Mechanic, R.A.F.   1907
SELWYN, Rev. H. E. C.F. 4th Class, R.A.C.D. *m.*   1885
SEWELL, F. C. Pte., R. Fusiliers, Army Pay Corps, and   1914
   Labour Corps
SHARMAN, Rev. G. H. Pte., S. African Infy.   1901
SHEARWOOD, Rev. G. F. F. C.F. 4th Class, R.A.C.D.   1909
SHEPHEARD, E. P. W. Pte., London Regt.; 2nd Lieut.,   1901
   King's Royal Rifle Corps. (W.) (P.)
SHILLAKER, E. C. H. Lieut., W. Yorks. Regt. and Tank   1913
   Corps. (W 2.) *M.C.*
SIMEON, Rev. J. P. Lieut., R.A.S.C.(M.T.) *M.*   1896
SMITH, H. A. Lieut., R.A.M.C.   1897
SMITH, Rev. S. T. 2nd Lieut., Labour Corps   1904
SMITH, W. G. Capt., Cranbrook School O.T.C.   1894
SPENCE, D. L. Capt., R.A.M.C.   1905
SPINNEY, Rev. M. H. C.F. 4th Class, R.A.C.D.   1906
STANDIDGE, C. Pte., W. Yorks. Regt. and Cameronians   1898
   (Scottish Rifles); Air Mechanic, R.A.F.
STANLEY, C. M. Capt., Army Cyclist Corps. *M.*   1904
✠STANTON, R. G. O. Lieut., R.M.L.I.   1914
   Died 28 *April* 1918 *of wounds received in action at*
   Zeebrugge 23 *April* 1918

✠STAUNTON, Rev. H. C.F. 4th Class, R.A.C.D. 1889
    Died in Mesopotamia 14 *Jan.* 1918
STEALEY, E. T. Lieut., Monmouthshire Regt. (P.) 1913
STOCKDALE, R. J. Capt., Durham L.I.(T.F.) (W 3.) *M.C.* 1914
STOKES, Rev. L. C.F. 4th Class, R.A.C.D. 1910
STONEMAN, W. E. Lieut., R.G.A. (W.) 1914
✠STRAUGHAN, T. A. Lieut., Northumberland Fus. 1910
    Died 17 *Feb.* 1918 *of wounds received in action in Galli-*
    poli 19 *Aug.* 1915
STRONG, P. N. W. 2nd Lieut., R.E. 1917
STROVER, E. J. Capt., 3rd Brahmans, Indian Army; attd. 1904
    R.F.C. (P.) *M.*
✠SUNDERLAND, G. Sergt., K. Edward's Horse; Capt., R. 1910
    Sussex Regt. (W.)
    Killed in action at Gricourt 24 *Sept.* 1918
SUTTON, L. J. Lieut., R.G.A. 1911
SWINEY, A. J. E. *See* MACSWINEY, Rev. A. J. E.
SYKES, Rev. F. M. C.F. 3rd Class, R.A.C.D. *O.B.E.* *M* 2. 1897

TADMAN, G. R. Major, R.A.S.C. (Camel Transport 1901
    Corps). *M.C.* *M.*
TANCOCK, E. O. 2nd Lieut., R.G.A. (W.) 1905
TAYLOR, J. F. Capt., R.A.M.C. 1905
TAYLOR, Rev. L. F. M. Chaplain, R.N. 1908
TELFER, A. C. 2nd Lieut., Cambridgeshire Regt.; Lieut., 1912
    The Queen's (R.W. Surrey Regt.) (W 2.)
TEMPEST, F. L. Capt., Suffolk Regt. and Gen. List 1912
    (Staff Capt.) *M.C.*
THOMAS, H. E. E. Lieut., R.A.S.C. and R.F.A. 1909
THORBURN, E. C. Lieut., M.G.C. *M.C.* [1914]
THORNEYCROFT, K. H. Lieut., The Queen's (R. W. 1912
    Surrey Regt.); Capt., Spec. List (cmdg. P. of W.
    Camp). (W.) *m.*
[1] THURSFIELD, R. M. R. Surgeon Lieut., R.N. 1903
TILBURY, Rev. H. F. C.F. 4th Class, R.A.C.D. 1895
TILSTON, Rev. H. E. C.F. 4th Class, R.A.C.D. 1901
TISDALL, E. G. ST. C. Capt., Monmouthshire Regt. 1914
    (W.) *M.C.*
TOMBLINGS, D. G. Capt., E. African Med. Service. *M.* 1908
TOMLINSON, H. Pte., R. Fusiliers 1906
✠TOVEY, D. 2nd Lieut., London Regt. (London Scottish) 1892
    and Gen. List
    Died 5 *May* 1918

    [1] Killed at sea after the armistice.

SELWYN COLLEGE   525

TRENCH, Rev. G. F. C.F. 4th Class, R.A.C.D. *M.*   1899
TRUMAN, Rev. M. G. C.F. 4th Class, R.A.C.D.   1909
TUDOR, O. C. O. Lieut., R.A.S.C.   1905
TUDOR, R. G. Capt., King's (Liverpool Regt.) (W 2.)   1910
    M.C. M.
TURNER, J. P. Pte., R.A.S.C.(M.T.)   1911
TURNER, J. S. Sub-Lieut., R.N.V.R.   1903
TYLER, H. H. F. M. Capt., I.A.R.O., attd. 9th Ghurkas. 1896
    (W.) *C.S.I. M.*

UNWIN, H. A. R. E. Capt., R.A.M.C. *m.*   1899
UNWIN, S. R. Capt., Unattd. List, T.F., attd. Devon   1895
    Regt.; Instructor, School of Musketry. *m.*

VIVIAN, G. L. Capt., I.A.R.O. (Cavalry)   1906

✠WADESON, E. Y. Lieut., Loyal N. Lancs. Regt. (W.)   1914
    Killed in action 22 March 1918
WADLEY, H. W. A. Pte., Canadian A.M.C.   1901
✠WAIT, C. F. W. Lieut., King's Own (Yorkshire L.I.)   [1914]
    Died 15 *July* 1916 *of wounds received in action*
WARD, J. G. Major, R.G.A.(T.F.) *M.*   1908
WARDLEY, D. J. Capt., R. Fusiliers; Capt. and Adjt.,   1912
    London Regt.; Staff Capt. *M.C. and Bar*
WEBER, W. E. Lieut., Spec. List (R.T.O.)   1896
WEBSTER, J. F. Capt., Norfolk Regt.; empld. Agricultural 1910
    Directorate, Mediterranean Exp. Force
WELCH, J. J. Lieut., R.G.A.   *1911
WELLER, Rev. C. H. C.F. 4th Class, R.A.C.D. (W.)   1898
    M.C.
WELLER, Rev. J. R. C.F. 4th Class, R.A.C.D.; empld.   1910
    Indian Army
WELLS, A. P. Sapper, R.E.   1906
WHARTON, C. H. L. Pte., Canadian A.M.C.   1905
✠WHITE, G. C. W. 2nd Lieut., Cheshire Regt.   1912
    Died 6 *Oct.* 1915 *of wounds received in action*
WHYTEHEAD, H. L. Pte., London Regt. (Artists Rifles)   1897
WILLIAMS, A. S. 2nd Lieut., Devon Regt.   1904
WILLIAMS, R. A. Cadet, R.G.A.   1898
WILLIAMS, R. F. Lieut., Canadian Infy.   1900
WILSON, H. L. Lieut., R.A.M.C.   1895
WILSON, J. S. 2nd Lieut., R. Warwickshire Regt. (W.)   1906
WINDSOR, J. F. Lieut., R.A.M.C.   1899
WING, T. 2nd Lieut., Wiltshire Regt. (W.)   1897

Wood, G. Capt. and Adjt., Cheshire Regt. (W.) *O.B.E.*   1913
M.C. M.
Wood, Rev. T. J. C.F. 4th Class, R.A.C.D.   1910
Woods, F. A. Lieut., Army Pay Dept.   1906
Woods, N. C. Pte., Army Pay Corps   1903
Woods, T. H. Lieut., R. Fusiliers   1910
Woolliscroft, F. H. Lieut., N. Staffs. Regt. (W.)   1912
✠Wordsworth, O. B. 2nd Lieut., Oxford and Bucks.   *1911
L.I.; Lieut., M.G.C.
Killed in action 2 April 1917
Wright, Rev. A. G. C.F. 4th Class, R.A.C.D.   1909
✠Wright, E. A. Sergt., London Regt. (London Scottish);   1896
Lieut., R.A.M.C.
Died at Alexandria 20 June 1915 of septic poisoning

✠Young, J. V. Pte., R. Fusiliers (P.S. Bn.); 2nd Lieut.,   1911
Somerset L.I.
Killed in action 2 July 1916

FITZWILLIAM HALL[1]
(NON-COLLEGIATE)

ADAM, W. A. Major, S. Staffs. Regt.(T.F.) (W 3.) (P.) 1901
✠ALFORD, A. C. G. 2nd Lieut., Gloucestershire Regt.; 1913
attd. Worcestershire Regt.
Killed in action 3 Sept. 1916
✠ALLISON, C. H. Capt., Suffolk Regt. 1914
Killed in action 13 Nov. 1916
ALLPRESS, H. G. Lieut., Monmouthshire Regt. (W.) 1909
ALNWICK, H. Lieut., W. Yorks. Regt. (W.) *M.C. M.* 1914
ARMOUR, J. 2nd Lieut., King's Royal Rifle Corps 1910

BAGNALL, J. M. V. Corpl., R.E. (Signals); Lieut., North- 1913
umberland Yeo.
BAKER, D. *See* BENDIGO, Rt. Rev. Bishop of
BAKER, E. 2nd Lieut., Norfolk Regt. 1917
BALL, S. H. Lieut., Coldstream Gds. and Gds. M.G. 1915
Regt.
BANYARD, F. E. Lieut., Cambridgeshire Regt. (W.) 1911
✠BARRAUD, V. H. A. Capt., French Army. (W.) *Chevalier,* 1910
Legion of Honour (France)
Killed in action 20 June 1915
BARRETT, R. O. Lieut., R. Welsh Fus. and Bedfordshire 1911
Regt.
✠BARTLETT, C. W. Capt., Sherwood Foresters (Notts. and 1913
Derby Regt.) (W.) *M.C. M.*
Killed in action 9 Oct. 1918

[1] The names of those who, after matriculating as Non-Collegiate students, joined one or other of the Colleges before the war, will be found under their adopted Colleges only.

BEARD, E. Lieut., Northamptonshire Regt. *m.* 1915
BEAUMONT, P. J. Gnr., R.G.A. 1903
✠BECK, C. B. H. 2nd Lieut., Cheshire Regt.(T.F.) *1913
    Died 18 *Aug.* 1915 *of wounds received in action in*
    Gallipoli 17 *Aug.* 1915
BENDIGO, Rt. Rev. Bishop of. C.F., Australian Chaplains' 1909
    Dept.
BIRD, Rev. E. G. Chaplain, R.N. 1900
BIRD, H. J. G. Capt., W. Yorks. Regt. (R. of O.); Major, 1895
    M.G.C. (Motor). *M.*
BOLTON, T. Sapper, R.E. (London Electrical Engineers, 1897
    T.F.)
✠BOUCHER, A. E. Lieut., R. Warwickshire Regt. (W.) [1914]
    M.C. M.
    Killed in action 18 *Nov.* 1916
✠BOWLER, S. 2nd Lieut., R.G.A. 1911
    Killed in action 21 *Oct.* 1917
BRADLEY, G. H. Cadet, O.C.B. 1917
BRIGGS, J. L. 2nd Lieut., Suffolk Regt. 1913
BRIGHT, F. T. Lieut., Suffolk Regt.; Capt. (A.), R.A.F. 1907
    (W.) *D.F.C.*
BRIGHT, W. J. Capt., R.F.A. *M.* 1911
BROOKES, A. Lieut., I.A.R.O., attd. 69th Punjabis; 1907
    Capt., Provost Marshal
BROOMER, A. 2nd Lieut., King's Own (R. Lancaster 1914
    Regt.); Lieut. (O.) and Capt. (Ad.), R.A.F.
BUCKLEY, A. ST D. Pte., R.A.S.C. 1910
BUTLER, E. W. 2nd Lieut., King's Royal Rifle Corps 1915
BUTLER, J. 2nd Lieut., R. Berkshire Regt. (W.) 1913
BYWATERS, Rev. F. J. C.F. 4th Class, R.A.C.D. 1911

CAIRNIE, J. B. Lieut., Seaforth Hdrs. 1913
✠CARTER, W. H. S. Lieut., King's (Liverpool Regt.) [1914]
    Killed in action 14 *July* 1916
CASSAN, Rev. A. W. M. C.F. 4th Class, R.A.C.D. (W.) 1903
    M.C. M.
CHAPPLE, C. J. Lieut., R. Sussex Regt. 1915
CHARLEY, L. W. Lieut., R. Warwickshire Regt.; Capt., 1908
    Gen. List (Intelligence). *O.B.E. M.*
CLEE, C. B. B. Capt. and Adjt., Suffolk Regt. (W.) *M.* 1914
CLEMENTS, P. M. H. Lieut., Essex Regt. (W.) [1914]
COHEN, M. 2nd Lieut., R.A.S.C.; attd. Serbian Army 1917
COOK, F. Pte., Training Res. Bn. 1915

COPPLESTONE, W. R. J. Lieut., E. Lancs. Regt. and 1912
Nigeria Regt., W. African Frontier Force; Liaison
Officer, attd. Belgian Gen. Staff
CROOKALL, Rev. E. C.F. 4th Class, R.A.C.D. 1906
CROSS, P. M. Lieut., Dartford Grammar School O.T.C. 1907

DALLING, W. E. Staff Sergt., R.A.M.C.(T.F.) 1913
DAVIES, J. R. Lieut., R.N.V.R. 1910
DAVIS, C. A. E. 2nd Lieut., R.F.A. 1914
Killed in action 31 July 1917
DE BRACONIER, L. Brigadier, Belgian Army. *Belgian* 1915
Croix de Guerre
DE CEULENEER, P. Belgian Army 1914
DEIGHTON, F. J. Capt., 124th Baluchistan Infy. and S. 1903
and T. Corps, Indian Army
DE LESTAPIS, H. Sous-Lieut., French Army 1914
DENNIS, W. J. M. 2nd Lieut., Durham L.I. 1903
DIXON, J. H. Lieut., Labour Corps 1913
DOWNMAN, B. V. R. 2nd Lieut., Sherwood Foresters 1914
(Notts. and Derby Regt.)
Killed in action 21 Sept. 1916
DUBOIS, H. A. Lieut., I.A.R.O., attd. 140th Patiala Infy. 1910
M.
DUNNING, G. C. Corpl., R.A.M.C.(T.F.) 1909
DUNSHEATH, P. Capt., R.E. *O.B.E. M* 2. 1910
DYSON, E. Lieut., R.F.A.(T.F.) (W.) 1912

EEMAN, J. Belgian Army 1915
ELLIOTT, O. C. F. 2nd Lieut., Gordon Hdrs. 1914
Killed in action 14 Oct. 1916
ELLIOTT, S. D. Pte., Sherwood Foresters (Notts. and 1917
Derby Regt.)
ELLIOTT, W. W. 2nd Lieut., R. Scots. (W.) 1906
EMTAGE, W. L. 2nd Lieut., Middlesex Regt.; Lieut., *1913
British W. Indies Regt.

FACEY, Rev. N. S. C.F. 4th Class, R.A.C.D. 1913
FANSHAWE, C. H. Major, R.A.S.C.; D. A. D. S. and T., 1893
W. Command. *m.*
FAWCETT, R. Lieut., R.G.A.(T.F.) (W.) *M.* 1911
FEW, H. C. Major, Cambridgeshire Regt. (W 2.) 1898
FLORY, P. J. 2nd Lieut., Bedfordshire Regt. 1916
Killed in action 22 Aug. 1918
FLOWER, Rev. W. J. Chaplain, R.N. 1903

✠FOSTER, R. Pte., N. Staffs. Regt.(T.F.); 2nd Lieut. (O.), 1912
R.F.C.
Killed in flying accident 3 Jan. 1918

GAMBLE, Rev. H. J. C.F. 4th Class, R.A.C.D. *M.* 1908
GARRETT, Rev. S. C.F. 4th Class, R.A.C.D. 1903
GAZE, Rev. A. M. B. Lieut., Bedfordshire Regt. and La- 1907
bour Corps. (W.)
GIBSON, Rev. H. C.F. 4th Class, R.A.C.D. *M.C. M.* 1903
GIRDLESTONE, Rev. F. S. P. L. C.F. 4th Class, R.A.C.D. 1900
D.S.O.
✠GLAISTER, G. F. Lieut., Tank Corps 1908
Killed in action 1 Aug. 1918
GLAISTER, S. E. Lieut., Tank Corps. (W 2.) [1914]
GOODCHILD, Rev. E. J. Capt., Essex Regt.(T.F. Res.) 1909
GORDON, J. E. Lieut., 5th Dragoon Gds. and M.G.C. 1904
(W 2.)
GOUGH, D. W. P. Rfn., King's Royal Rifle Corps 1917
GOULD, Rev. C. J. B. C.F. 4th Class, R.A.C.D. 1899
GREY, R. C. Lieut., Suffolk Regt.; attd. Indian Army 1913
GRIFFITHS, Rev. J. Lieut., R. Welsh Fus.; attd. R. Sussex 1912
Regt. (W.)

HALE, H. E. Trooper, Oxfordshire Yeo.; 2nd Lieut., 1899
Oxford and Bucks. L.I.
HARGREAVES, C. A. Capt., Manchester Regt.(T.F.) (W 2.) 1911
M.
HARRIS, F. W. Capt., R.F.A. (W.) *M.* 1913
HARRIS, Rev. G. H. C.F. 4th Class, R.A.C.D. *M. m.* 1910
✠HARRIS, T. W. S. Capt. (A.), R.A.F. 1913
Killed in action (21 Nov. 1918)
✠HASLAM, W. 2nd Lieut., Manchester Regt. 1915
Killed in action 21 March 1918
HASTINGS, Rev. W. Capt., Labour Corps 1881
✠HAYNES, W. G. 2nd Lieut., Suffolk Regt. [1914]
Killed in action 27 June 1917
✠HEATH, F. A. Pte., R.A.M.C. 1913
Died 12 Oct. 1917
HENDRY, C. W. 2nd Lieut., Gordon Hdrs.; Lieut., 1913
M.G.C. *M.C.*
HINTON, S. E. Capt., Cheshire Regt.(T.F.) 1914
✠HIRST, W. B. 2nd Lieut., Lincolnshire Regt.(T.F.) 1911
*Died 22 April 1915 of wounds received in action near
Ypres*

HOLLIS, W. P. B. Corpl., R.E. (Signals). (P.) 1912
HUDSON, T. E. 2nd Lieut., Hampshire Regt. 1910
HUME, D. B. M. Capt. (K.B.), R.A.F. *M.* 1912
HURRELL, G. W. 2nd Lieut., Tank Corps. (W 2.) [1914]
HURRELL, J. W. Capt. and Adjt., Bedfordshire Regt.; 1911
  Major, King's Royal Rifle Corps. (W.) *M.C.*
HUSSEY, Rev. R. L. C.F. 4th Class, R.A.C.D. 1907

ISON, L. J. Pte., London Regt.(Civil Service Rifles) 1911

JAMESON, T. S. Lieut., W. Yorks. Regt.; attd. E. Lancs. 1914
  Regt.(T.F.); empld. O.C.B.
JEFF, Rev. A. H. C.F. 4th Class, R.A.C.D. 1908
JENKINS, H. L. Lieut., M.G.C. (W.) 1910
JENKINSON, C. Pte., R.A.M.C.(T.F.) [1914]
JOHNSON, A. H. Pte., Suffolk Regt. (W.) 1915
JOHNSON, W. D. Cadet, O.C.B. 1918
JONES, Rev. D. M. C.F. 4th Class, R.A.C.D. *M.C.* 1914
JONES, Rev. E. C.F. 4th Class, R.A.C.D. 1914
JOSEPH, C. G. Lieut., Cambridge Univ. O.T.C. 1912

KEAY, K. D. Lieut., Cameronians (Scottish Rifles). (W.) 1913
KEELAN, Rev. V. L. Chaplain, R.N. 1890
KERRIDGE, W. A. L. Capt., D. of Wellington's (W. Riding 1911
  Regt.) (W.) *M.*
KING, R. R. Capt., London Regt. (Queen's). (W.) 1912
KNIGHT, J. H. Lieut., D. of Wellington's (W. Riding 1913
  Regt.) (W.)

LACY, H. C. 2nd Lieut., Suffolk Regt.; Draft Conducting 1917
  Officer
LEE, W. N. R. 2nd Lieut., E. Lancs. Regt.; attd. S. 1917
  Lancs. Regt.
LEGGE, P. A. Hon. Major, R.G.A. (R. of O.); Super- 1911
  visor of Customs, Gold Coast
LEGOUIS, P. A. E. Sous-Lieut., French Army 1913
LEWIS, A. T. Lce.-Corpl., R. Welsh Fus. 1916
LEWIS, H. G. Capt., Tank Corps. *M.* [1914]
LEWIS, O. G. Lieut., R.E.; empld. Ministry of Labour 1911
LITCHFIELD, G. Lieut., Devon Regt. (W.) 1911
LOCK, Rev. L. J. Capt., R.A.M.C. 1905
✠LONG, F. S. Lieut., Essex Regt. 1912
  Killed in action 26 Sept. 1915
LONGSTAFF, J. 2nd Lieut., Durham L.I. 1911

McCLIMENT, Rev. R. J.   C.F. 3rd Class, R.A.C.D.;   1912
   D.A.P.C. O.B.E. M 3.
MACKAY, R. F. B.   Capt., Essex Regt.(T.F.). m.   *1913
MAJOR, E.   Lieut., R.G.A. M.C.   1915
MALLETT, H. R.   R.S.M., R.A.M.C.   1907
MARIS, A. A.   Capt., Suffolk Regt.(T.F.) (W.)   1913
MARSH, A. W.   2nd Lieut., R.F.A. (W.)   1917
MARTIN, F.   Corpl., London Regt. (Civil Service Rifles)   1911
✠MARTIN, H. E.   Capt., Middlesex Regt.(T.F.)   1910
   Died 19 *June* 1916 *of wounds received in action*
MATTOCK, F. C.   Lieut., W. Yorks. Regt.   1912
MEAD, Rev. A.   C.F. 4th Class, R.A.C.D.   1913
MEIXNER, F.   Lieut., King's Own (R. Lancaster Regt.);   1910
   attd. R.E. (Signals)
MILLER, L. V.   Lieut., R.E. (Signals). (W.)   1912
MILLER, O. G.   2nd Lieut., I.A.R.O., attd. 23rd Sikhs   [1914]
MORGAN, G. E.   2nd Lieut., Welsh Regt.   1917
✠MORRIS, A. C.   Pte., Cheshire Regt.   [1914]
   Killed in action 1918
MORRIS, H. E. A.   Lieut., Cambridgeshire Regt. and   1913
   154th Infy., Indian Army
MORRISH, J.   *See* MURRISH, J.
MORTON, A. V.   Lieut., Gloucestershire Regt.; Lieut.   1914
   (A.), R.A.F. (W.)
MORTON, C. E.   Lieut., M.G.C. M.   1897
MORTON, Rev. J. G.   C.F. 4th Class, R.A.C.D.   1900
MUNCEY, A. P.   Telegraphist, R.N.V.R.   1915
MUNCEY, S. W. U.   Corpl., R.E. (Spec. Bde.)   1915
✠MUNRO, D.   Pte., R. Fusiliers   1912
   Died 14 *Jan* 1919 *of blood-poisoning contracted on*
   active service
MURRISH, J.   Lieut., D. of Cornwall's L.I. and R.E.   1911
   (Field Survey Bn.) (W.)

NEAL, R.   Cadet, O.C.B.   1908
NEWELL, Rev. H. W.   C.F. 4th Class, R.A.C.D.   1908
✠NORMAN, Rev. W. H.   Sergt., R.A.M.C.   1907
   Drowned on H.M. transport Transylvania 4 *May* 1917
✠NORTON-FAGGE, F. W. L.   Capt., I.A.R.O., attd. Punjabis.   1906
   M 2.
   Died 29 *Nov.* 1916

O'CONNELL, Rev. J. B.   C.F. 4th Class, R.A.C.D.   1912
OLDHAM, T. V.   Capt., R.A.M.C.(T.F.)   1914

O'RIORDAN, P. M. 2nd Lieut., I.A.R.O., attd. 75th Car- 1901
natic Infy.

PEACOCK, L. V. Lieut., Suffolk Regt. (Cyclist Bn., T.F.) 1913
and 46th Punjabis, Indian Army; attd. 18th Infy.
PECK, E. G. Lieut.-Col., R.A.M.C.(T.F.) *D.S.O. T.D.* 1872
M 2.
PECK, E. S. Capt., Cambridgeshire Regt.; Major, Gen. 1893
Staff, empld. British Military Mission. *m.*
PEEL, A. W. Lieut., Cambridgeshire Regt.; Capt., Gen. 1892
List (T.F. Res.), empld. Ministry of National Service.
M.B.E.
PEGG, H. E. Pte., London Regt. (Artists Rifles) 1914
PICKARD, Rev. H. G. C.F. 4th Class, R.A.C.D. 1910
✠PLAYER, E. N. Capt., Yorkshire Regt. 1911
Killed in action 6 Aug. 1916
POWELL, Rev. E. J. C.F. 4th Class, R.A.C.D. 1900
PRUST, T. W. Capt., Middlesex Regt. 1906
PRYKE, W. W. Pte., Suffolk Regt. 1915

REMNANT, G. L. 2nd Lieut., Lancs. Fus. 1917
ROBINSON, Rev. T. C.F. 4th Class, R.A.C.D. 1911
ROGERS, C. E. B. Capt., R. Berkshire Regt. (W.) *M.C.* 1913
✠ROLFE, P. Pte., R. Fusiliers (P.S. Bn.); Capt., R.A.S.C.; 1909
attd. Norfolk Regt.
Killed in action 24 Aug. 1918
✠ROSE, H. E. Capt., R.A.M.C. (W.) 1905
Died 7 July 1917 of wounds received in action
ROYSTON, H. R. 2nd Lieut., R. Fusiliers 1909

SALEEBEY, Rev. E. S. C.F. 4th Class, R.A.C.D. 1893
SAYER, S. D. Corpl., Suffolk Yeo. 1912
SCOTT, C. W. Major (A. and S.), R.A.F. *D.F.C. M 2.* 1914
✠SCOTT, F. Capt., Leicestershire Regt. (W 3.) *M.C.* 1913
Killed in action 27 May 1918
SCOTT, G. A. Lieut., Gloucestershire Yeo. 1909
SCOTT, R. F. M. Lieut., R.A.M.C. 1889
SCOTT, T. F. Lieut., Seaforth Hdrs.(T.F.) (W.) 1909
SEMPLE, Rev. E. G. C.F. 4th Class, R.A.C.D. (W 2.) 1909
✠SERGINSON, H. Capt., Northumberland Fus.; attd. 1915
T.M.B. *M.C.*
Killed in action 27 Feb. 1918
SEWELL, H. D. R.A.S.C.(M.T.) 1904
SHARP, G. G. Lieut., Border Regt. (W.) 1912

✠SHAW, W. Lieut., Cambridgeshire Regt. *M.* 1914
 Died in German hands 27 Sept. 1916 *of wounds received in action*
SHEEHAN, Rev. F. R. C.F. 4th Class, R.A.C.D. 1894
SHEPHERD, Rev. J. C.F. 4th Class, R.A.C.D. 1905
SHERLOCK, W. W. Lieut., I.A.R.O., attd. S. and T. Corps. 1900
 M 2.
SHILLAKER, G. Pte., London Regt. (W.) 1914
SHIPLEY, J. W. 2nd Lieut., York and Lancaster Regt.; 1912
 Lieut., M.G.C. (W 2.)
SHOVE, W. C. Lieut., R.F.A. *M.* 1912
SHREWSBURY, E. 2nd Lieut., R. Sussex Regt. 1913
¹SKINNER, C. E. Major, R.F.A. (W 2.) 1906
SLAWSON, W. N. 2nd Lieut., Leicestershire Regt. and 1912
 Worcestershire Regt.; Lieut., Gen. List, attd. R.A.F.
SLOMAN, H. Major, R.A.S.C. *M.* 1915
SMITH, Rev. E. H. C.F. 4th Class, R.A.C.D. (W.) *M.* 1912
✠SMITH, F. E. Lieut., Cambridgeshire Regt. and Suffolk 1909
 Regt.(T.F.) (W.) *M.*
 Died 18 *Nov.* 1918 *of pneumonia following influenza contracted on active service*
SMITH, Rev. G. L. C.F. 4th Class, R.A.C.D. (W.) 1906
SMITH, Rev. G. S. Cadet, R.G.A. 1913
SNOXELL, S. 2nd Lieut., Dorset Regt. 1917
SQUIRE, A. G. 2nd Lieut. (O.), R.A.F. (W.) 1917
STALEY, Rev. J. E. C.F. 4th Class, R.A.C.D. 1904
STANLEY, F. 2nd Lieut. (A.), R.A.F. 1917
STEPHENS, Rev. J. P. C.F. 4th Class, R.A.C.D. 1908
STEPHENSON, Rev. H. C.F. 4th Class, R.A.C.D. 1909
✠STOKES, W. H. Pte., R. Fusiliers (P. S. Bn.); 2nd Lieut., 1910
 R.G.A.
 Killed in action 18 *April* 1918
✠STOUT, G. F. 2nd Lieut., Lincolnshire Regt. and York- 1913
 shire Regt.
 Killed in action 30 *Sept.* 1916
STREAM, E. J. Major, Lincolnshire Regt. 1891
SUMNER, E. J. 2nd Lieut., Sedbergh School O.T.C. 1914
✠SWALLOW, J. R. 2nd Lieut., King's (Liverpool Regt.) 1907
 Killed in action 8 *Aug.* 1916
SWANN, P. W. 2nd Lieut., Hampshire Regt. (W.) 1913

TAYLOR, J. D. Capt., R.F.A. (W.) *M.C.* 1909

---

¹ Died on service in S. Russia after the armistice.

TEALE, Rev. E. C.F. 3rd Class, R.A.C.D. (W.) *M.C. M.* 1900
THATCHER, W. S. Lieut., I.A.R.O., attd. Baluchis. (W 3.) 1907
M.C.
THOMAS, Rev. R. E. C.F. 4th Class, R.A.C.D. *M.* 1908
TOMKINS, Rev. L. C. F. 2nd Lieut., Spec. List 1907
✠TYNDALL, A. G. 2nd Lieut., Rifle Brigade 1916
Killed in action at Passchendaele 18 *Nov.* 1917

VANCE, Rev. J. G. C.F. 4th Class, R.A.C.D. 1907
VAN GEHUCHTEN, P. Med. Corps, Belgian Army 1915
VINCENT, L. J. Capt., R.A.M.C. 1910
VINCENT, T. C. L. 2nd Lieut., M.G.C. 1916

WAITE, T. H. Cadet, O.C.B. 1917
WALKER, C. D. Corpl., Cameronians (Scottish Rifles). 1913
(W.)
WALTON, G. M. Lieut., S. Lancs. Regt. (W.) 1916
WARD, Rev. R. W. A. C.F. 4th Class, R.A.C.D. 1910
WARREN, C. Capt., Cambridgeshire Regt. 1915
WATKINS, M. Cadet, O.C.B. 1917
WATT, A. S. Corpl., R.E. (Spec. Bde.) 1914
WEAVER, J. Gnr., R.G.A. 1908
WESTBY, Rev. F. W. C.F. 4th Class, R.A.C.D. 1910
✠WHEELER, R. M. Lieut., Middlesex Regt.(T.F.) 1907
Killed in action 30 *Nov.* 1916
WHITE, Rev. A. J. C.F. 4th Class, R.A.C.D. 1915
WHITE, G. W. Capt., Spec. List (Officer i/c Wireless 1914
Repair Section, R.E.)
✠WHITE, H. A. Pte., R. Fusiliers (P.S. Bn.); 2nd Lieut., 1913
The Buffs (E. Kent Regt.) and R. Irish Fusiliers. (W.)
Died 22 *Nov.* 1917 *of wounds received in action*
WHITE, Rev. J. L. C.F. 4th Class, R.A.C.D. 1907
WHITFIELD, Rev. J. L. C.F. 3rd Class, R.A.C.D. 1897
D.S.O. M.
WHITMILL, G. H. Cadet, O.C.B. 1917
✠WILKINSON, E. F. Pte., Suffolk Regt. and M.G.C. 1917
Died in German hands 9 *June* 1918 *of wounds received*
in action at Jussy
WILLIAMS, Rev. T. C. L. C.F. 4th Class, R.A.C.D. *M.* 1900
WITNEY, Rev. T. C. C.F. 4th Class, R.A.C.D. 1906
WOLFF, C. H. Lieut., Somerset L.I.; Capt., R. Defence 1900
Corps, Suffolk Regt., Labour Corps, and Gen. List
(Education Officer)
✠WOODS, A. M. 2nd Lieut., R.F.A. 1913
Killed in action 26 *Feb.* 1917

WOODS, W. A. Capt., R.F.A. (W.) *M.*   1912
WORMALD, Rev. C. O. R. C.F. 4th Class, R.A.C.D.   1899
WORMELL, C. O. R. *See* WORMALD, Rev. C. O. R.
WORTHINGTON, W. R. Lieut., R. Warwickshire Regt. 1913
 (W 2.)

The following matriculated at CAVENDISH COLLEGE[1], which
was created a Public Hostel in 1882 and ceased to be such in 1892:

✠DATHAN, Rev. J. D. Chaplain, R.N.   1883
 Died 7 Jan. 1918

[1] The names of those who, after matriculating at Cavendish College, migrated
elsewhere, will be found under their adopted Colleges.

INDEX

Boyer, G. W. B.	74	Branston, C. A.	369	Brindle, W. S.	370
Boyle, G. E.	513	Branston, R.	4	Brinton, R. D.	74
Boyle, G. F.	369	Brash, E. J. Y.	321	Briscoe, F. E.	292
Boyle, G. L.	282	Brasnett, T. J. G.	4	Briscoe, F. E. T.	237
Boyle, J.	484	Brass, W.	369	Briscoe, J. R.	513
Boyle, R. F. R. P.	484	Bratton, A. B.	122	Briscoe, W. T.	513
Boyne, Viscount	220	Braun, G. C. P.	369	Brisley, C. E.	122
Boys, G. V.	369	Braunholtz, E. J. K.	194	Bristed, G. T.	194
Boyson, H. A.	121	Braunholtz, G. E. K.	88	Bristow, C. H.	4
Boyson, J. C.	121	Braunholtz, H. J.	321	Brittain, A. W.	4
Boyton, H. J.	165	Braunholtz, W.T.K.	370	Brittain, E. S.	122
Bozman, E. F.	369	Brawn, J. A.	4	Broad, A. M.	122
Brabazon, C. M. P.	484	Bray, E. F.	62	Broad, C. N. F.	237
Braby, H. W.	348	Bray, Sir E. H.	370	Broadbent, C. H.	370
Bracecamp, F. W.	165	Bray, F. E.	370	Broadbent, E. R.	122
Brachi, C. C.	308	Bray, J.	370	Broadbent, F. M.	220
Bracken, R. J. M. E.	121	Brayne, F. L.	237	Broadbent, H. G.	292
Brackett, A. W. K.	321	Brayne, W. F.	88	Broadbent, W.	370
Bradbury, J. B.	74, 121	Brearley, A. J.	88	Broadmead, H. H.	122
Bradbury, J. F.	194	Bree, H. R. S.	513	Brock, A. G.	237
Bradfield, L. G.	121	Breed, F. G.	165	Brock, E. G.	321
Bradfield, R.	121	Breese, W. L.	370	Brocklebank, J. J.	370
Bradford, Earl of	369	Bremner, F. D. H.	370	Brocklehurst, E. H.	485
Bradford, E. C.	237	Brenan, A. R. M.	370	Brocklehurst, H.	4
Bradley, A. S.	121	Brend, W. A.	348	Brocklehurst,	
Bradley, E. J. (Jesus)	165	Brereton, J. L.	370	Sir P. L.	485
Bradley, E. J. (Pem.)	237	Bretherton, H.	370	Brocklehurst, T. P.	485
Bradley, G. H.	528	Brett, J. H.	122	Brockman, E. P.	122
Bradley, G. M.	165	Breul, O. G. F. J.	370	Brockman, R. St L.	122
Bradley, H. E.	237	Brewer, C. H.	31	Brockman, W. D.	122
Bradley, M. G.	369	Brewer, F. G.	122	Brode, R. T.	4
Bradley, S. B.	121	Brewer, J.	88	Brodie, E. J.	370
Bradley, V. M.	165	Brewis, C. C.	74	Brodie, H. W.	31
Bradley, W. de W. H.	165	Brewster, G. W.	194	Brodie, M. M.	292
Bradney, J. A.	369	Brian, F. R. H.	321	Brodie, P.	31
Bradshaw, P. C.	369	Brice-Smith, H. F.	321	Brodsky, G. A.	370
Bradshaw, R. E. K.	369	Brice-Smith, J. K.	321	Brogden, G. A.	31
Bradshaw, T. B.	237	Brickwood, H.	282	Brogden, J. R. R.	31
Bradshaw, W. D.	369	Bridge, E. A.	485	Brölemann, P. W. A.	237
Bradshaw-Isherwood,		Bridgeman, R. O.	370	Bromet, E.	122
F. E.	31	Bridges, L. W.	513	Bromet, J. N.	31
Bradstock, G.	165	Bridgwater, H. N.	485	Bromhead, J. P.	348
Bragg, R. C.	369	Brierley, W. B.	4	Bromley, L.	122
Bragg, W. H.	308	Briggs, G. C.	31	Bromley-Davenport,	
Bragg, W. L.	369	Briggs, G. E.	321	H. R.	485
Brailey, A. R.	74	Briggs, G. R.	165	Brook, A. K.	165
Brailey, W. H.	292	Briggs, H. W.	88	Brook, R.	74
Brailsford, R. W.	121	Briggs, J. L.	528	Brooke, B. W. D.	370
Braimbridge, C. V.	74	Briggs, M.	348	Brooke, F. N.	237
Brain, F. S.	484	Briggs, P. J.	4	Brooke, H. K.	370
Braithwaite, C. F.	121	Briggs, R. S.	88	Brooke, J.	89
Braithwaite, J. G.	194	Briggs, W. A.	321	Brooke, J. C.	122
Braithwaite, P. P.	121	Briggs, W. R.	4	Brooke, R. C.	194
Bramall, E. H.	237	Briggs Gooderham,		Brooke, W. A. C.	194
Brameld, A. J. M.	308	E. J. R. see		Brooke, Z. N.	122, 321
Bramwell, B. S.	369	Gooderham, E. J. R. B.		Brooke Taylor, G. P.	237
Bramwell, J. C.	369	Bright, F. T.	528	Brooker, R. H. G.	237
Brandon, A. de B.	484	Bright, W. A.	122	Brookes, A.	528
Branson, F. H. E.	369	Bright, W. J.	528	Brookes, H. V.	89
Branson, J. R. B.	369	Brightman, E. W.	370	Brooks, C. D.	194
Branson, W. P. S.	369	Brigley, C. G.	308	Brooks, D. C. M.	194

C. U. W. L.

INDEX 557

INDEX

569

Newman, E. A. R.	146	Nicholson, R. S.	49	Northfield, H. D.	287
Newman, E. D.	501	Nicholson, W. N.	438	Northorp, F.	336
Newman, F. C.	80	Nickal, G. B.	17	Northrop, J. E.	50
Newman, F. H. C.	180	Nickels, R. N.	146	Norton, D. G.	146
Newman, J. B.	438	Nicklin, G. N.	336	Norton, E. H. P.	146
Newman, J. C. (Mag.)	228	Nicol, J.	438	Norton, G. P. .	146
Newman, J. C. (Trin.)	438	Nicoll, H. M. D.	146	Norton, H. E.	439
Newman, J. C. F.	521	Nicolls, G. E.	264	Norton, L. M.	287, 521
Newman, J. R. B.	438	Nicolson, L. G.	80	Norton, R. H.	209
Newman, J. S.	17	Nielsen, E. E. M.	49	Norton, V. E. B.	105
Newman, L. F.	80	Nightingale, A. D.	438	Norton-Fagge,	
Newmarch, J. G.	264	Nightingale, C. L.	301	F. W. L.	532
Newell, A.	314	Nightingale, D. A.	438	Nosworthy, J. L.	521
Newnes, Sir F. H.	49	Nightingale, H. P.	17	Nosworthy, P. C.	301
Newport, H.	521	Nihill, J. H. B.	104	Nott, H. P.	105
Newport, Viscount	438	Nisbet, A. T.	69	Nott, L. C.	105
Newson, W. A.	438	Niven, E. O.	264	Nott, T. W.	105
Newton, C. H. see		Nix, C. G. A.	438	Nowell-Rostron, S.	336
Herdman-Newton, C.		Nix, P. K.	264	Nowell-Usticke, G. W.	180
Newton, G. F.	17	Nixon, B. H.	439	Noyes, H. F. G.	147
Newton, H. A.	228	Nixon, J. A.	146	Noyes, J. C.	50
Newton, H. G. T.	336	Nixon, W. H.	17	Nunn, V. W. H.	301
Newton, H. W. G.	209	Nobbs, S. W.	105	Nurse, H. H.	336
Newton, R. H. H. see		Noble, A. H. (Clare)	49	Nutman, B. K.	180
Herdman-Newton, R.H.		Noble, A. H. (Qu.)	301	Nuttall, E. D.	17
Newton, T. H.	104	Noble, E. R.	354	Nuttall, W. L. F.	17
Newton, W. H.	104	Noble, H. B.	209	Nutting, A. R. S.	501
Newton Clare, E. T.	49	Noble, R. H.	17, 301	Oakden, W. M.	287
Newton Clare, H. J.	49	Noel, R. E. T. M.	439	Oakes, M. W.	105
Newton Clare, W. S.	49	Norbury, C. G.	439	Oakey, J. M.	439
Nibbs, C. A. J.	301	Norbury, F. C.	336	Oakshott, T. A.	439
Nichol, R. W.	146	Norby, R. H.	314	Oaten, E. F.	354
Nicholas, A. J.	17	Norden, F. L.	301	Oaten, W. S.	354
Nicholas, F.	104	Norman, A. C.	336	Oates, B. W. G.	439
Nicholas, F. P.	180	Norman, C.	49	Oates, J. S. C.	439
Nicholas, H. C.	438	Norman, C. L.	439	Oatfield, W. J.	209
Nicholas, T. C.	438	Norman, C. W.	439	Oats, G.	439
Nicholl, E. McK.	301	Norman, D. T.	105	Oats, W.	147
Nicholl, J. W. McK.	301	Norman, J.	105	O'Brien, J. C. P.	147
Nicholl, V.	264	Norman, N. F.	80, 105	O'Callaghan, T. F.	209
Nicholls, A. C.	336	Norman, R. E.	50	O'Connell, J. B.	532
Nicholls, G. B.	301	Norman, T. V.	180	O'Connor, A. C.	439
Nicholls, G. S.	80	Norman, W. H.	532	O'Connor, J.	314
Nicholls, L.	80	Norman-Lee, F.B.N.	336	Odell, R. E.	17
Nicholls, S. H.	146	Norquoy, F.	105	Odgers, F. W.	439
Nichols, C. W.	104	Norregaard, A. H.	336	Odgers, L. N. B.	336
Nichols, F. P.	314	Norris, C. G.	314	Odgers, R. B.	336
Nichols, W. H.	180	Norris, E. W. M.	521	Odling, F. C.	50
Nicholson, A. F.	438	Norris, W. F.	439	O'Driscoll, P. F.	439
Nicholson, B. D.	438	Norris, W. H. H.	69	O'Ferrall, C. L.	439
Nicholson, C. J.	146	North, G. D.	180	O'Flynn, D. R. C. D.	301
Nicholson, C. O. E.	438	North, J.	301	Ogden, H.	105
Nicholson, G. B.	49	North, J. B.	287	Ogilvie, A.	439
Nicholson, G. C. N.	49	North, J. F. A.	80	Ogilvie, G. L.	439
Nicholson, H. H.	521	North, W. G. B.	146	Ogilvie, H.	210
Nicholson, H. J.	438	Northcote, D. S.	439	Ogilvie, J.	17
Nicholson, J. E.	336	Northcote, T. F.	105	Ogilvie, N.	50
Nicholson, M.	501	Northcott, J. F.	336	Ogilvie, P. G.	264
Nicholson, O. W.	228	Northcott, W. W.	439	Ogilvy, L. W.	210
Nicholson, P. C.	438	Northen, E.	439	Ogle, K. W. S.	521
Nicholson, R.	438	Northen, F.	439	Oglethorpe, H. C.	264

INDEX

INDEX 613

Wiglesworth, G.	217	Willey, H.	217	Williams, O. St M.	115
Wigley, W. C. S.	114	Willey, H. L.	160	Williams, P.	475
Wigmore, J. B. A.	160	Willey, R. H. D.	160	Williams, R. (Magd.)	231
Wigram, C. K.	474	Williams, A.	25	Williams, R. (Joh.)	345
Wigram, H. F. E.	474	Williams, A. C.	160	Williams, R. A.	525
Wilberforce, H. H.	71	Williams, A. D. J. B.	160	Williams, R. A. W.	217
Wilcock, J. A.	83	Williams, A. F.	160	Williams, R. B. (Cai.)	160
Wilcox, A. G.	60	Williams, A. G.	160	Williams,R.B.(Pem.)	278
Wilcox, A. J.	114	Williams, A. J. (Cai.)	160	Williams, R. C. L.	290
Wild, J. A. P.	189	Williams, A. J. (Pet.)	290	Williams,	
Wilde, C. A. G.	189	Williams, A. K.	475	R. D. Garnons	475
Wilde, E. H. N.	217	Williams, A. L.	189	Williams, R. F. (Cai.)	160
Wilde, R. W.	474	Williams, A. S.	525	Williams,R.F.(Selw.)	525
Wilderspin, B. C.	83	Williams, C. (Caius)	160	Williams, R. G.	160
Wilding, A. F.	474	Williams, C. (Trin.)	475	Williams,S.C.(Cai.)	161
Wileman, G. W. B.	160	Williams, C. E. (Cai.)	160	Williams,S.C.(Trin.)	475
Wilenkin, C.	475	Williams,C.E.(Trin.)	475	Williams, S. R.	161
Wiles, H. H.	25	Williams, C. H.	358	Williams, T.	290
Wiles, J. J.	60	Williams, C. J.	60	Williams, T. B.	161
Wiles, J. W.	25	Williams, C. M.	25	Williams, T. C. L.	535
Wilkes, J. F.	475	Williams, C. S.	189	Williams, T. P.	83
Wilkin, A.	217	Williams, D. G.	25	Williams, T. R.	278
Wilkin, W. H.	278	Williams, E.	475	Williams, W. C. B.	278
Wilkin, W. R.	475	Williams, E. A.	278	Williams, W. D.	25
Wilkinson, C. A.	358	Williams, E. C.	25	Williams, W. E.	278
Wilkinson, C. F. W.	306	Williams, E. G.	475	Williams, W. F.	60
Wilkinson, C. L. G.	60	Williams, E. H. Y.	60	Williams, W. H.	345
Wilkinson, E.	317	Williams, E. K.	160	Williams, W. J.	83
Wilkinson, E. F.	535	Williams, F. F. S.	189	Williams, W. P.	161
Wilkinson, F.	358	Williams, F. J.	509	Williams, W. P. G.	83
Wilkinson,F.C.(Jes.)	189	Williams, F. L.	25	Williams, W. S.	317
Wilkinson,F.C.(Sid.)	358	Williams, G. (Emm.)	114	Williams-Ellis, B. C.	475
Wilkinson, G.	114	Williams, G. (Trin.)	475	Williams-Ellis, R. G.	358
Wilkinson, G. A. W.	306	Williams, G. A.	231	Williams-Freeman,	
Wilkinson, G. J.	160	Williams, G. C.	160	A. P.	475
Wilkinson, G. R.	475	Williams, G. D.	71	Williams-Green,W.T.	475
Wilkinson, H. A.	278	Williams, G. H.	475	Williams-Thomas,	
Wilkinson, H. E. T.	509	Williams, G. T.	475	F. S.	475
Wilkinson, H. R.	475	Williams, G. V.	290	Williams Wynn, W.	475
Wilkinson, J. R.	306	Williams, G. W.	345	Williamson, A. J. N.	278
Wilkinson, K.	278	Williams, H.	83	Williamson, C. G.	231
Wilkinson, M. L.	306	Williams, H. A.	115	Williamson, D. A.	475
Wilkinson, N.	160	Williams, H. B.	345	Williamson, F.	115
Wilkinson, R. du C.	60	Williams,H.F.F.	60, 189	Williamson, F. A.	306
Wilkinson, R. J.	475	Williams, H. G.	317	Williamson, F. L.	71
Wilkinson, S.	60	Williams, H. G. E.	217	Williamson, G. E.	476
Wilkinson, S. J.	25	Williams, H. H.	25	Williamson, G. H.	115
Wilkinson, V.	25	Williams,H.P.W.B.	115	Williamson, H.	345
Wilkinson, W. R.	231	Williams, I. A.	217	Williamson, J. B.	476
Wilks, E. L.	83	Williams, J. C. S.	160	Williamson, J. M.	161
Wilks, J. H.	160	Williams, J. E.	25	Williamson, J. N.	278
Will, J. G.	83	Williams, J. G.	306	Williamson, K. B.	345
Willan, G. T.	114	Williams, J. L. C.	160	Williamson,R.H.W.	218
Willans, E. T.	114	Williams, J. S.	160	Williamson, R. S.	25
Willans, R. St J.	475	Williams, K. G.	25	Williamson, S. K. G.	476
Willcocks, R. H.	217	Williams, L.	189	Williamson, T. R.	306
Willcocks, R. W.	160	Williams, M. B.	160	Willink, A. H.	278
Willett, E. W.	345	Williams, N. A.	160	Willink, A. J. W.	218
Willett, J. A.	345	Williams, N. D.	475	Willink, H. J. L.	161
Willett, W. L.	475	Williams, N. S.	60	Willink, H. U.	476
Willey, B.	290	Williams, O. H.	306	Willis, A. G. de L.	115

PRINTED IN ENGLAND BY J. B. PEACE, M.A.

AT THE CAMBRIDGE UNIVERSITY PRESS

Lightning Source UK Ltd.
Milton Keynes UK
UKOW05f1150230713

214230UK00001B/32/A